Employment Law
Eighth Edition

Books are to be returned on or before the

Offering comprehensive coverage of all the key aspects of individual and collective employment law in a clear and accessible way, *Employment Law* is ideal for both LLB and HRM students. Packed with a wealth of case law and legislation, this book will enable you to fully understand the intricacies of this fast-changing subject with ease. With features such as chapter summaries and further reading suggestions, *Employment Law* is well-suited to support you in your studies.

The eighth edition has been fully updated to include coverage of the latest legislative and case law developments, including:

- Issues around shared parental leave
- The national living wage
- Legal developments in the area of non-standard work

Malcolm Sargeant is Professor of Labour Law at Middlesex University and teaches discrimination law at both undergraduate and postgraduate levels. He is currently co-author of several student text books on employment law and has also authored and edited other books on aspects of discrimination law.

David Lewis is Professor of Employment Law at Middlesex University. He has written specialist and general books and has published articles in several countries. David has considerable experience as a consultant and is on the ACAS panel of arbitrators.

Employment Law
Eighth Edition

Malcolm Sargeant and David Lewis

Routledge
Taylor & Francis Group

LONDON AND NEW YORK

Eighth edition published 2018
by Routledge
2 Park Square, Milton Park, Abingdon, Oxon OX14 4RN

and by Routledge
711 Third Avenue, New York, NY 10017

Routledge is an imprint of the Taylor & Francis Group, an informa business

First edition published by Pearson 2001
Seventh edition published by Pearson 2014

British Library Cataloguing in Publication Data
A catalogue record for this book is available from the British Library

Library of Congress Cataloging in Publication Data
Names: Sargeant, Malcolm, author. | Lewis, David, 1949 March 24- author.
Title: Employment law / Malcolm Sargeant and David Lewis.
Description: 8. | Milton Park, Abington, Oxon ; New York, NY : Routledge,
2018. | Includes bibliographical references and index.
Identifiers: LCCN 2017046326| ISBN 9781138703209 (hbk) |
ISBN 9781138744929 (pbk) | ISBN 9781315203263 (ebk)
Subjects: LCSH: Labor laws and legislation—Great Britain.
Classification: LCC KD3009 .S27 2018 | DDC 344.4101—dc23
LC record available at https://lccn.loc.gov/2017046326

ISBN: 978-1-138-70320-9 (hbk)
ISBN: 978-1-138-74492-9 (pbk)
ISBN: 978-1-3152-0326-3 (ebk)

Typeset in Joanna MT
by Keystroke, Neville Lodge, Tettenhall, Wolverhampton

Printed and bound by CPI Group (K) Ltd, Croydon, CR0 4YY

Contents

Table of statutes

Table of cases

Table of statutory instruments

Table of European legislation

Treaties and conventions

Directives

Preface

The book is intended to be a comprehensive and supportive text for those studying employment law, whether they are law students or others. A particular feature of this new edition is a separate chapter on non-standard working in which we have tried to reflect upon the increase of this type of work and the development of the so-called gig economy.

The big imponderable in the writing of this edition has been the effect of the decision by the UK to leave the EU. Much of our employment law has its derivation in legislation enacted by the EU and we have reflected this in our writing. The government has stated that these employment rights will be incorporated into national law when we leave, but we must wait on developments.

Malcolm Sargeant
David Lewis

Publisher's acknowledgements

We are grateful to the following for permission to reproduce copyright material:

Tables 6.1 and 6.2 from Discrimination in the European Union, *Special Eurobarometer Survey* (2007), European Commission, © European Union, 1995–2013. http://ec.europa.eu/public_opinion/archives/ebs/ebs_263_sum_en.pdf.

In some instances we have been unable to trace the owners of copyright material, and we would appreciate any information that would enable us to do so.

Abbreviations

AC	Appeal Cases
ACAS	Advisory, Conciliation and Arbitration Service
All ER	All England Law Reports
AMRA	Access to Medical Reports Act 1988
ASTMS	Association of Supervisory, Technical and Managerial Staffs
AUEW	Amalgamated Union of Engineering Workers
CA	Court of Appeal
CAC	Central Arbitration Committee
CBI	Confederation of British Industry
CEEP	European Centre of Employers and Enterprises providing Public Services
CHR	European Convention on Human Rights
CJEU	Court of Justice of the European Union
CMLR	Common Market Law Reports
CO	Certification Officer
CPSA	Civil and Public Services Association
CRE	Commission for Racial Equality
CRTUPE	Collective Redundancies and Transfer of Undertakings (Protection of Employment) Regulations 2014
DDA	Disability Discrimination Act 1995
DBEIS	Department for Business, Energy and Industrial Strategy
DBIS	Department for Business, Innovation and Skills
DRC	Disability Rights Commission
DRCA	Disability Rights Commission Act 1999
EA	Equality Act 2010
EAT	Employment Appeal Tribunal
EC	European Community
ECHR	European Court of Human Rights
ECR	European Court Reports
EEA	European Economic Area
EEC	European Economic Community
EES	European Employment Strategy
EHRC	Equality and Human Rights Commission
EHRR	European Human Rights Reports
EIRR	European Industrial Relations Reports
EOC	Equal Opportunities Commission
EPA	Equal Pay Act 1970
ERA	Employment Rights Act 1996
ERelA	Employment Relations Act 1999
ERRA	Enterprise and Regulatory Reform Act 2013
ETA	Employment Tribunals Act 1996

ETEJO	Employment Tribunals (Extension of Jurisdiction) Order 1994
ETUC	European Trade Union Confederation
ETUI	European Trade Union Institute
EU	European Union
EWC	European Works Council
GCHQ	Government Communications Headquarters
GLAA	Gangmaster and Labour Abuse Authority
GMBATU	General, Municipal, Boilermakers and Allied Trades Union
HASAWA	Health and Safety at Work etc. Act 1974
HC	House of Commons
HL	House of Lords
HRA	Human Rights Act 1998
HSCE	Health and Safety (Consultation with Employees) Regulations 1996
IANA	Immigration, Asylum and Nationality Act 2006
ICE	Information and Consultation of Employees Regulations 2004
ICR	Industrial Cases Reports
IRLR	Industrial Relations Law Reports
LGBT	Lesbian, Gay, Bisexual or Transgender
MHSW	Management of Health and Safety at Work
MP	Member of Parliament
MPL	Maternity and Parental Leave etc. Regulations
NALGO	National Association of Local Government Officers
NEC	National Executive Committee
NGA	National Graphical Association
NGO	Non-Governmental Organisation
NIRC	National Industrial Relations Court
NMW	National minimum wage
NMWA	National Minimum Wage Act 1998
NUM	National Union of Mineworkers
NURMTW	National Union of Rail, Maritime and Transport Workers
ODI	Office for Disability Issues
OJ	Official Journal
ONS	Office for National Statistics
OPSI	Office of Public Sector Information
PTW	Part-time workers
QB	Queen's Bench
RRA	Race Relations Act 1976
SC	Supreme Court
SDA	Sex Discrimination Act 1975
SE	Societas Europaea
SI	Statutory Instrument
SNB	Special Negotiating Body
SOGAT	Society of Graphical and Allied Trades
SPA	State Pension Age
SRA	Standard retirement age
TFEU	Treaty on the Functioning of the European Union
TGWU	Transport and General Workers Union
TICE	Transnational Information and Consultation of Employees
TUC	Trades Union Congress

TULRCA   Trade Union and Labour Relations (Consolidation) Act 1992
TUPE   Transfer of Undertakings (Protection of Employment) Regulations 1981 and 2006
ULR   Union learning representative
WLR   Weekly Law Reports
WT   Working time

Chapter 1

The study of employment law

Chapter Contents

1.1 Introduction

The subject of employment law is the regulation of the relationship between employer and worker or, put in another way, the relationship between the user of labour and the supplier of labour. This regulation takes place at an individual level and at a collective level. At an individual level, the law takes the view that the contract of employment is like any other contract, namely a legally binding agreement that two equal parties have voluntarily entered into. At a collective level, workers and employers have banded together into trade unions and employers' associations in order, partly, to give themselves greater bargaining power with each other.

The sources of this regulation are diverse and, until Brexit takes effect, include:

1. Primary and secondary legislation initiated or supported by government.
2. The EU Treaties and legislation, usually, but not always, in the form of Directives.
3. The decisions of the courts, including the High Court, employment tribunals and the Employment Appeal Tribunal, but especially, as in other fields of law, decisions of the Court of Appeal and the Supreme Court.
4. The decisions of international courts, currently the Court of Justice of the European Union and the European Court of Human Rights.
5. Codes of practice and guidance issued by Ministers of the Crown and by individual bodies authorised by statute to do so. These latter include the Health and Safety Executive and the Equality and Human Rights Commission (EHRC).
6. The Advisory, Conciliation and Arbitration Service (ACAS) and the Central Arbitration Committee (CAC), which have been given a special role by governments in the field of dispute resolution between workers and employers, both individually and collectively.

A concern for students of employment law is how to access the large amount of information available in the most efficient and effective way. Books are one source of information but further study means accessing the law and its sources directly. The purpose of this chapter is to provide some information on accessing employment law and to show that a large amount of information is available free from the organisations mentioned above and others, much of which is accessible via the internet.

1.2 Primary and secondary legislation

The Acts of Parliament most often referred to in this book are the Employment Rights Act (ERA) 1996 and the Equality Act (EA) 2010. Both of these have been much amended by other statutes. There are other important Acts, such as the Trade Union and Labour Relations (Consolidation) Act (TULRCA) 1992 and the National Minimum Wage Act (NMWA) 1998. There are also a large number of statutory instruments that form an important source of employment law. For example, much EU legislation has been introduced via regulations under s. 2(2) European Communities Act 1972.

Study sources for both Acts of Parliament and secondary legislation are:

1. Office of Public Sector Information (OPSI) – the Stationery Office, which is the official publisher to Parliament, prints copies for sale of all primary and secondary legislation. These can be expensive but are often available in libraries.

    All such legislation since, and including, 1988 is available at: www.legislation.gov.uk. Here you can click on 'Browse Legislation', 'New Legislation' or 'Changes to Legislation' and you will be able to access all Acts of the UK Parliament adopted since 1988 together with draft legislation. If you click on 'Statutory Instruments', you will be able to access subordinate legislation. Bear in mind that there are several thousand statutory instruments adopted each year so it will help you if you know the year and the number that you are looking for. Thus SI 1998/1833 will lead you to statutory instrument number 1833 adopted in 1998, which will take you to the Working Time Regulations 1998.

2. Houses of Parliament – Hansard is the full verbatim report of debates in the Houses of Parliament and is kept by many libraries in microfiche format. There is also a large amount of information available on Parliament's website at: www.parliament.uk.

   If you click on this, you will be able to choose between the House of Commons and the House of Lords and explore at your leisure. Click on 'House of Commons' and then 'Publications & records', and you will see a section on 'Research publications'. If you click on these, you will be able to explore all the recent research papers written by House of Commons research staff. This will include papers on employment law issues and Bills before Parliament.

   Alternatively, the Parliament Home Page will give you access to the entire work of Parliament, including copies of Bills before Parliament and the current work of the House of Commons and the House of Lords. It will usefully give you access to the Committee System and the reports that Select Committees of both Houses have made. For example, you might follow this through to the Business, Energy and Industrial Strategy Committee.

   The government department that has the most relevance to the study of employment law is the Department for Business, Energy and Industrial Strategy. Its website can be found at: www.gov.uk/government/organisations/department-for-business-energy-and-industrial-strategy. The site has copies of all the consultations that have taken place about the introduction of many measures in the field of employment law and provides guidance on current legislation.

3. Other sources of statutes will be the same as for other law subjects studied, such as Halsbury's Statutes, Lexis Library and Lawtel.

1.3 The EU Treaties and legislation

Six countries adopted the Treaty of Rome in 1957 but the European Community has grown to 28 Member States at the time of writing. From December 2009 the two principal sources of EU law have been the Treaty on the Functioning of the European Union and the Treaty on European Union. The scope of the EU's activities has also grown from being concerned with a number of primarily economic objectives to a Union that has an important social dimension as well as an economic one.

As a result of this, there is a large amount of EU material available and it seemed to increase at a rate that alarmed even specialist students of EU law. Some of this material may still be relevant after Brexit has been effected so it is worth noting how it may accessed:

1. European Documentation Centres – a large number of libraries contain European Documentation Centres, which will normally have a specialist librarian in charge. These keep paper copies of both current and historical EU material. They are most useful if you know what you are looking for rather than starting a cold search.

2. The EU has a website with an enormous amount of material. It is not the easiest site to navigate but will reward those who know which document they are looking for or those with patience. It can be found at: http://europa.eu.

   Once you have clicked on the language you require, the next page provides a subject list of what the European Union does. Click on 'EU by topic' and the relevant area to choose is 'Employment and social affairs'. Here you will find useful summaries of legislation and policy as well as full texts of legislation and case law. You might also try the European Foundation for the Improvement of Living and Working Conditions (at www.eurofound.europa.eu). This site has extensive information about what is going on in the EU and individual Member States.

3. A good library will have other sources, such as those contained on various CDs, as well as access to relevant information via other commercial bodies.

1.4 The courts
1.4.1 Employment tribunals and the EAT

Section 1(1) Employment Rights (Dispute Resolution) Act 1998 renamed industrial tribunals as employment tribunals, so this is how they are referred to in this book. Unlike many other courts, employment tribunals and the Employment Appeal Tribunal (EAT) are created by statute[1] as is the subject matter in which they deal.[2] The composition of employment tribunals is set out in the Employment Tribunals Act 1996 and provision has recently been made for legal officers to determine certain claims if the parties have given their written consent.[3] An interesting issue with regard to tribunals and the Human Rights Act 1998 was raised in *Smith v Secretary of State for Trade and Industry*.[4] Article 6(1) of the European Convention on Human Rights gives everyone the right to an 'independent and impartial' tribunal.[5] The question raised was whether employment tribunals which were appointed by the Secretary of State could adjudicate in claims against the Secretary of State and still be an independent and impartial tribunal.

From 2013 fees were charged at two stages: the issue of the claim and prior to a hearing. Type A claims were for defined sums – for example, redundancy payments and unauthorised deductions from wages. The issue fee was £160 and the hearing fee was £230 in 2017. Type B claims were those involving more complex issues, including discrimination, whistleblowing and unfair dismissal. The issue fee was £250 and the hearing fee was £950 in 2017. There were arrangements for multiple claims and a remission system for those on low incomes.[6] After the Fees Order came into force there was a dramatic and persistent fall in the number of claims brought to employment tribunals and, in July 2017, the Supreme Court found that the fees: 'are in practice unaffordable by some people, and that they are so high as in practice to prevent even people who can afford them from pursuing claims for small amounts and non-monetary claims'.[7] It therefore quashed the Fees Order on the basis that it infringed both the common law constitutional right of access to justice and EU law. However, the effect is likely to be that the government will introduce a new fees regime as soon as possible.

Following evidence that employers were failing to pay sums awarded by tribunals, sections 37A–37Q ERA 1996 were introduced in 2016 to enable enforcement officers to issue a warning notice specifying a date by which an outstanding tribunal award and interest must be paid. An employer not complying with the notice may incur a financial penalty (payable to the Secretary of State) of 50 per cent of the sum owed, subject to a minimum of £100 and a maximum of £5,000. However, employers qualify for a reduction of 50 per cent of the penalty if they pay the reduced penalty and the whole unpaid amount within 14 days after the day on which notice of the decision to impose the penalty was sent.

Appeals from employment tribunals are normally to the EAT, which sits in Edinburgh and London. Proceedings are to be heard by a judge alone unless a judge directs otherwise.[8] Apart from

---

1 See ss 1 and 20 Employment Tribunals Act 1996.
2 Sections 2–3 and 21 Employment Tribunals Act 1996.
3 Sections 4 and 22–25 Employment Tribunals Act 1996 (as amended).
4 [2000] IRLR 6.
5 On the application of Article 6 to disciplinary proceedings, see *Mattu v University Hospitals of Coventry and NHS Trust* [2012] IRLR 661 CA.
6 The Employment Tribunals and the Employment Appeal Tribunal Fees Order 2013, SI 2013/1893.
7 *R (on the application of UNISON) v Lord Chancellor* (2017) UKSC 51 (para. 117).
8 Section 28(2)–(8) Employment Tribunals Act 1996.

TABLE 1.1 Employment tribunal cases sent to ACAS for conciliation in 2016/17

Subject matter	Number and percentage of applications	
Unfair dismissal	10,663	57%
Breach of contract	6,422	34%
Wages Act	6,043	32%
Working time (annual leave)	4,467	24%
Disability discrimination	3,643	20%
Sex discrimination	1,994	11%
Race discrimination	1,785	10%
Redundancy pay	1,542	8%
Public interest disclosure	1,369	7%
Maternity detriment	859	5%
Other	4,628	
Total jurisdictions	43,415	

challenges to the decision of the Certification Officer, an appeal to the EAT can only be made on a point of law and must be lodged within 42 days.[9] Prior to the Supreme Court's decision in *R v Lord Chancellor* (see above), the lodgement fee was £400 and the hearing fee was £1,200.

Table 1.1 provides a breakdown of the employment tribunal cases sent to ACAS for conciliation in 2016/17.[10]

1.4.2 Case reports

Paper reports of proceedings at the EAT, the Court of Appeal (CA) and the Supreme Court are published in:

● Industrial Cases Reports (ICR)
● Industrial Relations Law Reports (IRLR).

Wherever possible, these are the sources used in this book. Both carry good summaries of the cases in question. Cases may also be reported in non-specialist law reports, such as the All England Law Reports (All ER), the Weekly Law Reports (WLR), or in Appeal Cases (AC).

Other, more comprehensive, sources are:

● www.employmentappeals.gov.uk (the EAT)
● www.gov.uk/government/organisations/hm-court-service (the High Court and the Court of Appeal)
● www.supremecourt.uk/decided-cases (the Supreme Court).

Apart from the EAT, these sources are not restricted to employment law cases only and can be found via a number of other links. The advantage of all these sites over the paper reports is that the judgment of the court is reported in full in all cases. The Employment Tribunals Service website also

---

9 Rule 3 Employment Appeal Tribunal Rules 1993, SI 1993/2854.
10 See ACAS Annual Report 2016/17.

contains a lot of useful information and statistics. It can be found at: www.justice.gov.uk/tribunals/employment.

For employment law purposes, currently the two most important courts are the Court of Justice of the European Union (Court of Justice) and the European Court of Human Rights (ECHR). Significant and relevant cases in both are reported in the ICR and IRLR but they both have their own paper and electronic reports. These are:

- European Court Reports (ECR) for the Court of Justice
- European Human Rights Reports (EHRR) for the European Court of Human Rights.

Again, these reports cover all the work of the courts and will include a large number of cases that are not directly relevant to the study of employment law. In addition, both courts have websites that will provide access to the judgments of the court. These sites are:

- https://europa.eu/european-union/about-eu/institutions-bodies/court-justice_en (the Court of Justice)
- www.echr.coe.int (the ECHR).

1.5 Advisory, Conciliation and Arbitration Service

The Advisory, Conciliation and Arbitration Service (ACAS) was established by statute in 1975 to promote the improvement of industrial relations.[11] It operates as an independent publicly funded body and is not subject to direct ministerial control. It is run by a council of 12 individuals, which is made up of leading figures from business, unions, independent sectors and academics. ACAS operates in four key areas of activities. These are:

1. preventing and resolving disputes by means of collective conciliation and advisory mediation
2. conciliating in actual and potential complaints to employment tribunals
3. providing information and advice
4. promoting good practice and training.

Examples of its success are:

- In 2016/17,[12] 670 collective disputes were closed by outcome and another 253 were withdrawn; 615 cases were successfully completed and 55 unsuccessfully.
- In the same period, 18,220 individual conciliation case outcomes were explained. Of these, 16.7 per cent were withdrawn and 51.8 per cent settled, and 22.7 per cent made it to a tribunal hearing.

The ACAS annual report is a good source of statistical information and is free from the website. It also produces a wide range of publications that focus on good practice and explain the legal obligations of practitioners. Of considerable importance is its guide *Discipline and Grievances at Work* (see Chapter 4) and its codes of practice on:

- disclosure of information to trade unions for collective bargaining purposes 2003
- time off for trade union duties and activities 2010

---

11 See now s. 209 TULRCA 1992.
12 See the latest annual report available on the ACAS website, www.acas.org.uk.

- disciplinary and grievance procedures 2015
- settlement agreements 2013 and
- requests to work flexibly 2014.

ACAS has authority to issue these codes of practice under ss 199–202 TULRCA 1992. Sections 207 and 207A TULRCA 1992 provide that the contents of these codes will be taken into account at hearings before employment tribunals, courts or the Central Arbitration Committee (CAC). ACAS has a very useful website, which contains consultation and proposals on matters such as new codes of practice. It can be found at: www.acas.org.uk.

1.6 Central Arbitration Committee

The Central Arbitration Committee (CAC) is a permanent independent body with a number of roles:[13]

1. To adjudicate on applications relating to the statutory recognition of trade unions for collective bargaining purposes (see Chapter 12).
2. To determine disputes between employers and trade unions over the disclosure of information for collective bargaining purposes (see Chapter 12).
3. To determine claims and complaints regarding the establishment and operation of European Works Councils in Great Britain (see Chapter 10).
4. To provide voluntary arbitration in trade disputes, in certain circumstances.

In the period 2016/17 the CAC did not receive any applications concerning voluntary arbitration. However, it received seven applications concerning disclosure of information and 51 concerning trade union recognition.

The Committee consists of a chair and nine deputy chairs, together with 41 members experienced as representatives of employers or workers. Any determinations of the Committee are made by the chair, or deputy chair, plus two members.

The CAC has a useful website at: www.cac.gov.uk. This website contains information about the CAC and its statutory powers. It also contains information about decisions of the CAC and details about individual cases.

1.7 Certification Officer

The Certification Officer is appointed[14] to carry out particular functions[15] (see Chapter 11). He or she is responsible for maintaining a list of trade unions and employers' associations and, if an application is submitted, has to determine whether or not a listed union qualifies for a certificate of independence. The Certification Officer also:

- handles disputes which arise from trade union amalgamations and mergers and the administration of political funds
- enforces the annual return requirements and the provisions of Chapter IV TULRCA 1992 concerning trade union elections[16]

---

13 See ss 259–265 TULRCA 1992.
14 Sections 254–255 TULRCA 1992.
15 Part I TULRCA 1992 as amended.
16 See ss 256 and 32ZC TULRCA 1992.

- investigates breaches of a trade union's own rules relating to a union office, disciplinary proceedings, ballots (on any issue other than industrial action) and the constitution and proceedings of the executive committee or of any decision-making meeting.[17]

Under Schedule A3 of the Trade Union and Labour Relations (Consolidation) Act 1992, the Certification Officer has investigatory powers and can make enforcement orders, and Schedule A4 enables her or him to impose financial penalties. Schedule 2 of the Trade Union Act 2016 allows him or her to exercise certain powers without an application or complaint being made. In relation to all these jurisdictions, an appeal can be lodged on a question of fact or law.[18]

The Certification Officer produces a detailed and useful annual report that contains information on employers' associations and trade unions and on the work of the Certification Officer. The report and other material can be seen on the website at: www.certoffice.org.

1.8 Information Commissioner

The Office of the Information Commissioner was established by the Data Protection Act 1998, much of which came into effect on 1 March 2000.[19] The Commissioner oversees and enforces compliance with the Data Protection Act 1998 and the Freedom of Information Act 2000. It does this by, amongst other means:

- publishing guidance to assist with compliance
- providing a general inquiry service
- encouraging the development of codes of practice
- maintaining the public register of data controllers under the Data Protection Act 1998 and the list of public authorities with approved publication schemes under the Freedom of Information Act 2000
- prosecuting persons in respect of offences under the legislation.

There is an excellent website at: www.ico.org.uk. This provides legal guidance and compliance advice as well as links to the Data Protection Act 1998, codes of practice and consultation documents, including the code of practice on the use of personal data in employer/employee relationships.

1.9 Equality and Human Rights Commission (EHRC)

The Equality and Human Rights Commission was established by s. 1 Equality Act 2006. In addition to assuming responsibility for the work of the previous anti-discrimination Commissions (i.e. the Equal Opportunities Commission, the Commission for Racial Equality and the Disability Rights Commission), it has the duty to combat unlawful discrimination on the grounds of sexual orientation, religion or belief, and age.

Section 8 Equality Act 2006 provides that the EHRC must:

(a) promote understanding of the importance of equality and diversity,
(b) encourage good practice in relation to equality and diversity,

---

17 Section 108A TULRCA 1992.
18 See s. 21 Trade Union Act 2016.
19 Section 6(1) Data Protection Act 1998.

(c)   promote equality of opportunity,

(d)   promote awareness and understanding of rights under the Equality Act 2010,

(e)   enforce the equality enactments,

(f)   work towards the elimination of unlawful discrimination, and

(g)   work towards the elimination of unlawful harassment.

It must also monitor the effectiveness of equality and human rights legislation and report on progress made every three years.[20] As part of its general powers, the EHRC can provide advice and information, produce codes of practice, conduct inquiries, carry out investigations and issue unlawful act notices.[21]

The EHRC website is located at: www.equalityhumanrights.com.

1.10 Other useful websites

Some sites are useful because they provide good links to other legal sites, such as:

University of Kent	www.kent.ac.uk/lawlinks
Industrial Law Society	www.industriallawsociety.org.uk

Other useful sites include:

Business Europe	www.businesseurope.eu
Cabinet Office	www.cabinetoffice.gov.uk
Chartered Institute of Personnel and Development	www.cipd.co.uk
Confederation of British Industry	www.cbi.org www.etuc.org.uk
Emplaw Online	www.emplaw.co.uk
Employers Forum on Age	www.efa.org.uk
European Foundation for the Improvement of Living and Working Conditions	www.eurofound.europa.eu
European Trade Union Confederation	www.etuc.org
European Trade Union Institute	www.etui.org
Federation of Small Businesses	www.fsb.org.uk
Health and Safety Executive	www.hse.gov.uk
Incomes Data Services	www.incomesdata.co.uk
International Labour Organization	www.ilo.org
Labour Research Department	www.lrd.org.uk
Low Pay Commission	www.lowpay.gov.uk
National Statistics	www.statistics.gov.uk
Trades Union Congress	www.tuc.org.uk
UK Official Documents	www.official-documents.gov.uk
Unison	www.unison.org.uk
XpertHR	www.xperthr.co.uk

---

20 Sections 11–12 Equality Act 2006.
21 Sections 13–16, 20–21 Equality Act 2006.

Further reading

Davies, A. 'Judicial Self-Restraint in Labour Law' (2009) 38(3) *Industrial Law Journal* 278.

Hepple, B. 'Back to the Future: Employment Law under the Coalition Government' (2013) 42(3) *Industrial Law Journal* 203.

Tucker, E. 'Renorming Labour Law: Can We Escape Labour Law's Recurring Regulatory Dilemmas?' (2010) 39(2) *Industrial Law Journal* 99.

Chapter 2

The employment relationship

Chapter Contents

2.1 Introduction

A purely contractual approach to the employment relationship is unsatisfactory because it suggests that there are two equal parties agreeing the terms of a contract. The contractual approach was adopted by the courts in the 1870s, but it is still, in reality, an unequal relationship.[1] One party uses the labour or talents of another in return for providing remuneration. The payment of that remuneration, except in unusual circumstances, creates a labour force which is dependent upon the employer's goodwill and desire to continue with that relationship. It may be made less one-sided by statutes which limit the freedom of employers to take action against workers and may be made more equal by collective bargaining arrangements between employers and trade unions. In 1897 the Webbs wrote that:

> Individual bargaining between the owner of the means of subsistence and the seller of so perishable a commodity as a day's labour must be, once and for all, abandoned. In its place, if there is to be any genuine freedom of contract, we shall see the conditions of employment adjusted between equally expert negotiators acting for corporations reasonably comparable in strength.[2]

This was a call for effective collective bargaining with trade unions being able to negotiate with employers as equals.

Otto Kahn-Freund[3] described contracts of employment as concealing the realities of subordination behind the conceptual screen of contracts concluded between equals. The reality, he concluded, was that such contracts were between institutions and individuals. Freedom of contract is seen as a voluntary act of submission by the individual.[4] Later, Lord Wedderburn suggested that:

> The lawyer's model of a freely bargained individual agreement is misleading. In reality, without collective or statutory intervention, many terms of the 'agreement' are imposed by the more powerful party, the employer, by what Fox has called 'the brute facts of power'.[5]

Despite these limitations, the courts have not allowed the power of the employer to overcome the freedom that the parties have to enter voluntarily into contractual relations. *Nokes v Doncaster Collieries*[6] concerned an individual miner working for Hickleton Main Colliery Ltd who was apparently unaware that the company had been dissolved by a court order and that his contract of employment had been transferred to Doncaster Amalgamated Collieries Ltd. The issue was whether, in the circumstances, the contract automatically transferred to the new employer, even though the employee was ignorant of the change. Lord Atkin stated:

> My Lords, I should have thought that the principle that a man is not to be compelled to serve a master against his will . . . is deep seated in the common law of this country.

The employee needed to have knowledge of the employer's identity and to have given consent to the transfer. Without such knowledge and consent it would not be possible to say that the employee had freely entered into a contractual relationship with the employer.[7]

---

1 See the approach taken by the Supreme Court in *Autoclenz Ltd v Belcher* [2011] IRLR 820.
2 Sidney Webb and Beatrice Webb, *Industrial Democracy* (1897).
3 Professor Otto Kahn-Freund, who died in 1979, was an eminent and influential labour law academic.
4 See Paul Davies and Mark Freedland, *Kahn-Freund's Labour and the Law* (Stevens, 1983).
5 Lord Wedderburn of Charlton, *The Worker and the Law* (Sweet & Maxwell, 1986), Chapter 2.
6 *Nokes v Doncaster Amalgamated Collieries Ltd* [1940] AC 1014 HL.
7 For the statutory approach to employee rights during transfers, see Chapter 10.

Discussion about the importance of the contractual relationship also conceals the complexity and variety of working relationships that now exist. It is misleading to use a model of an employer/worker relationship consisting of a full-time employer and a full-time worker. Apart from the distinction between the employed and the self-employed, which in itself may be at times a difficult one (see below), contractual relationships will include those on part-time contracts, limited-term contracts, zero hours contracts, casual contracts and so on.

The contract of employment is also an unsatisfactory way of describing the employment relationship because it does not reflect the often informal relationship between employers and workers. This informal relationship is reflected, for example, in the number of hours that are worked in the United Kingdom, which are longer than elsewhere in the EU (see Chapter 8). The hours that many people work are often in excess of their contractual obligations and suggest that there is an informal expectation that this amount of work is required. Similarly it is difficult to incorporate quality and quantity of effort into a contract. During peak periods of work, employees may perform at a much more demanding level than in normal periods in order to cope with the extra workload. The contract of employment is not able to describe or incorporate this aspect of the employer/worker relationship.

2.2 Parties to the contract – employers

2.2.1 Employers' associations

Employers' associations are potentially important in their role as:

1. A representative of a particular industrial or commercial sector, such as the Engineering Employers' Federation, or as a representative of a particular type of employer, such as the Federation of Small Businesses, or as representatives of different employers working with common interests, such as the Business Services Association.[8]
2. A social partner, when they might be consulted by government on proposed policies or legislation. They may also have an international role and be able to influence EU decisions. One example of this is the Confederation of British Industry (CBI) which is a member of BusinessEurope, the European private employers' organisation, which is, in turn, a member of the Social Dialogue Committee in the EU.
3. A negotiator with trade unions on behalf of the members that they represent. It is perhaps less common than previously, with the decline in union membership, to have industry- or sector-wide agreements on pay and conditions. They are more common in the public sector than the private one. Where they exist they may regulate the pay and conditions of large numbers of employees, such as in the education or health service sectors. There is also a likelihood that such agreements will be incorporated into individuals' contracts of employment.[9]

Part II TULRCA 1992 is concerned with the regulation of employers' associations. They are defined as temporary or permanent organisations which consist mainly or wholly of either employers or individual owners of undertakings; or consist of constituent bodies or affiliated organisations, which are, in themselves, collections of employers or owners of undertakings; whose principal purposes include the regulation of relations between employers and workers or trade unions.[10] The Certification Officer has an obligation to keep lists of employers' associations and make them

---

8 Representing contracting businesses working in a variety of sectors.
9 See Chapter 10.
10 Section 122(1) TULRCA 1992.

available for public inspection at all reasonable hours, free of charge.[11] It is not mandatory, however, for associations to apply for listing.[12] According to the Certification Officer's annual report for 2016/17, there were 52 listed employers' associations at the end of March 2017.[13]

An employers' association may be either a body corporate or an unincorporated association.[14] If the latter, it will still be capable of making contracts, suing and being sued, as well as being capable of having proceedings brought against it for alleged offences committed by it or on its behalf.[15] As with trade unions (see Chapter 11), the purposes of employers' associations, in so far as they relate to the regulation of relations between employers and workers, are protected from legal actions for restraint of trade.[16]

2.2.2 Identifying the employer

Section 295(1) TULRCA 1992 defines an employer, in relation to an employee, as 'the person by whom the employee is (or, where the employment has ceased, was) employed'. Section 296(2) offers a similar definition in relation to workers.[17] In this case the employer is 'a person for whom one or more workers work, or have worked or normally work or seek to work'. These definitions are repeated elsewhere, such as in s. 54 National Minimum Wage Act 1998.[18] The differences between employees and workers are important and are discussed below.

The employer may be an individual, but is more likely to be a partnership or a business with limited liability. In equity partnerships the individual partners are likely to retain personal responsibility for the actions of the partnership.[19] In a business with limited liability there may be a separation of identity between the management of a company or business and the legal person that is that company or business. Thus, in some situations, management may make decisions affecting an employee, who will then have recourse against the business itself. The contract of employment or statement of particulars of employment will normally identify the employer.[20]

It is possible for the natural or legal person who is the employer to be changed if there is a transfer of the contract of employment. As will be explained in Chapter 10, the Transfer of Undertakings (Protection of Employment) Regulations 2006[21] enable the identity of the employer to be changed in such a manner that the employee will retain continuity of employment.[22] Unlike the case of *Nokes v Doncaster Collieries*[23] (discussed earlier), this may happen, in situations protected by these Regulations, even without the employee's knowledge.[24]

---

11 Section 123(1) and (2) TULRCA 1992; for information about the Certification Officer, see Chapter 1.

12 The processes for applying to have a name entered on the list, removing it from the list and appealing against the Certification Officer's decisions are contained in ss 124–126 TULRCA 1992.

13 See www.gov.uk/government/publications/annual-report-of-the-certification-officer-2016-2017.

14 Section 127(1) TULRCA 1992.

15 Section 127(2) TULRCA 1992. See *Barry Print v (1) The Showmen's Guild of Great Britain; (2) Bob Wilson & Sons (Leisure) Ltd*, unreported, 27 October 1999, where an unincorporated association was held to be without legal personality, save for s. 127(2) TULRCA 1992.

16 Section 128 TULRCA 1992; issues related to the property of and to the administration of employers' associations are contained in ss 129–134 TULRCA 1992.

17 See also s. 230(4) ERA 1996.

18 See Chapter 8.

19 On the status of partners see *Bates Van Winkelhof v Clyde & Co. LLP* [2014] IRLR 641.

20 Section 1(3)(a) ERA 1996.

21 SI 2006/246.

22 See also s. 218 ERA 1996 in relation to continuity of employment in certain changes of employer; discussed further below.

23 [1940] AC 1014 HL.

24 See *Secretary of State for Trade and Industry v Cook* [1997] IRLR 151 CA, which overturned a previous decision in *Photostatic Copiers (Southern) Ltd v Okuda* [1995] IRLR 12, and confirmed that such knowledge was not an essential prerequisite.

2.2.3 Employers as employees

The separation of the identity of management and the owners of an undertaking has some consequences for employees. The courts are reluctant to lift the veil of incorporation to look into the reality of that which lies behind it. In *Lee v Lee's Air Farming Ltd*[25] the controlling shareholder was also the company's sole employee. The court decided that:

> There appears no greater difficulty in holding that a man acting in one capacity can give orders to himself acting in another capacity than there is in holding that a man acting in one capacity can make a contract with himself in another capacity. The company and the deceased[26] were separate legal entities.

Thus it is possible for a controlling shareholder to be an employee of the same organisation. The Court of Appeal considered such a situation in *Secretary of State v Bottrill*[27] where an individual was appointed managing director of a company and, temporarily at least, held all the share capital. At the same time the individual signed a contract of employment which set out the duties of the post, the hours to be worked, holiday and sickness entitlement and details of remuneration. The issue was whether such a person was really an employee. The court did not accept a previous EAT decision which had concluded that a 50 per cent shareholder,[28] who was also a director, was not an employee. The EAT had concluded that a controlling shareholder could not be an employee because such a person would be able to control decisions that affected his or her own dismissal and remuneration and that there was a difference between an individual running a business through the device of a limited liability company and an individual working for a company subject to the control of a board of directors. The EAT stated that, in the context of employment protection legislation, *Lee's Air Farming* could not be relied upon to support the proposition that a shareholder with full and unrestricted control over a company could also be employed under a contract of service. The Court of Appeal, however, stated that all the factors that indicated an employer/employee relationship, or otherwise, needed to be examined. The fact that the person was a controlling shareholder was only one of those factors, albeit a potentially decisive one. Other factors to be considered were whether there was a genuine contract between the shareholder and the company, the reasons for the contract coming into existence and what each party actually did in carrying out their contractual obligations. The issue of control was important in deciding whether there was a genuine employment relationship: for example, were there other directors and to what extent did the employee become involved in decisions affecting them as employees?[29] More recently, in *Secretary of State v Neufeld*[30] the Court of Appeal thought that there was no reason why a shareholder and director cannot also be an employee. It does not matter that the shareholding provides total control of the company. Finally, in *Clark v Clark Construction Ltd*[31] the EAT identified three sets of circumstances

---

25 [1961] AC 12.

26 The applicant was the widow of the controlling shareholder and sole employee.

27 *Secretary of State for Trade and Industry v Bottrill* [1999] IRLR 326 CA.

28 *Buchan v Secretary of State for Employment* [1997] IRLR 80; the Court of Appeal preferred the decision of the Court of Session in *Fleming v Secretary of State for Trade and Industry* [1997] IRLR 682 where the court concluded that whether a person was an employee or not was a matter of fact and all the relevant circumstances needed to be looked at, rather than adopting a general rule of law.

29 See also *Sellars Arenascene Ltd v Connolly* [2001] IRLR 222 CA which also considered the position of a controlling shareholder of a business that had been taken over. The court held that the tribunal had placed too much reliance upon the individual's interest as a shareholder rather than as an employee. The fact that he would gain if the company prospered applied to employees as well as shareholders.

30 *Secretary of State for Business, Enterprise and Regulatory Reform v Neufeld* [2009] IRLR 475. In *Department of Employment and Learning v Morgan* [2016] IRLR 350 the Northern Ireland Court of Appeal held that an employee director who received a dividend as an alternative to remuneration for services rendered could be an employee.

31 [2008] IRLR 364.

where it might be legitimate not to give effect to what is alleged to be a binding contract of employment between a controlling shareholder and a company. First, where the company is itself a sham. Second, where the contract was entered into for some ulterior purpose – for example, to secure a payment from the Secretary of State. Third, where the parties do not in fact conduct their relationship in accordance with the contract.

2.2.4 Associated, superior and principal employers

One of the concerns of employment protection legislation is to ensure that, when necessary, two or more associated employers are treated as if they were one. This is especially important where there are exemptions for small employers, such as in the requirements for statutory recognition of trade unions.[32]

Section 297 TULRCA 1992 and s. 231 ERA 1996 define any two employers as associated if one is a company of which the other has, directly or indirectly, control or if both are companies of which a third person, either directly or indirectly, has control. This is a convenient definition when adding up numbers of employees to decide whether an employer or a group of employers crosses a threshold. However, it is important not to assume that groups of associated employers are to be treated as one employer for employment protection purposes in all situations. Each employer retains its distinct legal personality. In *Allen v Amalgamated Construction*,[33] for example, the Court of Justice held that a relevant transfer[34] of employees took place between two companies, who were distinct legal entities but who were part of the same group and would probably, under the statutory definitions, be treated as associated employers.

A superior employer, according to s. 48 National Minimum Wage Act 1998, is deemed to be the joint employer, with the immediate employer, of the worker concerned. This occurs where the immediate employer of a worker is in the employment of some other person and the worker is employed on the premises of that other person. This is a definition that seems to be aimed at stopping workers being sub-contracted to other workers so that the superior employer is liable for ensuring that the national minimum wage is paid.

Section 41 Equality Act 2010 makes it unlawful for a principal to discriminate against, harass or victimise a contract worker because of a protected characteristic. For these purposes a principal is defined as

> a person who makes work available for an individual who is – (a) employed by another person, and (b) supplied by that other person in furtherance of a contract to which the principal is a party (whether or not another person is a party to it).

Abbey Life Assurance Co Ltd v Tansell[35] involved a computer contractor who hired himself out via a company he had established for that purpose. He was placed as a contractor by an agency, so that there were two organisations between him and the ultimate hirer. The Court of Appeal held that the ultimate hirer was still the principal for the purposes of the Disability Discrimination Act 1995, as Parliament had probably intended that it should be the ultimate hirer who should be liable rather than the agency.

---

32 See Sch. A1 Part I, para. 7 TULRCA 1992 and Chapter 12.
33 Case C-234/98 GC *Allen v Amalgamated Construction Co Ltd* [2000] IRLR 119 CJEU; see also *Michael Peters Ltd v* (1) *Farnfield*; (2) *Michael Peters Group plc* [1995] IRLR 190 where the Group chief executive failed to persuade the EAT that the chief executive's post transferred with a number of subsidiaries to the transferee employer.
34 In relation to the transfer of undertakings, see Chapter 10.
35 [2000] IRLR 387 CA.

2.3 Parties to the contract – employees

2.3.1 Dependent labour

One of the features of employment law in the United Kingdom is the distinction between employees and workers. The latter tends to have a wider meaning. Section 230(1) ERA 1996 defines an employee as 'an individual who has entered into or works under (or, where the employment has ceased, worked under) a contract of employment'. Section 230(2) defines a contract of employment, for the purposes of the Act, as meaning 'a contract of service or apprenticeship, whether express or implied, and (if it is express) whether oral or in writing'. The meaning of worker can be the same, but it can also have a wider meaning, i.e. an individual who has entered into, or works under, a contract of employment or

> any other contract, whether express or implied and (if it is express) whether oral or in writing, whereby the individual undertakes to do or perform personally any work or services for another party to the contract whose status is not by virtue of the contract that of a client or customer of any profession or business undertaking carried on by the individual.[36]

Thus there are some individuals who will not have a contract of employment with a particular employer but are under a contract to perform personally any work or services. Often they will be treated as self-employed, which means, for example, that they would not receive the benefits of employment protection measures applicable to employees. Nevertheless, these workers may be as dependent on one employer as employees are.

In *Byrne Brothers (Formwork) Ltd v Baird*[37] the EAT held that the intention[38] was to create an intermediate class of protected worker who, on the one hand, is not an employee and, on the other hand, cannot be regarded as carrying on a business. In this case the EAT concluded that self-employed sub-contractors in the construction industry fitted into this category. The court stated:

> There can be no general rule, and we should not be understood as propounding one; cases cannot be decided by applying labels. But typically labour-only sub-contractors will, though nominally free to move from contractor to contractor, in practice work for long periods for a single employer as an integrated part of his workforce.

Not all the self-employed are people engaged in business on their own account and one way of distinguishing between the two is to ask what is the dominant purpose of the contract.[39] Is the contract to be located in the employment field or is it in reality a contract between two independent businesses? In *Inland Revenue v Post Office Ltd*[40] the EAT decided that sub-postmistresses and sub-postmasters were not workers for the purposes of the National Minimum Wage Act 1998 because they had a choice whether or not to personally perform the work.

The numbers of self-employed workers has grown significantly in the past 20 years and, in 2016, amounted to approximately 4.69 million people or 15 per cent of the workforce.[41] For some workers, self-employment is an illusion. They will be dependent upon one employer for their

---

36 Section 230(3) ERA 1996. In *Hospital Medical Group v Westwood* [2012] IRLR 834 the Court of Appeal held that the individual was a worker even though he was in business on his own account.

37 [2002] IRLR 96.

38 This case involved the definition of worker in reg. 2(1) of the Working Time Regulations 1998, which is identical to that contained in s. 230(3) ERA 1996.

39 See *James v Redcats (Brands) Ltd* [2007] IRLR 296.

40 [2003] IRLR 199. See also *Community Dental Centre v Sultan Damon* [2011] IRLR 124.

41 Information supplied by the Office for National Statistics; see www.ons.gov.uk.

supply of work and income, but may be lacking in certain employment rights because of their self-employed status. One study of freelancers in the publishing industry, for example, concluded that:

> Freelancers in publishing are essentially casualised employees, rather than independent self-employed . . . in objective terms they are disguised wage labour.[42]

Thus there is a real difficulty in distinguishing between those who are genuine employees and those who are self-employed, especially if they have the same dependence on one employer as do employees. To some extent this is recognised by the government when certain employment protection measures are applied to workers and others to employees only. The Working Time Regulations 1998,[43] for example, refer, in reg. 4(1), to a 'worker's working time', whilst the Maternity and Parental Leave etc. Regulations 1999 apply only to employees.[44] For the purposes of EU law, any person who was in an employment relationship, the essential features of which were that for a certain period of time they performed services for and under the direction of another person in return for remuneration, was a 'worker' if they pursued activities that were real and genuine and not on such a small scale as to be marginal and ancillary.[45]

2.3.2 The distinction between the employed and the self-employed

There are a number of reasons why it is important to establish whether an individual is an employee or self-employed:

1. Some employment protection measures are reserved for employees, although there are some which use the wider definition of worker, including the National Minimum Wage Act 1998 and the Working Time Regulations 1998. An example of protection being offered only to employees is contained in *Costain Building & Civil Engineering Ltd v Smith*,[46] where a self-employed contractor was appointed by the trade union as a safety representative on a particular site. The individual had been placed as a temporary worker with the company through an employment agency. After a number of critical reports on health and safety he was dismissed by the agency at the request of the company. He complained that he had been dismissed, contrary to s. 100(1)(b) ERA 1996, for performing the duties of a health and safety representative. In the course of the proceedings he failed to show that he was other than self-employed. This proved fatal to the complaint, as the relevant regulations only allowed trade unions to appoint safety representatives from amongst its members who were employees.[47] The EAT concluded that there was no contract of employment between the agency and the individual so he did not come within the protection offered to trade union health and safety representatives.

2. Self-employed persons are taxed on a Schedule D basis, rather than Schedule E which applies to employed earners. This allows the self-employed person to set off business expenses against income for tax purposes. A good example of the effect of this was shown in *Hall v Lorimer*.[48]

---

42 Celia Stanworth and John Stanworth, 'The Self Employed without Employees – Autonomous or Atypical?' (1995) 26(3) *Industrial Relations Journal* 221–229.

43 SI 1998/1833.

44 SI 1999/3312. See reg. 13(1) where employees with one year's continuous service, and responsibility for a child, are entitled to parental leave.

45 *Genc v Land Berlin* [2010] ICR 1108.

46 [2000] ICR 215. See also *Smith v Carillion Ltd* [2015] IRLR 467.

47 Regulation 3(1) Safety Representatives and Safety Committees Regulations 1977, SI 1977/500; employee is defined by reference to s. 53(1) HASAWA 1974, which defines employee as a person who works under a contract of employment.

48 *Hall (HM Inspector of Taxes) v Lorimer* [1994] IRLR 171 CA.

Mr Lorimer had been employed as a vision mixer working on the production of television programmes. He decided to become freelance and built up a circle of contacts. He worked on his own and was used by a large number of companies for a short period each. He worked on their premises and used their equipment. The Inland Revenue (now Her Majesty's Revenue and Customs) had assessed his income as being earned under a series of individual contracts of service and thus chargeable to Schedule E income tax. He claimed that he was self-employed and should have been taxed under Schedule D. It was important to him financially. In his first year his gross earnings were £32,875 and he had expenses of £9,250. If assessed under Schedule E, he would need to pay tax on the gross amount. If assessed under Schedule D, he would be able to offset his expenses and only be liable for tax on £23,625. In the event Mr Lorimer was successful and the Court of Appeal held that he was self-employed.

3. Employers are vicariously liable for the actions of their employees and normally not for independent contractors. Lord Thankerton summed up the test for vicarious liability at that time:

> It is clear that the master is responsible for acts actually authorised by him; for liability would exist in this case even if the relation between the parties was merely one of agency, and not one of service at all. But a master, as opposed to the employer of an independent contractor, is liable even for acts which he has not authorised, provided they are so connected with acts which he has authorised that they may rightly be regarded as modes – although improper modes – of doing them.[49]

This liability of the employer has been extended so that it continues even for acts of intentional wrongdoing which the employer could not have approved. Thus the employer of a house warden who sexually abused boarders at a school for maladjusted and vulnerable boys was held to be vicariously liable for the actions of the employee.[50] The Supreme Court held that the correct test for deciding whether an employee's wrongful act had been committed during the course of employment, so as to make the employer vicariously liable, is to examine the relative closeness of the connection between the nature of the employment and the employee's wrongdoing. In this case the employee's position as warden and the close contact with the boys that this entailed created a sufficiently close connection between the acts of abuse and the work which he had been employed to carry out.[51] Applying this test, the Court of Appeal has ruled that a club owner was vicariously liable for an act of violence committed by a security guard away from the club premises.[52] The Supreme Court subsequently stated that there is no relevant distinction between performing an act in an improper manner and performing it for an improper purpose or by improper means. Thus the mere fact that employees were acting dishonestly or for their own benefit is likely to be insufficient to show that they were not acting in the course of employment.[53]

More recently, the Court of Appeal has confirmed that the question is whether the torts are so closely connected with the employment that it would be fair and just to hold the employers vicariously liable. The sufficiency of the connection may be gauged by asking whether the wrongful act may be seen as a way of carrying out the work which the employer has authorised.

---

49 *Canadian Pacific Railway Co v Lockhart* [1942] AC 591 at p. 599 PC. See now Various Claimants v Barclays Bank [2017] IRLR 124.

50 *Lister v Hesley Hall Ltd* [2001] IRLR 472 HL.

51 See also *Balfron Trustees Ltd v Peterson* [2001] IRLR 758 where an employee of a firm of solicitors acted dishonestly; the crucial factor, according to the High Court, relying on *Lister*, was whether the employer owed some form of duty or responsibility towards the victim; if the answer was yes, then the employer cannot avoid liability because the duty or responsibility was delegated to an employee who failed to follow the employer's instructions.

52 *Mattis v Pollock* [2003] IRLR 603.

53 *Dubai Aluminium v Salaam* [2003] IRLR 608.

Importantly, the court acknowledged that the possibility of friction is inherent in any employment relationship and particularly in a factory when an instant instruction and quick reactions are required. Frustrations which lead to some violence in response are predictable and, in this case, an individual who had used moderate force in a spontaneous but deliberate reaction to a lawful instruction was acting in the course of employment.[54]

Historically, the doctrine of vicarious liability applied to employees, but not to the self-employed. However, a Supreme Court decision in 2016 means that employers will be liable for the tortious acts of non-employees in a wider range of circumstances:

> a relationship other than one of employment is in principle capable of giving rise to vicarious liability where harm is wrongfully done by an individual who carries on activities as an integral part of the business activities carried on by the defendant and for its benefit . . . and where the commission of the wrongful act is a risk created by the defendant by assigning those activities to the individual in question.[55]

In determining whether an employer is vicariously liable, the courts will focus on two questions. First, what functions or 'field of activities' have been entrusted to the person who was negligent? Second, was there a sufficient connection between the nature of the job and the wrongful conduct to make it right for the employer to be held liable under the principle of social justice? Thus, actions which are prohibited and unauthorised by the employer can still give rise to vicarious liability; for example, an assault by worker on a member of the public.[56]

4. The employer will also owe a duty of care to employees. This was demonstrated in *Lane v Shire Roofing*[57] where the claimant was held to be an employee (see below) rather than a self-employed contractor. As a result of this, damages in excess of £100,000 were awarded after a work-related accident which would not have been awarded if the claimant had been carrying out work as an independent contractor.[58] In *Waters v Commissioner of Police of the Metropolis*[59] a police constable complained that the Commissioner of Police had acted negligently in failing to deal with her complaint of sexual assault by a colleague and the harassment and victimisation that followed. The Supreme Court held that:

> If an employer knows that acts being done by employees during their employment may cause physical or mental harm to a particular fellow employee and he does nothing to supervise or prevent such acts, when it is in his power to do so, it is clearly arguable that he may be in breach of his duty to that employee. It seems that he may also be in breach of that duty if he can foresee that such acts will happen . . .

Thus the employer owes a duty of care to employees who may be at physical or mental risk or for whom it is reasonably foreseeable that there may be some such harm (see 3.4.3 in Chapter 3).[60]

---

54 *Weddall v Barchester Healthcare* [2012] IRLR 307.

55 *Cox v Ministry of Justice* [2016] IRLR 370.

56 *Mohamud v Morrison Supermarkets* [2016] IRLR 362. *See also Bellman v Northampton Recruitment Ltd* [2017] IRLR 194.

57 *Lane v Shire Roofing Co (Oxford) Ltd* [1995] IRLR 493 CA.

58 See also *Makepeace v Evans Brothers (Reading)* [2001] ICR 241 CA where a main site contractor was held not to have a duty of care to a contractor's employee who injured himself using equipment supplied by the main site contractor; responsibility rested with the employer alone.

59 [2000] IRLR 720 HL.

60 See *Wigan Borough Council v Davies* [1979] IRLR 127 on bullying and harassment by fellow employees.

2.4 Identifying the employee

The common law has developed a number of tests for distinguishing those who have a contract of employment from those who are self-employed. It is important not to see these tests as mutually exclusive, but rather developments in the law as a result of the courts being faced with an increasingly complex workplace and a greater variety of work situations.

2.4.1 The control test

An early test developed by the courts was the control test. In *Walker v Crystal Palace*[61] a professional footballer was held to have a contract of service with the club. He was paid £3 10s (£3.50) per week for a year's contract, in which he was expected to provide his playing services exclusively to the club. He was under the club's direction during training and was also expected to be available for matches. The club maintained that he did not have a contract of service because, it asserted, it was essential that in such a relationship the master should have the power to direct how work should be done. In *Yewens v Noakes*, Bramwell J had defined a servant as:[62]

> a person subject to the command of his master as to the manner in which he shall do his work.

It was argued that this definition could not be applied to professional footballers who were hired to display their talents and skills. The control of the club is limited to deciding whether the player is picked for the team or not. Farewell J dismissed this plea on the basis that many workmen displayed their own initiative, like footballers, but were still bound by the directions of their master. In this case the player had agreed to follow detailed training instructions and to obey his captain's instructions on the field:

> I cannot doubt that he is bound to obey any directions which the captain, as the delegate of the club, may give him during the course of the game – that is to say, any direction that is within the terms of his employment as a football player.[63]

The problem with this test for distinguishing the employed from the self-employed is that it is limited in its application. Employers, subject to statutory and common law restraints, are able to exercise considerable control over employees. This was recognised in *Market Investigations*[64] where the issue was whether a market researcher was employed under a contract of service (see below).

This test recognises the reality of many employment relationships and the level of control may still be a factor in deciding whether a person is working under a contract of employment or a contract for services. In *Lane v Shire Roofing Company* the Court of Appeal acknowledged this:[65]

> First, the element of control will be important; who lays down what is to be done, the way in which it is to be done, the means by which it is to be done, and the time when it is to be done? Who provides (i.e. hires and fires) the team by which it is to be done, and who provides the material, plant and machinery and tools used?

Although the concept of control is only one of a number of factors which might influence the final decision as to whether a person is an employee or not, it can still be crucial. In *Clifford v UDM*[66] the

---

61 *Walker v The Crystal Palace Football Club Ltd* [1910] 1 KB 87.
62 [1880] 6 QB 530 at p. 532.
63 *Walker v The Crystal Palace Football Club Ltd* [1910] 1 KB 87 at p. 93.
64 *Market Investigations Ltd v Minister of Social Security* [1968] 3 All ER 732.
65 [1995] IRLR 493 at p. 495.
66 *Clifford v Union of Democratic Mineworkers* [1991] IRLR 518 CA.

Court of Appeal approved the approach of an employment tribunal in deciding that in situations that lack clarity, control may be an important factor. The control need not be exercised directly. *Motorola Ltd v Davidson*[67] concerned an individual who was engaged by an agency to work at Motorola's premises. The individual was dismissed by the agency at the request of the company. This level of control, even though exercised via a third party, was sufficient to establish an employment relationship between the company and the individual. More recently, the Court of Appeal has confirmed that the key question is whether the employer has the contractual right to control rather than whether in practice the person has day-to-day control over his or her own work.[68]

2.4.2 The integration test

Early reliance on the control test alone proved inadequate, especially when considering more complex employment relationships. These relationships arise when there are highly skilled individuals carrying out work which, except in the most general sense, cannot be subject to any close control by an employer. Such examples might be a ship's captain[69] or the medical staff in a hospital, as in *Cassidy v Ministry of Health*.[70]

It is not entirely clear when a person is integrated into an organisation and when they are not. It was stated in *Stevenson, Jordan & Harrison v McDonald and Evans*[71] that:

> One feature that seems to run through the instances is that, under a contract of service, a man is employed as part of the business, and his work is done as an integral part of the business; whereas, under a contract for services, his work, although done for the business, is not integrated into it but is only accessory to it.

If an individual is integrated into the organisational structure, he or she is more likely to be an employee. The less the integration, the more likely the person is to be self-employed. In *Beloff v Pressdram Ltd*[72] Lord Widgery CJ approved Denning LJ's statement in *Stevenson, Jordan & Harrison*[73] and stated:

> The test which emerges from the authorities seems to me, as Denning LJ said, whether on the one hand the employee is employed as part of the business and his work is an integral part of the business, or whether his work is not integrated into the business but is only accessory to it, or, as Cooke J expressed it, the work is done by him in business on his own account.

It is difficult to anticipate where the dividing line may be drawn: for example, what of the dependent contractor? If a person is self-employed, but works continuously for one organisation, are they to be treated as integrated into the organisation or not? Much work is now outsourced. To what extent, for example, is the catering assistant who works for an outsourced company to be treated as an integrated part of the organisation in which he or she is located?

The integration test seemed to be an attempt to cope with the difficulties posed by the growth of technical and skilled work which may not be the subject of close control by an employer. Although

---

67 *Motorola Ltd v (1) Davidson; (2) Melville Craig Group Ltd* [2001] IRLR 4.
68 *White v Troutbeck SA* [2013] IRLR 949. On the need for subordination, see *Halawi v World Duty Free* [2015] IRLR 50 and *Windle v Secretary of State for Justice* [2016] IRLR 628.
69 See *Gold v Essex County Council* [1942] 2 KB 293.
70 [1951] 2 KB 343 CA.
71 [1952] 1 TLR 101, per Denning LJ.
72 [1973] 1 All ER 241.
73 [1952] 1 TLR 101.

it may be used as an indicator of a person under a contract of service, it cannot be conclusive. Indeed, the problem with this test and the control test is that they do not sufficiently distinguish between the employed and the self-employed. It is arguable that it is possible for workers without a contract of employment to be closely integrated into an organisation and closely controlled by that organisation.[74] To some extent this was recognised by the Court of Appeal in *Franks v Reuters Ltd*.[75] In this case it was held that a person who had worked for Reuters on a full-time permanent basis for more than four years on an assignment from an employment agency could be an employee of Reuters.

2.4.3 The economic reality test

This test was considered in *Market Investigations Ltd v Minister of Social Security*,[76] where the court considered not only the amount of control exercised over a part-time worker but also the question whether she was in business on her own account. The case concerned a market researcher who was employed to carry out specific time-limited assignments. The issue was whether she was employed under a contract of service or a contract for services. The court cited the case of *Ready Mixed Concrete*[77] in which MacKenna J stated that a contract of service existed if three conditions were fulfilled. These were:

1. whether the servant agreed that they would provide their own work and skill in return for a wage or other remuneration;
2. the individual agreed, expressly or impliedly, to be subject to the control of the master; and
3. that the other provisions of the contract were consistent with a contract of service.

In *Market Investigations* the court held that further tests were needed to decide whether the contract as a whole was consistent or inconsistent with there being a contract of service. The company argued that the researcher performed a series of contracts and that a master and servant relationship was normally continuous. This view was rejected by the court which doubted

> whether this factor can be treated in isolation. It must, I think, be considered in connection with the more general question whether Mrs Irving could be said to be in business on her own account as an interviewer.

It was concluded that she was employed by the company under a series of contracts of service. She was not in business on her own account, even though she could work for other employers (although she did not). She did not provide her own tools or risk her own capital, nor did her opportunity to profit depend in any significant degree on the way she managed her work. More recently, in a similar context the EAT confirmed that mutuality of obligation can arise in the course of individual assignments and the fact that a contract is terminable at will is not determinative of whether it is a contract of employment.[78]

This test of economic reality, i.e. looking at the contract as a whole to decide whether the individual was in business on his own account, was an important development in distinguishing between those under a contract of service and others. The element of control is still important, but there is a need to take into account the other factors that make up the contract of employment. Where there is ambiguity, it may be relevant to know whether the parties to the contract have labelled it a contract for services or a contract of service (see below on 'sham' relationships). There is, as Cooke J pointed

---

74 See *Smith v Carillion Ltd* [2015] IRLR 169 CA.
75 [2003] IRLR 423.
76 [1968] 3 All ER 732.
77 *Ready Mixed Concrete (South East) Ltd v Minister of Pensions and National Insurance* [1968] 2 QB 497.
78 *Drake v IPSOS Mori* [2012] IRLR 973.

out in *Market Investigations*, no exhaustive list of factors which can be taken into account in determining the relationship. More importantly, this test recognises the fact that the parties to the contract are independent individuals. The employee is not necessarily seen as merely someone under the control of another.

Thus a person who works for a number of different employers may be seen as an employee[79] or a self-employed contractor.[80] The economic reality test builds upon the control and integration tests and will view such matters as investment in the business or the economic risk taken as important considerations. Thus in *Quashie v Stringfellow Restaurants Ltd*[81] the employment tribunal inferred that the employer was under no obligation at all to pay a dancer. In reversing the EAT decision based on the level of control, the Court of Appeal ruled that the fact that the dancer took the economic risk was a powerful pointer against a contract of employment.

2.4.4 The multiple factor test

This test is a further recognition that there is no one factor that can establish whether a contract of service exists. In different situations, the various factors can assume greater or lesser importance. It is really a test that *Ready Mixed Concrete*[82] and *O'Kelly*[83] tried to come to terms with. In the first case, the court identified five factors which were inconsistent with there being a contract of service. In *O'Kelly* the court identified 17 possible factors which might influence the decision. More recently, the important factors appear to be that of personal performance and mutuality of obligation (see below). MacKenna J[84] illustrated the complexity of the decision:

> An obligation to do work subject to the other party's control is a necessary, though not always a sufficient, condition of a contract of service. If the provisions of the contract as a whole are inconsistent with it being a contract of service, it will be some other kind of contract, and the person doing the work will not be a servant. The judge's task is to classify the contract . . . he may, in performing it, take into account other matters than control.

The problem with this approach, which may be insoluble without a more precise statutory definition, is that it can lead to inconsistencies. It is employment tribunals that will decide what weight is to be given to specific factors in particular circumstances. It is not always clear whether such a decision is a question of fact or of law, which, in turn, affects the appeal court's opportunities to intervene in tribunal decisions to create uniformity of approach (see below).

2.4.5 Mutuality of obligation

One important factor the courts have examined in order to decide whether a contract of service exists or not is that of mutuality of obligation between employer and individual. In *O'Kelly v Trust House Forte plc*[85] a number of 'regular casual' staff made a claim for unfair dismissal. In order to make this claim they needed to show that they were working under a contract of service. The tribunal had identified a number of factors which were consistent, or not inconsistent, with the existence of a contract of employment. These included performing the work under the direction and control of

---

79 See *Lee v Chung and Shun Shing Construction & Engineering Co Ltd* [1990] IRLR 236.
80 See *Hall (HM Inspector of Taxes) v Lorimer* [1994] IRLR 171 CA.
81 [2013] IRLR 99.
82 *Ready Mixed Concrete (South East) Ltd v Minister of Pensions and National Insurance* [1968] 2 QB 497.
83 *O'Kelly v Trust House Forte plc* [1983] IRLR 369 CA.
84 *Ready Mixed Concrete (South East) Ltd v Minister of Pensions and National Insurance* [1968] 2 QB 497 at p. 517.
85 [1983] IRLR 369.

the appellants and, when they attended at functions, 'they were part of the appellants' organisation and for the purpose of ensuring the smooth running of the business they were represented in the staff consultation process'. These elements of control and integration were, however, not enough. One of the factors on which the tribunal had placed 'considerable weight' was a lack of mutuality of obligation between the two parties. The employer was under no obligation to provide work and the individuals were under no obligation to perform it.

In Carmichael[86] the Supreme Court approved the conclusion of an employment tribunal, which had held that the applicant's case 'founders on the rock of the absence of mutuality'. The case was about whether two tour guides were employees under contracts of employment and therefore entitled under s. 1 ERA 1996 to a written statement of particulars of the terms of their employment. The Supreme Court accepted that they worked on a casual 'as and when required' basis. An important issue was that there was no requirement for the employer to provide work and for the individual to carry out that work. Indeed, the court heard that there were a number of occasions when the applicants had declined offers of work. Thus there was an 'irreducible minimum of mutual obligation' that was necessary to create a contract of service. There needed to be an obligation to provide work and an obligation to perform it in return for a wage or some form of remuneration. Part-time home workers, for example, who had been provided with work and had performed it over a number of years could be held to have created this mutual obligation.[87] The obligation upon the employer is to provide work when it is available, not to provide work consistently. Thus a person who worked as a relief manager and had a contract which stated that there would be times when no work was available and he would not be paid on these occasions was still entitled to be treated as having a contract of employment. There was an obligation upon the employer to provide work when it was available.[88]

When this mutual obligation is absent in either party, then a contract of service, in some extreme cases, will not exist. In Express and Echo Publications Ltd v Tanton[89] the Court of Appeal stated that the test was a contractual one. It was necessary to look at the obligations provided, rather than what actually occurred. In this case an individual's contract enabled them to arrange, at their own expense, for their duties to be performed by another person when they were unable or unwilling to carry out their work. Such a term was incompatible with a contract of service, as it meant that the individual lacked a personal obligation to work in return for the remuneration. The obligation to work personally for another is, according to the EAT in Cotswold Developments,[90] at the heart of the relationship. This approach was somewhat qualified in Byrne Brothers (Formwork) Ltd v Baird,[91] which involved labour-only sub-contractors in the construction industry with a contract that allowed the worker to provide a substitute in limited and exceptional circumstances. This right was not inconsistent with an obligation of personal service. The same approach was applied to gymnasts working for a local authority who were able to provide substitutes for any shift that they were unable to work. The local authority paid the substitutes directly and the gymnasts could only be replaced by others on the council's approved list.[92] More recently, in Pimlico Plumbers Ltd v Smith[93] the Court of Appeal has confirmed that a conditional right to substitute is not necessarily inconsistent with personal performance.

---

86 Carmichael v National Power plc [2000] IRLR 43 HL.
87 Nethermere (St Neots) Ltd v Gardiner [1984] ICR 612 CA; see also Clark v Oxfordshire Health Authority [1998] IRLR 125 CA where the position of a nurse in the staff bank was considered and it was held that there was an absence of mutuality of obligation.
88 Wilson v Circular Distributors Ltd [2006] IRLR 38.
89 [1999] IRLR 367 CA. See also Stevedoring and Haulage Services Ltd v Fuller [2001] IRLR 627 where the documentation expressly provided that the individuals were being engaged on an ad hoc and casual basis with no obligation on the company to offer work and no obligation on the applicants to accept it.
90 Cotswold Developments Construction Ltd v Williams [2006] IRLR 181.
91 [2002] IRLR 96.
92 MacFarlane v Glasgow City Council [2001] IRLR 7.
93 [2017] IRLR 323.

Subsequently, the Court of Appeal stressed that both 'mutuality of obligation' and 'control' are the irreducible minimum legal requirements for the existence of a contract of employment. In *Windle v Secretary of State for Justice*[94] the Court of Appeal has stated that the absence of mutuality of obligation during a period when a person is not required to work may shed light on the character of the relationship when it is performed. The earlier case of *Montgomery v Johnson Underwood Ltd*[95] involved a temporary agency worker who, despite being on a long-term temporary assignment of over two years, wished to show that she was employed by the agency which had placed her. She failed because the court held that there was little or no control or supervision of her by the agency, and thus one of the essential prerequisites was missing.

On the other hand, in *Consistent Group Ltd v Kalwak*[96] the EAT found that there was sufficient mutuality of obligation between the worker and the agency to establish that the workers concerned were employees of the agency. Consistent Group Ltd provided staff from Poland to work in hotels and food processing. The recruits were given contracts headed 'Self-employed sub-contractor's contract for services'. The contracts contained clauses that stated that the sub-contractor was not an employee of the agency and was not entitled to sick pay, holiday pay or pension rights. The sub-contractor was able to work for others provided that the agency did not believe that it would interfere with any work provided by the agency; the sub-contractor agreed to provide services personally and, if he could not, had to inform Consistent and find an approved replacement. The EAT warned that tribunals must be alive to the fact that armies of lawyers will simply place substitution clauses, or clauses denying any obligation to accept or provide work in employment contracts, as a matter of form, even where such terms do not begin to reflect the real relationship.

The reality was that these workers had come from Poland expecting to work for the agency and their accommodation depended upon doing such work. There was no realistic chance of them working elsewhere whilst the agency required their services. Although they were able to provide substitutes rather than do the work personally, this only arose if they were unable to work, not if they did not wish to accept the work.[97] The contract, therefore, bore no relationship to the reality and there was sufficient mutuality of obligation to establish that an employment relationship existed.

Subsequently, the Court of Appeal has ruled that a sham may be found where the parties to a contract have a common intention that the document or one of its provisions is not intended to create the legal rights which they set out, whether or not there is a joint intention to deceive third parties or the court.[98] It has also stated that tribunals have to consider whether the words of a written contract represent the true intentions or expectations of the parties not only at the inception of the contract but, if appropriate, as time passes.[99]

2.5 Question of fact or law

Appeals from an employment tribunal may be based either on a question of law or against a decision that was so unreasonable as to be perverse. This means:

---

94 [2016] IRLR 628

95 [2001] IRLR 269 CA.

96 [2007] IRLR 560. This case was remitted to the employment tribunal by the Court of Appeal: [2008] IRLR 505.

97 This distinction between someone who was unable to work and someone who was unwilling to work was also considered in *James v Redcats (Brands) Ltd* [2007] IRLR 296; if the requirement is to provide a substitute when the individual was unable to work, this does not appear to suggest that there is no obligation to perform the work personally.

98 This was affirmed by the Supreme Court in *Autoclenz Ltd v Belcher* [2011] IRLR 820.

99 *Protectacoat Ltd v Szilagyi* [2009] IRLR 365.

that the primary facts as found by the fact-finding tribunal must stand, but also that the inferences of fact drawn by the tribunal from the primary facts can only be interfered with by an appellate court if they are insupportable on the basis of the primary facts so found.[100]

The reluctance of the appeal courts to interfere unless there is a point of law or a perverse decision may lead to inconsistencies between different employment tribunals. The problem of inconsistencies between the approaches of different employment tribunals was highlighted in O'Kelly[101] where the Court of Appeal stated:

> Without the Employment Appeal Tribunal being entitled to intervene where in its view the employment tribunal has wrongly evaluated the weight of a relevant consideration then it will be open to employment tribunals to reach differing conclusions, so long as they are reasonably maintainable, on essentially the same facts.

In such cases, the court concluded, it is only where the weight given to a particular factor shows a misdirection in law that an appellate court can interfere.

It is not always clear whether an issue is a question of law or a question of fact. In Carmichael,[102] for example, the Court of Appeal had held that the employment tribunal should have decided as a matter of law that an exchange of letters constituted an offer and acceptance which gave rise to a contract of employment in writing. The Supreme Court disagreed[103] and stated that the employment tribunal was entitled to find, as a fact, that the parties did not intend the letters to be the sole record of their agreement. The oral exchanges could also be taken into account. This difference in interpretation allowed the Court of Appeal to reverse the decision of the employment tribunal and the Supreme Court to restore it.

In Lee v Chung[104] the Privy Council had suggested that the decision whether a person was employed under a contract of service or not was often a mixed question of fact and law. It distinguished between those cases where the issue is dependent on the true construction of a written document[105] and those where the issue is dependent upon an investigation of factual circumstances in which the work is performed. This latter situation makes the decision a question of fact in which the appeal courts should not interfere.

This seems to be the approach adopted by the Supreme Court in Carmichael, except that in this case one of the differences with the Court of Appeal rested on whether reliance should be placed on a construction of the written documents (a question of law) or on the factual circumstances surrounding the agreement (a question of fact). One can appreciate that there might be a public policy issue related to allowing appeals on any issue other than a legal one, which might result in increased numbers of appeals. It is difficult, however, to escape the conclusion that the issue is flexible and that if an appeal court feels strongly enough, it will find ways of reviewing an employment tribunal's conclusions.

2.6 The intentions of the parties

What is the effect of the parties to the contract deciding that, for whatever reason, it should be for services, rather than of service? This clearly happens in different occupations, where there is an

---

100 Nethermere (St Neots) Ltd v Gardiner [1984] ICR 612 at p. 631, per Dillon LJ.
101 [1983] IRLR 369.
102 [1998] IRLR 301 CA.
103 [2000] IRLR 43 HL.
104 Lee v Chung and Shun Shing Construction & Engineering Co Ltd [1990] IRLR 236.
105 See Davies v Presbyterian Church of Wales [1986] IRLR 194 HL.

acceptance that individuals are to be treated as self-employed contractors, rather than employees. One study of the construction industry concluded that some 58 per cent of the workforce, excluding local government, was treated as self-employed. This was some 45 per cent of the total workforce. The author concluded that there 'is the strongest indication that self-employment, as an employment status, is an economic fiction'.[106] In *Ferguson v Dawson & Partners*[107] the claimant worked on a building site as a self-employed contractor. He had no express contract of any kind, although the court accepted that implied terms existed. Although the label of self-employment, as agreed by the parties, was a factor to be considered, it could not be decisive if the evidence pointed towards a contract of employment.[108]

In the financial services sector, salespeople are traditionally treated as self-employed, yet they have targets to fulfil and meetings to attend and cannot sell policies from businesses that compete with their employing company. In this industry, as in others, the parties have come to an arrangement based upon a particular employment relationship. In *Massey v Crown Life Assurance*[109] a branch manager with an insurance company changed his employment status from employee to self-employed, although he continued in the same job. Two years later the company terminated the agreement and he brought a complaint of unfair dismissal. He could only make this claim if he was an employee. Lord Denning MR summed up the Court of Appeal's approach:

> If the true relationship of the parties is that of master and servant under a contract of service, the parties cannot alter the truth of that relationship by putting a different label on it . . . On the other hand, if the parties' relationship is ambiguous and is capable of being one or the other, then the parties can remove that ambiguity, by the very agreement itself which they make with one another.[110]

Thus, the parties' views as to their relationship can be important if there is any ambiguity. (On sham relationships see above.)

2.7 Apprentices

Section 230(2) ERA 1996 defines a contract of employment as a contract of service or apprenticeship. The purpose of a contract of apprenticeship is to 'qualify the apprentice for his particular trade or calling'.[111] The execution of work for the employer is secondary.[112] Part 4 of the Enterprise Act 2016 now deals with apprenticeships. It established the Institute for Apprenticeship, introduced a definition of a 'statutory apprenticeship' in England and made it an offence to label any course or training 'an apprenticeship' unless it satisfies the statutory requirements or forms part of an individual's employment.[113]

---

106 Mark Harvey, *Towards the Insecurity Society: The Tax Trap of Self-Employment* (Institute of Employment Rights, 1995).
107 [1976] 1WLR 1213 CA.
108 See also *Young & Woods Ltd v West* [1980] IRLR 201 CA and *Lane v Shire Roofing Company (Oxford) Ltd* [1995] IRLR 493 CA where the courts relied upon the test in *Market Investigations Ltd*, note 64 above, to decide that the applicants in both cases were employees, even though treated as self-employed for tax purposes.
109 [1978] 1 WLR 676 CA.
110 Ibid. at p. 679.
111 *Wiltshire Police Authority v Wynn* [1981] 1 QB 95 CA. Section 25 of the Enterprise Act 2016 introduces a definition of a 'statutory apprenticeship' in England and makes it an offence to label any course or training 'an apprenticeship' unless it satisfies the statutory requirements or forms part of an individual's employment.
112 See *Wallace v CA Roofing Services Ltd* [1996] IRLR 435.
113 Sections 22 and 25 respectively.

Historically, apprenticeships were distinct from an ordinary contract of employment because:

> although a contract of apprenticeship can be brought to an end by some fundamental
> frustrating event or repudiatory act, it is not terminable at will as a contract of employment is
> at common law.[114]

Edmunds v Lawson QC[115] was a case that was of great interest to students wishing to progress to the Bar. It raised the question whether a person who was offered and accepted an unfunded pupillage at a barrister's chambers was under a contract of apprenticeship with the chambers. If this were so, then the consequence would be that the pupil would be entitled to be paid at least the national minimum wage.[116] It was accepted that there was an offer of a pupillage and an acceptance of that offer. The consideration was the claimant's promise to act as a pupil and this was held to be of value not only to the pupil but also to the chambers and the individual pupil masters. The last requirement to establish a contractual relationship was an intention to enter legal relations. The High Court, in the absence of any express provisions, implied this intention from the subject matter of the agreement. There is a distinction between agreements which regulate business relations and those which regulate social arrangements. The former were likely to have legal consequences.[117] An offer, as in this case, to provide professional training, was therefore likely to be a business relationship, thus establishing the necessary intent. The Court of Appeal agreed with the views of the High Court, except that it held that the resulting contract was not a contract of apprenticeship. The pupil could not therefore be treated as a worker for the purposes of the National Minimum Wage Act 1998. Such a relationship would require a mutual obligation on the part of the pupil master to provide training and on the part of the pupil to serve and work for the master and carry out all reasonable instructions. This latter obligation was missing from the relationship.

2.8 Employee shareholders

The Growth and Infrastructure Act 2013 inserted s. 205A into ERA 1996 in order to create the status of employee shareholder. Such persons will receive a minimum of £2,000 paid-up shares in the company but relinquish their general right to claim unfair dismissal,[118] the statutory rights to a redundancy payment and request flexible working,[119] and certain statutory rights in relation to time off for training. In addition, employee shareholders are required to give 16 weeks' notice of their intention to return to work after maternity, adoption or paternity leave.

Section 205A(5) ERA 1996 obliges the company to provide individual employee shareholders with a written statement of particulars which, inter alia, specifies:

(i)   that the employee shareholder will not have the statutory rights described above;
(ii) the notice periods which apply in relation to a return to work after maternity, adoption or paternity leave;
(iii) whether any voting rights are attached to the shares and whether they carry any rights to dividends;

---

114 *Wallace v C A Roofing Services Ltd* [1996] IRLR 435 at p. 436.
115 [2000] IRLR 391 CA.
116 Section 54(2) and (3) National Minimum Wage Act 1998 offers a definition of worker and a contract of employment for the purposes of the Act.
117 For further consideration of this, see *Rose and Frank Company v JR Crompton Brothers Ltd* [1925] AC 445.
118 See s. 205A(9)–(10) ERA 1996.
119 See s. 205A(8) in respect of returning from parental leave.

(iv) whether, if the company were wound up, the employee shares would confer any right to participate in the distribution of assets;

(v) if the company has more than one class of shares, explain how any employee shareholder rights differ from the equivalent rights that attach to the shares in the largest class;

(vi) whether the employee shares are redeemable and, if so, at whose option;

(vii) whether there are any restrictions on the transferability of the employee shares and, if so, what they are.

According to s. 205A ERA 1996, an employee shareholder agreement cannot be implemented unless, before it is concluded, the individual has received advice about the terms and effect of the proposed agreement and seven days have elapsed since the advice was given. In addition, the company must reimburse any reasonable costs incurred in obtaining this advice whether or not the individual becomes an employee shareholder. Finally, employees have the right not to suffer a detriment on the ground that they have refused to accept an employee shareholder contract and a dismissal for this reason will be automatically unfair (see Chapter 5).

At the time of writing it is uncertain how many employers will think it is in their interests to engage employees on a shareholder basis. What is clear is the inapplicability of this status to the public sector and the opposition of trade unions to the potential opting out of employment rights.

2.9 Continuity of employment

Continuity of employment is important because the right to claim unfair dismissal depends on having two years' continuous employment. Other rights, such as the right to take parental leave, depend upon the employee having one year's continuous employment with an employer.[120] The employment concerned must relate to employment with one employer,[121] although this can include associated employers. The test for control amongst such employers is normally decided by looking at who has the voting control, but there might be, in exceptional circumstances, a need to look at who has de facto control.[122]

2.9.1 Continuity and sex discrimination

The question of whether such a rule can amount to indirect sex discrimination or whether it can be objectively justified was considered in R v Secretary of State for Employment, ex parte Seymour-Smith and Perez (No 2).[123] In this case the complainants were individuals who were prevented from bringing a complaint of unfair dismissal because they did not have the necessary two years' continuous service. They claimed that the proportion of women who could comply with the two-year qualifying period was considerably smaller than the proportion of men. The Supreme Court referred a number of questions to the Court of Justice.[124] The Court of Justice ruled[125] that the entitlement to compensation and redress for unfair dismissal came within the scope of art. 119 EEC (now art. 157 of the Treaty on the Functioning of the European Union (TFEU)) and the Equal Treatment Directive,[126] but that the national court must verify whether the statistics showed that the measure in question has had a

---

120 Maternity and Parental Leave etc. Regulations 1999, SI 1999/3312.
121 Section 218(1) ERA 1996.
122 *Payne v Secretary of State for Employment* [1989] IRLR 352.
123 [2000] IRLR 263 HL.
124 [1997] IRLR 315 HL.
125 [1999] IRLR 253 CJEU.
126 Directive 76/207/EEC; see Chapter 6.

disparate impact between men and women. It is then up to the Member State to show that the rule was unrelated to any discrimination based upon sex and reflected a legitimate aim of its social policy. This case began with the dismissal of the applicants in 1991 and finally returned to the Supreme Court for a decision in 2000. The court accepted that the qualification period did have a disparately adverse effect on women. In the period between 1985 and 1991 the number of men and women who qualified for protection was in the ratio of 10:9. The court held that objective justification had to be determined as at 1985, when the qualifying period was raised to two years, and at 1991, when the individuals made their complaint. The court held that the onus was on the Member State to show:

1. that the alleged discriminatory rule reflected a legitimate aim of its social policy;
2. that this aim was unrelated to any discrimination based on sex; and
3. that the Member State could reasonably have considered that the means chosen were suitable for attaining that aim.

The government argued that the extension of the qualifying period should help reduce the reluctance of employers to take on more people. The court was sympathetic to the government's case and accepted objective justification:

> The burden placed on the government in this type of case is not as heavy as previously thought. Governments must be able to govern. They adopt general policies and implement measures to carry out their policies. Governments must be able to take into account a wide range of social, economic and political factors . . . National courts, acting with hindsight, are not to impose an impracticable burden on governments which are proceeding in good faith.

It was ironic that the judgment was arrived at after a new government had reduced the qualifying period to one year, but the two-year period has now been reinstated.

2.9.2 Continuity and the start date

An employee's period of continuous employment begins on the day on which the employee starts work. In *The General of the Salvation Army v Dewsbury*[127] a part-time teacher took on a new full-time contract which stated that her employment began on 1 May. As 1 May was a Saturday and the following Monday was a Bank Holiday, she did not actually commence her duties until the Tuesday 4 May. She was subsequently dismissed with effect from 1 May in the following year. The issue was whether she had one year's continuous employment. The EAT held that the day on which an employee starts work is intended to refer to the beginning of the person's employment under the relevant contract of employment and that this may be different from the actual date on which work commences. More recently, the EAT has rather contentiously suggested that continuity might be acquired from the time that a job offer is accepted. This is on the basis that the contract of employment may not require the performance of actual work but governed the relations between the parties (see below).[128]

There is a presumption that an individual's period of employment is continuous, unless otherwise shown.[129] Thus the onus is on those who wish to argue the point to show that there was not continuous service within the Act's definition. It is likely, however, that the presumption of

---

127 [1984] IRLR 222.
128 *Welton v De Luxe Retail Ltd* [2013] IRLR 166.
129 Section 210(5) ERA 1996.

continuity only applies to employment with one employer, unless the tribunal accepts that a transfer of the business, and, therefore, the contract of employment, has taken place.[130]

Section 212(1) ERA 1996 states that:

> Any week during the whole or part of which an employee's relations with his employer are governed by a contract of employment counts in computing the employee's period of employment.

A week is defined in s. 235(1) ERA 1996 as a week ending with Saturday or, for a weekly paid employee, a week ends with the day used in calculating the week's remuneration. Thus, if a contract of employment exists in any one week, using this formula, that week counts for continuity purposes. In *Sweeney v J & S Henderson*[131] an employee resigned from his employment on a Saturday and left immediately to take up another post. The individual regretted the decision and returned to work for the original employer the following Friday. The employee was held to have continuity of employment as a result of there not being a week in which the contract of employment did not apply. This was despite the fact that the employee worked for another employer during the intervening period.[132] The employee worked under a contract of employment with the employer during each of the two weeks in question and thus fulfilled the requirements of s. 212(1) ERA 1996.

If there is a period in the employment where the contract is tainted by illegality, continuity may not be preserved. In *Hyland v JH Barker (North West) Ltd*[133] an employee was paid a tax-free lodging allowance even though the employee did not stay away from home. The period of four weeks in which this happened did not count towards continuity of employment. Unfortunately for the employee, as this period fell within the 12-month period prior to dismissal, he was held not to have the necessary continuity of service to make a complaint of unfair dismissal. The EAT stated that 'continuously employed' meant 'continuously employed under a legal contract of employment'.

2.9.3 Continuity and absences from work

Absence from work means not performing in substance the contract that previously existed between the parties. Such a definition applied to a coach driver whose work was greatly reduced by the miners' strike in 1984. A substantial part of the individual's work was removed, but the employee was able to claim a temporary cessation of work (see below).[134]

There are a number of reasons for which a person can be absent from work without breaking their statutory continuity of employment. These are:

1. If the employee is incapable of work as a result of sickness or injury.[135] Absences of no more than 26 weeks under this category will not break continuity.[136] There needs to be a causal relationship between the absence and the incapacity for work in consequence of sickness or injury. The absence from work also needs to be related to the work on offer. If an injured

---

130 See *Secretary of State for Employment v Cohen and Beaupress Ltd* [1987] IRLR 169.
131 [1999] IRLR 306.
132 In *Carrington v Harwich Dock Co Ltd* [1998] IRLR 567 an employee resigned on a Friday and was re-employed on the following Monday. Despite a letter from the employer stating that, by resigning voluntarily, the employee's continuity of service was broken, the EAT held that there was continuity.
133 [1985] IRLR 403.
134 *GW Stephens & Son v Fish* [1989] ICR 324; the miners' strike lasted for about one year; the employee in this case had the normal duty of driving miners to work each day.
135 Section 212(3)(a) ERA 1996.
136 Section 212(4) ERA 1996; see also *Donnelly v Kelvin International Services* [1992] IRLR 496, where an employee who resigned on the grounds of ill health, but was then re-employed some five weeks later, was held to have continuity even though they had worked for another employer during the period.

employee was offered different work from that which he normally did but it was nevertheless suitable, the tribunal would have to decide whether the employee was absent from that newly offered work as a result of the sickness or injury.[137]

2. If there is a temporary cessation of work. Section 212(3)(b) ERA 1996 states that absence on account of a temporary cessation[138] of work will not break continuity of employment. According to the EAT, the reason for the cessation is irrelevant and the subsequent work could be in a different location.[139] The word 'temporary' indicates a period of time that is of relatively short duration compared to the periods of work. However, the decision as to whether the cessation is temporary is not a mathematical one only to be reached by comparing an individual's length of employment with the length of unemployment in a defined period.[140] Although it is possible to look back over the whole period of an individual's employment in order to come to a judgment, 'temporary' is likely to mean a short time in comparison with the period in work. Thus seasonal workers who were out of work each year for longer than they actually worked did not have continuity of employment.[141] Other seasonal workers who were regularly out of work for long periods were in the same position, even though, at the beginning of the next season, it was the intention of both parties that they should resume employment.[142] In contrast, an academic who was employed on regular fixed-term contracts to teach was held to have continuity, even though the individual was not employed during August and September each year. During this time the employee prepared for the coming year's teaching and the EAT decided that this amounted to a temporary cessation of work.[143]

3. Absence from work in circumstances that, by custom or arrangement, the employee 'is regarded as continuing in the employment of his employer for any purposes'.[144] In Curr v Marks and Spencer plc[145] the Court of Appeal ruled that a four-year absence under a child break scheme broke continuity because the ex-employee was not regarded by both parties as continuing in the employment of the employer for any purpose. Similarly, in Booth v United States of America[146] the employees were employed on a series of fixed-term contracts with a gap of about two weeks between each contract. On each return to work they were given the same employee number, the same tools and equipment and the same lockers. Despite the employees arguing that this arrangement was designed to defeat the underlying purpose of the legislation, the EAT could not find an arrangement. This would have required, in advance of the break, some discussion and agreement that continuity could be preserved. It was clear that the employers did not want such an arrangement. Neither is it likely that an agreement made subsequent to the absence could be used to preserve continuity. Section 212(3)(c) ERA 1996 envisages the arrangement being in place when the employee is absent. Thus an agreement between an employer and an employee that a break in work would not affect continuity was ineffective because it was made after the employee's return.[147]

---

137 See *Pearson v Kent County Council* [1993] IRLR 165.

138 Cessation of work means that work has temporarily ceased to exist; it does not mean that the work has been temporarily or otherwise reallocated to another employee. See *Byrne v City of Birmingham* [1987] IRLR 191 CA where the employer created a pool of casual employees to share the work; the absence then was not because of a cessation of work but because the employee was not offered any.

139 *Welton v Deluxe Retail* [2013] IRLR 166.

140 See *Ford v Warwickshire County Council* [1983] IRLR 126 HL.

141 *Berwick Salmon Fisheries Co Ltd v Rutherford* [1991] IRLR 203; see also *Flack v Kodak Ltd* [1986] IRLR 255 CA, where a group of seasonal employees in a photo finishing department tried to establish continuity of employment.

142 *Sillars v Charrington Fuels Ltd* [1989] IRLR 152 CA.

143 *University of Aston in Birmingham v Malik* [1984] ICR 492; see also *Hussain v Acorn Independent College Ltd* [2011] IRLR 126.

144 Section 212(3)(c) ERA 1996.

145 [2003] IRLR 74.

146 [1999] IRLR 16.

147 *Welton v Deluxe Retail* [2013] IRLR 166.

2.9.4 Continuity and industrial disputes

A week does not count for the purposes of computing continuity of service if during that week, or any part of it, the employee takes part in a strike.[148] In contrast, periods when the employee is subject to a lock-out do count for continuity purposes. However, in neither case is continuity itself broken.[149] *Bloomfield v Springfield Hosiery Finishing Co Ltd*[150] concerned a dispute that resulted in a strike by employees. They were summarily dismissed and the employer began to recruit replacement staff. As a result the strike ended and the employees returned to work. Subsequently, the employees were dismissed for redundancy. They did not receive redundancy payments because, it was said, they did not have sufficient continuity of employment as a result of being dismissed during the strike. The court held, however, that the term 'employee' should be given a wide meaning and that the strikers continued to be employees during the strike or until the employer engaged other persons or permanently discontinued the work that they were employed to do.

2.9.5 Continuity and change of employer

Although the continuity provisions normally apply to employment by one employer,[151] there are occasions where a transfer from one employer to another can preserve continuity of employment.[152] One such situation is when there is a relevant transfer under the Transfer of Undertakings (Protection of Employment) Regulations 2006[153] (see Chapter 10). These Regulations treat the original contract of employment as if it was agreed with the new employer. Thus an employee's period of service will transfer to the new employer.

Where the trade, business[154] or undertaking is transferred to a new employer, continuity is also preserved by s. 218(2) ERA 1996. The employee's length of service is deemed to be with the new employer, although, as pointed out in *Nokes v Doncaster Collieries*,[155] this is likely to require the knowledge and consent of the employee. There have been difficulties in identifying when a business has transferred rather than a disposal of assets taking place. In *Melon v Hector Powe Ltd*,[156] the employer disposed of one of two factories to another company. The disposal included the transfer of the work in progress and all the employees in the factory. The court held that there was a distinction between a transfer of a going concern, which amounted to a transfer of a business which remains the same business, but in different hands, and the disposal of part of the assets of a business.[157] It is employees in the former situation who are able to rely on s. 218 ERA 1996. There are a number of other specific situations where continuity is preserved:[158]

1. If a contract of employment between a corporate body and an employee is modified by an Act of Parliament so that a new body is substituted as the employer.
2. On the death of an employer, an employee is taken into employment by the personal representatives or trustees of the deceased.

---

148 Section 216(1) ERA 1996.
149 Section 216(2) ERA 1996.
150 [1972] ICR 91.
151 Section 218(1) ERA 1996.
152 See s. 218(2)–(10) ERA 1996.
153 SI 2006/246.
154 Business is defined in s. 235 ERA 1996 as including a trade or profession and includes any activity carried on by a body of persons (whether corporate or unincorporated).
155 [1940] AC 1014 HL.
156 [1980] IRLR 477 HL.
157 The court cited a speech to this effect by Lord Denning in *Lloyd v Brassey* [1969] ITR 199.
158 Section 218(3)–(11) ERA 1996.

3. If there is a change in the partners, personal representatives or trustees that employ a person.[159]
4. If the employee is taken into the employment of another employer who is an associated employer of the current employer.[160]
5. If an employee of the governors of a school maintained by a local education authority is taken into the employment of the authority, or vice versa.
6. If a person in relevant[161] employment with a health service employer is taken into such relevant employment by another such employer.

Section 219 ERA 1996 provides that the Secretary of State may make provisions for preserving continuity of employment. The current regulations are the Employment Protection (Continuity of Employment) Regulations 1996 (as amended),[162] which serve to protect continuity of employment where an employee is making a complaint about dismissal or making a claim in accordance with a dismissal procedures agreement.[163] Continuity is also protected as a result of any action taken by a conciliation officer or the making of a settlement agreement in relation to a dismissal (see Chapter 5).

 Further reading

Davidov, G. 'Who Is a Worker?' (2005) 34(1) *Industrial Law Journal* 57.

Freedland, M. 'From the Contract of Employment to the Personal Work Nexus' (2006) 35(1) *Industrial Law Journal* 1.

Kountouris, N. 'The Concept of "Worker" in European Labour Law: Fragmentation, Autonomy and Scope' (2017) *Industrial Law Journal*, dwx014, https://doi.org/10.1093/indlaw/dwx014

Leighton, P. and Wynn, M. 'Classifying Employment Relationships – More Sliding Doors or a Better Regulatory Framework?' (2011) 40(1) *Industrial Law Journal* 5.

www.direct.gov.uk/en/Employment/Employees/EmploymentContractsAndConditions/index.htm – official page on employment contracts, including employment status.

www.gov.uk/employee-shareholders – government guidance on employee shareholders.

www.hmrc.gov.uk/employment-status/index.htm – HM Revenue and Customs' view on employment status: employed or self-employed.

---

159 See *Stevens v Bower* [2004] IRLR 957.

160 See *Hancill v Marcon Engineering Ltd* [1990] IRLR 51; a transfer from an American company to one in the UK, where both were controlled by a Dutch company, was enough to ensure that the employee had transferred to an associated employer.

161 'Relevant' means those undergoing professional training who need to move employers for that training; s. 218(9) ERA 1996; s. 218(10) defines health service employers.

162 SI 1996/3147.

163 See s. 110 ERA 1996.

Chapter 3

Non-standard working

Chapter Contents

3.1 The gig economy

In the gig economy those who work in it carry out a series of 'gigs', i.e. one-off jobs, in order to create an income. They may be treated as self-employed, working for a single employer or a number of them. They are to be paid for a particular task, or tasks, rather than receive a guaranteed income. What is new about the gig economy is the development of technology that enables companies to claim not to employ those that work for them. It creates a pseudo employment market where workers are said to be independent self-employed receiving work from and providing services to a digital platform created by the company. A report by the Institute for Fiscal Studies[1] stated that there was no clear way to decide which jobs were part of the gig economy, 'but one of the characteristic features is the use of third-party digital platforms'. Companies provide a web-based platform which enables those selling their services to be linked with customers wishing to buy those services.

One of the important issues about this form of working for the study of employment law is that the workers involved, such as those delivering products for Deliveroo or driving minicabs for Uber, have been treated as self-employed. The question is whether this is really so or whether they fall into the group classified as workers (see s. 230(3)(b) ERA 1996).

Establishing the correct employment status is important as differing employment protections apply to each category. Workers, who are not employees, have the right to: the national minimum wage (or national living wage); protection against unlawful deductions from wages; paid annual leave; the statutory minimum length of rest break; protection from accidents at work; not having to work more than 48 hours on average per week; protection against unlawful discrimination; some protections for pregnant workers; protection for whistleblowing; not be discriminated against if working part-time; join a trade union and be accompanied in grievances and disciplinary actions.[2] All these rights plus others are also enjoyed by 'employees'. The self-employed, however, just benefit from some provisions on health and safety and protection from discrimination. It is the search for these additional protections which leads to challenges of false self-employment.

We discuss in Chapter 2 (2.3) those issues around employment status and the idea of the dependent worker. One case directly related to employment status and the gig economy is that of *Aslam and Farrar v Uber B.V.*[3] At the employment tribunal the claimants argued that the written terms between Uber and themselves should be read sceptically. They argued that the terms misrepresented the relationship and that in reality they worked for Uber and that they therefore fell within the definition found in s. 230(3)(b) ERA 1996 and were to be regarded as workers. Uber argued that this was not the case and that the terms reflected the reality of their relationship with the drivers. The fact that Uber makes and enforces rules about the way in which drivers may make use of the platform was 'unremarkable and unexceptional'. In its judgment the employment tribunal rejected all of Uber's claims, stating that 'it is plain to us that the agreement between the parties is to be located in the field of dependent work relationships'. All the authorities relied upon by Uber were rejected. They argued that the contract for the provision of transport services was between the driver and the user and not between Uber and the driver. This extract from para. 91 of the reasons shows this scepticism:

> Uber's case is that the driver enters into a binding agreement with a person whose identity he does not know (and will never know) and who does not know and will never know his identity, to undertake a journey to a destination not told to him until the journey begins, by a route prescribed by a stranger to the contract (UBV) from which he is not free to depart (at least not

---

1 www.parliament.uk/business/committees/committees-a-z/commons-select/business-energy-industrial-strategy/news-parliament-2015/the-future-world-of-work-and-rights-of-workers-launch-16-17

2 TUC – www.tuc.org.uk/employment-status-and-rights

3 Case No 2202550/2015 *Aslam and Farrar v Uber B.V.*; this can be found at www.judiciary.gov.uk/wp-content/uploads/2016/10/aslam-and-farrar-v-uber-reasons-20161028.pdf

without risk), for a fee which (a) is set by the stranger, and (b) is not known by the passenger (who is told only the total to be paid); (c) is calculated by the stranger (as a percentage of the total sum) and (d) is paid to the stranger.

The tribunal stated that the respondent's general case did not correspond with the practical reality. In its notice of appeal Uber disputed this and stated that there was 'no proper lawful basis for such a wholesale rejection of the written contracts'.

3.2 Part-time contracts

The European Directive on part-time work[4] was adopted as a result of a Framework Agreement reached by the social partners as part of the Social Dialogue process.

3.2.1 Discrimination against part-time workers

The treatment of part-time workers is a discrimination issue because the great majority of part-time workers are female.[5] About 42 per cent of women workers work part-time compared with about 12 per cent of men. In January 2017, according to ONS data, 7,010,000 of 26,832,000 employees worked part-time and 1,366,000 of the 4,804,000 self-employed were also part-timers.[6] Part-time self-employment grew by 88 per cent between 2001 and 2015, compared with 25 per cent for full-time self-employment. Part-time self-employment accounts for 1.2 percentage points of the 1.6 percentage point increase in the self-employment share of all employment between 2008 and 2015.[7] Over one million of those working part-time (12.8 per cent) did so because they could not find a full-time job.

3.2.2 The Framework Agreement on part-time work

The purpose of the Agreement, according to clause 1, is to provide for the removal of discrimination against part-time workers and to improve the quality of part-time work, as well as to facilitate the development of part-time work on a voluntary basis. The Agreement applies to those who are in an employment relationship[8] and a part-time worker is defined in clause 3.1 as:

> An employee whose normal hours of work, calculated on a weekly basis or on average over a period of employment of up to one year, are less than the normal hours of work of a comparable full-time worker.

Justification for the measure is contained in the preamble to the Agreement. It is a measure that:

- Promotes both employment and equal opportunities for men and women.
- Helps with the requirements of competition by creating a more flexible organisation of working time.
- Facilitates access to part-time work for men and women in preparation for retirement.
- Reconciles professional and family life.
- Facilitates the take-up of education and training opportunities.

---

4 Directive 97/81/EC of 15 December 1997 concerning the Framework Agreement on part-time work concluded by UNICE, CEEP and ETUC OJ L14/9 20.1.98.

5 See *R v Secretary of State, ex parte Equal Opportunities Commission* [1994] IRLR 176 HL.

6 Office for National Statistics *UK Labour Market* March 2017.

7 Office for National Statistics *Trends in self-employment in the UK: 2001 to 2015*.

8 *O'Brien v Ministry of Justice* [2013] IRLR 315 (SC).

The Agreement applies to part-time workers, but there is an express provision (clause 2.2) permitting Member States to exclude casual part-time workers for objective reasons.

The comparable full-time worker is narrowly defined. It is someone who is a full-time worker in the same establishment, having the same type of employment or employment relationship and who is engaged on the same or similar work as the part-timer. Due regard is to be given to other considerations which include seniority, qualifications and skill. Where there is no full-time comparator, there is still a comparison to be made. It is to be done by reference to:

> the applicable collective agreement or, where there is no applicable collective agreement, in accordance with national law, collective agreements or practice.
>
> (Clause 3.2)

It is difficult to give this any meaning in the United Kingdom where consultation with the social partners takes place less often than in many other countries in the European Union. Importantly, however, there is no suggestion that there should be a situation where there are no comparators. The Agreement states that the comparison should be with the full-time comparator and, if there is no such person, then in accordance with national law, collective agreements or practice. It does not appear to suggest that, in the absence of a full-time comparator, there should be no comparison at all.

Clause 4 establishes the principle that part-time workers should not be treated less favourably than their full-time comparators merely because they work part-time, unless the difference in treatment can be objectively justified. This applies to 'employment conditions', which is an expression that includes remuneration.[9] Objective justification presumably will mean a reason for the difference in treatment that is not related to the individual working part-time. In *Bilka-Kaufhaus*[10] the Court of Justice considered the position of part-time shop sales assistants who were excluded from an occupational pension scheme that included full-timers. The Court concluded that an employer may be able to justify the exclusion of part-timers, in relation to a sex discrimination claim, where it represents a real need on the part of the undertaking and the means chosen to meet this need are appropriate to achieving that objective.

Where appropriate, the principle of *pro rata temporis* should apply and, after consultation with the social partners, Member States may, where justified by objective reasons, make access to particular conditions of employment subject to periods of service, time worked or earnings. Opportunities for part-time work are to be encouraged. These would include the removal of obstacles to part-time work and giving consideration to requests from workers to transfer from full-time to part-time work and vice versa. A worker's refusal to transfer from full-time to part-time work, or vice versa, is not to be treated as a valid reason for termination of employment.

3.2.3 The Part-time Workers Regulations

The Part-time Workers (Prevention of Less Favourable Treatment) Regulations (the PTW Regulations) came into force on 1 July 2000.[11] The (former) Department of Trade and Industry's press release that accompanied the Regulations quoted the Secretary of State as saying that:

> The proposals I am putting forward today will ensure that part-timers are no longer discriminated against. This revised package safeguards the position of part-timers whilst avoiding unnecessary burdens on business.

---

9 According to the Court of Justice, remuneration covers pensions that are dependent on the employment relationship: INPS v Bruno [2010] IRLR 890.

10 Case 170/84 *Bilka-Kaufhaus GmbH v Weber von Hartz* [1986] IRLR 317 CJEU.

11 SI 2000/1551.

In an attempt to achieve these two somewhat contradictory aims, the Secretary of State stated that:

> the regulations will be introduced with a light touch by ensuring that comparisons can only be made between part-time and full-time workers with the same type of contract.

The effect of this is seen in the summary of the Regulatory Impact Assessment which accompanied the Regulations. The Assessment stated that there are some six million part-time employees in Great Britain. Of these the Department for Trade and Industry estimated that one million have a comparable full-time employee against whom it is necessary to compare the terms and conditions of part-timers. It was also thought that some 400,000 will benefit from the equal treatment provisions. Large numbers of low-paid part-time workers will be excluded because there are no full-time comparators. It is difficult to understand how this justifies the Secretary of State's assertion that the Regulations will 'ensure that part-timers are no longer discriminated against'.

Regulation 2(1) of the PTW Regulations identifies a full-time worker as someone who is paid wholly or partly by reference to the time worked and, having regard to the custom and practice of the employer in relation to their other workers, is identifiable as a full-time worker. Regulation 2(2) has the same definition for part-time workers, except that they must be identifiable as part-time workers. The definition of a full-time comparator follows closely the one in the Directive, although, in terms of stating where the comparator needs to be based, it does have a wider coverage.[12] Full-timers, in relation to the part-timers, need:

1. To be employed by the same employer under the same type of contract.
2. To be engaged in the same or broadly similar work having regard, where relevant, to whether they have similar levels of qualifications, skills and experience.
3. To be based at the same establishment or, if there is no full-time comparator at the same establishment, at a different establishment.

In *Matthews v Kent Fire Authority*[13] part-time retained fire-fighters alleged that they were treated less favourably than full-time fire-fighters. The Court of Appeal had concluded that although they were employed under the same type of contract, they did not carry out the 'same or broadly similar work'. The House of Lords disagreed and stated that, in making the assessment, particular attention should be given to the extent to which the work was exactly the same and to the importance of that work to the enterprise as a whole. If a large component of the work was the same, then the issue was whether the differences were so important that the work could not be regarded as the same or broadly similar. If part-time and full-time employees carry out the same work, but the full-timers do extra duties, this does not necessarily mean that the work is not the same or broadly similar.

It is a very demanding test for establishing whether an individual's job can be used as a comparator on which to base a claim for discrimination. The first issue is what happens if there is no full-time person who can meet the criteria. Where a workforce is made up entirely of part-time employees in a particular category, the Regulations will be of no assistance in enabling them to claim discrimination on the basis of being a part-timer.[14] One example might be a contract cleaning operation. All the employees concerned with cleaning might be part-time and all the supervisory, management and administration employees might be full-time. The result is that there is no full-time comparator on whom the cleaning staff can base a claim. These employees may be low-paid because

---

12 Hypothetical comparators are not permitted: see *Carl v University of Sheffield* [2009] IRLR 616.
13 [2006] IRLR 367.
14 In *Wippel v Peek & Cloppenburg GmbH* [2005] IRLR 211 the Court of Justice suggested that a part-time casual worker might be covered by the Framework Agreement. However, Ms Wippel could not find a full-time comparator who worked on a casual basis.

they are part-time and, perhaps, because they are not organised collectively. However, they are unable to base a claim using the PTW Regulations. Although there may be a prima facie case of discrimination, it could not be based upon the PTW Regulations. Even the government's own figures suggest that 80 per cent of part-time workers will not have a full-time comparator available to them.

Regulations 3 and 4 provide an exception to the need for such a comparator. Where a full-time worker, following the termination or variation of the contract of employment, works fewer hours, the worker will be able to use himself or herself as the comparable full-timer for the purpose of deciding whether there has been less favourable treatment. The same rule applies if a full-time worker returns to work and performs fewer hours in the same job or a job at the same level, for the same employer, after an absence of less than 12 months. This is regardless of whether the absence followed a termination of employment or not.[15] In *Fidessa v Lancaster*[16] the claimant returned to work just a few days before the end of the 12-month period, but then immediately took accrued annual leave. The respondent argued that this meant that she had not actually returned to work. The EAT did not accept this argument and held that the contract of employment was not in abeyance during periods of annual leave so she had returned from work even though she had then taken leave.

Regulation 5 establishes the principle of non-discrimination. A part-time worker has the right not to be treated less favourably than the employer treats a comparable full-timer as regards the terms of the contract or by being subject to detriment by any act, or failure to act, by the employer. The right only applies if the treatment is on the grounds that the worker is part-time and cannot be justified on objective grounds. In *Ministry of Justice v Burton*,[17] for example, less favourable treatment was held to have been shown when the claimants, who were part-time judges, were only paid for writing up cases as a matter of discretion. In contrast, full-time judges were paid for doing this as a matter of entitlement.

In determining whether a part-timer has been treated less favourably, the principle of pro rata temporis applies.[18] The one exception to this is overtime. Not paying overtime rates to a part-time worker until they have at least worked hours comparable with the basic working hours of the comparable full-timer is not to be treated as less favourable treatment. *McMenemy v Capita Business Services Ltd*[19] involved a part-time worker who worked only on Wednesdays, Thursdays and Fridays at a call centre which operated seven days a week. All employees had a contract of employment which entitled them to time off in lieu when statutory holidays coincided with one of their working days. This meant that Mr McMenemy was not entitled to time off for statutory holidays that occurred on Mondays. As other colleagues who worked full-time received this time off, he complained that he was being treated less favourably than a comparable full-timer. He failed in his claim because the court held that the reason why he was not given time off for Monday statutory holidays was not solely because he was a part-timer, but because he did not work on Mondays. In order to show less favourable treatment, he had to show that the employer intended to treat him less favourably solely because he was a part-time worker. The reason here for the less favourable treatment was that he had agreed not to work on Mondays. A full-time worker who worked from Tuesday to Saturday would also not be entitled to statutory holidays that fell on a Monday. Subsequently, in *Sharma v Manchester City Council*,[20] the EAT has ruled that the part-time nature of the claimant's work does not have to be the sole reason for the less favourable treatment. Additionally, the fact that not all part-timers are treated adversely does not mean that those who are cannot bring proceedings if being part-time is a reason for the discrimination experienced.

---

15 See also Chapter 8 on the flexible working provisions.
16 *Fidessa v Lancaster* [2017] UKEAT 0093_16_1601.
17 *Ministry of Justice v Burton* [2016] IRLR 100.
18 See *O'Brien v Ministry of Justice* [2013] IRLR 315.
19 [2007] IRLR 400.
20 [2008] IRLR 236. This approach was followed in *Carl v University of Sheffield* [2009] IRLR 616.

In the government's compliance guidance, accompanying the PTW Regulations, the following examples are given:

- Previous or current part-time status should not of itself constitute a barrier to promotion.
- Part-time workers should receive the same hourly rate as full-timers.
- Part-time workers should receive the same hourly rate of overtime pay as full-timers, once they have worked more than the normal full-time hours.
- Part-time workers should be able to participate in profit-sharing or share option schemes available for full-timers.
- Employers should not discriminate between full-time and part-time workers over access to pension schemes.
- Employers should not exclude part-timers from training simply because they work part-time.
- In selection for redundancy, part-time workers must not be treated less favourably than full-timers.

These examples apply only if the employer cannot objectively justify a distinction in treatment or if there is no full-time comparator meeting the criteria provided with whom the employee can be compared.

3.3 Fixed-term contracts

About 6 per cent of the UK workforce work under a fixed-term contract. There is a big variation in their usage amongst European countries, ranging from 1.5 per cent of the work force in Romania to 24 per cent in Spain. The EU average is about 14 per cent.[21] Some 28 per cent of those doing temporary work in the UK did so because they could not find a permanent job.[22] Of those that answered the question for an EU survey it emerged that 9.5 per cent of fixed-term contracts in the UK were for up to three months; 8.8 per cent for 4–6 months; 16 per cent for 7–12 months; 14.1 per cent for periods of 13–24 months and 10.2 per cent for more than 24 months.[23]

On 18 March 1999 the Social Partners at European Community level concluded a Framework Agreement on fixed-term work which became Directive 99/70/EC.[24] This Directive came after a lengthy period of attempts by the European Commission to obtain agreement amongst the Member States. Proposals were first introduced in 1990 and, until 1999, only one measure had been adopted.[25]

The purposes of the Framework Agreement are to:

(a) improve the quality of fixed-term work by ensuring the application of the principle of non-discrimination;
(b) establish a framework to prevent abuse arising from the use of successive fixed-term employment contracts or relationships.[26]

A fixed-term worker is defined by clause 3 of the Agreement as:

> a person having an employment contract or relationship entered into directly between an employer and a worker where the end of the employment contract or relationship is determined

---

21 DG for Internal Policies *Precarious Employment in Europe* (2016).
22 Office for National Statistics *UK Labour Market 2017*.
23 DG for Internal Policies *Precarious Employment in Europe* (2016).
24 Council Directive 99/70/EC of 28 June 1999 concerning the Framework Agreement on fixed-term work OJ L175/43 10.7.99.
25 Council Directive 91/383/EEC supplementing the measures to encourage improvements in the safety and health at work of workers with a fixed duration employment relationship or a temporary employment relationship OJ L206 29.7.91.
26 Clause 1 Framework Agreement.

by objective conditions such as reaching a specific date, completing a specific task, or the occurrence of a specific event.

The Agreement introduces a principle of non-discrimination against fixed-term workers,[27] with stricter controls over the renewal of such contracts. That such workers need to be protected is illustrated in *Booth v United States of America*.[28] Despite arguing that the arrangement for two-week breaks between contracts was designed to defeat the legislation, the applicants were unsuccessful in their claim for a redundancy payment, even though, apart from three two-week breaks, they had some five years' service. One of the consequences of the Fixed-term Work Directive is to require some objective justification for continuing fixed-term contracts of employment.

Section 18 Employment Relations Act 1999 was a first step by the government in implementing the requirements of the Fixed-term Work Directive. It removed s. 197(1) and (2) ERA 1996, which allowed individuals with a fixed-term contract of one year or more to opt out of the unfair dismissal provisions contained in Part X ERA 1996.[29]

Section 45 Employment Act 2002 provided authority for the introduction of the Fixed-term Employees (Prevention of Less Favourable Treatment) Regulations.[30] They define a fixed-term contract as either a contract of employment which is made for a specific term, or a contract that terminates automatically on the completion of a particular task, or the occurrence or non-occurrence of any specific event, except one resulting from the employee reaching normal retirement age.[31] The ability of the parties to give notice to terminate does not prevent the contract from being for a fixed term.[32]

The scope of the unfair dismissal provisions in the ERA 1996 has been widened to include these 'task' contracts of employment.[33] The ending of these contracts will be regarded as a dismissal for the purposes of the Act. As a result an individual on such a contract obtains a number of statutory rights which are enjoyed by permanent employees. These include the right not to be unfairly dismissed, the right to a written statement of reasons for dismissal and the right to statutory redundancy payments. The ERA 1996 was also amended so that those on 'task' contracts of less than three months will have the right to minimum notice periods in the same way as permanent employees.

A number of important decisions have been taken about which individuals are to be protected and which are to be excluded. The government has decided to apply the regulations to employees only. The approach is different from that taken by Part-time Workers Regulations (see 3.2 above). Those who are not treated as employees are to be excluded. Whilst recognising the problems associated with including non-employees, the decision does have the result of excluding significant numbers of individuals who work on fixed-term contracts and who, apart from their employment status, are indistinguishable from permanent employees or employees on fixed-term contracts.

The definition of comparator uses the same approach as that used by the Part-time Workers Regulations. The individual with whom a fixed-term worker is to be compared is someone who, at the time when the alleged treatment takes place, is employed by the same employer and is engaged on the same or broadly similar work, having regard to whether or not they have similar skills and qualifications, if this is relevant. The comparable permanent employee must work or be based at the

---

27 Clause 4 Framework Agreement. On the direct applicability of this clause see *Zentralbetriebsrat der Landeskrankenhauser Tirols v Land Tirol* [2010] IRLR 631 CJEU.

28 [1999] IRLR 16.

29 See Employment Relations Act 1999 (Commencement No 2 and Transitional and Savings Provisions) Order 1999, SI 1999/2830.

30 The Fixed-term Employees (Prevention of Less Favourable Treatment) Regulations 2002, SI 2002/2034, which came into force on 1 October 2002.

31 Regulation 1(2).

32 *Allen v National Australia Group Ltd* [2004] IRLR 847.

33 For these purposes they are referred to as limited-term contracts.

same establishment, although other locations will be considered if there is no one appropriate at the same establishment.[34]

The Regulations provide that a fixed-term employee has the right not to be treated by the employer less favourably than a comparable permanent employee with regard to the terms of the contract or by being subject to any other detriment related to being a fixed-term employee.[35] This includes less favourable treatment in relation to: first, any period of service qualification related to a condition of employment;[36] second, training opportunities; and, third, the opportunity to secure permanent employment in the establishment.

Importantly, however, the government has decided to include less favourable treatment in relation to pay and pensions. As a result, the rules on statutory sick pay, rights to guarantee payments and payments on medical suspension are amended to ensure that fixed-term employees and comparable permanent employees are treated in the same way. Similarly, where there are qualifying rules for membership of pension schemes, these rules should be the same for fixed-term and comparable permanent employees, unless the different treatment can be objectively justified. The government believes that this will help reduce pay inequalities because the majority of fixed-term employees are women, so the inclusion of pay and pensions will help reduce the inequality between the sexes.

There is a defence of objective justification in the Regulations.[37] Interestingly, the government has opted to allow the 'package' approach, as an alternative to the 'item by item' approach (compare Equality of terms in Chapter 6 at 6.6), when deciding whether an individual has been treated less favourably on the grounds of being a fixed-term employee. It will not be necessary to compare each part of the terms of employment and ensure that each individual part is comparable to the permanent employee, unless the employer so wishes. Such treatment is objectively justifiable if the terms of the fixed-term employee's contract of employment, as a whole, are at least as favourable as the permanent comparator. This presumably means that it will be permissible to pay a higher salary in compensation for other benefits such as holidays and pensions, as long as the value of the 'package' overall is equivalent or better than that of the permanent employee. It should be noted that the words 'objective grounds' in clause 4(1) of the Framework Agreement do not permit a difference in treatment to be justified on the basis that it is provided for by a general, abstract national norm, such as a law or collective agreement. According to the Court of Justice, unequal treatment must be justified by precise and concrete factors characterising the employment condition to which it relates, in the specific context in which it occurs and on the basis of objective and transparent criteria in order to ensure that there is a genuine need and that unequal treatment is appropriate for achieving the objective pursued and is necessary for that purpose.[38] The Court of Justice in Diego Porras[39] stated that the concept of 'objective grounds' required the unequal treatment to be justified by 'precise, specific factors' in order to ensure that the unequal treatment met a genuine need and was appropriate for achieving the objective and was necessary for that purpose. This case concerned termination payments which were higher for permanent employees than for those on fixed-term or temporary contracts.

An example of where temporary contracts were justified was given in another case at the Court of Justice. In Pérez López[40] the Court accepted that in the public health sector it was inevitable that

---

34 Regulation 2.
35 Regulation 3. In *Department of Work and Pensions v Webley* [2005] IRLR 288, the Court of Appeal ruled that termination by simple effluxion of time cannot, of itself, constitute less favourable treatment.
36 In *Gaviero v Xunte de Galicia* [2011] IRLR 504 the Court of Justice ruled that a length of service increment is an employment condition within clause 4 of the Framework Agreement.
37 Regulation 4.
38 *Alonso v Osakidetza-Servicio Vasco de Salud* [2007] IRLR 911. In *Impact v Ministry for Agriculture and Food* [2008] IRLR 552 the Court of Justice confirmed that clause 4(1) has direct effect.
39 *Diego Porras v Ministerio De Defensa* [2016] IRLR 964.
40 *Pérez López v Servicio Madrileño De Salud (Comunidad De Madrid)* [2016] IRLR 970.

there would be a need for temporary replacements to provide cover for staff who were on sick, maternity, parental or other leave. Fixed-term contracts and their renewal could not be justified when used to meet the permanent staffing needs of the employer. This was a Spanish case and the Court heard that up to 25 per cent of the 50,000 medical and healthcare staff in the Madrid region had been on fixed-term or temporary contracts for an average period of between five and six years. Some had been providing services continuously for more than 15 years. As a result the Court precluded the Spanish legislation that allowed for the employer to use these temporary contracts instead of recruiting persons on open-ended contracts of employment.

If employees consider that they have been treated less favourably on the grounds of being a fixed-term employee, then they are entitled to request a written statement giving particulars of the reasons for the treatment. This must be provided by the employer within 21 days of the request. Such a statement will be admissible in any future employment tribunal proceedings.[41] A dismissal connected to enforcing an employee's rights under the Regulations will be treated as an unfair dismissal.[42]

Unfortunately, the Regulations seem unlikely to stop the repeated use of fixed-term contracts, which is a rather strange outcome. Where there is a succession of fixed-term contracts resulting in the employee being continuously employed for four years or more, the contract will automatically be deemed a permanent contract, unless there is objective justification suggesting otherwise.[43] According to the Court of Justice, the contract of indefinite duration need not reproduce identically the principal terms in the previous contract. However, the conversion of a fixed-term contract must not involve material amendments that are overall unfavourable when the tasks and nature of the functions remain unchanged.[44] A major problem lies in the definition of continuous employment contained in the ERA 1996. Any week during which a contract of employment exists will count towards continuity of employment (s. 212(1) ERA 1996).[45] Thus, any sort of break not covered by ERA 1996 is likely to sever continuity and make the Regulations ineffective. The Court of Justice's decision in *Adeneler*[46] highlights the problems caused. This case involved workers employed by the Greek Milk Organisation, ELOG, who had been engaged on a number of fixed-term contracts. One of the issues in the case was that Greek legislation provided that continuity was broken if there was a gap of more than 20 days. The Court of Justice recognised that the decision as to what constituted continuity had been left to the Member State to decide. It held, however, that this discretion could not be exercised in such a way as to compromise one of the aims of the Directive, namely to prevent the misuse of fixed-term contracts. It therefore held that a gap of 20 days allowed such misuse to continue and was not in accord with the aims of the Directive.

If an employee considers that he or she has become a permanent employee because of the Regulations, then he or she may request a written statement from the employer stating that he or she is now a permanent employee or, if not, the reasons why the individual is to remain a fixed-term employee. This statement must be given within 21 days and is admissible in future employment tribunal proceedings.[47] Provision is made for some flexibility as the maximum qualifying period can be varied by collective or workforce agreements. However, this may be of limited benefit because the agreement will be reached with employee representatives, the majority of whom are likely to be permanent employees. This may not be a problem in situations where the employees are represented by a trade union and reach a collective agreement on the issue. Yet it might be

---

41 Regulation 5.
42 Regulation 6.
43 Regulation 8. See *Duncombe v Secretary of State for Children, Schools and Families* [2010] IRLR 331 where the Court of Appeal ruled that this Regulation applies irrespective of where contracts governed by English law are to be performed.
44 *Huet v Université de Bretagne Occidentale* (C-251/11) [2012] IRLR 703.
45 See *Sweeney v J & S Henderson* [1999] IRLR 306.
46 Case C-21/204 *Adeneler v Ellinikos Organismos Galaktos* [2006] IRLR 716.
47 Regulation 9.

difficult where employees elect their own representatives, the majority of whom will not be affected. It is more likely to be a problem if the workforce agreement is reached by a majority vote of the workforce (this can be done where there are fewer than 20 employees). It is questionable whether employees in such situations will resist management demands for a more flexible approach if the majority are unaffected by the proposals.

Employees will be able to claim unfair dismissal if they are dismissed for exercising their rights under the Regulations. They can take their claim for less favourable treatment to an employment tribunal which has the power to award compensation to the claimant and recommend that the employer takes action within a specific period in order to obviate or reduce the adverse effect complained about. The compensation is limited, however, as the tribunal is specifically forbidden to award damages for injury to feelings. The matters that will be taken into account will be the loss of benefit arising from the infringement and any reasonable expenses of the complainant as a result of the infringement.

3.4 Temporary agency workers

The employment agency industry is an important part of the UK economy with about 1.2 million agency workers – a little under 4 per cent of the workforce.[48] It grew from an industry that merely supplied domestic staff to the current-day one that supplies individuals with a wide range of skills.

3.4.1 The Temporary Agency Work Directive 2008/104/EC

Although the European Commission first published its proposal on this topic in 1982, the Directive was only adopted in November 2008. According to art. 2, the Directive has two aims. This first is to ensure the protection of temporary agency workers and to improve the quality of their work by ensuring that the principle of equal treatment is applied. Nowhere in the Directive is the word 'temporary' defined, so it would presumably apply to a very short-term posting of a few hours as well as a longer-term placement over a number of years. It is interesting to note that one of the objectives of the Fixed-term Work Directive was to stop the abuse of fixed-term contracts by limiting the number of such contracts before a person would be assumed to be a permanent employee. By way of contrast, there is no such issue with temporary agency work. Indeed, temporary work is to be encouraged and its status improved. Why is there this difference? The second aim contained in art. 2 is that the Directive aims to establish a suitable framework for the use of temporary work 'with a view to contributing effectively to the creation of jobs and to the development of flexible norms of working'.

Article 1(1) specifies that it applies to the contract of employment or the employment relationship that exists between a temporary agency and the worker who is posted to a user undertaking to work under its supervision and direction. The final decision about who will be covered is, as usual, left to the Member State, because the Directive defines a worker as someone who is protected as such under national law. It is likely that some temporary agency workers will not be covered. It may be difficult to show an employment relationship with those that work under the guise of a limited liability company. An example of such a complex employment situation is found in *Hewlett-Packard Ltd v O'Murphy*.[49] Here the individual concerned formed a private limited company, which then entered into a contract with the agency, which in turn had a contract with Hewlett-Packard. This case concerned the relationship between the worker and the user company.

---

48 World Employment Confederation *Economic Report* 2017 (2017).
49 [2002] IRLR 4.

The worker failed to show that there was an employment relationship between the two, but the relationship with the agency must also be clear. Article 3(2) specifies that people may not be excluded solely on the basis that they are part-time workers or on fixed-term contracts within the meaning of the Directives on part-time work and fixed-term contracts.

According to art. 5, the temporary worker is to receive at least as favourable treatment in terms of basic working and employment conditions as a person recruited directly by the user undertaking to do the same job. Basic working and employment conditions are those relating to working time, rest periods, overtime, breaks, night work, paid holidays, public holidays and pay. They also relate to work done by pregnant women, nursing mothers, children and young people, as well as any action taken to combat discrimination on other grounds. This seems an important list of terms yet there are some significant omissions. There is no mention of any notice period, so temporary staff can still, subject to any other issues, be removed at short notice. Neither is there any opportunity for any disciplinary or grievance appeals procedure. Presumably, this is an issue that is assumed to be between the worker and the agency employer, even though any disciplinary or grievance matters are likely to be between the individual and the user enterprise. Lastly, there is no mention of pension arrangements. The exclusion of these would make any attempt to lift the status of temporary agency workers to the same status as permanent workers meaningless.

Like the Directive and Regulations concerning part-time work, temporary agency workers are to be notified of permanent vacancies in the user enterprise to give them the opportunity to find permanent employment (art. 6). In addition, measures must be taken to improve access to training both in the agency employer and in the user enterprise. Finally, it should be noted that the Directive does not deal with the important issue of the employment status of agency workers.

3.4.2 The Temporary Agency Workers Regulations 2010

These were designed to implement Directive 2008/104/EC and introduced the principle of equal treatment for agency workers after they have been in 'the same role' with the same hirer for a qualifying period of 12 continuous calendar weeks.[50] Regulation 5 gives agency workers the right to the same 'basic working and employment conditions' as they would have been entitled to if they had been engaged directly by the hirer. The Regulation uses the expressions 'ordinarily included' and 'comparable employee' with the effect that individually negotiated terms are not covered. Regulation 6 makes it clear that it is terms and conditions relating to pay, the duration of working time, night work, rest periods, rest breaks and annual leave that are relevant. In relation to pay, reg. 5 does not apply where there is a permanent contract between the agency worker and a temporary work agency. There are a number of conditions that must be met in relation to the form and terms of this contract and there must be a minimum amount of pay between assignments.[51] Regulations 7 and 8 deal with the completion of the qualifying period and the effect of breaks during or between assignments. In essence, the individual must work 'in the same role with the same hirer' and a test of 'substantively different' will be applied. According to reg. 9, the qualifying period will be treated as satisfied if a worker is prevented from completion of the qualifying period by the structuring of assignments.

Regulations 12 and 13 both apply from the commencement of work. Regulation 12 provides a right to be treated no less favourably than a comparable worker in relation to 'collective facilities and amenities' provided by the hirer unless such treatment can be justified on objective grounds. Regulation 13 gives agency workers the right to be informed by the hirer of any vacant relevant posts and may be achieved by 'a general announcement in a suitable place in the hirer's establishment'. Regulation 14 states that a temporary work agency and hirer can both be liable to the extent that

---

50 Regulation 3 provides a definition of 'agency worker' and reg. 4 defines 'temporary work agency'.
51 See regs 10 and 11.

they are responsible for breaching reg. 5. The hirer is liable for breaches of regs 12 and 13. Agency workers also have the right to receive information from the temporary work agency or hirer as applicable about the rights and duties in regs 5, 12 and 13. Regulation 16 refers to written requests for a written statement to be supplied within 28 days. Regulation 17 introduces the right not to be unfairly dismissed or subjected to a detriment for a reason relating to the Regulations and reg. 18 offers remedies for breach. This includes a minimum award of two weeks' pay and an additional award of up to £5,000 where reg. 9 applies. There is no cap on compensation but no award can be made for injury to feelings. Finally, reg. 20 deals with the liability of employers and principals and reg. 15 restricts contracting out generally.

3.4.3 Agency/worker relationship

One of the issues for the courts has been to identify the employer of the staff concerned. Although the particular facts of each case will be important, the possible options are:

1. The individual is working under a contract for services.
2. There is a global contract of employment between the individual and the agency, covering all the assignments on which a temporary worker may be sent.
3. There is a contract of employment for each individual assignment.

In *McMeechan v Secretary of State for Employment*[52] a temporary worker completed a series of individual assignments through an employment agency. He was given a job sheet and a standard written statement of terms and conditions for each assignment. The statement specified that he was providing services as a self-employed worker and was not operating under a contract of service, although the agency did deduct tax and national insurance contributions. When the agency became insolvent, the individual made a claim to the Secretary of State for wages owed. The claim was refused because, it was argued, the individual was not an employee of the insolvent company. The Court of Appeal examined two aspects of the relationship between the agency and the individual. The first was the general relationship covering the whole period during which the individual was used by the agency and the second was the relationship during any specific engagement on which the agency had used the individual. The court considered[53] *Wickens v Champion Employment*[54] which looked at the general relationship and involved an attempt to show that all temporary staff of an agency were working under contracts of employment. This failed because:

> the relationship between the employers and the temporaries seems to us wholly to lack the elements of continuity, and care of the employer for the employee, that one associates with a contract of service.

The question for the court on the individual assignment was whether this could amount to a contract of service or not. The arguments for there being a contract for services were that there was an express statement that the individual was self-employed and there was freedom to work for a particular client on a self-employed basis. On the side of there being a contract of service were the power reserved by the agency to dismiss for misconduct, the power to bring any assignment to an

---

52 [1997] IRLR 353.
53 The court contrasted the judgments in *McLeod v Hellyer Brothers Ltd* [1987] IRLR 232, which concerned Hull trawlermen who worked on periodic agreements, and *Nethermere (St Neots) Ltd v Gardiner* [1984] ICR 612, which concerned home workers with no fixed hours who were paid by results.
54 [1984] ICR 365.

end, the establishment of a grievance procedure and the stipulation of an hourly rate of pay, which in turn was subject to deductions for unsatisfactory timekeeping, work, attitude or misconduct. The court concluded that:

> when those indications are set against each other, and the specific engagement is looked at as a whole in all its terms, the general impression which emerges is that the engagement involved in this single assignment gave rise, despite the label put on it by the parties, to a contract of service between the temporary worker and the contractor.

In *Dacas v Brook Street Bureau*[55] it was stated that formal written contracts between a woman and an agency and between that agency and the end user relating to the work to be done for the end user did not necessarily preclude the implication of a contract of employment between the woman and the end user. As a matter of law, when an issue is raised about the status of an applicant in unfair dismissal proceedings, an employment tribunal is required to consider whether there is an implied contract between the parties who have no express contract with one another. This view was supported by the Court of Appeal in *Cable & Wireless plc v Muscat*.[56] The court stated that in cases involving a triangular relationship consisting of a worker, an employment agency and an end user, the tribunal should consider the possibility of an implied contract between the worker and the end user. In this case such a contract was held to exist as the individual had been employed and then, at the employer's request, become a contractor via an employment agency. The court held that the end user was under an obligation to provide work and the worker was under an obligation to attend their premises and do the work, subject to their control and supervision. In *James v London Borough of Greenwich*[57] the Court of Appeal stated that the real issue in agency worker cases is whether a contract should be implied between a worker and the end user rather than whether an irreducible minimum of mutual obligations exist. The mutuality point is important in deciding whether a contract is a contract of employment or some other kind of contract. However, in agency cases the issue is whether a third contract exists at all between the worker and the end user.[58] Subsequently, the Court of Appeal has affirmed that the implication of a contract is a question of law but the parties' understanding that there was no such contract and their inability to reach agreement on the terms which a contract should contain were powerful factors militating against such an implication. Thus we reach the unsatisfactory conclusion that 'just because a claimant looked like an employee and was treated like one, does not mean that he was an employee'![59]

3.4.4 Employment agencies/businesses

The private employment industry has been regulated since 1973 when the Employment Agencies Act 1973 came into force. This contained a system for licensing and regular inspections by the (then) Department of Employment. The implementation of this Act was changed by the Conduct of Employment Agencies and Employment Businesses Regulations 2003,[60] and ss 15–16 of the Employment Act 2008.

The 1973 Act and the 2003 Regulations distinguish between employment businesses and employment agencies. Employment businesses are those that are concerned with the supply of temporary staff, whilst employment agencies are those that are concerned with the supply of work

---

55 [2004] IRLR 358.
56 [2006] IRLR 355.
57 [2008] IRLR 302.
58 See also *Muschett v HM Prison* [2010] IRLR 210 CA.
59 *Tilsom v Alstom Transport* [2011] IRLR 169 CA.
60 SI 2003/3319.

seekers to fill permanent vacancies with clients.[61] Many organisations are both employment businesses and employment agencies.

The main provisions of the Act and the Regulations are:

1. Neither an employment agency nor employment business may charge fees to work seekers for finding them work, or seeking to find them work. Neither an agency nor an employment business may make help to a work seeker conditional upon using other services which require a fee. There is a limitation on the terms in contracts between employment businesses and hirers preventing temporary workers from taking up permanent jobs unless a fee is first paid to the employment business.

2. An employment business may not introduce a work seeker to a hirer to perform the normal tasks carried out by a worker who is taking part in an industrial dispute or other industrial action, unless it is an unofficial strike or industrial action, i.e. one that does not take place within the rules governing such actions contained in the Trade Union and Labour Relations (Consolidation) Act 1992.

3. Employment businesses are not able to withhold pay owed to a temporary worker just because the worker has not obtained a signed worksheet from the hirer.

4. When an agency or business first offers to provide services to a work seeker, then the agency or business must provide the work seeker with details of their terms of business and fees (if any). The agency or business will obtain the agreement of the work seeker about fees (if any) and the type of work the agency or business will try to find for the work seeker.

5. Employment businesses must agree whether the work seeker is, or will be, employed under a contract of service or a contract for services (see above). The work seeker will also be given an undertaking that the business will pay him for the work that he does, regardless of whether the business is paid by the hirer. Other terms of business will include the rate of remuneration paid to the work seeker and the minimum rate of remuneration to be paid to the employment business, details of any entitlements to holidays and to payment in respect of holidays.

6. Similar requirements are imposed upon employment agencies to explain to work seekers what services will be provided and details of any fees to be paid to the agency for work-finding services, although fees may only be charged to work seekers wanting work in such areas as sport, music, dance and theatre.

7. Agencies and businesses are required to keep documentation showing the work seeker's agreement to the terms of business and any changes to them. Neither an agency nor a hirer may introduce or supply a work seeker unless the agency or business has sufficient information about the hirer, the dates on which the work seeker is required and the duration of the work, the position to be filled and the experience, training and qualifications necessary to work in the position, including the rate of remuneration to be paid to the work seeker. There are similar conditions in relation to obtaining information about a work seeker before that person can be introduced to a hirer. Agencies and employment businesses must obtain references on job seekers wishing to work with vulnerable persons.

8. Every advertisement must carry the full name of the agency or business and state the nature of the work, its location and the minimum qualifications necessary when advertising rates of pay.

9. Employment agencies must not introduce an employer to a young person under the age of 18 years if that person is attending school or has just left school, unless that person has received vocational guidance from their local careers service.

10. There are strict rules on record keeping.

---

61 See s. 13(1)–(3) Employment Agencies Act 1973.

The Regulations were amended in 2014[62] so that if an employment agency or employment business wish to advertise a GB-based vacancy in the EEA, they must first advertise it in English in Great Britain, unless they believe, on reasonable grounds, that this would be disproportionate. Breach of this requirement would constitute a criminal offence and may also give rise to an action in damages. Further amendments in 2016[63] reduced some of the 'regulatory burdens'. There is no longer a requirement for agencies or businesses to agree terms with clients and the record-keeping requirements have been relaxed. Anyone who contravenes the prohibition on charging fees to work seekers, fails to comply with regulations to secure the proper conduct of the agency or business, falsifies records or fails, without reasonable excuse, to comply with a prohibition order, will be guilty of an offence and subject to a fine not exceeding the statutory maximum. Section 16 EA 2008 has strengthened the powers of inspectors, and anyone obstructing an officer from carrying out enforcement functions can be fined.

An employment tribunal may make an order prohibiting a person (or company) from carrying on, or being concerned with, an employment agency or business for up to ten years on the grounds of the person being unsuitable because of misconduct or any other sufficient reason. In addition, terms of contracts with hirers or work seekers which are invalid in terms of the Act or Regulations will be unenforceable. Any contravention of the Act or Regulations which causes damage, including death or injury, will be actionable in civil law.

3.5 Zero hours contracts

A zero hours contract is a contract between an employer and a worker where the employer provides work but is not obliged to do so or provide any minimum hours and a worker who is not obliged to accept any work offered. Section 27A(1) ERA 1996 defines a zero hours contract as a contract under which 'the undertaking to do or perform work or services is an undertaking to do so conditionally on the employer making work or services available to the worker, and there is no certainty that any such work or services will be made available to the worker'.

They provide an opportunity for those wishing to have flexible employment to do so and enable employers to use workers as and when they need to. Indeed, according to the Office for National Statistics, some two-thirds of those working on zero hours contracts did not want to work more hours. About a third of all such workers are aged between 16 and 24 years, suggesting that it is a flexible type of contract used by young people in education.

The number of people working with zero hours contracts has increased significantly in recent years. In 2011 there were some 190,000, making up 0.6 per cent of the total workforce. By 2016 this had increased to 905,000 people, making up some 2.8 per cent of the total workforce.[64] According to ACAS,[65] the key points that one should note about these contracts are:

● Zero hours contracts normally mean there is no obligation for employers to offer work, or for workers to accept it.
● Most zero hours contracts will give staff 'worker' employment status.
● Zero hours workers have the same employment rights as regular workers, although they may have breaks in their contracts, which affect rights that accrue over time.
● Zero hours workers are entitled to annual leave, the national minimum wage and national living wage and pay for work-related travel in the same way as regular workers.

---

62 The Conduct of Employment Agencies and Employment Businesses (Amendment) Regulations 2014, SI 2014/3351.
63 The Conduct of Employment Agencies and Employment Businesses (Amendment) Regulations 2016, SI 2016/510.
64 All these statistics on zero hours work come from the Labour Force Survey: Zero hours contracts data tables (March 2017) which can be found at: www.ons.gov.uk/employmentandlabourmarket/peopleinwork/earningsandworkinghours/datasets/zerohourssummary datatables
65 ACAS 'Zero hours contracts', www.acas.org.uk/index.aspx?articleid=4468

Most people working on zero hours contracts will have worker status (see s. 230(3)(b) ERA 1996) but there is the potential for this to develop into employee status. Much will depend upon the contract and how it is put into practice (see Chapter 2, sections 2.3 and 2.4 on employment status).

There is always the potential for abuse by some employers such as workers feeling that they are obliged to work all the hours asked of them in order to ensure that they continue to receive work. One type of abuse that has now been made unenforceable was the inclusion of 'exclusivity' clauses in zero hours contracts so that workers were unable to take work from others even if not offered work from their usual employer. Section 27(3) ERA 1996 provides that any such exclusivity clause is unenforceable against the worker and in 2015 the government adopted regulations[66] making it an automatically unfair dismissal if a worker is dismissed for breaching an exclusivity clause and/or suffers detriment for doing so.

3.6 Gangmasters and labour abuse

Gangmaster is the word used to refer to individuals or groups of individuals who hire out 'gangs' of workers for the completion of certain tasks, most commonly in agriculture and parts of the fishing industry. Their activities had fallen outside the regulatory controls covering employment agencies and businesses. It appears that the individuals making up these gangs are often immigrants, sometimes illegal, who work long hours for low pay and are generally exploited. The worst incident in recent times was the drowning of 21 Chinese cockle pickers in Morecambe Bay in 2004. It has been estimated that there are up to 60,000 such workers living on very low pay in the United Kingdom.

In response to these issues the government adopted the Gangmasters (Licensing) Act 2004. This Act made provision for the licensing of activities concerning the supply of workers involved in agriculture, horticulture, shellfish gathering and associated processing industries.

The 2004 Act established the Gangmasters Licensing Authority (GLA) which issued licences to gangmasters and kept under review the activities of persons acting as gangmasters. A person or organisation may not be a gangmaster without a licence issued by the Authority and a register of licences is accessible to members of the public. The Immigration Act 2016 merged the GLA into a newly created Gangmasters and Labour Abuse Authority (GLAA). This new authority came into being on 1 October 2016. Overseeing its work is the newly created post of Director of Labour Market Enforcement. The Director will have responsibility for the GLAA, the National Minimum Wage Unit and the Employment Agency Inspectorate.

Persons who act as gangmasters without a licence or with false documents are guilty of an offence and can be fined plus imprisoned for up to 12 months. Similarly, a person may not knowingly use an unlicensed gangmaster. Such a person will also be liable to a fine and imprisonment for a period up to 51 weeks. The 2004 Act also allows the government minister to appoint enforcement officers who will ensure that only licensed gangmasters are operating. These officers have wide powers to inspect records and obtain information. Obstruction of such officers is a criminal offence, allowing fines and imprisonment of the obstructors.

---

66 The Exclusivity Terms in Zero Hours Contracts (Redress) Regulations 2015, SI 2015/2021.

Further reading

Adam, S., Miller, H. and Pope, T. *Tax, Legal Form and the Gig Economy* (Institute for Fiscal Studies, 2017).

Department for Business, Innovation and Skills *Understanding self-employment: BIS Enterprise Analysis research report* (2015), www.gov.uk/government/uploads/system/uploads/attachment_data/file/500305/understanding-self-employment.pdf

Trades Union Congress *Living on the Edge: The rise of job insecurity in modern Britain* (December 2016), www.tuc.org.uk/sites/default/files/Living%20on%20the%20Edge%202016.pdf

www.gla.gov.uk – the Gangmasters and Labour Abuse Authority website.

Chapter 4

The contract of employment

Chapter Contents

4.1 Express terms

In the same way that contract formation can be partly express and partly by implication,[1] the terms may be both express and implied. In the interests of transparency, the Contracts of Employment Act 1963 required employers to give each employee a written statement setting out certain particulars of the employee's terms of service. This Act, subsequently amended and now contained in the ERA 1996, preceded an EEC Directive[2] on this issue and, rather unusually, the adoption of European legislation required little change in domestic law. The Directive required Member States to ensure that all employees received information 'of the essential aspects of the contract or employment relationship'.[3]

The express terms of a written contract will normally be conclusive in the event of a dispute. In *Gascol Conversions Ltd v JW Mercer*[4] the Court of Appeal held that:

> it is well settled that where there is a written contract of employment, as there was here, and the parties have reduced it to writing, it is the writing which governs their relations. It is not permissible to say they intended something different.

In this case the employees had signed a written statement accepting a new contract of employment. By way of contrast, in *Systems Floors (UK) Ltd v Daniel*,[5] the EAT concluded that a statement of terms and conditions of employment, given to the employee as a result of the employer's statutory obligations,[6] was only evidence of a contract of employment. In this case the individuals had signed a document which, it was held, was an acknowledgement of the receipt of the statutory statement. The EAT held that this statement did not constitute a written contract between the parties. It was merely a document that stated the employer's view of the terms. It may provide strong *prima facie* evidence of what the terms are but it is not conclusive of the terms of the employment contract. However, there will be a heavy burden on the parties to show that the actual terms of the contract are different from those contained in the statement.

Article 2(2)(c) of the Directive specifies that the information given to the employee must include the title, grade or nature of the post and give a brief specification or description of the work. The Court of Justice has held that this provision is sufficiently precise and unconditional to allow individuals to rely on it before the national courts. Although the written statement of terms is important evidence, employers must be allowed to offer evidence that they have made a mistake and provided incorrect terms.[7]

4.2 The statutory statement

Section 1 ERA 1996 provides that employees should receive a written statement of the particular terms of employment not later than two months after the beginning of employment. This statement may be given in instalments but must be complete not later than the two months, even if the employment ends within that period.[8] If a person, before the two months have passed, is to work

---

1 See *Stack v Ajar-Tec* [2015] IRLR 474.

2 Council Directive 91/533/EEC on an employer's obligation to inform employees of the conditions applicable to the contract or the employment relationship OJ L288/32 18.10.91.

3 Ibid., art. 2(1).

4 [1974] IRLR 155 at p. 157 CA.

5 [1981] IRLR 475.

6 Now s. 1 ERA 1996.

7 Joined cases C-253/96 to 258/96 *Kampelmann v Landschaftsverband Westfalen-Lippe* [1998] IRLR 334.

8 Section 2(6) ERA 1996.

outside the United Kingdom for a period of at least one month, then the statement must be given to them before they leave the country.[9]

Sections 7A and 7B ERA 1996 provide that employers need not give a separate statement if they provide a letter of engagement or a contract of employment containing the information that would have been given if it were contained in such a statement.[10] This document still needs to be given within the two-month period or it can be given in the form of a letter of engagement prior to the start of employment. In such a case the effective date of the document will be the date on which employment begins.[11]

Section 11 ERA 1996 allows an employee to make a reference to an employment tribunal if a statutory statement or an alternative document is not received or if it is incomplete, or the employer has failed to provide a statement of any changes that take place.[12] However, the Court of Appeal has ruled that employment tribunals do not have jurisdiction to construe contractual terms contained or referred to in the statement of particulars of existing employees[13] (but see s. 3 Employment Tribunals Act 1996 which deals with the rights of those who have a breach of contract claim arising or outstanding on termination of employment). If the employment has ceased, the reference must be made within three months of the cessation or such further time as the employment tribunal thinks was reasonably practicable. If the lack of, or incompleteness of, a statutory statement or alternative document becomes evident upon a claim being made under certain employment tribunal jurisdictions, such as unfair dismissal or disability, sex or race discrimination, then the tribunal is required to increase the compensation awarded by an amount equivalent to between two and four weeks' pay.[14] Where compensation is not awarded, the employment tribunal must award a minimum of two to four weeks' pay.[15] In addition, it should be noted that s. 12A Employment Tribunals Act 1996 allows employment tribunals to impose a financial penalty on employers where there has been a breach of employment rights and the employment tribunal thinks that 'the breach has one or more aggravating features'.[16] Normally, the penalty must not be less than £100 or more than £5,000 but regard must be had to the employer's ability to pay and there is a 50 per cent discount if payment if made within 21 days.[17]

The ERA 1996 provides the following minimum list of contents for the statement of terms and conditions.

4.2.1 Names and addresses of employer and employee[18]

The identity of the employer may be the subject of dispute. This may be true of individuals who are placed by one employer to work in the premises and under the control of another employer, such as agency staff.[19] It may also be true of changes resulting from a reorganisation or a transfer of employees between employers. However, a transfer of a contract of employment needs the

---

9 Section 2(5) ERA 1996.

10 The information contained in ss 1(3)(a)–(c) and 4(a)–(c), (d)(i), (f) and (h).

11 Section 7B ERA 1996.

12 Section 4(1) ERA 1996.

13 *Southern Cross Healthcare Ltd v Perkins* [2011] IRLR 247.

14 Section 38 EA 2002; the complete list of such jurisdictions is contained in Sch. 5 to the Act; it includes, apart from those mentioned above, a wide range of issues such as those relating to the national minimum wage, working time and redundancy payments.

15 Subject to the maximum for a week's pay specified in s. 227 ERA 1996.

16 These 'features' are not defined but are clearly different to the circumstances in which aggravated damages might be awarded – for example, in discrimination cases.

17 Section 12A Employment Tribunals Act 1996 also deals with situations where there is more than one claim by a worker or more than one claimant against the same employer.

18 Section 1(3)(a) ERA 1996.

19 See *Dacas v Brook Street Bureau* [2004] IRLR 358 (Chapter 3 above).

employee's knowledge and, at least, implied consent.[20] In a case where two disabled employees were sponsored by Royal British Legion Industries to work in a 'host' organisation and remained there for nine years,[21] there was a dispute as to the identity of the employer. The EAT concluded that the correct approach was to start with the written contractual arrangements and decide whether these represented the true intentions of the parties. If they did, then the tribunal needed to discover if the situation had changed and when. There was a need to look at the reality of the situation in order to come to the correct conclusion.[22]

4.2.2 Date when employment began[23]

The date when employment begins can be important in establishing whether an employee has the minimum length of continuous service required for entitlement to various employment protection rights (see Chapter 2). For example, those individuals who are employed as temporary staff via an employment agency and are then employed on a permanent basis by the host company at which they work may need to clarify the precise start date of the new employment. The *Systems Floors*[24] case (see 4.1 above) involved a dispute about the employee's start date with the ability to make an unfair dismissal claim depending on the outcome.

4.2.3 Date on which continuous employment began[25]

For the purposes of assessing length of service, a person 'starts work' when their contract of employment commences rather than the date when they first undertake duties. This principle is likely to have a particular impact when the first day of the month is a Bank Holiday.[26] There is a requirement to take into account employment with a previous employer if that counts towards continuity. If there is a change of employer and a transfer of employment in accordance with s. 218 ERA 1996 or a relevant transfer takes place in accordance with the Transfer of Undertakings (Protection of Employment) Regulations 2006,[27] then service with the previous employer is likely to be added to the period of service with the new employer (see Chapter 10).

4.2.4 Remuneration[28]

The statement will need to contain information on the scale or rate of remuneration or the method of calculating it and the intervals at which it is paid. Remuneration can have a wider meaning than the payment of wages, although the term 'wages' itself is capable of a broad definition. It need not be confined to the payment of regular wages, but may include payment relating to work done.[29] Wages, according to s. 27(1) ERA 1996, means 'any sums payable to the worker in connection with his employment' (see below).[30]

---

20 See *Bolwell v (1) Redcliffe Homes Ltd; (2) O'Connor* [1999] IRLR 485 CA. On the impact of the Transfer of Undertakings (Protection of Employment) Regulations 2006, SI 2006/246, see Chapter 10.

21 *Secretary of State for Education and Employment v Bearman* [1998] IRLR 431.

22 See *Clifford v Union of Democratic Mineworkers* [1991] IRLR 518 CA.

23 Section 1(3)(b) ERA 1996.

24 *Systems Floors (UK) Ltd v Daniel* [1981] IRLR 475.

25 Section 1 (3)(c) ERA 1996.

26 See s. 211(1) ERA 1996 and *General of the Salvation Army v Dewsbury* [1984] IRLR 222.

27 See note 19 above.

28 Section 1(4)(a) ERA 1996.

29 See *New Century Cleaning Co Ltd v Church* [2000] IRLR 27 CA.

30 Section 27(1) ERA 1996 lists a number of items that are included in the term 'wages', such as statutory sick pay and statutory maternity pay; s. 27(2) lists a number of items that are excluded from the definition, such as payments for expenses and redundancy pay.

Employees also have the right to receive a written itemised pay statement from the employer. This is to be given before or at the time of payment and must contain information about: the gross[31] amount of wages or salary; the amount of any variable or fixed deductions and the purpose for which they are made; the net amount of wages payable; and, where different parts are payable in different ways, the amount and method of each part-payment.[32] The employer may give the employee a statement which contains an aggregate amount of fixed deductions, provided that the employer has given, at or before the time at which the pay statement is given, a standing statement of fixed deductions.[33] Such a standing statement must be in writing and contain details of the amount and purpose of each deduction and the intervals at which the deduction will be made. The statement can be amended in writing by the employer and must be renewed with amendments at least every 12 months.[34]

An employer may not receive a payment or payments from one of their workers, in their capacity as an employer, unless there is a pre-existing contractual agreement for such payment(s) to be made, or there is a statutory provision authorising such payment(s).[35] The exceptions to this rule are contained in s. 16 ERA 1996. These exceptions are:

1. Any payments that are a reimbursement of overpayment of wages or expenses paid to the worker.
2. A payment made by a worker as a consequence of any disciplinary proceedings resulting from a statutory provision.
3. Any payments required by the employer as a result of the worker taking part in industrial action.
4. A payment whose purpose is the satisfaction of an order of a court or tribunal requiring the payment to the employer.[36]

The employer does not have complete freedom to regulate remuneration as there is statutory regulation of wages. For example, the National Minimum Wage Regulations 1999[37] provide for a statutory minimum wage; the Equality Act 2010 attempts to stop discrimination in pay between women and men; and the Maternity and Parental Leave etc. Regulations 1999[38] define remuneration during leave. Other sources of regulation may include collective agreements incorporated into the contract of employment as well as custom and practice within a particular industry.

4.2.5 Hours of work[39]

Any terms and conditions relating to hours of work, including those relating to normal hours of work, need to be included.[40] Normal working hours are where there is a fixed number or a minimum number of hours stated.[41] Where there are no normal working hours, there is a formula for calculating a week's wage for statutory purposes. This involves averaging over 12 weeks, although weeks in which remuneration is not due are excluded from this period.[42]

---

31 Gross amount is defined in s. 27(4) ERA 1996 as the total amount of wages before deductions of whatever nature.
32 Section 8 ERA 1996.
33 Section 9(1) ERA 1996.
34 Section 9(2)–(5) ERA 1996.
35 Section 15 ERA 1996.
36 Section 16 ERA 1996.
37 SI 1999/584.
38 SI 1999/3312.
39 Section 1(4)(c) ERA 1996.
40 According to the Court of Justice in Case 350/99 *Lange v Georg Schünemann GmbH* [2001] IRLR 244, Directive 91/533 on proof of the employment relationship requires employers to notify employees of any term which obliges the employees to work overtime.
41 See s. 234 ERA 1996 which is concerned with the calculation of a week's pay as in Part XI ERA 1996.
42 Section 224 ERA 1996.

An example of the issues that might arise when there is a lack of clarity on working hours occurred in *Ali v Christian Salvesen Food Services Ltd*,[43] which involved a dispute over an annualised hours contract of employment. Employees were paid on a notional 40-hour week, but were not entitled to overtime until they had worked 1,824 hours in one year. The problem arose for employees who were terminated during the course of the year and wanted payment for hours they had worked in excess of the notional 40 hours per week. The Court of Appeal refused to imply a term to deal with this issue, because there was a likelihood that such a term had been deliberately left out of the agreement on annualised hours.

The Working Time Regulations 1998[44] also have an important bearing on the hours worked (see Chapter 8). An employee is given a contractual right not to be required to work more than a maximum of 48 hours work per week, averaged over a reference period, unless there has been agreement otherwise in writing. Thus, in *Barber v RJB Mining (UK) Ltd*[45] the High Court issued a declaration that the employees who had been required to work in excess of this during the reference period were not required to work again until the average fell to the maximum permitted.

The Part-time Workers (Prevention of Less Favourable Treatment) Regulations 2000[46] raise an important issue in relation to working time. They introduced the principle of non-discrimination between part-time workers and full-time comparators. Regulation 5 establishes the principle of non-discrimination (see Chapter 3). A part-time worker has the right not to be treated less favourably than the employer treats a full-time comparator. The principle of *pro rata temporis* applies, so a part-timer should receive a proportion of the benefits enjoyed by the full-time comparator in relation to hours worked. However, the one exception to this concerns overtime. Part-timers are not entitled to premium overtime rates until they have at least worked hours which are the same as the basic full-time hours of the comparator.

4.2.6 Entitlement to holidays and holiday pay[47]

The statement of terms and conditions must enable the employee to calculate any entitlement to accrued holiday pay on termination of employment. The minimum amount of holidays is regulated by the Working Time Regulations 1998 (see Chapter 8).[48] Regulation 13 provides for a minimum of 5.6 weeks' paid[49] leave during a leave year. The Regulations also contain detailed provisions for dealing with individuals who terminate their employment during the year, enabling the employee to receive payment for leave not taken.[50]

4.2.7 Sickness, injury and pensions[51]

Employees are entitled to know the arrangements for absence through sickness and incapacity, including sickness pay. This information can be included in a separate document, as can information about pension schemes.[52] The statement of terms and conditions need merely direct individuals to the appropriate document, which must be 'reasonably accessible to the employee'.[53] There is no

---

43 [1997] IRLR 17 CA.
44 SI 1998/1833 as amended by the Working Time Regulations 1999, SI 1999/3372.
45 [1999] IRLR 308.
46 SI 2000/1551.
47 Section 1(4)(d)(i) ERA 1996.
48 Note 43 above.
49 Regulation 16 Working Time Regulations 1998 concerns payment for periods of leave.
50 Regulation 14 Working Time Regulations 1998.
51 Section 1(4)(d)(ii) ERA 1996.
52 Section 1(4)(d)(iii) ERA 1996.
53 Section 2(2) ERA 1996.

requirement for the employer to provide information about pensions if the employee's pension rights derive from any statutory provision, when those statutory provisions provide for another body or authority to give the employee information about pension rights.[54]

In *Mears v Safecar Security Ltd*[55] the written terms of employment did not contain any reference to sick pay. The Court of Appeal concluded that where there was a gap in the terms of employment and the tribunal had insufficient information to fill that gap, then the question should be settled in favour of the employee. However, in this case the court held that, taking into account all the circumstances and evidence, there had been no intention to provide pay during periods of absence through sickness and that such a term should have been included in the written terms of employment.

4.2.8 Length of notice[56]

The statement needs to reflect the notice that the employee is required to give and is entitled to receive on termination of employment. Minimum periods to which an employee and an employer are entitled are contained in s. 86 ERA 1996. These are related to the length of continuous employment. After one month's employment an individual with less than two years' continuous service is entitled to a week's notice. Thereafter one week is added for each year of service up to and including 12 years (see Chapter 5).

4.2.9 Title of job or job description[57]

There is a need to provide the job title or a brief job description of the work to be done by the employee. The reliance that can be placed upon this job title or brief description was tested before the Court of Justice in *Kampelmann*.[58] Here the employers realised that a mistake had been made in the job information. The Court of Justice held that the job title or description could be factual evidence of the job duties, but that proof of the essential aspects of the relationship cannot depend solely upon the employer's notification. Employers must therefore be allowed to bring evidence to show that the notification is wrong.

4.2.10 Temporary contracts[59]

Where a position is not intended to be permanent, there is an obligation to include the period for which it is expected to continue and the date, if it is a fixed-term contract, upon which the contract is expected to end. This type of contract can include agency workers, who may be engaged on a week-to-week or even day-to-day basis, as well as those individuals who are employed directly on fixed-term contracts. Issues arise for the latter when either the term is extended or the contract is not renewed (see Chapter 3).

4.2.11 Place of work[60]

The location of the work needs to be written down. If the employee is required or permitted to work at various locations, there needs to be a note to this effect, together with the address of the

---

54 Section 1(5) ERA 1996.
55 [1982] ICR 626 CA.
56 Section 1(4)(e) ERA 1996.
57 Section 1(4)(f) ERA 1996.
58 Joined cases C-253/96 to 258/96 *Kampelmann v Landschaftsverband Westfalen-Lippe* [1998] IRLR 334 CJEU.
59 Section 1(4)(g) ERA 1996.
60 Section 1(4)(h) ERA 1996.

employer. The precise place of work can be extremely important. For example, the consultation requirements for collective redundancies depend upon the number of employees to be dismissed 'at one establishment'.[61] Many employers will want flexibility[62] and a requirement for the employee to be mobile written into the contract of employment. In *Aparau v Iceland Frozen Foods plc*[63] an employee was transferred to another branch after having several disagreements with the store manager. The employee disputed the employer's right to insist on the transfer and resigned, claiming constructive dismissal. The question was whether a mobility clause had become incorporated into the contract of employment. The EAT held that it had not and that it was not necessary to imply such a term. In certain occupations there may be an implication that mobility is necessary, but not in the contract of employment of a cashier working in a shop, where the nature of the work did not make such a clause necessary.[64]

4.2.12 Collective agreements[65]

Any collective agreements which directly affect the terms and conditions of employment are to be included in the statement. This includes, where the employer is not a party to the agreement, the identities of the parties by whom the agreement is made. This latter requirement will apply to collective agreements that are, for example, reached by employers' associations and trade unions. It is apparent from s. 2(3) ERA 1996, which allows reference to a collective agreement on periods of notice, that the terms of the collective agreement should be reasonably accessible to the employee (for issues relating to the incorporation of collective agreements into contracts of employment, see below).

4.2.13 Periods working outside the United Kingdom[66]

If an employee is to work outside the United Kingdom for a period of more than one month, the statement will need to contain information about the period they are to be working outside the country, the currency in which they are to be paid, any additional remuneration payable and any terms and conditions relating to their return to the United Kingdom. This information was of particular importance when certain rights, such as those connected with making a claim for unfair dismissal, were dependent upon a person not ordinarily working outside Great Britain. Although this requirement no longer applies, the courts still expect an employee to be working in Great Britain at the time of dismissal.[67]

The government introduced regulations[68] to implement the Posted Workers Directive[69] in 1999. The purpose of the Directive is to ensure that any legislation concerning the employment relationship in a Member State should be extended to include workers posted to that State. This protection is in relation to maximum working hours, paid holidays, minimum pay rates, rules on temporary workers, health and safety at work, the protection of pregnant women and provisions for ensuring equality of treatment between men and women.

---

61 Section 188(1) TULRCA 1992 and see Chapter 11.
62 See *Deeley v British Rail Engineering Ltd* [1980] IRLR 147.
63 [1996] IRLR 119 EAT.
64 See also *Jones v Associated Tunnelling Co Ltd* [1981] IRLR 477 and *White v Reflecting Roadstuds Ltd* [1991] IRLR 331.
65 Section 1(4)(j) ERA 1996.
66 Section 1(4)(k) ERA 1996.
67 See *Jeffery v British Council* [2016] IRLR 935.
68 Equal Opportunities (Employment Legislation) (Territorial Limits) Regulations 1999, SI 1999/3163.
69 Council Directive 96/71/EC concerning the posting of workers in the framework of the provision of services OJ L18/1.

4.2.14 General provisions

If there are no particulars to be described under any of the headings above,[70] there needs to be a statement to that effect.[71] All of the information needs to be contained in a single document with the exception of: s. 1(4)(d)(ii) and (iii) relating to incapacity for work, including sick pay provisions, and pension schemes; s. 1(4)(e) relating to periods of notice; s. 1(4)(g) relating to temporary contracts; s. 1(4)(j) relating to collective agreements; and s. 1(4)(k) on employment outside the United Kingdom. Thus these matters can be dealt with in separate documents. In relation to incapacity for work, pensions, periods of notice and the impact of collective agreements, all there needs to be is a reference to some other document which is readily accessible to the employee.[72]

4.2.15 Disciplinary and grievance procedures[73]

The statement also needs either to specify the disciplinary and dismissal[74] rules and procedures relevant to an individual or refer them to a reasonably accessible document containing the rules and procedures. For the purposes of statutory statements, 'reasonably accessible' means that the employee has reasonable opportunities to read the documents in the course of employment, or the documents being made reasonably accessible to the employee in some other way.[75] There also needs to be reference to a person to whom employees may apply if dissatisfied with any disciplinary or dismissal decision relating to them. Additionally, any rules concerning the steps necessary for the purpose of seeking redress of any grievance need to be stated as well as specifying the person to whom the employee should address grievances.[76] The disciplinary, dismissal or grievance requirements do not apply if the complaint relates to health and safety at work.

A failure to provide and/or implement a procedure may amount to a breach of contract entitling the employees to make a claim for constructive dismissal. In *W A Goold (Pearmak) Ltd v McConnell*,[77] two salespersons had their method of remuneration changed, which resulted in a substantial drop in their income. There was no established procedure for dealing with such grievances, but they talked to their manager initially. Nothing was done as a result of this. They then approached a new managing director, with whom they had a number of discussions. They were promised that something would be done, although nothing happened immediately. They then sought an interview with the chairman of the company, but were told that such interviews could only be arranged through the managing director. As a result they resigned and claimed constructive dismissal. Having considered Parliament's intentions in requiring employers to provide information about whom employees might approach if dissatisfied with a disciplinary matter or any grievance, the EAT concluded that the employer was in breach of the implied term to promptly afford a reasonable opportunity to obtain redress for a grievance.

Similarly, an attempt to use different procedures from those contractually agreed may entitle the employee to seek an injunction to stop the employer's action.[78] In *Raspin v United News Shops Ltd*[79] an employee was dismissed after the failure of the employer to follow agreed disciplinary procedures. The employee was awarded compensation by the employment tribunal to compensate for the period that would have been worked if the procedure had been followed.[80]

70 Under s. 1(3) or (4) ERA 1996.
71 Section 2(1) ERA 1996.
72 Section 2(2) and (3) ERA 1996.
73 Section 3 ERA 1996.
74 Section 3(1)(aa) ERA 1996.
75 Section 6 ERA 1996.
76 See Chapter 5 (section 5.4.5) below on the right to be accompanied at a disciplinary or grievance hearing.
77 [1995] IRLR 516.
78 See *Peace v City of Edinburgh Council* [1999] IRLR 417 and *Deadman v Bristol City Council* [2007] IRLR 888.
79 [1999] IRLR 9.
80 See also *Harper v Virgin Net Ltd* [2004] IRLR 390.

4.3 Implied terms

Guidance about the implication of terms was given in *Mears v Safecar Security Ltd*.[81] First, one needs to see if there is an express term. If not, one should decide if there was a term which could be said to have been agreed by implication. If this is not the case, then one looks to see whether such a term can be derived from all the circumstances, including the actions of the parties in the period during which the employment lasted. Finally, if none of this is possible, the employment tribunal may be required to invent a term. This last point was strongly disagreed with by the Court of Appeal in *Eagland v British Telecommunications plc*.[82] The case concerned a part-time cleaner who disputed her statement of terms and conditions. It omitted any terms relating to paid holidays, pay during absence for sickness and membership of a pension scheme which were included in the contracts of other part-time cleaners. The court held that it was not the task of employment tribunals to invent terms which had not been agreed between the parties. It distinguished between those terms which were mandatory and those which were non-mandatory. Amongst the latter are arrangements for disciplinary rules, pensions and sick pay schemes. Included in the former would be those legal necessities that arise out of a contract of employment – for example, minimum periods of notice. Although the employment tribunal will have the opportunity to include those terms arising out of legal necessities, they have no power to impose non-mandatory terms where there is no evidence of the parties' intentions.

4.3.1 Terms implied by statute

Employment legislation is often designed to affect the terms in contracts of employment. One group of statutes and regulations are those concerned with non-discrimination. The most overt example of such implication of a term is contained in s. 66 Equality Act 2010, which states that:

> If the terms of A's work do not (by whatever means) include a sex equality clause, they are to be treated as including one.

A second group of statutes and regulations is concerned with specific terms and with setting minimum standards. These include the Working Time Regulations 1998,[83] which, for example, impose rules about maximum working hours and holiday entitlement, and the National Minimum Wage Act (NMWA) 1998, which requires minimum rates of pay for certain workers.

The third category is concerned with allowing statutory bodies to regulate the contents of the contract. This will include the Central Arbitration Committee (CAC), which has powers under s. 185 TULRCA 1992 to deal with disputes over disclosure of information. The CAC may require the employer to observe certain terms and conditions that it specifies. The CAC also has extensive powers to require collective bargaining arrangements between employers and trade unions in relation to the contents of certain aspects of the contract of employment (see Chapter 12).

4.3.2 Terms implied in fact

These are intended to determine the true intentions of the parties. It is not a matter of law, but a matter of fact which the parties intended to be included in the contract. The two standard tests used to decide whether a term can be implied are the business efficacy test[84] and the officious bystander

---

81 [1982] ICR 626 CA.
82 [1992] IRLR 323 CA.
83 SI 1998/1833.
84 See *The Moorcock* (1889) 14 PD 64.

test, although these may be used as one. In *Shirlaw v Southern Foundries*[85] McKinnon LJ suggested that a term could be implied where it was so obvious that 'it goes without saying':

> If, while the parties were making their bargain, an officious bystander were to suggest some express provision for it in the agreement, they would testily suppress him with a common 'Oh, of course'.

Lord Wright in *Luxor (Eastbourne) Ltd v Cooper*[86] suggested that these tests allowed the implication of a term of which it can be predicated that 'it goes without saying', some term not expressed but necessary to give to the transaction such business efficacy as the parties intended.

One example in the employment context is *Jones v Associated Tunnelling Co Ltd*[87] where there was a dispute about whether an employee was required to work at a particular location. Browne-Wilkinson J stated that, in order to achieve business efficacy, the starting point must be that a contract of employment cannot simply be silent on the place of work:

> [I]n such a case, it seems to me that there is no alternative but for the tribunal or court to imply a term which the parties, if reasonable, would probably have agreed if they had directed their minds to the problem.[88]

In *Ali v Christian Salvesen Food Services Ltd*[89] the court refused to imply a term into an annualised hours contract, even though there was an apparent gap, because the parties may have intended to leave that gap in the agreement. The Court of Appeal concluded:

> The importation of an implied term depends, in the final analysis, upon the intention of the parties as collected from the words of the agreement and the surrounding circumstances.

The desirability of putting into effect the intentions of the parties was also illustrated in *Aspden v Webb Poultry & Meat Group (Holdings) Ltd.*[90] Here an employer introduced a generous permanent health scheme for employees, allowing incapacitated employees to receive an amount equivalent to 75 per cent of their annual salary, beginning 26 weeks after the start of the incapacity. The employee was dismissed during a prolonged absence as a result of a serious illness. He claimed that there was an implied term in his contract that he would not be dismissed during incapacity for work as this would frustrate the benefits of the health insurance scheme. Although there was an express term in the contract allowing the employer to dismiss as a result of prolonged incapacity, the court implied a term that a dismissal would not take place to stop an employee benefiting from the health scheme. This was because the contract was not written with the scheme in mind, and if the parties had stopped to consider the issue, it would have been their mutual intention not to frustrate the operation of the health scheme.[91]

More recently, in *Sparks v Department of Transport*[92] it was accepted that a sickness absence management clause in a staff handbook was apt for incorporation as an implied term. According to the

---

85 [1939] 2 KB 206 CA.
86 [1941] AC 108. See now *Ali v Petroleum Company of Trinidad and Tobago* [2017] IRLR 432.
87 [1981] IRLR 477.
88 See also *Courtaulds Northern Spinning Ltd v Sibson* [1988] IRLR 276 CA, which also concerned a change of work base for an employee.
89 [1997] IRLR 17 CA.
90 [1996] IRLR 521. See also *Briscoe v Lubrizol Ltd* [2002] IRLR 607.
91 In *Garratt v Mirror Group Newspapers Ltd* [2011] IRLR 591, the Court of Appeal held that an employee's entitlement to an enhanced redundancy payment was subject to an implied condition that he or she has signed a settlement agreement (see page 334 below).
92 [2016] IRLR 519.

Court of Appeal, there was no inconsistency in sickness management procedures being largely matters of guidance but with specific provisions having contractual force if that is the proper effect of the document as a whole.

4.3.3 Terms implied by law

These differ from implied terms of fact because they are not the result of identifying the intentions of the parties. In *Scally v Southern Health and Social Services Board*[93] the House of Lords stated:

> A clear distinction is drawn ... between the search for an implied term necessary to give business efficacy to a particular contract and the search, based on wider considerations, for a term which the law will imply as a necessary incident of a definable category of contractual relationship.

In *Malik and Mahmud v BCCI*[94] the court stated that such implied terms operated as 'default rules'.

4.4 Duties of the employer

4.4.1 Duty of mutual trust and confidence

There is a duty on the part of both the employer and the employee not to act in a manner which undermines an implied term of trust and confidence which enables the contract of employment to continue in the manner envisaged.[95] In *United Bank Ltd v Akhtar*[96] an employee had a mobility clause in his contract of employment which provided that he could be transferred to any of the bank's locations in the United Kingdom at short notice with only the possibility of a discretionary relocation payment. He was asked to move to Birmingham from Leeds with less than one week's notice, although he had difficult personal circumstances. The court held that this amounted to a fundamental breach of the implied term that employers will not conduct themselves in such a manner that will harm or destroy the relationship of confidence and trust between employer and employee. It was possible to imply a term which controls the exercise of discretion in a contract of employment. In this case there was an implied requirement that reasonable notice should be given in exercising the power to relocate the bank's employees.

An extreme example of employer behaviour can be found in the cases involving ex-employees of the Bank of Credit and Commerce International. This bank collapsed in 1991 after a period of trading insolvently and corruptly. In a series of cases, ex-employees claimed that the bank had been in breach of an implied term not to operate their business in a corrupt and dishonest manner. The House of Lords, in *Malik*,[97] accepted this argument and stated that:

> The conduct must, of course, impinge on the relationship in the sense that, looked at objectively, it is likely to destroy or seriously damage the degree of trust and confidence the employee is reasonably entitled to have in his employer.

---

93 [1991] IRLR 522 HL.

94 [1997] IRLR 462 HL.

95 See, for example, *Bliss v South East Thames Regional Health Authority* [1985] IRLR 308 CA, where the requirement that a consultant undergo a psychiatric examination was described by the court as an act which was calculated to destroy the relationship of confidence and trust which ought to exist between employer and employee.

96 [1989] IRLR 507; see also *Woods v WM Car Services (Peterborough) Ltd* [1982] IRLR 413 CA, where continual attempts to change an employee's terms and conditions of employment amounted to a breach of the duty of trust and confidence.

97 Consolidated cases *Malik v Bank of Credit and Commerce International SA, in liquidation; sub nom Mahmud v Bank of Credit and Commerce International SA* [1997] IRLR 462 SC.

Here the Supreme Court concluded that the manner in which the bank conducted itself impacted on the employment relationship and that the individuals were able to treat the employer's conduct as a repudiatory breach of contract, enabling them to leave and claim constructive dismissal. The court then went on to approve in principle a claim for what became known as 'stigma' damages. The employees' job prospects had been so damaged that they were entitled to compensation for the damage done. Many ex-employees of BCCI had signed compromise agreements[98] excluding further claims against the employer. However, the Supreme Court would not allow the employer to rely upon these agreements in order to exclude claims for stigma damages. The agreements were signed some eight years before the Supreme Court held that such claims were sustainable and the parties could not have intended to provide for the release from rights which they could never have contemplated as possible.[99]

Malik was further considered in Johnson v Unisys Ltd,[100] where an employee claimed damages for loss allegedly suffered as a result of the manner in which he was dismissed. The Supreme Court stated that a common law right in relation to the manner of dismissal could not co-exist alongside the statutory right not to suffer unfairness. It was not possible to imply a separate term into the contract of employment that a power of dismissal would be exercised fairly and in good faith. Thus, the employee could not rely upon the fact that he was dismissed without a fair hearing and in breach of the employer's disciplinary procedure to establish a claim for a breach of the implied term of trust and confidence. The court also stated that it was not appropriate to apply this implied term to dismissals, because it was about preserving the relationship between employer and employee and not about the way that the relationship is terminated.[101] Although it has a number of undesirable consequences – for example, requiring courts and tribunals to decide whether an employer's wrongful conduct formed part of the process of dismissal – this approach was followed in Eastwood v Magnox Electric plc.[102] In this case the claimants alleged that they had been victims of their employer's campaign to deprive them of their jobs by fabricating evidence and encouraging other employees to give false statements for the purpose of disciplinary proceedings. The Supreme Court held that in these circumstances the employees were not excluded from bringing common law claims for psychiatric injury based on a breach of trust and confidence prior to dismissal.

In Malik,[103] Lord Steyn stated:

> It is true that the implied term adds little to the employee's obligations to serve his employer loyally and not act contrary to his employer's interests. The major importance of the implied duty of trust and confidence lies in its impact on the obligations of the employer[104] . . . and the implied obligation as formulated is apt to cover the great diversity of situations in which a balance has to be struck between an employer's interest in managing his business as he sees fit and the employee's interest in not being unfairly and improperly exploited.

The affected employees still needed to establish that the bank's wrongdoing had stigmatised them in a way which undermined their prospects of finding alternative employment. In a subsequent decision[105] the Court of Appeal held that the question to be asked was: but for the breach of duty,

---

98 See Chapter 6.

99 Bank of Credit and Commerce International v Ali [2001] IRLR 292 HL.

100 [2001] IRLR 279 HL.

101 See Addis v Gramophone Company Ltd [1909] AC 488 HL, which prevents an employee in a case of wrongful dismissal from recovering damages for injured feelings, mental distress or damage to reputation arising out of the manner of the dismissal.

102 [2004] IRLR 733.

103 [1997] IRLR 462 at p. 468.

104 The court cited Douglas Brodie, 'The Heart of the Matter: Mutual Trust and Confidence' (1996) 25 Industrial Law Journal 121.

105 Bank of Credit and Commerce International SA v Ali (No 3) [2002] IRLR 460 CA.

what would the prospective employer have done and what would have been the result for the employee? This might mean looking at the whole history of a person's search for new employment, such as considering how many jobs have been applied for, how many interviews obtained and what the results were. It is for the claimant to show causation, but the judge should look at the whole picture in reaching a conclusion.

In *French v Barclays Bank plc*[106] the action of the employer in stopping an interest-free bridging loan to a relocated employee, as a result of the length of time it took to sell the employee's old house, was held to be a serious breach of this implied term. This was despite the fact that the loan facility was at the discretion of the employer. Similarly, the provision of a reference to a potential employer revealing information about which the employee was unaware is also likely to be a breach. In *TSB Bank plc v Harris*,[107] when a prospective employer approached the current employer for a reference, the latter revealed that 17 customer complaints had been made about the employee. It was the employer's practice not to discuss these with the employee concerned, which meant that the information, as a result of which a job offer was withdrawn, was unknown to the individual at the time of the reference. This failure to inform the employee and to discuss the complaints with her prior to revealing the information to a prospective employer amounted to a breach of the implied term of mutual trust and confidence.[108]

Logically, the duty of trust and confidence can also arise before the actual commencement of employment – for example, where there is a forward contract to work for an employer.[109]

It should also be noted that this implied term is dependent upon the alleged conduct of the employer being without reasonable and proper cause. Thus, if an employer has justifiable suspicions that an employee was dishonest, it would not be a breach of trust and confidence to remove responsibilities for cash from that individual's duties. This was the case in *Hilton v Shiner Ltd*,[110] where the EAT stated that a two-stage process had to be completed. First, whether there had been acts which seem likely to seriously damage or destroy the relationship of trust and confidence. Second, whether there is no reasonable or proper cause for those acts.

Sexual harassment by a senior employee against a more junior one is also likely to amount to a breach of the implied term. If the actions were such that, over a period of time, an employee found the workplace intolerable and felt that they had to resign over the unwanted harassment, that individual may then be entitled to claim constructive dismissal because of the breach.[111] More generally, the contract of employment requires the maintenance of self-esteem and dignity. Thus the use of foul and abusive language could be a breach of trust and confidence[112] as could allegations about the employee made to others if they are calculated to seriously damage the employment relationship.[113]

The process by which an employer deals with an employee who is to be investigated can itself lead to a breach of mutual trust and confidence. Thus the suspension of a care worker pending an inquiry about allegations of sexual abuse against a child in her care was interpreted as a breach of the implied term of trust and confidence.[114] The court held that just because an investigation was to

---

106 [1998] IRLR 646 CA.

107 [2000] IRLR 157; see also cases under duty of care below.

108 In *McBride v Falkirk Football and Athletic Club* [2012] IRLR 22 it was held that the club breached trust and confidence by imposing changes on the claimant without prior notice, consultation or discussion.

109 See *Tullett Prebon Plc v BGC Brokers LP* [2011] IRLR 420 CA.

110 [2001] IRLR 727.

111 See (1) *Reed*; (2) *Bull Information Systems Ltd v Stedman* [1999] IRLR 299.

112 See *Horkulak v Cantor Fitzgerald* [2003] IRLR 756.

113 See *RDF Group plc v Clements* [2008] IRLR 208 where the High Court acknowledged that 'garden leave' alters the nature and content of this implied term.

114 *Gogay v Hertfordshire County Council* [2000] IRLR 703 CA. See also *King v University Court of the University of St Andrews* [2002] IRLR 252, where the Court of Session confirmed that the duty of trust and confidence subsisted during an investigation into allegations of misconduct which might result in the employee's dismissal.

take place, it did not follow automatically that the employee must be suspended. The court described the employer's response as a 'knee-jerk reaction'. Similarly, in *Yapp v Foreign and Commonwealth Office*[115] it was held that the employer had breached the obligation of fair treatment in failing to conduct some basic analysis of the allegations of sexual misconduct against Yapp.

It remains to be seen how far the duty of trust and confidence imposes positive obligations on employers to ensure that employees are treated fairly. For example, the Supreme Court has accepted that in certain circumstances it will be necessary to imply an obligation on an employer to take reasonable steps to bring a contractual term to the employee's attention.[116] Similarly, in *Transco v O'Brien*[117] the Court of Appeal held that there was a breach of trust and confidence when, without reasonable excuse, an employee was denied the opportunity given to everyone else of signing a revised contract with enhanced redundancy payments. On the other hand, a failure to warn an employee who was proposing to exercise pension rights that the way he was proposing to act was not the most financially advantageous was not seen as breaching trust and confidence.[118] More recently, it was held that a refusal to allow a science professor to be accompanied by a specialist defence organisation representative at a misconduct investigation meeting breached the duty of trust and confidence. This was despite the fact that the university ordinances only expressly provided for accompaniment by a colleague or union. According to the judge, the investigator has discretion to add to the minimum levels of protection and here it was unfair to force the employee to attend the interview alone.[119]

Employees who believe that their employer has breached the duty of trust and confidence must decide what course of action to take. A resignation, which amounts to an acceptance of the employer's breach and the ending of the contract, may give rise to a claim for constructive dismissal. However, continuing to work and receive pay does not entitle the employee to disregard lawful and legitimate instructions from the employer because the duty to perform work and obey instructions is not dependent upon the employer's performance of its obligations.[120] If the employee resigns, the likely remedy for a successful claim will be compensation. Where there is a breakdown in mutual trust and confidence, it may be difficult for a tribunal to order reinstatement or re-engagement of the employee. In *Wood Group Heavy Industrial Turbines Ltd v Crossan*[121] an employee was dismissed for a genuine belief by the employer that the employee had been dealing in drugs at the workplace. The employment tribunal ordered re-engagement in the belief that the employers had not carried out sufficient investigations. The EAT allowed the employer's appeal against this remedy because it decided that:

> it is difficult to see how the essential bond of trust and confidence that must exist between an employer and an employee, inevitably broken by such investigations and allegations, can be satisfactorily repaired by re-engagement. We consider that the remedy of re-engagement has very limited scope and will only be practical in the rarest cases where there is a breakdown in confidence as between the employer and the employee.

4.4.2 Duty to provide work and pay

In *Beveridge v KLM UK Ltd*[122] an employee informed her employers that, after a long period of absence through sickness, she was fit to return to work. However, they refused to allow her to return until

---

115 [2013] IRLR 616.

116 *Scally v Southern Health Board* [1991] IRLR 522. Subsequently, in *Fraser v Southwest London St George's Mental Health Trust* [2012] IRLR 100, the EAT has confirmed that there is no duty on employers to advise employees of their rights as a matter of general law.

117 [2002] IRLR 444.

118 *University of Nottingham v Eyett* [1999] IRLR 87. See also *Outram v Academy Plastics* [2000] IRLR 499.

119 *Stevens v University of Birmingham* [2015] IRLR 899.

120 See *Macari v Celtic Football and Athletic Co Ltd* [1999] IRLR 787 at p. 795.

121 [1998] IRLR 680.

122 [2000] IRLR 765.

their own doctor had certified her fitness to do so. This process took six weeks, during which she was not allowed to work and was not paid. When she claimed that this amounted to an unauthorised deduction from her wages, the employment tribunal held that the employer was under no obligation to pay her as there was no express term of the contract to this effect. However, the EAT ruled that an employee who offers services to her employer is entitled to be paid unless there is an express provision of the contract providing otherwise. There was no such term in this case and the employee could do no more than attempt to fulfil her side of the contract.

There is also the question of whether there is an implied term in the contract of employment that the employer has a duty to provide work as well as pay. The traditional common law view was stated in *Collier v Sunday Referee Publishing Co Ltd*.[123] Here a newspaper subeditor was retained by his original employer after the newspaper for which he worked was taken over by another organisation. When he was not given any work to do, he claimed that his employer had breached his contract. Asquith J illustrated the general point graphically:

> Provided I pay my cook her wages regularly she cannot complain if I choose to take any or all of my meals out.

However, the court recognised that there were exceptions when there was an obligation to provide work. This would be the case where individuals earned their income from commission and where publicity is part of the bargain – for example, in the case of actors or singers.[124] This is especially important when employers seek to insist on employees serving out lengthy periods of notice whilst keeping them idle, in order to stop them going to work for what is perceived to be a rival organisation.[125] The purpose is to prevent the employee going to a rival company with up-to-date knowledge of the existing employer's business. This period of enforced idleness is sometimes referred to as 'garden leave'. It particularly affects individuals who are reliant upon continuing to work in order to maintain their skills or stay in the public eye. In *Provident Financial Group plc and Whitegates Estate Agency Ltd v Hayward*[126] there was a specific term in the contract of employment which provided that the employer need not provide work. Taylor LJ stated that:

> the employee has a concern to work and a concern to exercise his skills. That has been recognised in some circumstances concerned with artists and singers who depend on publicity, but it applies equally I apprehend, to skilled workmen and even to chartered accountants.

Thus the need to exercise and maintain skills could be widely interpreted as including those who are experts in their field. In *William Hill Organisation Ltd v Tucker*[127] an employee was put on six months' garden leave. In this case the court decided that the contract could be construed so as to give rise to an obligation on the employer to allow the employee to carry out his duties. This was not only because the individual held a 'specific and unique post' and needed to practise his skills regularly, but also because the terms of the contract pointed towards this conclusion, especially the obligation which required the employee to work the hours necessary to carry out the duties of the post in a

---

123 [1940] 2 KB 647.

124 See also *Breach v Epsylon Industries Ltd* [1976] IRLR 180 which emphasised that it was necessary to look at the background to the contract to consider how it should be construed, in order to decide whether there was a term to be implied concerning the provision of work.

125 The court is unlikely to give injunctive relief to an employer if the restriction stops the employee on 'garden leave' taking up employment with a non-competing organisation; see *Provident Financial Group plc and Whitegates Estate Agency Ltd v Hayward* [1989] IRLR 84 CA (below).

126 Ibid.

127 [1998] IRLR 313 CA.

full and professional manner. More recently, the High Court has introduced a qualification to the right to work. In *SG & R Valuation Service v Boudrais*[128] the judge stated that those who have the right to work hold it subject to the qualification that they have not, as a result of some prior breach of contract or other duty, demonstrated in a serious way that they are not ready and willing to work. For these purposes, the breach of contract or other duty must amount to wrongdoing by reason of which they will profit. In this case there had been evidence of poaching customers and the use of confidential information by two senior employees on garden leave whilst serving out their notice before joining a competitor.

4.4.3 Duty of care

This is a duty that might cover a variety of responsibilities. There are certain statutory requirements relating to health and safety matters. Section 2(1) HASAWA 1974 requires an employer 'to ensure, so far as is reasonably practicable, the health, safety and welfare at work of all his employees'. Similarly there is an obligation on employees to inform the employer, or any other person responsible for health and safety, of any work situation which might present a 'serious and imminent danger to health and safety'.[129]

There is an implied duty in every contract of employment that an employer will take all reasonable steps to provide and maintain a safe system of work so as not to expose the employee to unnecessary risks of injury. However, in *Greenway v Johnson Matthey*,[130] where the claimants suffered platinum sensitisation from exposure at work, the Court of Appeal held that in order to claim damages there must be an actionable injury and not purely economic loss. In *Wilsons and Clyde Coal Co Ltd v English*,[131] Lord Thankerton listed a number of duties of the master towards servants:

> If the master retains control, he has a duty to see that his servants do not suffer through his personal negligence, such as (1) failure to provide proper and suitable plant, if he knows, or ought to have known, of such failure; (2) failure to select fit and competent servants; (3) failure to provide a proper and safe system of working; and (4) failure to observe statutory regulations.

This obligation extends to responsibility for actions taken by employees and agents of the employer. The employer may be liable even if, centrally, they had taken all precautions as were 'reasonably practicable' but this had not been done by their employees elsewhere.[132] This general duty also extends to persons who are not directly employed.[133] However, provided that the employer had taken all steps that are reasonably practicable, they should not be held liable for the acts of their careless or negligent employees or agents. In *R v Nelson Group Services (Maintenance) Ltd*[134] gas fitters had not completed their tasks correctly and had thereby exposed customers to danger. The Court of Appeal allowed an appeal on the grounds that the judge's directions had not allowed the employer's defence of reasonable practicability to be decided by the jury.

Section 2(2)(e) HASAWA 1974 states that an employer has a duty to provide and maintain a working environment that is, as far as is reasonably practicable, safe and without risk to health. This is similar to the implied term in every contract of employment that employers have a duty to provide and monitor, as far as is reasonably practicable, a working environment which is reasonably

---

128 [2008] IRLR 770.
129 Regulation 14(2) Management of Health and Safety at Work Regulations 1999, SI 1999/3242.
130 [2016] IRLR 526.
131 [1938] AC 57 HL.
132 *R v Gateway Foods Ltd* [1997] IRLR 189 CA.
133 Section 3(1) HASAWA 1974 and *R v Associated Octel Co Ltd* [1997] IRLR 123 HL.
134 [1999] IRLR 646 CA.

suitable for employees to perform their contractual duties. This includes the right not to be required to work in a smoke-filled atmosphere, as in *Waltons & Morse v Dorrington*.[135] In this case a secretary objected to working in poorly ventilated accommodation with a number of smokers. Although the employer took some measures, they proved inadequate to solve the problem and the employee resigned and successfully claimed unfair constructive dismissal. In *Dryden v Greater Glasgow Health Board*[136] the introduction of a no-smoking policy by the employer, after consultation, had an adverse effect on a nurse who smoked 30 cigarettes a day. The EAT concluded that, where a rule is introduced for a legitimate purpose, the fact that it has an adverse effect on an employee does not enable that individual to resign and claim constructive dismissal. There was no implied term in the employee's contract of employment which entitled her to continue smoking.

The employer's duty of care is owed to the individual employee and not to some unidentified ordinary person. This is especially true in relation to psychiatric illness caused by stress at work. The stages in deciding whether employers have carried out their responsibilities are: first, whether the harm was foreseeable; second, what the employer did and should have done about it; and, third, where a breach has been shown, whether there is a causal relationship between the breach and the harm.

According to the Supreme Court,[137] the best statement of general principle remains that of Swanwick J in *Stokes v GKN Ltd*:[138]

> The overall test is the conduct of the reasonable and prudent employer taking positive thought
> for the safety of his workers in the light of what he knows or ought to know.

The test is the same whatever the employment. It is not the job that causes harm but the interaction between the individual and the job. There needs to be some indication to the employer that steps need to be taken to protect an employee from harm. Thus, if an employee returns to work after a period of illness and does not make further explanation or disclosure, then the employee is implying that he or she is fit to return to work. The employer is then entitled to take this at face value unless there is reason to think the contrary.[139] More recently, the Court of Appeal has emphasised the importance of distinguishing signs of stress and indicators of impending harm to health.[140]

Factors that are relevant to the question of foreseeability include: the nature and pressures of the job; is the workload more than normal for that job?; is the work particularly demanding for the employee?; are there signs of stress amongst others doing the same job?; is there a high level of absenteeism? The next stage is to consider whether there are signs of impending harm for the individual employee concerned, such as whether there are frequent or prolonged absences and whether the employee or his or her doctor has warned the employer about the risk of harm.[141]

Once harm is assessed as being foreseeable, attention focuses on what the employer should have done about it.[142] The actions that are reasonable will depend upon the employer's size and resources. It is then necessary to show that the breach was at least partly responsible for the harm. Thus, in *Corr v IBC Ltd*[143] the Supreme Court held that depression was the direct and foreseeable consequence of the accident and that suicide was the direct result of the deceased's depression.

---

135 [1997] IRLR 488. See the Smoke-free (Premises and Enforcement) Regulations 2006, SI/2006 3368.
136 [1992] IRLR 469.
137 *Barber v Somerset County Council* [2004] IRLR 475.
138 [1968] 1 WLR 1776.
139 See *Young v Post Office* [2002] IRLR 660.
140 *Dickins v O2 plc* [2009] IRLR 58.
141 See *Hone v Six Continents Ltd* [2006] IRLR 49 and *Intel Corporation v Daw* [2007] IRLR 355 CA.
142 See *Pratley v Surrey County Council* [2003] IRLR 794.
143 [2008] ICR 372.

The duty of care does not extend to medical practitioners who carry out health assessments on behalf of employers seeking to recruit staff. In *Baker v Kaye*[144] a medical practitioner concluded that an applicant was likely to consume excessive amounts of alcohol in a stressful work-related context. The employer withdrew a conditional offer of employment after receiving the medical report. Unfortunately, the applicant had already resigned from his previous post because he had not anticipated any problems with the report of the medical examination. The High Court was asked to consider whether there was a duty of care owed by the doctor to the applicant. The court relied upon *Caparo Industries*[145] and *Hedley Byrne & Co Ltd v Heller & Partners Ltd*[146] to reach the conclusion that it was clear that economic loss was a foreseeable consequence of a breach of this duty and that there was a sufficient proximity between the parties to give rise to a duty of care. However, in this case the court decided that the defendant was not in breach of that duty. In a subsequent decision, the Court of Appeal disagreed with this conclusion and held that there was no duty of care owed by a medical practitioner to a job applicant in these circumstances, even though the applicant might suffer economic loss as a result of a careless error in a doctor's report.[147] There was not sufficient proximity, as the duty of care will generally be owed to the person who commissions the report, not the subject of it. A medical practitioner is likely to be viewed, therefore, as an agent of the employer.[148]

In *Spring v Guardian Assurance plc*,[149] the Supreme Court held that an employer was under a duty of care to a former employee when providing a reference to a prospective employer. The duty was derived from the previous contractual relationship between the employer and the ex-employee. In this case the applicant sought damages for economic loss as a result of a failure to obtain work resulting from a reference written by a former employer. The question was whether the employer owed a duty of care to the applicant in the preparation of the reference. The Supreme Court decided that employees had a remedy in negligence if they could establish that the inaccurate reference was a result of the employer's lack of care. However, this does not mean that every reference needs to be full and comprehensive. In *Bartholomew v London Borough of Hackney*[150] the Court of Appeal needed to consider both the employer's duty to provide a reference for the individual and the obligation towards potential employers to provide a reference without being misleading or unfair.[151] The court accepted that a reference must not give 'an unfair or misleading impression overall, even if its discrete components are factually correct'. According to the High Court in *Kidd v Axa Equity & Law Life Assurance Society plc*,[152] it was not in the public interest to impose an obligation on employers to provide a full, frank and comprehensive reference. The court further held that to show a breach of the duty of care the claimant needed to show that:

1. The information provided in the reference was misleading.
2. The provision of such misleading information was likely to have a material effect on the mind of a reasonable recipient of the reference to the detriment of the claimant.
3. The defendants were negligent in providing such references.

The employer providing the reference is also under an obligation to carry out any necessary inquiries into the factual basis of any statements made in the reference. Unfavourable statements

---

144 [1997] IRLR 219.
145 *Caparo Industries plc v Dickman* [1990] 2 AC 605 HL.
146 [1964] AC 465 HL.
147 *Kapfunde v Abbey National plc* [1998] IRLR 583 CA.
148 See *London Borough of Hammersmith & Fulham v Farnsworth* [2000] IRLR 691, where the doctor's knowledge of an individual's disability was held to be enough for the employer to be held to have such knowledge.
149 [1994] IRLR 460 HL.
150 [1999] IRLR 246 CA.
151 The reference needs actually to have been given to a third party: see *Legal and General Assurance Ltd v Kirk* [2002] IRLR 124 CA.
152 [2000] IRLR 301.

should be confined to matters which had been investigated and for which there were reasonable grounds for believing that they were true.[153] In *Jackson v Liverpool City Council*[154] the Court of Appeal noted that accuracy and truth go to the facts, whereas fairness goes to the overall balance and opinion stated in the reference. In this case it was held that the reference and phone conversation together were not unfair because the latter made it clear that the allegations mentioned had not been investigated.[155] Indeed, it is worth noting that the EAT has held that a former employer could be liable for making negligent misstatements about an ex-employee to their current employer, even if those statements were not made in the reference.[156] However, a libel claim will fail if the defamatory imputations made were substantially true.[157]

Finally, if the employee has a safety grievance, there is an implied term that employers will act promptly and provide a reasonable opportunity for employees to obtain redress. This view was put forward in *Waltons & Morse v Dorrington*,[158] where a non-smoker's attempts to raise grievances about air quality were frustrated.

4.5 Duties of employees

4.5.1 Duty of obedience and co-operation

There is an implied duty to obey an employer's lawful and reasonable instructions and an employee's failure to do so might amount to a fundamental breach of contract.[159] However, it is possible for the failure to obey an unlawful instruction to result in a fair dismissal – for example, when an employer reasonably but mistakenly believed that they were giving a lawful instruction.[160] Certainly, a belief by the employee that the employer has breached an implied term is not justification for failing to obey other lawful and legitimate instructions.[161] This duty to obey might include the need to adapt to new technology. For example, in *Cresswell v Board of the Inland Revenue*[162] the introduction of computers into the administration of the PAYE system was held not to fall outside the job descriptions of the employees concerned. More recently, the EAT has ruled that there can be an implied term that an employee may be obliged to perform duties which are different from those expressly required by the contract or to perform them at a different place. However, an implied obligation to undertake work which is outside the express terms is only likely to be imposed where: the circumstances are exceptional; the requirement is plainly justified; the work is suitable; the employee suffers no detriment in terms of contractual benefits or status; and the change is temporary.[163]

The implied term to serve the employer faithfully also applies to managers who supervise others and exercise discretion in the carrying out of their duties. If the manager exercises that discretion in order to disrupt the work of the employer, then there may be a breach of this implied term. In *Ticehurst v British Telecom*,[164] as part of an industrial dispute, a supervisor refused to sign a declaration that she would work normally. This was seen as an intention not to perform the full range of duties

---

153 *Cox v Sun Alliance Life Ltd* [2001] IRLR 448 CA.
154 [2011] IRLR 1019.
155 See *Abdel-Khalek v Ali* [2016] IRLR 358; the Court of Appeal confirmed that the claimant has to demonstrate that the recipient was given the wrong impression.
156 *McKie v Swindon College* [2011] IRLR 575.
157 *Theedom v Nourish Ltd* [2016] IRLR 866.
158 [1997] IRLR 488.
159 See *Laws v London Chronicle (Indicator Newspapers) Ltd* [1959] 2 All ER 285 CA.
160 *Farrant v The Woodroffe School* [1998] IRLR 176.
161 See *Macari v Celtic Football and Athletic Co Ltd* [1999] IRLR 787.
162 [1984] IRLR 190.
163 *Luke v Stoke City Council* [2007] IRLR 305. However, see also the Court of Appeal's approach at [2007] IRLR 777.
164 [1992] IRLR 219 CA.

and amounted to a breach of the implied term to serve the employer faithfully. In *Wiluszynski v London Borough of Tower Hamlets*[165] local authority employees took partial industrial action and refused to answer queries from Members of the Council. Despite warnings, the employees carried on attending the place of work and completed all their other tasks. The employer refused to pay them for the period when they were not fulfilling all their contractual obligations. The Court of Appeal held that the employees were in repudiatory breach of their contracts but the employer had alternatives to accepting the breach and dismissing the employees. One of these alternatives was to tell them that they would not be paid during the period when they failed to carry out all the terms of their contracts.

This obligation to carry out duties in a full and professional manner was an issue in *Sim v Rotherham Metropolitan Borough Council*.[166] The National Union of Teachers instructed its members not to provide cover for absent colleagues. The union claimed that the system had operated on the basis of goodwill only. The High Court rejected this argument and stated that the teachers had a professional obligation which they owed to their pupils and the school in which they worked. The court accepted that there was no statement in the teachers' contracts to this effect but held that this was not to be expected in professional contracts of employment. Such contracts specified the nature of the work and these extra duties were simply part of the professional obligations of teachers.

4.5.2 Duty of fidelity

This duty is no more than an obligation to carry out loyally the job that the employee agreed to perform. This might require an employee to report a competitive threat of which they become aware,[167] although it is preferable for such an obligation to be imposed by an express term. There are two aspects to the duty of fidelity. The first is the implied duty not to compete with the employer and the second is not to disclose certain confidential information, except in certain circumstances. A further issue is the use of restrictive covenants to deter employees from working for competing businesses and using the knowledge and skills gained whilst in previous employment. According to the High Court, the necessity for non-compete provisions arises where non-solicitation and non-dealing covenants and restrictions on confidential information are difficult to police or there are material disputes about what information is confidential.[168]

4.5.2.1 Not competing

There is no general rule which, in the absence of an express term, restricts ex-employees from competing with their previous employer. If the former employer did not include an express term restricting the employees' activities,[169] then they are unlikely to be able to claim that there is any sort of implied term that achieves the same result.[170] The position is more complicated when considering existing employees who are contemplating or actively setting up a business to compete with their present employer. In *Lancashire Fires Ltd v SA Lyons & Co Ltd*,[171] the Court of Appeal cited with approval a judgment of Lord Greene MR[172] in which he warned against the danger of 'laying down any general proposition and the necessity for considering each case on its facts'. However, the High Court has ruled that where a contact address list is maintained on the employer's email system and is backed

---

165 [1989] IRLR 259 CA.

166 [1986] IRLR 391.

167 *Thomson Ecology v Apem Ltd* [2014] IRLR 184.

168 *Tradition Financial Services v Gamberoni* [2017] IRLR 698.

169 The validity of a non-competition clause is to be judged at the dates the acts relied on as constituting breaches took place: *Phoenix Group v Asoyag* [2010] IRLR 594.

170 *Wallace Bogan & Co v Cove* [1997] IRLR 453 CA.

171 [1997] IRLR 113 CA.

172 *Hivac Ltd v Park Royal Scientific Instruments Ltd* [1946] Ch 169.

up, that information belongs to the employer. Thus it cannot be removed or copied by employees for use outside.[173]

The obligations may be more extensive for some types of employees than others. In *Lancashire Fires* the younger brother of the company owner had obtained a loan from the company's principal supplier to set up in competition. He had also started to purchase the necessary premises and equipment. As a result he was held to have been in breach of the duty of fidelity. An individual does not breach an implied term of loyalty merely by indicating an intention to set up in competition with the employer, especially if any of the steps taken are in their own time. Thus two employees who wrote to a limited number of customers suggesting that they were about to start a competing business were held not to be in breach of such an implied term.[174] Other employers might find this a strange decision and understand why the employer in this case, having heard about the letter, dismissed the employees concerned. In *Adamson v B & L Cleaning Services Ltd*[175] an employee asked a customer to be put on a tendering list for a contract on which they were working when it was due for renewal. The EAT held that these actions amounted to a breach of the implied duty of fidelity.

Related to the issue of not competing is the making of secret profits from employment. Thus, if an employee acts in such a way that the employer loses trust and confidence in them, summary dismissal may be justified. In *Neary and Neary v Dean of Westminster*[176] the claimants were dismissed for using their positions in the organisation to make secret profits. This conduct was held to undermine fatally the relationship of trust between the parties. In *Nottingham University v Fishel*[177] the court distinguished between an individual's fiduciary duty and the individual's obligation to maintain trust and confidence. This case concerned the earnings of a university academic from organisations other than his employer. A feature of a fiduciary relationship is the duty to act in the interests of another. This is not necessarily the case in an employment relationship, where there is no obligation on the employee to pursue the employer's interests above their own.[178] To decide whether the employment relationship and the fiduciary relationship coincide requires an examination of the particular circumstances. In this case the individual did not have a fiduciary relationship because there was no contractual obligation to seek work on behalf of the university, rather than for himself.[179]

4.5.2.2 Restrictive covenants

In *Coppage v Safety Net Security Ltd*,[180] the Court of Appeal accepted that the following general principles apply. (i) Post-termination restraints are enforceable, if reasonable, but covenants in employment contracts are viewed more jealously than in other more commercial contracts, such as those between a seller and a buyer. (ii) It is for the employer to show that a restraint is reasonable in the interests of the parties and, in particular, that it is designed for the protection of some proprietary interest of the employer for which the restraint is reasonably necessary. (iii) Customer lists and other such information about customers fall within such proprietary interests. (iv) Non-solicitation clauses are therefore more favourably looked upon than non-competition clauses, for an employer is not entitled to protect himself against mere competition on the part of a former employee. (v) The question of reasonableness has to be asked as of the outset of the contract, looking forwards,

---

173 *Pennwell Publishing Ltd v Ornstein* [2007] IRLR 700. On the issue of employer property in emails see *Capital plc v Darch* [2017] IRLR 718.
174 See *Laughton and Hawley v Bapp Industrial Supplies Ltd* [1986] IRLR 245. On springboard relief against a team move, see *Dorma UK Ltd v Bateman* [2016] IRLR 616.
175 [1995] IRLR 193; see also *Marshall v Industrial Systems & Control Ltd* [1992] IRLR 294, where a company director making plans, and inducing another to join in those plans, to deprive their employer of their best customer, was held to have breached the duty of loyalty.
176 [1999] IRLR 288.
177 [2000] IRLR 471.
178 On the duty of employees to disclose their own misconduct, see *Item Software Ltd v Fassihi* [2004] IRLR 928.
179 However, he did have such a relationship in relation to other employees of the university out of whose work he made a profit.
180 [2013] IRLR 970.

as a matter of the covenant's meaning, and not in the light of matters that have subsequently taken place (save to the extent that those throw any general light on what might have been fairly contemplated on a reasonable view of the clause's meaning). (vi) In that context, the validity of a clause is not to be tested by hypothetical matters which could fall within the clause's meaning as a matter of language, if such matters would be improbable or fall outside the parties' contemplation. (vii) Because of the difficulties of testing in the case of each customer, past or current, whether such a customer is likely to do business with the employer in the future, a clause which is reasonable in terms of space or time will be likely to be enforced. Moreover, it has been said that it is the customer whose future custom is uncertain that is 'the very class of case against which the covenant is designed to give protection . . . the plaintiff does not need protection against customers who are faithful to him'. (viii) On the whole, cases in this area turn so much on their own facts that the citation of precedent is not of assistance.

Historically, the courts have drawn a distinction between 'objective knowledge', which is the property of the employer, and 'subjective knowledge', which is the property of the employee. This latter might consist of information in a person's memory, rather than confidential information kept by the employer. Even this subjective knowledge is capable of being protected, although the court will look at each case on its own facts. The names and addresses of customers may be legitimate information to be protected, even if it is innocently remembered by the ex-employee, rather than deliberately taken from the employer.[181] However, there is a distinction between those covenants against competition which follow a sale of a business, including its goodwill, and those covenants designed to prevent ex-employees entering into competition with their previous employers.[182] Covenants concerning the latter are more likely to be interpreted strictly by the courts and, as a matter of principle, all covenants should be clear so that those subject to them know what they can and cannot do.

The view that a restraint clause must not provide more protection than is necessary is illustrated in *TSC Europe (UK) Ltd v Massey*.[183] In this case an ex-employee was subject to a clause that stopped the inducement of employees to leave the company. The clause was held to be unreasonable and unenforceable for two reasons. First, it applied to all employees and not just those who had particular skills or knowledge that were important to the business. Second, it applied to any employee who joined the company during the prohibited period, including those who joined after the plaintiff had left. The test of reasonableness is applied by considering the substance and not the form of the transaction, and by reference to all the facts and surrounding circumstances.[184] In this case, it was held to be too wide[185] and, therefore, unenforceable.[186]

The same approach is taken with respect to contractual clauses which limit an individual's ability to compete with their ex-employer. According to the Court of Appeal, the employer needs to establish that at the time the contract was made the nature of the relationship was such as to expose the employee to the kind of information capable of protection beyond the term of the contract.[187] Thus a clause which, on its true construction, prohibited an employee engaging in any business in the same industry, rather than from any business competing with the ex-employer, was wider than necessary to protect the legitimate interests of that employer. It should also be noted that it is only

---

181 See *SBJ Stephenson Ltd v Mandy* [2000] IRLR 233.
182 See *Office Angels Ltd v Rainer-Thomas* [1991] IRLR 214.
183 [1999] IRLR 22.
184 Reasonableness must be interpreted in accordance with what was in the contemplation of the parties at the date the contract was made: *Patsystems v Neilly* [2012] IRLR 979. See also *Pickwell v Procam Ltd* [2016] IRLR 761 where injunctive relief was granted.
185 By way of contrast, a similar clause was held to be reasonable in *SBJ Stephenson Ltd v Mandy* [2000] IRLR 233, because the protection of the levels of investment in training employees and the stability of the workforce were legitimate subjects for a restrictive covenant.
186 See also *Bartholomews Ltd v Thornton* [2016] IRLR 432 where it was stated that it was contrary to public policy in effect to permit an employer to purchase a restraint.
187 *Thomas v Farr plc* [2007] IRLR 419.

possible to remove an offending part of a covenant if it is a separate obligation to that which can be enforced.[188]

In Rock Refrigeration[189] a restrictive covenant which took effect upon the ending of the contract of employment 'howsoever arising' was not necessarily unreasonable. Nevertheless, in the event of the termination resulting from the employer's repudiatory breach of the contract, the employee would be released from their obligations under the contract. Similarly, a covenant which 'restricts individuals from competing in any aspect of a company's business being carried on at the date of the termination in which the employees were actually involved during their employment' was held to be reasonable.[190] A non-solicitation clause which prevented an ex-employee from dealing even with potential clients who were negotiating with the employer at the time the individual left employment was also held not to be too vague to be relied upon. This was the situation in *International Consulting Services (UK) Ltd v Hart*,[191] where an ex-employee approached a potential customer who had held some preliminary discussions about the provision of services. In this context, the discussions were held to be negotiations and were caught by the non-solicitation clause.

4.5.2.3 Confidential information

In *Faccenda Chicken*[192] employees set up a business delivering chickens to butchers, supermarkets and catering operations and competed directly with their previous employer who had an identical operation. None of the employees had a restrictive covenant in their previous contracts. The Court of Appeal addressed the apparent conflict between the duty of an employee not to disclose confidential information which had been obtained in the course of employment with the *prima facie* right of any person to exploit the experience and knowledge which they have acquired for the purpose of earning a living. Neil LJ set out the following legal principles:

1. Where the parties were, or had been, linked by a contract of employment, then the obligations of the employee are to be determined by that contract.
2. In the absence of express terms, the obligations of the employee with respect to the use of information are the subject of implied terms.
3. Whilst the employee remains in the employment of the employer, these obligations are included in the implied term of good faith or fidelity.[193]
4. The implied term which places an obligation on the individual as to conduct after the ending of the employment is more restricted in its application than that which imposes a general duty of good faith.[194]
5. In order to decide whether a particular item of information falls within an implied term to prevent its use or disclosure after employment has ceased, it is necessary to consider all the circumstances of the case.

---

188 *Scully UK Ltd v Lee* [1998] IRLR 259 CA; see also *Hollis & Co v Stock* [2000] IRLR 712 CA, where a restriction on an employee not to work within ten miles of the ex-employer's office (a firm of solicitors) was interpreted as a restriction on working as a solicitor, rather than any employment, and was therefore not an unreasonable restraint of trade.

189 *Rock Refrigeration Ltd v Jones and Seward Refrigeration Ltd* [1996] IRLR 675 CA.

190 *Turner v Commonwealth & British Minerals Ltd* [2000] IRLR 114 – the fact that the employees were paid extra in return for agreeing to the restrictive covenant is not decisive, but is a legitimate factor to be taken into account.

191 [2000] IRLR 227.

192 *Faccenda Chicken Ltd v Fowler* [1986] IRLR 69 CA.

193 The duty of good faith will be broken if the employee makes, copies or memorises a list of the employer's customers for use after the end of employment. In *Warm Zones Ltd v Thurley* [2014] IRLR 791 a mandatory injunction was granted for the imaging and inspection of the ex-employee's computers following concerns about the misuse of confidential information.

194 The court relied upon the judgments in *Printers & Finishers Ltd v Holloway* [1965] RPC 253 and *E Worsley & Co Ltd v Cooper* [1939] 1 All ER 290 to distinguish between those secrets which are really trade secrets and not to be revealed and those matters which are confidential whilst the employment subsists.

In considering all the circumstances, a number of issues will be taken into account. First, the nature of the employment: if it is one that habitually uses confidential information, there may be a higher standard of confidentiality required. Second, the nature of the information itself: only information that can be regarded as a 'trade secret' can be protected, rather than looking at the 'status' of the information. Third, the steps that the employer had taken to impress upon the employee the confidentiality of the information. Finally, whether the relevant information can be isolated from other information which the employee is free to disclose or use.

For information to be classified as a trade secret, and therefore not to be disclosed, it is not incumbent upon an employer to point out to an employee the precise limits of what is sought to be made confidential. However, the closer an employee is to the 'inner circles' of decision making, the more likely they are to know that information is confidential.[195] This issue presents particular problems for employees who wish to work elsewhere. There is a distinction between knowledge which an employer can show to be a trade secret, and therefore the employer's property, and information which is the result of the skill, experience and know-how accumulated by an individual in the course of their employment.[196] To be protected the information needs to be precise and specific enough for a separate body of objective knowledge to be identified, rather than a general claim to an accumulated body of knowledge which an employer claims to be confidential.[197]

It is clear that an employer may be able to enforce an obligation of confidentiality against an individual who has made an unauthorised disclosure and used documents acquired in the course of employment. In *Camelot v Centaur Publications Ltd*[198] a copy of the draft accounts of the company which ran the National Lottery was sent by an unknown employee to an interested journalist. The information revealed, amongst other matters, increases in remuneration for some of the company's directors. The company asked the court to ensure that the leaked documents were returned, so that they could identify the individual who caused the leak. The Court of Appeal accepted that the case was not a whistleblowing one and held that it was in the public interest to enable the employer to discover a disloyal employee in their midst. More recently, the High Court ruled that a head of research and development was in breach of contract when she emailed confidential documents to her private address.[199] Finally, according to the Supreme Court, a person must have agreed or known that information is confidential. However, their state of mind when using the information is irrelevant to whether confidentiality has been abused. Indeed, if a person who directly misuses a trade secret does so in the course of employment by a third party, the third party could be liable for breach of confidence.[200]

4.5.2.4 Public Interest Disclosure Act 1998

The Public Interest Disclosure Act 1998 amended ERA 1996 to provide some protection for workers who disclose information about certain matters. Section 43J ERA 1996 makes void any provision in an agreement, including a contract of employment, which attempts to stop the worker from making a protected disclosure. Section 43A ERA 1996 provides that a 'protected disclosure' is a 'qualifying disclosure', as defined in s. 43B, which is made in accordance with ss 43C–43H. According to s. 43B, there is a qualifying disclosure if a worker reasonably believes that the information is in the public interest and tends to show one or more of the following: a criminal offence, a failure to comply with

195 As in *Lancashire Fires Ltd v SA Lyons & Co Ltd* [1997] IRLR 113 CA.
196 See *Crowson Fabrics Ltd v Rider* [2008] IRLR 288.
197 See *FSS Travel and Leisure Systems Ltd v Johnson* [1998] IRLR 382 CA and *Brooks v Olyslager OMS (UK) Ltd* [1998] IRLR 590 CA. On springboard relief until trial, see *UBS Ltd v Vestra LLP* [2008] IRLR 965.
198 [1998] IRLR 80 CA.
199 *Brandeaux Advisers Ltd v Chadwick* [2011] IRLR 224.
200 *Vestergaard Frandsen v Bestnet Ltd* [2013] IRLR 654.

any legal obligation,[201] a miscarriage of justice, a danger to health and safety and damage to the environment. A likelihood of any of these events occurring is also a qualifying disclosure, as well as any information about concealment, or attempts to conceal, such information. In relation to the public interest test, all the circumstances need to be considered but the following factors would normally be relevant: (i) the numbers in the group whose interests the disclosure served; (ii) the nature of the interests affected and the extent to which they are affected by the wrongdoing disclosed; (iii) the nature of the wrongdoing disclosed; and (iv) the identity of the alleged wrongdoer.[202]

The disclosure needs to be made to an individual's employer or to some other person who has responsibility for the matter disclosed, to a legal adviser or to a prescribed person[203] and ss 43G and 43H ERA 1996 impose strict rules about making disclosures in other circumstances. For example, the worker must reasonably believe that the information is true and not make disclosures for private gain. It must also be reasonable for the worker to make the disclosure.

Section 43K(1) ERA 1996 is designed to enable everyone who works to benefit from Part IVA, even if they do not fall within the section 230 ERA 1996 definition of 'employee' or 'worker'. Thus for these purposes the definition of 'worker' is extended to include certain agency workers; certain workers who would not otherwise be covered because they are not obliged to carry out all of their duties personally; NHS practitioners such as GPs, certain dentists, pharmacists and opticians; and certain trainees. Section 43K(2) ERA 1996 extends the definition of 'employer' accordingly.[204]

Those who make a protected disclosure have the right not to be subject to detriment by any act, or failure to act, on the part of the employer or a co-worker by reason of the individual making the disclosure.[205] Section 47B ERA 1996 imposes vicarious liability if a worker suffers a detriment at the hands of a co-worker and the employer did not take all reasonable steps to prevent this happening. A dismissal for the same reason will be automatically unfair[206] as will selection for redundancy.[207] One of the problems for workers seeking to rely on this legislation is that there are a number of hurdles which have to be overcome, including showing that they were acting in the public interest and had a reasonable belief in the existence of wrongdoing.[208] However, according to the Court of Appeal, the beliefs of the employer about whether or not there was a protected disclosure within the meaning of Part IVA ERA 1996 are irrelevant.[209] Good faith is no longer a requirement for making a protected disclosure but an award can be reduced by up to 25 per cent if it appears to an employment tribunal that a disclosure was not in good faith.[210]

---

201 See *Eiger Securities LLP v Korshunova* [2017] IRLR 115, *Parkins v Sodexho Ltd* [2002] IRLR 109, *Babula v Waltham Forest College* [2007] IRLR 346 and *Hibbins v Hesters Way Project* [2009] IRLR 198.

202 *Chesterton Global Limited v Nurmohammed* [2017] EWCA Civ 979.

203 See ss 43C–43F ERA 1996 and the Public Interest Disclosure (Prescribed Persons) Order 1999, SI1999/1549.

204 See *Day v Health Education England* [2017] IRLR 623 which confirmed that an agency and the end user may both be employers for these purposes.

205 The words 'subjected to' do not have any connotation of willfulness or control, but are concerned with causation. See *Abertawe University Health Board v Ferguson* [2014] IRLR 14. On compensation for injury to feelings, see *Virgo Fidelis School v Boyle* [2004] IRLR 268.

206 In *Miklaszewicz v Stolt Offshore Ltd* [2002] IRLR 344 an individual was dismissed, after the legislation came into effect, for making a disclosure some six years before. He was still held to be protected as the court held that it was the date of dismissal that triggered the employee's entitlement to protection, not the date of the disclosure. A protected disclosure may occur after the employment has terminated: see *Onyango v Berkeley* [2013] IRLR 338. On the burden of proof, see *Kuzel v Roche Ltd* [2008] IRLR 530 and *Fecitt v NHS Manchester* [2012] IRLR 64 CA.

207 See ss 103A and 105(6A) ERA 1996; Public Interest Disclosure (Compensation) Regulations 1999, SI 1999/1548 on the level of awards that may be given; there is no maximum figure set for compensation in such cases.

208 See *Bolton School v Evans* [2007] IRLR 140.

209 See *Beatt v Croydon Health Services NHS Trust* [2017] IRLR 748.

210 Section 123(6A) ERA 1996. On the possibility of obtaining stigma damages, see *Small v Shrewsbury and Telford Hospitals NHS Trust* [2017] EWCA Civ 882.

4.6 Other sources of terms

4.6.1 Custom and practice

It is possible for terms to become incorporated into the contract of employment as a result of custom and practice. In *Sagar v Ridehalgh & Sons Ltd*[211] a weaver challenged a long-accepted practice in the textile industry of deducting pay for poor work. The weaver failed in the complaint because the court held that the practice had prevailed at the place of work for over 30 years. The practice was judged to be 'reasonable, certain and notorious' and, therefore, to have legal effect. There was a question about whether the practice could have effect if the individual was unaware of its existence. In *Sagar*, the court found it difficult to believe that the complainant did not know of its existence.

In *Duke v Reliance Systems Ltd*[212] it was held that a management policy could not become incorporated into a contract of employment on the grounds of custom and practice unless it had been shown that the policy has been drawn to the employees' attention and had been followed without exception for a 'substantial period'. These factors were later referred to as 'to be among the most important circumstances to be taken into account', but all the other circumstances needed to be looked at. These included whether the 'substantial' period should be looked at in relation to these other circumstances to justify the inference that the policy had achieved the status of a contractual term. Additionally, the issue of communication with the employees was one of the factors which supported the inference that the employers intended to become contractually bound by it.[213]

The need for the custom and practice to be reasonable, certain and notorious was further illustrated in *Henry v London General Transport Services*.[214] In this case the trade union came to an agreement with the employers about changes to terms and conditions of employment in preparation for a management buy-out. These changes resulted in reductions in pay and other less advantageous terms and conditions. There had been a tradition of at least annual negotiations between the employer and the trade union where changes were agreed. However, there was no express agreement that changes would automatically be incorporated into employees' individual contracts of employment. A number of employees, unhappy at the reductions, claimed unlawful deductions from their wages. The EAT held that, once the reasonableness, certainty and notoriety of the custom and practice was established, it was to be presumed that the term represented the wishes and intentions of the parties concerned. This was not undermined by the fact that some individuals did not know of the practice or did not support it. Thus, in this case, the agreement was held to have become incorporated into the employees' individual contracts of employment.

4.6.2 Collective and workforce agreements

Collective agreements are defined in s. 178(1) TULRCA 1992 as 'any agreement or arrangement made by or on behalf of one or more trade unions and one or more employers or employers' associations' concerning matters listed in s. 178(2) TULRCA 1992 (see Chapter 11). The first item listed in s. 178(2)(a) includes terms and conditions of employment. Collective agreements are presumed not to be legally enforceable contracts unless the agreement is in writing and contains a provision to that effect.[215] The result is that the vast majority of such agreements are not legally binding in themselves (see Chapter 12). However, they achieve legal effect if they become incorporated into the contract of employment. If the contract states, for example, that:

---

211 [1931] 1 Ch 310 CA.
212 [1982] IRLR 347.
213 *Quinn v Calder Industrial Materials Ltd* [1996] IRLR 126.
214 [2002] IRLR 472.
215 Section 179(1) TULRCA 1992.

> The basic terms and conditions of your employment by this company are in accordance with and subject to the provisions of relevant agreements made between and on behalf of the Engineering Employers' Federation and the trade unions . . .[216]

then this is likely to be interpreted as an express provision incorporating the collective agreements negotiated between the employers and the trade unions (this issue is further considered in Chapter 12).[217]

Workforce agreements are an alternative mechanism for consulting and negotiating with employees when there is no trade union recognised for collective bargaining purposes (see Chapter 12). The specific requirements for reaching such agreements are contained in the Working Time Regulations 1998[218] and the Maternity and Parental Leave etc. Regulations 1999.[219] In both cases they are aimed at creating an opportunity for the parties to agree a more flexible approach to the implementation of the requirements of the Regulations. A workforce agreement[220] must apply to all the relevant members of a workforce or group and the agreement needs to be signed by all the individual members of the workforce or the group, or their representatives. The exception is in the case of smaller employers with 20 or fewer employees. In this case the agreement can be signed either by the appropriate representatives or by the majority of the workforce.

4.7 Variations in terms

Section 4 ERA 1996 provides rules for notifying changes in the s. 1 ERA 1996 statement of terms and conditions. The employer is required to give the employee a written statement of the changes at the earliest opportunity and, in any event, not later than one month after the change.[221] Section 4(3)(b) ERA 1996 provides for this to be done earlier if the person is required to work outside the United Kingdom for a period of more than one month. If the change relates to a change of employer and continuity of employment is not broken, then the new employer is not required to give a new statement, but merely to inform the employee of the change in circumstances,[222] specifying the date on which continuous employment began.[223]

There are a number of ways in which an employer may seek to change the terms of a contract of employment. The most straightforward would be to achieve mutual agreement to the changes with the employees and/or their representatives. If an employer is unable or unwilling to obtain this agreement, they may attempt to do so unilaterally.[224] One way is to dismiss the employees and then offer them new contracts of employment containing the new terms. The employer will have satisfied their common law obligations if they give the contractually required period of notice of termination to their employees. The danger with this approach is that employers may leave themselves open to claims for unfair dismissal and redundancy and a lack of consultation concerning

---

216 Quoted in *Alexander v Standard Telephones & Cables Ltd* [1991] IRLR 286.

217 Collective agreements can be arrived at, and incorporated into the contract of employment, by individual employers or by employers' associations negotiating with individual trade unions or groups of unions; see e.g. *Hamilton v Futura Floors Ltd* [1990] IRLR 478.

218 SI 1998/1833.

219 SI 1999/3312.

220 See Sch. 1 Maternity and Parental Leave etc. Regulations 1999.

221 Section 4(3)(a) ERA 1996.

222 Section 4(6) ERA 1996.

223 Section 4(8) ERA 1996.

224 In *Norman v National Audit Office* [2015] IRLR 634 the EAT observed that the employer's undertaking to 'notify' did not establish the right to make changes without the consent of the employee.

potential redundancies (see Chapter 10). In *GMB v Man Truck & Bus UK Ltd*[225] the respondent company had been formed by a merger of two other businesses. In order to harmonise terms and conditions, the employees were given notice of dismissal and then offered immediate re-employment on new terms and conditions. The EAT held that the employer had failed to consult as required by s. 188 TULRCA 1992, which applies where there are collective dismissals.[226]

If the employer seeks to impose new terms, then this may be interpreted as a repudiatory breach of contract, which the employee may decide to accept or not. One exception to this would be if the employer has a contractual right to make unilateral changes.[227] In *Farrant v The Woodroffe School*,[228] the employer tried to alter the job description of an employee on the mistaken advice that they were entitled to do so under the terms of the contract of employment. Even though the advice from the local authority was incorrect, the subsequent dismissal of the employee was held to be fair because it was reasonable for the employer to act on the advice received.[229] A second exception might be if the courts were willing to imply a term into the contract which permitted the employer to make a change. In *Jones v Associated Tunnelling Co Ltd*[230] the EAT concluded that there was an implied term to the effect that the employer had the right to change the employee's place of work to another location within reasonable daily commuting distance. The nature of the work required this change and the term was implied in order to give the contract business efficacy.

In *Jones*,[231] the employer also unsuccessfully claimed that the employee had assented to the change in the contract by continuing to work for another 12 months and not objecting. This argument was also used in *Aparau v Iceland Frozen Foods plc*,[232] where the EAT adopted the same approach. There was a need for

> great caution in reaching the conclusion that an employee has, by merely continuing an employment without any overt change or overt acceptance of terms which the employer is seeking to impose, truly accepted those terms so as to vary the contract.

In this case a shop worker was issued with a new contract containing a mobility clause, which was not activated for a further 12 months. It could not be said that the employee accepted the change by continuing performance when the impact of the change was some time away. Similarly, continuing to work under protest should not be construed as acceptance.[233] In *Harlow v Artemis Ltd*[234] the High Court confirmed that where an employer purports to change terms unilaterally that do not immediately impinge on the employee, then the fact that the employee continues to work does not mean that he or she can be taken to have accepted the variation. Here it was decided that an enhanced redundancy policy formed part of the contract of employment. More recently, the Court of Appeal decided that a claimant had not assented to a variation of his right to a performance-related bonus by his conduct. The relevant test is whether the employee's conduct, by continuing to work, was only referable to their having accepted the new terms imposed by the employer.[235]

---

225 [2000] IRLR 636.
226 See Chapter 10.
227 See *Airlie v City of Edinburgh District Council* [1996] IRLR 516.
228 [1998] IRLR 176.
229 See also *Port of Sheerness Ltd and Medway Ports Ltd v Brachers* [1997] IRLR 214, where the employer's legal advisers were held liable for giving negligent advice on handling redundancies.
230 [1981] IRLR 477.
231 Ibid.
232 [1996] IRLR 119 EAT; see also [2000] IRLR 196 CA on a separate point.
233 *Rigby v Ferodo Ltd* [1987] IRLR 516 HL.
234 [2008] IRLR 629.
235 *Khatri v Co-op Centrale* [2010] IRLR 715.

In some situations it may be vital to distinguish between the variation of an existing contract and the creation of a new one – for example, for the purposes of making a claim within a time limit which runs from the date of termination. According to the EAT, the task in each case is to determine the parties' intentions. Where it is clear from the documentation that the parties have agreed to implement changes via a fresh contract, that is decisive. However, if the change is not of a fundamental nature, the proper inference is that there is a variation unless the court or tribunal is satisfied that there was, objectively viewed, an express agreement that the mechanism to be adopted was the termination and new contract route.[236] Subsequently, the EAT has confirmed that fundamental as well as minor changes can be effected by consensual variation.[237]

In cases of pressing need, the employer may be justified in changing the employees' terms and conditions. In *Catamaran Cruisers Ltd v Williams*[238] a company was in financial difficulties and wanted to introduce less favourable terms and conditions. The EAT thought that they were able to do this but the lay members were obviously concerned about the outcome and stated that they wished

> to record that much of recent employment law has been to protect employees against arbitrary changes of their terms and conditions of employment and that this, as a principle, must stand . . . and that an employer must demonstrate . . . if he dismisses an employee for failing to accept changes of their terms and conditions of employment his actions must fall within the bounds of reasonableness.

Sometimes employers make changes which are the result of management policy rather than a change in the contract of employment. If an employer has a code of practice on staff sickness which, for example, included procedures for monitoring different types of absence, a decision to alter the procedure so that there were more frequent checks might amount to a change of policy which the employer could carry out unilaterally.[239] Lord Woolf summed up the approach:[240]

> The general position is that contracts of employment can only be varied by agreement. However, in the employment field an employer or for that matter an employee can reserve the ability to change a particular aspect of the contract unilaterally by notifying the other party as part of the contract that this is the situation. However, clear language is required to reserve to one party unusual power of this sort. In addition, the Court is unlikely to favour an interpretation which does more than enable a party to vary contractual provisions with which that party is required to comply.

The EAT applied this reasoning in *Bateman v ASDA Stores*[241] where the staff handbook enabled the employer to alter contractual terms without obtaining the consent of the staff. However, such a right should only be exercised in a way that does not breach the implied term of trust and confidence (see above).

---

236 *Cumbria County Council v Dow (No 2)* [2008] IRLR 109.
237 See *Potter v North Cumbria Acute NHS Trust* [2009] IRLR 900.
238 [1994] IRLR 386.
239 *Wandsworth London Borough Council v D'Silva* [1998] IRLR 193 CA. See now *Sparks v Department of Transport* [2016] IRLR 519.
240 *Wandsworth LBC v D'Silva* [1998] IRLR 193 at p. 197.
241 [2010] IRLR 370.

Further reading

Ashton, J. '15 Years of Whistleblowing Protection under PIDA 1998: Are We Still Shooting the Messenger?' (2015) *Industrial Law Journal* 29.

Barmes, L., Collins, H. and Fitzpatrick, C. 'Reconstructing Employment Contracts' (2007) 36(1) *Industrial Law Journal* 1.

Brodie, D. 'Mutual Trust and Confidence: Catalysts, Constraints and Commonality' (2008) 37(4) *Industrial Law Journal* 329.

Chapter 5

Termination of employment

Chapter Contents

5.1 Introduction

There are a number of ways in which a contract of employment, like any other contract, can be brought to an end. It can occur because the performance of the contract becomes impossible or because one of the parties brings it to an end. This may be done by voluntary notice given by the employee or by her or his employment being terminated, by notice or otherwise, by the employer. In addition, statute provides some protection for employees who are dismissed.

5.2 Termination of the contract not amounting to dismissal

5.2.1 Frustration

The common law doctrine of frustration deals with situations where, as a result of some event outside the control of the parties, the contract becomes impossible to perform, at least in the way that the parties intended. This view was stated by Lord Radcliffe in *Davies Contractors Ltd v Fareham Urban District Council*:[1]

> frustration occurs whenever the law recognises that without default of either party a contractual obligation has become incapable of being performed because the circumstances in which performance is called for would render it a thing radically different from that which was undertaken by the contract.

In *Paal Wilson & Co v Partenreederei Hannah Blumenthal*[2] the court held that there were two essential factors which must be present to frustrate a contract. These were that:

1. There must be some unforeseen change in the outside or extraneous circumstances, not provided for by the parties, which stopped the performance of the contract.
2. The outside or extraneous event should have occurred without the fault or default of either party to the contract.

Such a situation might be a custodial sentence. In *FC Shepherd & Co Ltd v Jerrom*[3] a contract of apprenticeship was held to be frustrated when an individual was sentenced to a period in a young offenders' institution for his part in a motorcycle gang fight. This was an event that was capable of rendering the performance of the contract impossible. The fact that the frustration must have occurred without the fault of either party means, according to the court, that the party who asserts that the performance of the contract has been frustrated must show that the frustration was not caused by his own act, and the person against whom frustration is asserted cannot rely on his own misconduct as an answer.

The following principles can be derived from these and other cases:[4]

1. The court must guard against too easy an application of the doctrine.
2. Although it is not necessary to decide that frustration occurred on a particular date, it may help the court to decide whether or not there was a true frustration situation.

---

1 [1956] AC 696 HL at p. 728.
2 [1983] 1 AC 854 HL.
3 [1986] IRLR 358 CA; see also *Four Seasons Healthcare Ltd v Maughan* [2005] IRLR 324.
4 See *Williams v Watson Luxury Coaches Ltd* [1990] IRLR 164.

3. There are a number of factors which may help to decide the issue:[5] the length of the previous employment; how long the employment would have continued;[6] the nature of the job; the nature, effect and length of the illness or disabling event; the needs of the employer for the work to be done and the need for a replacement to do it; the risk to the employer of incurring obligations related to redundancy or unfair dismissal of the replacement employee; whether wages have continued to be paid; the acts of the employer in relation to the employment, including dismissal of the employee; and whether in all the circumstances an employer could be expected to wait any longer.

4. The party alleging frustration should not be able to rely on that frustration if it were caused by that party.

Long-term sickness is capable of frustrating the contract of employment. However, an assessment needs to be made about whether any long-term incapacity has become a disability, thus providing the individual with protection under the Equality Act 2010 (see Chapter 7). If there are provisions in the contract about long-term sickness, it may be difficult to argue that the incapacity is an unforeseen event,[7] although it is unlikely that a total incapacity arising from an illness could have been foreseen. Frustration takes place because of events that have happened[8] so it is not possible to argue that a contract has been frustrated by the likelihood of an event happening in the future. Thus when an employee returns to work after a heart attack, it is not possible to argue frustration on the grounds that he might have a second heart attack in the future.[9]

5.2.2 Death of the employer

The death of either party may frustrate a contract but certain tribunal proceedings may continue and be defended by the personal representative of the deceased employer.[10] These include claims for itemised pay statements, guarantee payments, protection from detriment, time off work,[11] maternity rights, the right to a written statement of reasons for dismissal and those rights relating to unfair dismissal, redundancy payments and insolvency protection.[12] Where a claim under these headings accrues after the employer's death, then it will be treated as a liability of the deceased employer and as having accrued before the death.[13]

5.2.3 Voluntary resignation

This refers to a situation where the employee voluntarily resigns with or without notice.[14] It is not always clear whether an employee has resigned voluntarily or as a result of pressure from the employer.[15] As was held in *Sheffield v Oxford Controls Co Ltd*,[16] there is a principle of law which states that:

---

5 Some of which derive from *Egg Stores (Stamford Hill) v Leibovici* [1976] IRLR 376, which considered the issues connected with the fairness of dismissing absentees.

6 This is not to say that short-term contracts are not capable of being frustrated; see *Hart v RN Marshall & Sons (Bulwell) Ltd* [1977] IRLR 50.

7 See *Villella v MFI Furniture Centres Ltd* [1999] IRLR 468.

8 *Nottcutt v Universal Equipment Co (London) Ltd* [1986] IRLR 218 CA.

9 *Converform (Darwen) Ltd v Bell* [1981] IRLR 195.

10 See art. 9 Employment Tribunals (Extension of Jurisdiction) Order 1994, SI 1994/1623.

11 Excluding ss 58–60 ERA 1996 for time off for occupational pension trustees.

12 Section 206(1) ERA 1996.

13 Section 207 ERA 1996.

14 This may, in certain circumstances, amount to constructive dismissal: see below.

15 See *Martin v MBS Fastenings (Glynwed) Distribution Ltd* [1983] IRLR 198 CA; this was not the issue at the Court of Appeal but in the lower courts there was a question as to whether the employee had resigned in anticipation of the result of a disciplinary hearing or had been invited to resign by the employer.

16 [1979] IRLR 133 at p. 135. See now *Sandhu v Jan de Rijk Transport Ltd* [2007] IRLR 519 CA.

> where an employee resigns and that resignation is determined upon by him because he prefers to resign rather than be dismissed (the alternative having been expressed to him by the employer in the terms of the threat that if he does not resign he will be dismissed) the mechanics of the resignation do not cause that to be other than a dismissal.

This approach was followed by the Court of Appeal in *Jones v Mid-Glamorgan County Council*,[17] which described it as a 'principle of the utmost flexibility which is willing . . . to recognise a dismissal when it sees it'.[18] There was no dismissal, however, in *International Computers Ltd v Kennedy*,[19] which also involved a redundancy situation. Advice to employees to make every effort to find other jobs as quickly as possible was not equivalent to saying 'resign or be dismissed'. The invitation to resign was too imprecise in relation to the ultimate dismissal of individuals. It would also appear that there is no dismissal when an employee resigns on terms offered by an employer's disciplinary subcommittee. In *Staffordshire County Council v Donovan*[20] the EAT stated:

> It seems to us that it would be most unfortunate if, in a situation where the parties are seeking to negotiate in the course of disciplinary proceedings and an agreed form of resignation is worked out by the parties, one of the parties should be able to say subsequently that the fact that the agreement was reached in the course of disciplinary proceedings entitles the employee thereafter to say that there was a dismissal.

Two issues here are the extent to which employees must make clear their decision to resign and whether the employer has any obligations arising out of that decision. Often contracts of employment require a resignation to be effected in a certain way – for example, by putting it in writing or directing it to a certain individual. *Ely v YKK Fasteners*[21] involved an employee who was considering emigrating to Australia. The employee told his employer of his plans and that he had applied for a job there. Eventually, the employer took steps to replace him. When the individual decided not to emigrate, he informed his employers. By then he had been replaced and the employer regarded the individual's employment as being at an end. The question was whether there had been a resignation or a dismissal. It was held that there was a dismissal and that the reason for this was the employee's late notification to the employer that he had changed his mind about resigning. This dismissal was for 'some other substantial reason' (see below) within the meaning of s. 98(1)(b) ERA 1996.

Sometimes employees resign on the spur of the moment because they have become angry or discontented about some actions of the employer. This occurred in *Kwik-Fit (GB) Ltd v Lineham*[22] where, after an argument, the employee threw his keys down on to a counter and walked out. The EAT held that there was no ambiguity in the words used by the employee. When a resignation occurs, there is no obligation, except in special circumstances, for the employer to do anything but accept that decision. Words spoken in the heat of the moment or as a result of pressure on an employee may, however, amount to special circumstances. Where there are such special circumstances, the employer should allow a day or two to elapse before accepting the resignation at face value. During this time information may arise as to whether the resignation was really intended. Not to investigate may open the employer to the risk of new facts emerging at an employment tribunal hearing which may cast doubt on the intention to resign. Where there are no special circumstances arising out of a decision

---

17 [1997] IRLR 685 CA; [1997] ICR 815 CA.
18 See also *Allders International Ltd v Parkins* [1981] IRLR 68, where an employee was given the option of resigning or the employer calling in the CID to investigate allegations of theft.
19 [1981] IRLR 28.
20 [1981] IRLR 108.
21 [1993] IRLR 500 CA.
22 [1992] IRLR 156.

made in the heat of the moment or as a result of employer pressure, the employer is entitled to take the employee's words at face value and is not required to look behind them or interpret them as a 'reasonable employer' might. Thus, in *Sothern v Franks Charlesly & Co*[23] the words 'I am resigning' could be taken at face value, but in *Barclay v City of Glasgow District Council*[24] the resignation by an employee with learning difficulties was held to constitute a special circumstance even though unambiguous words of resignation had been used.[25]

5.2.4 Termination by agreement

Termination by mutual consent is an important concept that has been widely used by employers in order to reduce the number of staff. It will usually take the form of a financial inducement in excess of any statutory entitlement to make leaving attractive. One common form is that of early retirement, where older workers are induced to leave the workforce by the offer of enhanced retirement packages. This was the situation in *Birch and Humber v The University of Liverpool*[26] where the employer invited applications for early retirement as part of a staff reduction exercise. The two applicants were amongst those who applied and were accepted. Subsequently, they sought redundancy payments. The employment tribunal was first faced with the question of whether they had been dismissed. It was held that, because the retirement of any individual was subject to the employer's approval, then it was that approval which amounted to a dismissal; that is, when the employer wrote to the employees stating when their employment would end, a dismissal took place. The appeal to the EAT was successful and the Court of Appeal also held that there had been a mutual agreement to terminate. The acceptance of the applications could not be divorced from the formal applications to retire. Purchas LJ stated that 'in my judgment, dismissal . . . is not consistent with free, mutual consent, bringing a contract of employment to an end'.

The important question is whether the employer and the employee have freely agreed to end the contract of employment. In *Igbo v Johnson Matthey Chemicals Ltd*[27] there was a clause in a contract which an employee was required to sign before extended leave was granted. This stated that a failure to return on the due date would lead to the contract being automatically terminated. The employee was ill at the time she was due to return and, despite the submission of a medical certificate, the employer took the view that this failure terminated the contract. It was argued that there was no dismissal, but a consensual termination. The Court of Appeal rejected this because of its impact on (now) s. 203(1) ERA 1996, which provides that any agreement designed to exclude or limit the operation of the Act or stopping an individual from bringing proceedings before an employment tribunal was void. The clause that the employee had been required to sign attempted to limit her potential claim for unfair dismissal under the ERA 1996.[28] In *Logan Salton v Durham County Council*[29] an employee, after he became aware that a report recommended his summary dismissal, negotiated a written leaving agreement with the employer. He subsequently claimed that this agreement was made under duress. The EAT refused to accept this and distinguished the case from *Igbo*

---

23 [1981] IRLR 278 CA.

24 [1983] IRLR 313.

25 See also *Sovereign House Security Services Ltd v Savage* [1989] IRLR 115 CA, where the words 'jacking the job in' spoken in a heated moment were held not to be a resignation.

26 [1985] IRLR 165 CA; see also *Scott v Coalite Fuels and Chemicals Ltd* [1988] IRLR 131 which also involved individuals taking voluntary early retirement; the EAT followed *Birch and Humber* in holding that the decision as to whether someone had been dismissed was a question of fact for the employment tribunal to decide.

27 [1986] IRLR 215 CA.

28 See also *Tracey v Zest Equipment Co Ltd* [1992] IRLR 268, where the clause stated that 'the company will assume that you have terminated your employment with us' if there was a failure to return to work on the due date; this was held to be too imprecise to be legally binding.

29 [1989] IRLR 99.

by holding that the agreement was not part of the contract of employment or a variation of it, but a separate contract that was entered into willingly, without duress and after proper advice and for good consideration.

5.3 Termination of the contract by dismissal

5.3.1 Meaning of dismissal

For statutory purposes s. 95 ERA 1996 provides that a person is dismissed by the employer if:

1. The contract under which the individual is employed is terminated by the employer with, or without, notice.
2. The person is employed under a limited-term contract which terminates by virtue of the limiting event without being renewed under the same contract (see Chapter 3). There are three types of limiting event: the expiry of a fixed term; the performance of a specific task; or the occurrence of an event or failure of an event to occur.[30]
3. The employee terminates the contract, with or without notice, as a result of the employer's conduct. This last situation is commonly referred to as constructive dismissal.

As with cases involving voluntary resignation and mutual agreement (see above), employment tribunals may be asked to decide whether words used by an employer constitute dismissal. For example, in *Tanner v DT Kean*[31] an employer used the words: 'That's it, you're finished with me.' The employee claimed that this was a dismissal, but the employment tribunal held that the words were an expression of annoyance and a reprimand. They considered what a reasonable employee would take the words to mean in the circumstances. The EAT stated that, in order to arrive at the correct meaning of the words, one could look at events that preceded the words spoken as well as those which followed, in order to determine whether the employer intended to bring the contract to an end. More recently, the EAT has indicated that the fundamental question is whether the person to whom the words were addressed was entitled to assume that they amounted to a 'conscious rational decision'.[32]

5.3.2 Wrongful dismissal

The common law concept of wrongful dismissal may not be a fruitful avenue for employees to follow, unless, as in *Clark v BET plc*,[33] the individual is entitled to a long period of notice.[34] This is because damages will normally be limited to those losses arising out of the breach of contract – that is, the loss of the notice period.[35] However, this may include the loss of benefits that might have accrued during that notice period. In *Silvey v Pendragon plc*[36] the employee was dismissed for reasons of redundancy some 12 days before his 55th birthday, when certain pension rights would have accrued to him. Although the employee was given 12 weeks' pay in lieu of notice, there was no

---

30 'Limited term contracts' and 'limiting event' are defined in s. 235(2A) and (2B) ERA 1996 respectively.
31 [1978] IRLR 110.
32 *Willoughby v CF Capital plc* [2011] IRLR 198.
33 [1997] IRLR 348; the notice entitlement was three years.
34 See also *University of Oxford v (1) Humphries; (2) Associated Examining Board* [2000] IRLR 183 CA, which was a case where a university employee had a tenured post which would continue until he retired.
35 See *Smith v Trafford Housing Trust* [2013] IRLR 86 where there was a purported demotion.
36 [2001] IRLR 685 CA.

provision for such a payment in his contract of employment. The failure to give him 12 weeks' notice was held to be a repudiatory breach of the contract. The court held that he was not only entitled to damages consisting of wages or salary, but also to the value of any pension rights which would have accrued during the period of notice. There was no difference in principle between lost pension rights and lost pay. Second, any entitlement to non-contractual damages will be limited by the common law duty to mitigate one's losses. However, wrongful dismissal may be the only action possible if a person has less than two years' continuous employment and is thus debarred from pursuing a claim for unfair dismissal in accordance with Part X ERA 1996.

For many years it was not entirely clear what the effect of an employer's breach is. The alternatives were, first, that it results in an automatic termination of the contract of employment. This might seem reasonable because a breach which consists of a wrongful dismissal is likely to have the effect of destroying the basis of mutual trust and confidence between the employer and employee. The problem with this approach is that it makes wrongful dismissal a special case when compared with the way that the law of contract would normally treat a breach of contract. This 'normal' route is the second alternative, which is that it is the innocent party's choice as to whether to accept the repudiation and terminate the contract. In Société Générale v Geys[37] the Supreme Court ruled that the elective theory applies. Thus when an employer repudiates a contract, the employee must demonstrate a conscious intention to bring the contract to an end or do something that is inconsistent with its continuation.

Although an employee might refuse to accept that the contract is at an end, the reality is that they may have little choice in the matter. This dilemma was exemplified in Gunton v London Borough of Richmond upon Thames,[38] where it was held that the employer had repudiated the contract of employment and a wrongful dismissal had taken place. The Court of Appeal thought that the individual ought to be able to decide whether to accept the repudiation of the contract, but stated that:

> this practical basis for according an election to the injured party has no reality in relation to a contract of service where the repudiation takes the form of an express and direct termination of the contract in contravention of its terms. I would describe this as a total repudiation which is at once destructive of the contractual relationship.

The problem for the wronged individual is that the court will not allow them to claim pay for work not done – that is, after their contract has been repudiated.[39] Moreover, the claim for damages for wrongful dismissal cannot continue beyond the time when the employer could lawfully have brought the contract to an end.[40] This contrasts with the approach of the courts when an employer unilaterally varies a term of the contract of employment, such as a reduction of wages. Such an event is likely to be a repudiatory action by the employer. In Rigby v Ferodo Ltd[41] an employee elected to continue working after the employer reduced his wages. Although the employer's action was a repudiatory breach of the contract of employment, the contract did not automatically end unless the employee accepted the breach as a repudiation. The employee had made known his objections and so it could not be held that there was an implied acceptance of the breach. Unlike cases of outright dismissal and an employee walking out, there was no reason why the contract of employment should be treated any differently from any other contract. Generally, an unaccepted repudiation leaves the contractual obligations of the parties unaffected.

---

37 Société Générale (London Branch) v Geys [2013] IRLR 122 SC.
38 [1980] IRLR 321 CA.
39 See Alexander v Standard Telephones and Cables Ltd [1991] IRLR 286.
40 See Ralph Gibson LJ in Boyo v London Borough of Lambeth [1995] IRLR 50 CA.
41 [1987] IRLR 516 HL.

5.3.3 Notice

At common law employment is liable to be determined by 'reasonable' periods of notice.[42] If there is no express term to that effect in the contract of employment, then it may be implied.[43] Statute has limited the freedom of action of employers in giving, or not giving, notice of dismissal to their employees and does not allow the unilateral withdrawal of notice unless there are special circumstances.[44] The employee has statutory rights to a minimum notice period.[45] These are an entitlement to one week's notice for employees who have been continuously employed for at least one month and with less than two years' continuous employment, with an extra week for each year of continuous employment up to not less than 12 weeks' notice for continuous employment of 12 years or more. By way of contrast, employers are entitled to at least one week's notice of termination from employees who have been continuously employed for at least one month.[46] According to the EAT, unless the contract provides otherwise, oral or written notice given during the working day cannot take effect until the following day.[47] Additionally, any requirements for consultation with employees or their representatives, in redundancy or transfer situations (see Chapter 10), may inhibit the employer from giving notice until the appropriate time. None of this affects more generous contractual arrangements or the rights of either party to treat the contract as terminated without notice as a result of the other's conduct.[48]

The contract of employment continues to subsist during the notice period. The statutory rules contemplate the contract being brought to an end by one of the parties. It follows, therefore, that the ending of the contract through the doctrine of frustration, which occurs through no fault or design of the parties, will exclude any rules relating to notice periods.[49] Employees have the right to be paid during their notice period even if there is no work for them, provided that they are ready and willing to work. Pay is also protected if the notice period coincides with absence from work because of sickness, pregnancy, childbirth, parental, paternity or adoption leave or holiday leave.[50] An employer is not required, however, to pay for absences due to time off taken in accordance with Part VI ERA 1996,[51] or for trade union duties and activities specified in ss 168 and 170 TULRCA 1992, or for taking part in strike action during the notice period, if it is the employee that has given notice.[52]

The ERA 1996 does not prevent an employee from accepting a payment in lieu of notice but an employer must have contractual authority for insisting on such a payment. Without such authority a payment in lieu of notice will be construed as damages for the failure to provide proper notice.[53] Thus a payment in lieu can properly terminate a contract of employment if the contract provides for such a payment[54] or the parties agree that the employee will accept a payment in lieu.[55] The date of termination at common law is the day notice expires or the day wages in lieu are accepted. In *Société Général v Geys*[56] the Court of Appeal ruled that the bank could terminate a contract of employment by

---

42 See *McClelland v Northern Ireland Health Services Board* [1957] 2 All ER 129 HL.

43 See e.g. *Masiak v City Restaurants (UK) Ltd* [1999] IRLR 780.

44 In *Willoughby v CF Capital plc* [2011] IRLR 985 the Court of Appeal ruled that the employer could not unilaterally withdraw a notice of dismissal on the grounds of a mistaken expectation about the employee.

45 Section 86(1) ERA 1996.

46 Section 86(2) ERA 1996.

47 *Wang v University of Keele* [2011] IRLR 542.

48 Section 86(6) ERA 1996.

49 *GF Sharp & Co Ltd v McMillan* [1998] IRLR 632.

50 Sections 88–89 ERA 1996. See *Burlo v Langley* [2007] IRLR 145.

51 Such as time off for public duties, looking for work and care of dependants.

52 Section 91(1)–(2) ERA 1996.

53 *Cerberus Software Ltd v Rowley* [2001] IRLR 160.

54 In *Cavenagh v William Evans Ltd* [2012] IRLR 679 the company was obliged to make a payment in lieu despite subsequently discovering that Cavenagh had been guilty of misconduct.

55 *Locke v Candy & Candy Ltd* [2011] IRLR 163.

56 [2011] IRLR 482.

payment in lieu of notice without communicating that fact to the claimant. However, in reversing this decision, the Supreme Court stated that a party to an employment relationship must notify the other in clear and unambiguous terms that the right to bring the contract to an end is being exercised and how and when this is intended to happen.[57] Subsequently, the Court of Appeal has stated that where there is no contractual provision indicating when notice given by an employer takes effect, that notice is effective when the employee personally takes delivery of the letter.[58]

5.3.4 Summary dismissal

The right to dismiss summarily – that is, without giving notice – may be an express or an implied term of the contract of employment. If it is an express term, then the reason for the dismissal needs to come within the contractual definition of gross misconduct. Thus, in *Dietman v London Borough of Brent*[59] a clause in the contract defined gross misconduct, for which instant dismissal would result, as 'misconduct of such a nature that the authority is justified in no longer tolerating the continued presence at the place of work of the employee who commits the offence'. After an inquiry the employee was found grossly negligent in her duties. The court held, however, that gross negligence did not come within the contractual definition of gross misconduct and thus the employee had been wrongfully dismissed. More recently, the Court of Appeal has ruled that where gross misconduct is alleged, attention focuses on the damage to the relationship between the parties. Thus, in an appropriate case gross negligence can be treated as gross misconduct.[60] Nevertheless, summary dismissal remains an exceptional remedy which requires substantial justification. It will not be readily sustained for misconduct which only peripherally affects core duties. The repudiatory conduct must be so serious as to strike at the foundation of the employment relationship and make its continuance impossible. If an employer delays in reacting to the misconduct, there is a risk that it will be held to have affirmed the contract. Alternatively, a delay may make it more difficult to establish a genuine causal link between the misconduct and dismissal.[61]

The fact that a dismissal is without notice, or without sufficient notice, does not in itself render it unfair in statutory terms, but the lack of notice may render it a breach of contract and a wrongful dismissal.[62] It is likely that the summary nature of the dismissal can only be justified as a response to actions which breach an important term of the contract in such a way as to undermine the employment relationship, including the duty of mutual trust and confidence. In *Laws v London Chronicle (Indicator Newspapers) Ltd*[63] Lord Evershed MR stated that the question was 'whether the conduct complained of is such as to show the servant to have disregarded the essential conditions of the contract of service'. A more modern view was expressed in *Neary and Neary v Dean of Westminster*[64] where Lord Jauncey stated that:

> conduct amounting to gross misconduct justifying dismissal must so undermine the trust and confidence which is inherent in the particular contract of employment that the master should no longer be required to retain the servant in his employment.

57 *Société Générale v Geys* [2013] IRLR 122 SC.
58 *Newcastle upon Tyne NHS Foundation Trust v Haywood* [2017] IRLR 629.
59 [1988] IRLR 299 CA.
60 See *Adesokan v Sainsbury's Supermarkets Ltd* [2017] IRLR 346 where a regional manager was summarily dismissed for failing to take action after he became aware that the company's employee engagement procedure had been abused.
61 *McCormack v Hamilton Academical FC* [2012] IRLR 108.
62 See *BSC Sports & Social Club v Morgan* [1987] IRLR 391.
63 [1959] 2 All ER 285 CA. In *Farnan v Sunderland F.C.* [2016] IRLR 185 the employer was entitled to terminate without notice for serious breaches of an express term prohibiting the use of confidential information for non-business purposes.
64 [1999] IRLR 288. According to the Court of Appeal, there is no distinction between gross misconduct and conduct evincing an intention no longer to be bound by the contract: *Dunn v AAH Ltd* [2010] IRLR 709.

The conduct affecting the basis of mutual trust and confidence between the parties needs to be serious.[65] However, the gross misconduct must be examined in relation to the particular job and does not necessarily mean that the employee could not be employed elsewhere.[66] A situation where an employee appeared to be provoked into swearing at an employer and was then dismissed was held to be a wrongful dismissal, because the employer had already decided to dismiss the employee prior to the incident.[67] An example of where the courts have held a summary dismissal for gross misconduct to be acceptable is when an employee accesses confidential information, to which they are not entitled, for illegitimate purposes. In *Denco Ltd v Joinson*[68] an employee, who was a trade union representative, obtained information relating to the employer's business and other employees' salaries. The EAT held that this was no different from going into an office, for which he had no authorisation, picking up a key off the desk and unlocking a filing cabinet to take out confidential information.

If employers do not invoke the right to end the contract within a reasonable period, they will be taken to have waived their rights and can only seek damages. What is a reasonable period will depend on the facts of the particular case. In *Allders International v Parkins*[69] it was held that nine days was too long a period to be allowed to pass in relation to an allegation of stealing before deciding what to do about the alleged repudiatory conduct.

Finally, there may be an issue as to whether an individual is entitled to payment in lieu of notice after an instant ('on the spot') dismissal. In *T & K Home Improvements Ltd v Skilton*[70] a contractual term entitled the employer to terminate an employee's contract 'with immediate effect' if he failed to reach his sales targets in any one month. However, such a phrase was held not to deprive the employee of the right to the three months' notice to which the contract entitled him. There was evidence elsewhere in the contract of terms which specifically deprived him of the right to a payment in lieu in certain situations, but these did not apply in this case.

5.3.5 Remedies for wrongful dismissal

A wrongful dismissal is a dismissal without notice or with inadequate notice in circumstances where proper notice should have been given. The expression also covers dismissals which are in breach of agreed procedures. Thus, where there is a contractual disciplinary procedure, an employee may be able to obtain an injunction (interdict in Scotland) or declaration from the courts so as to prevent a dismissal or declare a dismissal void if the procedure has not been followed.[71] However, an injunction will only be granted if the court is convinced that the employer's repudiation has not been accepted, that the employer has sufficient trust and confidence in the employee, and that damages would not be an adequate remedy.[72]

Seeking an injunction to prevent an employer taking steps which might lead to a repudiatory breach might have the same effect as an order for specific performance; that is, stopping certain actions might have the same effect as ordering the employer to behave differently. This did not inhibit the granting of an interlocutory injunction in *Peace v City of Edinburgh Council*,[73] which involved a teacher who was subject to a disciplinary procedure. The employer was stopped from introducing a new procedure which would have been in breach of the contract of employment. The court

---

65 See *Williams v Leeds United F.C.* [2015] IRLR 383 which involved the emailing of pornographic images.
66 *Hamilton v Argyll and Clyde Health Board* [1993] IRLR 99.
67 *Wilson v Racher* [1974] ICR 428 CA.
68 [1991] IRLR 63.
69 [1981] IRLR 68.
70 [2000] IRLR 595 CA.
71 See *R (on the application of Shoesmith) v Ofsted* [2011] ICR 1195 CA and *Richards v IP Solutions Group Ltd* [2017] IRLR 133.
72 See *Dietman v London Borough of Brent* [1988] IRLR 299.
73 [1999] IRLR 417.

concluded that it was intervening in a choice between alternative schemes, rather than enforcing mutual co-operation. The individual was suspended, but the employment contract remained in existence. In *Anderson v Pringle of Scotland Ltd*[74] the employers wanted to change the method of selecting individuals for redundancy from a 'last in first out' basis to a more discretionary one. The 'last in first out' formula had been part of a collective agreement which was incorporated into the employees' contracts of employment. The court granted an interim interdict (injunction) prohibiting the employers from using any other method for selection. It acknowledged the issue of specific performance but held that the employment relationship continued and the decision was about the mechanisms of dismissal rather than the principle. Lord Prosser stated that:

> In the contemporary world, where even reinstatement is a less inconceivable remedy, intervention before dismissal must in my view be seen as a matter of discretion, rather than an impossibility.[75]

Since the courts are reluctant to enforce a contract of employment, in the vast majority of cases the employee's remedy will lie in damages for breach of contract. A person who suffers a wrongful dismissal is entitled to be compensated for such loss as arises naturally from the breach and for any loss which was reasonably foreseeable by the parties as being likely to arise from it. Hence an employee will normally recover only the amount of wages lost between the date of the wrongful dismissal and the date when the contract could lawfully have been terminated.[76] However, in a contentious decision the Supreme Court has ruled that, although an injunction or declaration can be sought, damages are not available where the employer has dismissed as a result of disciplinary proceedings which breached express contractual terms. Rather surprisingly, it was stated that if the disciplinary procedure is expressly incorporated into a contract of employment, its terms are not ordinary ones.[77]

The principle that damages resulting from a wrongful dismissal should put an individual in the same position as if the contract had been performed does not apply where the failure to give contractual notice results in the loss of opportunity to claim unfair dismissal.[78] If an employer has the option of paying for the notice period whilst it is being worked or paying a sum of money in lieu of notice, then the employer is able to make a payment in lieu even if it means that the employee will be stopped from having enough continuous employment to qualify to make a claim.[79] The courts will make the assumption that the employer will choose to perform the contract in the least burdensome way and that, had the contract been performed lawfully, the employee would have been dismissed at the earliest opportunity.[80] When looking at the failure to follow a disciplinary procedure, attention does not focus on whether or not an employee would have been dismissed if the procedure had been adhered to. The issue is how much longer the employee would have been retained before the employer could contractually give notice. It is this that will determine whether or not there has been a loss of opportunity.[81]

Damages are not awarded for distress or hurt feelings. In *Bliss v South East Thames Regional Health Authority*[82] Dillon LJ stated the general principle:

> The general rule laid down by the House of Lords is that where damages fall to be assessed for breach of contract rather than in tort it is not permissible to award general damages for

---

74 [1998] IRLR 64.
75 Ibid. at p. 67. See also *Irani v Southampton and South West Hampshire Health Authority* [1985] IRLR 203, where an interlocutory injunction was granted to restrain the employer from implementing an employee's notice before they had followed the disputes procedure.
76 See *Marsh v National Autistic Society* [1993] IRLR 453.
77 *Edwards v Chesterfield Royal Hospital NHS Foundation Trust* [2012] IRLR 129.
78 See *Harper v Virgin Net Ltd* [2004] IRLR 390.
79 *Morran v Glasgow Council of Tenants Associations* [1998] IRLR 67.
80 *Lavarack v Woods of Colchester Ltd* [1967] 1 QB 278 CA.
81 See *Janciuk v Winerite Ltd* [1998] IRLR 63.
82 [1985] IRLR 308 CA.

frustration, mental distress, injured feelings or annoyance caused by the breach. Modern thinking tends to be that the amount of damages recoverable for a wrong should be the same whether the cause of action is laid in contract or tort. But in *Addis*[83] Lord Loreburn regarded the rule that damages for injured feelings cannot be recovered in contract for wrongful dismissal as too inveterate to be altered.

It was argued in *French v Barclays Bank plc*[84] that a loan contract providing low-interest mortgage facilities should fall within the exceptions. Thus it was asserted that when an employer varied the terms of the loan there ought to be damages awarded for anxiety and stress. This argument was not accepted by the court who felt constrained by the authorities, such as *Addis* and *Bliss*.[85]

Employees have a duty to mitigate their losses, although there should be no set-off of any sums to which they are contractually entitled. This issue was considered in *Cerberus Software Ltd v Rowley*.[86] The contract of employment provided for the termination of the contract upon the giving of six months' notice by either side. The contract also allowed that the employer may make a payment in lieu of notice to the employee. In the event, the employee was dismissed without notice or payment in lieu. After five weeks he obtained alternative work at a higher salary. He then claimed damages for wrongful dismissal. One issue was whether he was entitled to six months' pay in lieu of notice as a contractual right or whether the measure of damages was the amount that the employee would have earned if the contract had continued. In the latter case, the employee would have a duty to mitigate losses. The court held that the contract gave the employer a choice of whether to make the payment in lieu or not, so the employee did not have a contractual right to the six months' pay and the normal rules concerning minimising losses should apply. The distinction between a claim for payments due under the contract and those which are damages for wrongful dismissal is important. In the former situation the court or tribunal is being asked to set a sum to be paid to the claimant, irrespective of any damage suffered as a consequence of the breach.[87] Where there is a failure to mitigate, the court will deduct a sum it feels the employee might reasonably have been expected to earn. As regards state benefits, it would appear that any benefit received by the dismissed employee should be deducted only where not to do so would result in a net gain to the employee.[88] Finally, the first £30,000 of damages is to be awarded net of tax, but any amount above this figure will be awarded gross since it is taxable in the hands of the recipient.

Proceedings may be brought before an employment tribunal in respect of:[89]

1. damages for a breach of contract of employment or other contract connected to employment;[90]
2. a claim for a sum due under such a contract;[91] and
3. a claim for the recovery of any sum, in pursuance of any enactment relating to the performance of such a contract.[92]

---

83 *Addis v Gramophone Company Ltd* [1909] AC 488 HL.
84 [1998] IRLR 646 CA.
85 See also *Johnson v Unisys Ltd* [2001] IRLR 279.
86 [2001] IRLR 160 CA.
87 See *Abrahams v Performing Rights Society* [1995] IRLR 486 CA.
88 See *Westwood v Secretary of State* [1984] IRLR 209.
89 Excluding those related to personal injuries (arts 3 and 4 Employment Tribunals (Extension of Jurisdiction) Order (ETEJO) 1994).
90 This includes the ability to enforce compromise agreements on terms connected with the end of employment: see *Rock-It Cargo Ltd v Green* [1997] IRLR 581.
91 In *Sarker v South Tees Acute Hospitals NHS Trust* [1997] IRLR 328 an employee was dismissed before she commenced work, but the court held that she was still entitled to make a claim for damages as the contractual relationship had come into existence.
92 Section 3(2) Employment Tribunals Act 1996.

Provided the claim arises or is outstanding on the termination of the employee concerned, such actions can be taken by both the employer and the employee.[93] Breach of contract claims are excluded if they are based on terms which:[94]

1. Require the employer to provide living accommodation for the employee.
2. Impose an obligation on the employer or the employee in connection with the provision of living accommodation.
3. Relate to intellectual property.[95]
4. Impose an obligation of confidence.
5. Are a covenant in restraint of trade.

Employees must present their claim to the employment tribunal within three months of the effective date of termination, or, if there is no such date, the last day on which the employee worked in the employment. The tribunal has discretion to lengthen this period if it decides that it was not reasonably practicable for the employee to present their complaint in time.[96] It is not possible to bring a claim for breach of contract to an employment tribunal before the effective date of termination.[97]

5.4 Unfair dismissal

The statutory concept of unfair dismissal was first introduced in the Industrial Relations Act 1971 and the right to claim is now contained in Part X ERA 1996. Section 94(1) ERA 1996 states that employees have the right not to be unfairly dismissed by their employer. In examining whether or not a dismissal is unfair, the following stages need to be completed. First, there is the issue of eligibility for protection. Second, it must be shown that a dismissal has taken place and the effective date of termination must be identified. Third, the reason for dismissal must be established. Finally, the question of reasonableness must be considered.

5.4.1 Eligibility

Before individuals can make a complaint of unfair dismissal they need to qualify for the right by overcoming some initial hurdles. These relate to their employment status and length of continuous service. Also considered here are contracts that are tainted by illegality. It should be noted that those who work abroad must show that their employment had much stronger connections both with Great Britain and British employment law than with any other system.[98]

5.4.1.1 Only employees qualify

Section 94(1) provides that it is employees that have the right. An employee is an individual who works under a contract of employment.[99] With an increasing number of rights accruing to workers,[100]

---

93 Articles 3 and 4 ETEJO 1994. See *Peninsula Ltd v Sweeney* [2004] IRLR 49.
94 Article 5 ETEJO 1994.
95 Defined as including copyright, rights in performance, moral rights, design rights, registered designs, patents and trade marks (art. 5 ETEJO 1994).
96 Article 7 ETEJO 1994.
97 *Capek v Lincolnshire County Council* [2000] IRLR 590.
98 See *Jeffery v British Council* [2016] IRLR 935.
99 Section 230(1)–(2) ERA 1996.
100 Section 230(3) ERA 1996.

it may seem less logical for those working under a contract to perform services personally to continue to be excluded from Part X ERA 1996.[101] Employment status is considered in Chapter 2.

5.4.1.2 Illegality

As has been stated before, the general rules of contract apply equally to contracts of employment and there is a general principle that the courts will not enforce an illegal contract, the *ex turpi causa non oritur actio* rule.[102] It is necessary not only to examine whether the contract of employment was performed legally but also to look at its purpose. If the contract has an illegal purpose, then it may not be relied upon (the 'reliance principle'). In *Colen v Cebrian Ltd*,[103] Waller LJ summarised the position as follows:

> an analysis needs to be done as to what the parties' intentions were from time to time. If the contract was unlawful at its formation or if there was an intention to perform the contract unlawfully as at the date of the contract, then the contract will be unenforceable. If at the date of the contract the contract was perfectly lawful and it was intended to perform it lawfully, the effect of some act of illegal performance is not automatically to render the contract unenforceable. If the contract is ultimately performed illegally and the party seeking to enforce it takes part in the illegality, that may render the contract unenforceable at his instigation. But not every act of illegality in performance even participated in by the enforcer, will have that effect. If the person seeking to enforce the contract has to rely on his illegal action in order to succeed then the court will not assist him. But if he does not have to do so, then in my view the question is whether the method of performance chosen and the degree of participation in that illegal performance is such as to 'turn the contract into an illegal contract'.

Knowledge of the illegality does not always appear to be relevant. In *Euro-Diam Ltd v Bathurst*[104] the Court of Appeal indicated that the issue of illegality should be approached pragmatically and with caution, especially where the defendant's conduct in participating in an illegal contract was so reprehensible, in comparison with the plaintiff, that it would be wrong to allow the defendant to rely upon it. Such a situation occurred in *Hewcastle Catering Ltd v Ahmed and Elkamah*.[105] This case involved a number of employees who were dismissed after co-operating with HM Revenue & Customs in an investigation of a fraud about VAT on customers' bills, for which their employer was prosecuted. The employees had participated in the fraud but only the employer had benefited. The court concluded that it would be wrong to allow the employer to rely on the argument that the fraud made the employees' contracts of employment illegal and prevented them bringing unfair dismissal claims.[106]

Thus the consequences of a strict application of the rules on illegality can be severe. *Salvesen v Simmons*[107] involved an employee who, at his request, was paid partly through an annual salary, with all the normal deductions for income tax and national insurance contributions, and partly through a consultancy which he operated with his wife. These latter payments were made without deductions. When a change of employer occurred, the new employer declined to continue with this

---

101 There are specific groups excluded from the right: these are the police (s. 200 ERA 1996) and share fishers (s. 199(2)) as well as those affected by a little-used opportunity to opt out of the provisions and replace them with a dismissal procedure agreement; see s. 110.

102 Action is not available on an illegal contract.

103 [2004] IRLR 210.

104 [1988] 2 All ER 23 CA.

105 [1991] IRLR 473 CA.

106 See also *Broaders v Kalkare Property Maintenance Ltd* [1990] IRLR 421, where the EAT stated that a fraud against an employer was quite different from one concerned with fraud against the tax authorities. The former did not make the contract illegal, even though the employee was receiving unofficial payments without the employer's knowledge.

107 [1994] IRLR 52.

arrangement. This was one of the issues that led the individual to resign and claim constructive dismissal. The EAT held that the contract had an illegal purpose, namely to defraud the Inland Revenue of tax. The result was that the employee was unable to rely upon it for the purposes of his claim even though the amount of tax lost to the Inland Revenue was small.[108] In *Hyland v JH Barker (North West) Ltd*[109] the giving of a tax-free lodging allowance for four weeks, whilst the employee commuted daily, was enough to taint the contract of employment with illegality. As a result the employee was unable to establish sufficient length of continuous employment to make an unfair dismissal claim. However, there is a difference between tax evasion and tax avoidance. Thus in *Lightfoot v D & J Sporting Ltd*[110] an arrangement to pay part of the salary to the employee's wife was held to be legitimate tax avoidance and did not make the employee's contract illegal.

It seems that such payments need to be part of an individual's regular remuneration and be more than occasional one-off payments without deductions. In *Annandale Engineering v Samson*[111] the occasional tax-free payments to a kennel hand by a greyhound trainer, made whenever one of their dogs won a race, could not be classified as part of the kennel hand's regular remuneration. The employer was not able to rely on the defence of illegality.

A different approach has been taken in relation to claims for unlawful sex discrimination. In *Leighton v Michael*[112] an ex-employee in a fish and kebab bar made a claim for sex discrimination. She had taken on extra work, and payment for this was made gross – that is, without any deductions for income tax and national insurance contributions. The employment tribunal had decided that it could not make a decision on sexual harassment claims because the contract was tainted with illegality. In the employment tribunal's view the individual needed to show that the discrimination was in the field of employment. In order to do this the claim had to be founded on the contract of employment, which was tainted. The EAT distinguished between actions based on dismissal, including constructive dismissal, and those based on discrimination. The former claims were concerned with enforcing rights based upon the contract of employment and in order to rely on the statutory rights the claimant had to establish not only that they were an employee, but also that they had been dismissed on the termination of a contract. By way of contrast, in a sex discrimination case, although there needs to be a reference to the contract to show that the claimant was employed, the right not to suffer unlawful discrimination does not involve relying upon, or basing a claim upon, the contract of employment. It is conferred by statute on persons who are employed.[113]

This distinction may seem artificial. Indeed, in *Chilton v HM Prison Service* (No 1),[114] which concerned another sex discrimination claim, Judge Peter Clark observed:

> We have grave reservations as to the correctness of *Leighton*. We are unable to appreciate the distinction between statutory claims of unfair dismissal and sex discrimination for the purpose of applying the public policy doctrine of illegality. Both statutory causes of action depend upon the contract as a prerequisite for the claim.

Despite this, because they had not heard full argument on the issue, the EAT again followed *Leighton*.

---

108 On the argument that the European Convention on Human Rights is infringed in these circumstances, see *Soteriou v Ultrachem Ltd* [2004] IRLR 870.
109 [1985] IRLR 403.
110 [1996] IRLR 64.
111 [1994] IRLR 59.
112 [1995] ICR 1091.
113 Rights to protection in employment under the Equality Act 2010 accrue to the wider definition of workers rather than just employees; see Chapter 6.
114 Employment Appeal Tribunal judgment delivered on 23 July 1999; not reported.

Hall v Woolston Hall Leisure Ltd[115] concerned an employee who was dismissed on the grounds of pregnancy and therefore had a claim under the Sex Discrimination Act 1975. She was paid part of her salary without the deduction of tax or national insurance contributions and she was aware of this illegality. The Court of Appeal confirmed the approach in *Leighton* and held that public policy grounds, that she should not be able to rely on the contract because of her knowledge of the illegality, were insufficient to defeat her claim. The court stated that it was undoubtedly correct that, where the complaint is of a discriminatory dismissal, the claimant must establish that she was employed and was dismissed from that employment, so that reliance must be placed on the contract. It further stated:

> It is the sex discrimination that is the core of the complaint, the fact of the employment and the dismissal being the particular factual circumstances which Parliament has prescribed for the sex discrimination complaint to be capable of being made . . . and the awareness of the employee that the employer was failing to deduct tax and NIC and to account to the Revenue does not of itself constitute a valid ground for refusing jurisdiction.

More recently, the EAT has stated that it does not consider that the authorities

> support the proposition that if the arrangements have the effect of depriving the Revenue of tax to which they were in law entitled then this renders the contract unlawful . . . there must be some form of misrepresentation, some attempt to conceal the true facts of the relationship, before the contract is rendered illegal . . .[116]

Where there is some illegality in the performance of the contract, the question for the court or tribunal is whether the right solution is to treat the whole contract as illegal or whether it is possible to sever the unlawful elements and allow the claimant to recover for the remainder. Thus in *Blue Chip Ltd v Helabawi*[117] a foreign student was only entitled to the national minimum wage for the weeks he was not in breach of a visa condition that prevented him working more than 20 hours a week. Finally, in a recent case the Supreme Court seems to have moved away from the 'reliance principle' and focused on the issues of proportionality and public policy.[118]

5.4.1.3 Continuous employment

Claimants must normally be continuously employed for a period of not less than two years, ending with the effective date of termination,[119] in order to qualify for the right not to be unfairly dismissed.[120] However, this does not apply if the reason or principal reason for dismissal was automatically unfair (see below) or relates to the employee's political opinions or affiliation. The length of this qualifying period has changed on a number of occasions. Initially, in 1971, the period was two years. It then became one year and subsequently six months. The Employment Act 1980 lengthened the period to two years again for smaller employers.[121] Continuity is to be calculated up to the effective date of termination in accordance with ss 210–219 ERA 1996 (see Chapter 2).

---

115 [2000] IRLR 578 CA.
116 *Enfield Technical Services Ltd v Payne* [2007] IRLR 840. The Court of Appeal upheld this decision: see [2008] IRLR 500.
117 [2009] IRLR 128.
118 *Patel v Mirza* [2016] UKSC 42.
119 Subject to the provisions in s. 97 ERA 1996 on the effective date; see s. 213(1) on continuity being preserved in accordance with that section.
120 Section 108(1) ERA 1996 as amended.
121 Those employing fewer than 20 employees.

5.4.2 The dismissal

5.4.2.1 Whether a dismissal has taken place

Having established that an employee has at least two years' continuous service and is not otherwise excluded, progress can be made to the next stage – that is, to establish that a dismissal has taken place. Section 95 ERA 1996 specifies the circumstances in which a dismissal takes place. The first of these is when a contract under which the individual is employed is terminated by the employer. Where there is a dispute as to whether a dismissal has taken place, the onus of proof is on the employee. Thus it is vitally important not to confuse a warning of impending dismissal – for example, through the announcement of a plant closure – with an individual notice to terminate.[122] For the giving of notice to constitute a dismissal at law the actual date of termination must be ascertainable. Where an employer has given notice to terminate, an employee who gives counter-notice indicating that he wishes to leave before the employer's notice has expired is still to be regarded as dismissed.[123]

There are occasions when there is a dispute as to whether the individual has been dismissed or whether they have resigned. This was the case in *Morris v London Iron and Steel Co Ltd*[124] where the employee claimed that he had been dismissed and the employer claimed that there had been a resignation. After hearing evidence, the employment tribunal was unable to decide which was the truth. Bearing in mind that the onus of proof was on the employee, the complaint was dismissed. This approach was approved in the Court of Appeal:

> the judge should at the end of the day look at the whole of the evidence that has been called before him, drawing inferences where appropriate, and ask himself what has or has not been shown on the balance of probabilities, and then, bearing in mind where the onus of proof lies, decide whether the plaintiff or the defendant, or both, succeeds.

More recently, in *Sandle v Adecco Ltd*[125] it was held that an agency worker had not been dismissed because the employer had not communicated an unequivocal intention to terminate the contract. According to the EAT, termination need not take the form of a direct express communication but there must be some form of communication.

A radical alteration to an employee's contract of employment may amount to a withdrawal of that contract and a conclusion that the individual was dismissed. *Hogg v Dover College*[126] was a drastic example of this. A teacher was informed by his employer that he would no longer be head of department, that he would be employed on a part-time basis only and his salary was to be halved. The EAT concluded that:

> both as a matter of law and common sense, he was being told that his former contract was from that moment gone ... It is suggested on behalf of the employers that there was a variation, but again, it seems to us quite elementary that you cannot hold a pistol to somebody's head and say 'henceforth you are to be employed on wholly different terms which are in fact 50 per cent of your previous contract'.

This was not a variation of the contract which might give the employee the opportunity to accept or reject a potential repudiation, but amounted to an express dismissal by the employer. This

---

122 See *Doble Firestone Tyre Co Ltd* [1981] IRLR 300.

123 Section 95(2) ERA 1996.

124 [1987] IRLR 182 CA.

125 [2016] IRLR 941.

126 [1990] ICR 39.

approach was applied in *Alcan Extrusions v Yates*[127] where the imposition of a continuous rolling shift system in place of a traditional shift system, contained in the employees' contracts, also amounted to an express dismissal by the employer. Alternatively, the unilateral variation of an employee's contractual working hours might amount to a breach of a fundamental term entitling the employee to resign and claim constructive dismissal. In *Greenaway Harrison Ltd v Wiles*[128] the threat to end the contracts of employment if the change of hours was not accepted amounted to an anticipatory breach giving rise to a constructive dismissal.

If an employer acts as a result of a genuine, but mistaken, belief that an employee has resigned, it may not be enough to prevent the conduct from amounting to a constructive dismissal. In *Brown v JBD Engineering Ltd*[129] an employer appointed a new employee and told customers that the previous employee was no longer employed, in the mistaken belief that the original employee had left as a result of an agreement. The mistake might be a relevant factor, but could not be enough to prevent the employee claiming that a dismissal had taken place.

5.4.2.2 Limited-term contracts

See 5.3.1 above and Chapter 3 on fixed-term contracts.

5.4.2.3 Constructive dismissal

Section 95(1)(c) ERA 1996 provides that an employee is to be treated as dismissed if the employee terminates the contract as a result of the employer's conduct. This is known as constructive dismissal. Lord Denning[130] provided a clear definition:

> If the employer is guilty of conduct which is a significant breach going to the root of the contract of employment; or which shows that the employer no longer intends to be bound by one or more of the essential terms of the contract; then the employee is entitled to treat himself as discharged from any further performance. If he does so, then he terminates the contract by reason of the employer's conduct. He is constructively dismissed.

Lord Denning went on to state that the employer's conduct must be sufficiently serious so as to entitle the employee to leave at once.[131] Subsequently, a number of additional principles have been developed. First, although the intention to dismiss is not a necessary part of an employer's repudiatory conduct, if such intention exists it is plainly material to the question of constructive dismissal.[132] Second, the duty of trust and confidence is not suspended because one party has broken it. Thus employees' own antecedent breaches will not prevent them from establishing a constructive dismissal claim.[133] Third, once a repudiatory breach has occurred, it cannot be cured by the contract breaker.[134]

An example of serious conduct which amounted to a repudiatory breach is shown in *Weathersfield v Sargent*.[135] The employee was given instructions to discriminate against ethnic minority customers. She was so upset by this policy that she telephoned the employer and told them that she was resigning, although she did not explain why. It was asserted that this failure to give a reason amounted to a failure to accept any repudiatory breach by the employer and so there could not be a constructive

---

127 [1996] IRLR 327.

128 [1994] IRLR 380.

129 [1993] IRLR 568.

130 *Western Excavations (ECC) Ltd v Sharp* [1978] IRLR 27 CA. For a more recent formulation of the test for repudiatory breach, see *Tullett Prebon plc v BGC Brokers LP* [2011] IRLR 420 CA.

131 See also *Woods v WM Car Services (Peterborough) Ltd* [1981] IRLR 413 CA, which followed *Western Excavations* in this respect.

132 *Grewals Ltd v Koo Seen Li* [2016] IRLR 638.

133 *Atkinson v Community Gateway Association* [2014] IRLR 834.

134 See *Buckland v Bournemouth University Higher Education Corporation* [2010] IRLR 445 CA.

135 [1999] IRLR 94 CA.

dismissal. The Court of Appeal did not accept this argument and held that it was quite clear what the real reason for the employee's departure was and the fact that the employee left for this reason amounted to an acceptance of the employer's repudiation.[136] Subsequently, the High Court has ruled that it is sufficient for a claimant to show that they have resigned in response at least in part to the employer's breach and the fact that employees are in reputiatory breach does not prevent them accepting an employer's breach as bringing their contracts to an end.[137]

The Court of Appeal has held that a series of acts can cumulatively amount to a breach of the implied duty of trust and confidence and thus a constructive dismissal. The 'final straw', however, does not have to be of the same character as earlier acts. It must contribute something to the breach but what it adds may be relatively insignificant. In *London Borough of Waltham Forest v Omilaju*[138] the complainant was employed by a local authority and issued five sets of proceedings alleging race discrimination and victimisation. These were heard in July and August 2001 but the employer refused to pay Mr Omilaju his full salary when he was absent without leave in order to attend the employment tribunal. It was the authority's rule that employees in his position were required to apply for special unpaid leave or annual leave. In September 2001 Mr Omilaju resigned and claimed unfair dismissal. The Court of Appeal upheld the tribunal's decision that the refusal to pay for the time attending the tribunal could not be regarded as the 'final straw' in a series of actions which together amounted to a breach of trust and confidence. According to the Appeal Court, a 'final straw' does not have to be of the same character as earlier acts. However, it must contribute something to the breach of the implied term even if what it adds may be relatively trivial.

It is not necessary for an employee to leave immediately in order to show that their departure is as a result of an employer's breach of contract. According to the EAT, where there is more than one reason why the employee left, the correct approach is to examine whether any of them was a response to the breach rather than identify which was the effective cause.[139] In *Jones v F Sirl & Son (Furnishers) Ltd*[140] the employee left some three weeks after the final event in a series of breaches of contract by her employer. She had obtained another job and left to take up the new position. The EAT concluded that the main cause of her leaving was the employer's actions, not because she had found another position to go to. A delay also occurred in *Waltons & Morse v Dorrington*[141] where the employer was held to be in breach of implied terms to provide a safe working environment and that the employer would reasonably and promptly afford employees a reasonable opportunity to obtain redress for any grievances.[142] In this case the employee strove to establish the right to sit in a smoke-free work environment. The failure of the employers to deal with her grievance led to the employee leaving and claiming constructive dismissal. She continued to work until she found alternative employment and it was argued that she had affirmed her contract in doing so. In rejecting the view that a delay in leaving negated the constructive dismissal, the EAT took into account her length of service and the fact that she needed to earn an income.[143]

Although in *Elsevier Ltd v Munro*[144] it was held that continuing in post until a new job was obtained amounted to affirmation of the contract, this will not always be the case. In *Aparau v Iceland Frozen Foods*

---

136 In *Moores v Bude-Stratton Town Council* [2000] IRLR 676 a local authority councillor's abusive conduct towards an employee of the authority amounted to a breach of the duty of trust and confidence such as to justify the employee resigning and claiming constructive dismissal.

137 *Tullett Prebon v BGC Brokers* [2010] IRLR 648.

138 [2005] IRLR 35.

139 *Wright v North Ayrshire Council* [2014] IRLR 4. See also *Ishaq v Royal Mail Group Ltd* [2017] IRLR 208 where it was held that the reason given in a letter of resignation was not genuine.

140 [1997] IRLR 493 EAT.

141 [1997] IRLR 488.

142 See also *Robins (UK) Ltd v Triggs* [2007] IRLR 857.

143 In *Dryden v Greater Glasgow Health Board* [1992] IRLR 469, where the employer introduced a no-smoking policy, the EAT held that there was no implied duty to provide facilities for smokers and no breach as a result of which the employee could claim constructive dismissal.

144 [2014] IRLR 766

plc[145] new contracts of employment were issued which contained a mobility clause. Some 18 months later the employee was given instructions to move to another branch. The employee denied that the employer had the right to issue such an instruction and successfully claimed that she had been constructively dismissed. The EAT accepted that the mobility clause had not been incorporated into her contract and a summary instruction to relocate was a repudiatory breach. By way of contrast, *White v Reflecting Roadstuds Ltd*[146] was about the transfer of an employee to an area of work where he earned less income. The employee resigned and claimed that he had been constructively dismissed. The claim failed because the EAT held that there was an express flexibility clause which permitted the employer to do this. There was no necessity to imply a reasonableness term into the clause as this would introduce a reasonableness test into the area of constructive dismissal.

An employer is not entitled to alter the formula whereby wages are calculated, but whether a unilateral reduction in pay or fringe benefits is of sufficient materiality to entitle the employee to resign is a question of degree. A failure to pay an employee's salary or wage is likely to constitute a fundamental breach if it is a deliberate act on the part of the employer rather than a mere break-down in technology. In *Gardner Ltd v Beresford*,[147] where the employee resigned because she had not received a pay increase for two years but others had, the EAT accepted that in most cases it would be reasonable to infer a term that an employer will not treat employees arbitrarily, capriciously or inequitably in relation to remuneration. However, if a contract makes no reference at all to pay increases, it is impossible to say that there is an implied term that there will always be a pay rise.[148]

The conduct complained about does not need to be taken by the employer. In *Hilton International Hotels (UK) Ltd v Protopapa*[149] a supervisor was severely reprimanded by her immediate superior in front of other employees. She resigned and claimed constructive dismissal. On appeal, the employer argued that there could not be a constructive dismissal because the immediate superior had no authority to sack her. The EAT did not accept this and reaffirmed the principle that an employer is to be held liable for the actions of employees for acts done in the course of their employment.[150] Finally, it should be noted that it is possible for an employer's repudiatory breach to result from the behaviour of the employee. In *Morrison*,[151] for example, the employer suspended an employee without pay as a result of the employee's behaviour. They had no contractual authority to suspend the employee who resigned and successfully claimed that there had been an unfair constructive dismissal. The employment tribunal decided that there should be a 40 per cent reduction in her compensation, because she had provoked the employer's unlawful reaction.

5.4.2.4 The effective date of termination of employment

The date on which a contract of employment terminates is important not just for reasons of calculating payments owed but also for calculating the start of the three-month period in which employees must make their complaint to an employment tribunal. The common law approach to the date of termination is that this will be when the notice given by the employer or employee expires, or the date that payment in lieu of notice is accepted. If an employer has given notice to an employee and, during that period, the employee resigns with the intention of leaving at an earlier

---

145 [1996] IRLR 119 EAT.

146 [1991] IRLR 331.

147 [1978] IRLR 63.

148 See *Murco Petroleum v Forge* [1987] IRLR 50.

149 [1990] IRLR 316.

150 See also *Warnes v The Trustees of Cheriton Oddfellows Social Club* [1993] IRLR 58, where an invalid resolution passed at a club's annual general meeting took away the secretarial duties of the club steward. Despite the invalidity of the resolution, this act amounted to a fundamental breach of contract justifying a claim for constructive dismissal.

151 *Morrison v Amalgamated Transport and General Workers Union* [1989] IRLR 361 CA.

date, the employee will still be treated as dismissed[152] but the effective date on which the contract ends will be that indicated by the employee's notice.[153]

Section 97(1) ERA 1996 provides a definition of the 'effective date of termination' in differing circumstances:

1. When a contract of employment is terminated by notice, the effective date is the date on which the notice expires. In *Hutchings v Coinseed Ltd*[154] an employee resigned and was told by her employer that she would not be required to work during her period of notice. She then started work for a competitor at a higher salary. The court rejected the employer's claim that this amounted to a repudiatory breach of contract entitling them not to pay the employee during the notice period, given the fact that they had not required her to do work for them during this period. Where there is a mutual variation of the notice to terminate, the notice and the contract of employment expire on the new date.[155]

2. Where a contract of employment is terminated without notice, then the effective date is the date on which the termination takes effect.[156] This is regardless of whether the employer followed all the contractual procedures to which the employee was entitled[157] or whether the dismissal was done in the correct manner.[158] In *Kirklees MBC v Radecki*[159] the Court of Appeal confirmed that the effective date of termination is the date of summary dismissal as long as the employee knows it. Thus the employer's communication that the employee was being taken off the payroll unequivocally conveyed that the employment was being terminated.

Where an employee is dismissed and no longer has the right to work and where the employer no longer has the obligation to pay, then the contract is at an end, unless there is an agreement to continue the relationship during any appeal proceedings.[160] *Drage v Governors of Greenford High School*[161] involved the dismissal of a school teacher. The question at issue was whether the effective date of termination was the date when he was told of the initial decision to dismiss him or the date when he was notified that his appeal against dismissal had failed. The Court of Appeal held that:

> The critical question arising, as in any similar case where contractual provision is made for an internal appeal, is whether during the period between the initial notification and the outcome of the appeal the employee stands (a) dismissed with the possibility of reinstatement or (b) suspended with the possibility of the proposed dismissal not being confirmed and the suspension thus being ended.

Thus if a contract is held to have been suspended during the appeals procedure, then the effective date will be the notification ending that procedure. The terms of the initial notification are likely to be important, although not necessarily decisive.[162]

---

152 Section 95(2) ERA 1996.

153 See *Thompson v GEC Avionics Ltd* [1991] IRLR 488, where an employee was given notice that her employment would cease on 9 November and she subsequently resigned and gave notice terminating her employment on 21 September. The earlier date was held to be the effective date of termination.

154 [1998] IRLR 190 CA.

155 See *Palfrey v Transco plc* [2004] IRLR 916.

156 *BMK Ltd and BMK Holdings Ltd v Logue* [1993] IRLR 477 considered the effective date of termination in constructive dismissals; the question to be asked is when did the termination take effect?

157 See *Batchelor v British Railways Board* [1987] IRLR 136 CA.

158 See *Robert Cort & Son Ltd v Charman* [1981] IRLR 437, which considered a summary dismissal without the contractual notice being given.

159 [2009] IRLR 555.

160 See *McMaster v Antrim Borough Council* [2011] IRLR 235 NICA and *Rabess v London Fire and Emergency Planning Authority* [2017] IRLR 147.

161 [2000] IRLR 315 CA.

162 See *Chapman v Letheby & Christopher Ltd* [1981] IRLR 440, where the EAT held that the construction to be put on a letter of dismissal should not be a technical one but one which an ordinary, reasonable employee would understand by the words used.

Even if the employee was contractually entitled to further payments, this may not delay the effective time or date of termination. Thus, as in *Octavius Atkinson & Sons Ltd v Morris*,[163] if an employee was summarily dismissed during the day, the effective time of the dismissal was when it was communicated to him. This was so even though the employee was entitled to further payments for travel to and from work.

3.   Where there is a limited-term contract which terminates as a result of the limiting event without being renewed under the same contract, the effective date is the date on which the termination takes effect.

Where the notice period is shorter than that required by s. 86 ERA 1996,[164] for the purposes of the qualifying length of service required to claim unfair dismissal and calculating the basic award for unfair dismissal,[165] the effective date of termination will be at the end of the period stipulated by s. 86 ERA 1996.[166]

Whether in a particular case the words of dismissal evince an intention to terminate the contract at once or only at a future date depends on the construction of those words. Such construction must not be technical but reflect what an ordinary, reasonable employee would understand by the language used. Moreover, words should be construed in the light of the facts known to the employee at the time of notification. If the language used is ambiguous, it is likely that tribunals will apply the principle that words should be interpreted most strongly against the person who uses them. It should also be observed that, where a dismissal has been communicated by letter, the contract of employment does not terminate until the employee has actually read the letter or had a reasonable opportunity of reading it.[167] Thus in *McMaster v Manchester Airport*,[168] the employer had posted a letter of dismissal to the applicant and had presumed that it was received and read. This was not an altogether unreasonable assumption, given that the employee was absent from work through sickness and might reasonably have been expected to be at home where the dismissal letter was sent. In fact he was away on a day trip to France and did not read the letter until the next day. The court held that it was the day that the employee read the letter which was the effective date of termination.

5.4.3 The reasons for dismissal

Having established that a dismissal has taken place and when it took effect, the next stage is to decide whether the reasons for dismissal can be treated as within those permitted by the ERA 1996 or whether they should be regarded as unfair.

5.4.3.1 Statement of reasons for dismissal

If an employer gives an employee notice of dismissal or terminates the employee's contract without notice, then the employee is entitled to be given a written statement giving particulars of the reasons for the dismissal. Employees engaged under a limited-term contract which expires without

---

163 [1989] IRLR 158 CA.

164 The minimum periods of notice required; see above.

165 Sections 108(1) and 119(1) ERA 1996.

166 Section 97(2)–(5) ERA 1996. In *Lanton Leisure Ltd v White and Gibson* [1987] IRLR 119 two employees were dismissed without notice for gross misconduct and, consequently, failed to have enough continuous service to qualify for making an unfair dismissal claim. The employees claimed that they were entitled to the protection of (now) s. 97(2) ERA 1996. The EAT concluded that the employment tribunal had a duty to consider first whether there had been conduct warranting a dismissal for gross misconduct, which had the effect of removing the employees' contractual rights to notice.

167 See *GISDA Cyf v Barratt* [2010] IRLR 1073 SC.

168 [1998] IRLR 112.

being renewed under the same contract are also entitled to such a statement.[169] There are some conditions attached to this right:

1. It only applies to employees who, at the effective date of termination,[170] have been continuously employed for a period of two years.[171]
2. The employee is entitled to the statement only if he or she requests it. Once requested, the statement must be provided within 14 days.[172]

It is acceptable for the statement to refer unambiguously to other letters already sent which contain the reasons for dismissal.[173] Special provision is made for those who are pregnant or who are on maternity or adoption leave, if this leave is brought to an end. If they are dismissed, there is no continuous service requirement before they are entitled to a statement, neither do they need to request it.[174] Written statements provided by the employer are admissible in evidence in subsequent legal proceedings.[175]

An employee may make a complaint to an employment tribunal if the employer unreasonably fails to provide the written statement or if the reasons given are inadequate or untrue.[176] The obligation on employers is to state what they genuinely believe to be the reason or reasons for the dismissal. There is no requirement for the employment tribunal to decide whether they were good reasons or justifiable ones.[177] This would happen at a later stage if unfair dismissal proceedings were brought. If the employment tribunal finds the complaint well founded, then it may make a declaration as to what it considers the employer's reasons for dismissing were and also make an award that the employer must pay the employee a sum equal to two weeks' pay.[178] Somewhat bizarrely, this right to complain only relates to statements that have been requested.[179]

5.4.3.2 Automatically unfair reasons

Dismissals for automatically unfair reasons do not require an employee to have worked continuously for a period of two years.[180] These dismissals relate to such matters as the following:[181]

1. Family reasons[182] – these are reasons relating to the Maternity and Parental Leave etc. Regulations 1999[183] and include reasons related to (a) pregnancy, childbirth or maternity, (b) paternity, parental or adoption leave. They also include the right to time off for dependants contained in s. 57A ERA 1996.
2. Health and safety matters[184] – where the reason for dismissal was that the employee:

---

169 Section 92(1) ERA 1996.
170 Section 92(6)–(8) ERA 1996 describes the meaning of effective date of termination; these provisions are identical to those in s. 97(1)–(2) described above.
171 Section 92(3) ERA 1996.
172 Section 92(2) ERA 1996.
173 See Gilham v Kent County Council (No 1) [1986] IRLR 56.
174 Section 92(4)–(4A) ERA 1996.
175 Section 92(5) ERA 1996.
176 Section 93(1) ERA 1996.
177 Harvard Securities plc v Younghusband [1990] IRLR 17.
178 Section 93(2) ERA 1996; see Part XIV Chapter II ERA 1996 for the meaning of a week's pay; considered below.
179 See Catherine Haigh Harlequin Hair Design v Seed [1990] IRLR 175.
180 Section 108(2)–(3) ERA 1996.
181 This should not be taken as a comprehensive list; the number of automatically unfair reasons seems to grow with each new piece of employment legislation. At the end of 2016 there were 28 automatically unfair reasons listed in Section 108(3) ERA 1996.
182 Section 99 ERA 1996.
183 SI 1999/3312.
184 Section 100 ERA 1996. On how this section should be applied, see Oudahar v Esporta Ltd [2011] IRLR 730.

- Carried out, or proposed to carry out, activities designated by the employer in connection with preventing or reducing risks to the health and safety of employees.
- Performed, or proposed to perform, any of his or her functions as a safety representative or a member of a safety committee.
- Took part or proposed to take part in consultation with the employer pursuant to the Health and Safety (Consultation with Employees) Regulations 1996 or in an election of representatives of employee safety within the meaning of those Regulations.
- Where there was no safety representative or committee or it was not reasonably practicable to raise the matter in that way, brought to the employer's attention, by reasonable means, circumstances connected with his or her work which she or he reasonably believed were harmful or potentially harmful to health and safety.
- Left or proposed to leave, or refused to return to (whilst the danger persisted), his or her place of work or any dangerous part of the workplace, in circumstances of danger which he or she reasonably believed to be serious and imminent and which she or he could not reasonably have been expected to avert.
- Took, or proposed to take, appropriate steps to protect himself or herself or other persons, in circumstances of danger which he or she reasonably believed to be serious and imminent. Whether those steps were 'appropriate' must be judged by reference to all the circumstances, including the employee's knowledge and the facilities and advice available at the time. A dismissal will not be regarded as unfair if the employer can show that it was, or would have been, so negligent for the employee to take the steps which she or he took, or proposed to take, that a reasonable employer might have dismissed on these grounds.

3. Protected shop workers and betting shop workers[185] who refuse to work on Sundays.
4. Working time[186] – where the reason for the dismissal is that an employee has refused to comply with instructions contrary to the provisions of the Working Time Regulations 1998,[187] refused to give up any rights under these Regulations, failed to sign a workforce agreement or is performing, or proposing to perform, the duties of an employee representative in relation to Sch. 1 to those Regulations.
5. Pension scheme trustees[188] – performing, or proposing to perform, the duties of a trustee of a relevant occupational pension scheme, which relates to the individual's employment.
6. Employee representatives[189] – being, or taking part in the elections for, an employee representative for the purposes of consultation on collective redundancies[190] or transfers of undertakings.[191]
7. Protected disclosures[192] – an employee dismissed for making a protected disclosure (see 4.5.2.4 above).
8. Assertion of a statutory right[193] – where an employee brings proceedings to enforce a statutory right or alleges that an employer has infringed a statutory right. These are rights associated with bringing complaints to an employment tribunal; rights to minimum notice;[194] matters concerned with deductions from pay, union activities and time off for trade union duties and

---

185 Section 101 ERA 1996.
186 Section 101A ERA 1996.
187 SI 1998/1833.
188 Section 102 ERA 1996.
189 Section 103 ERA 1996.
190 Part IV Chapter II TULRCA 1992.
191 Transfer of Undertakings (Protection of Employment) Regulations 2006, SI 2006/246.
192 Section 103A ERA 1996.
193 Section 104 ERA 1996. See *Mennell v Newell & Wright (Transport Contractors) Ltd* [1997] IRLR 519.
194 Section 86 ERA 1996.

activities;[195] matters connected with the right to be accompanied at disciplinary or grievance hearings;[196] and rights conferred by the Working Time Regulations 1998.[197] It is irrelevant whether the employee has the right or whether it has been infringed, as long as the employee acts in good faith.

9. The national minimum wage[198] – any action taken by, or on behalf of, an employee in connection with enforcing rights relating to the national minimum wage. Again it is irrelevant whether the employee has the right or whether it has been infringed, as long as the employee is acting in good faith.

10. Working family tax credits or disabled persons tax credits[199] – any action taken, or proposed to be taken, by or on behalf of the employee in connection with rights requiring employers to make payments and requiring employers to provide employees with information.

11. Participation in protected industrial action[200] – where an employee takes part in protected industrial action and is dismissed within the protected period. This protection does not extend to those who take part in unofficial industrial action (see Chapter 12).

12. Part-time work – where employees bring proceedings to enforce their rights under the Part-time Workers (Prevention of Less Favourable Treatment) Regulations 2000.[201]

13. Redundancy[202] – where the principal reason for a dismissal is redundancy and it is shown that the same circumstances apply to other employees in the same undertaking in similar positions and who have not been dismissed and it is shown that any of (1) to (12) apply.

14. Spent offences – where a conviction of less than two and a half years is spent[203] the employee is not under an obligation to disclose it. Section 4 of the Rehabilitation of Offenders Act 1974 stops employers from dismissing someone for not revealing the information to them. Certain sensitive occupations, such as nurses, police and social service workers, are excluded from these provisions.[204]

15. Transfers of undertakings – reg. 7(1) of the Transfer of Undertakings (Protection of Employment) Regulations 2006[205] makes a dismissal by reason of relevant transfer automatically unfair, unless the reason for the dismissal was an economic, technical or organisational one.[206]

16. Fixed-term work – where employees do anything to act on their rights under the Fixed-term Employees (Prevention of Less Favourable Treatment) Regulations 2002.

17. Flexible work – s. 104C ERA 1996 provides protection for a qualifying employee who applies, in accordance with s. 80F ERA 1996,[207] to change their hours, times or place of work to enable the employee to care for a child.

Other instances of automatically unfair dismissal are those which constitute discrimination made unlawful by the Equality Act 2010 (see Chapter 6).

---

195 Sections 68, 86, 146, 168–170 TULRCA 1992; see also s. 152 TULRCA 1992.

196 Section 12(3) Employment Relations Act 1999.

197 SI 1998/1833.

198 Section 104A ERA 1996.

199 Section 104B ERA 1996; see Sch. 3 Tax Credits Act 1999.

200 Section 238A(2) TULRCA 1992.

201 SI 2000/1551; see reg. 7.

202 Section 105 ERA 1996.

203 Meaning a period of time since the sentence was served; the length of this period depends upon the severity of the sentence.

204 See *Wood v Coverage Care Ltd* [1996] IRLR 264 which was about an employee, whose post was redundant, being refused alternative work because of a conviction that excluded her from the social work alternative positions.

205 SI 2006/246.

206 Regulation 7(2) Transfer of Undertakings (Protection of Employment) Regulations 2006; see *Dynamex Friction Ltd v AMICUS* [2008] IRLR 515 where the Court of Appeal accepted that employees had been dismissed for an economic reason when an administrator decided that he had no option but to sack them because the company had no money.

207 Inserted by s. 46 Employment Act 2002.

5.4.3.3 Fair or unfair reasons for dismissal

Having established that a dismissal has taken place, it is then for the employer to show that the reason for it was fair.[208] This is to be done by showing that the reason (or the principal reason if there is more than one), for the dismissal is that:

1. It relates to the capability or qualifications of the employee for performing work of the kind for which the employee was employed.
2. It relates to the conduct of the employee.
3. The employee was redundant.
4. The employee could not continue to work in the position for which the employee was employed without breaching a duty or restriction imposed by an enactment.[209]

There is a distinction between the first two of these reasons and the last two. It is a distinction, defined by the EAT, as that between the language of actuality and that of relationship. In *Shook v London Borough of Ealing*[210] the EAT considered this distinction:

> Two of them are couched in the language of actuality: the employee must be redundant or engaged under an unlawful contract, as the case may be. The other two are expressed in the language of relationship: the reason must relate to the capability for performing the work of the relevant kind or must relate to the conduct of the employee, as the case may be.

If the reason, or principal reason, does not fall into one of the four categories above it may still be fair if the dismissal takes place for

> some other substantial reason of a kind such as to justify the dismissal of an employee holding the position which the employee held.[211]

It follows that where no reason is given by the employer, a dismissal will be unfair simply because the statutory burden has not been discharged. Equally, if a reason is engineered in order to effect dismissal because the real reason would not be acceptable, the employer will fail because the underlying principal reason is not within s. 98(1) or (2) ERA 1996.[212]

No account is to be taken of any pressure exerted upon an employer to dismiss unfairly. If the employer is under pressure to dismiss an employee resulting from threats of, or actual, industrial action, this will not be taken into account. The tribunal will consider fairness as if there was no such pressure.[213] The exception to this rule is where an employer has been pressured to dismiss an individual for not joining a trade union. In such a case the employer may request the tribunal to add the person whom it is alleged exercised the pressure as a party to the proceedings. The effect of this is that the tribunal may order that part of any compensation owed is paid by the third party.[214]

The reason for the dismissal is the one known to the employer at the time of the dismissal. It is not acceptable for a tribunal to take into account matters which were not known to the employer

---

208 Section 98(1) ERA 1996.
209 Section 98(2) ERA 1996.
210 [1986] IRLR 46.
211 Section 98(1)(b) ERA 1996.
212 See *ASLEF v Brady* [2006] IRLR 76.
213 Section 107 ERA 1996.
214 Section 160 TULRCA 1992.

at the time of the dismissal.[215] In *W Devis & Sons Ltd v Atkins*[216] the employer attempted to introduce new evidence of a dismissed employee's serious misconduct. This failed because it was information that came to light after the dismissal had taken place for another reason, namely a failure to obey instructions. The court approved the approach taken in *Abernethy v Mott, Hay & Anderson*[217] where it was ruled that:

> A reason for the dismissal is a set of facts known to the employer, or it may be of beliefs held by him, which cause him to dismiss the employee. If at the time of the dismissal the employer gives a reason for it, that is no doubt evidence, at any rate as against him, as to the real reason.

Any extra information could, however, be taken into account when assessing compensation. The exception is information that may become available during an internal appeals procedure, although this material must relate to the original decision. To exclude this information would be to ignore important parts of the case, either in favour of the employer or the employee. Lord Bridge stated in *West Midlands Co-operative Society Ltd v Tipton*:[218]

> The apparent injustice of excluding . . . misconduct of an employee which is irrelevant to the real reason for dismissal is mitigated . . . by the provisions relating to compensation in such a case. But there is nothing to mitigate the injustice to an employee which would result if he were unable to complain that his employer, though acting reasonably on the facts known to him when he summarily dismissed the employee, acted quite unreasonably in maintaining his decision to dismiss in the face of mitigating circumstances established in the course of the domestic appeals procedure . . .[219]

Section 98(4)(a) ERA 1996 provides that once the employer has shown that the reason for the dismissal comes within the terms of s. 98(1) or (2), then the issue for the tribunal is whether the employer acted reasonably or unreasonably in treating it as a sufficient reason for dismissing the employee. This will partly depend upon the size and administrative resources of the employer's undertaking[220] and will be decided 'in accordance with equity and the substantial merits of the case'.[221]

5.4.3.4 Capability or qualifications

Capability is assessed by reference to skill, aptitude, health or any other physical or mental quality.[222] Assessing capability may well be subjective and an employer will need to be able to show that they had reasonable grounds for their belief. In *Taylor v Alidair Ltd*,[223] which concerned the competence of an airline pilot, Lord Denning MR stated:

> In considering the case, it must be remembered that . . . [the Act] contemplated a subjective test. The tribunal have to consider the employer's reason and the employer's state of mind. If the company honestly believed on reasonable grounds that the pilot was lacking in proper capability to fly aircraft on behalf of the company, that was a good and sufficient reason for the company to determine the employment then and there.

---

215 This includes considering the reasons throughout the notice period: see *Parkinson v March Consulting Ltd* [1997] IRLR 308 CA.
216 [1977] AC 931 HL.
217 [1974] IRLR 213.
218 [1986] IRLR 112 HL.
219 Similarly, defects in the disciplinary or dismissal procedures can be remedied on appeal: see *Whitbread & Co v Mills* [1987] IRLR 18.
220 Section 98(4)(a) ERA 1996.
221 Section 98(4)(b) ERA 1996.
222 Section 98(3)(a) ERA 1996.
223 [1978] IRLR 82 CA.

There are special considerations applicable when the individual could put people's safety at risk but the question as to when it is fair to dismiss an incompetent employee is an important one for employers.

(a) Incompetent employees

The employer has a right not to have their business harmed by an incompetent person, but the employee also has a right to be treated fairly. In *Whitbread & Co v Thomas*[224] three employees were dismissed as a result of their lack of competence in failing to prevent stock losses. This was despite the fact that the employer did not know which of the three might be responsible for the losses. The employer had, however, done everything possible to prevent the losses, including issuing warnings and transferring, temporarily, the staff to other locations. The EAT accepted that the employer had fulfilled three necessary conditions. These were, first, that if the act had been committed by an identified individual it would have led to dismissal; second, that the act was committed by one or more of the individuals in the group; and, third, that there had been a proper investigation to try to identify the person or persons responsible for the act.[225]

Treating an employee fairly does not necessarily mean not dismissing when they have many years of service. In *Gair v Bevan Harris Ltd*[226] a foreman was dismissed for unsatisfactory performance and this was held to be fair, even though the employee had 11 years' service. An unreasonable procedural delay, however, might turn an otherwise fair dismissal into an unfair one.[227]

According to para. 1 of the ACAS Code of Practice on Disciplinary and Grievance Procedures:[228]

> Disciplinary situations include misconduct and/or poor performance. If employers have a separate capability procedure they may prefer to address performance issues under this procedure. If so, however, the basic principles of fairness set out in this Code should still be followed, albeit that they may need to be adapted.

In addition, paras 19–21 and 23 provide:

> Where misconduct is confirmed or the employee is found to be performing unsatisfactorily it is usual to give the employee a written warning. A further act of misconduct or failure to improve performance within a set period would normally result in a final written warning.

> If an employee's first misconduct or unsatisfactory performance is sufficiently serious, it may be appropriate to move directly to a final written warning. This might occur where the employee's actions have had, or are liable to have, a serious or harmful impact on the organisation.

> A first or final written warning should set out the nature of the misconduct or poor performance and the change in behaviour or improvement in performance required (with timescale). The employee should be told how long the warning will remain current. The employee should be informed of the consequences of further misconduct, or failure to improve performance, within the set period following a final warning. For instance that it may result in dismissal or some other contractual penalty such as demotion or loss of seniority.

---

224 [1988] IRLR 43.
225 See *Monie v Coral Racing Ltd* [1980] IRLR 464 CA where this principle was established in situations of dishonesty. In *Whitbread* the EAT suggested that it would apply to situations concerning incompetence only exceptionally.
226 [1983] IRLR 368.
227 See *RSPCA v Cruden* [1986] IRLR 83, where an employee was dismissed for what was described, by the employment tribunal, as 'gross misjudgment and idleness quite incompatible with the proper performance of his duties'. Nevertheless, the dismissal was unfair because of a long delay in instituting proceedings.
228 2015. On the status of the Code, see below.

Some acts, termed gross misconduct, are so serious in themselves or have such serious consequences that they may call for dismissal without notice for a first offence. But a fair disciplinary process should always be followed, before dismissing for gross misconduct.[229]

It should be noted that in *Airbus Ltd v Webb*[230] the Court of Appeal held that an expired warning does not make the earlier misconduct an irrelevant circumstance under s. 98(4) ERA 1996. Subsequently, in *Wincanton Group v Stone*[231] the EAT suggested that employers are obliged to have regard to previous warnings. In this case the employment tribunal had wrongly looked at whether the warning was justified instead of considering whether the employer was entitled to rely on it. However, the Court of Appeal has accepted that warnings issued in bad faith should not be taken into account.[232]

(b) Ill health and absenteeism

A second and important aspect of capability is how employers deal with those who are absent from work as a result of ill health. Appendix 4 of the ACAS Guide provides advice on how to deal with persistent short-term absence, longer-term absence through ill health and special health problems.

According to the EAT, the cause of ill health is not a concern of the tribunal, only the question as to whether the employer was reasonable in dismissing the employee because of their unfitness for work. Thus, even when the employer may have some responsibility for the employee's lack of fitness for work, the matter is not relevant when considering whether the dismissal was fair on the grounds of capability.[233] Subsequently, the key question has been identified as whether in all the circumstances a reasonable employer would have waited any longer before dismissing on ill-health grounds.[234]

It is likely that a dismissal for ill health will not be fair if the employee has not been consulted. Discussions and consultation with the employee may bring out new facts which may influence the employer's decision. This is so even where the employer has received an independent medical report on the employee's state of health.[235] In *First West Yorkshire Ltd v Haigh*[236] the EAT ruled that where an employer provides an enhanced pension on retirement through ill health, it is expected to take reasonable steps to ascertain whether the employee is entitled to benefit from this scheme. There is a difference between situations where an employee becomes permanently unfit to carry out duties required by their post and occasions when the employer decides to dismiss as a result of a poor attendance record.

The issue of an individual becoming permanently unfit for work may also be an issue under the Equality Act 2010 (see Chapter 6).[237] In *Seymour v British Airways Board*,[238] for example, a registered disabled person was dismissed after the employer prepared and implemented a policy in relation to 'non-effective' staff, who might be restricted in their work for medical reasons. The EAT held that, although the disabled person was entitled to special consideration, this was not sufficient to give them priority over others in a redundancy situation. By way of contrast, in *Kent County Council v Mingo*[239] a disabled employee was held to have been discriminated against because priority was given

---

229 Pages 10–11 of the ACAS Guide *Discipline and Grievances at Work* (2016) describe the benefits of informality and pages 16–17 deal with formal disciplinary action.

230 [2008] IRLR 309.

231 [2013] IRLR 178.

232 *Way v Spectrum Property* [2015] IRLR 657.

233 See *McAdie v Royal Bank of Scotland* [2007] IRLR 895 CA.

234 *BS v Dundee City Council* [2014] IRLR 131.

235 See *East Lindsey District Council v GE Daubney* [1977] IRLR 181.

236 [2008] IRLR 182.

237 *Eclipse Blinds Ltd v Wright* [1992] IRLR 133 is an example of a case, prior to the Disability Discrimination Act 1995 (now replaced by the Equality Act 2010), which concerned a disabled person with deteriorating health.

238 [1983] IRLR 55.

239 [2000] IRLR 90.

to other redundant or potentially redundant employees who were not so disadvantaged. The unfitness needs to be in relation to the particular work which the individual was employed to undertake. Even where a contract gives the employer the right to transfer an employee to any other work at a similar level, the fitness of the individual needs to be assessed in relationship to the particular kind of work.[240]

Continued periodic absences may be a considerable problem for some employers. It is important that the individual is aware of the possible consequences of their absenteeism record. Formal warnings may not always be appropriate, nor will medical evidence where it is not possible to provide an accurate prognosis for the future. In *Lynock v Cereal Packaging*[241] the EAT held that the approach of the employer must be based upon 'sympathy, understanding and compassion'. Whilst each case must depend upon its own facts, important considerations will be:

> The nature of the illness; the likelihood of it recurring or some other illness arising; the length of the various absences and the spaces of good health between them; the need of the employer for the work done by the particular employee; the impact of the absences on others who work with the employee ... the important emphasis on a personal assessment in the ultimate decision and, of course, the extent to which the difficulty of the situation and the position of the employee has been made clear to the employee.

In *Devonshire v Trico-Folberth*[242] an employee received a formal warning about her number of absences from work due to ill health. After further monitoring showed no improvement in attendance she was dismissed, initially because of her unacceptable record. During the internal appeal procedure, an appellate body changed the reason for dismissal on compassionate grounds to one of being medically unfit to work. The tribunal stated that a dismissal for the original reason may well have been fair but not on grounds of being medically unfit. There had been insufficient investigation of her condition and inadequate consultation with the employee to justify dismissal on these grounds.[243] Consultation with the employee is necessary, so that the matter can be discussed personally. Only in the rarest of circumstances is a dismissal on the grounds of health likely to be fair if there has not been adequate consultation between the employer and the employee.[244]

(c) Qualifications

Qualifications means any degree, diploma or other academic, technical or professional qualification that is relevant to the position held.[245] The qualifications need to be considered in the light of the particular position that the employee held. Thus, depending upon the circumstances, even a failure to pass an aptitude test can be a reason for a dismissal under this heading.[246] Such qualifications might include the need for a driving licence, as in *Tayside Regional Council v Mcintosh*.[247] When the local authority advertised for vehicle mechanics they stipulated that applicants should have a clean driving licence, although this was not mentioned in the written offer of employment. The successful applicant met this criterion but, three years later, was disqualified from driving as a result of a motoring offence. The employer dismissed him as there was no alternative work available. Despite

---

240 See *Shook v London Borough of Ealing* [1986] IRLR 46.

241 [1988] IRLR 510.

242 [1989] IRLR 396 CA.

243 See also *Grootcon (UK) Ltd v Keld* [1984] IRLR 302 where lack of medical evidence was important and the real reason for dismissal may have been the insistence of a major customer.

244 See *East Lindsey District Council v GE Daubney* [1977] IRLR 181 for a fuller discussion of consultation requirements in such situations; this case was followed in *A Links Co Ltd v Rose* [1991] IRLR 353.

245 Section 98(3)(b) ERA 1996.

246 See *Blackman v The Post Office* [1974] IRLR 46 NIRC.

247 [1982] IRLR 272.

the lack of an express term in the contract, the EAT held that the need for a licence could be inferred and that it was an essential and continuing condition of the individual's employment.

5.4.3.5 Conduct

There may be a relationship between competence and conduct. For example, poor attendance at work might be seen as a lack of competence or a result of the employee's conduct.[248] In *Whitbread & Co v Thomas*[249] (above) the recurring stock losses in an off-licence raised issues about both the employees' competence in controlling the stock and their conduct in relation to their honesty or otherwise. Prior to the tribunal considering whether the employer acted reasonably in treating a reason as sufficient for dismissing an employee, it must first establish what the reason for dismissal was.[250] Issues about employee conduct are also issues about how an employer reacts to that conduct, so employee awareness of the conduct that is expected of them is important in establishing the reasonableness of the dismissal. *Lock v Cardiff Railway Co Ltd*[251] involved the dismissal of a train conductor who asked a teenage boy to leave the train when it was discovered that he had no ticket or money to pay. In this case the employer had failed to follow the ACAS Code of Practice by not making it clear which offences would be regarded as gross misconduct justifying summary dismissal.

As a general rule, if an order is lawful, a refusal to obey it will be a breach of contract and amount to misconduct even though similar refusals have been condoned in the past. Nevertheless, in disobedience cases the primary factor to be considered is whether the employee is acting reasonably in refusing to carry out an instruction.[252] Thus in *Robinson v Tescom Corporation*[253] the employee had agreed to work under the terms of a varied job description whilst negotiations were ongoing. His subsequent refusal to do so was held by the EAT to amount to disobedience of a lawful instruction.

Another area where there might be grounds for a fair dismissal is when a worker is dishonest. In *British Railways Board v Jackson*[254] a train buffet supervisor was dismissed because the employer believed that he was about to take his own goods on board the train to sell to customers, thus depriving the employer of revenue. There were no tills on train buffet cars, so the employer relied upon the honesty of its employees. The employer's action was held to be reasonable and the employer was entitled to take into account the prevalence of this type of dishonesty amongst employees and whether the dismissal would be a deterrent to others from following the same course. Dishonesty by employees against the employer is likely to be a breach of the fundamental relationship of mutual trust and confidence and a repetition of such a breach might lead to dismissal being within the range of reasonable responses (see below).[255] Providing evidence of the employee's dishonesty may be a problem, but if the employer has reasonable grounds for sustaining a genuine belief about the employee's guilt, after carrying out an investigation, this is likely to be sufficient.[256] Thus in *Rhondda CBC v Close*[257] the EAT accepted that it was not outside the band of reasonableness (see below) for the employer to choose not to carry out its own independent questioning in a disciplinary procedure but to rely instead on police statements. The Appeal Tribunal also expressed the view that it is not generally incumbent on an employer to allow the cross-examination of witnesses.

It may not be immediately apparent to an employee that their actions are dishonest. Using an employer's telephone to make personal calls, for example, may be viewed as dishonest by an

---

248 See e.g. *Devonshire v Trico-Folberth* [1989] IRLR 396.
249 [1988] IRLR 43.
250 See *Wilson v Post Office* [2001] IRLR 834.
251 [1998] IRLR 358.
252 See *UCATT v Brain* [1981] IRLR 224.
253 [2008] IRLR 804.
254 [1994] IRLR 235 CA.
255 See *Conlin v United Distillers* [1994] IRLR 169 CA where a repeated act of dishonesty led to such a dismissal.
256 See *British Leyland (UK) Ltd v Swift* [1981] IRLR 91 CA and *British Home Stores Ltd v Burchell* [1978] IRLR 379, considered further below.
257 [2008] IRLR 869.

employer but not by an employee. There may be a need for a proper investigation as to the purpose and circumstances of such calls. In *John Lewis plc v Coyne*[258] the court seemed to prefer a subjective approach rather than any absolute definition of dishonesty. An employee was dismissed for breaching company rules on the use of telephones but the lack of a sufficient investigation by the employer made it unfair. The court considered that there was a two-stage process in judging whether dishonesty had occurred. The first was that it must be decided whether, according to the ordinary standards of reasonable and honest people, what was done was dishonest. The second stage was to consider whether the person concerned must have realised that what he or she was doing was, by those standards, dishonest.

There is a distinction between misconduct at work and misconduct outside of it which has no relationship to the employment.[259] What, for example, is the position of an employer who has an employee facing criminal charges? In *Lovie Ltd v Anderson*[260] an employee was charged by the police with two separate offences of indecent exposure. It might be natural for an employer not to wish to retain an individual who faces such charges but there is still an obligation to carry out an investigation and give the employee an opportunity to state their case. Similarly, in *Securicor Guarding Ltd v R*[261] an employee was charged with sex offences against children, which he denied. The employer was concerned about the reaction of important customers and, after a disciplinary hearing, the employee was dismissed. This was held to be unfair, partly because the employer had not considered other options, such as suspension with full pay, in accordance with the company's own disciplinary code, or moving the individual to less customer-sensitive work. By way of contrast, an assistant schools groundsman who pleaded guilty to a sexual offence against his daughter was dismissed because of the possible risk to other children. According to the Court of Appeal, the employer had no choice but to dismiss the employee despite the lack of further investigation. The plea of guilty and the nature of the job were sufficient.[262] In *Mathewson v RB Wilson Dental Laboratories Ltd*[263] a dental technician was arrested during his lunch break and charged with being in possession of cannabis. The employers were held to have acted reasonably in treating this as a sufficient reason for dismissal, even though the offence was unconnected with his work. The employer argued that it was not appropriate to employ someone on highly skilled work who was using drugs, and that there was concern about the effect on younger staff members of continuing to employ him. A conviction itself, unless for a trivial or minor matter, would normally be sufficient to provide the employer with adequate grounds for believing that the employee had committed the offence and might be enough to dismiss the individual.[264]

Examples of misconduct at work include those that involve relationships with colleagues. *Hussain v Elonex*[265] concerned an allegation of head-butting and was part of a number of incidents between the complainant and another employee. This was considered grounds for dismissal, although there was an appeal on procedural grounds. The same result occurred in *Fuller v Lloyds Bank plc*[266] where, after an employer's investigation into an incident at a Christmas party that involved smashing a glass into another employee's face, the complainant was dismissed.

---

258 [2001] IRLR 139.

259 See *CJD v Royal Bank of Scotland* [2014] IRLR 25.

260 [1999] IRLR 164.

261 [1994] IRLR 633.

262 *P v Nottinghamshire County Council* [1992] IRLR 362 CA. In *A v B* [2016] IRLR 779 the Court of Appeal upheld a finding that a school's decision to dismiss a headteacher for misconduct was fair after she chose not to disclose a close personal relationship with a man convicted of making indecent images of children.

263 [1988] IRLR 512.

264 See *Secretary of State for Scotland v Campbell* [1992] IRLR 263, where a prison officer who was also treasurer of the officers' social club was found guilty of embezzling the club funds; this verdict was sufficient to justify his dismissal.

265 [1999] IRLR 420.

266 [1991] IRLR 336.

An employer is entitled to expect an employee not to compete for customers or contracts (see Chapter 4 on implied duties). Such competition may amount to a sufficient reason for dismissal. In *Adamson v B & L Cleaning Services*[267] a foreman for a contract cleaning firm refused to agree that he would not compete for a cleaning contract with his employer. The EAT distinguished between competing with the employer, which is more likely to be a sufficient reason, and merely indicating an intention to compete in the future,[268] or applying for a job with a competitor. The stage the plans for competing have reached may well be important for the employment tribunal in reaching a decision. Thus a managing director who had formed a plan with another senior manager and attempted to induce another employee to join them was held to have gone beyond merely indicating a plan to compete in the future and was held to have been fairly dismissed.[269]

5.4.3.6 Redundancy

In *Williams v Compair Maxam Ltd*[270] the EAT laid down some principles that a reasonable employer should follow if they were planning to dismiss on the grounds of redundancy. The EAT pointed out that these were not principles of law but standards of behaviour. However, the approach has been widely followed, even if the judgment now appears to reflect an industrial relations landscape that no longer seems to exist. The principles are:

1. The employer would try to give as much warning as possible, to employees and their representatives, of impending redundancies.
2. The employer would consult the employees' representatives and agree criteria for selection.
3. The criteria for selection would not, as far as possible, depend upon the personal opinion of the individual making the selection, but on objective criteria.
4. The employer would seek to ensure that the selection is made fairly against these criteria.
5. The employer would try to offer alternative employment, rather than dismissal.

If an employer has genuinely applied its mind to the issue of who should be in a redundancy pool, then it will be difficult to challenge the decision. However, there is no legal requirement that a pool should be limited to employees doing the same or similar work.[271] In selecting for redundancy, a senior manager is entitled to rely on the assessments of employees made by those who have direct knowledge of their work. However, where new roles are to be filled as a result of a reorganisation, the EAT has accepted that appointments are likely to involve something like an interview process.[272] Employers need to show that their method of selection was fair and applied reasonably.[273] An absence of adequate consultation with the employees concerned or their representatives might affect their ability to do this (consultation issues are considered below). It will not always be possible to call evidence to show that adequate consultation would not have made a difference to the decision about selection for redundancy. If the flaws in the process were procedural, it might be possible to reconstruct what might have happened if the correct procedures had been followed. Yet if the tribunal decides that the defects were more substantive, such a reconstruction may not be possible.[274]

Thus reasonableness will normally require a warning to and consultation with affected employees and/or their representatives, the establishment of a fair selection procedure and an

---

267 [1995] IRLR 193.
268 See *Laughton and Hawley v Bapp Industrial Supplies Ltd* [1986] IRLR 245 where the EAT held that an employee did not breach his duty of loyalty by indicating a future intention to compete.
269 *Marshall v Industrial Systems & Control Ltd* [1992] IRLR 294.
270 [1982] IRLR 83.
271 *Capita Hartshead Ltd v Byard* [2012] IRLR 814.
272 *Morgan v Welsh RFU* [2011] IRLR 376.
273 In *Northgate Ltd v Mercy* [2008] IRLR 222 the Court of Appeal ruled that the employment tribunal had been wrong to conclude that a glaring inconsistency produced in good faith could not amount to unfairness in the administration of a selection procedure.
274 See *King v Eaton (No 2)* [1998] IRLR 686.

attempt to avoid or minimise the redundancies. Nevertheless, a defect in this process is not necessarily fatal to the employer. In *Lloyd v Taylor Woodrow Construction*,[275] for example, there was failure to inform the employee of the selection criteria before the decision to dismiss was taken. This flaw was corrected at the appeal stage when the employee was given the opportunity to challenge the criteria. In these circumstances the EAT agreed that the dismissal had not been unfair. In *John Brown Engineering Ltd v Brown*[276] an employer agreed the selection criteria with the employees' representatives but then refused to publish the marks allocated to each employee. This was held to make the appeals procedure a sham, as individuals could not appeal against their selection without knowing their marks, and the dismissals were held to be unfair.

An employer will normally be expected to provide evidence as to the steps taken to select the employee for redundancy,[277] the consultation that has taken place with the employee or their representatives and the attempts to find alternative employment. Similarly, a tribunal would be expected to consider all these issues when reaching a decision on the reasonableness of the dismissal.[278]

'Last in, first out' is still used as a criterion for selection and it is assumed to be based on periods of continuous rather than cumulative service.[279] Arguably, this form of selection indirectly discriminates against women and younger staff and needs to be objectively justified. Selecting employees on part-time and/or fixed-term contracts may also be potentially discriminatory. Section 105 ERA 1996 makes it unfair to select for redundancy on a variety of impermissible grounds (see 5.4.3.2 above). In addition, s. 152 TULRCA 1992 offers special protection to those who are members of a trade union or take part in its activities.[280] Section 153 TULRCA 1992 provides that where the reason (or principal reason) for the dismissal was redundancy, but the circumstances constituting the redundancy applied equally to other employees holding similar positions and those employees have not been selected for redundancy, if the reason (or principal reason) was that the employee was a member of an independent trade union (or taking part in its activities), then that dismissal will be unfair. In *O'Dea v ISC Chemicals Ltd*[281] it was argued that an employee who spent half his time on trade union activities was in a special position and that, as a result, there were no other employees in a similar position with whom he could be compared. The Court of Appeal held that the trade union activities should be ignored when deciding whether the circumstances of the redundancy applied equally to others in a similar position.

It is well established that employers have a duty to consider the alternatives to compulsory redundancy.[282] As regards alternative employment, 'the size and administrative resources' of the employer will be a relevant consideration. Nevertheless, only in rare cases will a tribunal accept that a reasonable employer would have created a job by dismissing someone else.

Consultation may be directly with the employees concerned or with their representatives (see Chapter 9 for specific requirements in relation to collective redundancies). In *Mugford v Midland Bank plc*[283] the EAT held that a dismissal on the grounds of redundancy was not unfair because no consultation had taken place with the employee individually, only with the recognised trade union. The EAT described the position with regard to consultation as follows:

---

275 [1999] IRLR 782.
276 [1997] IRLR 90.
277 In *Watkins v Crouch* [2011] IRLR 382, the EAT rightly pointed out that 'the overall requirements of the business' is no more than a statement of the obvious.
278 See *Langston v Cranfield University* [1998] IRLR 172.
279 *International Paint Co v Cameron* [1979] IRLR 62.
280 This section also covers those who wish to make use of a union's services and those not wishing to be members or take part in the union's activities; see Chapter 11.
281 [1995] IRLR 599 CA.
282 See generally ACAS *Handling small-scale redundancies – A step-by-step guide*.
283 [1997] IRLR 208.

- Where no consultation about redundancy has taken place with either the trade union or the employee, the dismissal will normally be unfair, unless the reasonable employer would have concluded that the consultation would be an utterly futile exercise.
- Consultation with the trade union over the selection criteria does not of itself release the employer from considering with the employee individually the fact that he or she has been identified for redundancy.
- It will be a question of fact and degree for the tribunal to consider whether the consultation with the individual and/or the trade union was so inadequate as to render the dismissal unfair.

In deciding whether the employer acted reasonably or not, the tribunal must view the overall picture at the time of termination. The consultation must be fair and proper, which means that there must be:

- Consultation when the proposals are still at a formative stage.
- Adequate information and adequate time to respond.[284]
- A conscientious consideration by the employer of the response to consultation.[285]

Although proper consultation may be regarded as a procedural matter, it might have a direct bearing on the substantive decision to select a particular employee because a different employee might have been selected if, following proper consultation, different criteria had been adopted. It is not normally permissible for an employer to argue that a failure to consult or warn would have made no difference to the outcome in the particular case. It is what the employer did that is to be judged, not what might have been done. Nevertheless, if the employer could reasonably have concluded in the light of the circumstances known at the time of dismissal that consultation or warning would be 'utterly useless', he or she might well have acted reasonably. Whilst the size of an undertaking might affect the nature or formality of the consultation, it cannot excuse lack of any consultation at all. Finally, it should be noted that the EAT has taken the view that warning and consultation are part of the same single process of consultation, which should commence with a warning that the employee is at risk.[286]

5.4.3.7 Contravention of an enactment

An example of a statutory ban on employment might be the rules contained in the Immigration, Asylum and Nationality Act 2006.[287] Sections 15 and 21 provide penalties if an organisation employs an adult subject to immigration control if he or she has not been granted leave to enter or remain in the UK or such leave is invalid, has ceased to have effect or is subject to a condition preventing him from entering employment. However, a dismissal for the reason that the employer could not lawfully continue to employ someone without contravening a restriction under an enactment is not necessarily fair.[288]

5.4.3.8 Some other substantial reason

Section 98(1)(b) ERA 1996 includes a fifth potentially fair reason for dismissal. This is:

> Some other substantial reason of a kind such as to justify the dismissal of an employee holding the position which the employee held.

---

284 In *Pinewood Repro Ltd v Page* [2011] ICR 508 the EAT acknowledged that, while it might be too broad a principle to require employers always to provide an explanation as to why an individual received particular scores, fair consultation includes the provision of adequate information so that an employee can argue his or her case.

285 *King v Eaton* [1996] IRLR 199.

286 See *Elkouil v Coney Island Ltd* [2002] IRLR 174.

287 See *Hounslow London Borough Council v Klusova* [2008] ICR 396.

288 *Sandhu v (1) Department of Education and Science; (2) London Borough of Hillingdon* [1978] IRLR 208.

This provides flexibility for employers to introduce reasons other than the specific ones provided for in ERA 1996. In *RS Components Ltd v RE Irwin*,[289] which was about the dismissal of a salesperson who refused to accept a new contract of employment containing a restrictive covenant, the court held:

> There are not only legal but also practical objections to a narrow construction of 'some other substantial reason'. Parliament may well have intended to set out the common reasons for a dismissal but can hardly have hoped to produce an exhaustive catalogue of all the circumstances in which a company would be justified in terminating the services of an employee.

Thus 'some other substantial reason' is a general category which enables the courts to accept reasons as potentially fair that are not related to those in s. 98(2) ERA 1996. In Irwin's case the court was sympathetic to the employer's desire to protect its business by introducing non-competition covenants for its sales staff. The burden is on the employer to show a substantial reason to dismiss. The law is designed to deter employers from dismissing employees for a trivial reason or as a pretext to conceal the real reason.[290] However, if an employer can show that there was a fair reason in mind at the time the decision was taken, and that the employer genuinely believed it to be fair, then this might make it a dismissal for some other substantial reason. Thus this reason has covered a dismissal owing to: an irretrievable breakdown in work relationships,[291] pressure from a third party[292] and the removal of an incumbent chief executive following a takeover.[293] However, where allegations are unproved the employer should check the reliability of what it has been told and the integrity of the informant.[294]

This desire to help employers make difficult decisions for sound business reasons has typified the approach of the courts. *St John of God (Care Services) Ltd v Brooks*[295] involved a charity-owned hospital whose National Health Service funding was reduced. As a result the employer proposed to cut pay and benefits to staff in order to make the necessary savings to stop them getting into financial trouble. The proposals were eventually accepted by 140 of the 170 employees. The complainants were four of those who did not accept the changes and were dismissed. The EAT held that it was insufficient to look at the proposals alone. They were only one consideration and the reasonableness of the employer's actions had to be looked at in the context of sound business reasons and other factors – for example, that the majority of the employees had accepted the changes. Thus the employees had been dismissed for some other substantial reason.[296] The acceptance of new terms and conditions by the majority of employees was also a factor in *Catamaran Cruisers Ltd v Williams*.[297] In this case the employers wished to make substantial changes to improve safety and efficiency. The EAT held that:

> We do not accept as a valid proposition of law that an employer may only offer terms which are less or much less favourable than those which pre-existed if the very survival of his business depends upon acceptance of the terms.

The EAT remitted the matter back to the employment tribunal with an instruction that it should not look solely at the advantages and disadvantages to the employees – it was also necessary to look at the benefit to the employer of imposing the changes in the new contract of employment. In *Farrant*

---

289 [1973] IRLR 239 NIRC. See now *Willow Oak Ltd v Silverwood* [2006] IRLR 607.
290 See *Ezsias v North Glamorgan NHS Trust* [2011] IRLR 550.
291 *Phoenix House Ltd v Stockman* [2016] IRLR 848.
292 *Henderson v Connect Ltd* [2010] IRLR 466.
293 *Cobley v Forward Technology* [2003] IRLR 706.
294 *Z v A* [2014] IRLR 244.
295 [1992] IRLR 546.
296 The EAT followed the approach adopted by the Court of Appeal in *Hollister v National Farmers' Union* [1979] IRLR 238 CA.
297 [1994] IRLR 386. See also *Garside and Laycock v Booth* [2011] IRLR 735 on the meaning of equity in this context.

v The Woodroffe School[298] an employee was dismissed for refusing to accept organisational changes. The employer mistakenly believed that the employee was obliged to accept a new job description and that the dismissal was therefore lawful. The EAT held that dismissal for refusing to obey an unlawful order was not necessarily unfair. Of importance was not the lawfulness or otherwise of the employer's instructions but the overall reasonableness. In this case it was not unreasonable for the employer to act on professional advice even if that advice was wrong.

5.4.3.9 Reasonableness

According to s. 98(4) ERA 1996, the employment tribunal will need to decide whether in the circumstances the employer acted reasonably or unreasonably, having regard to the size and administrative resources of the employer, in treating the reason as sufficient to dismiss the employee. This is to be determined 'in accordance with equity and the substantial merits of the case'. At this stage the burden of proof is neutral.[299]

As a matter of law, a reason cannot be treated as sufficient where it has not been established as true or that there were reasonable grounds on which the employer could have concluded that it was true. Under s. 98(4) ERA 1996, tribunals must take account of the wider circumstances. In addition to the employer's business needs, attention must be paid to the personal attributes of the employee – for example, previous work record. Thus, when all the relevant facts are considered, a dismissal may be deemed unfair notwithstanding the fact that the disciplinary rules specified that such behaviour would result in immediate dismissal.[300] Conversely, employers may act reasonably in dismissing even though they have breached an employee's contract. In appropriate cases the test of fairness must be interpreted, so far as possible, compatibly with the European Convention on Human Rights.[301]

Employers will be expected to treat employees in similar circumstances in a similar way.[302] The requirement that the employer must act consistently between employees means that an employer should consider truly comparable cases which were known about or ought to have been known about. Nevertheless, the overriding principle seems to be that each case must be considered on its own facts and with the freedom to consider both aggravating factors and mitigating circumstances. The words 'equity and the substantial merits' also allow tribunals to apply their knowledge of good industrial relations practice and to ensure that there has been procedural fairness (see below). In West London Mental Health Trust v Sarkar[303] the EAT observed that where a disciplinary process includes an investigation, negotiation, disciplinary hearing and appeal, all material up to and including matters raised at the appeal are relevant in determining fairness. Indeed, there is no rule of law about holding a second set of disciplinary proceedings based on the same facts as the original proceedings. The issue is one of fairness and the circumstances in which it will be reasonable to embark on further proceedings are likely to be extremely rare.[304]

In Polkey v AE Dayton Services Ltd[305] Lord Bridge stated that there might be exceptional circumstances where an employer could reasonably take the view that these normal procedural steps would be futile and could not have altered the decision to dismiss. In such circumstances the test of reasonableness may have been satisfied.[306] This approach did not imply that the employer must have taken a deliberate

---

298 [1998] IRLR 176.

299 See Boys and Girls Welfare Society v McDonald [1996] IRLR 129 which concerned a residential social worker who allegedly hit a boy in his care and emphasised the error of placing the burden of proof on the employer.

300 See Arnold Clark Automobiles Ltd v Spoor [2017] IRLR 500.

301 See Garamukanwa v Solent NHS Trust [2016] IRLR 476 on art. 8 and respect for private life.

302 See Newbound v Thames Water Ltd [2015] IRLR 734.

303 [2009] IRLR 512. Reversed on other grounds by Sarkar v West London NHS Trust [2010] IRLR 508 (CA).

304 Christou v London Borough of Haringey [2013] IRLR 379.

305 [1987] IRLR 503 HL.

306 In Warner v Adnet Ltd [1998] IRLR 394 CA a failure to consult as a result of the appointment of a receiver, the dire financial straits of the company and the need to find a buyer urgently made the normal requirement to consult unnecessary; consultation could not have made a difference.

decision not to consult.[307] The test of reasonableness was based on what the employers knew at the time of the dismissal, irrespective of whether the decision not to consult was deliberate.[308]

British Home Stores v Burchell[309] concerned the dismissal of an employee for allegedly being involved in acts of dishonesty with a number of other employees. The EAT provided some guidance on the steps that need to be taken by employers who suspect one or more employees of misconduct:

> First of all, there must be established by the employer the fact of that belief; that the employer did believe it. Secondly, that the employer had in his mind reasonable grounds upon which to sustain that belief. And thirdly . . . that the employer, at the stage at which he formed that belief on those grounds, at any rate at the final stage at which he formed that belief on those grounds, had carried out as much investigation into the matter as was reasonable in all the circumstances of the case.

This three-step test has been used extensively since this judgment.[310] In *Linfood Cash & Carry Ltd v Thomson*,[311] for example, two employees were dismissed on suspicion of theft. The dismissals were held to be unfair because, applying the *Burchell* test, the court concluded that even though the employer genuinely believed in the employees' guilt, they had no reasonable grounds for that belief and had not carried out a sufficient investigation.[312] More recently, the Court of Appeal has emphasised that it is particularly important that employers take seriously their responsibility to conduct a fair investigation where the employee's reputation or ability to work in a chosen field is potentially at risk.[313]

A critical question in relation to investigations is 'whose knowledge or state of mind was for this purpose intended to count as the knowledge or state of mind of the employer?' According to the Court of Appeal, this will be 'the person who was deputed to carry out the employer's functions under Section 98'. The knowledge held by other employees cannot be imputed to that person if he or she could not reasonably have acquired that knowledge through the appropriate disciplinary procedure.[314]

Having followed the *Burchell* steps, the test is then whether it was reasonable for the employer to dismiss. *British Leyland UK Ltd v Swift*[315] involved an employee dismissed after being found guilty in a magistrates' court of fraudulently using a road fund licence belonging to a company vehicle on his own car. The question was whether a reasonable employer would have dismissed the employee. The court stated:

> It must be remembered that in all these cases there is a band of reasonableness, within which one employer might reasonably take one view; another quite reasonably take a different view . . . If it was quite reasonable to dismiss him, then the dismissal must be upheld as fair; even though some employers may not have dismissed him.

Thus there developed a test based on a band of reasonable responses. *Iceland Frozen Foods v Jones*[316] was about the dismissal of a night-shift foreman at a warehouse. The employee had failed to secure the

---

307 In *Ferguson v Prestwick Circuits Ltd* [1992] IRLR 266 the employers took a deliberate decision not to consult, claiming that the workforce had stated a preference for this approach after a previous redundancy exercise; this was held not to be a sufficient reason for failing to consult.

308 See *Duffy v Yeomans & Partners Ltd* [1994] IRLR 642 CA.

309 [1978] IRLR 379.

310 It was approved by the Court of Appeal in *Weddel v Tepper* [1980] ICR 286 CA.

311 [1989] IRLR 235.

312 See *Sainsbury's Supermarkets Ltd v Hitt* [2003] IRLR 23 CA.

313 See *Salford Royal NHS Trust v Roldan* [2010] IRLR 721.

314 *Orr v Milton Keynes Council* [2011] IRLR 317.

315 [1981] IRLR 91 CA.

316 [1982] IRLR 439.

premises after the shift and was held responsible by the employer for slow production on the shift. The tribunal held that the dismissal was unfair both for the reasons given and on procedural grounds. At the EAT Browne-Wilkinson J summarised the legal position:

1. The starting point should always be the words of the statute.
2. In applying the statute, the tribunal must consider the reasonableness of the employer's conduct, not simply whether the members of the tribunal thought the dismissal fair.
3. In considering the reasonableness of the employer's conduct, the tribunal must not substitute its own decision as to what was the right course for the employer to take.[317]
4. In many cases there was a band of reasonable responses to the employee's conduct with one employer taking one view and another employer a different view.
5. The function of the tribunal is to decide whether the decision to dismiss the employee fell within a band of reasonable responses which a reasonable employer might have adopted. If the dismissal falls within such a band, then it is fair.[318]

This approach was questioned in part by the EAT in *Haddon*,[319] *Wilson*[320] and *Midland Bank*.[321] The defects identified by the EAT were twofold. First, the expression 'range of reasonable responses' had become a mantra, so that nothing short of a perverse decision would be outside such a range. Second, it prevented members of employment tribunals from approaching the test of reasonableness by reference to their own experience in deciding what should be done. However, in *Post Office v Foley*[322] the Court of Appeal reaffirmed the previous approach. The range of reasonable responses test does not become one of perversity because the behaviour of an employer has to be extreme before it falls outside the range. There are cases where it will not apply and the court gave two examples. First, where an employee, without good cause, sets fire to the factory, burns it down and is dismissed. Second, where an employee says good morning to the line manager and is dismissed. In these cases there is unlikely to be a need to use the range of reasonable responses test as the first dismissal would be reasonable and the second not. It is in the range between these two examples that there is the possibility of disagreement about what action a reasonable employer would take. That is when the employment tribunal must apply the test. As for the suggestion that the members of the tribunal[323] ought to be able effectively to substitute their own views about what was the reasonable decision, the court held that:

> It was also made clear in Iceland Foods that the members of the tribunal must not simply consider whether they personally think that the dismissal is fair and they must not substitute their decision as to what was the right course to adopt for that of the employer. Their proper function is to determine whether the decision to dismiss the employee fell within the band of reasonable responses which a reasonable employer might have adopted.[324]

Finally, it should be remembered that there can only be an appeal to the EAT on a point of law and it goes without saying that the EAT cannot substitute its own judgment for that of the employment tribunal.[325]

---

317 See *Anglian Home Improvements Ltd v Kelly* [2004] IRLR 793.
318 For an example of a tribunal substituting its own view for that of the employer, see *Secretary of State v Lown* [2016] IRLR 22.
319 *Haddon v Van den Bergh Foods Ltd* [1999] IRLR 672.
320 *Wilson v Ethicon* [2000] IRLR 4.
321 *Midland Bank plc v Madden* [2000] IRLR 288.
322 *Post Office v Foley; HSBC plc (formerly Midland Bank) v Madden* [2000] IRLR 827 CA.
323 It should be noted that it is now normal for legally qualified employment judges to sit alone in unfair dismissal cases.
324 On the approach to be taken when human rights issues are raised, see *Turner v East Midland Trains* [2013] IRLR 107 CA.
325 See *Boardman v Nugent Care Society* [2013] ICR 927.

5.4.4 Procedural fairness (1): ACAS Code of Practice

The Code was first introduced in 1977 and the current version came into effect in 2015.[326] It was issued under s. 199 TULRCA 1992, which provides for the revision of the Code to bring it into line with statutory developments. Failure to observe the Code will not in itself render an employer liable to any proceedings.[327] However, it will be admissible in proceedings before employment tribunals and the Central Arbitration Committee and any relevant parts will be taken into account.[328] In addition, s. 207A TULRCA 1992 allows such tribunals to adjust compensation by up to 25 per cent for unreasonable failure to comply with any provision of the Code.[329] The Code covers disciplinary and grievance procedures and the right to be accompanied (see below).

The foreword to the Code emphasises that 'Employers and employees should always seek to resolve disciplinary and grievance issues in the workplace'. Paragraph 2 suggests that 'rules and procedures for handling disciplinary and grievance situations . . . should be set down in writing, be clear and specific'.[330] An example of the dangers of not ensuring that employees know what amounts to misconduct occurred in *W Brooks & Son v Skinner*.[331] After problems at a Christmas party at which a number of employees got drunk, the employer and the trade union negotiated an agreement that in future such behaviour would result in instant dismissal. Although normally such a collective agreement would be enough to show that the information had been communicated to the employees, it was not held to be so in this case. The following Christmas some employees became drunk and the complainant was sacked. The dismissal was held to be unfair because the complainant did not know of the agreement and it did not relate to conduct which any reasonable employee would realise would result in dismissal.[332]

Paragraph 4 of the ACAS Code identifies the following aspects of fairness:

- Employers and employees should raise and deal with issues promptly and should not unreasonably delay meetings, decisions or confirmation of those decisions.
- Employers and employees should act consistently.
- Employers should carry out any necessary investigations, to establish the facts of the case.[333]
- Employers should inform employees of the basis of the problem and give them an opportunity to put their case in response before any decisions are made.
- Employees should allow employees to be accompanied at any formal disciplinary or grievance meeting.
- Employers should allow an employee to appeal against any formal decision made.

The foreword to the Code advises employers to keep written records of the disciplinary cases they deal with. In addition, paras 5–29 discuss the following key steps to handling disciplinary issues in the workplace:[334]

---

326 It is important to note that, according to para. 1, this Code does not apply to dismissals owing to redundancy or the non-renewal of fixed-term contracts.

327 Section 207(1) TULRCA 1992.

328 Section 207(2)–(3) TULRCA 1992; see also the ACAS guide *Discipline and Grievances at Work* (2009) which does not form part of the Code.

329 This uplift does not apply to dismissals for ill health or some other substantial reason; see *Holmes v Qinetic Ltd* [2016] IRLR 664 and *Phoenix House Ltd v Stockman* [2016] IRLR 848 respectively.

330 See Appendix 2 of the ACAS Guide 2016 which provides sample disciplinary procedures.

331 [1984] IRLR 379.

332 Unlike that in the contrasting case of *Gray Dunn & Co Ltd v Edwards* [1980] IRLR 23.

333 On the propriety of human resources staff attempting to influence the report of an investigation officer see *Ramphal v Department for Transport* [2015] IRLR 985.

334 Further advice is contained in the ACAS Guide.

- Establish the facts of each case.
- Inform the employee of the problem.[335]
- Hold a meeting with the employee to discuss the problem.
- Allow the employee to be accompanied at the meeting.
- Decide on appropriate action.[336]
- Provide employees with an opportunity to appeal.

Paragraphs 30–31 of the ACAS Code suggest that special consideration be given to the way in which disciplinary procedures operate in relation to trade union officials and those charged or convicted of a criminal offence.

Finally, we must consider the impact of appeal procedures. In *West Midlands Co-operative Society Ltd v Tipton*[337] the Supreme Court confirmed that a dismissal is unfair if an employer unreasonably treats the reason for dismissal as sufficient, either when the original decision to dismiss is made or when it is upheld at the conclusion of an internal appeal.[338] A dismissal may also be unfair if the employer refuses to comply with the full requirements of an appeal procedure.[339] Whether procedural defects can be rectified on appeal will depend on the degree of unfairness at the original hearing.[340]

5.4.5 Procedural fairness (2): the right to be accompanied

Section 10 Employment Relations Act (ERelA) 1999 introduced the right for workers,[341] who are required or invited by the employer to attend a disciplinary or grievance hearing, to be accompanied by a single companion if the worker makes a reasonable request in writing. According to para.15 of the ACAS Code of Practice on Disciplinary and Grievance Procedures:

> To exercise the statutory right to be accompanied workers must make a reasonable request. What is reasonable will depend on the circumstances of each individual case. A request to be accompanied does not have to be in writing or within a certain timeframe. However, a worker should provide enough time for the employer to deal with the companion's attendance at the meeting. Workers should also consider how they make their request so that it is clearly understood, for instance by letting the employer know in advance the name of the companion where possible and whether they are a fellow worker or trade union official or representative

A disciplinary hearing, according to s. 13(4) ERelA 1999, is a hearing that could result in:

- The administration of a formal warning to a worker by the employer.
- The taking of some other action in respect of a worker by his employer.
- The confirmation of a warning issued or some other action taken.[342]

---

335 In *Spence v Department of Agriculture and Rural Development* [2011] IRLR 806 the Northern Ireland CA held that an employer must disclose the essence of its case to the employee and consider disclosing anything in its possession which may be of assistance in contesting the disciplinary action. However, it may be justified in withholding sensitive information – for example, the existence or identity of an informant.

336 In *Crawford v Suffolk Mental Health Trust* [2012] IRLR 402 the Court of Appeal stated that employment tribunals are entitled to look particularly carefully at procedures where careers as well as jobs are at stake.

337 [1986] IRLR 112.

338 See *O'Brien v Bolton St Catherine's Academy* [2017] IRLR 547.

339 See *Tarbuck v Sainsbury's Ltd* [2006] IRLR 664.

340 See *Adeshina v St George's University Hospitals Trust* [2015] IRLR 704.

341 With the exception of those in the security services, which includes the Security Service, the Secret Intelligence. Service and Government Communications Headquarters: s. 15 ERelA 1999.

342 A grievance hearing is one which concerns the performance of a duty by the employer in relation to a worker: s. 13(5) ERelA 1999. On redundancy meetings see *Heathmill Ltd v Jones* [2003] IRLR 856.

The right to be accompanied does not extend to more informal interviews which will not result in a formal warning. In *Harding v London Underground*,[343] where the employee had received an 'informal oral warning', the EAT ruled that a disciplinary warning becomes a formal warning if it becomes part of the employee's disciplinary record.

The right applies to workers, who are defined[344] as including those that come within the meaning of s. 230(3) ERA 1996 plus agency workers, home workers[345] and persons in Crown employment. It excludes those in the naval, military, air or reserve forces, and relevant members of the staff of the Houses of Parliament. Where this right is exercised, the employer must permit the worker to be accompanied at the hearing by a single companion chosen by the worker. The companion is to be permitted to address the hearing and confer with the worker during it. However, the employer does not have to allow the companion to: answer questions on behalf of the worker; address the hearing if the worker indicates that they do not wish the companion to do so; or use their position in a way that prevents the employer from explaining its case or prevents another person from making a contribution to the hearing.[346] Thus the companion is more than a witness to the proceedings but less than an advocate.[347] The companion can be:

1. An individual who is employed by a trade union and is an official[348] of that union.
2. An individual who is an official of a trade union whom the union has reasonably certified in writing as having experience of, or having received training in, acting as a worker's companion at such hearings.
3. Another of the employer's workers.[349]

An employer must also permit a worker to take paid time off during working hours for the purpose of accompanying another of the employer's workers to a hearing.[350] In addition, a worker has the right not to be subjected to detriment by the employer for exercising the right to ask for a companion or for being a companion. Any dismissal resulting from the assertion of these rights will be automatically unfair (see above).[351] A worker may present a complaint to an employment tribunal if the employer fails, or threatens to fail, to comply with these provisions. This complaint must be made within three months beginning with the date of the failure or threat, unless the tribunal is satisfied that it was not reasonably practicable to do so. If the employment tribunal finds the complaint well founded, it may order the employer to pay compensation to the worker, not exceeding two weeks' pay.[352]

5.4.6 Time limit for claiming unfair dismissal

Unless the 'time limit escape clause' applies,[353] claims must normally arrive at an employment tribunal within three months of the effective date of termination. A complaint can also be presented

---

343 [2003] IRLR 252.
344 Section 13(1) ERelA 1999.
345 Further definition of agency and home workers is provided in s. 13(2) and (3) ERelA 1999.
346 Section 10(2)(b)–(2)(c) ERelA 1999.
347 On the appropriateness of legal representation where an employee may be deprived of his or her right to practise a profession, see *R v Governors of X School* [2011] IRLR 756 SC.
348 Within the meaning of ss 1 and 119 TULRCA 1992.
349 Section 10(3) ERelA 1999; s. 10(4) provides an obligation on the employer to arrange alternative times for hearings if the companion has difficulties in attending.
350 Section 10(6) ERelA 1999.
351 Section 12(1)–(6) ERelA 1999.
352 Section 11(1)–(6) ERelA 1999.
353 Section 111(2) ERA 1996. The question of jurisdiction must be considered by an employment tribunal if it considers that the issue is a live one: see *Radakouits v Abbey National* [2010] IRLR 307.

before the effective date of termination provided it is lodged after notice has been given. This includes notice given by an employee who is alleging constructive dismissal.[354] What is or is not reasonably practicable is a question of fact and the onus is on the employee to prove that it was not reasonably practicable to claim in time. The meaning of 'reasonably practicable' lies somewhere between reasonable and reasonably capable of physically being done.[355] The tribunal will look at the issue in all the surrounding circumstances. Where a claimant has consulted skilled advisers, the tribunal will assess what the claimant could have done if he or she had been given the advice that should reasonably have been given.[356]

The courts have dealt with this jurisdictional point on several occasions and have taken the view that, since the unfair dismissal provisions have been in force for many years, tribunals should be fairly strict in enforcing the time limit. Nevertheless, the issue of reasonable practicability depends upon the awareness of specific grounds for complaint, not upon the right to complain at all. Thus there is nothing to prevent an employee who is precluded by the passage of time from claiming on one ground from proceeding with a second complaint on another ground raised within a reasonable period. According to the Court of Appeal, if employers want to protect themselves from late claims presented on the basis of newly discovered information they should ensure that the fullest information is made available to the employee at the time of dismissal.[357]

5.4.7 Pre-termination negotiations and settlement agreements, conciliation and arbitration

According to s. 111A ERA 1996, evidence of pre-termination negotiations normally cannot be heard by an employment tribunal. The exceptional circumstances are: where claimants assert that they have been dismissed for an automatically unfair reason; if the employment tribunal thinks that there has been improper words or behaviour and it would be just to allow information to be disclosed; and if an offer in relation to costs or expenses was made on the basis that the right to refer to it was reserved. For these purposes, pre-termination negotiations are defined as 'any offer made or discussions held' with a view to the employment being ended on agreed terms. ACAS has published a statutory Code of Practice[358] which explains, in particular, aspects of the confidentiality provisions which are associated with the negotiation of settlement agreements. This Code will be taken into account when employment tribunals consider relevant cases but there are no financial or other sanctions for non-compliance with it.

ACAS has an important role in conciliation and arbitration (see Chapter 1). In 2016/17, 55 per cent of applications[359] to employment tribunals were settled before reaching the stage of a formal tribunal hearing. These are not all a response to the intervention of ACAS, but clearly the organisation plays a significant part in reducing the burden on employment tribunals. As a result of the insertion of Section 18A into the Employment Tribunals Act 1996, most potential applicants must submit details of their case to ACAS before they can lodge an employment tribunal claim. The conciliation officer must endeavour to promote a settlement between the prospective parties within a prescribed period. If during this period the conciliation officer concludes that a settlement is impossible or the period elapses without a settlement being achieved, he or she will give the prospective claimant

---

354 Section 111(4) ERA 1996.
355 *Palmer v Southend Borough Council* [1984] IRLR 119. On the effect of the advice received, see *Marks & Spencer plc v Williams-Ryan* [2005] IRLR 562.
356 *Northamptonshire County Council v Entwhistle* [2010] IRLR 740.
357 See *Marley Ltd v Anderson* [1996] IRLR 163.
358 *Settlement Agreements* (July 2013). See also the ACAS booklet, *Settlement Agreements: A Guide* (July 2013).
359 See ACAS Annual Report 2016/17.

a certificate to that effect. A claim cannot be lodged without such a certificate[360] but a conciliation officer may continue to endeavour to promote a settlement. Even if it has not received information from a prospective claimant, s. 18B(1) Employment Tribunals Act 1996 obliges ACAS to promote a settlement where a person requests the services of a conciliation officer in relation to a dispute that is likely to result in employment tribunal proceedings against them.

In *Moore v Duport Furniture*[361] the House of Lords decided that the expression 'promote a settlement' should be given a liberal construction capable of covering whatever action by way of such promotion is appropriate in the circumstances. Where the complainant has ceased to be employed, the conciliation officer may seek to promote that person's re-employment (i.e. reinstatement or re-engagement) on terms that appear to be equitable. If the complainant does not wish to be re-employed, or this is not practicable, the conciliation officer must seek to promote agreement on compensation.[362] It should be noted that, according to the EAT, an ACAS officer must never advise on the merits of a case and has no responsibility to ensure that the settlement terms are fair to the employee.[363]

Where appropriate, a conciliation officer is to 'have regard to the desirability of encouraging the use of other procedures available for the settlement of grievances', and anything communicated to a conciliation officer in connection with the performance of the above functions is not admissible in evidence in any proceedings before a tribunal except with the consent of the person who communicated it.[364] It should be noted that an agreement to refrain from lodging a tribunal complaint is subject to all the qualifications by which an agreement can be avoided at common law – for example, on grounds of economic duress.

Section 203(1) ERA 1996 states that a provision in an agreement is void in so far as it attempts to exclude the operation of any part of the ERA 1996 or stops a person from bringing proceedings under the Act.[365] Exceptions to this are found in s. 203(2) and include a provision that any agreement to refrain from instituting or continuing proceedings has been reached where an ACAS conciliation officer has taken action under s. 18 Employment Tribunals Act 1996.[366] If an agreement is reached with the help of the conciliation officer, then it will be treated as an exception to s. 203(1) ERA 1996. Another exclusion is where an agreement to refrain from instituting or continuing proceedings has been reached in accordance with the conditions regulating settlement agreements.[367] The provisions on settlement agreements are contained in s. 203(3), (3A), (3B) and (4) ERA 1996 and are as follows:

1. The agreement must be in writing and relate to a particular complaint or proceedings.
2. The employee or worker must have received advice from a relevant independent adviser[368] on the terms and effect of the proposed agreement and its effect on the employee's ability to pursue a complaint or proceedings before an employment tribunal.
3. There must be an insurance policy in force to cover any claims from the employee in respect of any losses in consequence of the advice.
4. The agreement must identify the adviser.[369]

---

360 See *Compass Group v Morgan* [2016] IRLR 924 where it was held that a certificate obtained by a prospective claimant could cover future events.

361 [1982] IRLR 31.

362 Section 18A(9) Employment Tribunals Act 1996.

363 *Clarke v Redcar Borough Council* [2006] IRLR 324.

364 Section 18(6)–(7) Employment Tribunals Act 1996.

365 In *Sutherland v Network Appliance Ltd* [2001] IRLR 12 the EAT held that it was only those parts of the agreement that were in contravention of s. 203(1) ERA 1996 that would be void; not necessarily the whole agreement.

366 Section 203(2)(e) ERA 1996. On the meaning of 'taken action', see *Allma Construction Ltd v Bonner* [2011] IRLR 204.

367 Section 203(2)(f) ERA 1996. On the possibility of an agreement being irrationally generous, see *Gibb v Maidstone and Tunbridge Wells NHS Trust* [2010] IRLR 786. On misrepresentation, see *Industrials Ltd v Horizon Ltd* [2010] IRLR 204.

368 See *McWilliam v Glasgow City Council* [2011] IRLR 568.

369 See *Gloystarne & Co Ltd v Martin* [2001] IRLR 15, where the individual concerned denied having appointed a trade union official as his representative or agreeing to the compromise reached.

5. The agreement must state that these conditions regulating settlement agreements have been satisfied.

A person is an independent adviser if he or she is a qualified lawyer;[370] an officer, official, employee or member of an independent trade union who has been certified by the trade union as authorised and competent to give advice; an advice centre worker who is similarly certified by the advice centre, or some other persons identified by the Secretary of State. The effect of reaching a settlement agreement is to stop any further proceedings and is something that employers may use to prevent claims ending up at an employment tribunal.

Section 212A TULRCA 1992 is an attempt to provide an alternative to employment tribunals in unfair dismissal disputes. It allows ACAS to devise a scheme for arbitration in such cases.[371] The characteristics of the scheme are:

1. The arbitrators are independent individuals, at least some of whom will not be lawyers.
2. Parties to a dispute would both need to agree to go to arbitration.
3. In so agreeing, they would give up all their rights to go to an employment tribunal.
4. The parties would submit their cases in writing and legal representation would be discouraged at the hearing, which would take place locally.
5. The decision of the arbitrator, who would have all the relevant powers of an employment tribunal, is to be binding, with no appeal to the EAT.

The arbitrators will be heavily influenced by the ACAS Code of Practice on Discipline and Grievance Procedures. The advantage of the scheme is that it should, if used, speed up the process and be less formal than employment tribunals have become.

5.4.8 Remedies

The remedies following a finding of unfair dismissal by an employment tribunal are reinstatement, re-engagement or compensation.[372] There is also the opportunity to obtain interim relief.

5.4.8.1 Interim relief

An employee may apply for interim relief[373] if they have presented a claim for unfair dismissal by virtue of:

1. Dismissal on the grounds of trade union membership or activities.[374]
2. Being a designated employee to carry out activities connected with health and safety, or being a health and safety representative.[375]
3. Being an employee representative, or a candidate to be such a representative, for the purposes of the Working Time Regulations 1998.[376]
4. Being a trustee of an occupational pension scheme relating to the individual's employment.[377]

---

370 Section 203(4) ERA 1996 contains further definition of who is a qualified lawyer.
371 See ACAS Arbitration Scheme (Great Britain) Order 2004, SI 2004/753.
372 It should be noted that Section 12A Employment Tribunals Act 1996 allows employment tribunals to impose a financial penalty on employers where there has been a breach of employment rights and the employment tribunal thinks that 'the breach has one or more aggravating features'.
373 Section 128 ERA 1996.
374 Section 161(1) TULRCA 1992.
375 Section 100(1)(a)–(b) ERA 1996.
376 Section 101A(d) ERA 1996.
377 Section 102(1) ERA 1996.

5. Being an employee representative for the purposes of consultation on collective redundancies or transfers of undertakings.[378]

6. Being a reason connected with obtaining or preventing recognition of a trade union.[379]

7. Being a reason connected with making a protected disclosure.[380]

The application to the tribunal needs to be made within seven days immediately following the effective date of termination and the employer will be given seven days' notice of the hearing together with a copy of the application.[381] If it appears to the tribunal that it is 'likely',[382] after a full hearing, to find that there has been a dismissal for one of the impermissible reasons listed above, it will ask the employer if the employer is willing to reinstate or re-engage the employee. If the employer refuses or the employee reasonably refuses an offer of alternative employment,[383] the tribunal is able to make an order for the continuation of the contract.[384] It will stipulate the level of pay to be given to the employee, based on what the employee would normally have expected to earn in the period, but will take into account any payments already made by the employer as payments in lieu of notice or by way of discharging the employer's liabilities under the contract of employment.[385] Section 132 ERA 1996 enables the employment tribunal to award compensation if the employer does not comply with an order for continuation.

5.4.8.2 Reinstatement or re-engagement

If the employment tribunal finds the complaint well founded, it will explain to the complainant about its power to make an order for reinstatement or re-engagement and ask whether the complainant wishes the tribunal to make such an order. If the complainant expresses a wish for such an order, the tribunal will consider it.[386] An order for reinstatement is an order that the employer treat the employee as if he had never been dismissed. Thus the employee will return to the same job on the same terms and conditions as if there had been no interruption.[387] The employer will pay any amounts due, less any sums already paid to the employee in connection with the dismissal.[388] An order for re-engagement is an order that the employee be taken back by the employer into a position comparable to that from which he was dismissed, or other suitable employment. The employment tribunal will specify the terms and conditions upon which the employee will return.[389]

If at least seven days before the hearing the employee has expressed a wish to be re-employed but it becomes necessary to postpone or adjourn the hearing because the employer does not, without special reason, adduce reasonable evidence about the availability of the job from which the claimant was dismissed, the employer will be required to pay the costs of the adjournment or postponement.[390] In addition, s. 116(5) ERA 1996 states that where an employer has taken on a permanent replacement, this shall not be taken into account unless the employer shows either:

---

378 Section 103 ERA 1996.

379 Section 161(2) Sch. A1 TULRCA 1992.

380 Section 103A ERA 1996.

381 Section 128(2) and (4) ERA 1996.

382 See *Ministry of Justice v Sarfraz* [2011] IRLR 562.

383 Section 129 ERA 1996. There are issues about what terms and conditions might be offered on re-engagement.

384 Section 130(1) ERA 1996, but not an order that ensures the employee actually goes back to work.

385 Section 130(2)–(7) ERA 1996; this includes any payments made as damages for breach of contract.

386 Sections 112–113 ERA 1996.

387 See *McBride v Strathclyde Police* [2016] IRLR 633.

388 Section 114 ERA 1996.

389 Section 115 ERA 1996; the tribunal will, as far as is reasonably practicable, specify terms as favourable as reinstatement, the exception being where there is contributory fault by the employee (s. 116(4) ERA 1996). See *Lincolnshire County Council v Lupton* [2016] IRLR 576.

390 Section 13(2) Employment Tribunals Act 1996.

- that it was not practicable to arrange for the dismissed employee's work to be done without engaging a permanent replacement; or
- that a replacement was engaged after the lapse of a reasonable period without having heard from the dismissed employee that he wished to be reinstated or re-engaged, and that when the employer engaged the replacement it was no longer reasonable to arrange for the dismissed employee's work to be done except by a permanent replacement.

The employment tribunal has considerable discretion about making such orders and there are tests of practicability and justice. The tribunal will take into account the complainant's wishes and whether it is practicable for the employer to comply with an order for reinstatement. It will also take into account whether such an order would be just in circumstances where the employee contributed towards the dismissal.[391] In *Rao v Civil Aviation Authority*[392] an employee with an extremely poor attendance record was dismissed. The dismissal was held to be unfair on procedural grounds and the employment tribunal refused to order reinstatement or re-engagement because there was no evidence that, if he were re-employed, his absences would not continue, he would require retraining and his return might not be welcomed by his fellow employees. The EAT approved this decision and stated that 'practicable' is not the same as 'possible' or 'capable' and that the task of the employment tribunal was to look at what had happened and at what might happen and reach a decision on the basis of what would be fair and just for all parties. The issue of practicability was considered in *Port of London Authority v Payne*,[393] which involved a number of dockers who had been unfairly selected for redundancy because of their trade union activities. The employers claimed that it was not practicable for them to comply with the orders for re-engagement because they were going through a period of large-scale redundancies and there were no available job vacancies.[394] The Court of Appeal held:

> The employment tribunal, though it should carefully scrutinise the reasons advanced by the employer, should give due weight to the commercial judgment of the management … The standard [for re-engagement] must not be set too high. The employer cannot be expected to explore every possible avenue which ingenuity might suggest.

In *Wood v Crossan*[395] an employee was suspected of various offences, including dealing in drugs. The employers formed a genuine belief that he was guilty of the allegations and, after an investigation, the employee was sacked. The employment tribunal held that the dismissal was unfair because of an inadequate investigation and other procedural defects. The complainant's job had disappeared, so there was no possibility of reinstatement. Taking into account that the individual had 16 years' service and that there was no apparent animosity between him and the employer, the employment tribunal ordered that the complainant be re-engaged at the same salary. The appeal against this was allowed by the EAT, who held that the employer's belief in the guilt of the employee resulted in a breakdown of mutual trust and confidence. Without this bond the employment relationship could not exist. The EAT further concluded:

> We consider that the remedy of re-engagement has very limited scope and will only be practical in the rarest cases where there is a breakdown in confidence as between the employer and the

---

391 Section 116 ERA 1996. See *British Airways plc v Valencia* [2016] IRLR 633.

392 [1992] IRLR 303 EAT; the finding of the new tribunal on compensation was appealed at *Rao v Civil Aviation Authority* [1994] IRLR 240 CA.

393 [1994] IRLR 9 CA.

394 See *Clancy v Cannock Chase Technical College* [2001] IRLR 331, where the EAT confirmed a tribunal decision to decline to make a re-engagement order because of a worsening redundancy situation with the employer.

395 *Wood Group Heavy Industrial Turbines Ltd v Crossan* [1998] IRLR 680.

employee. Even if the way the matter is handled results in a finding of unfair dismissal, the remedy, in that context, invariably to our mind will be compensation.

Where a person is reinstated or re-engaged as the result of a tribunal order but the terms are not fully complied with, a tribunal must make an additional award of compensation of such amount as it thinks fit, having regard to the loss sustained by the complainant in consequence of the failure to comply fully with the terms of the order.[396] It is a matter for speculation how long re-employment must last for it to be said that an order has been complied with. If a complainant is not re-employed in accordance with a tribunal order, he or she is entitled to enforce the monetary element at the employment tribunal.[397] Compensation will be awarded together with an additional award unless the employer satisfies the tribunal that it was not practicable to comply with the order.[398] According to s. 117(3)(b) ERA, the additional award will be of between 26 and 52 weeks' pay. Within this range, the tribunal has discretion as to what additional compensation should be awarded but it must be exercised on the basis of a proper assessment of the factors involved. One factor would ordinarily be the view taken of the employer's conduct in refusing to comply with the order. Conversely, employees who unreasonably prevent an order being complied with will be regarded as having failed to mitigate their loss.

5.4.8.3 Compensation

Compensation for unfair dismissal is divided into two parts. The first is a basic award which, like redundancy payments, is related to age, length of service and pay. The second is a compensatory award, which is related to the actual loss suffered.

The basic award is arrived at by calculating the number of years of continuous service and allowing the appropriate amount for each year. This appropriate amount is:

- One and a half weeks' pay for each year of employment in which the employee was not below 41 years of age.
- One week's pay for each year of employment in which the employee was not below the age of 22 years.
- Half a week's pay for each year of employment in which the employee was not within either of the above.

Only 20 years' service can be taken into account, which results in a statutory maximum of 30 weeks' pay. A week's pay is to be calculated in accordance with Part XIV Chapter II ERA 1996 (see Chapter 8).[399] In certain cases there is a minimum award of £5,970.[400] This is where there has been unfair selection for redundancy or dismissal related to one of the reasons listed above in relation to interim relief. The basic award can be reduced by such proportion as the tribunal considers just and equitable on two grounds:

1. The complainant unreasonably refused an offer of reinstatement (such an offer could have been made before any finding of unfairness).
2. Any conduct of the complainant before the dismissal, or before notice was given.

---

396 Section 117(2) ERA 1996.
397 Section 124(4) ERA 1996.
398 Section 17(3)–(4) ERA 1996.
399 Section 119 ERA 1996; the maximum week's pay from April 2017 is £489, so the maximum basic award would be £14,670.
400 Section 120 ERA 1996; this amount is from April 2017.

This does not apply where the reason for dismissal was redundancy unless the dismissal was regarded as unfair by virtue of ss 100(1)(a) or (b), 101A(d), 102(1) or 103 ERA 1996. In that event the reduction will apply only to that part of the award payable because of s. 120 ERA 1996.[401]

A compensatory award is that which a tribunal 'considers just and equitable in all the circumstances having regard to the loss sustained by the complainant in consequence of the dismissal insofar as that loss is attributable to action taken by the employer'.[402] Thus tribunals will normally have to assess how long the claimant would have been employed but for the dismissal.[403] This requires the tribunal to ask whether the employer could have fairly dismissed and, if so, what were the chances that it would have done so.[404] However, the mere fact that the employer could have dismissed fairly on another ground arising out of the same factual situation does not render it unjust or inequitable to award compensation.[405] Employment tribunals will also have to consider whether the effect of subsequent employment was to break the chain of causation or not.[406] Thus in Dench v Flynn & Partners[407] an assistant solicitor was able to claim compensation for unemployment after a subsequent short-term job because it was attributable to the original dismissal.

Section 123(3) ERA 1996 specifically mentions that an individual whose redundancy entitlement would have exceeded the basic award can be compensated for the difference, whilst a redundancy payment received in excess of the basic award payable goes to reduce the compensatory award. The compensatory award can be reduced in two other circumstances: where the employee's action caused or contributed to the dismissal, and where the employee failed to mitigate his loss. Before reducing an award on the ground that the complainant caused or contributed to the dismissal, a tribunal must be satisfied that the employee's conduct was culpable or blameworthy – that is, foolish, perverse or unreasonable in the circumstances. Thus there could be a finding of contributory fault in a case of constructive dismissal on the basis that there was a causal link between the employee's conduct and the employer's repudiatory breach of contract.[408] According to the EAT, tribunals must consider the issue of contributory fault in any case where it is possible that there had been blameworthy conduct, whether or not this issue was raised by the employer.[409]

In deciding whether to reduce compensation, the tribunal must take into account the conduct of the complainant and not what happened to some other employee – for example, one who was treated more leniently. Not all unreasonable conduct will necessarily be culpable or blameworthy; it will depend on the degree of unreasonableness. Although ill-health cases will rarely give rise to a reduction in compensation on grounds of contributory fault, it is clear that an award may be reduced under the overriding 'just and equitable' provisions.[410] Having found that an employee was to blame, a tribunal must reduce the award to some extent, although the proportion of culpability is a matter for the tribunal. According to the Court of Appeal, tribunals should first assess the amount which it is just and equitable to award because this may have a very significant bearing on what reduction to make for contributory conduct.[411] The percentage amount of reduction is to be taken from the total awarded to the employee before other deductions – for example, offsetting what has already been paid by the employer. Complainants are obliged to look for work but the

---

401 Section 122 ERA 1996.
402 Section 123 ERA 1996.
403 See Software 2000 Ltd v Andrews [2007] IRLR 568.
404 Hill v Governing Body of Great Tey Primary School [2013] IRLR 274.
405 See Devonshire v Trico-Folberth [1989] IRLR 396.
406 See Aegon UK Corp Services Ltd v Roberts [2009] IRLR 1042.
407 [1998] IRLR 653.
408 See Frith Ltd v Law [2014] IRLR 510.
409 Swallow Security Services Ltd v Millicent [2009] Lawtel 25 March 2009.
410 See Slaughter v Brewer Ltd [1990] IRLR 426.
411 See Rao v Civil Aviation Authority [1994] IRLR 240.

tribunal must go through the following stages before it can decide what amount to deduct for an employee's failure to mitigate his or her loss:[412]

1. Identify what steps should have been taken by the applicant to mitigate loss.
2. Find the date on which such steps would have produced an alternative income.
3. Reduce the amount of compensation by the sum which would have been earned.

The onus is on the employer to prove that there was such a failure. Whilst acknowledging that the employee has a duty to act reasonably, the EAT has concluded that this standard is not high in view of the fact that the employer is the wrongdoer.[413] There is no duty to mitigate before dismissal and there is no principle that an offer of alternative employment from the same employer must be accepted or that it is unreasonable to reject such an offer.[414]

Section 123(5) ERA 1996 stipulates that no account is to be taken of any pressure that was exercised on the employer to dismiss the employee and s. 155 TULRCA 1992 provides that compensation cannot be reduced on the grounds that the complainant:

● Was in breach of (or proposed to breach) a requirement that he or she: must be, or become, a member of a particular trade union or one of a number of trade unions; ceases to be, or refrains from becoming, a member of any trade union or of a particular trade union or of one of a number of particular trade unions; would not take part in the activities of any trade union, of a particular trade union or of one of a number of particular trade unions; would not make use of union services.
● Refused, or proposed to refuse, to comply with a requirement of a kind mentioned in s. 152(3)(a) TULRCA 1992.
● Objected, or proposed to object, to the operation of a provision of a kind mentioned in s. 152(3)(b) TULRCA 1992.
● Accepted or failed to accept an offer made in contravention of s. 145A or 145B TULRCA 1992 (see Chapter 11).

The maximum compensatory award is £80,541 in 2017 or 52 weeks' pay if that amounts to less than this figure. Limits will only apply after credit has been given for any payments made by the employer and any deductions have been made,[415] but any 'excess' payments made by the employer over that which is required are deducted after the amount of the compensatory award has been fixed. As regards deductions, normally an employer is to be given credit for all payments made to an employee in respect of claims for wages and other benefits. Where an employee has suffered discrimination as well as unfair dismissal, s. 126 ERA 1996 prevents double compensation for the same loss.

It is the duty of tribunals to inquire into the various grounds for compensation, but it is the responsibility of the aggrieved person to prove the loss. The legislation aims to reimburse the employee rather than to punish the employer. Hence employees who appear to have lost nothing – for example, where it can be said that, irrespective of the procedural unfairness which occurred, they would have been dismissed anyway – do not qualify for a compensatory award. However, if the employee puts forward an arguable case that dismissal was not inevitable, the evidential burden

---

412 See *Savage v Saxena* [1998] IRLR 102.
413 *Fyfe v Scientific Furnishings Ltd* [1989] IRLR 331.
414 *F & G Cleaners Ltd v Saddington* [2012] IRLR 892.
415 Section 124(5) ERA 1996. For these purposes, a week's pay includes the employer's pension contributions: *University of Sunderland v Droussou* [2017] IRLR 1087.

shifts to the employer to show that dismissal was likely to have occurred in any event.[416] Additionally, a nil or nominal award may be thought just and equitable in a case where misconduct was discovered subsequently to the dismissal.

The possible heads of loss have been divided into the following categories.

(a) Loss incurred up to the date of the hearing

Here attention focuses on the employee's actual loss of income, which makes it necessary to ascertain the employee's take-home pay. Thus, tax and national insurance contributions are to be deducted, but overtime earnings and tips can be taken into account. Any sickness benefits received may be taken into account although, in *Sheffield Forgemasters Ltd v Fox*,[417] the EAT decided that the receipt of incapacity benefit (as it then was) did not preclude claimants from claiming compensation for loss of earnings during the same period. Being eligible for such benefits did not mean that the individual could not obtain paid work during that period.

It should also be noted that the loss sustained should be based on what the employee was entitled to, whether or not he was receiving it at the time of dismissal.[418] As well as lost wages, s. 123(2) ERA 1996 enables an individual to claim compensation for the loss of other benefits – for example, a company car or other perks. Similarly, 'expenses reasonably incurred' are mentioned in the statute – so, for example, employees will be able to recover the cost of looking for a new job or setting up their own business. However, complainants cannot be reimbursed for the cost of pursuing their unfair dismissal claims.

(b) Loss flowing from the manner of dismissal

Compensation can be awarded only if the manner of dismissal has made the individual less acceptable to potential employers. There is nothing for non-economic loss – for example, hurt feelings. However, economic loss may arise where the person is not fit to take up alternative employment as early as he would otherwise have done (or ever); or where by virtue of stigma damage,[419] loss of reputation or embarrassment no suitable employer was prepared to engage him, at least on terms that would not cause continuing loss.[420]

(c) Loss of accrued rights

This head of loss is intended to compensate the employee for the loss of rights dependent on a period of continuous service. However, because the basic award reflects lost redundancy entitlement, sums awarded on these grounds have tended to be nominal. Nevertheless, tribunals should include a sum to reflect the fact that dismissed employees lose the statutory minimum notice protection that they have built up.

(d) Loss of pension rights

There are two types of loss: the loss of the present pension position and the loss of the opportunity to improve one's pension position with the dismissing employer. When an employee is close to retirement, the cost of an annuity which will provide a sum equal to the likely pension can be calculated. In other cases the starting point will be the contributions already paid into the scheme and, in addition to having their own contributions returned, employees can claim an interest in

---

416 See *Britool Ltd v Roberts* [1993] IRLR 481.

417 [2009] IRLR 192.

418 For example, the minimum wage; see *Paggetti v Cobb* [2002] IRLR 861. On the issue of pay that should have been received during the notice period, the Court of Appeal has drawn a distinction between express and constructive dismissals; see *Peters Ltd v Bell* [2009] IRLR 941.

419 See *Uhr-Rehman v Ahmad* [2013] ICR 28 on the need for stigma to have a real or substantial effect.

420 See *Dunnachie v Kingston upon Hull City Council* [2004] IRLR 727.

their employer's contributions, except in cases of transferred or deferred pensions. However, in assessing future loss the tribunal must take into account a number of possibilities – for example, future dismissal or resignation, early death, and the fact that a capital sum is being paid sooner than would have been expected. Although employment tribunals have been given actuarial guidelines on loss of pension rights, in each case the factors must be evaluated to see what adjustment should be made or whether the guidelines are safe to use at all.[421]

(e) Future loss

Where no further employment has been secured, tribunals will have to speculate how long the employee will remain unemployed. Here the tribunal must utilise its knowledge of local market conditions as well as considering personal circumstances. According to the EAT, employees who have become unfit for work wholly or partly as a result of unfair dismissal are entitled to compensation for loss of earnings, at least for a reasonable period following the dismissal, until they might reasonably have been expected to find other employment.[422] However, in *Robins Ltd v Triggs*,[423] the Court of Appeal decided that the tribunal had erred in holding that the employee could claim for future loss of earnings resulting from illness that had been caused by the employer's breach of contract. In this case the illness pre-dated the constructive dismissal. If another job has been obtained, tribunals must compare the employee's salary prospects for the future in each job and estimate as best they can how long it will take the employee to reach the salary equivalent to that which would have been attained had he or she remained with the original employer.[424] Where the employee is earning a higher rate of pay at the time compensation is being assessed, the tribunal should decide whether the new employment is permanent and, if so, should calculate the loss as between the date of dismissal and the date the new job was secured.

Finally, mention must be made of the Employment Protection (Recoupment of Jobseeker's Allowance and Income Support) Regulations 1996,[425] which were designed to remove the state subsidy to employers who dismiss unfairly. Such benefits had the effect of reducing the losses suffered by dismissed persons. These Regulations provide that a tribunal must not deduct from the compensation awarded any sum which represents jobseeker's allowance or income support received, and the employer is instructed not to pay immediately the amount of compensation which represents loss of income up to the hearing (known as the 'prescribed element'). The National Insurance Fund can then serve the employer with a recoupment notice which will require him or her to pay the Fund from the prescribed element the amount which represents the jobseeker's allowance or income support paid to the employee prior to the hearing. When the amount has been refunded by the employer, the remainder of the prescribed element becomes the employee's property. It is important to note that private settlements do not fall within the scope of these Regulations.

5.5 Redundancy payments

Dismissal as a result of redundancy is a common feature of economies that are constantly changing and developing. Statutory protection for workers was first introduced by the Redundancy Payments Act 1965 and was seen as a way of encouraging mobility of labour. This Act provided for the establishment of the Redundancy Fund (now the National Insurance Fund) and for employees, with sufficient continuity of employment, to be entitled to a redundancy payment. The Employment

---

421 See *Port of Tilbury v Birch* [2005] IRLR 92.
422 See *Kingston upon Hull City Council v Dunnachie (No 3)* [2003] IRLR 843.
423 [2008] IRLR 317.
424 See *Wardle v Credit Agricole Corporate and Investment Bank* [2011] IRLR 604 CA.
425 SI 1996/2439.

Protection Act 1975 also introduced collective consultation requirements as a result of the then newly adopted EEC Directive (see Chapter 10). The provisions concerning the right to a redundancy payment are now contained in Part XI Chapter I ERA 1996.

Subject to various provisions (see below) an employer is obliged to make a payment to any employee who is dismissed by reason of redundancy or is eligible for a redundancy payment by reason of being laid off or kept on short-time.[426] Dismissal for redundancy purposes has essentially the same meaning as in cases of unfair dismissal[427] and includes the death of the employer.[428] A prerequisite to a claim for a payment is that there has been a dismissal and the reason for it is redundancy. In *Birch and Humber v The University of Liverpool*[429] the employer invited staff to apply for early retirement as a means of reducing numbers. The employees in this case applied and were accepted. They subsequently claimed that they had been dismissed by reason of redundancy, alleging that acceptance of their applications for early retirement amounted to dismissal. The Court of Appeal did not agree that the acceptances could be isolated from the formal applications to retire. There had not been a dismissal but a mutual determination of the contracts of employment, even though the situation might conveniently be called a redundancy situation.

Once notice has been given by the employer, the relevant date can be postponed by agreement without prejudicing the original reason for dismissal. Thus, in *Mowlem Northern Ltd v Watson*[430] an employee was given notice of dismissal by reason of redundancy, but was then kept on for a further three months on a temporary basis to help try to win another contract. When this failed, the employee left and the employer denied liability for making a redundancy payment on the grounds that there was no dismissal. The EAT held that the employee was entitled to the payment as the delay in leaving had been a result of a mutual agreement to postpone the date of termination by reason of redundancy.

According to s. 139(1) ERA 1996, employees are to be regarded as being redundant if their dismissals are attributable wholly or mainly to:

- the fact that the employer has ceased, or intends to cease, to carry on the business[431] for the purposes for which the employees were employed; or
- the fact that the employer has ceased, or intends to cease, to carry on that business in the place where the employees were so employed; or
- the fact that the requirement of that business for employees to carry out work of a particular kind, or for employees to carry out work of a particular kind in the place where they were so employed, has ceased or diminished or is expected to cease or diminish.

In this context 'cease' or 'diminish' means either permanently or temporarily and from whatever cause.[432]

In *High Table Ltd v Horst*[433] three waitresses worked for an agency and could be transferred to a variety of locations. In practice they worked for some years at one place. When a redundancy situation arose at that location, the employees sought to rely on their mobility clauses to argue that they were unfairly selected for redundancy. The Court of Appeal held that it defied common sense to expand the meaning of the place where an employee was employed. As these waitresses had worked permanently at that one location, that was their place of employment.

---

426 Section 135(1) ERA 1996.
427 See s. 136 ERA 1996.
428 Section 136(5) ERA 1996.
429 [1985] IRLR 165 CA.
430 [1990] IRLR 500.
431 'Business' is defined in s. 235(1) ERA 1996.
432 Section 139(6) ERA 1996.
433 [1997] IRLR 513 CA.

Lord Irvine LC, in *Murray v Foyle Meats Ltd (Northern Ireland)*,[434] stated:

[The statutory definition of redundancy] asks two questions of fact. The first is one of whether one or other of various states of economic affairs exists. In this case, the relevant one is whether the requirements of the business for employees to carry out work of a particular kind have diminished. The second question is whether the dismissal is attributable, wholly or mainly, to that state of affairs. This is a question of causation. In the present case, the Tribunal found as a fact that the requirements of the business for employees to work in the slaughter hall had diminished. Secondly, they found that that state of affairs had led to the appellants being dismissed. That, in my opinion, is the end of the matter.

This case was about the fact that some meat operatives from one part of the business were considered for dismissal by reason of redundancy and not operatives from the other parts who were less affected by the situation. The Supreme Court approved the EAT decision in *Safeway Stores plc v Burrell*,[435] which had considered different approaches to whether a dismissal for redundancy had taken place, specifically the 'function test' and the 'contract test'. The question arises as to whether there is a need to identify specific individuals, the requirements for whose work has ceased or diminished, or whether it is sufficient to state that there has been a reduction in the need for the numbers of employees needed. This latter approach might mean dismissing some employees whose work continues.

The function test required the tribunal to look at the work that the employee was required to do, and actually did, in order to decide whether or not the job had disappeared. The contract test required the tribunal to consider whether there was a diminishing need for the work which the employee could be required to do under the contract of employment. In *Safeway Stores* the EAT concluded that both these approaches were incorrect. There was a three-stage process:

1. The first question was: was the employee dismissed?
2. If so, the second question was: had the requirements of the employer's business for employees to carry out work of a particular kind ceased or diminished?
3. If so, the third question was: was the dismissal of the employee caused wholly or mainly by that state of affairs?

Thus the third stage is one of causation and in this case the court approved a method of selection known as 'bumping'. For example, if a fork-lift driver who was delivering materials to six production machines on the shop floor, each with its own operator, is selected for dismissal on the basis of 'last in, first out', following a decision of the employer that only five machine operators were required, and one machine operator with longer service is transferred to driving the fork-lift truck, the truck driver is dismissed for redundancy. This is the case even though the job of driving the fork-lift truck continues. There has been a diminished need for employees to carry out work of a particular kind and the dismissal of the employee was caused by this state of affairs.

The expiry of a limited-term contract may be a dismissal for reasons of redundancy. Thus the lecturers in *Pfaffinger v City of Liverpool Community College*,[436] who were employed during each academic year only, were dismissed for redundancy at the end of each academic term. Business reorganisations can lead to dismissals which are related to redundancy. Alternatively, they might be dismissals for

---

434 [1999] IRLR 562 HL.
435 [1997] IRLR 200.
436 [1996] IRLR 508.

'some other substantial reason'.[437] An employer cannot, however, argue a case based on redundancy and when this fails turn to some other substantial reason.[438]

5.5.1 Qualifications and exclusions

In order to qualify for a right to a redundancy payment an employee must have been continuously employed for two years at the relevant date.[439] There are a number of situations where employees will lose their right to a redundancy payment:

1. Employees who are dismissed with or without notice for reasons connected to their conduct.[440]

2. If an employee gives notice to the employer terminating the relationship with effect from a date prior to the date upon which the employer's notice of redundancy is due to expire, then the employee may lose their right to a redundancy payment.[441] This is provided that the employer serves a notice on the employee requiring him or her to withdraw their notice and to stay in employment until the employer's notice expires and warning the employee that he or she will lose their right to a payment.[442] An employee may ask an employment tribunal to decide whether it should be just and equitable to receive a payment, taking into account the reasons for which the employee seeks to leave early and the reasons for which the employer requires the individual to continue.[443]

3. If, before the ending of a person's employment, the employer or an associated employer makes an offer, in writing or not, to renew the contract or to re-engage under a new contract which is to take effect either on the ending of the old one or within four weeks, then s. 141 ERA 1996 operates in the following way. If the provisions of the new or renewed contract as to the capacity and place in which the person would be employed, together with the other terms and conditions, do not differ from the corresponding terms of the previous contract; or the terms and conditions differ, wholly or in part, but the offer constitutes an offer of suitable employment; and in either case the employee unreasonably refuses that offer, then he or she will not be entitled to a redundancy payment.

   The burden is on an employer to prove both the suitability of the offer and the unreasonableness of the employee's refusal. Offers do not have to be formal, nor do they have to contain all the conditions which are ultimately agreed. However, supplying details of vacancies is not the same as an offer of employment[444] and sufficient information must be provided to enable the employee to take a realistic decision.

   The suitability of the alternative work must be assessed objectively by comparing the terms on offer with those previously enjoyed. A convenient test has been whether the proposed employment will be 'substantially equivalent' to that which has ceased. Merely offering the same salary will not be sufficient but the fact that the employment will be at a different

---

437 See *Murphy v Epsom College* [1984] IRLR 271 CA for an example of a situation where a dismissal as a result of new technology might have been for reasons of redundancy or for some other substantial reason.

438 *Church v West Lancashire NHS Trust (No 2)* [1998] IRLR 492.

439 Section 155 ERA 1996. In most cases the relevant date is to be ascertained in the same way as the effective date of termination for unfair dismissal purposes (see above). However, where a statutory trial period has been served (see below), for the purpose of submitting a claim in time the relevant date is the day that the new or renewed contract terminated.

440 Section 140(1) ERA 1996; s. 140(2)–(3) provides protection for those dismissed, in certain circumstances, as a result of taking part in a strike.

441 If the employee leaves early by mutual consent, then the redundancy entitlement will not be affected; see *CPS Recruitment Ltd v Bowen* [1982] IRLR 54.

442 Section 142(1)–(2) ERA 1996.

443 Section 142(3) ERA 1996.

444 See *Curling v Securicor Ltd* [1992] IRLR 548.

location does not necessarily mean that it will be regarded as unsuitable. By way of contrast, in adjudicating upon the reasonableness of an employee's refusal, subjective considerations can be taken into account – for example, domestic responsibilities. In *Spencer and Griffin v Gloucestershire County Council*[445] the employees had refused offers of suitable employment on the grounds that they would not be able to do their work to a satisfactory standard in the reduced hours and with less staff. The Court of Appeal held that it was for employers to set the standard of work they wanted carried out but it was a different question whether it was reasonable for a particular employee, in all the circumstances, to refuse to work to the standard which the employer set. This is a question of fact for the tribunal.

If the new or renewed contract differs in terms of the capacity or place in which the employee is engaged or in respect of any other terms and conditions of employment, then the individual is given a trial period of up to four weeks in which to decide whether to accept the new or renewed contract.[446] If the employee or the employer terminates this new or renewed contract, then the entitlement to a redundancy payment for the original dismissal remains.[447] The four-week trial period is calendar weeks and not necessarily 'working' weeks. Thus, if public or other holidays come within the four-week period, they do not extend that period.[448] This trial can be extended by agreement if a period of retraining is necessary, provided that the agreement is in writing and specifies the date on which the retraining ends and the terms and conditions which will apply at the end of the retraining.[449] In *Cambridge & District Co-operative Society Ltd v Ruse*[450] a long-serving employee managed a butcher's shop which was eventually closed. The employee was then offered the position of butchery department manager in a larger store. He refused because he considered this to be a loss of status and therefore not suitable alternative employment. The argument was whether this was an unreasonable refusal. The EAT accepted that the offer of employment was to be assessed objectively but the reasonableness of an employee's refusal was more subjective and depended upon personal factors important to that person. The reasons did not necessarily need to be connected with the employment itself.

4. If an employee takes part in strike action after receiving notice of termination, the employer is entitled to issue a notice of extension. This notice, which must be in writing and indicate the employer's reasons, may request that the employee extends the contract beyond the termination date by a period equivalent to the number of days lost through strike action. Failure by employees to agree to this, unless they have good reasons – for example, sickness or injury – may justify the employer withholding a redundancy payment.[451]

5. The Secretary of State may make an exemption order excluding certain employees from any right to a redundancy payment. These are employees who, under an agreement between one or more employers and one or more trade unions or their associations, have the right to a payment on the termination of their contracts. The Secretary of State may act after receiving an application from all the parties to an agreement that an order be made. A condition of such orders is that any disputes about the right of an employee to a payment or a dispute about the amount should be submitted to an employment tribunal for resolution.[452]

---

445 [1985] IRLR 393.
446 See *Elliot v Richard Stump Ltd* [1987] IRLR 215 in which an employer's mistaken refusal to consider a four-week trial period was sufficient to enable an employee to reject an offer of alternative employment and claim unfair dismissal on the grounds of redundancy.
447 Section 138(2)–(4) ERA 1996.
448 See *Benton v Sanderson Kayser Ltd* [1989] IRLR 19 CA, where an employee lost their right to a redundancy payment because they gave their notice after a four-week period had ended, even though the period had included a seven-day Christmas break.
449 Section 138(6) ERA 1996.
450 [1993] IRLR 156.
451 Sections 143–144 ERA 1996.
452 Section 157 ERA 1996.

Finally, it should be noted sections 159–161 ERA 1996 also exclude the right to redundancy payments in respect of certain public offices, service in overseas government employment and certain domestic servants.

5.5.2 Lay-offs and short-time

For the purposes of the legislation, a person is laid off for a week if they work under a contract of employment where the remuneration depends upon work being provided by the employer and the employer does not provide any work during the week in question.[453] An employee is taken to be kept on short-time for a week if they earn less than half a week's pay as a result of a diminution of work provided by the employer during that week.[454] Employees are entitled to a redundancy payment by reason of being laid off or being kept on short-time if they are laid off or kept on short-time for a period of four consecutive weeks or for a series of six or more weeks within a period of 13 weeks.[455] In order to claim, the employee must resign[456] and give notice of the intention to seek a redundancy payment. An employer may resist the claim by issuing a counter-notice to the employee within seven days of receiving the notice of intention. In such circumstances the matter will be decided by an employment tribunal.[457]

5.5.3 Time off[458]

Section 52 ERA 1996 provides that an employee, with at least two years' service, who is given notice of dismissal by reason of redundancy, is entitled to time off to look for new employment or to make arrangements for training (see Chapter 8). An employee who is permitted such time off is entitled to be paid at the appropriate hourly rate.[459]

5.5.4 Level of payments

For those entitled to payment, once the number of years' service has been calculated[460] the 'appropriate amount' is calculated by allocating a certain sum of money to each of those years' service. The formula to be applied is:

1. One and a half weeks' pay for each year of employment in which the employee was not below the age of 41 years.
2. One week's pay for each year of employment (not in (1) above) in which the employee was not below the age of 22 years.
3. Half a week's pay for each year of employment not within (1) or (2).[461]

This calculation is subject to a number of restrictions. First, there is a maximum amount to a week's pay as defined in s. 227 ERA 1996.[462] This amount is £489 per week from 2017. There is also a

453 Section 147(1) ERA 1996.
454 Section 147(2) ERA 1996.
455 Section 148 ERA 1996. See *Dutton v Jones* [2013] ICR 559.
456 Section 150 ERA 1996.
457 Section 149 ERA 1996; if there is a likelihood of full employment for a period of at least 13 weeks within four weeks of the employee's notice, then there is no entitlement to a redundancy payment: s. 152 ERA 1996.
458 See Chapter 8 on working time.
459 Section 53 ERA 1996.
460 Section 162(1) ERA 1996.
461 Section 162(2) ERA 1996.
462 See Chapter 8 for further discussion on the concept of a week's pay.

maximum of 20 years' service to be taken into account.[463] Thus the maximum amount that can be claimed for a redundancy payment from 2017 is £14,670. It should be noted that s. 163(5) ERA 1996 enables employment tribunals to provide compensation for workers who suffer financial losses as a result of non-payment of redundancy payments.

Any questions as to the right of an employee to a redundancy payment, or the amount of such payment, are to be referred to an employment tribunal. There is a presumption in any such case that the individual employee has been dismissed by reason of redundancy.[464] An employee does not have any right to a redundancy payment unless, before the end of a period of six months beginning with the relevant date:[465]

1. The payment has been agreed and paid or the employee has made a claim for the payment by notice in writing given to the employer.
2. A question as to the employee's right to, or the amount of, the payment has been referred to an employment tribunal or a complaint has been made to a tribunal for unfair dismissal under s. 111 ERA 1996.[466]

The written notice to the employer does not have to be in a particular form. The test is whether it is of such a character that the recipient would reasonably understand in all the circumstances that it was the employee's intention to seek a payment. In this context the words 'presented' and 'referred' seem to have the same meaning – that is, an application must have been received by the employment tribunal within the six-month period. Nevertheless, if any of the above steps are taken outside this period but within 12 months of the relevant date, a tribunal has the discretion to award a payment if it thinks that it would be just and equitable to do so. In such a case a tribunal must have regard to the employee's reasons for failing to take any of the steps within the normal time limit.[467]

When making a redundancy payment,[468] otherwise than as a result of an employment tribunal decision, the employer is required to give the employee a written statement showing how the amount of the payment has been calculated. If the employer fails to do this, the employee may give the employer notice in writing requiring the employer to give the written statement within a period of not less than one week. Failure by the employer to provide such a notice, without reasonable excuse, will open the employer to the possibility of a fine.[469] Finally, it should be noted that Section 12A Employment Tribunals Act 1996 allows employment tribunals to impose a financial penalty on employers where there has been a breach of employment rights and the employment tribunal thinks that 'the breach has one or more aggravating features' (see Chapter 4, section 4.2 above).

Further reading

Cabrelli, D. and Zahn, R. 'The Elective and Automatic Theories of Termination in the Common Law of the Contract of Employment: Conundrum Resolved?' (2013) 76(6) *Modern Law Review* 1106.

---

463 Section 162(3) ERA 1996.
464 Section 163 ERA 1996.
465 See s. 145 ERA 1996 for the meaning of the relevant date.
466 Section 164(1) ERA 1996.
467 Section 164(2) ERA 1996.
468 If the employer fails to make the payment, then the employee may apply to the Secretary of State for payment: see ss 166–170 ERA 1996.
469 Section 165 ERA 1996.

Collins, H. *Nine Proposals for the Reform of the Law on Unfair Dismissal* (Institute of Employment Rights, 2004).

Mantouvalou, V. 'Human Rights and Unfair Dismissal: Private Acts in Public Spaces' (2008) 71(6) *Modern Law Review* 912.

www.acas.org.uk – Advisory, Conciliation and Arbitration Service.

www.bis.gov.uk – Department for Business, Energy and Industrial Strategy.

www.tuc.org.uk – Trades Union Congress.

Chapter 6

Equality: prohibited conduct and equality of terms

6.1 Equality

We need to consider the difference between the ideas of formal equality and substantive equality. The principle of *formal equality* requires the equal treatment of equal cases, so it does not take into account any material differences between those being compared. In this approach, discrimination against men is as bad as discrimination against women and there is no difference in the approach to the two groups. It does, however, ignore the fact that women are much more discriminated against than men. This approach is reflected in the legal definition of direct discrimination (see below). The principle of *substantive equality* takes into account the material differences between individuals or groups. This approach might be said to try to achieve de facto equality and thus will attempt to take into account the reality of women's position, rather than apply some universal standard. For example, women are much more likely to have a caring role in the family and a substantive approach to equality will take this into account. The formal equality approach allows bad treatment of individuals or groups as long as everyone is treated equally badly whereas a substantive equality approach might try to correct the wrong.

An equality approach perhaps requires that individuals are treated on individual merit rather than on the basis of a stereotypical approach. The problem with a merit-based approach is that it tends to be subjective rather than objective, and is likely to be measured against conventional norms of society, which tend to be those of the dominant group – white males. Conventional norms are often based upon stereotypical attitudes towards particular groups in society. One simple assumption, for example, might be that men are stronger than women. The result of this is that only men might be considered for physically demanding jobs, which, in turn, may be the higher-paid jobs in certain types of employment. The outcome is that women are discriminated against in the selection process and end up earning less than men. The assumption is patently false. Not all men are stronger than all women. Some women will be stronger than many men. The discrimination comes from the stereotyping of women in the first place. It is the allocation of a generalised characteristic to an identifiable group.

Another example might be the stereotypical attitudes that employers have towards the abilities of employees based upon their age. In one survey[1] of 500 companies, respondents were asked at what age someone would be too old to employ. Of the respondents 12 per cent considered people too old at 40, 25 per cent considered them too old at 50, 43 per cent considered them too old at 55, and 60 per cent felt they were too old at 60. The relationship of these judgements to conventional stereotypical attitudes can be shown in respondents' answers to questions about agreeing or not agreeing with statements. Figures such as the 36 per cent who thought that older workers were more cautious, the 40 per cent who thought that they could not adapt to new technology and the 38 per cent who thought that they would dislike taking orders from younger workers suggest that stereotypical attitudes remain strong. Research also indicates that there is little evidence that chronological age is a good predictor of performance.

6.2 Does discrimination still take place?

The simple answer to this is yes. A Eurobarometer survey[2] found that discrimination is widespread throughout the European Community. When citizens were asked about whether discrimination was widespread or rare, their answers were as shown in Table 6.1.

---

1 See P. E. Taylor and A. Walker, 'The Ageing Workforce: Employers' Attitudes towards Older People' (1994) 8 *Work, Employment and Society* 569.

2 Discrimination in the European Union, Special Eurobarometer Survey (2007) European Commission; http://ec.europa.eu/public_opinion/archives/ebs/ebs_263_sum_en.pdf

TABLE 6.1 Discrimination in the EU

Ground	Rare (%)	Widespread (%)	Don't know (%)
Ethnic origin	30	64	6
Disability	42	53	6
Sexual orientation	41	50	9
Age	48	46	7
Religion or beliefs	47	44	8
Gender	53	40	8

Source: Discrimination in the European Union, Special Eurobarometer Survey (2007) European Commission, © European Union, 1995–2013. http://ec.europa.eu/public_opinion/archives/ebs/ebs_263_sum_en.pdf

TABLE 6.2 Is belonging to one of these groups an advantage or a disadvantage or neither, in society at the current time?

Characteristic	Disadvantage (%)	Neither (%)	Advantage (%)
Being disabled	79	15	–
Being a Roma	77	15	–
Being aged over 50	69	24	–
Being of a different ethnic origin	62	30	–
Being homosexual	54	39	–
Being part of a different religion	39	54	–
Being a woman	33	54	1
Being aged under 25	20	38	39
Being a man	4	45	49

Source: Discrimination in the European Union, Special Eurobarometer Survey (2007) European Commission, © European Union, 1995–2013. http://ec.europa.eu/public_opinion/archives/ebs/ebs_263_sum_en.pdf

These figures record only the perceptions of individuals and are averages from across the EU. The survey report suggests that there are widespread differences between different Member States, but that generally the individuals surveyed thought that being disabled, being a Roma, being older, belonging to an ethnic minority or being homosexual tends to be a disadvantage in their country. This is reflected in a further analysis provided by the Eurobarometer survey (see Table 6.2).

There is no reason to assume that the situation is any different in the United Kingdom, although it is fair to say that the situation has improved over the years. Despite this improvement, inequalities do remain and obvious ones include the continuing gender pay gap for all full-time workers, which is still a little under 14 per cent,[3] and the employment rate for people with disabilities, which is just 48 per cent compared with about 80 per cent for the non-disabled population.[4]

---

3 See Fawcett Society website at www.fawcettsociety.org.uk
4 See 'Key statistics on people with disabilities in employment', House of Commons Library 2016.

6.3 European Union law

The principle of non-discrimination is a fundamental principle in European Community law. The Community has taken a number of initiatives to further this principle and here we limit ourselves to a consideration of the three most important Directives that further this principle in the field of employment.[5] It is worth remembering that although the EU has a long tradition of tackling sex discrimination and working for equal pay between men and women, its legislative enactments on discrimination in employment relating to other grounds of discrimination, including race, are much more recent.

6.3.1 The Equal Opportunities and Equal Treatment Directive

The Community has a long and effective record of measures combating sex discrimination and promoting equal treatment and equal pay. The original treaty establishing the European Economic Community, signed in Rome in March 1957, contained art. 119 which committed each Member State to the principle of 'equal remuneration for the same work as between male and female workers'. This was undoubtedly a far-reaching principle to have adopted in the 1950s. This commitment was contained in art. 141 EC and is now in art. 157 of the Treaty on the Functioning of the European Union (the TFEU). It includes the principle of equal pay for male and female workers for equal work or for work of equal value. It also provides for the Community to adopt measures to ensure the application of the principle of equal opportunities and equal treatment of men and women in matters of employment and occupation, including the principle of equal pay for equal work or work of equal value.[6]

The Equal Opportunities and Equal Treatment Directive[7] provides, in art. 1, that its purpose is to ensure the implementation of the principle of equal opportunities and equal treatment of men and women in matters of employment and occupation. Article 2(1) then provides some definitions of direct and indirect discrimination and harassment. It also provides for a wide definition of pay which is 'the ordinary basic or minimum wage or salary or any other consideration, whether in cash or in kind, which the worker receives either directly or indirectly, in respect of his/her employment from his/her employer'.

6.3.2 The Directive for Equal Treatment in Employment and Occupation

Council Directive 2000/78/EC established a general framework for equal treatment in employment and occupation.[8] The purpose of the Directive is to put into effect in the Member States 'the principle of equal treatment as regards access to employment and occupation ... of all persons irrespective of racial or ethnic origin, religion or belief, disability, age or sexual orientation'.[9] It is worth remembering that the provisions of the Directive are limited to employment and occupation

---

5 There are other more specialist books that consider this subject in much more depth, e.g. Evelyn Ellis and Philippa Watson, *EU Anti-Discrimination Law* (Oxford University Press, 2015).

6 Article 157(3).

7 Directive 2006/54/EC on the implementation of the principle of equal opportunities and equal treatment of men and women in matters of employment and occupation OJ L204/23, 26.7.2006. This Directive recast seven previous sex equality Directives, including the Equal Pay Directive 75/117, the Equal Treatment Directive 76/207 as amended by Directive 2002/73 and the Burden of Proof Directive 97/80, into one consolidated Directive from 15 August 2009.

8 OJ L303/16 2.12.2000.

9 Article 1 of the Directive.

and that there is a further Directive proposed to extend this protection to activities outside the field of employment.[10]

Article 3 is concerned with this scope and provides that the Directive applies to conditions for access to employment which includes selection criteria and recruitment conditions as well as promotion; access to vocational guidance, training and retraining, including practical work experience; employment and working conditions, including dismissals and pay as well as membership of workers' or employers' organisations.

There are two further very important articles which will be further considered along with each of the protected characteristics (see below). Article 5 provides for the duty of reasonable accommodation with respect to people with disabilities. This is more commonly referred to, in the United Kingdom, as the duty to make adjustments. Article 6 then provides for a very broad range of exceptions with respect to the prohibition on age discrimination, including the possibility of objective justification for direct and indirect discrimination, the effect of which is to considerably weaken the impact of the Directive in this field.

The great majority of cases at the Court of Justice regarding this Directive have been concerned with the age aspects of the prohibition on discrimination. A good example of this is *Mangold v Rüdiger Helm*[11] which concerned a national rule that permitted older people to be employed on fixed-term contracts with no restrictions. Prior to the transposition of Directive 1999/70, German law had placed a number of restrictions on fixed-term contracts of employment, requiring an objective reason justifying the fixed term or, alternatively, imposing limits on the number of contract renewals (a maximum of three) and on total duration (a maximum of two years).[12] These restrictions did not apply to contracts with people over the age of 52 years. Mr Mangold was employed on a fixed-term contract, at the age of 56. Thus the issue was that such a measure needed objective justification as required by art. 6 of Directive 2000/78/EC.

It was accepted that legislation which permitted employers to conclude, without restriction, fixed-term contracts with workers over the age of 52 did amount to a difference of treatment on the grounds of age. The Court readily accepted that the 'purpose of that legislation is plainly to promote the vocational integration of unemployed older workers' and that 'the legitimacy of such a public-interest objective cannot reasonably be thrown in doubt'. There is no indication in the published Opinion of AG Tizzano or the Court's judgment that any evidence was considered with regard to this. The real difficulty for the Court was whether the means adopted were appropriate and necessary. The national court had doubted whether the measure was in compliance with the Directive and the Court of Justice agreed. The problem was that the rule applied to all workers who have reached the age of 52, whether or not they had been unemployed before the contract was concluded and whatever the duration of any period of unemployment. The Court concluded:

> This significant body of workers, determined solely on the basis of age, is thus in danger, during a substantial part of its members' working life, of being excluded from the benefit of stable employment which, however, as the Framework Agreement makes clear, constitutes a major element in the protection of workers.

Thus the measure went beyond what was appropriate and necessary in order to achieve the legitimate aim.

---

10 Proposal for a Council Directive on implementing the principle of equal treatment between persons irrespective of religion or belief, disability, age or sexual orientation, COM2008 426.

11 Case C-144/04.

12 The facts of this case are taken from the Opinion of AG Tizzano.

In Maruko[13] the Court of Justice considered its first case concerning the sexual orientation provisions of the Directive. This case concerned Mr Maruko who had entered into a civil partnership in Germany. His life partner was a member of an occupational pension scheme and when he died Mr Maruko claimed a widower's pension from the scheme. He was refused on the grounds that only spouses were provided for under the scheme's rules. He claimed discrimination on the grounds of sexual orientation and the issue was whether the provisions of such a scheme came within the scope of the Directive. The Court held that such a pension, which was related to employment and service, was part of the individual's pay and therefore was covered. In this case, therefore, Mr Maruko had been less favourably treated than surviving spouses and, as a result, had been discriminated against on the grounds of sexual orientation.

6.3.3 The Race Directive

Council Directive 2000/43/EC implements the principle of equal treatment between persons irrespective of racial or ethnic origin.[14] This helped bring to an end the imbalance in the EU's anti-discrimination programme. In contrast to the EU's action on sex discrimination, it has taken fewer initiatives to combat race discrimination. It was not until the Amsterdam Treaty and the adoption of the new art. 13 that the Community had the authority to take such action. In its guide to the Directive the European Commission accepts that racial discrimination is widespread in everyday life and that legal measures are of 'paramount importance for combating racism and intolerance'.[15]

The purpose of the Directive, contained in art. 1, is 'to lay down a framework for combating discrimination on the grounds of racial or ethnic origin, with a view to putting into effect in the Member States the principle of equal treatment'. Article 2 is concerned with the meaning of direct and indirect discrimination and follows the Equal Treatment in Employment and Occupation Directive closely, including the addition of harassment. Its scope, of course, is wider than just employment, but those areas that are related to employment are also similar to the Equal Treatment in Employment Directive.

In Firma Feryn,[16] for example, one of the directors of the respondent company made a statement to the effect that, although the company was seeking to recruit, it could not employ 'immigrants' because its customers were reluctant to give them access to their private residences for the duration of the works. The Court of Justice held that such a statement concerning candidates of a particular ethnic or racial origin constituted direct discrimination under art. 2(2)(a) of Directive 2000/43. Such a public declaration was clearly likely to dissuade some candidates from applying for jobs with the employer.

6.4 The Equality Act 2010

The EA 2010 was designed to bring a more uniform approach to all the unlawful grounds of discrimination both in employment and in the provision of facilities, goods and services. It replaced much of the previously existing anti-discrimination legislation, including the Equal Pay Act 1970, the Sex Discrimination Act 1975, the Race Relations Act 1976, the Disability Discrimination Act 1995 and the Regulations concerned with stopping discrimination on the grounds of age, religion

---

13 Case C-267/06 Maruko v Versorgungsanstalt Der Deutschen Bühnen [2008] IRLR 405.

14 OJ L180/22 17 July 2000.

15 See also Council Regulation 1035/97 establishing a European Monitoring Centre on Racism and Xenophobia OJ L151 10 June 1997.

16 Case C-54/07 Centrum voor Gelijkheid van Kansen en voor Racismebestrijding v Firma Feryn NV [2008] IRLR 732.

or belief, and sexual orientation.[17] Most of the provisions relating to employment came into effect in October 2010. Alongside the Act is the Employment Statutory Code of Practice published by the Equality and Human Rights Commission. The Code explains its own status in law:

> The Code does not impose legal obligations. Nor is it an authoritative statement of the law; only the tribunals and the courts can provide such authority. However, the Code can be used in evidence in legal proceedings brought under the Act. Tribunals and courts must take into account any part of the Code that appears to them relevant to any questions arising in proceedings.

The Code also provides a detailed explanation of all parts of the Equality Act and can be used as an invaluable guide. It can be found on the Equality Commission's website.[18]

6.4.1 The protected characteristics

The EA 2010 lists nine protected characteristics and it is these that receive protection under the Act. It is important to remember that there are other grounds of discrimination and that the nine characteristics contained in the Act cannot be a comprehensive list. For example, s. 97 of the Enterprise and Regulatory Reform Act (ERRA) 2013 inserted a provision into the EA 2010 to add in the future discrimination on the grounds of caste as an aspect of race discrimination.[19] There are also other examples including appearance,[20] accent, etc. The nine protected characteristics are, however, as follows:

1. *Age* – a person belonging to a particular group is protected. Age group means persons of the same age or persons of a range of ages.
2. *Disability* – this defines who is to be regarded as having the protected characteristic of disability.
3. *Gender reassignment* – a person has this protected characteristic if the person is proposing to undergo, is undergoing or has undergone a process (or part of a process) for the purpose of reassigning the person's sex by changing physiological or other attributes of sex.
4. *Marriage and civil partnership* – this applies to those that are married or in a civil partnership, so just living together is not enough.
5. *Pregnancy and maternity* – traditionally, discrimination against women who are pregnant or have recently given birth has amounted to sex discrimination.
6. *Race* – this includes colour, nationality and ethnic or national origin. Those who have any of these characteristics can be described as a 'racial group' and such a group can consist of more than one racial group.
7. *Religion or belief* – religion means any religion or lack of religion; belief means any philosophical belief or lack of such belief. The guidance states that atheism or humanism would be included but not beliefs in communism, Darwinism, fascism, socialism or 'adherence to a particular football team'.
8. *Sex* – people having the protected characteristic of sex are men or women; men share this characteristic with other men and women with other women.
9. *Sexual orientation* – this is similar to the Employment Equality (Sexual Orientation) Regulations 2003, so sexual orientation means a sexual orientation towards people of the same sex, the opposite sex or either sex.

---

17 Employment Equality (Religion or Belief) Regulations 2003, SI 2003/1660, Employment Equality (Sexual Orientation) Regulations 2003, SI 2003/1661, Employment Equality (Age) Regulations 2006, SI 2006/1031.
18 www.equalityhumanrights.com
19 Section 9(5) EA 2010.
20 Sometimes known as 'lookism'.

It is normally only possible to claim discrimination on the basis of one of these protected characteristics at any one time. Sometimes, however, discrimination can take place on a number of characteristics; in other words, discrimination can be multiple. Indeed, the Equality Act 2010 included a provision for the possibility of dual discrimination claims,[21] but the government of the day decided not to bring the provision into effect. The current situation can lead to confusion about whether each characteristic complained about should be considered separately, as in *Bahl v The Law Society*[22] which concerned a case of both race and sex discrimination. The Court of Appeal stated that:

> In our judgment, it was necessary for the Employment Tribunal to find the primary facts in relation to each type of discrimination against each alleged discriminator and then to explain why it was making the inference which it did in favour of Dr. Bahl on whom lay the burden of proving her case.

It can also lead to confusion about remedies and whether there should be overall compensation – for example, with regard to injury to feelings – or whether each characteristic against which discrimination has been found should be compensated for separately. *Al Jumard v Clwyd Leisure Ltd*[23] concerned an individual who was an Iraqi by birth, with British nationality, and who was also disabled, with a hip injury. The employment tribunal found that he had been unfairly dismissed and had been subject to race discrimination, disability discrimination and victimisation. One of the questions for the EAT was whether the injury to feelings should be considered separately with respect to race and to disability discrimination. Its conclusion was that each was a separate wrong and there should be compensation for each wrong, although not necessarily the same amount for each.

6.4.2 Prohibited conduct

In relation to all the protected characteristics there are a number of unlawful acts. These are direct and indirect discrimination, harassment and victimisation, although the provisions on harassment do not apply to the characteristics of marriage and civil partnership or pregnancy and maternity. These unlawful acts are considered here, although there are a number of specific provisions that apply to individual protected characteristics which are considered in Chapter 7.

6.4.2.1 Direct discrimination

Section 13(1) of the Equality Act provides that direct discrimination takes place when a person (A) discriminates against another (B) if, because of a protected characteristic, A treats B less favourably than A treats, or would treat, others. The term 'on the grounds of' used in previous legislation is replaced by the term 'because of'. The guidance to the Act explains that this means the same thing but is designed to make it more accessible. It is not possible to justify direct discrimination, except with regard to the protected characteristic of age. The Act provides that direct discrimination in relation to age can be justified if shown to be a proportionate means of achieving a legitimate aim (s. 13(2)). In relation to pregnancy the claimant is able to claim unfavourable treatment rather than less favourable treatment (see above). The Code of Practice gives the following example:

> At a job interview, an applicant mentions she has a same sex partner. Although she is the most qualified candidate, the employer decides not to offer her the job. This decision treats her less

---

favourably than the successful candidate, who is a heterosexual woman. If the less favourable treatment of the unsuccessful applicant is because of her sexual orientation, this would amount to direct discrimination.

The less favourable treatment does not have to result in actual disadvantage. It is enough for the employee to be able to reasonably say that they would have preferred not to be treated differently from the way the employer treated, or would have treated, another person. The Code of Practice gives a further example:

> A female worker's appraisal duties are withdrawn while her male colleagues at the same grade continue to carry out appraisals. Although she was not demoted and did not suffer any financial disadvantage, she feels demeaned in the eyes of those she managed and in the eyes of her colleagues. The removal of her appraisal duties may be treating her less favourably than her male colleagues. If the less favourable treatment is because of her sex, this would amount to direct discrimination.

The definition of direct discrimination is also broad enough to include those treated less favourably because of their association with someone who has the characteristic or because the victim is thought to have it. This was the case in *Coleman v Attridge Law*,[24] which interpreted European Community law as extending protection from discrimination to those associated with an individual, rather than to just the individual alone. In this case a mother of a child with a disability claimed successfully that she was protected by the Disability Discrimination Act 1995 even though she was not herself disabled. She had been obliged to take a lot of time off work to look after her child.

The Code of Practice makes clear that it is direct discrimination if an individual is treated less favourably because of association with another person who has a protected characteristic. Examples given are:

> A lone father caring for a disabled son has to take time off work whenever his son is sick or has medical appointments. The employer appears to resent the fact that the worker needs to care for his son and eventually dismisses him. The dismissal may amount to direct disability discrimination against the worker by association with his son.

> A manager treats a worker (who is heterosexual) less favourably because she has been seen out with a person who is gay. This could be direct sexual orientation discrimination against the worker because of her association with this person.

The possibility of discrimination by association does not apply to the protected characteristics of marriage or civil partnership or pregnancy and maternity. It is also direct discrimination if the employer treats an applicant or worker less favourably because he or she mistakenly believed that the worker had the protected characteristic. This does not apply to marriage or civil partnership or pregnancy and maternity.

Thus, the two essential features of direct discrimination are, first, that it takes place in relation to a protected characteristic and, second, that it takes place when a person is treated less favourably than a person who does not share that protected characteristic. A comparative model of justice is used. The treatment given to the complainant by A is relative to the treatment given to the comparator B. It does not matter whether A has the protected characteristic as well.[25] If one takes sex discrimination as an example, one approach, according to the House of Lords in *James v Eastleigh Borough Council* is to

---

24 [2008] IRLR 722.
25 Section 24(1) EA 2010.

consider whether the complainant would have received the same treatment from the defendant but for his or her sex.[26] This 'but for' test can be applied where the treatment given derives from the application of gender-based criteria and where the treatment given results from the selection of the complainant because of his or her sex. Thus, when a local authority gave free use of its swimming pools to persons of pensionable age, then a male of 61 years who has not reached pensionable age is discriminated against in comparison with a woman who reached it at the age of 60 years. There need be no intention to discriminate and motives are not relevant. In *R v Birmingham City Council, ex parte Equal Opportunities Commission*[27] the local authority offered more places in selective secondary education to boys than to girls. This was held to be treating those girls less favourably on the grounds of their sex and the fact that the local authority had not intended to discriminate was not relevant.

The definition in s. 13(1) requires less favourable treatment in comparison with another or in comparison with the way that A 'would treat others'. Thus, in the absence of an actual comparator the court will need to construct a hypothetical one, in order for the complainant to show that she was treated less favourably than the hypothetical person. Inferences as to how this hypothetical person would have been treated can be gained from the surrounding circumstances and other cases which might not be exactly the same but would not be wholly dissimilar, although there must be no material differences to the circumstances relating to each case.[28] An exact comparator is not, of course, needed as it might be impossible to prove less favourable treatment, especially in isolated cases, if this were the case.[29]

This is not to suggest that there is a hypothetical reasonable employer who treats employees reasonably, so that it is possible to identify those treated less reasonably. In *Zafar v Glasgow City Council*[30] Lord Browne-Wilkinson stated that:

> In deciding that issue, the conduct of a hypothetical reasonable employer is irrelevant. The alleged discriminator may or may not be a reasonable employer. If he or she is not a reasonable employer, he/she might well have treated another employee in just the same unsatisfactory way as he treated the complainant, in which case he would not have treated the complainant less favourably . . .

Thus if an employer behaves in the same unreasonable way to all their employees it may not be possible for one individual to say that they have been treated less favourably, no matter how unreasonably they were treated. This situation also occurred in *Laing v Manchester City Council*[31] where a white supervisor was held not to have acted appropriately in her supervisory role to a subordinate who was black and of West Indian origin. The claimant failed to establish a *prima facie* case of discrimination because the supervisor's behaviour was not the result of any bias against the employee or other black employees, but was the result of her lack of experience, which resulted in her treating all employees in the same manner.

6.4.2.2 Indirect discrimination

Indirect discrimination is defined, in s. 19(1), as:

> A person (A) discriminates against another (B) if (A) applies to (B) a provision, criterion or practice which is discriminatory in relation to a relevant protected characteristic of (B)'s.

---

26 [1990] IRLR 288.
27 [1989] IRLR 173.
28 Section 23(1) EA 2010.
29 See *Balamoody v UK Central Council for Nursing* [2002] IRLR 288 CA.
30 [1998] IRLR 36 HL.
31 [2006] IRLR 748.

Section 19(2) then provides that a provision, criterion or practice is discriminatory if, in relation to a protected characteristic of B's:

- A applies, or would apply, it to persons with whom B does not share the characteristic;
- it puts, or would put, persons with whom B shares a characteristic at a particular disadvantage when compared with persons with whom B does not share it;
- it puts, or would put, B at that disadvantage; and
- A cannot show it to be a proportionate means of achieving a legitimate aim.

For indirect discrimination to take place the employer needs to apply (or would apply) a provision, criterion or practice to everyone in the affected group including a particular worker and

- the provision, criterion or practice puts, or would put, people who share the worker's protected characteristic at a particular disadvantage when compared with people who do not have that characteristic;
- the provision, criterion or practice puts, or would put, the worker at that disadvantage; and
- the employer cannot show that the provision, criterion or practice is a proportionate means of achieving a legitimate aim.

An example of indirect discrimination taken from the Code of Practice is:

> A factory owner announces that from next month staff cannot wear their hair in dreadlocks, even if the locks are tied back. This is an example of a policy that has not yet been implemented but which still amounts to a provision, criterion or practice. The decision to introduce the policy could be indirectly discriminatory because of religion or belief, as it puts the employer's Rastafarian workers at a particular disadvantage. The employer must show that the provision, criterion or practice can be objectively justified.

Indirect discrimination occurs when a policy which applies in the same way for everybody has an effect that particularly disadvantages people with a protected characteristic. Where a particular group is disadvantaged in this way, a person in that group is indirectly discriminated against if he or she is put at a disadvantage unless A can show that it is a proportionate means of achieving a legitimate aim. Indirect discrimination applies to all the protected characteristics except for pregnancy and maternity, although it might be possible to show indirect sex discrimination in relation to these.

If one uses sex discrimination as an example, then the process of deciding whether indirect sex discrimination has taken place is to examine the 'provision, criterion or practice' and assess, first, whether it would be to the detriment of a considerably larger proportion of women than of men, and, second, whether it is to the individual's detriment. This is provided that the application of the 'provision, criterion or practice' cannot be shown to be justifiable irrespective of the sex of the person to whom it is applied. Each situation needs to be looked at on its own merits. Just because a policy might be gender-neutral in some situations, it does not follow that it will be so in all situations. *Whiffen v Milham Ford Girls' School*,[32] for example, concerned a school that followed its local education authority's model redundancy policy. This required that the non-renewal of temporary fixed-term contracts should be the first step to be taken. In this particular case, however, the result was indirectly to discriminate against female employees because 100 per cent of male employees could satisfy the condition that an employee needed to be on a permanent contract in order not to be terminated early, but only 77 per cent of female employees could satisfy this condition.

---

32 [2001] IRLR 468 CA.

A provision, criterion or practice could be the necessity for previous management training or supervisory experience,[33] a contractual requirement that required employees to serve in any part of the United Kingdom at the employer's discretion,[34] or the imposition of new rostering arrangements for train drivers.[35] One might conclude that merely the imposition of such requirements under these circumstances would be sufficient for an employee to show that he or she had suffered a detriment, but there is a need for a detriment to be shown. In *Shamoon*,[36] for example, a female chief inspector was stopped from doing staff appraisals after some complaints about the manner in which she carried them out. When she complained of sex discrimination, the House of Lords ruled that a detriment occurs if a reasonable worker would or might take the view that they had been disadvantaged in the circumstances in which they had to work. However, it is not necessary to demonstrate some physical or economic consequence.

In *Seymour-Smith*[37] the House of Lords gave judgment in a long-running case that had begun with the dismissal of the applicants in 1991. The House of Lords had referred the case to the Court of Justice for guidance, amongst other matters, on the legal test for establishing whether a measure adopted by a Member State has such a degree of disparate effect as between men and women as to amount to indirect discrimination for the purposes of art. 119 EEC (now art. 157 TFEU) of the EC Treaty unless shown to be based on objectively justified factors other than sex. The Court of Justice responded[38] by stating that the first question, when attempting to establish whether there was indirect discrimination, was to ask whether the measure in question had a more unfavourable impact on women than on men. After this it is a question of statistics. This means considering and comparing the respective proportions of men and women that were able to satisfy the requirement of the two-year rule. The Court of Justice further stated:

> it must be ascertained whether the statistics available indicate that a considerably smaller percentage of women than men is able to satisfy the condition of two years' employment required by the disputed rule. That situation would be evidence of apparent sex discrimination unless the disputed rule were justified by objective factors unrelated to any discrimination based on sex.

In this case the House of Lords decided that the statistics did not indicate a significant difference, although it was accepted that such measures should be reviewed from time to time.[39] The government argued, as objective justification for the measure, that it would encourage recruitment as some employers were reluctant to employ new staff because of the lack of such a rule. This argument appeared to be accepted by the court, although it is somewhat ironic that the final decision was given some time after the qualifying period was reduced to one year with little apparent effect on recruitment. In *Rutherford v Secretary of State (No 2)*[40] the issue of statistics was considered in a case where a man complained that the inability to claim unfair dismissal and redundancy payments[41] after retirement age were indirectly discriminatory on grounds of sex. His argument was that a considerably higher proportion of men worked after the age of 65 years compared with women

---

33 *Falkirk City Council v Whyte* [1997] IRLR 560, where in practice the need for such experience became obligatory rather than desirable as at the beginning of the selection for promotion process.

34 *Meade-Hill and National Union of Civil and Public Servants v British Council* [1995] IRLR 478 CA.

35 *London Underground v Edwards* [1998] IRLR 364 CA.

36 *Shamoon v Chief Constable of the RUC* [2003] IRLR 285.

37 *R v Secretary of State for Employment, ex parte Seymour-Smith and Perez (No 2)* [2000] IRLR 263 HL.

38 Case C-167/97 [1999] IRLR 253 at p. 278.

39 The need to assess provisions periodically in the light of social developments was made by the Court of Justice in *Commission v United Kingdom* [1984] IRLR 29.

40 [2004] IRLR 892. This conclusion, for different reasons, was subsequently upheld by the House of Lords; [2006] IRLR 551.

41 Sections 109 and 156 ERA 1996.

and that, therefore, these rules indirectly discriminated against men. The Court of Appeal followed the approach taken in *Seymour-Smith* by insisting that the employment tribunal should have primarily compared the respective proportions of men and women who could satisfy the age requirement.

Although these cases concern sex discrimination, the same rules apply in cases concerning the other protected characteristics. In the case of racial discrimination, for example, the justification for any measure needs to be irrespective of the colour, race, nationality or ethnic or national origins of the persons concerned. In *JH Walker Ltd v Hussain*[42] an employer had banned employees from taking non-statutory holidays during its busy period of May, June and July. Their justification for this was a business-related one. About half the company's production workers were Muslims of Indian ethnic origin. The holiday period ban coincided with an important religious festival when many of the employees traditionally took time off. Seventeen employees took the day off despite the ban. When they returned to work they were given a final written warning. The 17 employees successfully complained of indirect racial discrimination. The employment tribunal and the EAT held that the rule was discriminatory and that the business justification put forward was not adequate.

Judgments of the European Court of Human Rights have indicated that indirect discrimination may not be just a result of group disadvantage. In *Eweida and others v United Kingdom*[43] the Court of Justice held that a failure to allow Ms Eweida to wear her religious symbol of a cross was a denial of her right to manifest her religious belief as provided for in art. 9 of the ECHR. The denial of her right to manifest her religious belief had, according to the Court, caused her individually 'considerable anxiety, frustration and distress'.

According to the Code of Practice, the question of whether the provision, criterion or practice is a proportionate means of achieving a legitimate aim should be approached in two stages:

- Is the aim of the provision, criterion or practice legal and non-discriminatory, and one that represents a real, objective consideration?
- If the aim is legitimate, is the means of achieving it proportionate – that is, appropriate and necessary in all the circumstances?

In *Pendleton v Derbyshire County Council*[44] a school teacher with strong religious beliefs decided to stay with her husband after he was convicted of downloading indecent images of children. She had a strong belief in the sanctity of marriage and wanted to stay with him if he repented. Her school, however, had a policy (provision, criterion or practice) of dismissing employees who were associated with those convicted for such reasons. She claimed that she had suffered indirect discrimination because of her religious beliefs. The EAT held that the school's policy placed an additional burden on those with a strong religious belief compared with those that did not share that faith, resulting in indirect discrimination.

A legitimate aim might relate to the needs of the business but, as this example from the Code of Practice shows, reducing costs cannot be a justifiable reason for discrimination:

> Solely as a cost-saving measure, an employer requires all staff to work a full day on Fridays, so that customer orders can all be processed on the same day of the week. The policy puts observant Jewish workers at a particular disadvantage in the winter months by preventing them from going home early to observe the Sabbath, and could amount to indirect discrimination unless it can be objectively justified. The single aim of reducing costs is not a legitimate one; the employer cannot just argue that to discriminate is cheaper than avoiding discrimination.

---

42 [1996] IRLR 11.
43 [2013] IRLR 231.
44 [2016] IRLR 580

The term 'proportionate' is equivalent to the words 'appropriate and necessary' which are used in EU directives. The decision on whether the means to achieving the legitimate aim are appropriate and necessary is likely to lead to a consideration by the court of the needs of the employer or business balanced against the rights of the individual. A good example from the Code of Practice is:

> A food manufacturer has a rule that beards are forbidden for people working on the factory floor. Unless it can be objectively justified, this rule may amount to indirect religion or belief discrimination against the Sikh and Muslim workers in the factory. If the aim of the rule is to meet food hygiene or health and safety requirements, this would be legitimate. However, the employer would need to show that the ban on beards is a proportionate means of achieving this aim. When considering whether the policy is justified, the Employment Tribunal is likely to examine closely the reasons given by the employer as to why they cannot fulfil the same food hygiene or health and safety obligations by less discriminatory means, for example by providing a beard mask or snood.

6.4.2.3 Harassment

An employer has a duty not to harass applicants or employees.[45] According to s. 26(1) EA, a person (A) harasses another (B) if

(a) A engages in unwanted conduct related to a relevant protected characteristic and
(b) The conduct has the purpose or effect of –

    (i) Violating B's dignity.
    (ii) Creating an intimidating, hostile, degrading, humiliating or offensive environment for B.

There are three types of harassment provided for in s. 26 EA. The first is harassment in relation to a protected characteristic. The relevant protected characteristics here are age, disability, gender reassignment, race, religion or belief, sex or sexual orientation. The second is sexual harassment[46] and the third is less favourable treatment of a worker because they submit to, or reject, sexual harassment or harassment related to sex or gender reassignment.[47] Examples of harassment might include witnessing abusive action or language against a colleague which creates an offensive environment or an employer displaying material of a sexual nature, such as topless calendars, which may create an offensive environment for female or male employees. An example given in the Code of Practice is:

> In front of her male colleagues, a female electrician is told by her supervisor that her work is below standard and that, as a woman, she will never be competent to carry it out. The supervisor goes on to suggest that she should instead stay at home to cook and clean for her husband. This could amount to harassment related to sex as such a statement would be self-evidently unwanted and the electrician would not have to object to it before it was deemed to be unlawful harassment.

Section 26(2) also specifically states that unwanted conduct of a sexual nature which has the outcome in s. 26(1)(b) above also amounts to harassment. If B rejects, or refuses to submit to, such conduct (relating to sex or gender reassignment), then any subsequent less favourable treatment resulting from the rejection or refusal to submit may also amount to harassment.[48] The essential characteristic of sexual harassment is that it is words or conduct which are unwelcome to the

---

45 Section 40(1) EA 2010; s. 40(2)–(4) concerned third party harassment, but these provisions were repealed by s. 65 ERRA 2013.
46 Section 26(2) EA 2010.
47 Section 26(3) EA 2010; see also para. 7.3 Code of Practice on Employment.
48 Section 26(3) EA 2010.

recipient and it is for the recipient to decide for themselves what is acceptable to them and what they regard as offensive.[49] A characteristic of sexual harassment is that it undermines the victim's dignity at work. It creates an 'offensive' or 'hostile' environment for the victim and an arbitrary barrier to sexual equality in the workplace.

It follows from this that because a tribunal would not find an action or statement offensive, but the applicant does, the complaint should not be dismissed. There still needs to be evidence of the harassment, however. In a one-to-one counselling interview between a male manager and a female clerical officer, it was alleged that the manager was sexually aroused and that the woman was effectively trapped in the interview room with him.[50] She claimed that this amounted to sexual harassment. The employment tribunal accepted that the manager was not sexually aroused, but decided that the atmosphere at the interview was sexually intimidating. There was, for example, only one copy of the appraisal report, so that it had to be read jointly. The EAT allowed the appeal. Proof of sexual harassment would cause a detriment, but having rejected the evidence on which the claim was made – that is, that the manager was sexually aroused – it could not be said that there was sexual harassment. The EAT did not think that it was necessary or desirable for all female employees to be required to have a female chaperone every time they had an interview with a male manager.

The EAT stated that there were three elements to the liability of the employer (this case concerned s. 3A of the Race Relations Act (RRA) 1976). In *Richmond Pharmacology Ltd v Dhaliwal*,[51] Ms Dhaliwal was British and had lived in England all her life. She resigned and, during her notice period, relationships with her employer deteriorated. Her manager made the statement: 'We will probably bump into each other in future, unless you are married off in India.' She brought proceedings for racial harassment and was successful but was only awarded £1,000. The three elements of liability, according to the EAT, were:

1. Whether the employer engaged in unwanted conduct.
2. Whether the conduct had (a) the purpose, or (b) the effect of either violating the claimant's dignity or creating an adverse environment for her.
3. Whether the conduct was on the grounds of the claimant's race.

There is much overlap between these three elements, but a tribunal should look at each in turn.

The Code of Practice states that in deciding whether the conduct has this effect the following need to be taken into account:

a) The perception of the worker; that is, did they regard it as violating their dignity or creating an intimidating (etc.) environment for them. This part of the test is a subjective question and depends on how the worker regards the treatment.
b) The other circumstances of the case; circumstances that may be relevant and therefore need to be taken into account can include the personal circumstances of the worker experiencing the conduct; for example, the worker's health, including mental health; mental capacity; cultural norms; or previous experience of harassment; and also the environment in which the conduct takes place.
c) Whether it is reasonable for the conduct to have that effect; this is an objective test. A tribunal is unlikely to find unwanted conduct has the effect, for example, of offending a worker if the tribunal considers the worker to be hypersensitive and that another person subjected to the same conduct would not have been offended.[52]

---

49 Section 26(4) EA 2010.
50 *British Telecommunications plc v Williams* [1997] IRLR 668.
51 [2009] IRLR 336.
52 Para. 7.18 Code of Practice.

6.4.2.4 Victimisation

The Equality Act, in s. 27, provides that person A victimises person B if A subjects B to a detriment because B has done a protected act or A believes that B has done, or may do, a protected act. A protected act is:

(a) bringing proceedings under the Equality Act;
(b) giving evidence or information connected to such proceedings;
(c) doing anything else for the purposes of, or in connection with, this Act;
(d) making an allegation that A, or another person, has contravened the Act.

It is also unlawful to instruct someone to discriminate against, or harass or victimise another because of a protected characteristic.[53]

Giving false evidence or making a false allegation is not a protected act if the evidence is given, or the allegation made, in bad faith.[54] Examples given in the guidance include:

- A woman makes a complaint of sex discrimination against her employer. As a result, she is denied promotion. The denial of promotion would amount to victimisation.
- An employer threatens to dismiss a staff member because he thinks she intends to support a colleague's sexual harassment claim. This threat could amount to victimisation.

In *HM Prison Service v Ibimidun*[55] the complainant had a successful claim for discrimination against the employer; he then launched a number of other claims, some of which resulted in cost orders being made against him (five cost orders in total). He was eventually dismissed by the prison service and brought claims of victimisation and unfair dismissal. His claims failed because, although the bringing of the claims were protected acts, the reason for his dismissal was that he had brought the claims in order to harass the employer. The provisions of the Act (in this case the RRA 1976) were designed to protect bona fide acts, not ones brought with a view to harassment.

Withholding a reference is one way in which an employer might be held to victimise an employee or ex-employee. In *Chief Constable of West Yorkshire Police v Khan*[56] a sergeant in the police applied for promotion in another force at the same time as having an outstanding employment tribunal application alleging racial discrimination by his employer. The employer refused to give a reference until the proceedings were completed. The employee then complained that he had been unlawfully victimised contrary to s. 2 RRA 1976. The court acknowledged that such references were normally given on request, but decided that in this case the reference had not been withheld because the employee had brought proceedings. It had been withheld so that the employer's position could be protected with regard to the proceedings. This was a legitimate action for the employer, acting honestly and reasonably, and should not result in a charge of victimisation. In contrast, the failure of an employer to provide a reference to an ex-employee who had settled a complaint of sex discrimination after alleging that she had been dismissed because of her pregnancy was entitled to bring a complaint of victimisation against her previous employer.[57]

In *Bullimore*[58] an individual had a job offer withdrawn after her ex-employer gave her a poor reference. Her claim of victimisation was upheld by the employment tribunal, but the tribunal held

53 Section 111(1) EA 2010.
54 Section 27(3) EA 2010.
55 [2008] IRLR 940.
56 [2001] IRLR 830 HL.
57 *Coote v Granada Hospitality Ltd (No 2)* [1999] IRLR 452. See now s. 20A SDA 1975 and s. 27A RRA 1976 on discrimination after the employment relationship has ended.
58 *Bullimore v Pothecary Witham Weld (No 2)* [2011] IRLR 18.

that she was not entitled to compensation for loss of earnings, because that loss was too remote. The initial offer of employment by a new employer had broken 'the chain of causation'. The EAT reversed this decision stating that the modern approach to causation was to ask whether the damage would have occurred 'but for' the defendant's wrongful act. It was, according to the EAT, hard to see how the loss in this case could be regarded as being too remote to attract compensation.

There has been an issue about the extent to which ex-employees are protected from victimisation from previous employers. The problem is that, since the EA 2010 came into force, victimisation is not to be treated as a form of discrimination. Section 108 of the Act concerns relationships that have come to an end and provides that an employer may not discriminate against or harass those ex-employees. Section 108(7), however, provides that 'conduct is not a contravention of this section in so far as it also amounts to victimisation'. The question is whether they are also still to be inhibited from victimising them. Onu v Akwiwu[59] concerned an ex-employee who claimed that she had been victimised by her ex-employers. The EAT held that the provision for post-termination victimisation was not explicit but that the actions in the case did constitute actionable victimisation. This was in opposition to an earlier EAT decision that held that the provisions of the legislation did not include this victimisation.[60]

In St Helens Metropolitan Borough Council v Derbyshire[61] a number of staff had brought an equal pay claim. About two months before the equal pay claims were due to be heard the employers sent letters to the staff stating that they were concerned about the impact of the claim on staff. The House of Lords agreed with the court in Khan (see above) that employers acting honestly and reasonably ought to be able to take steps to preserve their position in discrimination proceedings, but it emphasised that it was primarily from the perspective of the alleged victim that one decides whether any detriment has been suffered, not from the perspective of the alleged discriminator.

6.4.3 Asylum and immigration

A potential issue for migrant workers is whether any discrimination or harassment suffered because of their migrant status is protected by the legislation. This is illustrated in the Supreme Court's decision in Onu v Akwiwu.[62] This case concerned the abuse of a domestic worker who entered the UK on a migrant domestic workers' visa. Such visas, according to the court, meant that the worker concerned depended upon the employer for their right to remain and work in the UK. Ms Onu was of Nigerian nationality and suffered much physical and verbal abuse at the hands of her employer. A claim for race discrimination failed because the court held that, although nationality came within the definition of race in the Equality Act, they suffered this abuse because of their vulnerable immigration status and not because of their nationality.

The rules on employing those who are subject to immigration control and who do not have permission to stay and work in the United Kingdom are strict. Section 15 of the Immigration, Asylum and Nationality Act (IANA) 2006 provides that it is not permitted to employ an adult subject to immigration control if the person has not been given leave to enter or remain in the United Kingdom; or the person's leave is invalid, ceased to have effect or is subject to a condition preventing them from accepting employment. An employer will be liable to a penalty if he breaks this rule. An employer may be excused the penalty if he can show that he has complied with the prescribed requirements in relation to the employment of such persons. An employer who knew, at

---

59 [2013] IRLR 523.
60 *Rowstock v Jessemey* [2013] IRLR 439.
61 [2007] IRLR 540.
62 [2016] IRLR 719.

any time during the period of employment, that the person was subject to the limitations in s. 15 cannot be excused the penalty.

Section 21 of the IANA 2006 provides that a person who employs another knowing either that the individual concerned is subject to immigration control and has not been given leave to enter or remain in the United Kingdom, or that the individual's leave is invalid, ceased to have effect or is subject to a condition preventing him from accepting employment will be subject to the possibility of both a fine and a term of imprisonment. Section 23 IANA 2006 provides that the Secretary of State will issue a code of practice[63] specifying what an employer should or should not do in order to ensure that, whilst avoiding liability to a penalty under s. 15 IANA 2006 and whilst avoiding the commission of an offence under s. 21, he or she also avoids contravening the EA 2010. It is important, therefore, to treat all candidates in the same way in order to avoid any actions that might constitute unlawful discrimination.

6.4.4 Discrimination in employment

Employment is defined as 'employment under a contract of employment, a contract of apprenticeship or a contract personally to do work'.[64] According to the Code of Practice on Employment, this is a wider definition of employment than that contained in the Employment Rights Act.

In relation to employment it is unlawful to discriminate in relation to the protected characteristics in the arrangements made for the purpose of determining who should be offered employment, in the terms on which employment is offered, or by not offering employment (s. 39(1) EA). These arrangements can include the interviewing and assessing of candidates for a post. If racial grounds, for example, are the reason for the less favourable treatment resulting from the arrangements made, then direct discrimination is established. The reason for the discrimination is not relevant.[65] Harassment of an applicant for employment for reasons connected to the protected characteristics is specifically covered by the legislation (s. 40) as is victimisation (s. 39(3)). In X v Mid Sussex Citizens Advice Bureau[66] the claimant argued that the Framework Directive on Equal Treatment (2000/78/EC) protected voluntary workers from discrimination on the grounds of disability. She was a volunteer and she further argued that really the volunteering arrangements with the Citizens Advice Bureau were for the purpose of deciding to whom employment should be offered. The Supreme Court held that Directive 2000/78/EC did not cover voluntary activity. Of importance was that the European Commission had not suggested that the Directive had been inadequately implemented by the failure of the UK or other governments to include voluntary activity.

In respect of applicants and employees, the employer has a duty to make reasonable adjustments (s. 39(5)). This subject is discussed further when disability discrimination is considered (see Chapter 7). The Equality Act does specifically state, in order to limit the potential for discrimination, that an employer must not ask about the health of an applicant, except for certain specific reasons, until the applicant has been either offered a job or has been included in a pool of successful applicants to be offered a job when a position arises (s. 60(1)). The specific occasions when health enquiries can be made are:

- establishing whether there is a need to make reasonable adjustments to enable the person with a disability to participate in the selection process;
- establishing whether an applicant could participate in all parts of the selection process;

---

63 See Immigration (Restrictions on Employment) Order 2007/3290.

64 Section 83(2) EA 2010.

65 *Nagarajan v London Regional Transport* [1999] IRLR 572.

66 [2013] IRLR 146.

- discovering whether an applicant could undertake a function that is specific to the job;
- monitoring diversity in applicants;
- supporting positive action for disabled people; and
- enabling an employer to establish whether the applicant has a disability where there is an occupational requirement for someone with a disability.

Employers will therefore need to be careful not to have general health questions as part of the selection process unless it can be shown that they are for one of these specific purposes. If a candidate is asked a question which cannot be shown to be so, and they subsequently fail to get the job, they will be able to make a claim of direct disability discrimination.

It is also unlawful to discriminate against an employee in relation to the protected characteristics during a person's employment. This includes the individual's terms of employment, access to opportunities for promotion, training or transfer, dismissal and any other detriment (s. 39(2)). Obvious examples of discrimination in this respect given in the guidance, are:

- An employer decides not to shortlist for interview a disabled job applicant because of her disability. This would be direct discrimination.
- An employer enforces a 'no beards' policy by asking staff to shave. This could be indirect discrimination, because it would have a particular impact on Muslims or Orthodox Jews.
- An employer refuses to interview a man applying for promotion, because he previously supported a discrimination case against the employer brought by another employee. This would be victimisation.

A good example of the care that needs to be taken in recruitment is shown in a case where it became known that an employer would not employ people of a certain ethnic origin. There will then be a presumption of discriminatory practices, as happened in *Firma Feryn* where the employer publicly stated that this was its position.[67]

There are also specific provisions concerning harassment of employees and applicants in s. 40 EA. An employer must not harass his or her employees or persons who have applied for employment. The provisions on harassment also provide that an employer will be treated as harassing an employee where a third party harasses the employee or applicant in the course of employment (see below) and the employer fails to take steps which are reasonably practicable to stop the third party harassment.[68] According to s. 40(3) EA, however, this provision only applies when the employer knows that the employee has been harassed during the course of employment on at least two other occasions and it does not matter whether the third party is the same person or a different person on each occasion. An example of this can be found in the Code of Practice on Employment:[69]

> An employer is aware that a female employee working in her bar has been sexually harassed on two separate occasions by different customers. The employer fails to take any action and the employee experiences further harassment by yet another customer. The employer is likely to be liable for the further act of harassment.

Section 108 EA also provides that discrimination or harassment which arises in connection with a relationship that used to exist is also to be treated as prohibited conduct.

---

67 Centrum voor Gelijkheid van Kansen en voor Racismebestrijding v Firma Feryn [2008] IRLR 732.
68 Section 40(2) EA 2010.
69 Para. 10.21 Code of Practice.

'Employment' covers engagement under a contract of service or a contract personally to execute any work or labour (s. 83(1)). According to the Court of Appeal, the legislation contemplates (referring, of course, to pre-EA legislation) a contract of which the dominant purpose is that the party contracting to provide services under it personally performs the work or labour which constitutes the subject matter of the contract.[70]

It would seem to follow that human resource managers need to ensure that application forms and interviewers ask only questions about and insist on minimum qualifications that are relevant to the requirements of the job. Thus a height requirement and certain conditions relating to past experience (e.g. having served an apprenticeship) might be difficult to justify under either Act. Clearly, word-of-mouth recruitment is suspect, and refusing to employ those who live in a particular geographical area could amount to indirect discrimination if there was a racial imbalance in the population residing there.

6.4.5 Burden of proof

One of the problems with discrimination cases is the ability of the complainant to show that discrimination has actually taken place. In order to make the task for complainants of sex discrimination less onerous, Council Directive 97/80/EC on the burden of proof in cases of discrimination based on sex[71] was adopted by the other Member States in 1997. It was adopted by the United Kingdom, via an extension Directive,[72] in 1998. The purpose of the Directive is summarised in art. 1:

> The aim of this Directive shall be to ensure that the measures taken by the Member States to implement the principle of equal treatment are made more effective, in order to enable all persons who consider themselves wronged because the principle of equal treatment has not been applied to them to have their rights asserted by judicial process after possible recourse to other competent bodies.

It has been extended to cover other protected characteristics, so, for example, art. 10(1) of the Equal Treatment in Employment and Occupation Directive states:

> Member States shall take such measures as are necessary, in accordance with their national judicial systems, to ensure that, when persons who consider themselves wronged because the principle of equal treatment has not been applied to them establish, before a court or other competent authority, facts from which it may be presumed that there has been direct or indirect discrimination, it shall be for the respondent to prove that there has been no breach of the principle of equal treatment.

Section 136 EA provides for this reversal of the normal requirements to prove a complaint. Section 136(2) states that if there are facts from which the court could decide, in the absence of any other explanation, that a person (A) contravened the provisions, then the court must hold that a contravention occurred, unless A can show that A did not contravene the provision. Thus it is up to the employer to show that he or she did not contravene the provision once the facts of the case have established that a contravention had occurred. The reason for this approach is, of course, the difficulty that complainants might have in proving discrimination.

---

70 See *Mirror Group Ltd v Gunning* [1986] IRLR 27 and *Percy v Church of Scotland* [2006] IRLR 195. Section 41 EA 2010 makes discrimination against contract workers unlawful.

71 OJ L14/6 20.1.98 (Burden of Proof Directive).

72 Council Directive 98/52/EC OJ L205/66 22.7.98.

According to the Court of Appeal, very little direct discrimination is overt or deliberate. Often the employment tribunal will need to draw inferences as to the conduct of individuals in a particular case. In *King v The Great Britain-China Centre*[73] an applicant who was Chinese, but educated in Britain, failed to be shortlisted for a post of deputy director of the Centre, even though her qualifications on paper seemed to meet the selection criteria. In such a situation the tribunal was entitled to look to the employer for an explanation. In this case, none of the five ethnic Chinese candidates was selected for interview and the Centre had never employed a person with such an ethnic background. The Court of Appeal supported the approach of the employment tribunal in inferring that there was discrimination on racial grounds.[74] In *King*, Neill LJ set down some principles and guidance that could be obtained from the authorities.[75] These were that:

1. It is for the applicant who complains of racial discrimination to make out his case.
2. It is unusual to find direct evidence of racial discrimination.
3. The outcome of a case will therefore usually rely upon what inferences it is possible to draw from the primary facts as found by the tribunal.
4. There will be some cases where it is possible to draw the inference of discrimination and in such cases the tribunal is entitled to look to the employer for an explanation.
5. It is unnecessary to introduce shifting evidential burdens of proof. Having adopted this approach then it is open to the tribunal to reach a conclusion based on the balance of probabilities.

Whether it is possible to draw an inference of discrimination on the basis of sex or race depends upon whether it is possible to show that a person has been subject to less favourable treatment than another person of a different sex or different racial group. In *Martins v Marks & Spencer plc*[76] an applicant of Afro-Caribbean ethnic origin applied, unsuccessfully, four times for a post as a trainee manager with Marks & Spencer. She settled a race discrimination claim on the last occasion and as part of the arrangement was allowed to take a selection test and was given an interview. She failed her selection interview with poor marks. The employment tribunal had found the selection panel 'biased' in its treatment of the candidate. This, the Court of Appeal decided, was not a meaningful conclusion. The real question was whether they were treating this candidate less favourably than they would treat another candidate in the same circumstances, and, second, whether one could infer that this less favourable treatment was on racial grounds. The Court of Appeal found that there was insufficient evidence for this.

There is a need to establish a causal relationship between the detriment and the racial or sexual discrimination. Mummery J discussed causation in *O'Neill*:[77]

> The basic question is: what, out of the whole complex of facts before the tribunal, is the 'effective and predominant cause' or the 'real or the efficient cause' of the act complained of? As a matter of common sense not all the factors present in a situation are equally entitled to be treated as a cause of the crucial event for the purpose of attributing legal liability for consequences.

The tribunal's approach to the question of causation should be 'simple, pragmatic and commonsensical', although this approach needs to be qualified by the fact that the event complained of need not be the only or the main cause of the result complained of.

---

73 [1991] IRLR 513 CA.
74 See *Igen Ltd v Wong* [2005] IRLR 258.
75 See now s. 63A SDA 1975 and s. 54A RRA 1976.
76 [1998] IRLR 326 CA.
77 *O'Neill v Governors of St Thomas More Roman Catholic Voluntarily Aided Upper School* [1996] IRLR 372.

Igen Ltd v Wong[78] was an important case where the Court of Appeal considered a number of questions in relation to the interpretation of the statutes concerning the shifting of the burden of proof. The court held that the provisions required an employment tribunal to go through a two-stage process. The first stage is for the applicant to prove facts from which the tribunal could conclude, in the absence of an adequate explanation, that the respondent has committed an act of discrimination against the applicant. The second stage, which only comes into effect if the complainant has proved these facts, requires the respondent to prove that he did not commit the unlawful act. This case actually contains a 13-point guidance to the decision-making process in relation to the burden of proof. It includes:

1. The claimant must prove on the balance of probabilities facts so that, in the absence of an adequate explanation, the tribunal could conclude that the act of discrimination had taken place against the applicant.
2. It is unusual to find evidence of direct discrimination.
3. It could mean that at this stage the tribunal does not have to have reached a final conclusion.
4. The respondent must prove on the balance of probabilities that the treatment was not on a discriminatory ground.

It is not always necessary to go through this two-stage procedure. In Brown v LB of Croydon[79] the court held that it was not obligatory, but good practice to do so. In some circumstances it was possible to go straight to the second stage. In this case the emphasis was on the reasons for the treatment, so it was natural to do so.

Shifting the burden of proof to the respondent once a prima facie case of discrimination has been established is of great importance. In Madarassy v Nomura International plc[80] the Court of Appeal stated that it did not underestimate the significance of the reversal of the burden of proof. It stated that 'there is probably no other area of civil law in which the burden of proof plays a larger part than in discrimination cases'. A good example of establishing a prima facie case of discrimination can be found in the case of McCorry v McKeith[81] which concerned a case of associative disability discrimination. The claimant had a daughter who was disabled. She was made to stay at home by her employer to look after her daughter and was eventually made redundant. The Northern Ireland Court of Appeal stated that:

> The tribunal set out a number of facts which concerned the claimant having been sent home on previous occasions because of her disabled daughter, the manager's belief that the claimant should have been at home with her disabled daughter, the reluctant piecemeal and incomplete nature of discovery, that two other persons who were made redundant at the same time had been first re-engaged as volunteers and then rehired, evasive and unconvincing evidence of the manager, and non-compliance with statutory dismissal procedures. The tribunal stated '. . . if this is not a case where the burden of proof should shift, no such case exists'.

6.4.6 Liability of employers and employees

According to s. 109(1) EA:

> Anything done by a person (A) in the course of A's employment must be treated as also done by the employer.

---

78 [2005] IRLR 258.
79 [2007] IRLR 259.
80 [2007] IRLR 246.
81 McCorry v McKeith [2017] IRLR 253.

Thus the employer is liable for any acts done by the employee in the course of his or her employment and s. 109(2) provides that it does not matter whether this has been done with the employer's knowledge or approval.

There is sometimes an issue as to whether an act is done during 'the course of employment'. In Jones v Tower Boot Co Ltd[82] the employer argued that the acts of racial harassment were outside the normal course of employment. The employment tribunal took the view that this would amount to saying that no act could become the liability of the employer unless it was expressly authorised by the employer. The Court of Appeal supported this approach and took the view that the words ought to be given their everyday meaning. In Sidhu[83] the event, which consisted of a racially motivated assault on an employee by another employee, took place at a family day out organised by the employers. This was held not to be 'in the course of employment', but subjecting a female police officer, by a male police officer, to inappropriate sexual behaviour during an after-work gathering of police officers in a pub and during a leaving party for a colleague amounted to actions done in the course of employment.[84] When there is a social gathering of work colleagues, it is for the employment tribunal to decide whether the gathering was an extension of employment. Whether a person was, or was not, on duty and whether the events occurred on the employer's premises are just two indicators that need to be considered. In this case the two police officers could not have been said to be merely socialising with each other.[85]

The employer does have a defence if they can show they 'took all reasonable steps' to prevent the employee from doing the thing. The employer needs to show that they have taken steps to prevent the employee from doing the act or other acts of a similar description. In Martins v Marks & Spencer plc[86] (see above at 6.4.5) the Court of Appeal stated that:

> There can be no doubt that Marks & Spencer made out the defence on the findings of fact about the effective arrangements made for the 'special interview' to ensure that the members of the panel had no knowledge of the reason for the interview; their equal opportunities policy; their compliance with the Code of Practice issued by the Commission for Racial Equality in relation to selection procedures, criteria and interviewing; and their selection of the interviewing panel to include Mr Walters as a person with an interest in recruiting from ethnic minorities.

All these actions amounted to a sufficient defence for the employer. It is no defence to say that all possible steps were not taken because the taking of those steps would not have made any difference. This might be true in some extreme forms of harassment, such as the sexual assault that took place in Canniffe v East Riding of Yorkshire Council.[87] Even though there may have been little the employers could have done to stop this action, the fact that they did not take further possible measures was enough to stop them being able to rely on s. 41(3) SDA 1975. The proper approach for the employment tribunal, according to the EAT, was:

1. to identify whether the respondent had taken any steps at all to stop the employee from committing the act or acts complained of and then,
2. having identified what steps, if any, had been taken, to decide whether there were any further steps that could have been taken which were reasonably practicable.

---

82 [1997] IRLR 168 CA.

83 Sidhu v Aerospace Composite Technology Ltd [2000] IRLR 602 CA.

84 Chief Constable of the Lincolnshire Police v Stubbs [1999] IRLR 81.

85 The matter was also considered in Waters v Commissioner of Police of the Metropolis [2000] IRLR 720 HL where an alleged sexual assault in a section house was deemed to be in the course of employment; see also Lister v Hesley Hall Ltd [2001] IRLR 472 HL, above Chapter 2, section 2.3.2.

86 [1998] IRLR 326 CA.

87 [2000] IRLR 555.

Whether these further steps would have stopped the acts is not decisive.

Section 110 EA also provides that the employee will also have contravened the provisions, even if the employer has been found liable for the employee's actions. The employee has a defence if they can show that they relied upon a statement by the employer that the thing done did not contravene the Act and it was reasonable for the employee to rely on the statement.

6.4.7 Relationships that have come to an end

Sections 108(1) and 108(2) EA make it unlawful for employers to discriminate against or harass employees after a relationship has ended. An employer will be liable for acts of discrimination or harassment arising out of the work relationship and which are closely connected to it. The phrase 'closely connected to it' is not defined by the Act. The protection includes the failure to make reasonable adjustments for a person with a disability.[88] An employee will be able to enforce their rights as if the relationship had not ended.[89]

6.4.8 Aiding contraventions

Section 112(1) EA provides that A must not knowingly help another (B) to do anything that contravenes the provisions of the Act in relation to work and other matters (a basic contravention), although it is not a contravention if A relies on a statement by B that the help which is being given does not contravene the Act and it is reasonable for A to do so.[90] The making of such a statement by B is an offence if it is made knowingly or recklessly and is false or misleading.[91]

The concept of 'knowingly aiding' (previous legislation used the word 'aid' rather than 'help') was considered in *Anyanwu and Ebuzoeme v South Bank Students Union*.[92] This concerned two black students who were elected as paid officers of the students' union. They were subsequently expelled from the university for other reasons and barred from the students' union building. This led to the termination of their employment with the students' union. They complained that, amongst other matters, their employer had discriminated against them in terminating their employment. They also complained that the university had knowingly aided this unlawful act. The House of Lords held that the word 'aids' did not have any special or technical meaning in this context and that there was an arguable case that the university had 'knowingly aided' the students' dismissal from employment by the students' union. The university had brought about a state of affairs in which the employment contracts were bound to be suspended. In *Gilbank v Miles*[93] a pregnant hairdresser was subject to a campaign of bullying and discrimination which led to the salon manager being made jointly and severally liable with the company employer as she had helped create the growth of a discriminatory culture.

In *Hallam v Cheltenham Borough Council*[94] the police had concerns about a wedding reception that was to be held at a council-owned hall. The father of the bride was of Romany origin. The Council reacted by imposing new contractual conditions, including admittance only to those with pre-issued tickets. The hirer treated this as repudiatory conduct and held the reception elsewhere. The Council were subsequently found to be guilty of racial discrimination. One further question was whether the police officers concerned had knowingly aided the Council in this discriminatory act. The House of Lords held that each situation should be looked at on its merits. In this case the police officers had

---

88 Section 108(4) EA 2010.
89 Section 108(3) EA 2010.
90 Section 112(2) EA 2010.
91 Section 112(3) EA 2010.
92 *Anyanwu and Ebuzoeme v South Bank Students Union and South Bank University* [2001] IRLR 305 HL.
93 [2006] IRLR 538.
94 [2001] IRLR 312 HL.

not been a party to, neither had they been involved in, the Council's decision. There were a number of ways in which the Council could have reacted to the information, some of which would have been lawful, so more than a general attitude of helpfulness and co-operation was required.

May & Baker v Okerago[95] raised the question of whether an employer was responsible for the racial act of a temporary worker. In this case the temporary worker had asked Mrs Okerago whether she would support England or her own country in a World Cup football match. She had answered that she would support her own country and the result was abuse directed at her by the temporary worker. Although the claimant complained about this, nothing specific was done. The EAT held that it was not possible for an employer to 'aid' an act after it was done. Thus the lack of action could not be called 'aiding'.

6.4.9 Lawful discrimination

The Equality Act provides for a number of exceptions that are permitted to the principle of non-discrimination. We deal in more detail with those that are specific to individual protected characteristics in Chapter 7. Here we deal with some more general exceptions.

6.4.9.1 Occupational requirements

Schedule 9 para. 1 provides that a person (A) does not contravene the provisions concerning non-discrimination in recruitment, termination or in matters concerning access to promotion, transfers, training or for receiving any other benefit, facility or service by applying, in relation to work, a requirement to have a particular protected characteristic. A will have to show that, having regard to the nature or context of the work:

- there is an occupational requirement;
- the application of the requirement is a proportionate means of achieving a legitimate aim;
- the person to whom A applies the requirement does not meet it; and
- except in the case of sex, the employer has reasonable grounds for not being satisfied that the applicant or worker meets the requirement.[96]

Schedule 9 para. 1(3) also provides that, in the case of gender reassignment and marriage and civil partnership, the requirement is not to be a transsexual person, married or a civil partner.

The Code of Practice on Employment gives examples of situations where an occupational requirement might be justifiable. These are, first, that a unisex gym could rely on an occupational requirement to employ a changing room attendant of the same sex as the users of that room; and, second, a women's refuge which lawfully provides services to women only can apply a requirement for all members of its staff to be women. Here is another relatively straightforward example given by the Code:

> A local council decides to set up a health project which would encourage older people from the Somali community to make more use of health services. The council wants to recruit a person of Somali origin for the post because it involves visiting elderly people in their homes and it is necessary for the post-holder to have a good knowledge of the culture and language of the potential clients. The council does not have a Somali worker already in post who could take on the new duties. They could rely on the occupational requirement exception to recruit a health worker of Somali origin.

---

95 [2010] IRLR 394.

96 Schedule 9 para. 1(1) EA 2010; previous legislation referred to 'genuine' occupational requirement, but the word 'genuine' was dropped for the Equality Act.

6.4.9.2 Positive action

This is only a limited provision and positive action needs to be distinguished from positive discrimination, as can be seen from some decisions of the Court of Justice. The issue, for example, of whether there could be positive discrimination in favour of women in terms of access to work was tested in *Marschall*,[97] where the complainant was a male comprehensive school teacher who had applied for promotion to a higher grade. He was told that an equally qualified female applicant would be given the position as there were fewer women than men in the more senior grade. The Court of Justice considered previous judgments[98] which concluded that the Equal Treatment Directive did not permit national rules which enabled female applicants for a job to be given automatic priority. Article 2(4) of the Equal Treatment Directive 76/207 (now art. 3 of the Equal Treatment and Equal Opportunity Directive 2006), provided for the possibility of positive action so that Member States may, within the limits of the Directive, maintain or adopt measures with a view to ensuring full equality in practice between men and women in working life. The Court of Justice considered whether this could alter the outcome. It distinguished between those measures which were designed to remove the obstacles to women and those measures which were designed to grant them priority simply because they were women. The latter measures, as in *Kalanke* and *Marschall*, conflicted with the Directive. There was a difference between measures concerned with the promotion of equal opportunities and measures imposing equal representation. This situation appears unchanged despite art. 157(4) of the TFEU that states:

> With a view to ensuring full equality of practice between men and women in working life, the principle of equal treatment shall not prevent any Member State from maintaining or adopting measures for providing for specific advantages in order to make it easier for the under-represented sex to pursue a vocational activity or to prevent or compensate for disadvantages in professional careers.

In *Abrahamsson and Anderson v Fogelqvist*[99] the Court of Justice held, somewhat disappointingly, that this did not permit measures positively to discriminate in favour of women in a selection process. Preference could not be given to one sex merely because they were under-represented. There had to be an objective assessment of the relative qualifications for the job in question in order to establish that the qualifications of the two sexes were similar before any preference could be given to one sex over the other.[100]

Section 159 Equality Act deals with the issue of positive action in recruitment and promotion. This allows an employer to take into account a protected characteristic when deciding upon whom to recruit and whom to promote. Thus, if the employer thinks that persons who share a particular protected characteristic suffer a disadvantage connected to that characteristic or the participation of persons who share a particular characteristic is disproportionately low, then the employer is not prohibited from taking positive action in favour of the disadvantaged candidate. This can only be done where the candidates are as qualified as each other and the positive action taken is a proportionate means of achieving the aim of helping those disadvantaged to overcome or minimise that disadvantage. An employer may not therefore have a policy of automatically treating people who share a particular protected characteristic more favourably than those who do not have it. Two contrasting examples contained in the guidance are:

1. A police service which employs disproportionately low numbers of people from an ethnic minority background identifies a number of candidates who are as qualified as each other for

97 Case C-409/95 *Marschall v Land Nordrhein-Westfalen* [1998] IRLR 39.
98 See Case C-450/93 *Kalanke v Freie Hansestadt Bremen* [1995] ECR 660 CJEU and Case C-312/86 *Commission v France* [1998] ECR 6315.
99 Case 407/98 [2000] IRLR 732.
100 See Case 158/97 *Application by Badeck* [2000] IRLR 432.

recruitment to a post, including a candidate from an under-represented ethnic minority background. It would not be unlawful to give preferential treatment to that candidate, provided the comparative merits of other candidates were also taken into consideration.

2. An employer offers a job to a woman on the basis that women are under-represented in the company's workforce when there was a male candidate who was more qualified. This would be direct discrimination.

6.4.9.3 The general duty to promote equality

Prior to the Equality Act 2010 there was a public sector duty in relation to disability, race and sex only. The Act now provides for this public sector equality duty also to include the other protected characteristics. The duty is set out in s. 149(1) so that a public authority must, in the exercise of its functions, have due regard to the need to:

1. eliminate discrimination, harassment, victimisation and any other conduct prohibited by the Act;
2. advance equality of opportunity between persons who share a relevant protected characteristic and persons who do not share it;
3. foster good relations between persons who share a relevant protected characteristic and persons who do not share it.

The last two points do not apply to the protected characteristic of marriage and civil partnership. Section 149(3) spells out these duties further by stating that public authorities must have due regard for the need to:

1. remove or minimise disadvantage suffered by persons who share a relevant characteristic;
2. take steps to meet the needs of persons who share a relevant protected characteristic that are different from the needs of people who do not share it;
3. encourage persons who share a relevant protected characteristic to participate in public life or in any other activity in which participation by such persons is disproportionately low.

There is therefore a real need to be proactive and it is clear that just keeping records of diversity will not be enough to satisfy the requirements of the legislation.

The public authorities affected by this measure are listed in Sch. 19 to the Act, and the list covers a wide range of bodies, including local authorities, health boards and trusts, education authorities, government departments, the armed forces and the police.

In R (Brown) v Secretary of State for Work and Pensions[101] the court considered what a relevant body has to do to fulfil its obligation to have due regard to the aims set out in the general equality duty. The six 'Brown principles' it set out have been accepted by courts in later cases. These principles are that:

1. Decision makers must be made aware of their duty to have 'due regard' to the identified goals.
2. The due regard duty must be fulfilled before and at the time that a particular policy is being considered by the public authority in question.
3. The duty must be exercised in substance, with rigour and with an open mind.
4. The duty imposed on public authorities is a non-delegable duty.
5. The duty is a continuing one.
6. It is good practice for those exercising public functions in public authorities to keep an adequate record showing that they had actually considered their duties and pondered relevant questions.

---

101 [2008] EWHC 3158

6.5 Remedies

Section 120 Equality Act 2010 provides that employment tribunals have jurisdiction to determine complaints relating to contraventions of the Act's provisions in relation to work. An employment tribunal will not consider the complaint unless it is presented within a period of three months starting with the date of the act to which the complaint relates,[102] unless the tribunal thinks it is 'just and equitable'.[103] A broad approach was shown in *Derby Specialist Fabrication Ltd v Burton*,[104] where an employee resigned after a period of racial abuse and harassment. Although the discriminatory acts took place before this constructive dismissal, the EAT approved of the tribunal's decision that the three-month period ran from the date of the resignation. If the employee is making a complaint as a result of suffering a detriment from the employer, then the three months commences from when he heard of the detriment.[105] Where an employment tribunal finds that there has been a contravention, then it has a choice of what action to take. It may make:

1. an order declaring the rights of the claimant and the respondent in relation to the act complained of;
2. an order requiring the respondent to pay compensation to the claimant;
3. a recommendation that the respondent takes action, within a specified period of time, for the purpose of obviating the adverse effect on the complainant of any act of discrimination to which the complaint relates.[106]

According to the Code of Practice, provided that the employee has two or more years continuous employment at the date of termination, a dismissal that amounts to a breach of the Act will almost inevitably be an unfair dismissal as well. In such cases, a person can make a claim for unfair dismissal at the same time as a discrimination claim.[107] The Code provides the following example:

> An employee who has worked with his employer for five years provides a witness statement in support of a colleague who has raised a grievance about homophobic bullying at work. The employer rejects the grievance and a subsequent appeal. A few months later the employer needs to make redundancies. The employer selects the employee for redundancy because he is viewed as 'difficult' and not a 'team player' because of the support he gave to his colleague in the grievance. It is likely that the redundancy would amount to unlawful victimisation and also be an unfair dismissal.

In *Prestcold Ltd v Irvine*[108] it was held that actions (2) and (3) above were exclusive. The first should take care of losses of wages, whilst the second is concerned with taking steps other than payment of wages in order to obviate or reduce the adverse effects of discrimination. If the respondent fails, without reasonable justification, to comply with the recommendation, then the tribunal may increase the level of compensation.[109] It is important to note that there is no upper limit on compensation that can be awarded.

---

102 Section 123(1)(a) EA 2010. On acts extending over a period, see s. 123(3) EA 2010 and *Hendricks v Commissioner of Police for the Metropolis* [2003] IRLR 96.
103 Section 123(1)(b).
104 [2001] IRLR 69.
105 Delays in internal procedures do not necessarily justify delaying the presentation of the complaint to an employment tribunal: it is one factor that will be taken into account; see *Robinson v Post Office* [2000] IRLR 804.
106 Section 124(2) EA 2010.
107 Para. 10.16 Code of Practice.
108 [1980] IRLR 67.
109 Section 124(7) EA 2010.

In *Essa v Laing Ltd*[110] the Court of Appeal ruled that a victim of racial abuse was entitled to be compensated for the loss which arises naturally and directly from the wrong. It was not necessary for the particular type of loss to be reasonably foreseeable. Individuals can recover for both physical and psychiatric injury[111] and obtain aggravated damages.[112]

6.5.1 Contracts

A term of a contract is unenforceable if it promotes or provides for treatment that is prohibited by the Act.[113] According to the Code of Practice, this will not stop a person relying on the unenforceable term to get any benefit to which they are entitled.[114] Section 144(1) EA also provides that a term of a contract that tries to limit or exclude a provision of the Act is unenforceable. This does not prevent the parties coming to an agreement to settle a claim via a compromise agreement with the help of an ACAS official.[115]

An example of a clause that was unenforceable can be found in *Clyde v Winkelhof*.[116] This concerned a solicitor expelled from the firm for which she worked and who started formal proceedings claiming, amongst other matters, pregnancy and sex discrimination. The firm applied for an injunction in the High Court to stop her proceeding as she had not gone through an internal dispute resolution procedure as required by clause 41.1 of the firm's agreement. The clause provided that this arbitration was to be the final resolution of a dispute and there could only be appeals to courts on points of law. The High Court found that such a clause fell foul of s. 144(1) and was therefore unenforceable.

Section 145(1) also applies the same principle of unenforceability to terms in collective agreements that promote or provide for treatment prohibited by the Act.

6.6 Equality of terms

The Equal Pay Directive[117] built upon art. 119 EEC (now art. 157 TFEU) and established that the principle of equal pay meant:

> for the same work or for work to which equal value is attributed, the elimination of all discrimination on grounds of sex with regard to all aspects and conditions of remuneration.[118]

Pay is given a broad definition and actions which have been held to be discriminatory include when retired male employees receive travel concessions not available to female retirees;[119] when part-time employees do not receive pay during sickness when it is paid to full-time employees;[120] and when men and women receive different payments, including pensions, resulting from compulsory redundancies.[121]

---

110 [2004] IRLR 313.
111 See *Sheriff v Klyne Tugs* [1999] IRLR 481.
112 See *British Telecom plc v Reid* [2004] IRLR 327.
113 Section 142(1) EA 2010.
114 Para. 10.64 Code of Practice.
115 Section 144(4) EA 2010.
116 *Clyde & Co LLP v Bates Van Winkelhof* [2011] IRLR 467.
117 Council Directive 75/117/EEC of 19 February 1975 on the approximation of the laws of the Member States relating to the application of the principle of equal pay for men and women OJ [1975] L45/19.
118 Article 1 Directive 75/117/EEC.
119 Case 12/81 *Garland v British Rail Engineering Ltd* [1982] IRLR 111.
120 Case 171/88 *Rinner-Kühn v FWW Spezial-Gebaudereinigung GmbH* [1989] ECR 2743.
121 Case C-262/88 *Barber v Guardian Royal Exchange Assurance Group* [1990] ECR I-1889.

The Equal Pay Act was passed by Parliament in 1970, but there was a long introductory period before it came into effect in 1975. Although one cannot doubt that the legislation has had an impact on the relative pay of men and women, a significant pay gap of some 14 per cent still remains with respect to male and female full-time workers.[122] The Equal Pay Act has now been replaced by the Equality Act 2010. The Equality and Human Rights Commission have also produced a statutory Code of Practice on Equal Pay and this can be found on the Commission's website. As the Code explains,[123] it does not itself impose legal obligations but tribunals and courts considering an equal pay claim are obliged to take into account any part of the Code that appears relevant to the proceedings.

The provisions previously in the Equal Pay Act are now contained in Chapter 3 of the Equality Act. The principle of equality is established by s. 64(1)(a) which states that its equality of terms provisions apply 'where a person (A) is employed on work that is equal to the work that a comparator of the opposite sex (B) does'. Section 65(1) further provides that A's work is equal to B's work if it is:

- like B's work;
- rated as equivalent to B's work;
- of equal value to B's work.

There is also a sex equality clause implied into terms of employment where one does not already exist.[124] A sex equality clause, according to s. 66(2) has the following effect:

- if a term of A's contract is less favourable to A than a corresponding term of B's is to B, then A's term is modified so as not to be less favourable;
- if A does not have a term which corresponds to a term of B's that benefits B, A's terms are modified so as to include such a term.

So the need for equality applies to each individual term, not the contract as a whole, although the employer does have the opportunity to justify the difference by showing that there is a material factor defence (see below). Here is an example given in the Code of Practice:

> A female sales manager is entitled under her contract of employment to an annual bonus calculated by reference to a specified number of sales. She discovers that a male sales manager working for the same employer and in the same office receives a higher bonus under his contract for the same number of sales. She would bring her claim under the equality of terms (equal pay) provisions.

> However, if the female sales manager is not paid a discretionary Christmas bonus that the male manager is paid, she could bring a claim under the sex discrimination at work provisions rather than an equal pay claim because it is not about a contractual term.

Thus, if any term of the woman's contract, apart from the equality clause, is less favourable to the woman than the comparable man, it should be modified so as to be not less favourable. Similarly, if the woman's contract does not contain a term conferring a benefit on her that is contained in the comparable man's contract, then the woman's contract shall be deemed to include the term.[125] Equal pay must, therefore, be calculated not on the basis of the worth of the overall contract in comparison with the man's contract, but on the basis of each individual item taken in isolation.

---

122 See the Fawcett Society website: www.fawcettsociety.org.uk
123 Code of Practice on Equal Pay, Commission for Equality and Human Rights at para. 16.
124 Section 66(1) EA 2010.
125 Section 66(2)(b) EA 2010.

In Brunnhofer,[126] for example, two bank employees were employed on the same grade and on the same basic salary. The comparable man, however, was paid a higher supplement than Mrs Brunnhofer. This was subsequently justified on the grounds that the man carried out more important functions and was said to do work of a higher quality. The higher supplement, however, was paid from when they were recruited. It was not possible to justify the differences in pay by factors that became known only after the employees had taken up their employment and had been assessed.

In *Hartlepool Borough Council v Dolphin*[127] the EAT summarised the approach to be applied to equal pay claims:

(i) The complainant must produce a gender-based comparison showing that women doing like work, or work rated as equivalent, or work of equal value to men, are being paid or treated less favourably than men; this would produce a rebuttable claim of sex discrimination.

(ii) The employer must then show that the variation between the woman's contract and the man's contract is not tainted with sex, that is, that it is due to a material factor that is not the difference of sex. To do this the employer must show:

(a) That the explanation for the variation is genuine.
(b) That the more favourable treatment of the man is due to that reason.
(c) That the reason is not the difference of sex.

(iii) If the employer cannot show that the reason was not due to the difference of sex, he or she must show objective justification for the disparity between the woman's contract and the man's contract.

The result may not always seem fair. *Evesham v North Hertfordshire Health Authority*[128] was an appeal against the remedy awarded by an employment tribunal as a result of a long-running claim by speech therapists that their work was of equal value to that of a district clinical psychologist. The claimant was a district chief speech therapist with six years' experience in her post. The comparator was a newly appointed clinical psychologist in his first year and near the bottom of the pay scale. Ms Evesham argued that she should be placed at a point on the incremental scale that reflected her experience. The Court of Appeal held that to do this would be to entitle her to pay in excess of that received by the male comparator, with whom she had established equal value. The EA 2010 requires an identified comparator with whom the value of the applicant's work can be compared. It was a comparison between the work of individuals, rather than a comparison between what speech therapists do and what clinical psychologists do.[129]

6.6.1 The comparator

The comparator needs to be selected by the complainant[130] and be in the same employment as the claimant. Section 79 EA provides that the complainant must be employed:

● by the same or an associated employer at the same establishment or workplace, or
● by the same or an associated employer at a different establishment or workplace, provided that common terms and conditions apply either generally between employees or as between the woman and her comparator.

---

126 Case 381/99 *Brunnhofer v Bank der Österreichischen Postsparkasse AG* [2001] IRLR 571.
127 [2009] IRLR 169.
128 [2000] IRLR 257 CA.
129 The Court of Justice held, in Case 236/98 *Jämställdhetsombudsmannen v Örebro läns landsting* [2000] IRLR421, that the proper comparison between the two groups is the basic monthly pay, excluding supplements; no account is to be taken of different working hours, although these might constitute reasons unrelated to sex.
130 See *Ainsworth v Glass Tubes and Components Ltd* [1977] IRLR 74, where an employment tribunal was held to have erred by selecting the comparator they wished to use.

The claimant and the comparator must be 'employed', which means being employed under a contract of service, a contract of apprenticeship or a contract personally to execute any work or labour.[131]

The comparators need to be employed by the same employer as the claimant at the same establishment or other establishments in Great Britain which, including the one at which the claimant is employed, have common terms and conditions of employment generally or for particular relevant classes of employees.[132] This appears to be interpreted widely, so if there is a sufficient connection in a 'loose and non-technical sense' between the different employments, then this might be sufficient. *Dumfries and Galloway Council v North*[133] concerned a claim by classroom assistants and others employed at the council's schools under a set of terms and conditions deriving from a collective agreement known as the 'blue book' agreement. They sought to compare themselves with male manual workers such as road workers and refuse workers, who were employed in various depots and governed by a separate collective agreement contained in the 'green book'. The question was whether the claimants and their comparators were employed in the 'same employment' as required by s. 1(6) EPA 1970. The EAT stated that where a woman seeks to use a male comparator who is not employed at her establishment, she has to show a real possibility that he would be employed there in the job he carries out at the other establishment, or in a broadly similar job. Having the same or associated employers does not mean necessarily that they are in the same employment. The purpose of s. 1(6) was to allow a woman to compare herself with a man in another of her employer's establishments, but only where there are factors which show a commonality or uniformity of employment regime between them. If there is no possibility of a person being employed to perform the comparator's job at the complainant's establishment, then this would suggest that there is no commonality of regime; thus here it would be wrong to conclude that the claimant and the comparator were in the same establishment.

The claimant cannot just choose an artificial or arbitrary group, although, in principle, the comparison should be between the advantaged and the disadvantaged group. In *Somerset County Council v Pike*,[134] for example, a retired teacher who came back to work part-time found that the part-time work was not pensionable. The question was who the correct comparator should be. The employment tribunal said that it should be the entire teaching profession, and therefore the statistical evidence did not show disparate impact. The EAT said the pool should not consist of people who have no interest in the advantage or disadvantage in question; it should consist of retired teachers who had returned to work and then disparate impact could be shown.

Where there is no actual comparator doing equal work, the sex equality clause cannot apply. In such a case the woman may be able to claim sex discrimination if there is evidence of this in relation to contractual pay. The Code of Practice gives the following example:

> A woman's employer tells her that she would be paid more if she were a man. There are no men employed on equal work so she cannot claim equal pay using a comparator. However, she could claim direct sex discrimination as the less favourable treatment she has received is clearly based on her sex.

6.6.2 Like work

A woman is to be regarded as employed on like work with a man if her work is the same or 'broadly similar' to his.[135] It may not be enough that the two groups being compared appear to do identical work. Section 65(3) EA 2010 provides that, when comparing one person's work with another, it is necessary to have regard to the frequency with which differences between their work occur in

---

131 Section 1(6)(a) EPA 1970.
132 Section 1(6)(c) EPA 1970, added by the SDA 1975.
133 [2009] IRLR 915.
134 [2009] IRLR 870.
135 Section 65(2) EA 2010.

practice and the 'nature and extent of the differences'. In a case that considered a health authority that employed both graduate psychologists and medical doctors as psychotherapists, the Court of Justice held that a difference could be identified between the two groups even though they carried out similar functions. In treating their patients, both groups drew upon their training and experience. The doctors had a very different training and experience. That, combined with the ability to employ doctors on a greater range of duties, was sufficient to justify a difference in treatment in their remuneration.[136] The level of responsibility, together with the severity of the consequences of one's actions, may be a factor that distinguishes two jobs where the work may otherwise be identical. In *Eaton v Nuttall*,[137] for example, although the complainant and the male comparator were employed on like work, the consequences of an error by the male comparator were much more serious than the consequences of an error by the female complainant.[138]

Thus there is likely to be a two-stage process in deciding such an equal pay claim:

(i)   First, the question is whether the woman and her male comparator are employed in work that is the same or of a broadly similar nature.

(ii) If the woman shows that the work is broadly similar, the second question is whether any differences between her work and that done by her comparator are of practical importance having regard to:

- the frequency with which any differences occur in practice, and
- the nature and extent of those differences.[139]

Without this approach a tribunal may fail to recognise that, although a woman and a man may be doing work of a broadly similar nature, they may not actually be employed on like work.[140] All the duties done by a complainant and a comparator need to be examined and it is unlikely that some duties could be ignored even if they take only a little time.[141] The Code of Practice on Equal Pay[142] gives a good example of where these differences matter:

> A woman working as a primary school administrator claimed equal pay with a male secondary school administrator. The courts found they were not doing like work. Although the work was broadly similar, the latter role carried greater financial and managerial responsibilities and was in a much larger school. The primary school administrator had more routine, term-time tasks while the secondary school administrator's work was year round and more strategic. These differences were considered to be of practical importance so the equal pay for like work claim failed.[143]

6.6.3 Work rated as equivalent

Section 65(4) EA provides that A's work is rated as equivalent to B's work if a job evaluation study

- gives an equal value to A's job and B's job in terms of the demands made on the worker; or
- would give an equal value to A's job and B's job in those terms were the evaluation not made on a sex-specific system.

---

136 Case C-309/97 *Angestelltenbetriebsrat der Wiener Gebietskrankenkasse v Wiener Gebietskrankenkasse* [1999] IRLR 804.
137 [1977] IRLR 71.
138 See also *De Brito v Standard Chartered Bank* [1978] ICR 650 that also compared a trainee with more experienced employees.
139 See para. 35 Code of Practice on Equal Pay.
140 *Waddington v Leicester Council for Voluntary Service* [1977] IRLR 32.
141 In *Dance v Dorothy Perkins Ltd* [1978] ICR 760 the EAT held that, where a comparator was chosen as representative of a wider group, then it was important to examine the duties in the context that they were representative.
142 Para. 37.
143 This example was taken from *Morgan v Middlesbrough Borough Council* [2005] EWCA Civ 1432.

Section 65(5) then explains that a 'sex-specific system' is one that sets different values for men and women. The Code of Practice on Equal Pay gives an example[144] of this:

> A job evaluation study rated the jobs of female classroom teaching assistants and their better paid male physical education instructors as not equivalent. This was because the study had given more points to the physical effort involved in the men's jobs than it had to the intellectual and caring work involved in the jobs predominantly done by women. Because it uses a sex-biased points system, this job evaluation would not prevent the women succeeding in an equal pay claim.

The Code then helpfully explains[145] that a job evaluation system is 'a way of systematically assessing the relative value of different jobs'. Thus a woman is to be regarded as employed on work rated as equivalent with that of a man only if her job has been given an equal value with his job in a job evaluation study undertaken with a view to evaluating the jobs in an undertaking or group of undertakings.

Alternatively, it would have been given an equivalent rating if the evaluation system was not flawed by having a system that gives different values for men and women under the same heading. The factors used in the assessment of any job under a job evaluation system need to be objective. The criteria used should be common to both men and women, but must also not be such as to discriminate against women. This does not necessarily mean that criteria involving physical strength, viewed as a male characteristic, should be excluded. If a job is seen objectively as requiring a certain amount of strength, then this may be included as a criterion. It is important, however, to view the overall picture to ensure that any particular attributes, conventionally seen as female, needed for the job are also taken into account. Not to do this and leave, as part of the criteria, a factor associated with one sex might open the door to a discrimination claim.[146]

There is a problem when jobs are just slotted in against benchmark jobs and given a consequent grading. It might be possible to claim that such jobs have not properly been considered against the various criteria. The onus is upon the employer to show that there had been a job evaluation study that satisfied the requirements of s. 65(4) EA.[147]

In O'Brien v Sim-Chem Ltd[148] the three appellants complained that a job evaluation study had given their jobs an equal rating with that of their male counterparts. Apparently, because of a government incomes policy the employer did not apply the new job grade or salary range to the individuals in question. Although a job evaluation study required the co-operation of both employees and an employer, the consequences of a study were that, where jobs were found to be rated as equivalent, there should be a comparison of the respective terms and conditions. The job evaluation system does not, in itself, determine any terms of the women's contract. This is done in the subsequent comparison. Even where the results of the job evaluation study are not entirely accepted by the parties to the study, the existence of a prima facie valid job evaluation study would be enough for an employment tribunal to be bound by s. 1(5).[149]

6.6.4 Work of equal value

Section 65(6) EA states that A's work is equivalent to B's work if it is:

- neither like B's work nor rated as equivalent to B's work, but
- nevertheless equal to B's work in terms of the demands made on A by reference to factors such as effort, skill and decision making.

---

144 Para. 43.
145 Para. 39.
146 See Case 237/85 Rummler v Dato Druck GmbH [1987] IRLR 32.
147 See Bromley v H & J Quick Ltd [1988] IRLR 249.
148 [1980] IRLR 373.
149 See Green v Broxtowe District Council [1977] ICR 241.

This category applies if a woman is employed on work which, not being work falling into the categories of like work or work rated as equivalent, is nevertheless, in terms of the demands made on her, of equal value to that of a man in the same employment.

Where an issue arises in the proceedings as to whether one person's work is of equal value to another's, then the tribunal may ask for a report by an independent expert.[150]

6.6.5 Defence of material factor

Paragraph 74 of the Code of Practice states that there are three possible defences to an equal pay claim. These are:

1. the woman and her comparator are not doing equal work;
2. the chosen comparator is not one allowed by law (for example, he is not in the same employment);
3. the difference in pay is genuinely due to a material factor, which is not related to the sex of the jobholders.

Section 69 Equality Act provides a 'material factor' defence to an equal pay claim. This defence will assist an employer if they are able to show that the difference in pay is genuinely due to a material factor which is not the difference of sex.[151]

Glasgow City Council v Marshall[152] concerned an equal pay claim between instructors and teachers in certain specialist schools. A number of female instructors claimed that they were employed on like work with male teachers and a male instructor claimed that he was employed on like work with a female teacher. After a long hearing, over some 52 days, the instructors won their case at an employment tribunal. The employers appealed against the tribunal's decision on their defence under s. 1(3) EPA 1970. Their case was based upon the fact that the sets of employees had their terms and agreements settled by different collective bargaining structures. The employers also, with the help of statistics, sought to show an absence of sex discrimination. This latter argument was not appealed against. It was this presumed lack of sex discrimination that undermined the instructors' case, however. The House of Lords held that to exclude matters of sex discrimination would mean that the legislation was concerned with one employee being paid less than another, rather than with arguments about whether a female employee was paid less than a male comparator.

The burden of proof, according to the court, then passes to the employer who needs to show that the reason for the differences is not tainted with sex. In order to satisfy the employment tribunal the employer must show that:

1. The explanation or reason offered is genuine, and not a sham or pretence.
2. The less favourable treatment is due to this reason – that is, it is a material factor.
3. The reason for the difference is not the difference of sex. In order to do this, the employer will need to show that there is an absence of direct or indirect sex discrimination.
4. Finally, the employer will need to show that the factor relied upon is a 'material difference' – that is, a significant and relevant difference between the woman's case and the man's case.[153] If there is evidence of sex discrimination, the employer will need to show that the difference in

---

150 Section 131(2) EA 2010.
151 See *Ministry of Defence v Armstrong* [2004] IRLR 672.
152 [2000] IRLR 272.
153 See *McGregor v GMBATU* [1987] ICR 505 which considered that the work of the applicant was of equal value to the comparator, but that the comparator's long experience and exceptional knowledge was a material factor which justified the difference in pay.

pay can be objectively justified. If, however, as in this case, the employer shows an absence of sex discrimination, then the employer will not be required to justify the pay disparity.[154]

An example given in the Code of Practice[155] is:

> If an employer argues that it was necessary to pay the comparator more because of a skill shortage, they will have to provide evidence of actual difficulties in recruiting and retaining people to do the job being done by the higher-paid man. The employer will also need to monitor the discrepancy to ensure it is still justified.

A material factor is said to be a 'significant and relevant' factor which is 'material' in a causative sense, when considering a pay difference.[156] Thus an employer can establish a defence by identifying the factors causally relevant to the pay disparity and showing that they are free of sex discrimination. One result of this was the somewhat surprising decision of the Court of Justice in *Cadman*[157] where the Court held that where there was a disparity of pay between men and women as a result of using length of service as a criterion, then the employer did not need to establish specifically that using this criterion was appropriate in order to achieve a legitimate objective. The Court did add that where a worker can show evidence that casts serious doubt as to whether recourse to the criterion of length of service was appropriate in the circumstances, then the employer may have to justify in detail how length of service leads to experience which enables the worker to perform his duties better. The problem, of course, is that generally women are often unable to achieve the same length of service as men, because it is women who are more likely to have career breaks as a result of caring responsibilities.

In *Strathclyde Regional Council v Wallace*[158] a group of nine female teachers claimed to be doing like work with higher-paid principal teachers. They were part of a group which consisted of 134 teachers, comprising 81 men and 53 women. The difference in sex was not a factor that could be relied upon. The material factor was, amongst other matters, the financial constraints that the education authority found itself under. There is nothing, according to the court, in s. 1(3) that requires the employer to justify the factors causing the disparity by showing that there was no other way in which they could have taken action to avoid the difference.

Nevertheless, if a sexually discriminatory practice is the cause of the disparity, the employer may still be able to rely on objective justification. In *Seymour-Smith*,[159] the effect of the, then, two-year continuous service qualification before a claim for unfair dismissal could be made was held to have had a disparate effect on women and amounted to indirect discrimination for the purposes of art. 141 EC (157). It could, nevertheless, be objectively justified as a legitimate method of encouraging employers to recruit.[160] It will not be enough for the employer to show that they had no intention of discriminating against a woman on the grounds of her sex. Thus an employer who mistakenly placed a male employee at a point on a salary scale higher than that to which they were entitled could not use this mistake as evidence of a material factor when a female employee made a claim for equal pay.[161]

---

154 See *Nelson v Carillion Services Ltd* [2003] IRLR 428 and *Parliamentary Commissioner for Administration v Fernandez* [2004] IRLR 22.

155 Para. 76.

156 See *Rainey v Greater Glasgow Health Board* [1987] IRLR 26 HL.

157 Case C-17/05 *Cadman v Health and Safety Executive* [2006] IRLR 969.

158 [1998] IRLR 146 HL.

159 *R v Secretary of State for Employment, ex parte Seymour-Smith and Perez (No 2)* [2000] IRLR 263.

160 See also Case 170/84 *Bilka-Kaufhaus v Weber von Harz* [1986] IRLR 317 where excluding part-timers from membership of a pension scheme was held to be justifiable on the grounds that the employer wished to discourage part-time recruitment; this decision would now have to take into account Directive 97/81/EC on part-time work. In Case 96/80 *Jenkins v Kingsgate (Clothing Production) Ltd* [1981] IRLR 228, the Court of Justice also stated that the differences between the pay of part-timers and full-timers was only contrary to art. 119 if it also amounted to indirect sex discrimination.

161 *McPherson v Rathgael Centre for Children and Young People* [1991] IRLR 206; it was suggested, *obiter*, that the employment tribunal might have considered whether the applicant was able to select an anomalous employee, rather than four other male employees who were on the same salary as her.

6.6.6 Enforcing equal pay

6.6.6.1 Gender pay gap reporting

New Regulations[162] came into effect in April 2017 requiring employers with 250 or more employees to publish information about pay between men and women in their organisations. Employees in this case means those employees with a contract of service, workers and agency with a contract to do work or provide services and some self-employed people who have to personally perform the work.[163] Employers are required to publish six sets of figures. These are outlined in regulation 2 as:

(a) the difference between the mean hourly rate of pay of male full-pay relevant employees and that of female full-pay relevant employees (see regulation 8);

(b) the difference between the median hourly rate of pay of male full-pay relevant employees and that of female full-pay relevant employees (see regulation 9);

(c) the difference between the mean bonus pay paid to male relevant employees and that paid to female relevant employees (see regulation 10);

(d) the difference between the median bonus pay paid to male relevant employees and that paid to female relevant employees (see regulation 11);

(e) the proportions of male and female relevant employees who were paid bonus pay (see regulation 12); and

(f) the proportions of male and female full-pay relevant employees in the lower, lower middle, upper middle and upper quartile pay bands (see regulation 13).

Regulation 3 provides that ordinary pay includes basic pay; allowances; pay for piecework; pay for leave; and shift premium pay; and regulation 4 defines bonus pay as any remuneration that is in the form of money, vouchers, securities, securities options, or interests in securities; and that which relates to profit sharing, productivity, performance, incentive or commission.

The information must be published on the employer's website and a government website and must be accompanied by a signature authorising the correctness of the information. The whole exercise is obviously aimed at encouraging employers to take the necessary action to correct any imbalances in pay.

6.6.6.2 Enforcement

Any claim, including a claim for arrears of remuneration and damages, relating to equal pay may be made to an employment tribunal.[164] Compensation for non-economic loss is not recoverable in an equal pay claim, unlike claims under the Sex Discrimination Act. Thus there can be no damages for injury to feelings under the Equal Pay Act.[165] An employer may also apply to an employment tribunal, where there is a dispute about the effects of the equality clause in s. 132 EA 2010, for a declaration as to the rights of the employer and employees.[166] Section 129 EA provides that claims must be lodged before a qualifying date. This is normally six months after the last day on which the claimant was employed. Where the proceedings relate to a period during which a stable employment relationship subsists, the qualifying date is six months after the day on which that relationship ended.

Section 139 EA provides for a questionnaire procedure into equal pay claims. The questions and replies can be admitted as evidence in any subsequent employment tribunal proceedings. If the

---

162 The Equality Act 2010 (Gender Pay Gap Information) Regulations 2017, SI 2017/172.
163 See Managing Gender Pay Gap Reporting, ACAS March 2017.
164 See Part 9 Chapter 4 EA 2010.
165 *Council of the City of Newcastle upon Tyne v Allan* [2005] IRLR 504.
166 Section 2(1A) EPA 1970.

employment tribunal considers that the respondent deliberately, or without reasonable excuse, failed to reply to the questions in the time limit, then it can draw any inference that it thinks just and equitable.

Further reading

Fredman, S. *Discrimination Law*, 2nd edn (Oxford University Press, 2011).
Hepple, B. *Equality: The New Legal Framework* (Hart Publishing, 2011).
Sargeant, M. *Discrimination and the Law* (Taylor & Francis, 2017).
www.gov.uk/government/policies/equality – Government Equalities Office.
www.equalityhumanrights.com/en – Equality and Human Rights Commission.

Chapter 7

Equality: the protected characteristics

Chapter Contents

7.1 Employment Tribunal claims

It is interesting to look at the relative numbers of claims for the different protected characteristics (Table 7.1). The figures, of course, do not reflect the relative levels of discrimination that take place in the workplace and the absolute numbers have been affected by the government decision to introduce tribunal fees for those making claims, now ruled unlawful after the UNISON case.[1]

Sex discrimination continues to have the highest levels of complaint and it is interesting that this is so, given that we have had legislation making it unlawful at work since 1975.

The six grounds of discrimination that existed prior to the Equality Act 2010 have now been expanded to nine protected characteristics (see section 6.4.1 in Chapter 6).

7.2 Age

People of all ages can suffer from age discrimination, but it appears to manifest itself mostly in discrimination against older people and young people. Article 1 of the Equal Treatment in Employment and Occupation Directive provides that the Directive's purpose is to lay down a general framework for combating discrimination in relation to a number of grounds including that of age.

Article 4 provides for the possibility that a difference of treatment may be justified where there is 'a genuine and determining occupational requirement, provided that the objective is legitimate and the requirement is proportionate'. Article 6 refers to the justification of differences of treatment on the grounds of age. Differences in treatment on the basis of age may be justified if 'they are objectively and reasonably justified by a legitimate aim including legitimate employment policy, labour market and vocational treatment'. Examples given of such differences are:

● The setting of special conditions for access to employment and training, including dismissal and remuneration for young people, older workers and persons with caring responsibilities in order to promote their integration into the workforce.
● The fixing of minimum conditions of age, professional experience or seniority for access to employment or certain advantages linked to employment.
● The fixing of a maximum age for recruitment which is based either on the training needs of a post, or the need for a reasonable period before retirement.

TABLE 7.1 Employment tribunal receipts by subject matter

Discrimination	2013/14	2014/15	2015/16
Age	1,994	1,087	12,635[1]
Disability	5,196	3,106	3,468
Race	3,064	1,858	2,001
Religion or belief	584	339	340
Sex	13,722	4,471	5,371
Sexual orientation	361	189	188

Source: Figures taken from the website of the Ministry of Justice Tribunal Statistics, March 2017.

1 The spike in age discrimination claims seems to have resulted from a large number of multiple discrimination claims in which age was included.

---

1 R (*on the application of* UNISON) v *Lord Chancellor* [2017] UKSC 51.

It is interesting that it was felt necessary to spell out these exceptions to age discrimination in the Directive. It is perhaps symptomatic of the way that age discrimination is treated differently from other forms of discrimination. These provisions effectively state that some age discrimination is benign. There appears to be an economic or business imperative that suggests that more harm will be done if discrimination does not take place, rather than an imperative that states that age discrimination is wrong and can only be justified in exceptional circumstances. Effectively, discrimination is not to be allowed to continue except those forms which are held to be for the economic good of business.

The Directive was due to be transposed into national law by December 2003, but there was a provision, in art. 18, for Member States to have an additional period of three years. The United Kingdom took advantage of this flexibility and finally transposed the Directive in October 2006 by adopting the Employment Equality (Age) Regulations 2006.[2] These Regulations were subsequently substantially incorporated into the Equality Act 2010.

7.2.1 The ageing population

The population of the United Kingdom is ageing. The percentage of the population aged 65 and over increased from 14.1 per cent in 1975 to 17.8 per cent in 2015. Over the same period the percentage of the population aged under 16 decreased from 24.9 to 17.7 per cent. This trend is likely to continue and, by 2045, some 24.6 per cent of the population will be aged 65 and over compared with just 17.7 per cent aged 15 or younger. A consequence of this is the reducing number of people able to support an increasing older population. In 2016, for example, there were about 308 people of pensionable age for every 1,000 people of working age. By 2037 this is projected to increase to 365 people.[3]

The relevance of these statistics here is that whilst the population is ageing, the proportion of older workers is also increasing. The numbers in employment for those aged between 50 and 64 years have increased from 62 per cent in 2001 to 70.8 per cent in 2017. The figure for those over 65 years who have continued to work increased during the same period from 4.9 to 10.5 per cent. Older workers are, however, much more likely to be self-employed and/or working part-time compared with other groups. In 2012, for example, some 13 per cent of those aged 25 to 49 were self-employed, compared with a figure of 19 per cent for those aged between 50 and 64, and 37 per cent for those aged 65 and over. The figures for part-time work are 22 per cent for 25 to 49 year olds, 29 per cent for those aged 50 to 64, and 67 per cent for those aged 65+. Thus, although the trend is for larger numbers of older people to stay in the workforce, they are less likely to be in full-time employment than younger age groups.[4]

The government consultation document on its Code of Practice on Age Diversity in Employment[5] concluded that 'it is clear that age discrimination against older workers does exist'. It is interesting to speculate at what age a person becomes an older worker. One study, albeit quite an old one now, asked this question of organisations.[6] Five companies put 40 years as the starting point, four suggested 45 and five said 50 years. One company stated that anyone over 30 years was in the category of older worker. Further information suggested that these generalisations were qualified by consideration of occupation and gender. Forty-something was not necessarily old for a management position, but might be for another occupation. Similarly, women seemed to become 'older' at an earlier age. One respondent suggested that when women returned to work after children in their mid-thirties that they might be classified as an older worker.

---

2 SI 2006/1031.

3 *Overview of the UK population*: Office for National Statistics, March 2017

4 Information taken from *Older Workers Statistical Information Booklet* (Office for National Statistics, 2012).

5 First published in 1999 and subsequently updated.

6 Hilary Metcalf and Mark Thompson, *Older Workers: Employers' Attitudes and Practices* Report No 194 (Institute of Manpower Studies, 1990).

7.2.2 The Equality Act 2010

The EA 2010, as with the other protected characteristics, makes direct discrimination, indirect discrimination, harassment and victimisation on the characteristic of age unlawful (see Chapter 6). The Act substantially superseded the Equal Treatment in Employment (Age) Regulations 2006. The main exception was in relation to Sch. 6 of the Regulations which had provided for a procedure whereby workers could be given notice of retirement and could then request the right to continue working. The decision was left entirely to the employer, who was not required to give any reason for their decision. This procedure had been necessary because the government in 2006 had introduced a default retirement age. This was usually age 65 years and meant that the employer could retire employees against their will. The default retirement age was abolished in 2011, thus rendering the process contained in Sch. 6 redundant. Schedule 5 Equality Act provides that a reference to a person who has, or shares, a particular protected characteristic is a reference to a person of a particular age group or persons of the same age group. So those affected can be individuals or groups of people of the same or similar age or who are part of an age range.

The most striking feature about the Equality Act in relation to age is the number of exceptions to the general principle of non-discrimination that exist. As with the other protected characteristics, protection is offered against direct and indirect discrimination, harassment and victimisation. The difference is that, unlike other forms of discrimination,[7] it is permissible to directly discriminate on the grounds of age in some circumstances. There is a requirement to show that the less favourable treatment is a 'proportionate means of achieving a legitimate aim'. All three of these exceptions are, of course, debatable, but they do effectively permit direct discrimination on the grounds of age in the interests of both diversity and, perhaps, acceptability.

Two important cases at the Supreme Court tested the boundaries of direct and indirect discrimination based on age. In *Seldon*,[8] the claimant was a senior partner in a law firm where the partnership deed contained a mandatory retirement clause at the age of 65 years. Mr Seldon did not wish to retire and claimed that his compulsory retirement amounted to direct age discrimination.

After a review of the case law at the Court of Justice of the EU, the Supreme Court concluded that two kinds of legitimate aims had been identified. These were *inter-generational fairness* and *dignity*. The first of these, which was stated as being 'comparatively uncontroversial', meant various things depending upon the particular circumstances of the employment, and could include facilitating access to employment for young people, but it could also mean enabling older people to remain in the workforce. It can also mean sharing limited opportunities to work in a particular profession fairly between the generations. The second general type of legitimate aim identified was dignity. It is concerned with avoiding the need to go through lengthy disciplinary and competence procedures when some older workers decline in performance and capacity. Retirement is seen as a way for older workers to exit the workforce with dignity rather than being dismissed for other reasons. Thus, in this case, retirement was seen as a proportionate means of achieving these legitimate aims.

Homer[9] was a case about indirect age discrimination. This case concerned a retired police officer who subsequently obtained a position as a legal adviser with the Police National Legal Database (PNLD). In 2005 the PNLD introduced a new grading structure with three 'thresholds' above the starting grade. In order to reach the third threshold it was necessary to have a law degree or 'similar fully completed'. In 2006, Mr Homer was regraded to the first and second thresholds, but not to the third as he did not have a law degree, although he met the criteria in all other respects. The issue was that the earliest he could have graduated would have been the summer of 2010, after his planned retirement date. The court held that such 'a requirement which works to the comparative

---

7 Except in relation to genuine occupational qualification.
8 *Seldon v Clarkson, Wright and Jakes* [2012] IRLR 590.
9 *Homer v Chief Constable of West Yorkshire Police* [2012] IRLR 601.

disadvantage of a person approaching compulsory retirement age is indirectly discriminatory on grounds of age'.

Schedule 9 Part 1 Equality Act also contains an exception, as do other grounds of discrimination, for an occupational requirement. The government has stated that it was likely to be construed narrowly and in one consultation gave the example of the acting profession. Part 2 of Schedule 9 is devoted to exceptions relating to age. These are in addition to that in respect of direct discrimination and these exceptions are considered below.

7.2.2.1 Benefits based on length of service

Service-related pay and benefits may include salary scales, holiday entitlement, company cars, etc., all or some of which may be related to length of service. Without some action, benefits linked to length of service may amount to age discrimination as younger people who have not served the necessary time required may suffer detriment. Paragraph 10(1) of Schedule 9 provides that:

> It is not an age contravention for a person (A) to put a person (B) at a disadvantage when compared with another (C), in relation to the provision of a benefit, facility or service in so far as the disadvantage is because B has a shorter period of service than C.

Thus an employer may award benefits using length of service as the criterion for selecting who should benefit from the award. First, there is no need to justify any differences related to service of less than five years. Where it exceeds five years it needs to fulfil a business need of the undertaking.[10] What makes this exception even wider is the fact that the length of service can be the entire length of time (less absences) that an employee has worked for an employer or it can be the length of time worked at a particular level. Thus if a person were promoted to a new grade at regular intervals this period of five years could be considerably extended.[11]

The argument is that having pay scales of a certain length is justified to recognise experience and, perhaps, seniority. It can also be argued strongly that workers who have been with an employer for five years should receive some preferential treatment compared with those who have just joined an organisation. These are, however, exceptions to a rule requiring the principle of equal treatment. It has been an important issue in relation to redundancy payments and there have been a number of cases concerning whether relating redundancy payments to length of service amounts to discrimination in favour of older workers at the expense of younger ones.

1. *Rolls Royce v Unite the Union*[12] considered two collective agreements which had an agreed matrix to be used to choose who should be selected for redundancy. There were five criteria against which an individual could score between 4 and 24 points. In addition there was a length-of-service criterion which awarded 1 point for each year of continuous service. Thus older employees would have an important advantage over younger ones. It was, unusually, the employer who claimed that the age elements amounted to age discrimination and the union which, successfully, resisted this claim.
2. *MacCulloch v ICI plc*[13] concerned a redundancy scheme which had been in existence since 1971. The amount of payment was linked to service up to a maximum of ten years, and the size of the redundancy payment increased with age. The claimant was 37 years old and received 55 per cent of her salary as a payment, but she claimed that someone aged between 50 and 57 years would have received 175 per cent of salary under the scheme.

---

10 Schedule 9 para. 10(2) EA 2010.
11 Schedule 9 para. 10(3) EA 2010.
12 [2009] IRLR 576.
13 [2008] IRLR 846.

3. *Loxley v BAE Systems*[14] had a contractual redundancy scheme in which each employee received two weeks' pay for the first five years of employment, three weeks' pay for each of the next five years and four weeks' pay for each year after ten years. There was also a further age-related payment of two weeks' pay for each year after the age of 40 years. All this was subject to a maximum of two years' pay. The scheme was amended for older workers approaching retirement when the retirement age was raised, but essentially the claimant, who was 61 years of age, was not entitled to any enhanced payments for voluntary redundancy as he had an entitlement to a pension. Indeed, the EAT stated that preventing such a windfall could be a legitimate aim.

7.2.2.2 National minimum wage

There is also a general exemption concerning the national minimum wage so that employers can pay the lower rate for those under 21 and under 18 years without it amounting to age discrimination.[15] It is, of course, age discrimination against the younger person, but he or she will be prevented from claiming this. The intention is to help younger workers to find jobs, by making them more attractive to employers. One question is whether such a measure is a proportionate response to the problem. In *Mangold v Helm*[16] the Court of Justice considered a German law which restricted the use of fixed-term contracts, but did not apply these restrictions to those aged 52 years and over. The Court accepted that the purpose of this legislation was to help promote the vocational integration of unemployed older workers and that this was a 'legitimate public-interest objective'. It is not only the objective that needs to be legitimate, but the means used to achieve the objective need to be 'appropriate and necessary'. The problem with the German law was that it applied to all workers of 52 years and above, whether unemployed or not. The result was that a significant body of workers was permanently excluded from 'the benefit of stable employment' available to other workers. The Court then stated:

> In so far as such legislation takes the age of the worker concerned as the only criterion [for the application of a fixed-term contract of employment], when it has not been shown that fixing an age threshold, as such, regardless of any other consideration linked to the structure of the labour market in question or the personal situation of the person concerned, is objectively necessary to the attainment of the objective [which is the vocational integration of older workers], it must be considered to go beyond what is appropriate and necessary in order to attain the objective pursued.

There must be a question about whether the application of a universal lower minimum wage for younger people is an appropriate and necessary response to the problem of youth unemployment.

7.2.2.3 Redundancy payments

One of the difficult issues for the Age Regulations was the question of what to do about the age-related aspects of redundancy payments (see Chapter 10). The government had proposed removing these and paying a uniform rate per year for all. Presumably, when faced with the prospect of levelling upwards, so that no group would be worse off, the government decided that the age-related aspects could be objectively justifiable. The lower and upper age limits to entitlement were therefore removed and employers are allowed to enhance payments.[17]

---

14 *Loxley v BAE Systems (Munitions and Ordnance) Ltd* [2008] IRLR 853.
15 Schedule 9 para. 11 EA 2010.
16 Case C-144/04 [2006] IRLR 143.
17 Schedule 9 para. 13 EA 2010.

7.2.2.4 Retirement

The Framework Directive does not say a great deal about retirement ages. Paragraph 14 of the Preamble states that the Directive shall be 'without prejudice to national provisions laying down retirement ages'. Article 6.2 allows for the fixing of ages for invalidity and retirement schemes, and the use of ages for actuarial calculations, without it constituting age discrimination. Article 8.2 provides that any measures implementing the Directive shall not lessen the protection against discrimination that already exists in the Member State.

The United Kingdom, in implementing the Directive, adopted a default retirement age of 65 years. Retirement below the age of 65 years needed to be objectively justified and presumably this will be entirely possible and proper in some cases. Section 98 of the Employment Rights Act 1996 was amended to add another fair reason for dismissal which was the 'retirement of the employee'. As a result it was possible to compulsorily retire workers at the age of 65 years without the employer risking actions for unfair dismissal or for age discrimination. This provision was challenged by the age NGO, Age Concern,[18] in the High Court.[19] Aspects of the case were referred to the Court of Justice,[20] but the challenge was unsuccessful. In the event the government, in 2011, abolished the default retirement age,[21] so that any compulsory retirement that now takes place would need to be justified by the employer as having a legitimate aim and that the means of achieving that aim (i.e. retirement) were appropriate and necessary. It is believed that this would only be possible in exceptional circumstances.[22]

7.2.2.5 Child care, life assurance and personal pensions

Paragraphs 14–16 of Schedule 9 provide for a limited number of further exceptions relating to age. Paragraph 14 permits an employer to treat employees differently in relation to life assurance if they are under or over the age of 65 years or the state retirement age, whichever is greater. Paragraph 15 protects employers from any age claims if they provide assistance with child care for a certain age of children (below the age of 17 years) and para. 16 allows the use of age as a factor in relation to contributions to personal pension schemes.

7.3 Disability

The Framework Directive on Equal Treatment in Employment and Occupation included proposals to combat discrimination on the grounds of disability 'with a view to putting into effect in the Member States the principle of equal treatment'.[23] In particular it provided[24] that employers should have a duty of 'reasonable accommodation'. This means that employers are obliged to take steps, when needed, to ensure that a person with a disability could have access to, participate in, have advancement in employment and undergo training. The only possible exception to this duty, according to the Directive, is if this places a 'disproportionate burden' on the employer. Thus the Directive permits, in certain circumstances, positive discrimination in favour of the disabled employee or applicant.

The Disability Discrimination Act (DDA) 1995 was the first measure to outlaw discrimination against disabled people in the United Kingdom and included an obligation upon the employer to

---

18 Now Age UK.
19 R (on the application of Age UK) v Secretary of State for Business, Innovation and Skills [2009] IRLR 1017.
20 Case C-388/07 R (on the application of the Incorporated Trustees of the National Council on Ageing) v Secretary of State for Business, Enterprise and Regulatory Reform [2009] IRLR 373.
21 The Employment Equality (Repeal of Retirement Age Provisions) Regulations 2011, SI 2011/1069.
22 See Seldon v Clarkson, Wright and Jakes [2012] IRLR 590.
23 Council Directive 2000/78/EC OJ L303/16.
24 Article 5.

make reasonable adjustments (see below).[25] The Act, which preceded the Framework Directive, gave disabled people rights in employment and other areas. The Act provided originally for a National Disability Council,[26] whose task was to advise the government 'on matters relevant to the elimination of discrimination against disabled persons and persons who have a disability'. One of the criticisms of the Act was that this was an advisory body, which did not have the powers of investigation and enforcement held then by the Equal Opportunities Commission and the Commission for Racial Equality. The position was changed with the Disability Rights Commission Act (DRCA) 1999, which abolished the National Disability Council and replaced it with a Disability Rights Commission.[27] The Disability Rights Commission itself has now been absorbed into the Equality and Human Rights Commission, which was established by the Equality Act 2006.

The need for action is illustrated by the fact that although disabled people are now more likely to be employed than they were in the past, they remain significantly less likely to be in employment than non-disabled people. In mid-2016, 49 per cent of disabled people aged 16–64 were in employment compared with 81 per cent of working-age non-disabled people. There is therefore a 32 percentage point gap between disabled and non-disabled people, representing over 2 million people. The disability employment gap has increased from 30 percent in 2010, although it has closed marginally in more recent times.[28]

Research for the Equality and Human Rights Commission found that on all key employment measures examined, disabled people were at a disadvantage compared with non-disabled people. They are less likely to be economically active, and those who are economically active are more likely to be unemployed and unemployed for longer. Disabled people in work are more likely to work in part-time, lower-skilled and lower-paid jobs.[29] Employment rates do, however, vary with the type of disability. Some types, such as those concerned with diabetes, skin conditions and hearing problems, are associated with relatively high employment rates. Other types, such as those associated with mental illness and learning disabilities, have much lower employment rates.

7.3.1 The Equality Act 2010

The EA 2010, as with the other protected characteristics, makes direct discrimination, indirect discrimination, harassment and victimisation on the characteristic of disability unlawful (see Chapter 6). It also provides protection against discrimination arising from a disability.

In British Sugar plc v Kirker, for example,[30] an individual selected for redundancy claimed that they had been discriminated against because of a visual impairment, suffered since birth. The employers had carried out an assessment exercise in order to select those to be dismissed. This had consisted of marking employees against a set of factors. The complainant claimed that the marks attributed to them were the result of a subjective view arising out of the disability. The employee had scored 0 out of 10 for promotion potential and 0 for performance and competence. The EAT observed that such marks would indicate that the employee did not always achieve the required standard of performance and required close supervision. Yet the employee had never been criticised for poor performance and did not have any supervision. It was clear that this individual had been undermarked by reason of their disability. The fact that many of the relevant events took place before

---

25 The approach prior to the DDA 1995 had been to establish quotas of disabled people in an employer's workforce: see Disabled Persons (Employment) Act 1944; this approach failed.

26 Section 50 DDA 1995.

27 Section 1 DRCA 1999.

28 Disability Employment Gap; House of Commons Work and Pensions Committee session 2016/17 HC56.

29 Nick Coleman, Wendy Sykes, and Carola Groom, *Barriers to employment and unfair treatment at work: a quantitative analysis of disabled people's experiences*, Equality and Human Rights Commission Research report 88 (2013).

30 [1998] IRLR 624.

the coming into force of the DDA 1995 did not stop the employment tribunal from looking at them in order to help draw inferences about the employer's conduct.[31]

Similar provisions apply to contract workers.[32] It is unlawful for a 'principal', in relation to contract work, to discriminate against a disabled person. In *Abbey Life Assurance Co Ltd v Tansell*[33] the principal was described as the 'end user' in a situation where there was an unbroken chain of contracts between a person 'A' who makes work available for doing by individuals who are employed by another person who supplies them under a contract made with 'A'. In this case a contract computer person was employed by their own limited liability company which had a contract with a consultancy who supplied their services to an end user. Taking a purposive approach to the statute, the EAT and the Court of Appeal concluded that it was the end user who should be the target for the complaint as the agency would simply justify their actions by reference to the instructions of 'A'. Similar rules apply to office holders,[34] partnerships,[35] barristers and advocates.[36]

In addition the Act also makes unlawful discrimination arising from disability and imposes upon employers a duty to make reasonable adjustments (see below). Prior to 2004 there was an exemption for small employers, employing fewer than 15 employees, but this was subsequently removed.

Section 6(1) EA 2010 provides that a person (P) has a disability, or has had a disability,[37] if

(a) P has a physical or mental impairment, and
(b) the impairment has a substantial and long-term adverse effect on P's ability to carry out normal day-to-day activities.

Thus the tests for whether a person has a disability are, first, that there must be a physical or mental impairment; second, that it must have a substantial adverse effect; third, that it must have a long-term adverse effect; and, finally, this adverse effect must relate to the ability to carry out normal day-to-day activities. Schedule 1 Equality Act provides some meaning to these terms. The government's Office for Disability Issues also issued guidance on the definition of disability in 2011.[38] This guidance does not impose any legal obligations, but tribunals are required to take it into account where relevant.[39]

7.3.1.1 Long-term impairment

According to the guidance, the term impairment should be given its everyday meaning.[40] *Greenwood v British Airways plc*[41] considered a complaint from an employee who was told that one of the reasons for a failure to gain promotion was the employee's sickness record. The employee suffered flashbacks which could prevent him from working and affected his ability to concentrate. After a failure to gain promotion the employee was absent through depression. The employment tribunal decided to look only at matters at the time when the employee was rejected for promotion. The tribunal held that the applicant was not disabled at the time of the act complained of. The EAT concluded that the employment tribunal had erred in law and had wrongly decided that events subsequent to the act complained

---

31 See also *Kent County Council v Mingo* [2000] IRLR 90 where a redeployment policy that gave preference to redundant or potentially redundant employees, in preference to those with a disability, amounted to discrimination in accordance with the DDA 1995.
32 Section 41 EA 2010.
33 [2000] IRLR 387 CA.
34 Section 49.
35 Sections 6A–6C DDA 1995.
36 Sections 7A–7D DDA 1995.
37 Section 6(4) EA 2010.
38 The website for the Office for Disability Issues is http://odi.dwp.gov.uk
39 Schedule 1 para. 12 EA 2010.
40 *Goodwin v The Patent Office* [1999] IRLR 4 contains a substantial analysis of these various tests.
41 [1999] IRLR 600.

of were not relevant. The EAT concluded that one needed to look at the whole period up to the employment tribunal hearing to assess whether a person had a long-term impairment. Considering the whole period does not necessarily mean an investigation of the causes of the disability.

In *Power v Panasonic UK Ltd*[42] an area sales manager had the geographical area for which she was responsible expanded, following a reorganisation. She became ill and was eventually dismissed after a long period of absence. It was not disputed that during her long absence she was both depressed and drinking heavily. The tribunal concerned itself with whether the drinking or the depression came first, but the EAT stated that it was not necessary to consider how the impairment was caused. What was relevant was to discover whether the person had a disability within the meaning of the Act at the relevant time.

The important issue with regard to the Equality Act and disability concerns the effect of the impairment upon the individual's ability to carry out day-to-day activities. The guidance provides two examples to illustrate this:

- A woman is obese. Her obesity in itself is not an impairment, but it causes breathing and mobility difficulties which substantially adversely affect her ability to walk.
- A man has a borderline moderate learning disability which has an adverse impact on his short-term memory and his levels of literacy and numeracy. For example, he cannot write any original material, as opposed to slowly copying existing text, and he cannot write his address from memory.

Thus it is the effect, not the cause, of the disability that is important. The tribunal needs to look at the underlying facts which amounted to the disability rather than the condition itself.[43]

One route to establishing the existence of a mental impairment has traditionally been to show proof of a mental illness classified in the World Health Organisation International Classification of Diseases (WHOICD). Many parts of its classification require specific symptoms to manifest themselves over a specified period. Thus just claiming 'clinical depression' without further clarification is unlikely to be sufficient.[44] Similarly, a failure to establish that back pain was the result of a physical or mental impairment put it outside the scope of the Act.

Schedule 1 para. 2 explains that 'long term' means that an impairment has lasted, or is likely to last, at least 12 months. If it were to cease having a substantial impairment, then it would still be treated as having that effect if there was a possibility of recurrence in the future.[45] For the avoidance of doubt, there are a number of specific disabilities which are to be taken as being a disability. These are severe disfigurement,[46] cancer, HIV infection and multiple sclerosis.[47] The effect of medical treatment is not to be taken into account, so if a disabled person is able to carry out day-to-day activities whilst under medication, that will not alter the fact that he or she will be regarded as having a disability.[48] For example, according to the guidance, if a person with a hearing impairment wears a hearing aid, the question as to whether his or her impairment has a substantial adverse effect is to be decided by reference to what the hearing level would be without the hearing aid.

Certain addictions and conditions are not to be treated as impairments for the purposes of the disability provisions of the Equality Act. These include: addictions to alcohol, nicotine or any other substance (unless the addiction was originally the result of medically prescribed drugs or treatment);

---

42 [2003] IRLR 151.
43 *Urso (appellant) v Department for Work & Pensions* [2017] IRLR 204.
44 *Morgan v Staffordshire University* [2002] IRLR 190.
45 Schedule 1 para. 2(2) EA 2010.
46 Schedule 1 para. 3 EA 2010.
47 Schedule 1 para. 6 EA 2010.
48 Schedule 1 para. 5 EA 2010; this section also excludes sight deficiencies which can be corrected by wearing glasses.

hay fever, except where it affects others; a tendency to set fires, to steal or to physical or sexual abuse of other persons; exhibitionism and voyeurism; and severe disfigurement that results from tattooing or piercing. The guidance gives an example:

> A young man has Attention Deficit Hyperactivity Disorder (ADHD) which manifests itself in a number of ways, including exhibitionism and an inability to concentrate. The disorder, as an impairment which has a substantial and long-term adverse effect on the young person's ability to carry out normal day-to-day activities, would be a disability for the purposes of the Act. The young man is not entitled to the protection of the Act in relation to any discrimination he experiences as a consequence of his exhibitionism, because that is an excluded condition under the Act.

> However, he would be protected in relation to any discrimination that he experiences in relation to the non-excluded effects of his condition, such as inability to concentrate. For example, he would be entitled to any reasonable adjustments that are required as a consequence of those effects.

7.3.1.2 Day-to-day activities

According to the guidance issued by the government's Office for Disability Issues, the Act does not define day-to-day activities because it is not possible to provide an exhaustive list. Generally, they are activities that people do on a regular basis, such as 'shopping, reading and writing, having a conversation or using the telephone, watching television, getting washed and dressed, preparing and eating food, carrying out household tasks, walking and travelling by various forms of transport'. This will include the impairments that affect the individual's ability to carry out duties at work, particularly if they include these 'normal day-to-day activities'.[49] In *Banaszczyk*[50] the claimant was involved in a car accident, suffering an injury to his spine. He worked as a picker – filling and loading cases of goods. After the accident he could not reach the minimum pick rate and was eventually dismissed on the grounds of incapability. He successfully claimed disability discrimination. It was the picking and loading that was the day-to-day activity which was to be focused on, not the pick rate. One needed to be careful not to confuse the day-to-day activity with a particular requirement of the employer.

In *Hewett v Motorola Ltd*[51] the complainant, an engineer, was diagnosed as having autism in the form of Asperger's Syndrome. He argued that, without medication or medical treatment, his memory would be affected and he would have difficulties in concentrating, learning and understanding. The EAT held that one had to have a broad view of the meaning of understanding and that any person who had their normal human interaction affected might also be regarded as having their understanding affected. What is 'normal' may be best defined as anything that is not abnormal or unusual. It does not depend upon whether the majority of people do it – for example, there may be some activities that only women usually do and the fact that men do not do them does not stop them being 'normal day-to-day activities'.[52]

7.3.1.3 Substantial adverse effect

The fact that an applicant can still carry out day-to-day activities does not mean that the individual's ability has not been impaired. If the individual can only carry them out with difficulty, then there may be an adverse effect. This can be seen in *CC of Dumfries and Galway*[53] where a policeman had

---

49 *Law Hospital NHS Trust v Rush* [2001] IRLR 611, where the work of a nurse was stated to include some normal day-to-day activities.
50 *Banaszczyk v Booker* [2016] IRLR 273.
51 [2004] IRLR 545.
52 *Ekpe v Commissioner of Police* [2001] IRLR 605.
53 *Chief Constable of Dumfries and Galloway Constabulary v Adams* [2009] IRLR 612.

difficulty in carrying on night work because he had ME. Night work was held to be a 'normal day-to-day activity'.

If an impairment is likely to have a substantial adverse effect upon the ability of the person concerned to carry out normal day-to-day activities, but the person does not do so because of measures taken to treat or correct it, it is still to be treated as having the adverse effect.[54] Such measures can include counselling sessions for an individual who was suffering from a form of depression. This was held to be the case in *Kapadia v London Borough of Lambeth*[55] where an employment tribunal failed to find that a person was disabled within the terms of s. 1(1) DDA 1995, despite uncontested medical opinion. The EAT held that the employment tribunal had erred in doing so and had arrived at a judgment based on how the complainant seemed when giving evidence, although in *Goodwin* the EAT stated that this was something that the employment tribunal could take into account. The Court of Appeal, in this case, confirmed this approach and held that just because the symptoms are kept under control by medication, this does not stop a person suffering a substantial adverse effect on their day-to-day activities,[56] although there is a need for the individual to show that they would suffer from this effect without the medication or treatment.[57] The guidance gives the following as an example:

> A man has a hearing impairment which has the effect that he cannot hold a conversation with another person even in a quiet environment. He has a hearing aid which overcomes that effect. However, it is the effect of the impairment without the hearing aid that needs to be considered. In this case, the impairment has a substantial adverse effect on the day-to-day activity of holding a conversation.

7.3.1.4 Long term

According to Schedule 1 para. 2(1) Equality Act, the effect of an impairment is long term if:

(a) it has lasted for at least 12 months,
(b) it is likely to last for at least 12 months, or
(c) it is likely to last for the rest of the life of the person affected.

The House of Lords, in *SCA Packaging Ltd v Boyle*,[58] concluded that the word 'likely' means 'could well happen', rather than 'probable' or 'more likely than not'. The court stated, *obiter*, that where someone is following a course of treatment on medical advice, in the absence of any indication to the contrary, an employer can assume that, without the treatment, the impairment is 'likely' to recur. Similarly, if it had a substantial effect on the individual's day-to-day life before it was treated, the employer can also assume that, in the absence of any contra-indication, if it does recur, its effect will be substantial. The ODI guidance follows this wording and states that the word 'likely' should be interpreted as meaning 'could well happen'.[59]

The cause of an impairment is not relevant to deciding whether there is an impairment or not, so when one impairment develops into another they should be taken as cumulative for the purposes of deciding whether the impairment is long-term or not. *Patel v Oldham Metropolitan Borough*

---

54 Schedule 1 para. 2 EA 2010.
55 [2000] IRLR 14.
56 [2000] IRLR 699 CA; see also *Leonard v Southern Derbyshire Chamber of Commerce* [2001] IRLR 19 where the EAT held that a tribunal should concentrate on what a person could not do or had difficulty doing.
57 *Woodrup v London Borough of Southwark* [2003] IRLR 111 where an individual failed to produce medical evidence that the discontinuation of her psychotherapy treatment would have a substantial adverse effect.
58 [2009] IRLR 746.
59 Para. C3.

Council,[60] for example, concerned a primary school teacher who suffered from mild inflammation of the spinal cord. She then developed a secondary syndrome which affected the same parts of her body. She had a phased return to work but then suffered an injury whilst restraining a pupil in a swimming lesson. This further aggravated her pain and after a long period of further absence she was dismissed. The employment tribunal decided that she was not disabled because she suffered from two different impairments over two different periods lasting less than 12 months. The Employment Appeal Tribunal disagreed and remitted the case for further consideration of whether one impairment arose out of the other, in which case they combined to last for more than 12 months and the teacher would therefore meet the legislation's definition of disability.

7.3.2 Discrimination arising from disability

Section 15(1) Equality Act provides that a person (A) discriminates against a disabled person (B) if:

(a) A treats B unfavourably because of something arising in consequence of B's disability, and

(b) A cannot show that the treatment is a proportionate means of achieving a legitimate aim.

Discrimination arising from disability is different to direct discrimination because it only requires a person to be treated 'unfavourably' because of something related to the disability rather than 'less favourably'. The Code of Practice on Employment gives the following example:

> An employer dismisses a worker because she has had three months' sick leave. The employer is aware that the worker has multiple sclerosis and most of her sick leave is disability-related. The employer's decision to dismiss is not because of the worker's disability itself. However, the worker has been treated unfavourably because of something arising in consequence of her disability (namely, the need to take a period of disability-related sick leave).

Discrimination arising from disability is also different from indirect discrimination. When showing indirect discrimination, there is a need to show that there has been a provision, criterion or practice which puts, or would put, people sharing a disability at a particular disadvantage when compared with others. This is not the case with showing discrimination arising from disability. Thus a really important characteristic of this form of discrimination is that there is no requirement for a comparator. There is only a need to show unfavourable treatment arising from the disability. However, s. 15(2) disapplies the provision if the employer (A) did not know, and could not reasonably be expected to know, that B had a disability. The Code of Practice provides an example of unfavourable treatment arising in consequence of an employee's disability:

> A woman is disciplined for losing her temper at work. However, this behaviour was out of character and is a result of severe pain caused by cancer, of which her employer is aware. The disciplinary action is unfavourable treatment. This treatment is because of something which arises in consequence of the worker's disability, namely her loss of temper.
>
> There is a connection between the 'something' (that is, the loss of temper) that led to the treatment and her disability. It will be discrimination arising from disability if the employer cannot objectively justify the decision to discipline the worker.

This definition of discrimination arising from disability tackled some confusion which previously existed. Prior to the Equality Act, the DRC Code of Practice used the term 'disability-related

---

60 [2010] IRLR 280.

discrimination'. The whole effectiveness of the concept of disability-related discrimination was thrown into doubt by a decision of the House of Lords in a housing-related disability discrimination case. In *London Borough of Lewisham v Malcolm*[61] an individual suffering from schizophrenia sublet his council home. The Council took possession proceedings against him and he claimed that this was contrary to the DDA as it was the disability that made him decide to sublet – that is, a disability-related reason. The court, however, said that the correct comparison was with a non-disabled person who had decided to sublet. The result was to considerably weaken the effectiveness of protection from disability-related discrimination. In *Child Support Agency v Truman*[62] the EAT confirmed that the approach in *Malcolm* should equally apply in the employment context. The position has now been restored with the introduction of the concept of discrimination arising from disability contained in the Equality Act.

7.3.3 The duty to make reasonable adjustments

The importance of the need to make reasonable adjustments is shown in one survey,[63] which stated that over 25 per cent of people who left their job because of their disability said that adaptations would have enabled them to stay in work, but less than 20 per cent of these people were offered such changes.

The employer discriminates against a disabled person if the employer fails to comply with a duty to make reasonable adjustments in relation to the disabled person.[64] According to s. 20 Equality Act, the duty to make reasonable adjustments consists of three requirements. These are:

1. where a provision, criterion or practice puts a disabled person at a substantial disadvantage in comparison with those who are not disabled, then the employer must take reasonable steps to avoid the disadvantage;
2. where a physical feature puts a disabled person at a substantial disadvantage, then the employer must alter or remove that feature, or provide a reasonable means of avoiding such a feature;[65]
3. the provision of an auxiliary aid where a disabled person would, but for the provision of that aid, be put at a substantial disadvantage.

Thus, where the disabled person is placed at a substantial disadvantage compared with persons who are not disabled because of a provision, criterion or practice applied by or on behalf of an employer, or any physical feature of premises occupied by an employer,[66] it is the duty of the employer to take reasonable steps, in all the circumstances of the case, to prevent the provision, criterion, practice or feature from having that effect.

According to para. 6.12 of the Code of Practice on Employment, physical features can include:

steps, stairways, kerbs, exterior surfaces and paving, parking areas, building entrances and exits (including emergency escape routes), internal and external doors, gates, toilet and washing facilities, lighting and ventilation, lifts and escalators, floor coverings, signs, furniture and temporary or moveable items.

---

61 [2008] IRLR 700.

62 [2009] IRLR 277.

63 See Office for National Statistics 'Disability and the Labour Market', *Labour Market Trends*, September 1999, p. 467.

64 Section 21(2) EA 2010.

65 Section 20(9) EA 2010.

66 Physical feature includes any feature arising from the design or construction of a building, approaches to it, access or exits, fixtures, fittings, furnishings, furniture, equipment or material in the building: any other physical element or quality of the premises: s. 20(10) EA 2010.

The term 'provision, criterion or practice' is not specifically defined in the Equality Act but, according to the Code of Practice on Employment, it is likely to be construed widely to include such matters as formal and informal policies, rules, practices, arrangements, etc. The arrangements referred to will include the arrangements for determining who should be offered employment, and any term, condition or arrangements on which employment, promotion, transfer, training or any other benefit is offered. These arrangements are strictly job-related. Employers are required to make adjustments to the way that the job is structured and organised so as to accommodate those who cannot fit into the existing arrangements. This appears to exclude providing assistance with personal arrangements and care so as to enable an individual to attend work.[67] Examples of steps which may need to be taken are:[68]

1. Making adjustments to premises.
2. Allocating some of the disabled person's duties to another person.
3. Transferring the disabled person to an existing vacancy.
4. Altering his hours of work or training.
5. Assigning him to a different place of work or training.
6. Allowing him to be absent during working or training hours for rehabilitation, assessment or treatment.
7. Giving, or arranging to give, training or mentoring.
8. Acquiring or modifying equipment.
9. Modifying instructions or reference manuals.
10. Providing a reader or interpreter.
11. Providing supervision or other support.

This obligation applies in respect of applicants for employment as well as in respect of existing employees. There is, however, no obligation placed upon the employer if the employer does not know, or could not have reasonably been expected to know, that the applicant or employee had a disability. The position was summarised in *Eastern and Coastal Kent Primary Care Trust v Grant*[69] which concerned an applicant with dyslexia. The EAT stated that an employer is exempted from the duty to make adjustments if each of four matters can be satisfied. These were that the employer:

1. does not know that the disabled person has a disability;
2. does not know that the disabled person is likely to be at a substantial disadvantage compared with persons who are not disabled;
3. could not reasonably have been expected to know that the disabled person had a disability;
4. could not reasonably be expected to know that the disabled person is likely to be placed at a substantial disadvantage in comparison with people who are not disabled.[70]

These matters are cumulative and not alternatives. In *Secretary of State v Alam*[71] the employer was held not to have known of the employee's disability (which was depression) but ought to have known that he had a disability which might put him at a substantial disadvantage in relation to any provision, criterion or practice applied by the employer. There was no indication, however, that the particular provision – that is, asking for permission to finish work early to attend an interview – was a feature of the claimant's disability. It followed, therefore, that the employer was exempt from the

---

67 See *Kenny v Hampshire Constabulary* [1999] IRLR 76.
68 Para. 6.33 Code of Practice on Employment.
69 [2009] IRLR 429.
70 Schedule 8 para. 20(1) EA 2010.
71 *Secretary of State for the Department for Work and Pensions v Alam* [2010] IRLR 283.

duty as he could not be reasonably expected to know that the disabled person was likely to be placed at a substantial disadvantage in comparison with those not suffering from a disability.

The question of whether an employer had made sufficient arrangements in the light of their knowledge is one of fact for the employment tribunal. *Ridout v TC Group*[72] concerned an applicant with a rare form of epilepsy who may have been disadvantaged by the bright fluorescent lighting in the interview location. The EAT held that no reasonable employer could be expected to know, without being told, that the arrangements for the interview might place the applicant at a disadvantage. The EAT held that the DDA 1995:

> requires the tribunal to measure the extent of the duty, if any, against the assumed knowledge of the employer both as to the disability and its likelihood of causing the individual a substantial disadvantage in comparison with persons who are not disabled.

In *G4S Gas Solutions v Powell*[73] an individual who became disabled was put into an alternative job which carried a 10 per cent reduction in pay. He claimed that the reduction in pay would amount to disability discrimination. The EAT disagreed and held that the Act should not be read in such a way as to protect an employee's pay in conjunction with other measures to meet the employee's disadvantage arising from disability. The question should be whether it was reasonable for the employer to take that step. The extent of the adjustments needed is subject to a reasonableness test. This first requires an employer to carry out a proper assessment of what is needed to eliminate a disabled person's disadvantage. This might include a proper assessment of the individual's condition, the effect of the disability on her and her ability to perform the duties of the post, and the steps that might be taken to reduce or remove the disadvantages to which she was subjected.[74] In deciding whether it is reasonable for an employer to have to take a particular step, regard may be had to the nature of the employer's activities and the size of the undertaking, as well as the extent to which the step would prevent the effect or barrier that existed and the practicability of taking the step in the first place. It may mean creating a new job for an individual, such as in *Southampton City College v Randall*[75] where a reorganisation of work would have enabled the employer to create a new job for a lecturer whose voice had broken down. The employers were guilty of disability discrimination because they did not consider this option and others as possible reasonable adjustments. Similarly, it might be that swapping jobs between a person with a disability and a person without disability might amount to a reasonable adjustment as happened in *Jelic*.[76] Here the EAT held that swapping the jobs of two police officers would have been a reasonable adjustment. The EAT warned, however, that this would not always be the case. In some instances job swapping would not be a way of fulfilling the duty to make reasonable adjustments; for example, it would not be reasonable to require a woman working flexible hours because of child care responsibilities to swap jobs with a person with a disability working longer hours.

A further example of the scope of the duty to make reasonable adjustments arose in *Archibald v Fife Council*.[77] This concerned an employee of Fife Council who was employed as a road sweeper. As a result of a complication during surgery she became virtually unable to walk and could no longer carry out the duties of a road sweeper. She could do sedentary work and the Council sent her on a number of computer and administration courses. Over the next few months she applied for over 100 jobs within the Council but she always failed in a competitive interview situation. Eventually,

---

72 [1998] IRLR 628.

73 *G4S Gas Solutions v Powell* [2016] IRLR 820.

74 *Mid Staffordshire General Hospitals NHS Trust v Cambridge* [2003] IRLR 566.

75 [2006] IRLR 18.

76 *Chief Constable of South Yorkshire Police v Jelic* [2010] IRLR 744.

77 [2004] IRLR 651 CA.

she was dismissed as the redeployment procedure was exhausted. The issue for the court was the limits of the duty to make reasonable adjustments. It was agreed that the DDA 1995 required some positive discrimination in favour of disabled people, but did this include finding them another job if their disability stops them from performing their current one? The court held that the DDA 1995, to the extent that the provisions of the Act required it, permitted and sometimes obliged employers to treat a disabled person more favourably than others. This may even require transferring them to a higher-level position without the need for a competitive interview.[78]

The Equality Act does not provide for justification for failing to make reasonable adjustments, except insofar as there is a reasonableness test. The duty is for employers to make reasonable adjustments. The Code of Practice on Employment makes some suggestions as to some of the factors which might be taken into account when deciding whether a particular action is reasonable for an employer to take. These are:

- whether taking any particular steps would be effective in preventing the substantial disadvantage;
- the practicability of the step;
- the financial and other costs of making the adjustment and the extent of any disruption caused;
- the extent of the employer's financial or other resources;
- the availability to the employer of financial or other assistance to help make an adjustment; and
- the type and size of the employer.

A failure to make reasonable adjustments over a period of time would be almost bound to lead to a breach of the implied term of trust and confidence, which would then entitle the employee to treat it as a repudiatory breach of contract (see Chapter 5).[79] *Nottinghamshire County Council v Meikle*[80] concerned a local authority school teacher. Her vision deteriorated until she lost the sight in one eye and some vision in the other. She made a number of requests for adjustments, including to her classroom location, the amount of preparation time she was given, and that notices and written materials should be enlarged. There were delays in responses from the employer and eventually Mrs Meikle resigned. The Court of Appeal agreed with her that the continuing failure of the local authority to deal with the disability discrimination amounted to a fundamental breach of contract and that she had been constructively dismissed.

7.4 Gender reassignment

Gender dysphoria is a condition where people feel that they are trapped in a body of the wrong sex and a transsexual is someone with an extreme and long-term case of gender dysphoria, who seeks to alter their biological sex to match their gender identity. It is estimated that there are some 4,000 people in the UK who are receiving medical help for gender dysphoria, indicating a total of some 15,000 in all. This cannot, of course, be an accurate measure of the number of transsexual people, but it does suggest that it is a substantial number of people.[81] Studies carried out in the Netherlands suggest that the prevalence of transsexualism is between 1:11,900 and 1:17,000 in men over 15 years of age. The number of female-to-male transsexual people is far smaller, possibly in the region

78 This was one of the problems for the employer. Most positions were at a higher level than that of a road sweeper and the local authority assumed that it had an obligation to make all promotion interviews competitive.
79 *Greenhof v Barnsley Metropolitan Borough Council* [2006] IRLR 99.
80 [2004] IRLR 703.
81 See the NHS website at www.nhs.uk/conditions/gender-dysphoria/Pages/Introduction.aspx?url=Pages/What-is-it.aspx

of 1 to every 5 male-to-female transsexual people. A further study carried out in primary care units in Scotland estimated the prevalence in men over 15 years at 1:12,400, with an approximate sex ratio of 1 to 4 in favour of male-to-female patients. These studies suggest that in the UK there are between 1,300 and 2,000 male-to-female and between 250 and 400 female-to-male transsexual people. Press for Change, however, estimate the figures at around 5,000 post-operative transsexual people.[82] On perhaps a wider definition, one study for the Equality and Human Rights Commission estimated that there were some 300,000–500,000 trans people (those who experience some degree of gender variance) in the UK.[83]

The Equality Act, as with the other protected characteristics, makes direct discrimination, indirect discrimination, harassment and victimisation on the characteristic of gender reassignment unlawful. Section 7(1) EA provides that a person has the protected characteristic of gender reassignment if the person is 'proposing to undergo, is undergoing or has undergone a process (or part of a process) for the purpose of reassigning the person's sex by changing physiological or other attributes of sex'. This is a widening of the protection previously offered in the Sex Discrimination Act 1975[84] where the definition referred to someone who 'intended', rather than 'proposed' to undergo the process. The Act protects people who have, at least, proposed to go through all or part of the process. There is now no requirement for them to actually undergo surgery or treatment. The Code of Practice on Employment also makes the point that people who have gender dysphoria may also be protected as having a disability if the disorder has a substantial adverse long-term effect on their ability to carry out day-to-day activities.

Section 16 EA provides that less favourable treatment in relation to absences from work, because of sickness, injury or some other reason connected to the person proposing or undergoing (or having undergone) the gender reassignment process, also amounts to discrimination on the protected characteristic of gender reassignment. The Code of Practice on Employment[85] also states that there is no requirement for an individual to inform their employer of their gender reassignment status, but that they may want to discuss it with the employer if they are proposing to go through the gender reassignment process, in order to obtain the support of the employer.

As mentioned, prior to the Equality Act, gender reassignment was treated as a sex discrimination issue. *P v S and Cornwall County Council*,[86] for example, concerned an employee who informed the employer of an intention to undergo gender reassignment. The first part of this was to undertake a 'life test', which consisted of spending a year living in the manner of the proposed gender. Whilst on sick leave for initial surgery, the employee was dismissed. The employment tribunal decided that the individual had been dismissed because of the gender reassignment, but decided that the SDA 1975 did not apply to these circumstances. They referred the matter to the Court of Justice with the question as to whether the Equal Treatment Directive provided for this situation. The Court of Justice held that the Directive sought to safeguard the principle of equality and applied, although not exclusively, to discrimination on the grounds of sex. The Court held that discrimination on the basis of gender reassignment was to treat a person less favourably than persons of the sex to which the individual had been deemed to belong before the gender reassignment and was therefore contrary to art. 5(1) Equal Treatment Directive.

Another pre-Equality Act example of discrimination on this ground was in *Chessington World of Adventures Ltd v Reed*[87] where an individual announced a change of gender from male to female and, as

---

82 Report of the Interdepartmental Working Group on Transsexual People (2000) at www.oocities.org/transforum2000/Resources/wgtrans.pdf

83 M. Mitchell and C. Howarth *Trans Research Review* (Equality and Human Rights Commission, 2009).

84 Section 82(1) SDA 1975.

85 Para. 2.27.

86 Case 13/94 [1996] IRLR 347.

87 [1997] IRLR 556.

a result, was subjected to continuous harassment from her work colleagues. She eventually was absent through sickness and then dismissed. The EAT confirmed the employment tribunal's view that the employer, who had known of the harassment, was directly liable for the sex discrimination that had taken place.

The Gender Recognition Act 2004 provides that a person over the age of 18 years may make an application for a gender recognition certificate. The application will be reviewed by a Gender Recognition Panel who will grant a certificate if certain conditions are met. These are that the applicant has or has had gender dysphoria, has lived in the acquired gender throughout the period of two years ending with the date on which the application is made and intends to continue to live in the acquired gender until death. The numbers applying for recognition are limited, although this should not put in doubt the importance of the legislation for transgender people. In the year 2015/16 there were some 374 applications for a certificate. The great majority of those granted are for male-to-female transition. In the year 2015/16 some 223 certificates were given for those who were male at birth, whilst just 109 for those who were female at birth.[88]

The effect of obtaining such a certificate is to legally acquire the sought-for gender. The Code of Practice on Employment states[89] transsexual people should not be routinely asked to produce their gender recognition certificate to prove their legal gender as this would compromise the person's right to privacy. If the employer requires proof of a person's legal gender, then their new birth certificate should be treated as sufficient.

7.5 Marriage or civil partnership

Section 8 EA makes marriage or civil partnership a protected characteristic and s. 13(4) ensures that it is only people who are married or in a civil partnership who are protected. Single people are not protected nor are those who intend to get married or enter a civil partnership. Those who have divorced or had their civil partnership dissolved are not protected either.

The Equality Act, as with the other protected characteristics, makes direct discrimination, indirect discrimination and victimisation on the characteristic of marriage or civil partnership unlawful. Note that this protected characteristic is not included amongst those characteristics that are protected from harassment in s. 26 EA and that discrimination by association is not included for this protected characteristic. Also direct discrimination only covers less favourable treatment of a worker because the worker themselves is married or a civil partner.[90]

There is an issue about how narrowly this protected characteristic is defined. Is it the fact of marriage itself that is protected or an individual who is identified as married? In *Hawkins v Atex Group Ltd*[91] a person was held to have been dismissed not because she was married, but because of her close relationship with another employee. An unmarried person would equally have been dismissed if in the same relationship. There had not, therefore, been less favourable treatment on the grounds of marriage because an unmarried comparator would have been treated in the same way. The court referred to another case where this distinction between the fact of marriage and the relationship between two individuals which was in the form of a marriage was less than clear and disagreed with some of the resulting conclusions.[92]

---

88 Tribunals and gender recognition statistics at https://data.gov.uk
89 Para. 2.30.
90 Section 13(4) EA 2010.
91 [2012] IRLR 807.
92 *Dunn v Institute of Cemetery and Crematorium Management* [2012] All ER (D) 173 (Feb) EAT.

There have in the past been a number of cases related to married women being treated less favourably than married men because they are married, sometimes based upon outdated assumptions about the roles of men and women, both within and outside marriage. In *Coleman v Sky Oceanic Ltd*,[93] for example, two competing travel firms employed one member each of what became a married couple. There was a concern about confidentiality of each business's information. The two companies consulted and decided to dismiss the female because the man was assumed to be the breadwinner. Such an assumption, according to the Court of Appeal, was an assumption based upon sex and amounted to discrimination under the SDA 1975. *Chief Constable of the Bedfordshire Constabulary v Graham*[94] also concerned a married couple. Inspector Margaret Graham had a promotion rescinded by the Chief Constable because she was married to a chief superintendent in the same division. It was considered that there would be difficulties arising from having the couple working together at these levels. The EAT upheld the employment tribunal's decision that the complainant was treated less favourably than a single person would have been, for reasons connected to her marital status.

The possibility of having a civil partnership took effect in December 2005 when the Civil Partnership Act 2004 came into effect. Section 1 of this Act provides that civil partnerships are between same-sex couples. It gave same-sex couples the right to form legally recognised relationships giving the participants similar rights to heterosexual couples who get married.

The Marriage (Same Sex Couples) Act 2013 finally allowed same-sex couples to marry in the same way as heterosexual couples, although it also provided that services could not be carried out by the Church of England or the Church in Wales.

7.6 Pregnancy and maternity

Prior to the Equality Act 2010, the dismissal of a female worker on account of pregnancy was, and still is, likely to constitute direct sex discrimination.[95] This is because only women can become pregnant, so discrimination related to pregnancy and maternity is likely to be discrimination on the grounds of sex.

In 2015 the Equality and Human Rights Commission carried out research into pregnancy and maternity discrimination.[96] As part of the study they interviewed 3,034 employers and 3,254 mothers. Their main findings included the following information:

- Around one in nine mothers (11 per cent) reported that they were either dismissed; made compulsorily redundant, where others in their workplace were not; or treated so poorly they felt they had to leave their job; if scaled up to the general population this could mean as many as 54,000 mothers a year.
- One in five mothers said they had experienced harassment or negative comments related to pregnancy or flexible working from their employer and/or colleagues; if scaled up to the general population this could mean as many as 100,000 mothers a year.
- 10% of mothers said their employer discouraged them from attending antenatal appointments; if scaled up to the general population this could mean as many as 53,000 mothers a year.

---

93 [1981] IRLR 398 CA. On assumed ethnic characteristics, see *Bradford NHS Trust v Al-Shahib* [2003] IRLR 4.
94 [2002] IRLR 239.
95 See e.g. Case C-177/88 *Dekker v Stichting Vormingscentrum voor Jonge Voluiassen* [1991] IRLR 27 and Case C-32/93 *Webb v EMO Air Cargo (UK) Ltd* [1994] IRLR 482.
96 www.equalityhumanrights.com/en/managing-pregnancy-and-maternity-workplace/pregnancy-and-maternity-discrimi nation-research-findings

Article 10(1) of the Pregnant Workers Directive[97] provides that dismissal should be prohibited during the period from the beginning of pregnancy to the end of maternity leave, save in exceptional circumstances unrelated to the worker being pregnant, breastfeeding or having recently given birth. In *Brown v Rentokil Ltd*[98] the Court of Justice considered the dismissal of a female employee who was absent through most of her pregnancy and was dismissed under a provision of the contract of employment which allowed for dismissal after 26 weeks' continuous absence through sickness. The Court held that arts. 2(1) and 5(1) of the Equal Treatment Directive 'preclude dismissal of a female worker at any time during her pregnancy for absences due to incapacity for work caused by an illness resulting from that pregnancy'.

Absences after pregnancy and maternity leave are to be treated in the same way as any other sickness is treated under the employee's contract of employment. Measures which impose length-of-service conditions before an employee is eligible for promotion, when time spent on maternity leave is excluded from the calculations as to that length of service, will also be excluded by art. 2(3) Equal Treatment Directive.[99] The Directive will allow national provisions which give women specific rights because of pregnancy,[100] but the provision of such rights is intended to ensure the principle of equal treatment. Thus the refusal to appoint a pregnant woman to a permanent position because there was a statutory restriction on her employment in that position during her pregnancy amounted to sex discrimination. This was the situation in *Mahlberg v Land Mecklenburg-Vorpommern*[101] where a pregnant woman was refused an appointment as an operating theatre nurse because German law banned pregnant women from being employed in areas where they would be exposed to dangerous substances. The financial loss that the employer might suffer because they could not employ the woman in the position for the duration of her pregnancy was not an acceptable reason for the unfavourable treatment. Similarly, in *P & O Ferries Ltd v Iverson*[102] a woman was stopped from going to sea once she reached week 28 of her pregnancy. Pregnancy was one of a number of lawful reasons for stopping an individual going to sea, but it was the only one for which, with this employer, there was no pay. All the other reasons, including sickness, resulted in suspension with pay. The fact that this was not available to pregnant women was held to be discriminatory.[103]

Whether the employee concerned is on a permanent contract or a fixed-term contract is of no consequence. In *Tele Danmark A/S*,[104] for example, the Court of Justice held that art. 5 of the Equal Treatment Directive and art. 10 of the Pregnant Workers Directive precludes a worker who was recruited for a fixed period who failed to inform her employer that she was pregnant even when she was aware of this when recruited, and then was unable to work during much of the period because of her pregnancy, from being dismissed on the grounds of her pregnancy. Expiry of the fixed term would not amount to a dismissal, according to the Court of Justice, but a non-renewal of the fixed-term contract on the grounds of pregnancy would.[105]

---

97 Directive 92/85/EEC on the introduction of measures to encourage improvements in the safety and health of pregnant workers and workers who have recently given birth or are breastfeeding OJ L348/1 28.11.92.

98 Case C-394/96 [1998] IRLR 445.

99 Case C-136/95 *Caisse Nationale d'Assurance Vieillesse des Travailleurs Salariés v Thibault* [1998] IRLR 399.

100 See Case C-179/88 *Handels-og Kontorfunktionaerernes Forbund i Danmark (acting for Hertz) v Dansk Arbejdsgiverforening (acting for Aldi Marked A/S)* [1991] IRLR 31.

101 Case C-207/98 [2000] IRLR 276.

102 [1999] ICR 1088.

103 See also *British Airways (European Operations at Gatwick) Ltd v Moore and Botterill* [2000] IRLR 296 for a similar approach in relation to air crew grounded because of pregnancy.

104 Case 109/100 *Tele Danmark A/S v Kontorfunktioncerernes Forbund i Danmark* [2001] IRLR 853.

105 Case 438/99 *Jiménez Melgar v Ayuntamiento De Los Barrios* [2001] IRLR 848.

The Code of Practice provides a list[106] of examples of situations where to treat a woman less favourably might amount to pregnancy and maternity discrimination:

- the fact that, because of her pregnancy, the woman will be temporarily unable to do the job for which she is specifically employed whether permanently or on a fixed-term contract;
- the pregnant woman is temporarily unable to work because to do so would be a breach of health and safety regulations;
- the costs to the business of covering her work;
- any absence due to a pregnancy-related illness;
- her inability to attend a disciplinary hearing due to morning sickness or other pregnancy-related conditions;
- performance issues due to morning sickness or other pregnancy-related conditions.

This is not an exhaustive list.

7.6.1 The Equality Act 2010

Section 4 EA now specifically makes pregnancy and maternity a protected characteristic and ensures that such discrimination is now dealt with under this heading rather than sex discrimination (but discrimination by association is not included for this protected characteristic).[107] Sections 72–74 EA are concerned with a maternity equality clause. Section 73(1) states:

> If the terms of the woman's work do not (by whatever means) include a maternity equality clause, they are to be treated as including one.

The Equality Act defines a protected period during which the rules concerning this protected characteristic are effective. The protected period begins with the pregnancy and has two possible end points.[108] The first is if the woman has the right to ordinary and additional maternity leave, then the end point is when that leave period ends or when she returns to work, if that is earlier. The alternative end point is if she does not have the right to such leave, then it is at the end of a period of two weeks beginning with the end of the pregnancy (in Chapter 9 we consider the rights attached to maternity leave). When a pregnancy begins can be the subject of dispute. Mayr[109] concerned a waitress who was undergoing in vitro fertilisation treatment. During her treatment she was dismissed. At the time of dismissal two ova had been taken from her and fertilised but had not yet been transferred to her uterus. That procedure was carried out three days after her dismissal. The real question in the case was whether she was protected by the Pregnant Workers Directive. Article 10 provides that the protection from dismissal starts with the beginning of the pregnancy. The question was whether Ms Mayr was a pregnant worker. The Court of Justice held that, for reasons of legal certainty, the fact that the process had not been completed meant that she was not protected. The problem is that sometimes the transfer back to the woman can be delayed for a considerable period of time – for example, when the eggs are frozen and preserved. It is not possible, according to the Court, to give the worker protection for a number of years.

---

106 Para. 8.22.
107 Section 18(7) EA 2010.
108 Section 18(6) EA 2010.
109 Case C-506/06 Mayr v Bäckerei und Konditorei Gerhard Flöckner OHG [2008] IRLR 387.

Section 18 EA also follows the pattern described above in relation to disability discrimination, in that it provides for unfavourable treatment, rather than less favourable treatment. There is no need to try to find a comparator to show less favourable treatment. Thus s. 18(2) EA states that:

A person (A) discriminates against a woman if, in the protected period in relation to a pregnancy of hers, A treats her unfavourably –

(a) because of the pregnancy, or

(b) because of illness suffered by her as a result of it.

If the woman is unfavourably treated after the protected period because of a decision taken during the protected period, then the unfavourable treatment will still be treated as occurring during the protected period.[110] Discrimination related to pregnancy or maternity outside the protected period is likely to be sex discrimination. The same section then further specifies that discrimination takes place if a woman is treated unfavourably because she is on compulsory maternity leave or if she is exercising, or seeking to exercise her right to ordinary or additional maternity leave (see Chapter 9).[111] Further examples of discrimination given in the Code of Practice are:

- failure to consult a woman on maternity leave about changes to her work or about possible redundancy;
- disciplining a woman for refusing to carry out tasks due to pregnancy-related risks;
- assuming that a woman's work will become less important to her after childbirth and giving her less responsible or less interesting work as a result;
- depriving a woman of her right to an annual assessment of her performance because she was on maternity leave;
- excluding a pregnant woman from business trips.

7.7 Race

The ethnic minority population of the United Kingdom has grown significantly in the latter part of the twentieth century and the first part of this one. In England and Wales, for example, in 1991 the white ethnic group accounted for 94.1 per cent of the population; by the 2011 census this had decreased to 86 per cent. Within the white ethnic group, white British had decreased from 87.5 per cent in 2001 to 80.5 per cent in 2011. The 'Any Other White' category had the largest increase across the ethnic groups, with an increase of 1.1 million (1.8 percentage points) between the 2001 and 2011 censuses. This included people with Poland as a country of birth, who were the second-largest group of non-UK born residents in 2011. The Asian/Asian British ethnic group categories had some of the largest increases between the 2001 and 2011 censuses. People identifying as Pakistani and Indian each increased by around 0.4 million (0.5 percentage points and 0.6 percentage points respectively). The number with an Indian ethnic origin was some 1.4 million people (2.5 per cent) and those with a Pakistani ethnicity amounted to some 2 per cent. The remaining ethnic groups each showed small increases of up to 1 per cent.[112]

Unemployment rates for the non-White population are significantly higher than for the White population. The UK unemployment rate (the proportion of the economically active population who are unemployed) was 5 per cent in mid-2016. The unemployment rate was 5 per cent for

---

110 Section 18(5) EA 2010.
111 Sections 18(4) and 18(5) EA 2010.
112 Figures taken from the website of the Office for National Statistics.

TABLE 7.2 Unemployment by ethnic background: UK; July 2015 to June 2016

	Total 16+	
	000s	%
White	1,310	5
Black/African/Caribbean/Black British	120	12
Indian	60	6
Pakistani	50	10
Mixed/Multiple ethnic group	40	12
Other ethnic group	40	9
Bangladeshi	20	11
Any other Asian background	20	6
Chinese	10	6

Source: House of Commons Briefing Paper 6385 which sourced it from the ONS *Annual Population Survey* microdata.

white people compared with 9 per cent for people from a BAME (Black, Asian, and Minority Ethnic) background.[113] It is not the same for all ethnic minority groups, however.

The first Race Relations Act was enacted in 1965, but did not include employment or the concept of indirect discrimination. There was a further Race Relations Act in 1968, which was eventually followed by the 1976 Race Relations Act (RRA), which distinguished between direct and indirect discrimination. In 2000 the Race Relations (Amendment) Act introduced the Race Equality Duty to the RRA. Also in 2000 the EU adopted Directive 2000/43/EC implementing the principle of equal treatment between persons irrespective of racial or ethnic origin. All these provisions are now incorporated into the Equality Act 2010.

7.7.1 The Equality Act 2010

Section 4 EA 2010 provides that race is one of the protected characteristics. The Equality Act, as with the other protected characteristics, makes direct discrimination, indirect discrimination, harassment and victimisation on the characteristic of race unlawful. Section 9(1) provides that the term 'race' includes colour, nationality and ethnic or national origins. A reference to a person sharing one of these characteristics with others is a reference to a racial group.[114] Interestingly, there is also provision for a further protected characteristic to be included, namely that of caste.[115]

It is possible for a person to be unfavourably treated on racial grounds even if the claimant is not a member of the group being discriminated against. In *Weathersfield v Sargent*[116] a person of White European ancestry was instructed to discriminate against black and Asian people in the hiring out of vehicles. She resigned and claimed constructive dismissal on the grounds that she had been unfavourably treated on racial grounds. The Court of Appeal held that it was appropriate to give a broad meaning to the expression 'racial grounds'. It was an expression that should be capable of covering any reason or action based on race. In *Redfearn v SERCO Ltd*[117] a white man was employed as a bus driver

---

113 *Unemployment by Ethnic Background*, House of Commons Library Briefing Paper No 6385 (November 2016).

114 Sections 9(2) and 9(3) EA 2010.

115 Section 9(5) EA 2010.

116 [1999] IRLR 94 CA.

117 [2006] IRLR 623.

and escort for children and adults with special needs. It emerged that he was a candidate for the British National Party at the local elections. Membership of this party was restricted to white people only. Some 70–80 per cent of the bus passengers were of Asian origin and also some 35 per cent of the employer's workforce in this instance. He was dismissed on health and safety grounds because of the feared reaction of other employees and passengers. The Court of Appeal supported the view that he had not been dismissed on racial grounds, although it did state that discrimination on racial grounds is not restricted to less favourable treatment on the grounds of the colour of the applicant. White persons could be treated less favourably than other white persons on the grounds of colour – for example, in the case of a white person being dismissed after marrying a black person or a white publican refusing to admit or serve a white customer on the grounds that he is accompanied by a black person. The court also held that although the circumstances leading to the dismissal included racial considerations, this did not necessarily mean that the dismissal itself was 'on racial grounds'.

According to the Code of Practice, the term 'nationality' describes the legal relationship between a person and a state, resulting from birth or naturalisation.[118] This is to be distinguished from the reference to national origins. These, according to the Code of Practice, 'must have identifiable elements, both historic and geographic, which at least at some point in time indicate the existence or previous existence of a nation'.[119] So the English and Scots have separate national origins because England and Scotland were once separate nations. National origin is to be distinguished from nationality – for example, those who have a Chinese national origin may be citizens of China, but may also be citizens of another country.[120] In Onu[121] the claimant was a Nigerian national. She entered the UK on a domestic worker's visa obtained by her employers. She suffered a lot in their employ – she was not given enough food or adequate rest periods or breaks. She was also subject to both physical and mental abuse. Eventually, she escaped and, amongst other matters, made claims for direct and indirect discrimination. She failed in these claims. First, the court held that the treatment took place because of her immigration status and not because of her Nigerian nationality. As for the indirect discrimination claim, this also failed because the court was unable to identify a provision, criterion or practice.

Everyone has an ethnic origin, but to be protected by the Equality Act a person needs to belong to an ethnic group.[122] Mandla v Dowell Lee[123] resulted from a school refusing to change its school uniform policy to allow the wearing of turbans. This stopped a boy's application to join the school, because his father wished him to be brought up as a practising Sikh, which in turn required the wearing of a turban. The boy's father complained to the Commission for Racial Equality (now the Equality and Human Rights Commission) which took up the case that finally went to the House of Lords to consider. In order to establish that racial discrimination had taken place, in terms of the Act, it was necessary for Sikhs to be defined as a racial group. The argument centred on whether they were an ethnic group. The court decided that there were a number of conditions to be met before a group could call itself an ethnic group. Lord Fraser stated:

> The conditions which appear to me to be essential are these: – (1) a long, shared history, of which the group is conscious as distinguishing it from other groups, and the memory of which it keeps alive; (2) a cultural tradition of its own, including family and social customs and manners, often but not necessarily associated with religious observance. In addition to those two essential characteristics the following characteristics are, in my opinion, relevant; (3) either a common geographical origin, or a descent from a small number of common ancestors; (4) a common language, not necessarily peculiar to the group; (5) a common literature peculiar

---

118 Para. 2.38.
119 Para. 2.43.
120 Paras 2.43 and 2.44 Code of Practice.
121 ONU v Akwiwu [2016] IRLR 719.
122 Para. 2.39.
123 [1983] IRLR 209 HL.

to the group; (6) a common religion different from that of neighbouring groups or from the general community surrounding it; (7) being a minority or being an oppressed or a dominant group within a larger community.

Such a group could include converts to it or persons who have married into it. Thus the term 'ethnic' could have a wide meaning.

This definition is adopted by the Code of Practice on Employment which states, in para. 2.40, that the two essential elements in defining an ethnic group are a long shared history and the group having a cultural tradition of its own. In addition the group may share one or all of having a common language; a common literature; a common religion; a common geographical origin; or being a minority; or an oppressed group.

Surprisingly, this definition did not extend to Rastafarians (discrimination on the grounds of religion or belief is discussed below). In *Dawkins*[124] an applicant for a job was turned away because he was a Rastafarian and would not comply with a requirement for short hair. His complaint of discrimination was rejected by the Court of Appeal on the grounds that Rastafarians could not be defined as a racial group under the Race Relations Act 1976. They did not fulfil the criteria laid down in *Mandla v Dowell Lee* because they did not have a long shared history,[125] and could not be compared as a racial group to the Jamaican community or the Afro-Caribbean community in England. In contrast, Jews, Romany Gypsies, Irish Travellers, Scottish Gypsies, and Scottish Travellers have been held to be protected ethnic groups by the courts, although an attempt to define English-speaking Welsh people as a separate ethnic group from Welsh-speaking Welsh persons failed. This was because it was insufficient to identify a separate group on the basis of language alone.[126]

R v Governing Body of JFS[127] concerned an application for admission to the Jewish Free School (JFS). It was described as a school that was Orthodox Jewish in character. The school had a policy of giving preference to those whose status as Jews was recognised by the Chief Rabbi's office. An important aspect of this is that the child of a Jewish mother is automatically Jewish. The problem for the applicant was that his father was born Jewish, but his mother was a convert to Judaism. Conversion to Orthodox Judaism was a long and difficult process, but conversion to other denominations of Judaism was a shorter process and this was the route followed by the applicant's mother. He was then refused admission to the school on the basis that his mother's conversion was not in accordance with Orthodox standards. The House of Lords upheld his complaint of racial discrimination. The conversion of the mother had, using the *Mandla* definition, brought her within the Jewish ethnic group and it followed that the applicant had been refused admission because of his membership of the ethnic group. It was irrelevant that this was done to comply with religious law rather than a concern with the ethnicity of the candidate.

7.7.2 Segregation

Section 13(5) EA provides that:

> If the protected characteristic is race, less favourable treatment includes segregating B from others.

Thus, when the protected characteristic is race, deliberately segregating a worker or group of workers from others of a different race automatically amounts to less favourable treatment. There is

---

124 *Dawkins v Department of the Environment; sub nom Crown Suppliers PSA* [1993] IRLR 284 CA.
125 Only 60 years was suggested by the court.
126 *Gwynedd County Council v Jones* [1986] ICR 833.
127 *R v Governing Body of JFS and the Admissions Appeal Panel of JFS* [2010] IRLR 136.

no need to identify a comparator, because racial segregation is always discriminatory.[128] The Code of Practice provides the following example:

> A British marketing company which employs predominantly British staff recruits Polish nationals and seats them in a separate room nicknamed 'Little Poland'. The company argues that they have an unofficial policy of seating the Polish staff separately from British staff so that they can speak amongst themselves in their native language without disturbing the staff who speak English. This is segregation, as the company has a deliberate policy of separating staff because of race.

7.8 Religion or belief

Religious discrimination can be closely linked to racial discrimination, but religious discrimination was not expressly made unlawful until 2003. A good example of a case predating regulation was *Ahmad v ILEA*.[129] This concerned a Muslim school teacher who required a short time off on Friday afternoons to attend prayers at a nearby mosque. He resigned and claimed unfair dismissal when his employers refused him paid time off. They had offered him a part-time position working four and a half days per week. The United Kingdom had not at the time incorporated the European Convention on Human Rights into national law, but, as Lord Denning stated in this case, 'we will do our best to see that our decisions are in conformity with it'. In this case it still meant rejecting the claim as it would give the Muslim community 'preferential treatment'. The court held that art. 9(2) of the Convention did not give an employee the right to absent himself from work in breach of the contract of employment. Lord Scarman dissented, stating that the issue began, but did not end, with the law of contract. The judgment would mean that any Muslim, who took their religious duties seriously, could never be employed on a full-time contract as a teacher. This is an old case and one must doubt whether the same decision would be reached today. It does, however, illustrate how it is possible to penalise someone for carrying out the activities and ritual connected to their religious beliefs. Another example is *Mandla v Dowell Lee*[130] where the Sikhs were identified as an ethnic group, and were thus protected under the Race Relations Act 1976.

The 2011 census[131] showed that Christianity was the largest religion in England and Wales, with some 33.2 million people (59.3 per cent of the population). The second-largest religious group was Muslims with 2.7 million people (4.8 per cent of the population). Some 14.1 million people, around a quarter of the population, stated that they had no religion. Between 2001 and 2011 there had been a decrease in people who identified as Christian (from 71.7 per cent to 59.3 per cent) and an increase in those reporting no religion (from 14.8 per cent to 25.1 per cent). There were increases in the other main religious group categories, with the number of Muslims increasing the most, from 3.0 per cent to 4.8 per cent.[132]

The Framework Directive was transposed into national law by the Employment Equality (Religion or Belief) Regulations 2003,[133] which have now been absorbed into the Equality Act 2010.

---

128 Para. 3.8 Code of Practice.
129 [1977] ICR 490.
130 [1983] IRLR 209.
131 The religion question was the only voluntary question on the 2011 census and 7.2 per cent of people did not answer the question.
132 Information from the website of the Office for National Statistics.
133 SI 2003/1660.

7.8.1 The Equality Act 2010

Section 4 EA provides that religion or belief is one of the protected characteristics. The Equality Act, as with the other protected characteristics, makes direct discrimination, indirect discrimination, harassment and victimisation on the characteristic of religion or belief unlawful.

Religion means any religion and includes a lack of religion.[134] The Code of Practice explains, for example, that this means that Christians are protected because of their Christianity, but non-Christians are also protected because they are not Christians. Mainstream religions are, of course, covered, such as Buddhism, Christianity, Hinduism, Islam, Judaism, Rastafarianism and Sikhism. Non-mainstream religions are not excluded provided they have, according to the Code of Practice, a clear structure and belief system. Denominations within groups, such as Methodists within Christianity or Sunnis within Islam, are also likely to be regarded as religions within the scope of the Act.

Belief means any religious or philosophical belief and also includes having a lack of belief.[135] According to the Code of Practice, a belief which is not a religious belief may be a philosophical belief, such as Humanism and Atheism. A belief need not include faith or worship, but must affect how a person lives their life or perceives the world. For a philosophical belief to be protected under the Act:

- it must be genuinely held;
- it must be a belief and not an opinion or viewpoint based on the present state of information available;
- it must be a belief as to a weighty and substantial aspect of human life and behaviour;
- it must attain a certain level of cogency, seriousness, cohesion and importance;
- it must be worthy of respect in a democratic society, not incompatible with human dignity and not conflict with the fundamental rights of others.[136]

This listing was repeated in the case of *Grainger plc v Nicholson*[137] where a belief in manmade climate change was held to be a philosophical belief for the purposes of the legislation.[138] The EAT stated that to be a belief that is protected by the legislation, the belief did not have to be something that governed the entirety of one's life. Examples given by the court were vegetarianism or pacifism. Both of these would be protected philosophical beliefs, so the belief did not have to be a fully-fledged system of thought.

There is a particular difficulty with outward manifestations of religious belief, as shown in *Eweida v British Airways plc*.[139] Mrs Eweida was a devout Christian who regarded the cross as the central image of her belief; she wanted to wear it over her uniform in her role as a part-time check-in member of staff. The company's rules only permitted the wearing of visible religious symbols where there was a 'mandatory' religious requirement. Mrs Eweida complained that this amounted to indirect discrimination. Ms Eweida lost at the Court of Appeal but her appeal to the European Court of Human Rights was successful.[140] She successfully argued that her right to freedom of thought, conscience and religion and the manifestation of that belief under art. 9 of the ECHR had not been protected. In a parallel case, however, the Court of Human Rights said that in the case of Ms Chaplin, a nurse who was forbidden to wear a cross at work, there had been no violation of art. 9 on health

---

134 Section 10(1) EA 2010.
135 Section 10(2) EA 2010.
136 Code of Practice para. 2.59.
137 [2010] IRLR 4.
138 Much reliance is placed on art. 9 of the European Convention on Human Rights, which protects the right to freedom of thought, conscience and religion; and judicial decisions of the European Court of Human Rights.
139 [2010] IRLR 322.
140 *Eweida and others v United Kingdom* [2013] IRLR 231.

and safety grounds. The right to manifest one's beliefs had to be matched against the need for health and safety on a hospital ward.

The Code of Practice points out, however, that restrictions on some manifestations of belief may amount to indirect discrimination. Such manifestations could include the treating of certain days as days for worship or rest or the following of a particular dress code or diet. The Code provides an example:

> An employer has a 'no headwear' policy for its staff. Unless this policy can be objectively justified, this will be indirect discrimination against Sikh men who wear the turban, Muslim women who wear a headscarf and observant Jewish men who wear a skullcap as manifestations of their religion.

In *Wasteney*[141] the claimant, who was employed by East London NHS Foundation Trust, was a born-again Christian who attended an evangelical church. There was an initiative whereby the church provided religious services at the facility. A woman of Pakistani heritage and Muslim faith started work at the trust as an occupational therapist in her first 12-month placement post-training. Subsequently, she complained that the claimant had tried to impose her religious views on her: inviting her to services at the church, praying with her and, on one occasion, laying hands on her. She said that she felt 'groomed' by the claimant, who had abused her managerial position. She described how the claimant's attention had begun to make her feel ill and had 'completely ruined her first year of practice'.

The EAT held that art. 9 of the ECHR does not merely protect the right to hold a particular belief but also to manifest it. Decisions of the European Court of Human Rights, interpreting the right under Article 9, have shown that the freedom to manifest religion or belief can extend, in principle, to the right to attempt to convince others of the tenets of that religion or belief, and to bear witness in words and deeds. That said, the freedom to manifest one's religion or belief as guaranteed by art. 9 is qualified and may be limited in accordance with art. 9.2.

The EAT concluded that the claimant was not subjected to disciplinary process or sanction because she manifested her religious belief in voluntary and consensual exchanges with a colleague but because she subjected a subordinate to unwanted and unwelcome conduct. The treatment of which the claimant complained was because of, and related to, those inappropriate actions, not any legitimate manifestation of her belief.

7.8.2 Occupational requirements relating to organised religion and belief

The Equality Act provides that an employer may be permitted to require an applicant or employee to be of a particular sex or not to be a transsexual. There are also circumstances where the employer may be permitted to have rules with regard to marriage, civil partnership or sexual orientation.[142] The employer will need to show that:

(a) the employment is for the purposes of an organised religion,
(b) the application of the requirement engages the compliance or non-conflict principle, and
(c) the person to whom A applies the requirement does not meet it (or A has reasonable grounds for not being satisfied that the person meets it).

---

141 *Wasteney v East London NHS Foundation Trust* [2016] IRLR 388.
142 Schedule 9 para. 2(1); see also 13.12–13.18 Code of Practice on Employment.

The compliance principle relates to a requirement to comply with the doctrines of the religion in question; and the non-conflict principle relates to a requirement, because of the nature or context of employment, to avoid conflicting with strongly held religious views of a significant number of the religion's followers.[143] According to the Code of Practice, the requirement must be a proportionate way of meeting the compliance or non-conflict principle and should only be used for a limited number of positions, such as ministers of religion. Additionally, an employer with an ethos based on religion or belief may be able to apply, in relation to work, a requirement to be of a particular religion or belief if the employer can show, having regard to that ethos and to the nature or context of the work, that:

(a) it is an occupational requirement,

(b) the application of the requirement is a proportionate means of achieving a legitimate aim, and

(c) the person to whom the employer applies the requirement does not meet it (or the employer has reasonable grounds for not being satisfied that the person meets it).

The Code of Practice gives the example of a lawful exception which might be a Humanist organisation which promotes Humanist philosophy and principles applying an occupational requirement for their chief executive to be a Humanist.

There is a potential conflict between the right to practise one's religious beliefs and the right to be free from discrimination on the grounds of sexual orientation. Two cases that illustrate this issue are *Ladele* and *McFarlane*.[144] Ms Ladele was a registrar of births, deaths and marriages who objected to carrying out same-sex partnership ceremonies. Mr McFarlane was a marriage counsellor who objected to counselling homosexual couples. Both individuals' objections were on the grounds that homosexuality was incompatible with their Christian beliefs. Both cases were lost at the European Court of Human Rights which held that there had not been a violation of art. 9 ECHR because of the need for the organisations concerned to carry out their policies in a non-discriminatory way. These cases illustrate the difficulty in protecting the rights of individuals when there is a clash between two of the protected characteristics, namely religion or belief and sexual orientation. The rules on occupational exceptions try to deal with this by limiting the occasions when exceptions to the general rule of non-discrimination can be made.

7.9 Sex

Recently, the gender pay gap has been decreasing, although it is still substantial. For full-time employees the pay gap in 2016 was 9.4 per cent, down from 17.4 per cent in 1997. For all employees, including part-timers, the gap was 18.1 per cent, down from 27.5 per cent in 1997. This is, of course, more than 40 years since the first Sex Discrimination Act in 1975 and even longer since the Equal Pay Act 1970, and is an example of the continuing disadvantage suffered by women. Now s. 4 EA provides that sex is one of the protected characteristics.

Section 78 of the Equality Act 2010 enabled the Minister to make regulations requiring employers with at least 250 employees to publish information about the differences in pay between their male and female employees. The Gender Pay Gap Regulations[145] were introduced with effect from 6 April 2016. An obligation is placed upon a relevant employer to produce certain information

---

143 Schedule 9 paras 2(5)–2(6).

144 *Ladele v London Borough of Islington* [2010] IRLR 211 and *Ladele and McFarlane v United Kingdom* [2011] ECHR 737; see *Eweida and others v United Kingdom* [2013] IRLR 231.

145 The Equality Act 2010 (Gender Pay Gap Information) Regulations 2017, SI 2017/172.

annually. A relevant employer is one that employs at least 250 people on the snapshot date (5 April). Regulation 2(1) provides that the employer must publish for 2017 and subsequent years:

(a) the difference between the mean hourly rate of pay of male full-pay relevant employees[146] and that of female full-pay relevant employees (see regulation 8);
(b) the difference between the median hourly rate of pay of male full-pay relevant employees and that of female full-pay relevant employees (see regulation 9);
(c) the difference between the mean bonus pay paid to male relevant employees and that paid to female relevant employees (see regulation 10);
(d) the difference between the median bonus pay paid to male relevant employees and that paid to female relevant employees (see regulation 11);
(e) the proportions of male and female relevant employees who were paid bonus pay (see regulation 12); and
(f) the proportions of male and female full-pay relevant employees in the lower, lower middle, upper middle and upper quartile pay bands (see regulation 13).

Regulation 14 provides that the information must be accompanied by a signed written statement confirming that the information is accurate. The information must be published on the employer's website and a further one designated by the government (reg. 15).

According to para. 7.3 of the explanatory memorandum accompanying the Regulations, the aim of compulsory gender pay gap reporting is 'to use transparency as a tool for raising awareness, to incentivise employers to analyse the drivers behind their gender pay gap and to explore the extent to which their own policies and practices may have contributed to that gap'. The passing of time will show whether this is effective or not.

B v A[147] concerned an executive in a local authority who claimed that she had been raped by a colleague and that this was the culmination of a period of sexual harassment. She did not make a formal complaint to the police, but the CEO dismissed the alleged rapist. Subsequently, the police decided not to take further action, so he made a complaint, amongst other matters, of sex discrimination; namely that the employer had been motivated by a gender stereotype that a complaint by a woman against a man for rape had to be well founded. The employment tribunal rejected this but still found sex discrimination because the employer had not gone through any form of due process. It applied the process from another case, *Igen Ltd v Wong*,[148] which provided that there was a two-stage process to be gone through: first, whether there was evidence from which it could be reasonably concluded that the employer had discriminated and, second, whether the employer had proved that there had been no discrimination on the grounds of sex. The EAT overturned the decision – the CEO had been motivated by a fear of further violence towards the claimant, but the EAT said that this was not necessarily due to gender stereotyping. If he would have acted in the same way if the alleged attacker had been a woman and the victim a man, then there was no case for less favourable treatment.

MOD v DeBique[149] was a case concerning, amongst other matters, indirect sex discrimination. Ms DeBique came from a Commonwealth country, St Vincent and the Grenadines. In 2001 she joined the British army and moved to the United Kingdom. As a serving soldier she had to be available 24/7. In 2005 she gave birth to a daughter. She arranged with her unit that she would not

---

146 According to ACAS, a wider definition of who counts as an employee is used here (from the Equality Act 2010). This means that workers are included, as well as some self-employed people. Agency workers are included, but counted by the agency providing them. www.acas.org.uk/index.aspx?articleid=5768
147 [2010] IRLR 400.
148 [2005] IRLR 258; see Chapter 6.
149 *Ministry of Defence v DeBique* [2010] IRLR 471.

undertake weekend duties or those between 8.30 and 4.30 during the week. There were various incidents including being late appearing on parade for childcare reasons. As punishment, she was given two extra night shifts but pointed out that she could not do this because of her child. She was given a formal warning about her unsuitability to serve as a soldier and was put on three months' monitoring. In order to solve her problems she wanted to bring her sister over to help look after the child but her sister was unable to come to the United Kingdom owing to immigration rules. She brought a grievance procedure on sex and race discrimination on the basis that British soldiers could have an adult relative living with them to help with childcare but this was not available to foreign and Commonwealth soldiers. Tribunal cases eventually resulted. The provision, criterion or practice in question was the need to be available 24/7. The employment tribunal said this was reasonable in isolation, but it failed to reflect the claimant's situation. The fact that she could not have relatives stay with her was also regarded as an immigration provision, criterion or practice. The pool for comparison was single parent soldiers and that those of St Vincent origin suffered in comparison because they could not bring over their extended family.

Although the provisions of the Equality Act, with regard to sex, have as a primary purpose the removing of gender imbalances between men and women, it does not necessarily require the same treatment as between men and women. The aim is to ensure that one gender is not treated less favourably than another. One area of contention in the employment field has been the imposition of dress codes that might have the effect of discriminating against one particular sex. In *Smith v Safeway plc*,[150] for example, a male employee was dismissed because his ponytail grew too long to keep under his hat. The store had a code which required men to have hair not below shirt-collar level, but female employees were permitted to have hair down to shoulder length. Phillips LJ stated that:

> I can accept that one of the objects of the prohibition of sex discrimination was to relieve the sexes from unequal treatment resulting from conventional attitudes, but I do not believe that this renders discriminatory an appearance code which applies a standard of what is conventional.

The result was that the court held that the employer was imposing a dress code that reflected a conventional outlook and that this should not be held to be discriminatory. The effect of such a decision was, however, that a male employee was dismissed because of the length of his hair, which would have been permissible in a female employee.[151]

Section 11(a) EA also makes it clear that this characteristic applies to men as well as women. A good example of this occurred in *Eversheds v De Belin*.[152] The employer in this case was in a difficult situation. The claimant was one of two solicitors of whom one would be made redundant. The choice for the employer was between the claimant, who was a man, and another solicitor who was absent on maternity leave at the time. The employer adopted a points scheme to decide on which person was to go. One of the factors gaining points was called 'lock up'. This was the amount of time between undertaking a piece of work and receiving payment. The claimant was scored on his actual performance, but the absent person, on maternity leave, was given the maximum possible points for lock up, even though she did not have any payments during the chosen period. This enabled her to gain marginally more points than the claimant and so he was made redundant. He then claimed sex discrimination and unfair dismissal. Given the restrictions on acting against pregnancy or people on maternity leave, the employer argued that they had fulfilled their responsibility

---

150 [1996] IRLR 457 CA.

151 In *Burrett v West Birmingham Health Authority* [1994] IRLR 7, female nurses were required to wear caps but male nurses were not. The EAT held that the important issue was that they both had to wear uniforms, not that those uniforms differed.

152 *Eversheds Legal Services Ltd v De Belin* [2011] IRLR 448.

to the maternity leave employee (if they had taken an alternative route, it is possible that they could have faced a sex discrimination claim from the, then, redundant female employee absent on maternity leave). The EAT held, in the event, that the law which gave pregnant women and those on maternity leave special treatment and protection still required the treatment to be a proportionate means of achieving a legitimate aim. In this case the treatment given to the absent employee was disproportionate and thus amounted to direct sex discrimination against the male employee.[153]

7.10 Sexual orientation

There are difficulties in estimating what proportion of the population is lesbian, gay or bisexual (LGB), but the estimate used by the government and others is that between 5 and 7 per cent of the UK population are LGB.[154] This is a large number of people, many of whom have suffered and continue to suffer discrimination because of their sexual orientation. In order to meet its obligations under the Equal Treatment in Employment and Occupation Directive,[155] the government adopted the Employment Equality (Sexual Orientation) Regulations 2003 (the Sexual Orientation Regulations).[156] These came into force on 1 December 2003. These are now incorporated into the Equality Act 2010. Prior to these Regulations there were few provisions protecting people at work from being discriminated against because of their sexual orientation.

Until the government relaxed its approach in 2000 this absence of protection posed a particular problem for members of the armed services. The Court of Appeal refused to construe the Equal Treatment Directive in order to include sexual orientation and suggested that any proscription of discrimination on the grounds of sexual orientation might need to be achieved by a specific Directive.[157] The government's change of approach occurred after the European Court of Human Rights reached a decision in *Smith and Grady*.[158] Prior to this decision the policy of the Ministry of Defence had been that 'homosexuality, whether male or female, is considered incompatible with service in the armed forces'.[159] After the European Court of Human Rights held that the rights of the individuals under art. 8 (right to privacy) and art. 13 (right to an effective domestic remedy) of the European Convention on Human Rights had been violated, the ban on homosexuals in the armed forces was lifted. The Ministry of Defence issued a new Code of Social Conduct[160] which banned unacceptable social conduct, which applied to heterosexuals as well as homosexuals. The 'service test' was introduced to determine when it was necessary to intervene in the personal lives of employees. This test consists of the commanding officer considering whether 'the actions or behaviour of an individual adversely impacted or are likely to impact on the efficiency or operational effectiveness of the service'.

There is a distinction between discrimination against homosexuals on the grounds of their sexuality and discrimination on the grounds of their sex. In *Smith v Gardner Merchant Ltd*[161] a male homosexual complained that he was subjected to threatening and abusive behaviour by a female

---

153 *Nelson v Newry and Mourne DC* [2009] IRLR 548 was also a case where a man claimed direct sex discrimination. This case concerned two council employees, one male and one female, who were investigated for misusing council property. They were treated in different ways with regard to the disciplinary process and the man was given a much more severe sanction than the female.

154 See Stonewall's website at www.stonewall.org.uk.

155 Directive 2000/78/EC.

156 SI 2003/1661; the government estimates that between 1.3 and 1.9 million people are affected by the Regulations.

157 See *R v Secretary of State for Defence, ex parte Perkins* (No 2) [1998] IRLR 508 where a medical assistant was discharged from the Royal Navy because of his sexual orientation; see also *Secretary of State for Defence v MacDonald* [2001] IRLR 431 CS, which concerned a member of the RAF who was excluded because of his sexual orientation.

158 *Smith and Grady v United Kingdom* [1999] IRLR 734 ECHR.

159 Ministry of Defence Guidelines on Homosexuality, December 1994.

160 *The Armed Forces Code of Social Conduct: Policy Statement*, 1999.

161 [1998] IRLR 510 CA.

colleague. He was subsequently dismissed and the employment tribunal decided that it did not have jurisdiction to hear claims of discrimination on grounds of sexual orientation. The appeal was won at the EAT and upheld by the Court of Appeal who concluded that such discrimination against a male homosexual could amount to discrimination against him as a male. In this case the correct comparator, under s. 5(3) SDA 1975,[162] in relation to the treatment by the work colleague could be with a homosexual woman and whether she would have been treated in the same way. For comparison concerning a complaint about the employer's handling of the situation, the female colleague could be used as the comparator. This approach did not help a lesbian school teacher who was subject to homophobic verbal abuse by pupils at the school. *Pearce v Governing Body of Mayfield Secondary School*[163] followed the approach in *Smith v Gardner Merchant Ltd* to conclude that it could not be said that she had received less favourable treatment than a hypothetical homosexual male teacher, as there was no evidence that such a teacher would have been treated any differently. The change brought about by the Regulations is illustrated in *English v Thomas Sanderson Blinds Ltd*[164] where Mr English claimed that for many years he had been subject to homophobic abuse as a result of having attended a public school and living in Brighton. He was not homosexual and he accepted that his work colleagues did not really believe him to be homosexual. The Court of Appeal held that a person being tormented by homophobic abuse could rely on reg. 5 of the Sexual Orientation Regulations even though he was not gay or perceived as being gay by his colleagues.

Section 4 EA provides that sexual orientation is one of the protected characteristics. The Equality Act, as with the other protected characteristics, makes direct discrimination, indirect discrimination, harassment and victimisation on the characteristic of sexual orientation unlawful. Section 12(1) defines sexual orientation as a sexual orientation towards persons:

- of the same sex – thus covering both gay men and gay women;
- of the opposite sex – which provides for heterosexual relationships;
- of the same sex and opposite sex – which covers bisexual men and women.

Grant v HM Land Registry[165] concerned an individual who complained that a number of incidents occurring during his employment amounted to discrimination and harassment on the grounds of his sexual orientation. This included the dissemination of the fact that he was homosexual. Direct discrimination is unlawful when it results in an employee's dismissal or subjects him to any detriment. The court held that the disclosure of someone's sexual orientation would amount to a detriment and could be a case of humiliating treatment so constituting harassment. In this case Mr Grant had himself 'come out' and revealed his homosexuality, albeit when he worked at a different location, and this was held to be important when there were references to his sexual orientation. Any grievance that he then had about this information being disseminated to others could not amount to a detriment. Nor could it amount to harassment. The dissemination may have been unwanted but could not be said to amount to creating an environment which was intimidating, hostile, degrading or offensive.

According to para. 2.66 of the Code of Practice, sexual orientation discrimination includes discrimination connected with manifestations of that sexual orientation. These may include someone's appearance, the places they visit or the people they associate with.

---

162 Section 5(3) SDA 1975 provides that a comparison of persons of different sex or marital status, or of the cases of discrimination and gender reassignment, must be such that the relevant circumstances in the one case are the same as, or not materially different from, those in the other.
163 [2001] IRLR 669 CA.
164 [2009] IRLR 206.
165 [2012] IRLR 748.

Further reading

Bisom-Rapp, S. and Sargeant, M. *Lifetime Disadvantage, Discrimination and the Gendered Workforce* (Cambridge University Press, 2016).

Colgan, F. and Wright, T. 'Lesbian, Gay and Bisexual Equality in a Modernizing Public Sector 1997–2010: Opportunities and Threats' (2011) 18(5) *Gender, Work and Organization* 548.

Hepple, B. 'Enforcing Equality Law: Two Steps Forward and Two Steps Backwards for Reflexive Regulation' (2011) 40(4) *Industrial Law Journal* 315.

Lawson, A. 'Disability and Employment in the Equality Act 2010: Opportunities Seized, Lost and Generated' (2011) 40(4) *Industrial Law Journal* 359.

Sargeant, M. *Age Discrimination and Diversity* (Gower Publishing, 2011).

Sargeant, M. *Discrimination and the Law* (Taylor & Francis, 2017).

www.edf.org.uk – Equality and Diversity Forum.

www.equalityhumanrights.com – Equality and Human Rights Commission.

www.homeoffice.gov.uk/equalities – Government Equalities Office.

Chapter 8

Time and pay

Chapter Contents

8.1 Working time

The discussion about the regulation of a person's working time encapsulated the arguments about the degree to which governments should intervene in the employment relationship and the extent to which such regulation should originate with the EU. The British government, in *United Kingdom v Council of Ministers*,[1] argued that such matters were an issue of subsidiarity and should be settled within Member States rather than by the Community. The Council argued that the justification for the Working Time Directive[2] was a health and safety one and that the Community had competence in this field. In the event, the United Kingdom finally transposed the Directive into national law some two years late.[3]

8.2 Young Workers' Directive

The Working Time Regulations include the transposition of parts of the Young Workers' Directive[4] into national law. This Directive came into effect on 22 June 1996, but the United Kingdom was permitted to delay this process. The final parts of the Directive were transposed into national law in 2002. This Directive was also adopted under art. 137 EC (now art. 153 of TFEU) concerning health and safety. It applies to any person under the age of 18 years who has an employment contract or an employment relationship. Subject to minor exceptions, the Directive prohibits the employment of children. These are defined as persons of less than 15 years of age, or the minimum school leaving age, whichever is higher. The minor exceptions include work experience, work in the theatre and light work.[5]

Articles 6 and 7, which describe the general obligations placed upon employers and the prohibition of certain types of employment of young people, were implemented by the Health and Safety (Young Persons) Regulations 1997.[6] Those parts concerning the employment of children were implemented by the Children (Protection at Work) Regulations 1998 (see below).[7] The provisions on working hours, night work, rest periods, periodic and annual breaks are included in the Working Time Regulations.[8]

The number of young people working is significant, despite the expansion of numbers in further and higher education. Many will be part-time workers helping to finance their education.[9] According to the Management of Health and Safety at Work Regulations 1999 (MHSW Regulations 1999),[10] an employer of a young person[11] must carry out a risk assessment which takes particular account of a number of factors.[12] These are:

1. The inexperience, lack of awareness of risks and immaturity of young persons.
2. The fitting-out and the layout of the workplace and the workstation.

---

1 Case C-84/94 [1997] IRLR 30.
2 Council Directive 93/104/EC concerning certain aspects of the organisation of working time OJ L307/18 13.12.93. This was significantly amended by the European Parliament and Council Directive 2003/88/EC.
3 Working Time Regulations 1998, SI 1998/1833.
4 Council Directive 94/33/EC on the protection of young people at work OJ L216/12 20.8.94.
5 Articles 4–5 Young Workers' Directive.
6 SI 1997/135.
7 SI 1998/276.
8 There were also provisions relating to young people working on sea-going ships, which were dealt with by the Fishing Vessels (Health and Safety) (Employment of Children and Young Persons) Regulations 1998, SI 1998/2411.
9 See Chapter 2 on the Part-time Workers Regulations 2000.
10 SI 1999/3242.
11 Young person means any person who has not attained the age of 18 years; see reg. 1(2) MHSW Regulations 1999.
12 Regulation 3(5) MHSW Regulations 1999.

3. The nature, degree and duration of exposure to physical, biological and chemical agents.
4. The form, range and use of work equipment and the way in which it is used.
5. The organisation of processes and activities.
6. The extent of the health and safety training provided or to be provided to young persons.
7. The risks from agents, processes and work listed in the annex to the Young Workers' Directive.

Regulation 10(2) of the MHSW Regulations 1999 provides that, before employing a child,[13] any employer must provide a parent[14] of the child with 'comprehensible and relevant information' on any risks to the child's health and safety that have been identified by the risk assessment and the preventive and protective measures that have been taken. Employers have a general responsibility for protecting young persons from any risks to their health and safety which are

> a consequence of their lack of experience, or absence of awareness of existing or potential risks or the fact that young persons have not fully matured.[15]

The Children (Protection at Work) Regulations 1998 amended the Children and Young Persons Acts 1933 and 1963 to give effect to the Young Workers' Directive. They impose restrictions on the working hours and the type of work that can be undertaken by individuals under the compulsory school leaving age.

8.3 Working Time Directive

The justification for the Working Time Directive in 1993 was art. 118a EC (now art. 153 TFEU), which stated at the time that:

> Member States shall pay particular attention to encouraging improvements, especially in the working environment, as regards the health and safety of workers, and shall set as their objective the harmonisation of conditions in this area, while maintaining the improvements made.

It was also justified, in the preamble to the Directive, by the following extract from the Community Charter of the Fundamental Social Rights of Workers:[16]

> The completion of the internal market must lead to an improvement in the living and working conditions of workers in the European Community. This process must result from an approximation of these conditions while the improvement is being maintained, as regards in particular the duration and organisation of working time . . .

Thus the measure was intended to harmonise the approach of Member States to 'ensure the safety and health of Community workers'.[17] One problem for the United Kingdom was that many other Member States already had statutory rules on weekly and daily hours, which preceded the Working

---

13 Someone who is not over compulsory school leaving age.
14 A parent is someone who has parental responsibility according to s. 3 Children Act 1989; the same definition as in the Maternity and Parental Leave etc. Regulations 1999; see Chapter 9.
15 Regulation 19(1) MHSW Regulations 1999.
16 Adopted on 9 December 1989 by all the then Member States with the exception of the United Kingdom.
17 The preamble states: 'Whereas, in order to ensure the safety and health of Community workers, the latter must be granted minimum daily, weekly and annual periods of rest and adequate breaks . . .'

Time Directive. Belgium, France, Greece, Ireland, Italy and Portugal all had existing rules which limited working hours.[18] One of the consequences of using art. 118a EC (now art. 153 TFEU) was that it could be adopted using the 'co-operation procedure' in art. 189c EC (now repealed). This needed only a qualified majority by the Council of Ministers to adopt a common position with regard to the proposal. In the event the United Kingdom abstained, but indicated that it would challenge the legal basis for the Directive.

The subject matter of the Directive related to minimum periods of daily and weekly rest, breaks in work, annual leave, maximum weekly working time and patterns of work, such as night work and shift work. Subject to certain derogations permitted in art. 17, the Directive applies to the same public and private sectors as the Health and Safety at Work Directive.[19] There were a number of specific exceptions to this, which included air, rail, road and sea, as well as the activities of doctors in training.[20]

The Directive was due to be transposed into national law by 23 November 1996 but, partly because of the United Kingdom government's legal challenge, it came into effect with the Working Time Regulations in October 1998. This challenge[21] was through proceedings for annulment of the Directive, or of certain parts of arts. 4, 5, 6 and 7. The action was brought under art. 173 EC (now art. 263 TFEU), which gives the Court of Justice jurisdiction in actions brought by Member States or certain EU institutions, to review the legality of acts of the EU

> on grounds of lack of competence, infringement of an essential procedural requirement, infringement of this Treaty or any rule of law relating to its application, or misuse of powers.

The UK action was based on the following four claims:

1. The Directive had a defective legal basis i.e. it should have been adopted on the basis of art. 100 EC (now art. 115 TFEU) or art. 235 EC (now art. 352 TFEU), which required unanimity in the Council of Ministers.
2. The Directive did not comply with the principle of proportionality, because its provisions went beyond the minimum requirements permitted under art. 118a EC (now art. 153 TFEU). Specifically, overall reductions in working hours or an overall increase in rest periods were not 'minimum requirements', the desired level of protection could have been attained by less restrictive measures and the proposed measures were not justified by scientific research. Additionally, it had not been shown that the Directive's objectives could be better achieved at Community level, rather than at Member State level.
3. The Directive contained a number of measures which were unconnected with its purported aims and were, therefore, a misuse of powers.
4. Finally, it was claimed that there was an infringement of essential procedural requirements. This arose because there was a failure to show a causal relationship between the proposals and health and safety, which meant that it had failed to state the reasons on which it was based. Alternatively, it was argued, the reasoning was flawed as there was a failure to explain that many of the measures were concerned with matters other than health and safety.

---

18 *European Industrial Relations Review* 280, May 1997, p. 18.
19 Council Directive 89/391/EEC on the introduction of measures to encourage improvements in the safety and health of workers at work OJ LI1 83/1 29.6.89.
20 Article 1 Working Time Directive; see below for current exclusions.
21 Case C-84/94 *United Kingdom v Council of Ministers* [1997] IRLR 30.

The United Kingdom lost on every point, except where the Court of Justice annulled a proposal that, in principle, the weekly rest period should be on a Sunday. The Court of Justice held that the principal purpose of the Directive was the protection of the health and safety of workers and that it was, therefore, adopted under the correct part of the Treaty and that it was not in breach of the principle of proportionality. It stated that the concept of 'minimum requirements' is not about setting minimum standards but refers to the individual State's ability to impose more stringent standards than that set by Community action. The Council also dismissed the claims of misuse of powers or inadequate reasoning.

As a result, there was a period when the United Kingdom had failed to transpose the Directive. In *Gibson v East Riding of Yorkshire Council*[22] a local authority employee claimed that she could rely on art. 7[23] of the Directive having direct effect during the period between 23 November 1996, the date by which it should have been implemented, and 1 October 1998, the date when the Working Time Regulations came into effect. She was an employee of an emanation of the State and the EAT held that she could rely on the Directive, as art. 7 in particular met the requirements for having direct effect[24] by being sufficiently precise and unconditional. However, the Court of Appeal disagreed with this approach and allowed the appeal.[25] The court held that certain provisions were not sufficiently precise, especially the definition of working time itself. The court stated:

> The first basic question for the national court is: what is the period of 'working time' for which the worker must have worked before he becomes entitled to annual leave under Article 7? Annual leave is leave from 'working time'. The concept of 'working time' is not precisely defined. To what period of 'working time' does the specified period of annual leave relate? The question is not answered by Article 7 itself or by any other provisions in the Directive. How then is it possible for a national court to decide which workers are entitled to annual leave?

8.4 Working Time Regulations

The Working Time Regulations 1998 have been amended on a number of occasions.[26] One effect of these amendments is to weaken the 1998 Regulations even further, making it much easier for the employer and worker to agree to exclude the provisions of the maximum weekly working time of an average of 48 hours. There were also fresh exclusions from certain provisions for those whose working time is not measured or predetermined.

8.4.1 Scope and definition

The 1998 Regulations, which apply to Great Britain, offer protection to workers who are defined, in reg. 2(1), as those having a contract of employment or any other contract where the individual undertakes to do or perform personally any work or services for another party.[27] 'Young worker' is someone who is over the compulsory school age but is under 18 years of age.[28] Regulation 36 of

---

22 [2000] IRLR 598 CA.

23 Concerning annual leave; see below.

24 See also *R v Attorney General for Northern Ireland, ex parte Burns* [1999] IRLR 315 which also considered this issue in relation to night work.

25 *Gibson v East Riding of Yorkshire Council* [2000] IRLR 598 CA.

26 For example, the Working Time Regulations 1999, SI 1999/3372; the Working Time (Amendment) Regulations 2001, SI 2001/3256; the Working Time (Amendment) Regulations 2003, SI 2003/1684. The 2003 Regulations are concerned with finally implementing the working time provisions of Directive 94/33/EC on the protection of young people at work.

27 See s. 230(3) ERA 1996. See *Redrow Homes Ltd v Wright* [2004] IRLR 720.

28 On the position of children see *Addison v Ashby* [2003] IRLR 211.

the Regulations 1998[29] specifically provides for agency workers to be included. Where an individual is provided by an agency to do work for another, unless there is an agreement to different effect between the agency and the principal, the person who pays the agency worker in respect of the work is to be treated as the employer.[30]

The following three conditions must be satisfied for a period to constitute 'working time':

1. any period during which the worker is working;
2. any period when the worker is at the employer's disposal; and
3. any period when the worker is carrying out his duties and activities.

According to the EAT, reg. 2(1) should not be read as requiring that the duties and activities are contractual or normal working duties. Thus attendance at union meetings by union officials could constitute working time.[31]

Thus in *FSPSO v Tyco Security*[32] the CJEU held that the time security system technicians spent travelling between their homes and the employer's first and last customers of the day constituted working time.

The definition of working time also includes any period during which the worker is receiving relevant training.[33] Relevant training is defined as meaning work experience which is part of a training course or programme, training for employment, or both of these. It does not include work experience or training provided by an educational institution or a person whose main business is the provision of training or courses provided by such bodies. Presumably, this is conditional upon the employer's relationship with the training provider. If an institution provides a training course, defined by the employer as relevant to work, on the employer's premises and during normal working hours, it is difficult to see how this could not be 'relevant training', even though provided by this third party.

Lastly, working time means any additional period which is to be treated as working time under a 'relevant agreement'.[34] A 'relevant agreement' is any workforce agreement or any contractually binding part of a collective agreement or any other legally enforceable agreement between the worker and the employer (see below).

8.4.2 Exclusions

The 1998 Regulations follow the Directive closely in listing the exceptions to its coverage. Regulation 18 (as amended) excludes certain categories entirely. These are seafarers covered by Directive 1999/63 and those on board a sea-going vessel or a ship or hovercraft 'employed by an undertaking that operates services for passengers or goods by inland waterways or lake transport'. In addition, mobile staff in civil aviation who are covered by Directive 2000/79 and those performing mobile road transport activities who are covered by Directive 2002/15 are excluded from certain provisions. Other special categories are doctors in training[35] and those occupations where the characteristics of

---

29 Regulations 37–43 Working Time Regulations 1998 concern the position of other groups of workers, such as those in Crown employment and the armed forces and the police service.
30 Regulation 36(2) Working Time Regulations 1998.
31 *Edwards v ENCIRC Ltd* [2015] IRLR 528.
32 [2015] IRLR 935.
33 Regulation 2(1) Working Time Regulations 1998.
34 Regulation 2(1) Working Time Regulations 1998.
35 On doctors' maximum hours, see below.

the activities are likely to be incompatible with the Regulations, such as the armed services or the police.[36]

8.4.3 The 48-hour week

Regulations 4 and 5 are concerned with placing a 48-hour limit on the average amount of time worked per week. Unless an employer has first obtained the person's agreement in writing, a worker's working time (including any overtime) in any reference period must not exceed 48 hours for each seven days.[37]

Regulation 2(1) defines a day as a period of 24 hours commencing at midnight. The fact that working time is averaged means that it is possible for people to work long hours for sustained periods. In *King v Scottish & Newcastle*,[38] an individual was required to work for between 50 and 60 hours over the Christmas period, but there was no breach of the regulations as her hours were to be averaged over the reference period. The reference period is normally 17 weeks but can be varied by a collective or workforce agreement up to a maximum of 52 weeks.[39] This extension must be for 'objective or technical reasons'. It is not clear what these are likely to be but reg. 4(2) imposes an obligation on employers to take all reasonable steps 'in keeping with the need for health and safety of workers' to ensure that the limit specified is adhered to.[40] The obligation in reg. 4(2) is a separate obligation from the limit of 48 hours imposed by reg. 4(1). This was discussed in *Barber v RJB Mining (UK) Ltd*[41] where a trade union asked the High Court for a declaration that its members need not work again until their average working week fell to the 48-hour level. The trade union succeeded because the right in reg. 4(1) is a contractual obligation upon the employer. Subsequently, the Court of Justice has ruled that public sector workers can obtain reparation from their employer for breaches of the 48-hour limit in art. 6(6) of the Directive.[42]

The reference period can also be lengthened to 26 weeks for a number of special cases contained in reg. 21. These are situations where, for example, continuity of services needs to be maintained – for example, in hospitals or airports – or where there are peaks of work, such as in agriculture or tourism, or where the workers' activities are affected by events or accidents outside the control of the employer. Finally, for new workers, who have worked for less than the reference period, the period to be counted will be the actual time worked.[43]

The 1998 Regulations provide a formula for calculating the hours worked for each seven days during a reference period.[44] They are calculated as

$$\frac{A + B}{C} = \text{average hours per week during reference period}$$

The purpose of this formula is not to count the days that are not worked during the reference period, but to include an equivalent number of days from the next period in order to make up for those lost days. In this formula:

---

36 On emergency workers, see *Pfeiffer v Deutsches Rotes Kreuz* [2005] IRLR 137.
37 Regulation 4(1) Working Time Regulations 1998. On time spent 'on call', see *Landeshauptstadt Kiel v Jaeger* [2003] IRLR 804.
38 IDS Brief 641, 10 May 1999.
39 Regulation 23(b) Working Time Regulations 1998.
40 It does mean that annualised contracts are catered for within the 1998 Regulations.
41 [1999] IRLR 308.
42 *Fuss v Stadt Halle (No 2)* [2011] IRLR 177.
43 Regulation 4(4) Working Time Regulations 1998.
44 Regulation 4(6) Working Time Regulations 1998.

A is the aggregate number of hours in the worker's working time during the course of the reference period.

B is the aggregate number of hours in the worker's working time in the period immediately after the end of the reference period, equivalent to the number of days excluded in A.[45]

C is the number of weeks in the reference period.

❖ EXAMPLE

An individual has two periods of employment during the 17-week reference period as follows: working ten hours per day for five weeks, then a break of two weeks before a further period of eight hours per day for ten weeks (working a five-day week). In the next reference period the individual works an average of nine hours per day. Thus:

A = (10 hours × 5 days × 5 weeks) + (8 hours × 5 days × 10 weeks) = 650 hours worked;

B = 9 hours × 5 days × 2 weeks = 90

The formula is now:

$$\frac{650 + 90}{17} = 43.53 \text{ hours}$$

If the employee has agreed in writing to perform their work outside the scope of the regulations, then this formula cannot apply. If there is agreement to exclude for a limited period of time, then that period will count as excluded days. According to reg. 5, the agreement may apply for a specific period or for an indefinite period. It may also be subject to termination by the worker via the giving of notice, subject to a maximum of three months. If there is no such provision, then reg. 5 applies a seven-day notice period by default. Formerly, employers were required to maintain records of those who had opted out, specifying the numbers of hours worked during each reference period. All that an employer must now do is keep up-to-date records of the employees who have signed such an agreement.[46]

8.4.4 Night work

Regulations 6 and 7 deal with limits on night working and related obligations placed upon the employer.[47] As with the rules on the 48-hour average week, the employer has a duty to take all reasonable steps, in keeping with the need to protect the health and safety of workers, to ensure that the limits specified are complied with.[48] Night work is defined as being work during 'night time'. Night time has a specific meaning, which is a period of at least seven hours that includes

---

45 Regulation 4(7) Working Time Regulations 1998; excluded days means days taken for the purposes of annual leave, sick leave, maternity leave and any days in which the limit does not apply as agreed in writing between employer and worker; see below.
46 See Working Time Regulations 1999, SI 1999/3372.
47 Regulation 6A Working Time Regulations 1998 deals with young workers.
48 Regulations 4(2) and 6(2) Working Time Regulations 1998.

the period between midnight and 5 am. There are two alternative meanings given to the term 'night worker':

1. An individual who, as a normal course, works at least three of the normal daily working hours during night time. 'Normal course' means if the individual works such hours on the majority of days they work. This is said to be without prejudice to the generality of the expression, which suggests that there might be circumstances when 'normal course' can mean something else, such as working for at least three hours every day, rather than just the majority of days.
2. A worker who is likely, during night time, to work at least such a proportion of annual working time as may be specified in a collective or workforce agreement.[49]

In *R v Attorney General for Northern Ireland, ex parte Burns*[50] the High Court in Northern Ireland considered the meaning of the term 'normal course' as defined in art. 2(4) of the Working Time Directive. The employee had been asked to change to a shift system, which meant working a night shift between 9 pm and 7 am one week in three. The court held that the requirement for someone to work at least three hours during night time as a normal course meant no more than that this should be a regular feature of their work. According to the court, it was inconceivable that the protection should be confined to someone who works night shifts exclusively or predominantly.

In any applicable reference period, a night worker's normal hours must not exceed an average of eight hours for each 24 hours. There is a default reference period of 17 weeks and it is possible to agree to successive periods of 17 weeks[51] via a collective or workforce agreement. Where the individual has worked for the employer for less than 17 weeks, the reference period is the period since they started the employment.[52]

There is a formula for calculating a night worker's average normal hours for each 24 hours during a reference period. It is:

$$\frac{A}{B - C} = \text{average normal hours for each } 24 \text{ hours}$$

where:

A is the number of hours during the reference period which are normal working hours for that worker.

B is the number of days during the reference period.

C is the total number of hours during the reference period comprised in rest periods spent by the worker in pursuance of entitlement under reg. 11,[53] divided by 24.[54]

---

49 Regulation 2(1) Working Time Regulations 1998.
50 [1999] IRLR 315.
51 Regulation 6(1) and (3) Working Time Regulations 1998.
52 Regulation 6(4) Working Time Regulations 1998.
53 Weekly rest periods; see below.
54 Regulation 6(5) Working Time Regulations 1998.

❖ **EXAMPLE**[55]

A night worker normally works four 12-hour shifts per week. With a 17-week reference period,

A is 17 × (4 days × 12 hours) = 816 hours.

B is 17 × 7 days = 119 days.

The number of 24-hour weekly rest periods to which the worker is entitled under reg. 11 is 17; thus

C is (17 × 24 hours) divided by 24 = 17.

The formula will now look like this:

$$\frac{816}{119 - 17} = 8 \text{ hours}$$

The important difference between this formula and that applied to the 48-hour average is that this one deals with a worker's normal hours rather than their actual hours.

8.4.4.1 Special hazards

There is an additional obligation on an employer contained in reg. 6(7) and (8). This is to ensure that no night worker whose work involves special hazards or heavy physical or mental strain works for more than eight hours in any 24-hour period in which the worker does night work. Thus the focus is on actual rather than normal working hours. A worker is to be regarded as being involved in such hazards and strain either if it is identified as such in a collective or workforce agreement which takes into account the specific effects and hazards of night work, or it is recognised in a risk assessment carried out in accordance with reg. 3 MHSW Regulations 1999.

8.4.4.2 Health care

The other aspect of an employer's obligations with regard to night work relates to the worker's health and well-being. An employer must not assign an adult to night work without ensuring that the worker has the opportunity of a free[56] health assessment prior to taking up the assignment, unless the worker has had a health assessment on a previous occasion and the employer has no reason to believe that it has been become invalid. The employer also has a duty to ensure that each night worker has the opportunity for a free health assessment at regular and appropriate intervals.[57] Young workers are entitled to a free assessment of their 'health and capacities' before being assigned to work during the restricted period,[58] unless they had one on a previous occasion and the employer had no reason to believe that it has been become invalid[59] and unless the work is itself of an exceptional nature.[60] It is not clear if there is a difference between 'health assessment' and

---

55 Taken from the DTI (now DBIS) guidance to the Regulations.
56 Free means being of no cost to the workers to whom it relates: reg. 7(3) Working Time Regulations 1998.
57 Regulation 7(1) Working Time Regulations 1998.
58 The restricted period is between 10 pm and 6 am: reg. 7(2)(a) Working Time Regulations 1998.
59 Regulation 7(2) Working Time Regulations 1998.
60 Regulation 7(5) Working Time Regulations 1998.

an 'assessment of health and capacities'. Health assessment does not appear to mean the same as a medical examination. In its guidance to the Working Time Regulations 1998, the DBIS (now DBEIS) suggested that a health assessment should take place in two stages. First, workers should be asked to complete a questionnaire which asks specific questions about their health which are relevant to the type of night work which they will be doing. Second, if the employer is not certain that they are fit for night work following the questionnaire, the worker should be asked to have a medical examination.

There is an obligation of confidentiality associated with the health assessment. There is to be no disclosure of an assessment, apart from a statement that the worker is fit to be assigned to or continue with night work, to anyone but the worker to whom the assessment relates. The only exception is if the worker has given permission for disclosure.[61] If a registered medical practitioner advises an employer that a worker is suffering from health problems associated with night work, then the employer is under an obligation to transfer that person. There are two conditions attached to this obligation. First, it must be possible to transfer the individual to work which is not categorised as night work and, second, it must be work to which that person is suited.[62]

The employer must keep adequate records relating to regs 4(1), 6(1), (7), 7(1) and (2).[63] These records must relate to each worker employed and must be kept for a minimum of two years from the date that they were made.[64]

8.4.5 Time off

Regulation 8 imposes a general obligation on an employer to give workers adequate rest breaks where the pattern of work is such that the health and safety of the individuals may be put at risk, in particular if the work is monotonous or its rate is predetermined. Apart from this general obligation on an employer, regs 10–17 Working Time Regulations 1998 give the worker a number of specific entitlements to different types of breaks. These entitlements only and there is no obligation upon the worker to take advantage of them.[65]

8.4.6 Daily rest periods and rest breaks

Put simply, a rest period is a period between shifts and a rest break is a break during a shift. According to reg. 10(1) Working Time Regulations 1998, an adult worker is entitled to a rest period of at least 11 consecutive hours in each 24-hour period during which the person works for the employer.[66] The 24-hour period rather than an 11-hours-per-day rule means that, if necessary, the 11 hours can be over two working days. There is special provision for young workers who are entitled to a rest period of 12 consecutive hours in any 24-hour period that the young person works for the employer, although this period may be interrupted in the case of activities that are split up during the day or are of short duration.[67]

Additionally, where an adult worker's daily working time exceeds six hours, then the individual will be entitled to a rest break which can be spent away from the workstation if they have one.[68]

---

61 Regulation 7(6) Working Time Regulations 1998.
62 Regulation 7(6) Working Time Regulations 1998.
63 Maximum weekly working time, length of night work, length of night work involving special hazards or strain, health assessments for adult and young workers.
64 Regulation 9 Working Time Regulations 1998; reg. 25 excludes this requirement in relation to workers in the armed forces.
65 However, in order to meet the common law duty of care an employer may impose a contractual duty on employees to take breaks.
66 On the impact of periods spent 'on call', see *McCartney v Overley House Management* [2006] IRLR 514.
67 Regulation 10(2) and (3) Working Time Regulations 1998.
68 See *Gallagher v Alpha Catering Services Ltd* [2005] IRLR 102 on the difference between 'downtime' and rest breaks.

Indeed, according to the EAT, employers must not only permit the taking of rest breaks but they should proactively ensure working arrangements allow for those breaks to be taken.[69]

This break can be agreed by a collective or workforce agreement but, in default of such an agreement, it will be for 20 minutes. In *Martin v Southern Health and Social Care Trust*[70] the Northern Ireland Court of Appeal drew a distinction between rest breaks that are uninterrupted subject to exceptional circumstances arising from the demand for continuity of services and 'on call' duty in the course of which the employee remains at the disposal of the employer. In *Corps of Commissionaires Management Ltd v Hughes*[71] the EAT held that the entitlement was to one rest break of 20 minutes no matter how much longer than six hours the individual worked. The rules for young workers are that where their daily working time is more than four and a half hours[72] they will be entitled to a rest break of at least 30 minutes. This break should be continuous, if possible, and can be spent away from the workstation. Interestingly, and perhaps impracticably, there is a provision that where the young person works for more than one employer, then the daily working time should be aggregated for the purposes of determining the entitlement to a rest break.[73]

8.4.7 Weekly rest periods

Adult workers are entitled to uninterrupted rest of not less than 24 hours in each seven-day period during which they work for an employer.[74] At the employer's discretion, this can be taken as one uninterrupted period of 48 hours in each 14-day period. Young people are entitled to a rest period of not less than 48 hours in each seven-day period that they work.[75] Unlike adults, this period is not required to be uninterrupted. According to reg. 8, the period may be interrupted in the case of activities involving periods of work that are split up over the day or are of short duration and may be reduced where it is justified by technical or organisational reasons.[76]

The seven- or 14-day periods can begin on a day established by a relevant agreement; if there is no such agreement, then at the commencement of the week (or every other week) beginning at the start of the week in which employment began.[77] A week starts at midnight between Sunday and Monday.[78] Note that there is no requirement for a Sunday to be part of the rest period.

8.4.8 Annual leave

The Working Time Regulations 1998 introduced a statutory entitlement to paid annual holidays. Regulation 16 specifies that a worker is entitled to be paid in respect of their annual leave. Sections 221–224 ERA 1996 apply for the purpose of determining a week's pay, except for any references to a maximum limit. In *British Airways v Williams*[79] the Court of Justice interpreted 'paid annual leave' in Article 7 of the Directive to mean normal remuneration for the period of rest. In the same case, the Supreme Court noted that some work costs would not be incurred during holiday periods.[80] In a

---

69 *Grange v Abellio London Ltd* [2017] IRLR 108.

70 [2010] IRLR 1048.

71 [2009] IRLR 122.

72 Note that there is no requirement for these hours to be consecutive.

73 Regulation 12 Working Time Regulations 1998.

74 This is not to include any rest periods to which the worker is entitled under reg. 10(1) (daily rest periods) unless justified by objective or technical reasons concerning the organisation of work: reg. 11(7) Working Time Regulations 1998.

75 Regulation 11(1)–(3) Working Time Regulations 1998.

76 It may not be reduced for technical or organisational reasons to less than 36 consecutive hours.

77 Regulation 11(4) and (5) Working Time Regulations 1998.

78 Regulation 11(6) Working Time Regulations 1998.

79 [2011] IRLR 948.

80 [2012] IRLR 1014.

subsequent case, the Court of Appeal has ruled that the Working Time Regulations require results-based commission earnings to be taken into account in calculating holiday pay.[81]

The leave year begins on the date on which employment starts and subsequent anniversaries, unless otherwise fixed by a relevant agreement.[82] If a worker joins during the leave year, they have a pro rata entitlement. The leave may be taken in instalments but cannot be replaced by a payment in lieu. Any statutory leave in excess of four weeks can be carried over into the following year.[83] It should be noted that there is no statutory entitlement to bank or public holidays in addition to the leave arrangements in the Working Time Regulations 1998. Thus it is possible for an employer to count bank or public holidays against the entitlement to leave. However, a unilateral decision by one employer to reduce the hourly rate of its employees in order to assist in meeting the costs of paid holidays introduced by these Regulations was held to be impermissible by the EAT.[84] In *Caulfield v Marshalls Products*[85] it was accepted that a contractual provision for 'rolled up' holiday pay, which identifies an express amount or percentage by way of addition to basic pay, does not infringe the regulations. According to the Court of Appeal, there is nothing in the Directive which imposes an obligation to pay workers in respect of their holiday at the time it is taken. Nevertheless, a reference was made to the Court of Justice for its opinion. In the subsequent case of *Robinson-Steele v RD Retail Ltd*,[86] the Court of Justice ruled that 'rolled up' holiday pay was precluded by the Directive. However, it suggested that such payments could be offset against a worker's entitlement if the employer could prove that the sums were paid transparently and comprehensibly. Thus, in *Lyddon v Englefield Ltd*[87] the EAT allowed 'rolled up' holiday pay to be set off. According to the Appeal Tribunal, the fundamental question is whether there is a consensual agreement identifying a specific sum properly attributable to holiday periods.

A worker may take their leave entitlement by giving notice to the employer. This is subject to the employer being able to give notice to the worker when to take leave or not to take leave.[88] Thus, in *Russell v Transocean Ltd*[89] the employer was entitled to insist that offshore workers take paid annual leave during periods when they were onshore on field breaks. The Supreme Court observed that the Court of Justice has not ruled that a pre-ordained rest period can never constitute annual leave.

A notice given by the worker or the employer must fulfil three conditions. These are:

1. It may relate to all or part of the leave to which the worker is entitled in a leave year.
2. It shall specify the days on which leave is to be, or not to be, taken.
3. It shall be given to the employer, or the worker, by the 'relevant date'.[90]

The 'relevant date' is a date which is twice as many days in advance of the earliest day specified in the notice as the number of days or part-days to which the notice relates. If the notice relates only to the employer requiring the worker not to take leave, then this notice needs to be given as many days in advance of the earliest day specified as the number of days or part-days to which the notice relates.[91] It should be observed that employers are not required to consult with a worker before

81 *Lock v British Gas (No.2)* [2016] IRLR 946. On the inclusion of overtime pay, see *Bear Scotland Ltd v Fulton* [2015] IRLR 15 and *Dudley MBC v Willetts* [2017] IRLR 870.

82 Regulation 15A Working Time Regulations 1998.

83 See *FN v SDN* [2006] IRLR 561 and the Working Time (Amendment) Regulations 2007, SI 2007/2079.

84 See *Davies v MJ Wyatt (Decorators) Ltd* [2000] IRLR 759.

85 [2004] IRLR 564.

86 [2006] IRLR 386.

87 [2008] IRLR 198.

88 Regulation 15(1) and (2) Working Time Regulations 1998. See *Sumsion v BBC (Scotland)* [2007] IRLR 678 and DBIS's 'Your Guide to the Working Time Regulations'.

89 *Russell v Transocean International Resources Ltd* [2012] IRLR 149.

90 Regulation 15(3) Working Time Regulations 1998.

91 Regulation 15(4) Working Time Regulations 1998.

refusing a request for leave and the whole notice period may be varied or excluded by a relevant agreement.[92] If a worker is entitled to a rest period, rest break or annual leave under the provisions of the Working Time Regulations 1998 and also has a contractual right, the worker may take advantage of whichever right is more favourable.[93]

In *Stringer v HM Revenue & Customs*[94] the Court of Justice established that the right to paid annual leave cannot be made subject to a condition that the worker has actually worked during the leave year. Thus the right continues to accrue during sick leave and, on termination of employment, a worker who has been on sick leave and unable to take paid annual leave is entitled to payment in lieu. More generally, the Court of Justice stated that the Directive does not preclude national legislation prohibiting workers on sickness absence from taking paid annual leave during that absence, provided they can exercise their right during another period. Equally, national legislation could allow workers on sickness absence to take paid annual leave during this absence. Subsequently, the Court of Justice has ruled that, irrespective of precisely when the incapacity for work arises, workers who are off sick must be allowed to carry over their holiday even if that is to a different leave year.[95] In the UK, reg. 13A(7) Working Time Regulations 1998 now provides that a relevant agreement may allow any leave to which a worker is entitled under reg. 13A (the additional 1.6 weeks' annual leave in the UK) to be carried forward into the leave year immediately following the leave year in respect of which it is due. In *KHS AG v Schulte*[96] the Court of Justice pointed out that annual leave had the dual purpose of providing rest and a period of leisure and that these purposes have to be borne in mind where an employee is sick for several reference periods. In such circumstances the carry-over period must be substantially longer than the reference period.[97] Finally, according to the Court of Appeal, there is no legal requirement that a person on sick leave who wishes to carry forward their entitlement to paid annual leave must give notice of that fact during the period of sickness.[98]

8.4.9 Special cases

Regulation 19 excludes those employed as domestic servants in a private household from the provisions on the maximum working week and those concerning night work and health assessments for night workers.

Those whose working day is not measured or predetermined or who decide their own hours are also excluded.[99] Examples of this last category are managing executives, family workers or those officiating at religious ceremonies in churches and religious communities. Also excluded are those who partly decide their own hours and partly have them determined for them. This group only have that part of their work which is predetermined counting for the purposes of the Working Time Regulations 1998, which seems to undermine the protection afforded.

There are a number of situations, in addition to the other exclusions, to which the regulations on night work, daily rest periods and weekly rest periods do not apply.[100] These exclusions are subject to compensatory rest periods being given.[101] There are six such situations:

---

92 Regulation 15(5) and (6) Working Time Regulations 1998. See *Lyons v Mitie Security Ltd* [2010] IRLR 288.
93 Regulation 17 Working Time Regulations 1998.
94 [2009] IRLR 214.
95 See *Asociación Nacional de Grandes Empresas de Distribución (ANGED) v Federación de Asociaciones Sindicales (FASGA)* [2012] IRLR 779 and *Pereda v Madrid Movilidad SA* [2009] IRLR 959.
96 [2012] IRLR 156.
97 See *Plumb v Duncan Print Group* [2015] IRLR 711.
98 *NHS Leeds v Larner* [2012] IRLR 825.
99 Regulation 20 Working Time Regulations 1998.
100 Regulation 21 Working Time Regulations 1998.
101 Regulation 24 Working Time Regulations 1998. See *Hughes v Corps of Commissionaires (No 2)* [2011] IRLR 915 where the Court of Appeal held that Regulation 24(a) on 'equivalent period of compensatory rest' applied.

1. Where the worker's activities are such that the place of work and the place of residence are distant from each other, or there are different places of work which are distant from each other.
2. Where the worker is engaged in security and surveillance operations, requiring a permanent presence to protect property and persons. Examples of this may be security guards or caretakers.
3. Where the worker's activities require continuity of service or production. This results in a large number of exceptions.[102]
4. Where there is a foreseeable surge in activity, such as in agriculture, tourism and the postal services.
5. Where the worker's activities are affected by unusual and unforeseeable circumstances, exceptional events, accidents or the imminent risk of accidents.
6. Where people work in railway transport and their activities are intermittent, they spend their working time on board trains or their activities are limited to transport timetables and to ensuring the continuity and regularity of traffic.

Regulation 22 provides that shift workers changing shift are excluded from the provisions on daily and weekly rest periods when it is not possible for them to take such rest between those shifts.[103] Neither do these rest periods apply to workers whose activities involve work split up over the course of the day. An example of this may be cleaning staff.[104] In addition, the rules about daily rest periods and rest breaks for young workers[105] can be varied if the employer requires a young person to undertake work for which there is no adult available[106] and the need is the result of unusual or unforeseeable circumstances beyond the employer's control or occasioned by exceptional events which could not have been foreseen. The need for the young person's services must also be immediate and of a temporary nature. In such circumstances the worker is entitled to compensatory rest to be taken within the following three weeks.

8.4.10 Relevant agreements

Regulation 2(1) defines 'relevant agreement' as a:

> workforce agreement which applies to him, any provision of a collective agreement which forms part of a contract between him and his employer, or any other agreement in writing which is legally enforceable as between the worker and the employer.

The term is therefore an umbrella one which includes collective and workforce agreements as well as any other written agreements such as a contract of employment. A collective agreement is one within the meaning of s. 178 TULRCA 1992 and is an agreement between an employer and an independent trade union within the meaning of s. 5 of that Act.[107] In a move opposed by the TUC but supported by the CBI, the 1998 Regulations introduced the concept of workforce agreements, the requirements for which are set out in Sch. 1 (see Chapter 10). The importance of these

---

102 Regulation 21(c) Working Time Regulations 1998 states that this is in relation to services provided by hospitals, residential establishments and prisons; work at docks or airports; press, radio, television, cinema, postal and telecommunications services and civil protection services; gas, water and electricity production, transmission and distribution; household refuse collection; industries that cannot be interrupted on technical grounds; research and development; agriculture.

103 Regulation 25(2) and (3) Working Time Regulations 1998 also exclude, subject to compensatory rest, young workers serving in the armed forces.

104 Regulation 22(1)(c) Working Time Regulations 1998.

105 As in regs 10(2) and 12(4) Working Time Regulations 1998.

106 Regulation 27 Working Time Regulations 1998.

107 Regulation 2(1) Working Time Regulations 1998.

requirements is that reg. 23 provides that collective or workforce agreements may modify or exclude the application of certain regulations. These are:

- Regulation 4 – the possible extension of the reference period to a maximum of 52 weeks.
- Regulation 6 – length of night work.
- Regulations 10, 11 and 12 – minimum daily and weekly rest periods and breaks in relation to adult workers.

Regulation 24 provides for compensatory rest when rest periods or breaks are excluded or modified.

8.4.11 Enforcement

The provisions of the Working Time Regulations 1998 which impose obligations upon employers[108] are generally to be enforced by the Health and Safety Executive.[109] An employer who fails to comply with any one of the relevant requirements will be guilty of an offence and subject to a fine. The Health and Safety Executive has wide powers for their inspectors to enter premises and investigate and it is an offence to obstruct them in their investigations.[110] A worker may present a complaint to an employment tribunal relating to an employer's refusal to permit the exercise of those parts of the Working Time Regulations 1998 which provide entitlements,[111] or an employer's refusal to pay for all or any part of the annual leave.[112] The complaint must be presented within three months, or such further period as the tribunal considers reasonable, beginning with the date on which the exercise of the right should have been permitted or payment made. Where the employment tribunal finds such a complaint well founded, it will make a declaration and award compensation or order the employer to pay the worker the amount the tribunal finds is due to the individual. The amount of compensation will be such as the employment tribunal finds just and equitable and will take into account the employer's default in refusing to permit the worker to exercise the right and any loss sustained by the worker in relation to the matters complained of.[113] However, in *Santos Gomes v Higher Level Care Ltd*[114] the EAT ruled that compensation for injury to feelings is not available where an employer has failed to provide rest breaks.

Any agreements to exclude or limit the operation of the Regulations, including limiting the right of a worker to bring proceedings before an employment tribunal, will be void unless it results from action taken by an ACAS conciliation officer under s.18 Employment Tribunals Act 1996 or it meets the statutory requirements for settlement agreements.[115]

8.4.12 Protection from detriment

Section 45A ERA 1996 provides that a worker has the right not to be subjected to any detriment by an act, or failure to act, by the employer on a number of grounds. These are:

---

108 Regulations 4(2) (48-hour week), 6(2) and (7) (night work and special hazards), 7(1), (2) and (6) (health assessment provisions), 8 (pattern of work) and 9 (record keeping).

109 Regulation 28(2) Working Time Regulations 1998; although, in relation to workers employed in those premises for which local authorities are responsible, by the Health and Safety Executive issuing guidance to the local authorities.

110 See reg. 29 Working Time Regulations 1998 referring to parts of s. 33(1) HASAWA 1974.

111 These are the provisions concerning daily and weekly rest periods, rest breaks and annual leave.

112 Regulation 30 Working Time Regulations 1998. In *HM Revenue & Customs v Stringer* [2009] IRLR 677, the House of Lords held that a failure to pay holiday pay can also constitute an unauthorised deduction from wages under ERA 1996 (see 8.6.1 below).

113 Regulation 30(3)–(5) Working Time Regulations 1998. It should be noted that Section 12A Employment Tribunals Act 1996 allows employment tribunals to impose a financial penalty on employers where there has been a breach of employment rights and the employment tribunal thinks that 'the breach has one or more aggravating features' (see Chapter 4.2 above).

114 [2016] IRLR 678.

115 Regulation 35 Working Time Regulations 1998; see also Chapter 5.

1. That the worker refused, or proposed to refuse, to comply with a requirement imposed by the employer in contravention of the Working Time Regulations 1998.
2. That the worker refused, or proposed to refuse, to forgo a right conferred by the 1998 Regulations.
3. For failing to sign a workforce agreement, or any other agreement, with the employer in relation to the 1998 Regulations.
4. For performing, or proposing to perform, any of the functions or activities of an employee representative for the purpose of the 1998 Regulations.
5. That the worker brought proceedings against the employer to enforce a right conferred by the 1998 Regulations.
6. That the worker alleged that the employer had infringed such a right.[116]

If the detriment is dismissal within the meaning of Part X ERA 1996 and the person is an employee, then those who are qualified must claim unfair dismissal rather than claiming a detriment under s. 45A. Dismissal for relying on the rights conferred by the Regulations as an employee or an employee representative will be automatically unfair.[117] Otherwise a worker may complain to an employment tribunal that they have been subjected to a detriment.[118] If the claim is well founded, the tribunal will make a declaration and award compensation. If the claim relates to the termination of a worker's contract, which is not a contract of employment, then the compensation must not exceed the maximum amount that can be awarded to an employee under Part X ERA 1996.[119]

8.5 Statutory right to time off work

There are a number of reasons for which an employee is entitled to time off work, sometimes with pay. These are, apart from time off for trade union duties and activities and for being a union learning representative, contained in Part VI ERA 1996.

8.5.1 Time off for public duties

There are a large number of statutory bodies that rely on part-time contributors. This in turn is dependent upon employees obtaining leave of absence in order to take part in the activities of these bodies. As a matter of public policy and to help ensure a mixture of people that reflect the make-up of the population, it must be in the interests of government to ensure that it is possible for individuals to take time off work to perform public duties.

Section 50(1) ERA 1996 provides that an employer must permit an employee who is a Justice of the Peace to take time off during working hours to carry out any of their duties. There are no conditions as to length of service with an employer before an employee may take time off during working hours but there is no right to be paid for this activity. Working hours are defined as any time, in accordance with the contract, that the employee is required to be at work.[120] Section 50(2) describes other bodies whose members qualify for time off. These include members of a local

---

116 In *Fuss v Stadt Halle* [2010] IRLR 1080 the Court of Justice ruled that art. 6(b) of the Directive precludes national rules that allow a public sector employer to compulsorily transfer workers to another service on the ground that they had requested compliance with the limit on weekly hours. On the protection of the rights of full-timers who move to part-time work, see *Land Tirol case* [2010] IRLR 631.
117 Section 101A ERA 1996; similarly s. 105(4A) makes selection for redundancy on these grounds an unfair dismissal.
118 Section 48(1ZA) ERA 1996.
119 Section 49(5A) ERA 1996. On the possible imposition of financial penalties, see note 113 above.
120 Section 50(11) ERA 1996.

authority,[121] a statutory tribunal, an independent monitoring board for a prison, a relevant health body,[122] a relevant education body,[123] the Environment Agency or the Scottish Environment Protection Agency, Scottish Water. Time off in relation to these bodies is for the following purposes: (i) attendance at a meeting of the body or of any of its committees or sub-committees; (ii) the doing of something approved by the committee or body for the purpose of the discharge of the functions of the body or committee.[124] Section 50(10)(a) provides the Secretary of State with the power to add organisations to the list in order to bring attendance at their meetings and other work into these provisions.

The amount of time off that an employee is to be permitted to take is that which is reasonable having regard to all the circumstances; in particular, to how much time is required, how much the employee has already been permitted under ss 168 and 170 TULRCA 1992,[125] and the circumstances of the employer's business and the effect of the employee's absence on the running of that business.[126] In *Borders Regional Council v Maule*[127] the EAT considered the situation of a school teacher who was a member of a number of public bodies, including the Borders Social Security Appeal Panel. During the previous year she had taken 22 days' leave of absence for such duties and 24 days in the year preceding that. The employer tried to regulate and limit the absences to two days a month. During one month when she had already taken two days, her request for an extra day to attend training was turned down. The EAT held that all the circumstances needed to be taken into account, including the number and frequency of other absences permitted by the employer, in order to assess whether there was a breach of the statute. The EAT also observed that where an employee was undertaking public duties to which the statute applies, there should be a discussion between the employer and the individual to establish a pattern of absences by agreement. An employee who was undertaking a number of such absences also had a duty to plan their level of commitment and produce a schedule that was reasonable in the circumstances.

An employee may present a complaint to an employment tribunal that an employer has failed to permit them to take time off. The complaint needs to be made within three months beginning with the date on which the failure occurred, unless it was not reasonably practicable to do so. If the tribunal finds the complaint well founded, then it will make a declaration to that effect and award compensation.[128] The amount of compensation will take into account the employer's default and any attributable loss suffered by the employee.[129]

8.5.2 Time off to look for work or arrange training[130]

An employee who has been given notice of dismissal by reason of redundancy is entitled to take reasonable time off during working hours[131] for the purpose of looking for new employment or making arrangements for training. This applies to those who have two years' continuous service at

---

121 Section 50(5) ERA 1996 offers a definition of a local authority.

122 A National Health Service trust or health authority: see s. 50(8) ERA 1996.

123 The managing or governing body of an educational establishment: see s. 50(9) ERA 1996.

124 Section 50(3) ERA 1996.

125 Time off for trade union duties and activities.

126 Section 50(4) ERA 1996.

127 [1993] IRLR 199.

128 It may not make conditions about what time off an individual may be permitted to have in the future: see *Corner v Buckinghamshire County Council* [1978] IRLR 320.

129 Section 51 ERA 1996. On the possible imposition of financial penalties, see note 113 above.

130 Section 52 ERA 1996.

131 Defined in the same way as for time off for public duties: see s. 52(3) ERA 1996.

the time the notice was due to expire or would have expired if given in accordance with s. 86(1) ERA 1996.[132]

An employee who has time off under s. 52 ERA 1996 is entitled to be paid at the appropriate hourly rate. The hourly rate is arrived at by taking the amount of one week's pay divided by the number of normal working hours for that employee under the contract in force at the time notice of dismissal was given. If the working hours vary from week to week, then the average over a 12-week period, ending with the last complete week before the day on which notice is given, is taken.[133]

If the employer unreasonably refuses to allow an employee to take time off, the latter is entitled to make a complaint to an employment tribunal within three months of the date on which time off should have been given. The tribunal, if it finds the complaint well founded, may make a declaration and order the employer to pay an amount equal to the remuneration the individual would have received if they had taken the time off, provided that this does not exceed 40 per cent of a week's pay for the employee concerned.[134]

8.5.3 Time off for antenatal care

A pregnant employee is entitled to time off during working hours if she has, on the advice of a registered medical practitioner, a registered midwife or a registered nurse, made an appointment for the purposes of receiving antenatal care.[135] The woman may be required to produce a certificate from one of the above stating that she is pregnant as well as an appointment card or some other document showing that an appointment has been made.[136] This evidence is not required for the first appointment during the pregnancy. A woman is entitled to be paid by her employer during the period of absence from work.[137] It is important that pregnant women are not treated less favourably than others in the period before maternity leave begins. In *Pederson v Kvickly Skive*[138] Danish employees absent from work through pregnancy-related sickness prior to their maternity leave were paid less than other workers who were absent for non-pregnancy-related illnesses. The Court of Justice held that to treat pregnant women in this way was contrary to art. 141 EC and the Equal Pay Directive and thus discriminatory.

If time off is refused or if the employer fails to pay the whole or any part of any amount to which the employee is entitled, then the latter may complain to an employment tribunal. This claim must be made within three months of the appointment, or longer if an employment tribunal is satisfied that it was not reasonably practicable for the complaint to be presented within the three-month deadline. The tribunal may award compensation equivalent to the amount that the woman would have received if she had taken the time off, or an amount equal to the non-payment or underpayment of remuneration due.[139]

---

132 This provides for minimum levels of notice to be given.

133 Section 53(1)–(3) ERA 1996.

134 Sections 53(4), (5) and 54 ERA 1996. On the possible imposition of financial penalties, see note 113 above.

135 It should be noted that Section 57ZA provides a right to time off for ante-natal care for agency workers, s. 57ZE provides a person in a qualifying relationship with a right to time off to accompany a woman to ante-natal appointments, s. 57ZJ provides a right to paid time off to attend adoption appointments and s. 57ZS applies to the placement of looked after children with prospective adopters.

136 Section 55(1)–(2) ERA 1996.

137 Section 56(1) ERA 1996.

138 Case C-66/96 [1999] IRLR 55.

139 Sections 56–57 ERA 1996. On the possible imposition of financial penalties, see note 113 above.

8.5.4 Time off for dependants

Clause 3 of the Framework Agreement on parental leave[140] states:

> Member States and/or management and labour shall take the necessary measures to entitle
> workers to time off from work, in accordance with national legislation, collective agreements
> and/or practice, on grounds of *force majeure* for urgent family reasons in cases of sickness or
> accident making the immediate presence of the worker indispensable.

The provisions implementing this are contained in ss 57A and 57B ERA 1996.[141] They permit an
employee to take a 'reasonable' amount of time off during working hours to deal with specified
emergencies in relation to designated people. No definition of the word 'reasonable' is offered in
the legislation and it is likely that the reasonableness of the amount of time taken off will vary
according to circumstances.

There is no indication in the statutory provisions as to whether this time off should be with or
without pay. There is also no requirement to keep records of the time off taken by employees.
However, employers might feel that it is wise to do so because such records might be of assistance
in showing that the amount of time taken was reasonable or not.

Section 57A ERA 1996 refers to employees being permitted to take a reasonable amount
of time off 'in order to take action which is necessary'. *Royal Bank of Scotland plc v Harrison*[142] involved
a mother who worked three days a week and cared for two young children. She learned on
8 December that her regular childminder would not be able to care for her children on 22 December.
When her attempts to make alternative arrangements failed, she asked to take one day's leave. This
was turned down but she took it anyway. The question for the EAT was whether an event that was
known about and would not happen for another two weeks could be called 'unexpected'. The
Appeal Tribunal held that the word 'unexpected' did not necessarily require the event to be sudden
or an emergency so Ms Harrison was covered by the legislation.

Generally, the right is for the care of dependants, although this is given a generous meaning in
the statute. For these purposes dependants are: a spouse or civil partner; a child; a parent; a person
who lives in the same household as the employee and is not employed by the employee, tenant,
lodger or boarder; any person who reasonably relies on the employee either for assistance on an
occasion when the person falls ill or is injured or assaulted, or relies on the employee to make
arrangements for the provision of care in the event of illness or injury. Section 57A(6) also makes it
clear that illness or injury in the above definitions includes mental conditions.

8.5.4.1 Situations that qualify

The ERA 1996 specifies the following situations which entitle the employee to time off:[143]

1. to provide assistance when a dependant falls ill, gives birth or is injured or assaulted;
2. to make provision for the care of a dependant when they fall ill or are injured;
3. as a result of the death of a dependant;[144]
4. to deal with unexpected disruption or termination of care arrangements made for a dependant;
   and
5. to deal with any incidents involving a child of the employee whilst at school.

---

140 See Chapter 9.
141 Added to the ERA 1996 by Sch. 4 Part II Employment Relations Act (ERelA) 1999.
142 [2009] IRLR 28.
143 Section 57A(1) ERA 1996.
144 See *Foster v Cartwright Black* [2004] IRLR 781.

The Department of Business, Innovation and Skills (now DBEIS) has given examples of situations that are likely to qualify – for example, when a dependant falls ill or has been involved in an accident or assaulted, including where the victim is hurt or distressed rather than injured physically, or when a partner is having a baby, or to make longer-term care arrangements for a dependant who is ill or injured.

It is clear that the government's view was that such a right to time off should be linked to genuine emergencies, rather than a need to deal with more mundane domestic issues – for example, awaiting the arrival of a plumber to carry out repairs. During the report stage of the Employment Relations Bill, Lord Sainsbury stated on behalf of the government:

> The statutory right will be restricted to urgent cases of real need. The emergency must involve a dependant who is either a family member or someone who relies upon the employee for assistance in the particular circumstances.

He then gave some examples of what the right to time off was intended to cover:

> We intend the right to apply where a dependant becomes sick or has an accident, or is assaulted, including where the victim is distressed rather than physically injured . . . reasonable time off if an employee suffers a bereavement of a family member, to deal with the consequences of that bereavement . . .

> Employees will be able to take time off in the event of the unexpected absence of the carer, where the person is a dependant of the employee. So if the childminder or nurse does not turn up, the employee will be able to sort things out without fearing reprisals at work . . .

> Employees may have to take time off to attend to a problem arising at their children's school or during school hours . . .

> A father will have the right to be on hand at the birth of his child . . .[145]

The ERA 1996 gives no indication about the length of time that should be permitted. It is likely to vary according to the type of incident and the only condition is that the employee is entitled to a 'reasonable' period of time off work. There will clearly be difficulties for employers in defining what is reasonable and whether each incident needs to be looked at on its merits or whether one can take into account the number of absences taken by an employee.

8.5.4.2 Notice requirements

Employees qualify for time off to deal with these emergencies if they tell their employer the reason for the absence and how long they plan to be away as soon as is reasonably practicable.[146] Failure to allow an employee time off may result in a complaint to an employment tribunal. The employee must claim within three months beginning with the date when the refusal occurred or longer if the tribunal considers that it was not reasonably practicable to do so.[147] If the tribunal upholds the complaint, it must make a declaration to that effect and may award compensation. The amount will

---

145 HL Report stage, HL Deb, 8 July 1999, cols 1083–1089.
146 Section 57A(2) ERA 1996. See *Truelove v Safeway* [2005] IRLR 589.
147 Section 57B(2) ERA 1996.

take into account the circumstances surrounding the employer's refusal and any loss sustained by the employee.[148]

8.5.4.3 Protection from detriment and dismissal

According to reg. 19 Maternity and Parental Leave etc. Regulations 1999, an employee is entitled not to be subjected to any detriment[149] by any act, or failure to act, by the employer for taking time off under s. 57A ERA 1996. Additionally, an employee who is sacked when the reason (or the principal reason) for the dismissal is taking time off under s. 57A ERA 1996 will be regarded as unfairly dismissed.

Similarly, if an employee is dismissed for reasons of redundancy and it is shown that the circumstances constituting the redundancy applied equally to one or more employees in the same business holding similar positions who have not been made redundant, and the reason (or principal reason) for the employee being selected for dismissal was connected with taking time off under s. 57A ERA 1996, the dismissal will be unfair.

In *Qua v John Ford Morrison Solicitors*[150] the claimant was a single mother whose young son had medical problems. As a result she was away from work for 17 days until she was dismissed ten months after her employment started. According to the EAT, s. 57A(1)(a) ERA 1996 is dealing with something unforeseen and does not allow employees to take time off in order to provide care themselves beyond the reasonable amount necessary to enable them to deal with the immediate crisis.[151] To determine whether action is 'necessary', factors to be taken into account include: the nature of the incident; the closeness of the relationship between the employee and the dependant; and the extent to which anyone else was available to assist. However, the EAT thought that for these purposes the inconvenience caused to the employer's business was irrelevant.

8.5.5 Time off for pension scheme trustees[152]

Employees who are trustees of the employer's 'relevant occupational pension scheme'[153] must be permitted time off during working hours[154] for the purpose of: (i) performing any of the duties of a trustee; (ii) undergoing training relevant to the performance of those duties.[155] The amount of time off and any conditions attached to it must be reasonable having regard to how much time is required for the performance of the duties or training, as well as the circumstances of the business and the effect of the employee's absence on the running of that business.

An employer who permits an employee to take time off under s. 58 ERA 1996 must pay the employee for the time taken off, for which permission had been given, as if they had been at work. If the remuneration for the work which they would normally be doing varies with the amount of work done, the employee must be paid by calculating the average hourly earnings.[156] An employee may make a complaint to an employment tribunal that there has been a failure to allow time off or to pay for it within three months beginning with the date when the failure occurred, unless the tribunal decides it was not reasonably practicable. The tribunal may make a declaration and award

---

148 Section 57B(4) ERA 1996.
149 See s. 47C ERA 1996.
150 [2003] IRLR 184.
151 Section 57A(1)(b) ERA 1996 permits reasonable time off to make longer-term arrangements for care.
152 Sections 58–60 ERA 1996.
153 Relevant occupational pension scheme is one defined in s. 1 Pensions Act 1993 and established under trust: s. 58(3)(a) ERA 1996.
154 Working hours is any time, in accordance with the contract of employment, that the employee is required to be at work: s. 58(4) ERA 1996.
155 Training can be on the employer's premises or elsewhere: s. 58(3)(c) ERA 1996.
156 The average hourly earnings of the employee or of persons in comparable employment with the same employer; if none of these, then an average figure which is reasonable in the circumstances: s. 59(4) ERA 1996. Sections 61–63 ERA 1996.

compensation to be paid. Again the amount will depend on the extent of the employer's default and any attributable loss suffered by the employee.[157]

8.5.6 Time off for employee representatives[158]

In certain circumstances, an employee elected for the purpose of representing employees in discussions with the employer has a statutory right to be paid reasonable time off during working hours for the purpose of carrying out the functions of a representative. Section 61 ERA 1996 provides that the employee representatives with whom an employer should consult when proposing collective redundancies[159] and a transfer of an undertaking[160] are entitled to time off. Candidates for election as employee representatives also have such an entitlement. Similarly, the Transnational Information and Consultation of Employees Regulations 1999 (TICE Regulations 1999)[161] provide that an employee who is a member of a Special Negotiating Body, a member of a European Works Council, an information and consultation representative, or a candidate in an election for any of these, is also entitled to reasonable time off with pay. Working hours are any time that the employee is required to be at work in accordance with his contract.[162]

Employee representatives or candidates for election are entitled to be paid at the appropriate hourly rate for the time off. This rate is a week's pay divided by the normal working hours specified in the contract in force on the day that leave is taken. Where there are no normal working hours or the number of hours varies, then the average over a 12-week period is taken. Where an employee has been employed for less than 12 weeks, then reference is made to the normal working hours of other employees of the same employer in comparable employment.[163]

An employee may make a complaint to an employment tribunal that the employer unreasonably refused time off or failed to pay the whole or part of the remuneration to which the individual was entitled. The complaint must be made within three months of the day when time off should have been permitted, unless it was not reasonably practicable to do so. If the tribunal finds the complaint well founded, then it must make a declaration to this effect and order the employer to pay the employee an amount equal to that which would have been paid if the time off had been permitted. Where the complaint is about non-payment, the employer will be required to pay the amount due to the employee.[164]

8.5.7 Time off for a young person for study or training[165]

Certain employees are entitled to time off with pay during working hours for the purpose of undertaking study or training leading to a relevant qualification. If the employee is someone supplied to another employer (the principal) to work in accordance with a contract between the employer and the principal, then the obligations under the Regulations fall upon the principal.[166] The employee must: (i) be 16 or 17 years of age; (ii) not be receiving full-time secondary[167] or

---

157 On the possible imposition of financial penalties, see note 113 above.
158 Sections 61–63 ERA 1996.
159 See Part IV Chapter II TULRCA 1992.
160 See regs 10 and 11 Transfer of Undertakings (Protection of Employment) Regulations 1981, SI 1981/1794.
161 SI 1999/3323 regs 25–27; see Chapter 11.
162 Section 61(2) ERA 1996; reg. 25(2) TICE Regulations 1999.
163 Section 62 ERA 1996; reg. 26 TICE Regulations 1999.
164 Section 63 ERA 1996; reg. 27 TICE Regulations 1999. On the possible imposition of financial penalties, see note 113 above.
165 Sections 63A–63C ERA 1996.
166 Section 63A(3) ERA 1996.
167 Secondary as in the Education Act 1996.

further[168] education; and (iii) not have attained such standard of achievement as is prescribed by Regulations made by the Secretary of State.[169] However, for these purposes an employee does not include a person to whom Part 1 of the Education and Skills Act 2008 (duty to participate in education or training for 16 and 17 year olds in England) applies.[170] A 'relevant' qualification is an external[171] qualification which would contribute to the attainment of the standard prescribed in the Regulations issued by the Secretary of State and would be likely to enhance the individual's employment prospects (whether with their employer or otherwise). Where an employee is 18 years of age and began study or training leading to a relevant qualification before that age, then the provisions as described continue to apply.[172]

The amount of time to be permitted needs to be reasonable in all the circumstances, taking into account the requirements of the employee's study or training, the circumstances of the business of the employer or the principal and the effect of the time off on the running of the business.[173] Pay is to be at the appropriate hourly rate. This rate is a week's pay divided by the normal working hours of the employee according to the contract in force on the day that leave is taken. Where there are no normal working hours or the number of hours varies, then the average over a 12-week period is taken. If an employee has been employed for less than 12 weeks, then reference is made to the normal working hours of other employees of the same employer with relevant comparable employment.[174]

An employee may make a complaint to an employment tribunal that the employer or principal unreasonably refused time off or failed to pay the whole or part of the remuneration to which the employee was entitled. The complaint must be made within three months of the day when time off should have been permitted, unless it was not reasonably practicable to do so. If the tribunal finds the complaint well founded, it must make a declaration to this effect and order the employer or principal to pay the employee an amount equal to that which would have been paid if the time off had been permitted, or, if the complaint is about not being paid, order the employer or principal to pay the amount due to the employee.[175]

Since April 2010 employees in organisations with 250 or more employees have had a new right to request time off to undertake training. This is modelled on the flexible working provisions (see Chapter 9) which means that employers must consider requests seriously but can refuse time off if there is a good reason for doing so.[176]

8.5.8 Time off for trade union duties, activities and union learning representatives

Sections 168–170 TULRCA 1992 provide that an employer must permit officials and members of independent trade unions, recognised by the employer, to take time off during working hours for the purpose of carrying out the duties[177] of, or taking part in the activities of, the trade union.[178]

---

168 Further as described in Sch. 2 Further and Higher Education Act 1992.
169 Right to Time Off for Study or Training Regulations 2001, SI 2001/2801; reg. 3 specifies standards of achievement.
170 Section 63A(5A) ERA 1996.
171 An external qualification is an academic or vocational qualification awarded or authenticated by a body as specified by the Secretary of State in the Schedule to reg. 4 Right to Time Off for Study or Training Regulations.
172 Section 63A(4) ERA 1996.
173 Section 63A(5) ERA 1996.
174 Section 63B ERA 1996.
175 Section 63C ERA 1996. On the possible imposition of financial penalties, see note 113 above.
176 Part VIA ERA 1996.
177 This includes accompanying workers, at their request, to disciplinary and grievance hearings: see s. 10(7) ERelA 1999.
178 The employee needs to ensure that a request for time off has been made and that the employer has refused the request, ignored it or failed to respond before they can establish a right to compensation: see *Ryford Ltd v Drinkwater* [1996] IRLR 16.

There is a distinction between carrying out union duties and carrying out union activities. The former relates to duties carried out by officials, whilst the latter is concerned with the activities of union members. The statutory provisions allowing trade union officials a right to a reasonable amount of time off with pay to carry out their trade union duties and to undergo trade union training originated in the Employment Protection Act 1975. The right for an employee who is an official of an independent trade union recognised by the employer to take time off during working hours[179] is now contained in s. 168 TULRCA 1992. 'Official' means either an officer[180] of the union, or of a branch or section of the union, or a person elected or appointed to be a representative of the members or some of them.[181] The right is to enable the official to carry out duties relating to the following:

1. Those duties concerned with negotiations or matters related to collective bargaining[182] for which the trade union is recognised by the employer.[183] This appears to be a test of proximity, i.e. to what extent are the duties undertaken by the official related to negotiations or collective bargaining. In *Adlington v British Bakeries*,[184] union officials wanted time off to attend a workshop on government proposals to repeal 1954 legislation that regulated working hours, etc. The employer had agreed to give them time off but not with pay. The Court of Appeal held that the proximity of meetings to actual negotiations was a matter of degree and therefore a question of fact. In this case the purpose of the workshop was to acquaint union representatives with the implications of repeal, which would lead to negotiations, rather than any attempt to prevent the repeal. In contrast, an unofficial preparatory meeting of shop stewards was held to be outside the scope of the statute. It was not convened or authorised by the union, neither did the union ask that its shop stewards be given leave to attend.[185]

2. Those duties[186] connected with the performance, on behalf of the employees, of functions related to collective bargaining matters to which the employer has agreed. Section 199 TULRCA 1992 provides that ACAS has a duty to provide practical guidance on the time off to be permitted by an employer.[187] Paragraph 9 of the ACAS Code of Practice gives a number of examples of trade union duties for which time off should be given. These include functions connected with terms and conditions of employment, matters of discipline and the machinery for negotiation or consultation. However, time off to attend a conference about collecting information from employers may not fall within the terms of the legislation where there is already a means for obtaining that information.[188]

3. Those duties[189] concerned with the receipt of information from the employer and consultation by the employer concerning collective redundancies and transfers of undertakings.[190]

---

179 Working hours are those hours when, in accordance with the contract of employment, the individual is required to be at work: s. 173(1) TULRCA 1992.

180 Officer means any member of the governing body of a trade union or any trustee of any fund applicable for the purposes of the union: s. 119 TULRCA 1992.

181 Section 119 TULRCA 1992.

182 Section 168(2) TULRCA 1992. See *Beal v Beecham Group Ltd* [1982] IRLR 192 CA where duties connected with collective bargaining were held to include duties in preparation for that bargaining.

183 See s.178 TULRCA 1992 and Chapter 12.

184 [1989] IRLR 218 CA.

185 *Ashley v Ministry of Defence* [1984] IRLR 57, where, in addition, a union/MOD advisory committee was held to be too remote from the actual negotiations.

186 Section 168(2)(b) TULRCA 1992.

187 ACAS Code of Practice on Time Off for Trade Union Duties and Activities 2010. See *Depledge v Pye Telecommunications Ltd* [1981] ICR 82.

188 See *Depledge v Pye Telecommunications Ltd* [1981] ICR 82.

189 Section 168(2)(c) TULRCA 1992.

190 Section 188 TULRCA 1992 and Transfer of Undertakings (Protection of Employment) Regulations 2006, SI 2006/246; see Chapter 10.

4.   For the purpose of undergoing training in industrial relations.[191] This training needs to
     be relevant to the carrying out of the duties for which recognition is given and needs to be
     approved by the TUC or the union of which the individual is an official. Paragraph 24 of the
     ACAS Code of Practice gives examples of the types of training that might be included, such as
     the structure of the union or the role of the official. Paragraph 26 of this Code also makes it
     clear that an official will be more effective if they possess the skills and knowledge that might
     come from this training.

The time off for officials is with pay on the basis that the individual should receive what they would
have earned if they had worked during the time off.[192] The guidance given by ACAS[193] on this subject
is that there is no statutory requirement to pay for time off where training is undertaken at a time
when the official would not normally have been at work. This was a problem especially for union
officials who were part-time employees or worked shifts because they appeared to be excluded
from receiving pay for union duties during the hours when they were not at work. In *Hairsine v
Kingston-upon-Hull City Council*[194] a swimming pool attendant was a shop steward who worked a shift
system. The employee was given time off with pay to attend a training course, only some of which
clashed with the working hours. This individual was unable to substitute the daytime hours spent
on the course for the evening shift hours they were expected to work. However, part-timers are
more likely to be protected.[195] *Davies v Neath Port Talbot Borough Council*[196] concerned a council employee
who worked a 22-hour week. The individual was a health and safety representative who was given
time off to attend two five-day courses run by the union. The employer agreed to pay for the usual
working hours, not the 40 and 32.5 hours actually spent on the courses. In these circumstances the
employee made an equal pay claim under art. 119 EEC. The EAT agreed that part-time workers had
a right, under art. 119, to be paid on the same basis as full-timers when attending union-run
courses. As the great majority of part-timers are female, to do otherwise would amount to indirect
sex discrimination. The EAT concluded that s. 169(2) TULRCA 1992 which provides for the
individual to be paid what they would have earned if they had been at work was, in so far as it
applied to part-timers, in conflict with art. 119 and therefore could not be relied on.[197]

8.5.8.1 Taking part in trade union activities

Section 170 TULRCA 1992 provides that employees who are also members of an independent trade
union recognised by the employer are entitled to time off during working hours for the purpose
of taking part in any activities of the trade union or any activities in relation to which the employee
is acting as a representative of the union. This right excludes time off for activities in relation to
industrial action, whether or not in contemplation or furtherance of an industrial dispute.[198] There
is no statutory right to pay during this period of time off. Examples of trade union activities are
contained in paras 37–38 ACAS Code of Practice. They include attending workplace meetings
to discuss and vote on the outcome of negotiations or voting in union elections. Examples of
acting as a representative are attending branch, area or regional meetings of the union to discuss
union business or attending meetings of official policy-making bodies, such as the union's annual

---

191   Section 168(2) TULRCA 1992.
192   Section 169 TULRCA 1992.
193   Paragraph 19 the Code of Practice.
194   [1992] IRLR 211.
195   See the Part-time Workers (Prevention of Less Favourable Treatment) Regulations 2000 (Chapter 2 above).
196   [1999] IRLR 769.
197   The EAT also refused to follow *Manor Bakeries v Nazir* [1996] IRLR 604, which had held that attendance at a union conference was
      not 'work' under art. 119.
198   Section 170(2) TULRCA 1992; see Chapter 12.

conference. In some way the activity needs to be linked to the employment relationship and the union. Thus a TUC lobby of Parliament against an Education Reform Bill was not an activity which entitled a number of teachers, who were members of the National Union of Teachers, to time off under s. 170 TULRCA 1992. Such a lobby was to express political and ideological objections to the proposed statute and was not part of the employment relationship.[199]

Sections 168(3) and 170(3) TULRCA 1992 state that the amount of time off, and the purposes for which it is taken, should be 'reasonable in all the circumstances' having regard to the relevant provisions of the ACAS Code of Practice. In *Wignall v British Gas Corporation*[200] the EAT held that each application need not be looked at in isolation. It would be reasonable for an employer, when considering a request for time off, to consider this in the light of time off already taken. The Code states that trade unions should be aware of the variety of difficulties for employers and take into account the size of the organisation, the number of workers, the production process, the need to maintain a service to the public and the need for safety and security at all times. Equally, employers should be aware of the difficulties for trade unions in ensuring effective representation for a variety of workers, such as those who are shift workers, part-timers, employed at dispersed locations and workers with particular domestic commitments.[201] Trade union officials and members requesting time off should give as much notice as possible, giving details of the purpose of the time off, the intended location and the timing and duration of the time off.[202]

The remedy for employees is to present a complaint to an employment tribunal.[203] The claim needs to be made within three months of the date when the failure occurred, unless the tribunal finds that it was not reasonably practicable to do so.[204] If the tribunal finds the complaint well founded, it may make a declaration and award compensation. This compensation will be such as the tribunal decides is just and equitable and will take into account any losses suffered by the employee as a result of the employer's actions, including unpaid wages.[205]

Finally, it should be noted that s. 13 of the Trade Union Act 2016 inserted s. 172A into TULRCA 1992 and requires specified public sector employers to report annually on paid time off provided to trade union representatives for trade union duties and activities.

The Trade Union (Facility Time Publication Requirements) Regulations 2017 activates this but only applies where the employer has at least one trade union representative and 50 or more employees for seven months during the reporting period.[206] The first report must be published by 31 July 2018 on the employer's website and, where the employer publishes an annual report, it must be included in that document.

8.5.8.2 Union learning representatives

Section 168A(1) TULRCA provides that an employee who is a member of an independent trade union recognised by the employer must be given time off with pay to perform the duties of being a union learning representative (ULR).[207] The employer has this obligation if notice has been received from the trade union that the employee is a ULR and has undergone (or will undergo)

199 *Luce v London Borough of Bexley* [1990] IRLR 422.
200 [1984] IRLR 493.
201 Paragraph 45 ACAS Code of Practice.
202 Paragraph 50 ACAS Code of Practice.
203 Sections 168(4), 169(5) and 170(4) TULRCA 1992.
204 Section 171 TULRCA 1992.
205 Section 172 TULRCA 1992; see *Skiggs v South West Trains Ltd* [2005] IRLR 459. On the possible imposition of financial penalties, see note 113 above.
206 This is the period of 12 months beginning 1 April each year.
207 Paras 28–33 of the ACAS Code of Practice on Time Off for Trade Union Duties and Activities provides guidance on time off for union learning representatives.

sufficient training for the role.[208] The employee is also to be permitted time off to undergo training for the role.[209]

The functions of a ULR are, in relation to members of the trade union and others, to:

1. analyse learning or training needs;
2. provide information about learning or training matters;
3. arrange learning or training; and
4. promote the value of learning or training.

This will include consultations with the employer about carrying out these activities and any necessary preparations.[210]

8.6 Protection of wages

One major aspect of the relationship between the worker and the employer is payment for the work carried out, or time spent at the employer's disposal. Thus workers who are ready and willing to perform their contracts but are unable to do so owing to sickness, injury or other unavoidable impediment are entitled to wages.[211] Section 27 ERA 1996 provides a statutory definition of the meaning of wages, etc. 'Wages' include any fee, bonus,[212] commission,[213] holiday pay,[214] or other emolument relating to the employment, whether or not payable under the worker's contract. It can also include statutory sick pay[215] and statutory maternity pay.[216]

8.6.1 Unauthorised deductions

Workers have a right not to suffer deductions of pay by their employer, unless the deduction is authorised by statute,[217] a relevant provision of the worker's contract or by the worker previously signifying their agreement in writing.[218] A 'relevant provision' of a contract is a term of the contract which has been notified to the worker prior to the employer making the deduction.[219] In *Kerr v The Sweater Shop (Scotland) Ltd*[220] it was held that an individual need not agree in writing to the deduction because it was possible for consent to be given through continuing to work once the change had been brought to the individual's attention.

---

208 Section 168A(3) TULRCA 1992.

209 Section 168A(7) TULRCA 1992.

210 Section 168A(2) TULRCA 1992.

211 See Burns v Santander UK plc [2011] IRLR 639.

212 In *Farrell Matthews and Weir v Hansen* [2005] IRLR 160 the EAT held that an employee suffered an unlawful deduction when the employer refused to pay the balance of a non-contractual discretionary bonus which was payable in monthly instalments. See now *Small v Boots plc* [2009] IRLR 328.

213 See *Kent Management Services Ltd v Butterfield* [1992] IRLR 394, which held that the withholding of commission was an unlawful deduction, even though the commission might be on a discretionary and non-contractual basis.

214 See HMRC v Stringer [2009] IRLR 677 HL.

215 See *Taylor Gordon Ltd v Timmons* [2004] IRLR 180.

216 For a full list of what is included and excluded, see s. 27 ERA 1996.

217 For example, income tax and national insurance contributions.

218 Section 13(1) ERA 1996; s. 15(1) ERA 1996 is similarly concerned with the rights of employees not to have to make payments to an employer. On the lawful recovery of recruitment and training costs when employees are dismissed for misconduct, see *Cleeve Ltd v Bryla* [2014] IRLR 86.

219 Section 13(2) ERA 1996; 'to the worker' means some written notification, not just the displaying of a notice; see *Kerr v The Sweater Shop (Scotland) Ltd* [1996] IRLR 424; also see s. 15(2) on 'relevant provision' concerning the right not to have to make payments to an employer.

220 [1996] IRLR 424.

The deduction in wages is to be treated as the difference between the amount owed to the worker[221] and the amount actually paid.[222] This can be calculated on each occasion that wages are paid. Thus, where a person receives a regular salary, each occasion that the salary is paid can be considered for the purposes of whether there has been an unlawful deduction of wages.[223] The conditions that must be satisfied in order to show that workers have given their consent to deductions are: (i) there must be a document which clearly states that the deductions are to be made from wages; (ii) it must be clear that the worker agrees to the deduction.[224]

Section 14 ERA 1996 provides a list of deductions which are excluded from s. 13 ERA 1996.[225] These are if the deduction is:

1. A reimbursement of overpayment of wages or expenses[226] paid by the employer.[227]
2. Made as a result of disciplinary proceedings resulting from a statutory provision.[228]
3. As a result of a statutory requirement to deduct sums and pay them over to a public authority.[229]
4. Where there is prior contractual agreement, or other prior written agreement, for the deduction of money to be paid over to a third person, after notification by the third person of the amount owed by the worker.
5. As a result of the worker taking part in industrial action.[230]
6. A deduction, made with prior written consent of the worker, resulting from the order of a court or tribunal.

There are special provisions for dealing with cash shortages and stock deficiencies in retail employment.[231]

It is not permissible to make a complaint about a threatened deduction from wages.[232] Section 23(1) ERA 1996 states that a worker may present a complaint to an employment tribunal that the employer *has made* a deduction from wages in contravention of s. 13 ERA 1996 or received a payment in contravention of s. 15 ERA 1996 (see above). The complaint must be made within three months of the date of the deduction or payment. This date is the last date on which the payment could have been made in accordance with the contract, rather than from the date when it was actually made.[233] Where the complaint relates to a series of deductions or payments, then it must be within three months of the last deduction or payment, subject to the employment tribunal being satisfied that this was not reasonably practicable.[234] If the tribunal finds the complaint well founded, it may issue a declaration and order the employer to repay the unauthorised deductions or payments to the

---

221 This can be what is 'properly payable' in terms of employee expectations.

222 Section 13(3) ERA 1996.

223 See *Murray v Strathclyde Regional Council* [1992] IRLR 396, where a deduction in one month for a series of alleged overpayments was held to be a deduction in salary in terms of the statute.

224 See *Potter v Hunt Contracts* [1992] IRLR 108, which concerned the deduction of the balance of a loan made to the employee from wages due on termination of employment.

225 Section 16 ERA 1996 provides similar exceptions concerning the right of an employee not to have to make payments to an employer.

226 Expenses are not to be subject to too much scrutiny; if there is a profit element in expenses, this would not necessarily stop the whole amount from being expenses; it is not the tribunal's job to try to apportion sums in order to be precise about what are expenses and what are not: *London Borough of Southwark v O'Brien* [1996] IRLR 420.

227 See *Murray v Strathclyde Regional Council* [1992] IRLR 396.

228 It has been suggested that this provision refers not to private employers but to such services as the police or fire service: see *Chiltern House Ltd v Chambers* [1990] IRLR 88.

229 See *Patel v Marquette Ltd* [2009] IRLR 425.

230 See *Hartley v King Edward VI College* [2017] IRLR 763.

231 Sections 17–22 ERA 1996.

232 See *Mennell v Newell & Wright (Transport Contractors Ltd)* [1997] IRLR 519 CA.

233 See *Group 4 Nightspeed Ltd v Gilbert* [1997] IRLR 398.

234 Section 23 ERA 1996. See *List Design Ltd v Douglas & Catley* [2003] IRLR 14.

worker. It cannot consider a complaint about deductions made before the period of two years ending with the date of presentation of the claim but it can compensate a worker who suffers financial losses.[235]

A failure to make a payment in lieu of notice is unlikely to be treated as a deduction in wages, although it might amount to a breach of contract. In *Delaney v Staples t/a De Montfort Recruitment*[236] the Supreme Court dealt with a case where an employee was summarily dismissed and given a cheque as payment in lieu of notice. The employer subsequently stopped the cheque, claiming that the employee had taken confidential information with her. The employee then claimed an unlawful deduction had been made from her wages. The court held that a payment in lieu was not wages where it relates to the period after employment. Wages are payments in respect of rendering services during employment. All payments relating to the termination of the contract are excluded unless expressly provided for in the legislation. However, payments paid after termination in relation to work done before the termination are wages. In *Robertson v Blackstone Franks Investment Management Ltd*[237] the payment of commission earned during employment but paid after the employee had left was held to be wages within the meaning of the Act.

Any variations in contractual terms to allow deductions does not provide authorisation for a deduction until the variation takes effect.[238] If there is a variation in pay resulting from a change in work patterns permitted by the contract, then a related variation in pay may not be treated as a deduction. Thus, when there is a change in shift patterns permitted by the contract which results in the payment of a lower shift premium, this could not be treated as an unauthorised deduction from wages.[239] If the contractual variation is a result of the employer's unilateral decision, then any resulting reduction in wages may contravene s. 13 ERA 1996. In *McCree v London Borough of Tower Hamlets*[240] the employer introduced a new bonus system which absorbed a previously paid supplement to an employee. The unilateral abolition of this supplement resulted in a breach of these provisions.[241]

Where the employer makes an error in calculating the gross amount of pay due to a worker, the shortfall is not to be treated as a deduction.[242] For these purposes, an error is not one that is based upon a misunderstanding of the law. In *Morgan v West Glamorgan County Council*[243] an employee was demoted for disciplinary reasons and suffered a reduction in salary. The employer wrongly thought that they had the contractual authority to do this. This was not an error in terms of s. 13(4) ERA 1996 but the result of a deliberate decision to demote and reduce salary. Thus the shortfall in salary was to be treated as a deduction for these purposes.[244]

8.6.2 Normal working hours and a week's pay

Sections 220–229 ERA 1996 define a week's pay. For such purposes as the basic award of compensation for unfair dismissal[245] and the calculation of protective awards resulting from a failure to

---

235 Sections 24–26 ERA 1996. On the possible imposition of financial penalties, see note 113 above.
236 [1992] IRLR 191 HL.
237 [1998] IRLR 376 CA.
238 Section 13(5) ERA 1996.
239 See *Hussman Manufacturing Ltd v Weir* [1998] IRLR 288.
240 [1992] IRLR 56.
241 See also *Bruce v Wiggins Teape (Stationery) Ltd* [1994] IRLR 536, where there was a unilateral reduction in overtime rates; the EAT stated that no distinction was to be drawn between a deduction and a reduction in wages.
242 Section 13(4) ERA 1996.
243 [1995] IRLR 68.
244 See also *Yemm v British Steel* [1994] IRLR 117, which also concerned a mistaken belief that the employer could change contractual duties with a resulting reduction in pay.
245 Section 119 ERA 1996.

consult in collective redundancy situations,[246] a week's pay is subject to a maximum. This was set at £489 per week from April 2017.[247]

Normal working hours are usually determined by reference to the contract of employment. If the contract stipulates a minimum number of fixed hours, then those are to be taken as the normal working hours.[248] If the contract requires overtime to be worked, these may become part of the normal working hours provided that there is an obligation to work the hours and they are guaranteed by the employer.[249] It is not enough to show that an employee regularly worked extra hours. There needs to be an obligation upon the employer to pay for the hours and a duty on the employee to carry them out. This was the case in *Lotus Cars Ltd v Sutcliffe and Stratton*[250] where employees were expected to work a 45-hour week but contractually had a basic working week of 40 hours. They were paid a premium rate for the extra five hours worked each week. The court followed *Tarmac*[251] and concluded that the element of obligation was absent for these purposes.

The calculation date depends upon the purpose of the calculation.[252] There are a number of different categories:

1. If the employee's remuneration for normal working hours does not vary with the amount done in that period, then the amount of a week's pay is the amount payable by the employer under the contract in force on the calculation date if the employee works the normal working hours.[253] There are additional rules for those who do not have regular hours or are not paid according to the time they work (see below).

2. In cases where the remuneration varies in relation to the amount of work done, remuneration will be calculated by using the average hourly rate paid by the employer in respect of the 12 weeks ending with the last complete week before the calculation date or, if the calculation date is the last day of the week, then that week. This can include those whose remuneration includes commission or similar payment which varies in amount, but will exclude overtime premium rates.[254]

3. Where the normal hours worked vary from week to week, perhaps as a result of shift work, then the amount of a week's pay is the amount of remuneration for the average number of weekly normal working hours at the average hourly rate of remuneration. The average number of hours is to be calculated by totalling the number of hours worked over the previous 12 weeks and dividing by 12.[255]

4. Where there are employments with no normal working hours, then the weekly pay will be the average weekly remuneration in the period of 12 weeks ending with the calculation date. This is the last complete week before the calculation date or, if the date is the last day of the week, then that week. No account is to be taken of weeks when there was no remuneration and, in such cases, earlier weeks will be used to bring the total to 12.[256]

---

246 Section 190 TULRCA 1992.

247 See s. 227(1) ERA 1996.

248 Section 234 ERA 1996.

249 *Tarmac Roadstone Holdings Ltd v Peacock* [1973] IRLR 157 CA.

250 [1982] IRLR 381 CA.

251 [1973] IRLR 157 CA.

252 See ss 225–226 ERA 1996.

253 Section 221(2) ERA 1996.

254 Section 221(3)–(4) ERA 1996; see *British Coal Corporation v Cheesebrough* [1990] IRLR 148 HL.

255 Section 222 ERA 1996; the hourly rate and calculation date is as for s. 221(3) above; if there has been no pay in any of the weeks for the purposes of ss 221 and 222, then earlier weeks are to be used to bring the total to 12, but any overtime hours included will not take into account any premium rates paid: see s. 223.

256 Section 224 ERA 1996.

5. If an employee does not have sufficient service to calculate the 12 weeks, then there are a number of factors used to calculate the amount 'which fairly represents a week's pay' contained in s. 228 ERA 1996. Those employees who have maintained continuity of employment may use time served and remuneration earned with the previous employer if necessary.[257]

8.6.3 Guarantee payments

An employee is entitled to be paid an amount by the employer for any day,[258] or part of a day, during which they would normally be required to work in accordance with the contract, and they have not been provided with work. In *Abercrombie v Aga Ltd*[259] the Court of Appeal held that the claimants were entitled to payments in respect of Fridays despite there being a temporary arrangement for Monday to Thursday working. According to the Appeal Court, the relevant question is whether the employee would normally be contractually required to work on that day. It is immaterial whether the normal state of affairs is covered by an agreement which expressly varies the contract. The workless days must be as a result of:

1. a diminution in the requirements of the employer's business for work of the kind that the employee was hired to do; or
2. any other event affecting the normal working of the employer's business in relation to such work.[260]

There is a statutory maximum payable to an employee, which makes the provision of little value to many people. The maximum daily figure set in 2017 was £27[261] and the maximum number of days for which payment must be made is five in any three-month period.[262] This right does not, however, affect any contractual rights to payment and any such payment can be offset against the statutory requirement.[263] In practice, this provision is of most use to those who have a contract which allows them to be laid off without pay or those who are paid by the amount of work that they produce (piece workers, commission-only workers).

There are a number of exceptions to entitlement:[264]

1. An employee must have been continuously employed for at least one month ending with the day before the day for which a guarantee payment is claimed.
2. Employees are not entitled to payment for 'workless days' if the failure to be provided with work results from a strike, lock-out or other industrial action[265] involving any employee of the employer or associated employer.
3. If the employee has been offered suitable alternative work by the employer for that day and has unreasonably refused that offer.
4. If the employee has not complied with reasonable requirements of the employer ensuring the employee's availability for work.

---

257 Section 229 ERA 1996.
258 Section 28(4) ERA 1996; day means the 24-hour period between midnight and midnight; see also s. 28(5) dealing with situations where the day extends through midnight.
259 [2013] IRLR 953.
260 Section 28(1) ERA 1996.
261 Section 31(1) ERA 1996.
262 Section 31(2)–(6) ERA 1996; see s. 30 for guidance in calculating the amount due, subject to this maximum.
263 Section 32 ERA 1996.
264 Sections 29 and 35 ERA 1996.
265 'Other industrial action' is to be given its natural and ordinary meaning; e.g. it can include a refusal to work overtime: see *Faust v Power Packing Casemakers Ltd* [1983] IRLR 117 CA.

5.	Situations where there is a collective agreement or an agricultural wages order concerning guaranteed payments and the Minister to whom an application is made issues an order excluding the obligation under s. 28 ERA 1996.

An employee may complain to an employment tribunal if the employer fails to pay all or part of the entitlement. The complaint must be made within three months of the failure to pay unless the tribunal accepts that it was not reasonably practicable to do so. In the event of the tribunal finding the complaint well founded, it may order the employer to pay to the employee the amount due.[266]

8.6.4 Suspension from work on medical grounds

Employees have the right to be paid by the employer if they are suspended from work on medical grounds.[267] A person is suspended on medical grounds if the suspension is as a result of a requirement or provision imposed under any enactment, or a recommendation in a code of practice issued or approved under s. 16 Health and Safety at Work etc. Act 1974.[268]

This suspension, with the right to remuneration, is subject to a maximum of 26 weeks. An employee is to be regarded as suspended only for as long as employment continues and the employer does not provide work or the individual does not perform the work normally performed before the suspension.[269] There is no entitlement to payment if:

1.	Employees have not been continuously employed for at least one month ending with the day before the suspension begins.
2.	It is a period during which the employee is incapable of work because of a disease or other physical or mental impairment.
3.	The employee has been offered suitable alternative work and has unreasonably refused that offer.
4.	The employee does not comply with reasonable requirements imposed by the employer to ensure that the employee is available for work.[270]

Complaints about a failure to pay the whole or part of the amount due may be made to an employment tribunal within three months of the failure, unless the tribunal accepts that this was not reasonably practicable. Where the tribunal finds the complaint well founded, it will order the employer to make the payment.[271]

8.7 National minimum wage

Section 1(1) of the National Minimum Wage Act (NMWA) 1998 places an obligation upon employers and provides that any person who qualifies should be remunerated, in any pay reference period, at a rate which is not less than the national minimum wage.[272] The pay reference period is

---

266	Section 34 ERA 1996. On the possible imposition of financial penalties, see note 113 above.
267	Section 64(1) ERA 1996. On maternity grounds see Chapter 9.
268	Section 64(2)–(3) ERA 1996; the Health and Safety Executive has the power to issue or approve codes of practice relating to health and safety regulations.
269	Section 64(5) ERA 1996.
270	Section 65 ERA 1996.
271	Section 70(1)–(3) ERA 1996. On the possible imposition of financial penalties, see note 113 above.
272	In *Revenue and Customs Commissioners v Annabel's Ltd* [2008] ICR 1076 it was decided that customer tips had become the property of a 'troncmaster'. Thus the payments to employees from the tronc were not 'payments paid by the employer'.

one month, or a shorter period if the worker is paid at shorter intervals.[273] An 'employer' is defined in s. 54 NMWA 1998 as the person by whom the employee or worker is employed, but there are provisions to ensure that a superior employer is identified as the person responsible.[274] The Act was brought into effect on 1 April 1999 with the adoption of the National Minimum Wage Regulations (NMW Regulations) 1999.[275]

The Act established the Low Pay Commission,[276] which is given responsibility for advising the government on the amount to be paid. However, it is HM Revenue & Customs that has the role of enforcing the payment and prosecuting offenders (see below). The national living wage (£7.50 from April 2017) applies to those aged at least 25 years.[277] The minimum wage for those aged 21–24 was set at £7.05[278] per hour from April 2017 although three groups of workers are only entitled to a reduced rate. First, those workers who have attained the age of 18 years and are less than 21 years old are entitled to £5.60 in 2017. Second, the hourly rate for those 16–17 years is £4.05 in 2017.[279] The third group, apprentices who are either under 19 years or over this age but in the first year of their apprenticeship,[280] are entitled to £3.50 per hour from April 2017.

8.7.1 Who qualifies for the national minimum wage?

An individual qualifies for the national minimum wage (NMW) if they are a worker[281] who is working, or is ordinarily working, in the United Kingdom under a contract and who has ceased to be of compulsory school age.[282] Agency workers and homeworkers qualify. In the case of agency workers, if there is confusion as to who is the employer because of the lack of a contract between the worker and the agency or the principal, the person providing the wages or salary has the responsibility for paying the NMW.[283] 'Homeworkers' are defined as individuals who contract to carry out work in a place not under the control or management of the person with whom they have contracted.[284] The following groups do not qualify:

1. Workers participating in schemes to provide training, work experience or temporary work, or to assist them in finding work.[285]
2. A worker participating in a trial period with an employer in the circumstances specified in Regulation 52(2) NMW Regulations 2015.
3. Workers attending a higher or further education course who are required before the course ends to complete a period of work experience not exceeding one year do not qualify for the NMW for work done as part of that course – for example, sandwich students who spend part of their course gaining work experience.[286]
4. Workers participating in a traineeship in England if the conditions specified in Regulation 54(2) NMW Regulations 2015 are satisfied.

---

273 Regulation 6 National Minimum Wage Regulations 2015, SI 2015/621.
274 Section 48 NMWA 1998; see also s. 34 NMWA 1998 on the employer of agency workers.
275 SI 1999/584. These Regulations were replaced by the National Minimum Wage Regulations 2015, SI 2015/621.
276 Sections 5–8 NMWA 1998.
277 Regulation 4 National Minimum Wage Regulations 2015.
278 Most benefits in kind, apart from living accommodation, are not to be treated as payments to the worker for the purposes of calculating the NMW: reg.10 NMW Regulations 2015.
279 Regulation 4A NMW Regulations 2015.
280 Regulation 5 NMW Regulations 2015
281 Worker is defined in s. 54(3) NMWA 1998 and is given the same meaning as in s. 230(3) ERA 1996.
282 Section 1(2) NMWA 1998.
283 Section 34 NMWA 1998.
284 Section 35(2) NMWA 1998.
285 Regulation 51 NMW Regulations 2015.
286 Regulation 53 NMW Regulations 2015.

5. Workers who are homeless or residing in a hostel for the homeless, are eligible for income support and are participating in a voluntary or charitable scheme.[287]
6. Workers participating in the EU programmes set up in Regulation 56(2) NMW Regulations 2015.
7. Share fishers.[288]
8. Workers employed by a charity or a voluntary organisation, or similar, who only receive expenses in respect of work done. These expenses can include subsistence income for the worker concerned.[289]
9. Workers who are residential members of religious or charitable communities in respect of work done for those communities. Exempt from this are communities that are independent schools or those that provide courses in further or higher education.[290]
10. Workers who are prisoners do not qualify for the NMW in respect of any work done in pursuance of prison rules.[291]

Work is also defined as excluding any work relating to the employer's family household if the worker lives in the employer's family home, is treated as a member of the family, does not pay for the living accommodation and, if the work had been done by a member of the employer's family, it would not have been treated as being work.[292] In *Nambalat v Taher*[293] the Court of Appeal stated that Regulation 2(2) NMW Regulations 1999 (now Regulation 57 NMW Regulations 2015) requires an overall approach to family membership and that accommodation is only one factor. The way in which the household tasks are shared is an important indicator as is the extent of the duties exclusively done by the worker.

8.7.2 Calculating the hourly rate

The hourly rate paid to a worker is calculated by finding the total remuneration paid in that period and dividing it by the total number of hours of time work, salaried hours work, output work and unmeasured work in the pay reference period (these categories are discussed below).[294] The total remuneration in such a period is calculated[295] by adding together:

1. All money paid by the employer to the worker in the pay reference period.
2. All money paid in the following reference period that relates to the pay reference period.
3. Any money paid by the employer later than the following reference period in respect of work done in the pay reference period.[296]
4. Any amount permitted to be taken into account for the provision of living accommodation.[297]

We now discuss the meaning of time work, salaried hours work, output work and unmeasured work.

---

287 Regulation 55 NMW Regulations 2015.
288 Section 43 NMWA 1998.
289 Section 44 NMWA 1998.
290 Section 44A NMWA 1998.
291 Section 45 NMWA 1998. See also Sections 45A and 45B NMWA 1998.
292 Regulation 57 NMW Regulations 2015.
293 [2012] IRLR 1004; see also *Onu v Akwiwu* [2013] IRLR 523.
294 Regulation 7 NMW Regulations 2015.
295 Regulation 8 NMW Regulations 2015.
296 There are further conditions related to whether a worker is obliged to complete records of the amount of work done: reg. 9 NMW Regulations 2015.
297 Reg. 14 NMW Regulations 2015

8.7.2.1 Time work[298]

Time work is when workers are paid for the number of hours that they are at work. It also applies if a worker is contracted to perform a particular job but is paid for the hours done each week or month and where a person is on piece work but is expected to work a certain number of hours per day. Whatever the level of the piece work, the worker must receive, on average, at least the NMW for each hour during the pay period.

Time work includes[299] time when the worker is available at or near the place of work (other than at home) for the purpose of doing time work. Regulation 32(2) provides that a person is only available when they are awake for the purposes of working, even if by arrangement he or she sleeps at or near a place of work and the employer provides suitable sleeping facilities.[300] This does not apply to situations where an employee is required to be on the premises for a specific number of hours and who may sleep, if she or he chooses to, when the designated tasks have been completed.[301] It only applies where the employer gives specific permission to the worker to take a particular amount of time off for sleep.[302] More recently, the EAT has explained the relationship between Regulations 30 and 32 and indicated that it is only if the worker cannot be said to be working that Regulation 32 falls for consideration. In deciding whether a person is working by being present, four factors were said to be relevant: (i) the employer's purpose in engaging the worker; (ii) the extent to which the worker's activities are restricted by being present and at the employer's disposal; (iii) the extent of responsibility undertaken by the worker; (iv) the immediacy of the requirement to provide services if something untoward occurs.[303] Similarly, in *British Nursing Association v Inland Revenue*[304] staff providing a night-time booking service from home were entitled to have the entire period that they were available to answer the phone counted as time work. This was so even though they were able to undertake other activities during these hours, such as watching TV or reading. The Court of Appeal stated that it would make a mockery of the national minimum wage to conclude that the employees were only working when they answered the telephone and that all the time spent waiting for a call should be excluded. Time spent travelling can also be time work although, unsurprisingly,[305] time work does not include periods when the worker is absent or taking part in industrial action.[306] According to the DBIS (now DBEIS) guide to the NMW, most workers who are not on an annual salary will be on time work.

8.7.2.2 Salaried hours work

Salaried hours work is where a worker is paid under a contract for a set number of hours worked per year, is entitled to an annual salary and is paid in equal weekly or monthly instalments during the year regardless of the number of hours worked. Variations as a result of the payment of a performance bonus, a pay increase, excess hours payments or because the worker left partway through the week or month do not stop the hours being salaried hours. According to the EAT,

---

298 Regulation 30 NMW Regulations 2015.
299 Regulation 32(1) NMW Regulations 2015.
300 See *Shannon v Rampersad* [2015] IRLR 982.
301 See *Esparon v Slavikovska* [2014] IRLR 598 where the worker as entitled to the national minimum wage while on 'sleep in' duty at a care home.
302 *Scottbridge Construction Ltd v Wright* [2003] IRLR 21. In *Burrow Down Ltd v Rossiter* [2008] ICR 1172 the EAT held that since the employee was required to undertake tasks during the time when he was otherwise permitted to sleep, he was actually working and engaged in time work for the whole of the shift.
303 *Focus Care Agency Ltd v Roberts* [2017] IRLR 588.
304 [2002] IRLR 480 CA.
305 Regulation 34 NMW Regulations 2015. See *Whittlestone v BJP Home Support Ltd* [2014] IRLR 176.
306 Regulation 35 NMW Regulations 2015.

the issue is whether the contract provides the period in question to be part of the employee's working hours. It is unnecessary to establish what work is actually done – the question is what the contract provides for.[307]

The provisions relating to salaried workers are similar to those for time workers,[308] except that absences count if the worker is paid the normal pay during the absence. Absences such as lunch breaks, holidays and sickness absence count if they form part of the worker's basic minimum hours. Periods paid at a lesser rate do not count – for example, when the worker is absent as a result of long-term sickness; neither do periods of unpaid leave and time on industrial action.[309] The basic number of hours for a salaried worker is the basic number of hours in respect of which a worker is paid, under the contract, on the first day of the reference period.[310]

8.7.2.3 Output work

Output work is work that is paid for by reference to a worker's output, be it the number of tasks performed or the value of sales made.[311] It is sometimes known as piece work or can be work that is paid by commission. Time travelling can be included, except for travelling to the premises from which work is performed and, in the case of a home worker, the premises to which the worker reports.[312] Again, time spent in taking industrial action does not count.[313]

There are two ways in which the hours of an output worker can be calculated.[314] These are: (i) by counting the number of hours spent in output work, or (ii) by applying a complicated system called 'rated output work'. This requires employers to give their workers a notice containing specified information and to test them in order to identify 'the mean hourly output rate'. The number of hours taken by a worker in producing the relevant pieces or performing the relevant tasks during a pay reference period is deemed to be the same number of hours that a person working at the mean hourly output rate would have taken to produce the same number of pieces or perform the same number of tasks during the pay reference period. Employers must pay their workers producing that piece or performing that task an amount per piece or task which, given that the workers are deemed to have worked at the mean hourly output rate, is at least equivalent to the hourly national minimum wage. Since April 2005, the number of hours spent by a worker on rated output work has been treated as being 120 per cent of the number of hours that a person working at the mean hourly output rate would have taken.

8.7.2.4 Unmeasured work

Unmeasured work is work that is not time work, salaried hours work or output work. It is work that has no specified hours and the person is required to work when needed or when work is available – for example, a carer.[315] There are two methods of identifying the number of hours to be worked and for which the NMW should be paid.[316] These are, first, to pay the NMW for every hour worked. The second is for the employer and the worker to come to a 'daily average' agreement, to determine the average number of daily hours the worker is likely to spend on unmeasured work. The agreement

307　*Binfield School v Roll* [2016] IRLR 670.
308　Regulations 21–29 NMW Regulations 2015.
309　Regulation 23 NMW Regulations 2015.
310　Regulation 22 NMW Regulations 2015.
311　Regulation 36 NMW Regulations 2015.
312　Regulation 39 NMW Regulations 2015.
313　Regulation 40 NMW Regulations 2015.
314　Regulations 37 and 43 NMW Regulations 2015.
315　Regulation 44 NMW Regulations 2015. See *Walton v Independent Living Organisation* [2003] IRLR 469.
316　Regulations 45 and 49–50 NMW Regulations 2015.

must be made before the start of the pay reference period that it covers, be in writing, set out the average daily number of hours, and ensure that the daily average is realistic.

8.7.3 Record keeping

An employer of a worker who qualifies for the NMW has a duty to keep records.[317] These records need to be sufficient to establish that the worker is being remunerated at a rate at least equal to the NMW. They must also be kept in such a way that the information relating to a worker in a pay reference period can be produced in a single document. In addition, the employer is required to keep copies of any agreements entered into with the worker concerning unmeasured work. These records must be kept for at least three years, beginning with the day upon which the pay reference period immediately following that to which they relate ends.[318] The records may be kept on computer.[319]

If workers believe, on reasonable grounds, that they are being remunerated, in any particular reference period, at a rate less than the NMW, they have the right to request that the employer produce any relevant records and have the right to inspect them.[320] The inspection can be by the worker alone or accompanied by another person of their choice. The request to inspect records must be done by the worker giving a 'production notice' to the employer requesting the production of relevant records[321] relating to a specific period. If the worker is to be accompanied, this must be stated in the 'production notice'. When this notice has been given, the employer must give the worker reasonable notice of the place[322] and time when the records will be produced. However, the records must be produced within 14 days of the employer receiving the 'production notice' unless otherwise agreed with the worker.[323]

If the employer fails to provide some or all of the records requested or fails to allow the worker to inspect the records or be accompanied by another person of the worker's choice, then the worker may make a complaint to an employment tribunal.[324] The complaint must be made within three months of the end of the 14-day period allowed for the provision of the records, or at the end of any other period agreed by the worker and the employer according to s. 10(9) NMWA 1998, unless the tribunal accepts that this was not reasonably practicable. Where an employment tribunal finds the complaint well founded, it may issue a declaration and make an award that the employer pays the worker a sum equal to 80 times the amount of the NMW in force at the time.

8.7.4 Enforcement

HM Revenue & Customs has the task of ensuring that workers are remunerated at a rate at least equivalent to the NMW. HM Revenue & Customs officers are given wide powers to inspect and take copies of records, require relevant persons to provide information[325] and to enter any relevant

---

317 Section 9 NMWA 1998 and reg. 59 NMW Regulations 2015.
318 Regulation 38(7) NMW Regulations 1999.
319 Regulation 38(8) NMW Regulations 1999.
320 Section 10 NMWA 1998.
321 'Relevant' means those records which will establish whether or not the worker has been remunerated at a level equivalent to the NMW in any pay reference period: s. 10(10) NMWA 1998.
322 The place must be the worker's place of work, any other place that is reasonable for the worker to attend or any further place agreed with the worker: s. 10(8) NMWA 1998.
323 Section 10(9) NMWA 1998.
324 Section 11 NMWA 1998.
325 Although no person may be required to provide information that will incriminate themselves or their spouse: s. 14(2) NMWA 1998. On disclosure of information by officers see s.16A NMWA 1998.

premises for the purpose of exercising their powers.[326] According to s. 14(4) NMWA 1998, a relevant person can be the employer or the employer's agent, the supplier of work to the individuals or the workers themselves. 'Relevant premises' means the premises at which the employer carries on business or premises that the employer, or employer's agent, uses in connection with the business.[327]

The Employment Act 2008 amended s. 17 NMWA 1998 in order to provide a fairer method of calculating arrears for workers and a penalty for employers who fail to pay the NMW. If a notice of underpayment is not complied with, HM Revenue & Customs is able to take civil proceedings for the recovery of the money or present a complaint to an employment tribunal, on behalf of the worker, that there has been an unlawful deduction of wages in contravention of s. 13 ERA 1996 (see above).[328] In such proceedings the burden of proof is on the employer to show that the worker was remunerated at the appropriate level.[329]

A failure to comply with certain requirements of the NMWA 1998 can lead to prosecution for a criminal offence and can result in a fine. The offences in question are a refusal or wilful neglect to pay the NMW; failing to keep NMW records; keeping false records; producing false records or information; intentionally obstructing an enforcement officer; and refusing or neglecting to give information to an enforcement officer.[330] In April 2016 the maximum penalty that could be enforced was raised to an amount equal to 200% of the underpayment, subject to a maximum of £20,000 per worker. For those employers who deliberately and persistently fail to comply with the NMW, the government has created a new type of enforcement order, a Labour Market Enforcement Order, supported by a criminal offence for non-compliance. Other penalties include the public naming of underpayers.

8.7.5 Right not to suffer detriment

Section 104A ERA 1996 provides that the dismissal of an employee shall be unfair if the reason, or the principal reason, for the dismissal is entitlement to the NMW or any reason related to the enforcement of it. It is immaterial whether the employee has the right or whether the right has been infringed, although any claim must be made in good faith.

Section 23 NMWA 1998 provides that workers have the right not to be subjected to detriment because of entitlement to the NMW or any reason related to the enforcement of it. Again, good faith is required for complaints and it is immaterial whether the worker has the right or whether it has been infringed. In this context, 'detriment' includes workers who are not protected from unfair dismissal by Part X ERA 1996. The complaint to an employment tribunal must be made within three months beginning with the act, or failure to act, that is to be complained of, unless the tribunal considers that it was not reasonably practicable to do so. If the tribunal finds the complaint well founded, it may make a declaration and award compensation.[331]

---

326 Section 14(1) NMWA 1998.
327 Section 14(5) NMWA 1998.
328 Section 19D NMWA 1998. On the possible imposition of financial penalties, see note 113above.
329 Section 28 NMWA 1998.
330 Sections 31–33 NMWA 1998.
331 Sections 48–49 ERA 1996. On the possible imposition of financial penalties, see note 113 above.

Further reading

Barnard, C., Deakin, S. and Hobbs, R. 'Opting Out of the 48 Hour Week: Employer Necessity or Individual Choice?' (2003) 32(4) *Industrial Law Journal* 223.

Bogg, A. 'Of Holidays, Work and Humanisation: A Missed Opportunity?' (2009) 34 *European Law Review* 738.

Davies, A. 'Getting More Than You Bargained For? Rethinking the Meaning of "Work" in Employment Law' (2017) *Industrial Law Journal*, https://doi.org/10.1093/indlaw/dwx006

Simpson, R. 'The National Minimum Wage Five Years On' (2004) 33(1) *Industrial Law Journal* 22.

www.acas.org.uk – Advisory, Conciliation and Arbitration Service.

www.lowpay.gov.uk – Low Pay Commission.

www.tuc.org.uk – Trades Union Congress.

Chapter 9

Parental and maternity rights

Chapter Contents

9.1 EU Directives

9.1.1 The Pregnant Workers Directive[1]

The Pregnant Workers Directive identified pregnant workers and workers who have recently given birth, or who are breastfeeding, as workers who face particular risks in the workplace. The Directive makes such workers a particular case for protection and makes provisions regarding the health and safety of this group, and adopts certain employment rights connected with pregnancy. The Directive[2] defines a pregnant worker as a woman who informs her employer of her condition, in accordance with national laws and practice. The employer is required to complete an assessment of the risk of exposure to a non-exhaustive list of agents,[3] processes or working conditions and then to inform the worker or her representatives of the results and the measures intended to be taken concerning health and safety at work.[4] It also contains protective provisions concerning night work, maternity leave and protection against dismissal relating to pregnancy or maternity. Member States are required to 'take the necessary measures to prohibit the dismissal of workers . . . during their pregnancy to the end of their maternity leave . . . save in exceptional cases not connected with their condition . . .'.[5] As a result all countries provide protection against dismissal for pregnant workers or those that have recently given birth, although much of this protection emanated from previous anti-sex discrimination legislation. One issue for the national courts was whether there was a necessity to compare a pregnant woman's absence with that of a man to show that discrimination had taken place. *Webb v EMO*[6] was a case where an applicant was employed initially to cover for another employee who was to go on maternity leave. It was envisaged that the new employee would continue to be employed after the pregnant employee returned from her maternity leave. Shortly after starting work, the new employee discovered that she was pregnant also and the employer dismissed her. She complained of sex discrimination contrary to s. 1(1) Sex Discrimination Act 1975. When the case reached the House of Lords it was referred to the CJEU for a decision on whether the dismissal constituted sex discrimination. The CJEU held that it was contrary to the Equal Treatment Directive and that one could not compare a pregnant woman who was not capable of performing the task for which she was employed with a male who was absent through sickness and incapable therefore of carrying out his tasks.

In the Danish case of *Hertz*,[7] the male comparator was of importance, however. Ms Hertz was a part-time cashier and saleswoman. She gave birth to a child after a difficult pregnancy during which she was mainly on sick leave. When her statutory maternity leave period ended she returned to work. After a further period of about six months she was ill and was absent for 100 days. The illness had arisen out of her pregnancy and confinement. Eventually, her employers dismissed her on the grounds of repeated absence due to illness. A question for the CJEU was whether this dismissal contravened art. 5 of the Directive as the illness had resulted from the pregnancy. The Court held that dismissal because of absence during maternity leave would constitute direct discrimination. With regard to an illness that appears some time after, however, there was no reason to distinguish between an illness that had its origin in pregnancy and one

---

1 Directive 92/85/EC on the introduction of measures to encourage improvements in the health and safety at work of pregnant workers and workers who have recently given birth or are breastfeeding OJ L348 28.11.92 p. 1.

2 Article 2(a) Pregnant Workers Directive.

3 Article 4 Pregnant Workers Directive.

4 A failure to carry out a risk assessment amounts to sex discrimination: *Hardman v Mallon* [2002] ICR 510.

5 Article 10 Pregnant Workers Directive.

6 Case C-32/93 *Webb v EMO Air Cargo (UK) Ltd* [1994] ICR 770.

7 Case C-179/88 *Handels og Konturfunktionærernes Forbund i Danmark (acting for Hertz) v Dansk Arbejdsgiver forening (acting for Aldi Marked A/S)* [1991] IRLR 31 CJEU.

from any other cause. If such sickness absence would have led to the dismissal of a male worker under the same conditions, then there is no discrimination on the grounds of sex.[8]

A refusal to employ results in direct discrimination when the most important reason for the refusal applies only to one sex, rather than to employees, without distinction, of both sexes. Only women can be refused employment because of pregnancy, so a decision not to employ someone because they are pregnant is directly discriminatory against the woman concerned. *Dekker*,[9] which was a reference to the CJEU from the Dutch Supreme Court, concerned a woman who had applied for a post of training instructor in a youth centre. She was pregnant when she applied and she informed the selection committee of this. The committee recommended her as the most suitable candidate, but the board of the youth centre declined to employ her. The reason given was that their insurer would not compensate them for payments which would be due to Ms Dekker during her maternity leave. The CJEU concluded that the refusal to employ had been a reason connected with the pregnancy and that this was contrary to the Equal Treatment Directive. As only women can be refused employment because of pregnancy, the fact that there were no male candidates for the post was not seen as relevant. In *Mayr*[10] the CJEU considered the case of a woman undergoing in vitro fertilisation treatment. She was dismissed during the treatment period, but before the fertilised ovum was transferred to her uterus. That procedure was carried out three days after her dismissal. The CJEU stated that the purpose of art. 10 was to protect pregnant women at the earliest possible moment from dismissal for reasons linked to the pregnancy. In the case of in vitro treatment, however, the protection commenced when the ovum was actually transferred. To do otherwise might give protection over a period of many years as there can be a gap of years before the actual transfer.

Article 11(1) Pregnant Workers Directive provides for rights under the employment contract including the maintenance of a payment whilst a woman is granted leave from work because of risks to her health or that of her baby, or when she is granted leave from night work. Article 11(2) provides similar rights for workers during maternity leave as exist for health and safety reasons. The case of *North Western Health Board v McKenna*[11] at the CJEU concerned a sickness scheme which guaranteed full pay for the first 183 days of sickness in any one year and half pay for the remaining period. The scheme also expressly stated that sickness related to maternity-related illness prior to the taking of maternity leave would be treated in the same way as sickness for any other reason. Mrs McKenna was absent because of maternity-related sickness for virtually the whole of her pregnancy and also after her maternity leave. She spent some time, as a result, on half pay. She claimed that this was sex discrimination. The Court of Justice did not agree with this and stated that Community law does not require the maintenance of full pay for absences related to maternity-related illness, provided that the payment is not so low as to undermine the Community law objective of protecting female workers, especially before giving birth.

9.1.2 The Parental Leave Directive[12]

A new Parental Leave Directive came into effect from March 2012.[13] This replaced Directive 96/34/EC on the same subject. The proposals for having Community rules on parental leave had been in existence for some time. They were first introduced as a proposed Directive in 1983,[14] but the

---

8 See Case 394/96 *Brown v Rentokil Ltd* [1998] IRLR 445 CJEU, which also distinguished between the protected period during pregnancy and maternity leave compared with the period after that leave.

9 Case C-177/88 *Dekker v Stichting Vormingscentum voor Jonge Volwassen* [1991] IRLR 27 CJEU.

10 Case C-506/06 *Mayr v Bäckerei und Konditorei Gerhard Flöckner OHG* [2008] IRLR 387.

11 Case C-191/03 [2005] IRLR 895.

12 Council Directive 96/34/EC on the Framework Agreement on parental leave concluded by UNICE, CEEP and the ETUC OJ L145 19.6.96 p. 4; applied to the United Kingdom by Directive 97/75/EC OJ L10 16.1.98 p. 24.

13 Council Directive 2010/18/EU implementing the revised Framework Agreement on parental leave; repealing Directive 96/34/EC.

14 Proposal for a Directive on parental leave and leave for family reasons COM(83) 686 as amended by COM(84) 631.

British government opposed them and was able effectively to veto them as adoption required a unanimous vote in the Council of Ministers. In 1994 the proposals were again put forward, but this time under the Social Chapter, from which the United Kingdom had excluded itself. These led to the Framework Agreement which was adopted by all the other Member States (excluding the United Kingdom) in 1996. After the 1997 general election, and a change of government, the United Kingdom signed up to the Social Chapter. As a result, Directive 97/75/EC was adopted on 15 December 1997 extending the Parental Leave Directive to the United Kingdom. In order to comply, the Maternity and Parental Leave etc. Regulations[15] and ss 57A and 57B Employment Rights Act 1996 came into effect on 15 December 1999.[16]

Men and women workers are given the individual right to parental leave on the grounds of the birth or adoption of a child,[17] in order to enable them to take care of that child, for at least four months (this was a period of three months in the 1996 Directive), until an age of up to eight years. The actual age is left to individual Member States. Clause 2(2) states that, in principle, these rights should be given on a non-transferable basis, although the new Directive provides that it is at least one of the four months that must be taken on a non-transferable basis. Thus one parent could transfer their right of up to three months' leave to the other parent. There are also provisions for countries to:

1. Protect workers against less favourable treatment or dismissal for taking parental leave.
2. Ensure that workers are able to return to the same job, or an equivalent, at the end of their leave period.
3. Ensure the maintenance and continuation of rights accrued to the start of the leave period.
4. Define the status of the contract of employment during the leave period.[18]

Clause 7.1 of the Framework Agreement 2010 provides that Member States should take measures to entitle workers to time off from work on grounds of 'force majeure for urgent family reasons in cases of sickness or accident making the immediate presence of the worker indispensable'. This led to the rules on the right to time off for dependants being introduced in the Employment Relations Act 1999.[19] Thus an employee is entitled to take a reasonable amount of time off in order to take action which is needed:

1. To provide assistance when a dependant falls ill, gives birth, is injured or assaulted.
2. To make arrangements for care for a dependant who is ill or injured.
3. As a result of the death of a dependant.
4. As a result of the unexpected disruption of arrangements for the care of a dependant.
5. To deal with unexpected incidents resulting from a child being at school.[20]

The definition of dependent is restricted to a spouse, a child, a parent or a person living in the same household as the employee who is not an employee, lodger, tenant or boarder.[21] There is an obligation for the employee to tell the employer the reason for the absence and the likelihood of its length as soon as is reasonably practicable.[22] Complaints for a failure to grant reasonable time off are made to an employment tribunal within three months of the date the refusal was made, unless not reasonably practicable. The tribunal may make a declaration and award compensation that it

---

15 SI 1999/3312; subsequently amended by the Maternity and Parental Leave (Amendment) Regulations 2002, SI 2002/2789.
16 See Employment Relations Act 1999 (Commencement No 2 and Transitional and Savings Provisions) Order 1999, SI 1999/2830.
17 Clause 2(1) Framework Agreement 2010 on parental leave.
18 Clause 5.5 Framework Agreement 2010 on parental leave.
19 Now contained in ss 57A and 57B ERA 1996.
20 Section 57A(1) ERA 1996.
21 Section 57A(3) ERA 1996.
22 Section 57A(2) ERA 1996.

considers just and equitable.[23] *Qua v John Ford Morrison Solicitors*[24] concerned a legal secretary who had a large number of absences during a relatively short period of employment. She stated that most of these absences were due to medical problems experienced by her son. The EAT held that there was no statutory maximum to the number of occasions that an employee could be absent in accordance with s. 57A ERA 1996, but there was no entitlement to an unlimited amount of time off. The right to time off was to deal with the unexpected. When it was known that the employee's dependant was suffering from a medical condition which was likely to result in regular lapses, then it no longer came within the provisions of s. 57A, because it was no longer unexpected.

9.2 Maternity protection in the United Kingdom

Special measures to benefit pregnant women and women who had recently given birth were first introduced in the United Kingdom during the post-Second World War period. The National Insurance scheme, in 1948, introduced a maternity allowance for women contributors who gave up work to have a baby. This was paid for 13 weeks. The period was increased to 18 weeks in 1953. In 1975 the Employment Protection Act introduced six weeks' maternity pay for women who contributed to the Maternity Fund. This maternity pay equalled 90 per cent of normal weekly earnings less the amount of the maternity allowance. Maternity allowance and maternity pay were amalgamated in 1987 and became statutory maternity pay.[25] This is paid by employers, who then recover their costs by deductions from their tax and national insurance contributions. Small employers can claim an additional amount in respect of such pay.[26]

The Employment Protection Act 1975 also introduced the right to return to work for up to 29 weeks after confinement for women who had been employed for two years continuously with the same employer. In 1994, changes were made as a result of the Pregnant Workers Directive. These changes concerned the right for women to have at least 14 weeks' maternity leave, regardless of their length of service or hours of work. Two weeks of this were to be compulsory. They also concerned the payment to women of an 'adequate allowance', equal at least to State rules on sickness benefit, during their maternity leave period, although this could be limited to those with at least one year's continuous service. The changes were made in ss 23–25 Trade Union Reform and Employment Rights Act 1993 and various regulations.[27]

Prior to the Employment Relations Act 1999 and the Maternity and Parental Leave etc. Regulations 1999 all women were entitled to 14 weeks' maternity leave, although confusingly they were also likely to be entitled to 18 weeks' maternity pay. Some, with two years' continuous employment, were also entitled to extended maternity leave. One of the aims of the government in making the changes contained in the 1999 legislation, and subsequently, was to remove some confusion, especially with respect to the procedures for giving notice, arrangements for return to work and the definition of remuneration. Importantly, the number of women likely to benefit is large. It is estimated that there are about 370,000 pregnant employees in any one year in the United Kingdom. Despite all the measures taken by the EU and the UK discrimination still takes place. A survey by the Equality and Human Rights Commission in 2015 stated that around one in nine mothers (11 per cent) reported that they were either dismissed; made compulsorily redundant, where others in their workplace were not; or treated so poorly they felt they had to leave their job; if scaled up to the

---

23 Section 57B ERA 1996.

24 [2003] IRLR 184.

25 See House of Commons Research Paper 98/99, *Fairness at Work*.

26 See Statutory Maternity Pay (Compensation of Employers) (Amendment) Regulations 1999, SI 1999/363.

27 Maternity Allowance and Statutory Maternity Pay Regulations 1994, SI 1994/1230 and Social Security Maternity Benefits and Statutory Sick Pay (Amendment) Regulations 1994, SI 1994/1367.

general population, this could mean as many as 54,000 mothers a year. In addition, one in five mothers said that they had experienced harassment or negative comments related to pregnancy or flexible working from their employer and/or colleagues; if scaled up to the general population, this could mean as many as 100,000 mothers a year. Finally, some 10 per cent of mothers said their employer discouraged them from attending antenatal appointments; if scaled up to the general population, this could mean as many as 53,000 mothers a year. This needs to be borne in mind when considering the effectiveness of the legislation protecting pregnant employees.

9.3 Maternity and Parental Leave etc. Regulations 1999

The Maternity and Parental Leave etc. Regulations 1999[28] were amended in 2002,[29] 2006[30] and 2008[31] (the MPL Regulations). Further provision was also made by the Work and Families Act 2006. These provide for three types of maternity leave: ordinary maternity leave, compulsory maternity leave and additional maternity leave, although the distinction between ordinary and additional maternity leave has been somewhat reduced by the 2008 Regulations. These are periods of leave, before and after childbirth, to which a pregnant employee, or one that has recently given birth, is entitled. The dates of leave are calculated as being periods before or after the 'expected week of childbirth'. Regulation 2(1) MPL Regulations defines this as the week, beginning with midnight between Saturday and Sunday, in which it is expected that childbirth will occur. This regulation also defines childbirth as 'the birth of a living child or the birth of a child whether living or dead after 24 weeks of pregnancy'. This means, of course, that a woman who gives birth to a stillborn child after 24 weeks of pregnancy will be entitled to the same leave as a person who gave birth to a live child.

Similar rules exist for ordinary and additional adoption leave and are contained in the Parental and Adoption Leave Regulations 2002.[32]

9.3.1 Statutory maternity leave[33]

The rules on maternity and parental leave apply to employees only. Regulation 2(1) MPL Regulations defines an employee as an individual who has 'entered into or works under (or, where the employment has ceased, worked under) a contract of employment'. A contract of employment is further defined as a 'contract of service or apprenticeship whether express or implied, and (if it is express) whether oral or in writing'. This is the same definition as in s. 230(1) and (2) ERA 1996 and is narrower than the definition of worker. It is the narrower definition that applies in the case of maternity or parental leave.

The MPL Regulations define employer, simply, as the person by whom an employee is (or, where the employment has ceased, was) employed.[34] The regulations also define associated employer, which assumes importance in certain respects, such as rights in a redundancy situation during maternity leave (see below). Two employers are treated as associated if one is a company of which the other (directly or indirectly) has control, or both are companies of which a third person (directly or indirectly) has control.[35]

28 SI 1999/3312.
29 SI 2002/2789.
30 The Maternity and Parental Leave etc. and the Paternity and Adoption Leave (Amendment) Regulations 2006, SI 2006/2014.
31 The Maternity and Parental Leave etc. and the Paternity and Adoption Leave (Amendment) Regulations 2008, SI 2008/1966.
32 SI 2002/2789, as amended by the 2006 Regulations – see above.
33 Regulation 2(1) of the MPL Regulations states that statutory maternity leave means ordinary and additional maternity leave.
34 Regulation 2(1) MPL Regulations.
35 Regulation 2(3) MPL Regulations.

An employee may be entitled to ordinary and additional maternity leave if she satisfies certain conditions. These are:[36]

1. No later than the end of the 15th week before her expected week of childbirth she notifies her employer of her pregnancy, the expected week of childbirth and the date on which she intends to start her ordinary maternity leave. If it is not reasonably practicable to inform the employer by that time, then she must inform the employer as soon as is reasonably practicable.

2. The employee must give this notice in writing if the employer so requests.[37] The employee is entitled to change her mind about the date for commencement of her maternity leave, provided she notifies the employer at least 28 days before the new date or the date varied.[38]

3. The employer is able to request, for inspection, a certificate from a registered medical practitioner or a registered midwife stating the expected week of childbirth, and the employee is required to provide it.

4. As a response to the notice the employer must, within 28 days, notify the employee of the date when her additional maternity leave will end.[39]

5. If the leave period commences because of absence from work on a day after the fourth week before the expected week of childbirth (see below),[40] then the employee is not expected to have given the required notice, but she will lose her entitlement if she does not inform her employer as soon as is practicable that she is absent from work wholly or partly because of her pregnancy.[41] This notice must give the date upon which her maternity leave now commences and must be in writing if the employer requests it.

6. If the leave period commences on the day which follows the childbirth (see below), then she is not required to give the specified notice in order to keep her entitlement. Whether or not she has given that notice, however, she is not entitled to ordinary or additional maternity leave unless she notifies the employer as soon as is reasonably practicable after the birth that she has given birth and the date on which this took place.[42] This notice must be in writing if the employer requests it.

Ordinary maternity leave can be started in a number of ways.[43] First, the employee may choose the start date, provided the notice requirements are met and provided that she does not specify a date earlier than the beginning of the 11th week before the expected week of childbirth.[44] Second, if the employee is absent from work on any day after the beginning of the fourth week before the expected week of childbirth, for a reason wholly or partly because of the pregnancy, then the ordinary leave period will automatically begin on that day. Third, when the child is born. If the ordinary maternity leave period has not begun by this time, then it will begin on the day after childbirth occurs.

Ordinary maternity leave continues for a period of 26 weeks from its commencement, or until the end of the compulsory maternity leave period, whichever is later.[45] This period can be further extended if there is a statutory provision that prohibits the employee from working after the end of

---

36 Regulation 4(1)(a) MPL Regulations.
37 Regulation 4(2)(a) MPL Regulations.
38 Regulation 4(1A) MPL Regulations.
39 Regulation 7(6) and (7) MPL Regulations.
40 See Case C-411/96 *Boyle v Equal Opportunities Commission* [1998] IRLR 717 CJEU, which held that a rule which required a woman who is absent on a pregnancy related illness within six weeks of the expected date of childbirth should take paid maternity leave, rather than be given sick pay, was not precluded by the Pregnant Workers Directive.
41 Regulation 4(3)(b) MPL Regulations.
42 Regulation 4(4)(b) MPL Regulations.
43 Regulation 6 MPL Regulations.
44 Regulation 4(2)(b) MPL Regulations.
45 Regulation 7(1) MPL Regulations.

the ordinary maternity leave period, for a reason related to the fact that she had recently given birth. The period of leave may end early if the employee is dismissed during the period of her leave. In the event of such a dismissal, the period ends at the time of that dismissal.[46]

An employee's additional maternity leave period commences on the day after the last day of her ordinary maternity leave period and continues for 26 weeks, meaning that all affected employees are entitled to a total of 52 weeks' leave.[47] The period of leave may end early if the employee is dismissed during the period of her leave. In the event of such a dismissal, the period ends at the time of the dismissal.[48]

It is also worth mentioning here the effect of the Additional Paternity Leave Regulations 2010 (see below) which provide the possibility of fathers taking between two and 26 weeks' additional paternity leave providing that the mother has returned to work. This enables couples to share the maternity leave period if they so desire.

9.3.2 Compulsory maternity leave

Section 72 ERA 1996 provides that an employer must not allow a woman who is entitled to ordinary maternity leave to work during the compulsory leave period. The compulsory leave period is for two weeks commencing with the day on which childbirth occurs.[49] These two weeks fall within the ordinary maternity leave period, so are part of the 26 weeks permitted for such leave. An employer who contravenes this requirement will be guilty of an offence and liable to a fine if convicted.[50]

9.4 Employment rights before and during maternity leave

Certain special rights are accorded to pregnant workers and those who have recently given birth or are breastfeeding.

9.4.1 Time off for antenatal care

Sections 55–57 ERA 1996 provide that an employee who is pregnant and has, on the advice of a registered medical practitioner, registered midwife or registered health visitor, made an appointment to attend at any place for antenatal care is entitled to time off with pay during the employee's working hours in order to keep the appointment.

9.4.2 Suspension from work on maternity grounds

Regulation 3(1) Management of Health and Safety at Work Regulations 1999 (MHSW Regulations 1999)[51] requires an assessment by the employer of the risks to health and safety of employees and others. Regulation 16(1) MHSW Regulations 1999 requires special attention in the event of there being female employees of childbearing age. The assessment is to decide whether the work is of a kind which would pose a risk, by reason of her condition, to the health and safety of a new or expectant mother or that of her baby. The obligation to carry out this risk assessment is not confined

---

46 Regulation 7(5) MPL Regulations.
47 Regulation 6(3) MPL Regulations.
48 Regulation 7(4)–(5) MPL Regulations.
49 Regulation 8 MPL Regulations.
50 Section 72(3)(b) and (5) ERA 1996.
51 SI 1999/3242.

to situations where the employer has a pregnant employee. The employment of a woman of childbearing age should be enough to set off the need for such an assessment.[52] If it is reasonable to do so, the employer can change the working hours or working conditions in order to avoid the risks.[53] If it is not reasonable to do so, then the employer must suspend the pregnant employee for as long as the risk persists. This suspension can only take place where a risk cannot be avoided. Avoiding risk does not mean the complete avoidance of all risks, but their reduction to the lowest possible level.[54] The EAT has stated that there is no general obligation to carry out a risk assessment on pregnant employees except where there are particular circumstances. These are, first, that the employee has notified the employer that she is pregnant; second, that the work is of a kind which could involve a risk of harm or danger to the health and safety of the expectant mother or her baby; third, that the risk arises from 'either processes or working conditions or physical, biological, or chemical agents in the workplace at the time'. Where the duty is triggered, a failure to carry out the risk assessment would amount to sex discrimination.[55]

Sections 66–68 ERA 1996 provide that an employee who is suspended from work as a result of a statutory prohibition or as a result of a recommendation contained in a code of practice issued or approved under s. 16 Health and Safety at Work etc. Act 1974, is entitled to be paid during that suspension, or offered alternative work. The alternative work needs to be both suitable and appropriate given the employee's circumstances and the terms and conditions offered to her must not be substantially less favourable than her previous terms and conditions.

Failure to provide alternative work and/or remuneration[56] can lead to a complaint to an employment tribunal by the employee. *British Airways (European Operations at Gatwick) Ltd v Moore and Botterill*[57] concerned cabin crew who could not fly during their pregnancies and who succeeded in their claim for their full allowances whilst employed on alternative work. They were employed on alternative ground-based work, but were not given the flying allowances to which they had previously been entitled when working as cabin crew. If a statutory prohibition were to prevent the employment of a pregnant woman from the outset and for the duration of the pregnancy, then that prohibition might be held to be discriminatory.[58]

The complaint about pay is required to be made within three months, unless not reasonably practicable, of the day on which there was a failure to pay. Complaints about not being provided with alternative work need to be made within three months, unless not reasonably practicable, of the first day of the suspension.[59] The amount of compensation to be paid will be such as the tribunal decides is just and equitable in all the circumstances.

9.4.3 The contract of employment during maternity leave

The status of the employment contract during maternity leave has not always been clear. *McPherson v Drumpark House*[60] was a case that concerned an employee who went on maternity leave without

---

52 See *Day v T Pickles Farms Ltd* [1999] IRLR 217.

53 Regulation 16(2) MHSW Regulations 1999.

54 See *New Southern Railway Ltd v Quinn* [2006] IRLR 267, where managers became concerned about the safety of an employee who had been appointed to the post of station manager. The tribunal stated that the managers had jumped to the conclusion that the employee could not continue in this role because of their personal feelings and had then attached a health and safety label to it.

55 O'Neill v Buckinghamshire County Council [2010] IRLR 384.

56 See Case C-66/96 *Handels og Kontorfunktionærernes Forbund i Danmark (acting for Høj Pedersen) v Fællesforeningen for Danmarks Brugsforeninger (acting for Kvickly Skive)* [1999] IRLR 55 CJEU, which held that national legislation which permitted the sending home of a pregnant woman, in such a situation, without paying her salary in full was contrary to the Equal Treatment Directive; legislation that only affects pregnant employees is in breach of art. 5 of the Directive.

57 [2000] IRLR 296.

58 Case C-207/98 *Mahlberg v Land Mecklenburg-Vorpommern* [2000] IRLR 276 CJEU.

59 Section 70 ERA 1996.

60 [1997] IRLR 277.

fulfilling all the statutory requirements for taking such leave and returning afterwards. When she indicated to her employers that she was returning to work, they informed her that, in their view, she was no longer employed under a contract of employment. The issue for the EAT was whether the contract of employment continued during the period of maternity leave. The EAT concluded that it was not clear and that the payment of maternity pay was not in itself enough to show a continuation of the contract without some express or implied agreement to that effect.

9.4.3.1 Work during the maternity leave period

An employee may carry out up to ten days' work for her employer during her statutory maternity period (excluding the compulsory maternity period)[61] without bringing her maternity leave period to an end.[62] This is part of a policy designed to encourage employers and those on maternity leave to keep in touch with each other and, of course, to ease the moment of return to work. Any work carried out on any day shall constitute a day's work and the work can include training or any activity designed for the purpose of keeping in touch with the workplace.[63] Regulation 12A(6) MPL Regulations makes it clear that this does not mean that the employer has the right to require this work or that the employee has a right to work. It clearly needs to be a mutually agreed option, but one which many employers and those on maternity leave may be interested in using. The period spent working does not have the effect of extending the total duration of the maternity leave period.[64]

9.4.3.2 Employment rights

Section 71(4) ERA 1996 provides that an employee on ordinary maternity leave is, first, entitled to the benefit of the terms and conditions of employment which would have applied had she not been absent. This does not include terms and conditions about remuneration,[65] although reg. 9 MPL Regulations limits the definition of remuneration to sums payable to an employee by way of wages or salary.[66] A failure to reflect a pay increase in calculating earnings-related statutory maternity pay, for an employee on maternity leave, was likely to be a breach of art. 141 EC on equal pay and the employee would have an entitlement to make a claim for unlawful deduction from her wages.[67]

Second, the employee is bound by obligations arising out of those terms and conditions, and, third, she is entitled to return from leave to the job in which she was employed before her absence (for discussion on the right to return to work, see below).[68] Indeed, where the contract of employment continues during pregnancy, to afford a woman less favourable treatment regarding her working conditions during that time would constitute sex discrimination within the terms of the Equal Treatment Directive.[69]

The rules for the period of additional maternity leave changed for employees whose expected week of childbirth began on or after 5 October 2008. Section 73(4) ERA 1996 provides that those on such leave are entitled to the benefit of the terms and conditions which would have applied had they not been absent, and are bound, subject to any regulations, by obligations arising under those terms and conditions and entitled to return to a job of a prescribed kind. The 2008 Regulations

---

61 Regulation 12A(5) MPL Regulations.
62 Regulation 12A(1) MPL Regulations.
63 Regulation 12A(2) and (3) MPL Regulations.
64 Regulation 12A(7) MPL Regulations.
65 Section 71(5) ERA 1996.
66 Case C-333/97 *Lewen v Denda* [2000] IRLR 67 CJEU where a voluntarily given Christmas bonus was held to be 'pay' within the meaning of art. 119 EEC (now art. 157 TFEU); thus an employer may not take into account periods when a mother was prohibited from working in order to reduce proportionately the amount awarded.
67 See *Alabaster v Woolwich plc and Secretary of State for Social Security* [2000] IRLR 754.
68 Following s. 17(2) EA 2002, this is changed to the right to return 'to a job of a prescribed kind'.
69 See e.g. Case C-136/95 *Caisse National d'Assurance Vieillesse des Travailleurs Salariés v Thibault* [1998] IRLR 399 CJEU, where a woman on maternity leave was not given an annual appraisal and was, as a result, deprived of a merit pay award.

removed the distinction between ordinary and maternity leave so that an employee taking additional maternity leave is also entitled to the benefit of (and bound by any obligations arising from) all the terms and conditions of employment which would have applied had she not been absent. This does not include remuneration, as defined in reg. 9 MPL Regulations. The employee is entitled, like the person returning from ordinary maternity leave, to protection of her seniority, pensions and similar rights on her return.

All contracts of employment have an implied term of mutual trust and confidence which the employee and employer have a duty to maintain. This continues during the period of additional maternity leave.[70] The authors of the Regulations obviously had a concern that employees might use periods of additional maternity leave or parental leave to participate in rival businesses (see Chapter 2). These provisions ensure that contractual obligations restricting this continue during the period of absence, as well as the employer's and the employee's rights and obligations concerning notice periods. An example of a situation where an employer's treatment of an employee returning from maternity leave amounted to a breach of the duty of mutual trust and confidence can be seen in *Shaw v CCL*.[71] Mrs Shaw became pregnant and took maternity leave. Whilst on leave she submitted an application to return to work on a part-time basis. She was flexible about which days and what hours to work but wanted the total to be no more than 14 hours per week. Her application was refused by her employer. She brought claims which included direct and indirect sex discrimination and that she had been constructively dismissed. The Tribunal found in her favour on the discrimination claims. She had suffered direct sex discrimination as a result of not being allowed to return to work on a part-time basis and indirect discrimination as a result of the rule requiring her to work full-time on her return from maternity leave. The EAT also held that this discrimination amounted to a fundamental breach of contract, specifically the duty of mutual trust and confidence (see Chapter 2) and thus allowed her claim for constructive dismissal.

9.4.3.3 Shared parental leave

The Shared Parental Leave Regulations[72] came into effect in December 2014 and includes all those with children born on or after 5 April 2015. Their purpose is to enable parents and their partners to choose how to share time off during the first year after the birth or adoption of a child.[73] The issue for maternity leave is that it can only be taken by mothers and this re-enforces the image of the mother as the main carer of children. Shared parental leave is aimed at tackling this and perhaps reducing the disadvantages suffered by women at work that come from being regarded as the main child carer in any family unit. It is important to note that maternity leave is still the mother's or adopter's entitlement and it is their decision as to whether it is shared with a partner.

To qualify for shared parental leave (SPL), the mother[74] needs to be entitled to statutory maternity leave and be the main carer for the child (reg. 2). She must pass the continuity of employment test (reg. 35) which means that she must have worked for the same employer for at least 26 weeks at the end of the 15th week before the week in which the child is due (or at the week in which an adopter was notified of having been matched with a child for adoption) and is still employed in the first week that Shared Parental Leave is to be taken. The other parent must meet the employment and earnings test (reg. 36) which means that the person must have worked for at least 26 weeks in the 66 weeks leading up to the due date and have earned above the maternity allowance threshold in 13 of the 66 weeks.

---

70 Regulation 17 MPL Regulations.
71 *Shaw v CCL Ltd* [2008] IRLR 284.
72 The Shared Parental Leave Regulations 2014, SI 2014/3050.
73 See ACAS guidance on shared parental leave: www.acas.org.uk/index.aspx?articleid=4911
74 Although we refer to 'mother' here, the same rules also apply to those adopting.

The rules are complex but the mother or adopter makes the decision as to whether to use SPL. It can be used at any time from the date the child is born (or placed) and finishes 52 weeks after that date. An employee is entitled to submit three separate notices to book leave and it must be taken in complete weeks and may be taken either in a continuous period, which an employer cannot refuse, or in a discontinuous period, which the employer can refuse. If a request for discontinuous leave is refused, then the total amount of leave requested in the notice will automatically become a continuous block unless it is withdrawn.[75]

A CIPD survey in May 2016 revealed that just over 20 per cent of organisations had received requests from male staff to take SPL and in two-thirds of organisations where mothers were eligible for SPL there has been no take-up at all.[76] This low take-up meant that just 5 per cent of new fathers and 8 per cent of new mothers had taken SPL.

9.5 Protection from detriment

Regulation 19 MPL Regulations provides that an employee is not to be subjected to any detriment by any act, or failure to act, by her employer[77] for a number of specified reasons. It is important to note that deliberately failing to act can also be a detriment, such as giving benefits to employees, but failing to give those benefits to persons included in the categories below. The specified reasons include that the employee is pregnant, has given birth to a child, took, or sought to take, the benefits of ordinary maternity leave, took, or sought to take, additional maternity leave or failed to return after a period of ordinary or additional maternity leave and undertook, considered undertaking or refused to undertake work that is allowed (see 9.4.3.1 above) during the maternity leave period. (According to reg. 19(6), if the act that leads to a detriment in this case takes place over a period of time, then the date of the act is the last day of the period. A failure to act takes place on the date it was decided upon.[78])

In *Abbey National plc v Formoso*[79] an employee was held to have suffered detriment when her employer proceeded to hold a disciplinary hearing without the attendance of the employee, who was absent on a pregnancy-related illness. The employee had given notice of the date when she wished her maternity leave to begin, whilst she was absent through pregnancy-related sickness. The employers wished to resolve the matter prior to the maternity leave and proceeded with the hearing even though the employee's doctor considered that she was unfit to attend the meeting and would be so until the end of her pregnancy. The EAT confirmed the employment tribunal's view that pregnancy was the effective cause of the disciplinary hearing and that her treatment had amounted to sex discrimination. Similarly, in *Gus Home Shopping Ltd v Green and McLaughlin*,[80] two employees who were absent from work because of their pregnancy were held to have been discriminated against when they did not receive a discretionary loyalty bonus payable to all employees who remained in their posts until a business transferred to a new location. The different treatment meant that they had been unlawfully discriminated against on the grounds of sex.

---

75 See ACAS Guidance.
76 CIPD: www.personneltoday.com/hr/shared-parental-leave-take-woefully-low-cipd-reveals
77 See s. 47C ERA 1996.
78 Regulation 19(7) MPL Regulations states that, in the absence of any other evidence, a failure to act is when the employer does an act which is inconsistent with doing the failed act or, if no inconsistent act takes place, when the period expires in which the employer might reasonably have been expected to do the failed act.
79 [1999] IRLR 222.
80 [2001] IRLR 75.

9.6 Protection from dismissal

9.6.1 Redundancy

It may be that, during an employee's ordinary or additional maternity leave periods, it is not practicable for the employer to continue to employ her during her existing contract of employment, by reason of redundancy (see Chapter 5). If this happens, then the employee is entitled to be offered any suitable alternative vacancy before the end of her employment under a new contract of employment, which takes effect immediately upon ending employment under the current contract. This applies to vacancies with the employer, their successor or an associated employer (see above). The new contract of employment must be such that the work to be done is of a kind which is both suitable in relation to the employee and appropriate for her to do in the circumstances, and the terms and conditions of employment and the capacity and location in which she is to be employed are not substantially less favourable than had she continued to be employed under her previous contract of employment.[81] If the employee is not offered available alternative employment, then she may be regarded as being unfairly dismissed for the purposes of Part X ERA 1996.

Regulation 20(2) MPL Regulations provides that if an employee is dismissed for reasons of redundancy and it is shown that the circumstances constituting the redundancy applied equally to one or more other employees in the same undertaking who held similar positions to the dismissed employee, and those other employees have not been dismissed, and the reason, or the principal reason, for the employee being selected for dismissal was related to her pregnancy (as in protection from detriment above), then the dismissal will be unfair for the purposes of Part X ERA 1996 (unfair dismissal).

In *Eversheds Legal Services Ltd v De Belin*[82] the employer was faced with a choice between dismissing a male employee or a woman on maternity leave for reasons of redundancy. The employer awarded notional points to the employee on maternity leave which enabled her to score more points with the result that the male employee was made redundant. He brought and succeeded in a claim for sex discrimination. The EAT held that the means used to compensate for the disadvantage of being absent on maternity leave were not proportionate. The court stated that the words 'special treatment afforded to women in connection with pregnancy or childbirth' referred only to treatment given to a woman

> so far as it constitutes a proportionate means of achieving the legitimate aim of compensating her for the disadvantages occasioned by her pregnancy or her maternity leave.

It was pointed out during the case that the employer was in a difficult position and likely to face a complaint no matter what decision was taken. If the employer had made the woman on maternity leave redundant, then it may have faced a claim from her.

9.6.2 Unfair dismissal

There are a number of relevant reasons for dismissal which will be regarded as unfair. If the reason, or the principal reason, for the dismissal is:

1. the pregnancy of the employee or the fact that she has given birth to a child, during her ordinary or additional maternity leave period; or
2. the application of a relevant requirement, or a relevant recommendation in accordance with s. 66(2) ERA 1996 (see suspension from work on maternity grounds above); or

---

81 Regulation 10(2)–(3) MPL Regulations.
82 *Eversheds Legal Services Ltd v De Belin* [2011] IRLR 448.

3. the fact that she undertook, considered undertaking or refused to undertake work in accordance with reg. 12A (see 9.4.3.1 above),[83] or
4. the fact that she took or availed herself of the benefits of ordinary maternity leave, or the fact that she took additional maternity leave;

then the dismissal is unfair.[84] A dismissal during pregnancy for reasons connected with the pregnancy is likely to amount to direct sex discrimination. In *Brown v Rentokil Ltd*[85] the employers dismissed a female employee for sickness absences related to her pregnancy. The employer was applying a rule which meant that any male or female employee could be dismissed if absent for more than 26 weeks. The CJEU held that the situation of a pregnant worker absent because of her pregnancy could not be equated to the absences of a male worker due to incapacity for work.[86]

9.7 The right to return to work

An employee who wishes to return early from her additional maternity leave period must give her employer at least eight weeks' notice of the date on which she intends to return. If the employee tries to return early without giving this notice, then the employer may delay her return for eight weeks.[87] 'Job' is defined, in relation to a person returning to work after additional maternity leave, as meaning 'the nature of the work which she is employed to do in accordance with her contract and the capacity and place in which she is so employed'.[88]

An employee's right to return from leave to the job in which she was employed before her absence[89] means that she has a right to return both with her seniority, pension and other similar rights intact, as if she had not been absent, and with terms and conditions no less favourable than those that would have applied had she not been absent.[90] Except where there is a genuine redundancy situation leading to the dismissal, an employee who takes ordinary or additional maternity leave is entitled to return to the job in which she was employed before her absence.[91] If it is not reasonably practicable for an employer to permit her to do so, then she may return to another job which is both suitable and appropriate for her in the circumstances. This right to return is to return on terms and conditions no less favourable than would have been applicable had she not been absent from work at any time since the beginning of the ordinary maternity leave period. This includes returning with her seniority, pension rights and similar rights as if she had been in continuous employment during the periods of leave and not any less favourable than if she had not been absent through taking additional maternity leave after the ordinary maternity leave period.[92] There is not necessarily a right to return to a different job or to a job with different hours. Women of newly born children might need, for example, flexible working arrangements or part-time hours. Except in so far as they are affected by the Part-time Workers (Prevention of Less Favourable Treatment) Regulations 2000[93] or the Flexible Working Regulations 2002,[94] the legislation does not

---

83 Regulation 19 MPL Regulations.
84 Regulation 20 MPL Regulations.
85 Case 394/96 [1998] IRLR 445 CJEU.
86 See also Case C-32/93 *Webb v EMO Air Cargo (UK) Ltd* [1994] IRLR 482 ECJ.
87 Regulation 11 MPL Regulations.
88 Regulation 2(1) MPL Regulations.
89 Section 71(4)(c) ERA 1996.
90 Section 71(4)(c) ERA 1996.
91 Regulation 18(2) MPL Regulations.
92 Regulation 18(5) MPL Regulations.
93 See Chapter 2.
94 Flexible Working (Eligibility, Complaints and Remedies) Regulations 2002, SI 2002/3236.

provide this flexibility as a legal right. An example of the problems experienced in the past is that contained in *British Telecommunications plc v Roberts and Longstaffe*[95] which concerned two full-time employees who wished to return to work after their maternity leave on a job-share basis. They were unable to comply with an 'operational requirement' that the work should include Saturday mornings, and complained of indirect sex discrimination. On the issue of whether they had a right to return to work on a job-share arrangement, it was held that this was not covered by the special protection given to women during their pregnancy and maternity leave. When a woman returns to work the statutory protection is ended.

If the employer offers an alternative post with an associate employer and this is unreasonably turned down by the employee, then the employee is likely to lose her protection from unfair dismissal under these regulations. In both these cases, the onus is on the employer to show that the provisions in question were satisfied in relation to any individual in question.[96]

If an employee has a statutory right to maternity leave as well as a contractual right, in her contract of employment, to such leave, then she is able to take advantage of whichever right, in any particular respect, is the more favourable.[97] Employees are not permitted to take advantage of the statutory right in addition to the contractual right. The regulation does suggest, however, in the use of the term 'in any particular respect', that an employee is able to select those aspects in each which are most favourable to her.

Regulation 22 MPL Regulations also provides an amendment to Part XIV Chapter II ERA 1996 in respect of a week's pay. When, for the purposes of that section, a calculation is being made on the basis of 12 weeks' average pay, then weeks in which the employee is taking ordinary or additional maternity leave and is paid less than her normal entitlement will be disregarded for the calculation purposes.

9.8 Flexible working

The Flexible Working Regulations 2014[98] gave the right to all those who have been continuously employed for a period of 26 weeks to make an application for flexible working. This measure came into effect in June 2014 and amended previous regulations which confined this right to parents who needed more flexible working to care for children. No more than one application every 12 months is permitted and the rules specifically exclude their application to agency workers, which may seem surprising in a wider context of making non-standard work attractive (see Chapter 3). The request must be in writing, be dated and state whether a previous application has been made to the employer and, if so, when.[99] Within 28 days[100] of the request, the employer, unless he agrees to the request, must hold a meeting with the employee to discuss the application.[101] The employee has the right to be accompanied by another employee of the same employer. This companion has the right to address the meeting and confer with the applicant employee during the meeting.[102] After this meeting there are a further 14 days for the employer to give the employee notice of the decision reached. This decision needs to be in writing and can either be an agreement to the employee's request, specifying

---

95 [1996] IRLR 601.
96 Regulation 20(7)–(8) MPL Regulations.
97 Regulation 20(2) MPL Regulations.
98 The Flexible Working Regulations 2014, SI 2014/1398.
99 Regulation 4 Flexible Working Regulations 2014.
100 All the periods referred to here can be extended by mutual agreement between the employer and the employee: reg. 12 Flexible Working (Procedural Requirements) Regulations 2002, SI 2002/3207.
101 Regulation 3 Flexible Working (Procedural Requirements) Regulations 2002.
102 Regulation 14 Flexible Working (Procedural Requirements) Regulations 2002.

the contract variation which is to take place, or a rejection of the request. In the latter case the employer must give the grounds for refusal together with a sufficient explanation. *Commotion Ltd v Rutty*[103] concerned an individual who was employed as a warehouse assistant. After she became legally responsible for the care of her grandchild she made an application to work three days a week instead of five. Her request was turned down on the grounds that it would have a detrimental impact on performance in the warehouse. The EAT, however, supported her claim that the employer had failed to establish that they had refused the request on one of the grounds permitted by s. 80G(1)(b) ERA 1996. Tribunals were entitled to investigate to see whether the decision to reject the application was based on facts and whether the employer could have coped with the change without disruption. In this case the EAT found that the evidence did not support the employer's assertion and that the employer had not carried out any investigations to see whether they could cope with what the claimant wanted.

Section 80G(1)(b) ERA 1996 provides that an employer may refuse such a request only if one or more of the following grounds applies:

- the burden of additional costs;
- an inability to reorganise work amongst existing staff;
- an inability to recruit additional staff;
- a detrimental impact on quality;
- a detrimental impact on performance;
- detrimental effect on ability to meet customer demand;
- insufficient work for the periods the employee proposes to work;
- a planned structural change to the business.[104]

An employee is entitled to appeal against any refusal by the employer. This appeal needs to be in writing, set out the grounds for the appeal and be dated. It must be done within 14 days after the date of the employer's notice giving the decision on the original application. Again within 14 days of this meeting the employer must give the employee a decision. If the appeal is dismissed, then the employer must state the grounds for dismissal and give a sufficient explanation as to why those grounds apply.[105]

Failure of an employer to respond in relation to one of these grounds or a decision by an employer to reject the application on incorrect facts may lead to a complaint to an employment tribunal and the award of compensation of up to eight weeks' pay.

9.9 Parental leave

Two important features of parental leave are, first, that it is available to fathers as well as mothers and, second, that it is unpaid.[106] This latter feature affects the take-up of the benefit, especially amongst those who cannot afford the cost of taking time off from work on an unpaid basis.

9.9.1 Entitlement

Certain employees are entitled to parental leave. This is in addition to any entitlement to statutory maternity or paternity leave. The employees who qualify for parental leave are those who have been continuously employed for a period of not less than one year, and have, or expect to have, responsibility for a child.

---

103 [2006] IRLR 171.
104 See ACAS, *The Right to Request Flexible Working*, www.acas.org.uk/index.aspx?articleid=1616
105 Regulations 9 and 10 Flexible Working (Procedural Requirements) Regulations 2002.
106 See 9.10 below for provisions relating to paid paternity leave.

The second condition raises the question of who has responsibility for a child. A 'traditional view' of children with a male and a female parent sharing responsibility for a child is not an acceptable model. The MPL Regulations go some way towards offering a definition. Regulation 13(2) states that an employee has responsibility for a child if they meet one of the following tests:

1. If the employee has parental responsibilities for a child.
2. If the employee has been registered as the child's father under any provision of ss 10(1) or 10A(1) Births and Deaths Registration Act 1953 or of s. 18(1) or (2) Registration of Births and Deaths and Marriages (Scotland) Act 1965.

9.9.2 Meaning of parental responsibility

Parental responsibility is defined in s. 3 Children Act 1989. Section 3(1) provides that:

> parental responsibility means all the rights, duties, powers, responsibilities and authority which by law a parent of a child has in relation to the child and his property.

Section 2(1) Children Act 1989 states that where a child's father and mother were married to each other at the time of the birth, they shall each have parental responsibility for the child. Thus parental responsibility is automatically acquired by both parents if married at the time of birth. It can also be automatically acquired by both parents if they marry subsequent to the birth.[107] Where they are not married, the mother has parental responsibility, unless the father acquires that responsibility in accordance with the provisions of the Act.[108] Where the child's father and mother were not married to each other, parental responsibility can be achieved by the father on an order of the court resulting from an application by the father, or by entering into a parental responsibility agreement with the mother, which provides for the father to have parental responsibility for the child.

Parental responsibility is therefore automatically acquired by the mother, but this cannot be said of the father if not married to the mother at the birth or subsequently. Parental responsibility does not necessarily mean that a father is making day-to-day decisions about a child or, indeed, having the same responsibility for a child's welfare as the mother may have. It suggests, as stated by Lady Justice Butler-Sloss[109] in a case concerning a father's application for a parental responsibility order:

> A father who has shown real commitment to the child concerned and to whom there is a positive attachment, as well as a genuine *bona fide* reason for the application, ought in a case such as the present, to assume the weight of those duties and cement that commitment and attachment by sharing the responsibilities for the child with the mother. This father is asking to assume that burden as well as that pleasure of looking after his child, a burden not lightly to be undertaken.

As the MPL Regulations make clear, this includes having responsibility for an adopted child or a child who is placed with the employee for the purposes of adoption.

9.9.3 Leave entitlement

An employee is entitled to 18 weeks' leave in respect of any individual child or adopted child up to their 18th birthday.[110] The leave entitlement is of 'any individual child', so that an employee/parent

---

107 See s. 1 Family Reform Act 1987.
108 Section 2(2) Children Act 1989.
109 Re S (A Minor) (Parental Responsibility) [1995] 3 FCR 225.
110 Regulation 14(1) MPL Regulations and reg. 14(1A) added by the Maternity and Parental Leave (Amendment) Regulations 2001, SI 2001/4010.

of multiple-birth children will be entitled to 18 weeks in respect of each. Similarly, employees/parents with more than one child, of differing ages, will be entitled to 18 weeks' leave in respect of each child. Section 76(1) ERA 1996 states that the absence from work is with the 'purpose of caring for a child'. Although the ERA 1996 suggests that the regulations may 'specify things which are, or are not, to be taken as done for the purpose of caring for the child',[111] they do not. It is, presumably, left to the employer and employee to decide.

A week's leave has different meanings in different circumstances. First, it can mean that where the employee is required, under the contract of employment, to work the same period each week, then a week's leave is equal in duration to that period. Thus if an employee works from Monday to Friday each week, then a week's leave will be a period from Monday to Friday. Second, where the employee is required, under the contract of employment, to work different periods in different weeks, or works in some weeks and not others, then a week's leave is calculated by adding the total periods that the employee is required to work in a year and dividing by 52. Thus, for example, if an employee works for five days every alternate week, then a week's leave will be 5 x 26, divided by 52, making it 2.5 days.[112] If an employee takes leave in shorter periods than a week, according to the definitions, then an employer will need to total the leave taken to aggregate it into weekly periods.

The entitlement to 18 weeks' leave is dependent upon one year's continuous employment with the same, or an associated, employer, so, if an individual changes employers, that individual will be required to establish one year's continuous service with the new employer before being able to acquire rights to parental leave again. This raises the question of transferring the balance on an employee's entitlement between employers. If an individual, for example, takes four weeks' parental leave with employer A and then moves to employer B, they will have a balance of nine weeks' leave to which they will be entitled after one year's continuous service with employer B. The problem for employer B is to know how much of an entitlement the individual has left. This information can only come from employer A or from the employee. There is no requirement for employers to keep records of parental leave taken, although it will surely be a matter of good practice to do so.

9.9.4 Procedural rules[113]

If there are no contractual rules to the contrary or any collective or workforce agreements affecting the procedures, then the MPL Regulations lay down a number of default procedures which apply before the employee can take their parental leave entitlement. There are essentially three conditions that an employee needs to comply with before their parental leave may commence. These are the evidence condition, the notice condition and the postponement condition. It should be noted that, under the default arrangements, employees may not take leave in periods of less than one week, except where the child is entitled to a disability living allowance. To fulfil the evidence condition, an employer may request from the employee such evidence as may be reasonably required of the employee's responsibility or expected responsibility for the child in question and the age of that child. It is interesting that the employee is not required to show any evidence of leave previously taken in respect of that child.

To fulfil the notice condition, employees are required to give notice to the employer specifying the dates on which the period of leave is to start and finish. This notice is to be given to the employer at least 21 days before the start date. There are special rules for certain employees. The first applies to an employee who is the father and wishes his parental leave to commence on the date on which the child is born. In this situation the employee must give at least 21 days' notice before the

---

111 Section 76(5)(a) ERA 1996.
112 Regulation 14(2)–(3) MPL Regulations.
113 Schedule 2 MPL Regulations.

beginning of the expected week of childbirth, specifying when the expected week of childbirth is and the duration of the period of leave. The second is where the leave is in respect of a child to be placed with the employee for adoption; then the notice needs to specify the week in which the placement is expected to occur and the duration of the leave. It needs to be given to the employer at least 21 days before the beginning of the placement week, or, if that is not reasonably practicable, as soon as is reasonably practicable.

The employer cannot delay the taking of parental leave unless the employer has a significant reason, such as the leave would cause serious disruption to the business.

This is an important safeguard for employers who may be faced with a number of employees wishing to take time off at the same time of the year (e.g. school holidays). The employer may postpone leave for up to six months as long as, at the end of the postponement period, the employee is permitted to take the same length of leave as originally requested. The employer is required to give notice to the employee of the postponement, in writing, stating the reasons for the delay and specifying the dates on which the delayed leave may commence and end. The employer's notice of postponement must be given to the employee not more than seven days after the employee's notice was given to the employer. This means, of course, that employees will have a minimum of 14 days' notice of the employer's decision to postpone the leave. No delay is possible if it is being taken by the father or partner immediately after the birth or adoption of the child or if it meant that the employee would no longer qualify for parental leave – for example, if it were postponed until after the child's 18th birthday.[114]

9.9.5 Limitations on parental leave

An employee may not take more than four weeks' leave in respect of a particular child in any one year and that leave must be taken in periods of at least one week. This is rather an inflexible approach and can mean that a person will need to take a week's parental leave when they actually need less. This happened in *Rodway v South Central Trains Ltd*[115] where an employee needed a Saturday off in order to look after his son. His application for parental leave was turned down because of the lack of available cover. In the event he took the day off anyway and was subsequently disciplined. The EAT held that the individual could not have suffered a detriment because of a reason related to parental leave, because such leave could only be taken in periods of one week and not just for one day.

A week is here defined as in reg. 14 (see above). The definition of a year is interesting. It is a 12-month period commencing with the date, except in certain cases, on which the employee first became entitled to parental leave in respect of the child in question. This presumably means, for example, 12-month periods from the birth of a child. Alternatively, where a period of continuous employment is interrupted, then at the date when the employee newly qualifies after a further period of continuous employment.

It is important to note that these procedural rules can be varied by agreement between employers and employees or their representatives, in the form of collective or workforce agreements.[116]

9.9.6 Complaint to an employment tribunal

Section 80(1) ERA 1996 provides that an employee may complain to an employment tribunal if the employer has unreasonably postponed a period of parental leave or has prevented, or attempted to prevent, the employee from taking parental leave. The complaint needs to be made within three

---

114 See www.gov.uk/parental-leave/delaying-leave
115 [2005] IRLR 583.
116 For collective agreements, see Chapter 12.

months beginning with the date of the matter complained about, or such further period as the tribunal agrees if this was not reasonably practicable. If the tribunal agrees with the complaint, it may make a declaration to that effect and award compensation to the employee, having regard to the employer's behaviour and any loss sustained by the employee as a result of the matters complained of.

9.9.7 Employee rights during parental leave

An employee who is absent on parental leave is entitled to the benefit of the terms and conditions of employment which would have applied if they had not been absent. This includes any matters connected with the employee's employment, whether or not they arise under the contract of employment, except for matters relating to remuneration.[117] The employee is also entitled to the benefit of the employer's implied obligation of trust and confidence and any terms and conditions of employment relating to notice of the termination of the employment contract by his employer, compensation in the event of redundancy, disciplinary or grievance procedures.

The absent employee is bound by any obligations arising under their terms and conditions of employment. Additionally reg. 17(1) MPL Regulations states that the employee is bound by an implied obligation of good faith and any terms and conditions of employment relating to notice of the termination of the employment contract by the employee, the disclosure of confidential information, the acceptance of gifts or other benefits, or the employee's participation in any other business.[118]

9.9.8 The right to return to work

There are important differences in this right, depending upon the length of leave taken:

1. An employee who takes parental leave for a period of four weeks or less, other than immediately after additional maternity leave, is entitled to return to work to the job in which they were employed before the absence.
2. An employee who takes more than four weeks' parental leave is also entitled to return to the job in which they worked prior to the absence. If, in this latter case, it is not reasonably practicable to return to that job, then an employer must permit the employee to return to another job which is both suitable and appropriate in the circumstances. The exception to this will be as a result of a redundancy situation.
3. An employee who takes parental leave of four weeks or less immediately after additional maternity leave is entitled to return to the job in which she was employed prior to the absence, unless it would not have been reasonably practicable for her to return to that job at the end of her additional maternity leave, and it is still not reasonably practicable for the employer to permit her to return to that job at the end of parental leave. In such a situation she will be entitled to return to another job which is both suitable and appropriate in the circumstances. There is also an exception for redundancy situations.[119]

This right to return is on terms and conditions, with regard to remuneration, which are no less favourable than those which would have applied if the employee had not been absent from work on parental leave, with seniority, pension rights and similar rights preserved as if the employee had

---

117 In Case C-218/98 *Abdoulaye v Régie Nationale des Usines Renault SA* [1998] IRLR 811 CJEU the trade unions claimed that new fathers should be entitled to the same bonus given to women taking maternity leave; this view was rejected by the ECJ (now CJEU) who held that they were not comparable situations.

118 Section 77(1) ERA 1996.

119 Regulation 18(1)–(3) MPL Regulations.

been in continuous employment; otherwise on terms and conditions no less favourable than those which would have applied if there had been no period of absence.

The MPL Regulations also make provision for a person who takes parental leave immediately after the period of additional maternity leave. In that case they are entitled to return with all the above as if they had not been absent during the period of ordinary maternity leave, additional maternity leave and parental leave combined.

9.9.9 Protection from detriment and dismissal

An employee who has taken parental leave is not to be subjected to detriment by any act, or any deliberate failure to act, by the employer.[120] An employee who is dismissed for reasons connected to the fact that they took parental leave is to be treated as unfairly dismissed in accordance with Part X ERA 1996 (the provisions relating to unfair dismissal).[121] If there is a complaint of unfair dismissal and the question arises as to whether the reason, or principal reason, is related to the fact that the employee took, or sought to take, parental leave, then it is for the employer to show that the provisions have been complied with.[122]

An employee shall also be regarded as unfairly dismissed if the reason, or the principal reason, for their dismissal is that they were redundant and it can be shown that the circumstances causing the redundancy applied equally to one or more employees in the same business and holding similar positions to that held by the dismissed employee, and who have not been dismissed by the employer, and the reason, or the principal reason, for the selection of the employee for dismissal was that they had taken parental leave.[123] Thus an employee selected for redundancy, where it can be shown that other employees in similar positions were not selected for redundancy and the selected employee was chosen because of their parental leave, will automatically be entitled to make a claim for unfair dismissal. If, however, the employer, or an associated employer, offers the employee a position that is both appropriate and suitable, but the employee unreasonably turns it down, then the employee will lose any right to claim unfair dismissal by reason of taking parental leave.[124]

9.9.10 Additional provisions

If an employee has a statutory right to parental leave and also a contractual right, in their contract of employment, to parental leave, then they are able to take advantage of whichever right, in any particular respect, is the more favourable.[125] They are not permitted to take advantage of the statutory right in addition to a contractual right. The regulation does suggest, however, when it uses the term 'in any particular respect', that it is permissible to 'cherry-pick' – that is, pick out the best features of both schemes and take advantage of those.

Regulation 22 MPL Regulations also provides an amendment to Part XIV Chapter II ERA 1996 in respect of a week's pay. When, for the purposes of that regulation, a calculation is being made on the basis of 12 weeks' average pay, then weeks in which the employee is taking parental leave should be ignored.

---

120 Regulation 19(1) MPL Regulations.
121 Regulation 20(1)(a) MPL Regulations.
122 Regulation 20(8) MPL Regulations.
123 Regulation 20(2) MPL Regulations.
124 Regulation 20(7) MPL Regulations.
125 Regulation 21(2) MPL Regulations.

9.10 Paternity leave

The rules on paternity leave are governed by the Paternity and Adoption Leave Regulations 2002.[126] These provide an entitlement to one or two week's consecutive leave which has to be taken within 56 days of the child's birth. Other rules, such as the evidential requirements and protection offered, were similar to those concerned with parental leave (see above). An example of a dismissal during paternity leave took place in *Atkins v Coyle Personnel plc*.[127] Mr Atkins had taken paternity leave but still carried out work and was available for contact by phone whilst at home. One phone call was from his manager on an issue related to his commission earnings. He was asleep at the time, having only had three hours' sleep the previous night because of the new baby. He was not pleased at being woken up; there was an escalating and angry email correspondence and a heated telephone call with his manager which resulted in Mr Atkins being sacked. His unfair dismissal claim included the claim that he had been dismissed for a reason connected with the taking of paternity leave. Regulation 29 of the Paternity and Adoption Leave Regulations 2002[128] provides that an individual is unfairly dismissed in accord with s. 99 ERA 1996 if the reason or principal reason for the dismissal was one connected with taking, or seeking to take, paternity leave. He failed in his claim because the employment tribunal decided that the reason for the dismissal was the frustration of his manager which had grown during the heated exchange between the two. Although he was dismissed during paternity leave, there was no evidence that the reason for the dismissal was connected with the taking of that leave.

9.11 Adoption leave

The right to adoption leave was introduced by the Employment Act 2002 and the Paternity and Adoption Leave Regulations 2002. Some amendments were made by the 2006 Regulations, and in addition the Work and Families Act 2006 provided for regulations to introduce additional adoption leave under certain circumstances. An employee who meets the necessary conditions and complies with the notice and evidential requirements is entitled to adoption leave. As with maternity leave, this is divided into ordinary and additional adoption leave, although, of course, there is no equivalent of compulsory maternity leave.

An employee is entitled to adoption leave if the employee, if he is the child's adopter, has been continuously employed for a period of not less than 26 weeks ending with the week in which the employee was notified of being matched with the child, and has notified the agency that he agrees that the child should be placed with him on the date of placement.[129] An employee's entitlement to adoption leave is not affected by the placement for adoption of more than one child as part of the same arrangement.

Ordinary adoption leave will normally last for 26 weeks. It may be less, of course, if the employee is dismissed before the end of this period. It may also end early if the placement is disrupted. The other matters concerning adoption leave are identical to those concerning maternity leave, which are outlined earlier in this chapter. These matters concern the right to return to work, notice periods for early return, matters concerning terms and conditions during adoption leave, and contact between the employer and employee during adoption leave, including the right to carry out up to ten days' work with the employer without bringing the statutory adoption leave period to an end.

---

126 SI 2002/2788; these were amended by the Maternity and Parental Leave etc. and the Paternity and Adoption Leave (Amendment) Regulations 2006, SI 2006/2014 and by the Maternity and Parental Leave etc. and the Paternity and Adoption Leave (Amendment) Regulations 2008, SI 2008/1966.

127 [2008] IRLR 420.

128 SI 2002/2788.

129 Regulation 15(2) Paternity and Adoption Leave Regulations 2002.

Further reading

Bisom-Rapp, S. and Sargeant, M. *Lifetime Disadvantage, Discrimination and the Gendered Workforce* (Cambridge University Press, 2016).

Fawcett Society, Parents, *Work and Care: Striking the Balance*, www.fawcettsociety.org.uk/parents-work-and-care-striking-the-balance

Smith, I. and Baker, R. *Smith and Wood's Employment Law* (Oxford University Press, 2017).

www.gov.uk/shared-parental-leave-and-pay – Shared Maternity Leave and Pay.

Chapter 10

Business restructuring

Chapter Contents

10.1 Consultation and information – the international model

The European Commission has a long history of introducing measures to encourage employee involvement and employee consultation in the enterprises in which they are employed. The Commission's attempts to adopt measures which included employee involvement, rather than measures aimed at consultation and information, have not been successful. The measures concerning employee involvement were associated with the Community's attempts to set up new legal instruments such as the European company statute.[1] This was one of a number of statutes aimed at setting up European legal entities which would help organisations to carry out their business in different Member States within the Community without being hindered by a legal organisation based on the rules of just one Member State. Other entities included a European co-operative society and a European mutual society. The Commission included proposals for employee involvement in these organisations. Initially, a German model of two-tier company boards was proposed, so that employee representatives would have membership of the supervisory board and have, therefore, some involvement in the running of the business. At various times since then the Commission has modified its proposals, but, as the Commission accepted, the proposals were never agreed because they were suggesting worker participation, rather than worker consultation.[2] It was only after, finally, adopting a much more flexible approach that the Directives were adopted, providing for a range of employee involvement in new legal entities, known as a European company (or Societas Europaea)[3] and a European co-operative society.[4] The European Commission has proposed to harmonise the approach of Member States on two levels to the issues of consultation of employees. These are, first, at the transnational level, as exemplified by the introduction of European Works Councils and the statute on European companies, and, second, at the national level, with the adoption of the Information and Consultation Directive.

10.1.1 European Works Councils

The European Works Council Directive[5] (EWC Directive) was finally adopted after some 14 years of debate. It was originally adopted under the Agreement on Social Policy 1992 and so did not bind the United Kingdom. After the 1997 general election, and a willingness of the United Kingdom to accept the Social Policy Agreement, the Council adopted an extension Directive with a requirement for it to be transposed into national law by 15 December 1999.[6] The Directive has now been recast and replaced by Directive 2009/38/EC.[7] The purpose of Directive 2009/38 is

> to improve the right to information and to consultation of employees in Community-scale undertakings and Community-scale groups of undertakings.[8]

---

1 See OJ C176 8.7.91.
2 See Communication from the Commission on worker involvement and consultation COM (95) 547.
3 Council Directive 2001/86/EC supplementing the Statute for a European company with regard to the involvement of employees OJ L294/22 10.11.2001.
4 Council Directive 2003/72/EC supplementing the statute for a European Co-operative Society with regard to the involvement of employees OJ L207/25 18.8.2003.
5 Council Directive 94/45/EC on the establishment of a European Works Council or a procedure in Community-scale undertakings and Community-scale groups of undertakings for the purpose of informing and consulting employees OJ L254/64.
6 Council Directive 97/74/EC OJ L010/22.
7 Directive 2009/38/EC on the establishment of a European Works Council or a procedure in Community-scale undertakings and Community-scale groups of undertakings for the purpose of informing and consulting employees.
8 Article 1(1) EWC Directive.

A Community-scale undertaking is one that has at least 1,000 employees within the Member States and at least 150 employees in each of at least two Member States. A Community-scale group of undertakings is one where a group of undertakings[9] has at least 1,000 employees within the Member States with at least two group undertakings in different Member States employing at least 150 employees.[10] The lack of effectiveness of the previous Directive was shown in the Vilvoorde crisis in 1997. This was where the French car maker Renault announced the closure of its Belgian plant without any consultation whatsoever with its Belgian workers or its European Works Council. The Renault EWC met once a year, but was not called together until after the company had announced the closure. Although Renault subsequently agreed amendments to its EWC agreement to consult on future transnational structural changes, the whole process perhaps reflects the weakness of the requirements and of any potential sanctions. A similar lack of consultation appeared to take place when BMW of Germany sold its Rover car-making subsidiary in the United Kingdom in 1999. Consultation appeared to take place with German workers represented on the company's supervisory board, but not with British workers represented by eight members of its EWC.[11]

10.1.1.1 Transnational Information and Consultation of Employees Regulations 1999 and 2010

The 1994 EWC Directive was transposed into national law by the TICE Regulations 1999, which came into effect on 15 January 2000. By this time many British employees were already represented in EWCs set up by multinational companies, influenced by the law of other Member States which had already transposed the Directive. The Regulations did not have effect if there is already in existence an art. 6 or an art. 13 agreement, unless the parties have decided otherwise.[12] An art. 6 agreement was one that established an EWC in accordance with the Directive. An art. 13 agreement was one that established their own information and consultation procedures before the Directive was transposed into national law. The Regulations were amended in 2010 (the revised TICE Regulations 1999) in order to transpose the revised EWC Directive 2009.[13] These amendments mostly came into effect in June 2011.

Consultation is defined in the revised TICE Regulations 1999 as meaning the exchange of views and the establishment of a dialogue in the context of an EWC or in the context of an information and consultation procedure.[14] The central management of an undertaking is responsible for creating the conditions and the means necessary for setting up an EWC, where the central management is situated in the United Kingdom; where it is situated outside the country, but has its representative agent based in the United Kingdom; or, if neither of these, has its biggest group of employees in the United Kingdom.[15] The number of UK employees is to be calculated by taking an average over a two-year period, with provision for counting some part-timers as a half number. The number of employees in undertakings in other Member States is to be calculated in accordance with whatever formula that State has adopted in its law transposing the EWC Directive. Employee representatives are entitled to information on these calculations so that they can decide whether the employer qualifies. If the information given to them is incomplete or inadequate, they may present a complaint to the Central Arbitration Committee (CAC).[16]

---

9 Meaning a controlling undertaking and its controlled undertakings: art. 2(b) EWC Directive.

10 Article 2(a) and (c) EWC Directive.

11 The workers employed at Luton by Vauxhall Motors also complained about the absence of consultation when the company announced the plant's closure in December 2000.

12 Regulation 42 TICE Regulations 1999 as amended.

13 The Transnational Information and Consultation of Employees (Amendment) Regulations 2010 SI 2010/1088.

14 Regulation 2 TICE Regulations 1999 as amended.

15 Regulation 5 TICE Regulations 1999 as amended.

16 Regulations 6–8 TICE Regulations 1999 as amended.

If central management does not act on its own initiative, the whole process of establishing an EWC can be started with a request from 100 employees, or their representatives, in two undertakings in two Member States. If there is a dispute as to whether a valid request has been made, this can be referred to the CAC for a decision.[17]

The first stage is the establishment of a special negotiating body (SNB), whose task is to negotiate, with central management, a written agreement covering 'the scope, composition, functions and terms of office' of an EWC or the arrangements for implementing an information and consultation procedure.[18] The SNB must consist of at least one representative from each Member State and there is a weighting formula to increase representation from bigger units in different States. The United Kingdom representatives are to be elected by a ballot of United Kingdom employees and any complaints about the ballot are to be made to the CAC. Where there is already an elected body in existence with whom consultation takes place, then that body can nominate the representatives from its membership.[19]

The contents of the agreement to be reached between the SNB and the central management are set out in art. 6 EWC Directive and are reflected in Part IV TICE Regulations 1999. The two parties are to negotiate in 'a spirit of co-operation with a view to reaching an agreement'.[20] They may negotiate an agreement to set up an EWC or to establish an information and consultation procedure.[21] The EWC agreement must include agreement on such matters as the undertakings which are covered by the agreement, the composition of the EWC, the procedures of information and consultation, the frequency of meetings and the financial resources to be allocated to the EWC, as well as the arrangements to link information and consultation of the EWC with information and consultation of any national employee representation bodies.[22] An information and consultation procedure must specify the method by which employee representatives are able to meet and discuss the information given to them. Regulation 18A of the amended Regulations provides that management must give the information to employee representatives in a way that enables them to:

(a) acquaint themselves with and examine its subject matter;
(b) undertake a detailed assessment of its possible impact; and
(c) where appropriate, prepare for consultation.

These measures are, of course, designed to ensure that the opportunity for consultation is real and that the employee representatives have the time to consider all the information provided.

Complaints about the failures of management in relation to setting up the EWC or information and consultation procedure can be referred to the CAC, and the CAC can make an order requiring the management to take such steps as are necessary to comply. Complaints about the failure to establish an EWC or information and consultation procedure can also be referred to the CAC. The maximum penalty payable is £100,000.

One of the major worries about requiring employers to provide employee representatives with information has been the issue of confidentiality. Regulation 24(1) of the amended TICE Regulations provides that:

> The central management is not required to disclose any information or document to a recipient when the nature of the information or document is such that, according to objective criteria,

---

17 Regulations 9–10 TICE Regulations 1999 as amended.
18 Regulation 11 TICE Regulations 1999 as amended.
19 Regulations 12–15 TICE Regulations 1999 as amended; the BMW EWC Agreement mentioned above, for example, had a membership of eight German representatives, eight British representatives and four Austrian representatives.
20 Regulation 17(1) TICE Regulations 1999 as amended which copies the wording in art. 6(1) EWC Directive.
21 Regulation 17(3) TICE Regulations 1999 as amended.
22 Regulation 17(4) TICE Regulations 1999 as amended.

the disclosure of the information or document would seriously harm the functioning of, or would be prejudicial to, the undertaking or group of undertakings concerned.

Thus there is some protection for management if they do not wish to disclose confidential information, but there appears to be a strict test for withholding disclosure, the meaning of which will need to be left to the courts. There is also an obligation for employee representatives, or their advisers, not to disclose confidential information[23] and any disputes about confidentiality can be resolved by appealing to the CAC.

Information and consultation representatives, members of EWCs, SNBs and candidates for relevant elections have the right to reasonable time off with pay during working hours,[24] protection from dismissal in carrying out their functions and the right not to be subject to detriment.

10.1.2 European Company Statute

On 20 December 2000 the Council of Ministers also reached agreement on a Regulation establishing a European Company Statute.[25] This gives companies operating in more than one Member State the option of establishing themselves as 'European companies' (Societas Europaea or SE) operating under EU rules rather than a variety of national rules as at present. An SE can be established by the merger or formation of companies with a presence in at least two different Member States.

Information here is defined as informing the representatives of the employees

> in a manner and with a content which allows the employees' representatives to undertake an in-depth assessment of the possible impact and, where appropriate, prepare consultations with the competent organ of the SE.[26]

Consultation is defined as:

> The establishment of dialogue and exchange of views between the body representative of the employees . . . and the competent organ of the SE, at a time, in a manner and with a content which allows the employees' representatives, on the basis of information provided, to express an opinion on measures envisaged by the competent organ which may be taken into account in the decision-making process within the SE.[27]

When the SE is created, there will need to be a special negotiating body to discuss the arrangements for employee involvement. In the absence of any agreement there will be standard rules established by the Directive which will need to be followed. These require information and consultation on matters such as:

- The structure, economic and financial situation.
- The probable development of the business and of production and sales.
- The situation and probable trend of employment and investment.
- Substantial changes concerning organisation, introduction of new working methods or production processes.

---

23 Regulation 23 TICE Regulations 1999 as amended.
24 Regulations 25–26 TICE Regulations 1999 as amended.
25 Directive 2001/86/EC supplementing the Statute for a European company with regard to the involvement of employees OJ [2001] L294/22.
26 Article 2(i).
27 Article 2(j).

- Transfers of production, mergers, cutbacks or closures of undertakings, establishments or important parts thereof.
- Collective redundancies.

There are also provisions for employee participation for those SEs which include companies from countries where there are such rules. Participation can include the right to elect or appoint, or oppose the election or appointment of, members of the supervisory or administrative board.

10.1.2.1 The European Public-Liability Company (Employee Involvement) (Great Britain) Regulations 2009[28]

These Regulations are concerned with implementing the Directive on the European Company Statute. They provide for, amongst other matters, the establishment of a special negotiating body, the selection of UK members for that body, the negotiation of an employee involvement agreement, the treatment of confidential information and employee protection. Essentially, when a decision is made to form an SE there is a duty to provide information on the participating companies and the number of employees, and then to set up a special negotiating body with the objective of reaching an employee involvement agreement.[29]

The employee involvement agreement is similar to that of the agreement required to set up an EWC. There are standard rules for information and consultation contained in Part 2 of the Schedules to the Regulations. These state that the competence of an employee representative body is limited to questions that concern the SE itself plus subsidiaries. For the purpose of informing and consulting the employees, the SE must:

(a) prepare and provide to the representative body regular reports on the progress of the business of the SE and the SE's prospects;
(b) provide the representative body with the agenda for meetings of the administrative, management or supervisory organs of the SE;
(c) inform the representative body when there are exceptional circumstances affecting the employees' interests to a considerable extent, particularly in the event of relocations, transfers, the closure of establishments or undertakings, or collective redundancies.[30]

10.2 Information and consultation – the national model

Models of consultation vary between the Member States of the European Community. In many, works councils are an established way of channelling information, consultation and, sometimes, negotiation between management and employees.

In the United Kingdom, prior to the Information and Consultation with Employees Regulations 2004[31] (ICE Regulations), there were only a limited number of occasions during which there was a statutory requirement to consult. These included those concerned with collective redundancies and transfers of undertakings (see below). Prior to 1995 the only requirement was for this consultation to take place when there were trade unions recognised for the purpose. Following on from

---

28 SI 2009/2401.
29 Regulations 5–8.
30 These Regulations are complex and only a brief summary is attempted here.
31 SI 2004/3426.

Commission v United Kingdom,[32] when the Court of Justice held this to be an inadequate application of the relevant Directives, this liability to consult was widened to include appropriate representatives.[33] Thus, in certain situations there is a requirement to consult even if there is not a trade union recognised for that purpose. A similar requirement is imposed by the Health and Safety (Consultation with Employees) Regulations 1996 (HSCE Regulations 1996).[34] Prior to these regulations there was a requirement for health and safety representatives nominated by the recognised trade union.[35] The 1996 Regulations were intended to provide for situations where there were no such safety representatives. The employer has a duty to consult, in good time, on a range of safety matters, including the introduction of any measure at the workplace which might substantially affect the health and safety of the employees.[36] The consultation must be with the employees directly or their elected representatives.[37]

The result of this approach has been extended to other regulations concerned with the transposition of Community law. These include the Working Time Regulations 1998[38] and the Maternity and Parental Leave etc. Regulations 1999.[39] In both sets of regulations there is a default agreement, one concerned with varying aspects of the rules on working time and the other concerned with the rules on parental leave. These default arrangements may be varied by a collective agreement or by a workforce agreement. The former occurs where there are independent trade unions recognised for the purpose. The latter occurs when there are employee representatives, either elected or appointed by the workforce.

Thus an employer has an obligation to consult employee representatives if they wish to adopt a more flexible approach to working time or parental leave. These consultations can result in workforce agreements.[40] An agreement is a workforce agreement if:

1. It is in writing.
2. It has effect for a specific period not exceeding five years.
3. It applies to all the relevant members of the workforce or all those who belong to a particular group.
4. It is signed by the representatives of the workforce; if the employer employs fewer than 20 workers, then there is the option for the majority of the workers to sign the agreement.
5. Before the agreement is made available for signature, the employer provides all of the workers to whom it is intended to apply with a copy of the agreement and such guidance as the workers might reasonably require in order to understand it fully.

The two Schedules also contain provisions for the election of employee representatives. These 'representatives of the workforce' are workers who have been elected to represent the relevant members of the workforce.[41] Thus, even prior to the 2004 Regulations there existed within the

---

32 Cases 382/92 and 383/92 [1994] IRLR 392 and [1994] IRLR 412.
33 Collective Redundancies and Transfers of Undertakings (Protection of Employment) (Amendment) Regulations 1995, SI 1995/2587, as amended by regulations of the same name in 1999, SI 1999/1925.
34 SI 1996/1513.
35 Safety Representatives and Safety Committees Regulations 1977, SI 1977/500.
36 Regulation 3(a) HSCE Regulations 1996.
37 Regulation 4(1) HSCE Regulations 1996.
38 SI 1998/1833.
39 SI 1999/3312.
40 See Sch. 1 Working Time Regulations 1998, SI 1998/1833 and Sch. 1 Maternity and Parental Leave etc. Regulations 1999, SI 1999/3312.
41 Relevant members of the workforce are all those workers employed by a particular employer, excluding any worker whose terms and conditions of employment are provided for, wholly or in part, by a collective agreement: see Sch. 1 para. 2 Working Time Regulations 1998; para. 3 contains rules concerning the election of such representatives.

United Kingdom an alternative model for employee consultation. It applied to a very limited number of circumstances and was introduced as a result of the requirement imposed by the appropriate Directives to consult on specific issues.

10.2.1 The Information and Consultation Directive

Directive 2002/14/EC of the European Parliament and of the Council establishing a general framework for informing and consulting employees in the European Community[42] was finally unanimously adopted by the Council of Ministers in December 2001 after some years of debate. It suffered delays because of opposition from a number of countries, including the United Kingdom. The final version was much weaker than the original 1998 proposal, especially in terms of sanctions and of the implementation timetable. Nevertheless it is likely to have an important impact on employer/employee relations in the United Kingdom.

It is the first EU Directive to introduce a generalised requirement to provide information and to consult with employees or their representatives. All other information and consultation measures have been concerned with specific situations, such as collective redundancies, transfers of undertakings or in situations where companies have a European Works Council. The Directive applies to all undertakings with 50 or more employees. This represents less than 3 per cent of all EU companies, but about 50 per cent of all employees.

In the preamble to the Directive the European Commission provides the justification for the measure. Some of the reasons given are that:

1. The existence of current legal frameworks at national and Community level concerning the involvement of employees has not always prevented serious decisions, that affect employees, from being taken and made public without adequate consultation.[43]
2. There is a need to strengthen dialogue in order to promote trust within undertakings. The result of this will be an improvement in risk anticipation, making work organisation more flexible, and to facilitate employee access to training within the undertaking. It will also make employees more flexible in their approach and involve them in the operation and future of the undertaking, as well as increasing its competitiveness.[44]
3. Timely information and consultation is a prerequisite for successful restructuring and adaptation of undertakings to the needs of the global economy, especially through the new forms of organisation at work.[45]
4. The existing legal frameworks for employee information and consultation are inadequate, because they 'adopt an excessively *a posteriori* approach to the process of change, neglect the economic aspects of decisions taken and do not contribute either to genuine anticipation of employment developments within the undertaking or to risk prevention'.[46]

There are perhaps some, even amongst those who support the aims of the Directive, who might be a little sceptical about such grand claims for the result of the introduction of employee consultation procedures. Nevertheless these justifications give rise to the purpose of the Directive. This is to establish minimum requirements for information and consultation, whilst not preventing Member States from having or introducing provisions more favourable to employees. The Directive only applies to undertakings with a minimum size of 50 employees or establishments with at least 20

---

42 OJ L80/29 23.3.2002.
43 Preamble para. (6).
44 Preamble para. (7).
45 Preamble para. (9).
46 Preamble para. (13).

employees. This is to avoid any action which might hinder the creation and development of small and medium-sized undertakings.[47]

The purpose is set out as being to establish a general framework for the right to information and consultation of employees in undertakings or establishments within the European Community. The practical arrangements for defining and implementing this are to be left to the Member States, who must carry out their obligations in such a way as to ensure their effectiveness. In doing this the employer and the employees' representatives must work 'in a spirit of co-operation'.

There are some interesting definitions, particularly with regard to the distinction between undertakings and establishments.

An *undertaking* is a public or private undertaking carrying out an economic activity (whether or not for gain) which is located within the territory of the Member States. An *establishment* is a unit of business where an economic activity is carried out on an ongoing basis with human and material resources.

Information means transmission by the employer to the employees' representatives of data to help them acquaint themselves with the subject matter and to examine it. *Consultation* means the exchange of views and establishment of dialogue between the employer and the employees' representatives.

The importance of the definitions of undertaking and establishment are relevant because the Directive will apply either to undertakings employing at least 50 employees in any one Member State or to establishments employing at least 20 employees in any Member State. The method for calculating the thresholds of employees is left to the Member State.

It may be possible to make special arrangements for political, religious and charitable bodies where special rules already exist in the Member State and, as ever, Member States may exclude crews of ships 'plying the high seas'.

As mentioned above, the practical arrangements are to be left to the individual Member State. There are, however, rules concerning what information and consultation will cover, when it is to take place and what its objectives are. The subject matter is to be:

1. Information on the recent and probable development of the undertaking's or establishment's activities and economic situation.
2. Information and consultation on the situation, structure and probable development of employment and on any anticipatory measures envisaged, especially those that threaten employment.
3. Information and consultation on decisions likely to lead to substantial changes in work organisation or in contractual relations (including those covered in art. 9 below).

Information shall be given at such time, and in such fashion, as to enable employee representatives to conduct an adequate study and, where necessary, prepare for consultation. *Consultation* shall take place:

● Whilst ensuring that timing, method and content are appropriate.
● At the relevant level of management, depending upon the subject under discussion.
● On the basis of information provided by employer and of the opinion of employee representatives.
● In such a way as to enable employee representatives to meet the employer and obtain a response, and the reasons for that response, to the employee representatives' opinion.
● With a view to reaching agreement on decisions within the scope of the employer's powers.

As with the European Works Council Directive, there is the opportunity for management and labour to negotiate their own information and consultation arrangements, provided that they meet the

---

47 Preamble paras (18) and (19).

requirements of the Directive and national legislation. Thus any agreements existing at the transposition date of 23 March 2005 were able to continue, as were any other agreements subsequently negotiated. Presumably, the UK regulations will provide a framework for such individually negotiated arrangements.

Confidential information has always been an important concern of employers, and the question of what is confidential and what is not will be part of the interest in watching this Directive put into practice. There are two aspects to confidentiality. One is imposing an obligation upon the parties to maintain a confidence. The second is the decision as to what material is so confidential that it cannot be revealed at all. In dealing with the first of these, Member States may provide that employee representatives, and any experts who assist them, may not reveal information to employees or third parties if provided in confidence 'in the legitimate interest of the undertaking or establishment', unless that other party is bound by a duty of confidentiality. This obligation may continue after the expiry of a term of office.

Member States may also provide that the employer need not provide information or consult when the nature of the information or consultation is such that, 'according to objective criteria', it would seriously harm the functioning of the undertaking or establishment or would be prejudicial to it.

Member States shall provide for judicial review of situations where the employer requires confidentiality or does not provide information or consult in accordance with the above. This is the case with the TICE Regulations implementing the European Works Council Directive. The independent body is the Central Arbitration Committee.

Article 8 obliges Member States to have suitable judicial processes in place to enable the obligations of employers and employees to be enforced. It also requires adequate sanctions to be available for infringement of the Directive. These sanctions must be 'effective, proportionate and dissuasive'. This is going to be an interesting provision of any UK regulations. There are potentially large sums of money which may be involved in, for example, a merger or an acquisition. If an employer decided that it wished not to consult the employees, is a fine of the sort contained in the TICE Regulations going to be a sufficient deterrent? If it is not, then there might be an issue related to a bigger fine as to whether it would be proportionate.

10.2.2 The Information and Consultation of Employees Regulations[48]

Although art. 11 of the Information and Consultation Directive stipulated 23 March 2005 as the deadline for transposition, there was an extension for Member States who did not have a general, permanent and statutory system of information and consultation, such as the United Kingdom. The ICE Regulations took effect over a period of three years and now affect all employers with at least 50 employees. There is a narrow definition of employee, so only those who work under a contract of employment are included.[49] The number of employees is worked out by taking the average number employed in the previous 12 months.[50] Employees, or their representatives, have the right to ask for the data on employee numbers,[51] and if the employer fails to provide the information, or provides incorrect information, within one month, then the employee, or the employee representatives, can complain to the CAC. After this the CAC can order the employer to produce the

---

48 SI 2004/3426.
49 Regulation 2 ICE Regulations 2004.
50 Regulation 4 ICE Regulations 2004.
51 Regulation 5 ICE Regulations 2004.

information.[52] This information is, of course, crucial. It settles if and when the employer is covered by the Regulations.

The Regulations are complex and the process has a similar approach to that which is used in the statutory recognition of trade unions (see Chapter 12). The process can begin in one of two ways. Either the employer can initiate the process or it starts with a request from the employees. There is a duty of co-operation as stated in reg. 21:

> The parties are under a duty, when negotiating or implementing a negotiated agreement or when implementing the standard information and consultation provisions, to work in a spirit of co-operation and with due regard for their reciprocal rights and obligations, taking into account the interests of both the undertaking and the employees.

According to *Darnton v Bournemouth University*[53] the duty to co-operate was placed on the parties once the negotiating representatives commenced negotiations. In this case it was concluded that the employer was under no obligation to disclose its own legal advice not to make arrangements for the employees to receive such advice.

Stage 1 The request

At least 10 per cent of the employees, either together or separately, need to make the request to the employer to open negotiations to reach an Information and Consultation Agreement in order for it to be a valid request. This 10 per cent is subject to a minimum of 15 employees and a maximum of 2,500. Thus an employer with only 50 employees could require at least 15 employees to make the request, and, in larger organisations, of 25,000 or more, there is a cap on the numbers who need to be involved.[54] The issue of what constituted an undertaking arose in the case of *Moyer-Lee*[55] where 28 of the 210 employees working on a University of London contract made a request for an information and consultation procedure. Although the numbers exceeded 10 per cent of the site workforce, they only constituted some 0.3 per cent of the whole workforce. The EAT held that the term 'undertaking' in the Regulations meant that there had to be a legal entity capable of being the employer of employees under a contract of employment, and not just a section or division of the undertaking. The grouping of employees here could not be seen as a legal entity capable of entering into such contracts. The undertaking therefore was the whole of the company's employees and the request failed.

The request or requests must be in writing and sent to the employer's head office or principal place of business. It can be sent to the CAC if the employees wish to act anonymously.[56] If there is already an Information and Consultation Agreement in operation, the employer may decide to hold a ballot of all employees to find out if they endorse the application for a new agreement.[57]

In *Stewart v Moray Council*[58] the employer claimed that three existing agreements covered all employees, even though each only covered part of the workforce. The EAT accepted this argument but then stated that one of the agreements, that covering teachers, was not detailed enough. Where more than one agreement is relied upon, each of them has to cover all the requirements of the Regulations. In this case there was not sufficient information on one of the agreements concerning

---

52 Regulation 6 ICE Regulations 2004.
53 [2009] IRLR 4.
54 Regulation 7(1), (2) and (3) ICE Regulations 2004.
55 *Moyer-Lee v Cofely Workplaces Ltd* [2015] IRLR 879.
56 Regulation 7(4) ICE Regulations 2004.
57 Regulations 8–10 ICE Regulations 2004; the employer can only initiate a ballot if less than 40 per cent of the employees had endorsed the original request.
58 [2006] IRLR 592.

reg. 8(1)(d) where there is a requirement to set out how the employer is to give information and seek the views of the employee representatives.[59]

In *University of London v Morrissy*[60] the employer received a request to set up an information and consultation procedure from at least 10 per cent of its employees. The employer already recognised two trade unions (who represented about 25 percent of the workforce) and decided to meet the request by setting up a procedure just involving those two unions. The CAC and the EAT found this unsatisfactory and the EAT stated that the arrangements put in place 'should be with a view for the effective representation of all employees, rather than a section of employees'. It is not for the employer to set up and appoint a process with employee representatives. This must be done with the involvement of the employees who must be able to elect or appoint the representatives.

Stage 2 The negotiations

The employer may initiate negotiations without waiting for the employees to request action.[61] Whether it is done on his own initiative or as a result of an employee request, the obligations upon the employer are the same. Regulation 14 sets out the procedure. As soon as is reasonably practicable the employer must make arrangements for the appointment or election of 'negotiating representatives'. The employees need to be informed of who these representatives are (in writing) and then invite the negotiating representatives to enter into negotiations to reach a negotiated agreement. All employees need to be entitled to take part in the appointment or election of representatives and all employees in the undertaking need to be represented by a representative.[62] As with the statutory recognition procedures for trade unions, there are strict time limits to be applied to the process. The negotiation must not last more than six months, unless both sides agree, from a time of three months after the employee request was made or the employer initiated the process.[63] In *Darnton*[64] the EAT rejected the argument that this meant that the employer's obligations had to be completed in three months. The wording was 'as soon as reasonably practicable', although there was a maximum period of six months for completion.

Stage 3 The negotiated agreement

A negotiated agreement must be in writing, be dated and cover all employees. It must set out the circumstances in which the employer must inform and consult the employees.[65] It must provide for the appointment of the Information and Consultation Representatives who are to be informed or consulted. Alternatively, it may provide for the information and consultation of all employee representatives.[66] It must be approved by all the negotiating representatives signing it or at least 50 per cent of them if a ballot of all employees is held which approves the agreement.[67]

10.2.2.1 Standard information and consultation provisions

If the employer fails to initiate negotiations, then the standard provisions will apply from six months of the date the employee request was made or within six months of the date that representatives were appointed or elected (whichever is sooner). Similarly, if the parties fail to reach agreement within the allowed time limit, then six months from that time limit expiry the standard

59 In *Amicus v Macmillan Publishers Ltd* [2007] IRLR 378 the employers had a pre-existing agreement covering only one site. The CAC held that this could not be relied upon to meet the requirements of the Regulations.

60 [2016] IRLR 487.

61 Regulation 7(1) ICE Regulations 2004.

62 Regulation 15 ICE Regulations 2004 provides for complaints about these requirements to the CAC.

63 This period does not take into account the delays caused by a ballot or by complaints to the CAC.

64 *Darnton v Bournemouth University* [2010] IRLR 294.

65 Regulation 16(1) ICE Regulations 2004.

66 Regulation 16(1)(g) ICE Regulations 2004.

67 Regulation 16(2) ICE Regulations 2004; Sch. 2 specifies the electoral process for the election of representatives.

provisions apply.[68] In practice this means that the standard provisions will normally be the minimum provisions agreed in any negotiated agreement. There is no need for the information and consultation representatives to agree to anything less as all they need do is wait for the period to expire and the standard provisions will automatically apply.

The standard provisions first itemise what information must be provided to the representatives.[69] These are:

(i)   the recent and probable development of the undertaking's activities and economic situation;
(ii) the situation, structure and probable development of employment within the undertaking and on any anticipatory measures envisaged, in particular, where there is a threat to employment;
(iii) decisions likely to lead to substantial changes in work organisation or in contractual relations.[70]

Where there is a failure to comply with any of the terms of a negotiated agreement or a standard provision, a complaint may be made to the CAC within three months beginning with the date of the failure.[71] The CAC may then issue an order for compliance. Failure to carry this out within three months may lead to a further complaint, this time to the EAT which has the power to issue a penalty of up to £75,000.[72]

10.2.2.2 Confidential information

Regulations 25 and 26 deal with the issue of confidentiality. If the employer issues material to employees that is confidential, then the employee owes the employer a duty not to disclose the information.[73] This is always a difficult issue for employee representatives, when they are given information that they are not allowed to disclose to the people who elected or appointed them in the first place. If the recipient does not believe that it is genuinely confidential, then he may apply to the CAC to decide whether it was reasonable for the employer to impose a confidentiality condition.

Similarly, the employer need not disclose information at all where 'according to objective criteria, the disclosure of the information or document would seriously harm the functioning of, or would be prejudicial to, the undertaking'. Again any information and consultation representative, or, where there are no representatives, any employee or their representative, may apply to the CAC for a declaration as to whether it is confidential or not.

10.2.2.3 Employee protection

An employee who is a negotiating representative or an information and consultation representative is entitled to reasonable paid time off during working hours.[74] Employees may take a complaint to an employment tribunal for an employer's failure in this regard within a period of three months beginning with the day of the alleged wrongdoing.

A dismissal of any employee for carrying out activities in relation to the ICE Regulations will be an automatically unfair dismissal. The rules on minimum service or maximum age do not apply in these circumstances.[75] Similarly, employees or representatives are protected from detriment.[76]

---

68 Regulation 18(1) ICE Regulations 2004.
69 Regulation 20(1) ICE Regulations 2004.
70 The employer need not inform or consult under these regulations in relation to this section if the employer tells the representatives that he will be complying with the information and consultation obligations under s. 188 TULRCA on collective redundancies or reg. 10 of the TUPE Regulations 1981 on transfers of undertakings.
71 Regulation 22 ICE Regulations 2004.
72 Regulation 23 ICE Regulations 2004.
73 Unless the recipient reasonably believes the disclosure to be a 'protected disclosure' under s. 43A ERA 1996.
74 Regulations 27–28 ICE Regulations 2004.
75 Regulation 30 ICE Regulations 2004.
76 Regulation 32 ICE Regulations 2004.

10.3 Collective redundancies

Redundancy is one of the potentially 'fair' reasons for dismissal listed in s. 98(2) of the ERA 1996. It is therefore dealt with in Chapter 5.

Council Directive 98/59/EC on the approximation of the laws of the Member States relating to collective redundancies (the Collective Redundancies Directive) is a consolidation Directive. It consolidated Directives 75/129/EEC as amended by Directive 92/56/EEC on the same subject. The original Directive was adopted in 1975 and transposed into British law very quickly. It was included in the Employment Protection Act 1975 and has been part of national law, subject to various amendments, ever since. The provisions are now contained in Part IV Chapter II TULRCA 1992, which outlines the procedure for handling collective redundancies. The legislation has been targeted towards consultation and information, as distinct from negotiations, on the subject. The duty to consult rests upon an employer who is proposing to dismiss 20 or more employees at one establishment within a period of 45 days or less for reasons of redundancy.[77] This may include situations where the employer is proposing to dismiss a workforce and then immediately re-employ them as part of a reorganisation.[78] The Court of Justice, in *Pujante Rivera*[79] also confirmed that where an employer makes significant detrimental changes to essential elements of the contract of employment for reasons not related to the individual employee, then this falls within the definition of redundancy in the context of the Collective Redundancies Directive. The consultation shall begin 'in good time' and in any event at least 30 days before the first dismissal takes effect, or at least 45 days before the first dismissal takes effect if the employer is proposing to dismiss 100 or more employees at one establishment within a period of 90 days.[80]

A debatable issue here, of course, is at what point in time is the employer 'proposing to dismiss'. It is likely that, except, for example, in a disaster situation, there is a period of time over which the decision to dismiss employees by reason of redundancy is reached. There is, perhaps, first the decision in principle to dismiss employees. There may be a second stage where the parts of the organisation in which the redundancies are to take place are identified, followed by a further stage when particular employees are identified. In *R v British Coal Corporation and Secretary of State for Trade and Industry, ex parte Price*[81] the court approved an approach to fair consultation which meant that it began when the proposals were still at a formative stage. Glidewell LJ cited the tests proposed in *R v Gwent County Council, ex parte Bryant*, that fair consultation meant:[82]

(a)   consultation when the proposals are still at a formative stage;
(b)   adequate information on which to respond;
(c)   adequate time in which to respond;
(d)   conscientious consideration by an authority of the response to consultation.

The court in *Griffin v South West Water Services Ltd*[83] disagreed with this, expressing instead the view that the employer's obligation arose only when the employer was able to identify the workers and be in a position to supply the information required by the Directive.

---

77   Section 188(1) TULRCA 1992; s. 195 defines dismissal for redundancy as dismissals not related to the individual and there is a presumption of redundancy in any proceedings unless the contrary is shown.

78   See *GMB v Man Truck & Bus UK Ltd* [2000] IRLR 636.

79   *Pujante Rivera v Gestora Clubs Dir SL* [2016] IRLR 51.

80   Section 188(1A) TULRCA 1992. Prior to April 2013 the requirement was for the consultation to begin at 90 days before, but this figure was reduced to 45 days by the Trade Union and Labour Relations (Consolidation) Act 1992 (Amendment) Order 2013 SI 2013/763.

81   [1994] IRLR 72.

82   [1988] COD 19.

83   [1995] IRLR 15.

This issue was considered in *Hough v Leyland DAF Ltd.*[84] This case concerned security staff at a number of the employer's premises. The security manager was asked to prepare a report on the possibility of contracting out the security function. The manager produced a report recommending that it should be contracted out. It was a further six months before the employer approached the trade union informing them of the employer's intention to contract out security services. The issue was at what stage the employers could be said to have been proposing to dismiss. The EAT held that this occurred at the time of the security manager making his report recommending the contracting out. The employers had argued that the proposals needed to be at a far more advanced stage before the statutory obligation to consult took effect. The EAT held:

> We agree that [s. 99] read as a whole contemplates that matters should have reached a stage where a specific proposal has been formulated and that this is a later stage than the diagnosis of a problem and the appreciation that at least one way of dealing with it would be by declaring redundancies.

The EAT then went on to state that it would not be more helpful to seek a more precise definition because of the large variety of situations that might arise. Article 2(1) Collective Redundancies Directive states that consultation should begin when the employer is 'contemplating' collective redundancies. This was considered in *Re Hartlebury Printers Ltd*[85] where the court held that proposing redundancies cannot include merely thinking about the possibility of redundancies. Contemplating redundancies in the sense of proposing them meant 'having in view or expecting' them. It is, therefore, likely to be at an early stage, but not so early that it is merely an idea that the company is thinking about. If, however, the employer's decision making has progressed to the stage of contemplating two options for the future, one of which is closing down the business and the other is selling it as a going concern, then the employer has reached the stage of 'proposing to dismiss as redundant'.[86]

There are additional complications when an employer is part of a group of companies and the decisions leading to the redundancies are taken elsewhere, such as in the holding company. In *Akavan*[87] the parent company decided to close a factory and consultations were begun by a subsidiary company which was the employer. The Court of Justice held that the employer's obligation to consult arises when strategic decisions are made within a group of undertakings compelling the employer to contemplate or plan collective redundancies. Consulting prematurely may defeat the purpose of the Directive, by restricting the flexibility available to businesses when restructuring, creating heavier administrative burdens and causing unnecessary anxiety to workers about the safety of their job. It is the employer that has the responsibility for consultation, not the holding company, so the obligation is triggered when the strategic decision compels the employer to contemplate or plan redundancies. This has led the Court of Appeal to refer the matter to the Court of Justice for further clarification as to when the obligation to consult is triggered by the Directive.[88]

The Court of Justice[89] held that the notice of dismissals shall not take place until after some of the consultation had taken place. The Court suggested that art. 2 meant that consultation with a view to reaching an agreement really meant 'negotiation'. Such negotiation would not be meaningful if it took place entirely after the notice period had commenced. This resulted in an amendment to s. 193 TULRCA which ensures that notification of any proposals takes place prior to notice being given.[90]

---

84 [1991] IRLR 194.
85 [1992] ICR 704.
86 See *Scotch Premier Meat Ltd v Burns* [2000] IRLR 639.
87 Case C-44/08 *Akavan Erityisalojen Keskusliitto AEK RY v Fujitsu Siemens* [2009] IRLR 944.
88 *United States of America v Nolan* [2011] IRLR 41.
89 Case C-188/03 *Junk v Kühnel* [2005] IRLR 310.
90 The Collective Redundancies (Amendment) Regulations 2006, SI 2006/2387.

10.3.1 Meaning of establishment

The obligation to consult rests upon 20 or more people being made redundant at one establishment. The Court of Justice considered the meaning of this term in *Rockfon A/S v Specialarbejderforbundet i Danmark*.[91] This case considered the Danish legal interpretation of the term 'establishment',[92] which provided that an establishment needed an independent management 'which can independently effect large-scale dismissals'. The Court of Justice held that the existence of such separate management was not necessary. The term applied to the unit to which the workers who have been made redundant are assigned to carry out their duties. This was further developed by the Court of Justice in a Greek case *Athinaiki v Chartopoiia AE*,[93] where it was stated that an establishment

> may consist of a distinct entity, having a certain degree of permanence and stability, which is assigned to perform one or more given tasks and which has a workforce, technical means and a certain organizational structure allowing for the accomplishment of those tasks.

The link is not necessarily a geographical one, but one concerned with the employment relationship. It is likely in many circumstances to be less than the whole undertaking of the employer. If it were the whole undertaking, then there would be no need for reference to one establishment. This was the view of the EAT in *Renfrewshire Council v Educational Institute of Scotland*[94] where some teachers were unable to show that the whole educational authority should be taken as one establishment. The EAT held that it was not necessary to focus on where the claimants' employment was controlled and that individual schools could be identified as distinct entities. In a much earlier case[95] the EAT had held that one should adopt a commonsense approach and use the word in a way in which ordinary people would use it. In this case this meant that 14 building sites administered from one base amounted to one establishment, rather than 14 separate ones. Establishment and employer are not synonymous, so if three distinct employers are making employees redundant, albeit at one location, the numbers cannot be aggregated to come within the terms of the statute.[96] In contrast, two field forces being restructured as a result of the merger of the two parent companies were held to be assigned to their branch offices, rather than to the field force as a whole. This meant that, when calculating whether the 20-person threshold had been exceeded, the establishment should be the field office rather than any other.[97] Which workers to count in working out whether the numbers threshold has been met can be quite broad and does, for example, include directors of the company and publicly funded trainees.[98]

10.3.2 Appropriate representatives

The employer must consult with the appropriate representatives of any of the employees who may be affected by the proposed dismissals or by any measures taken in connection with those dismissals.[99] The appropriate representatives are the employees' trade union representatives if an independent trade union is recognised by the employer.[100] If there is no such trade union, then they

---

91 Case C-449/93 [1996] IRLR 168.
92 Used in art. 1(1)(a) Collective Redundancies Directive.
93 Case C-270/05 *Athinaiki v Chartopoiia AE v Panagiotidis* [2007] IRLR 286.
94 [2013] IRLR 76.
95 *Barratt Developments (Bradford) Ltd v UCATT* [1977] IRLR 403.
96 *E Green & Sons Ltd v ASTMS* [1984] IRLR 134.
97 *MSF v Refuge Assurance plc* [2002] IRLR 324.
98 See *Balkayav. Kiesel Abbruch- und Recycling Technik GmbH* [2015] IRLR 771.
99 Section 188(1) TULRCA 1992.
100 The Secretary of State may, on the application of the parties, vary the statutory provisions in favour of a collective agreement concluded by the parties themselves: s. 198 TULRCA 1992.

may be either employee representatives appointed or elected by the affected employees for some other purpose, but who have authority to receive information and be consulted about the proposed dismissals, or they may be employee representatives elected by the employees for the purpose of such consultation.

The choice of which of these two alternatives should be consulted is left to the employer.[101] Prior to 1995 there had only been a requirement to consult trade union representatives if they were recognised by the employer. Where there were no recognised trade unions, there had been no requirement to consult. This approach had been challenged by the European Commission in *Commission v United Kingdom*.[102] As a result the Court of Justice held that the United Kingdom had not adequately transposed the Directive. The legislation was then amended in 1995 to allow the employer to choose whether to consult a trade union or other appropriate representatives.[103] This was then amended again in 1999, so that an employer could choose between the alternative appropriate representatives only if there was not a recognised trade union with whom to consult.[104]

Section 188A TULRCA 1992 sets out the requirements for the election of employee representatives where this is necessary.[105] The onus is on the employer to make such arrangements as are reasonably practical to ensure fairness. The election is to be conducted, so far as is reasonably practicable, in secret. The employer's duties include deciding on the number of representatives to be elected, what constituencies those representatives should represent and the term of office of those representatives. The term needs to be long enough to enable the information and consultation process to be completed. The candidates for election must be affected employees at the date of the election.[106] All affected employees have the right to vote and no affected employee must be unreasonably excluded from standing for election. Employees must be entitled to vote for as many candidates as there are representatives to be elected. The elected representatives are to be allowed access to the affected employees and given such accommodation and other facilities as are necessary.[107] They are also entitled to reasonable time off during working hours to carry out their functions as a representative or candidate, or in order to undergo training for the performance of these functions.[108] Where, after the election, one of those elected ceases to be a representative, then there may be a need for the election of a replacement.[109]

The consultation itself is to include consultation about ways of avoiding the dismissals, reducing the number of employees to be dismissed, and mitigating the consequences of the dismissals. It is necessary for the employer to consult on each of these three aspects and not on just some of them. Thus, if an employer genuinely consults with employee representatives about ways of reducing the numbers involved and mitigating the consequences of the dismissals, they will still have failed in their duty if they have not also consulted about ways of avoiding the dismissals.[110] There is an obligation for the employer to undertake such consultations with a view to reaching

---

101 Section 188(1B) TULRCA 1992.

102 Case 383/92 [1994] IRLR 412.

103 Collective Redundancies and Transfers of Undertakings (Protection of Employment) (Amendment) Regulations 1995, SI 1995/2587.

104 Collective Redundancies and Transfers of Undertakings (Protection of Employment) (Amendment) Regulations 1999, SI 1999/1925.

105 An election can be deemed to have taken place if there are the exact number of candidates for the places available and there is no need for an election; *Phillips v Xtera Communications Ltd* [2011] IRLR 724.

106 They must also be employed by the employer at the time when they were elected: s. 196(1) TULRCA 1992.

107 Section 188(5A) TULRCA 1992.

108 Section 61 ERA 1996.

109 Note that s. 47 ERA 1996 provides protection against detriment for employee representatives and s. 103 ERA 1996 makes their dismissal unfair if it is related to their candidacy or position as an employee representative.

110 *Middlesbrough Borough Council v TGWU* [2002] IRLR 332.

agreement with the appropriate representatives.[111] There is certain information that the employer must disclose in writing to the appropriate representatives. This information consists of:

1. the reasons for the proposals;
2. the numbers and descriptions of employees whom it is proposed to dismiss;
3. the total number of employees of any description employed by the employer at the establishment;
4. the proposed method of selecting those to be dismissed and the proposed method of carrying out the dismissals; and
5. the proposed method of calculating payments if different from those required by statute.

This information must be delivered to each of the appropriate representatives.[112] Whether sufficient information has been given is a question of fact for the employment tribunal to decide, although there is no rule that states that full and specific information under each of these heads should be given before consultation could begin.[113] It is not sufficient, however, for the employer to argue that the information can be gleaned from the surrounding circumstances and other documents and that any consultation would have had no effect upon the decision to close the workplace.[114] Nor is it enough for the employer just to supply a list of those to be affected.

In *Lancaster University v UCU*[115] the employer was in the habit of providing the trade union with a regular list of fixed-term contracts which were to come to an end. Even though the employer had extensive individual consultation with those affected, it was not enough to mitigate the failure to enter into meaningful consultation collectively. Similarly in *University of Stirling v UCU*[116] the EAT held that it could not be concluded that dismissals at the ending of fixed-term contracts were redundancies. In this case those academics on this sort of contract had accepted that there would be an end date and did not have any reasonable justification for an expectation that their employment would continue after that date.

10.3.3 Special circumstances

There are two 'escape' clauses for employers unable to comply with their obligations under s. 188 TULRCA 1992:

1. Where there are special circumstances which make it not reasonably practicable for an employer to comply with the consultation and information requirements, they are to take all steps towards compliance that are reasonably practicable in the circumstances.[117]
2. Where they have invited affected employees to elect representatives and the employees have failed to do so within a reasonable time, then the employer must give all the affected employees the information set out above.[118]

In *The Bakers' Union v Clarks of Hove Ltd*[119] the court held that there were three stages to deciding whether there was a defence in any particular case. First, were there special circumstances; second, did they

---

111 Section 188(2) TULRCA 1992.
112 Section 188(4)–(5) TULRCA 1992.
113 See *MSF v GEC Ferranti (Defence Systems) Ltd* [1994] IRLR 113.
114 See *Sovereign Distribution Services Ltd v TGWU* [1989] IRLR 334.
115 *Lancaster University v University and College Union* [2011] IRLR 4.
116 *University of Stirling v University and College Union* [2012] IRLR 266.
117 Section 188(7) TULRCA 1992.
118 Section 188(7B) TULRCA 1992.
119 [1978] IRLR 366 CA.

render compliance with the statute not reasonably practicable; and, third, did the employer take all the reasonable steps towards compliance as were reasonably practicable in the circumstances? In this case even an insolvency was not a special enough circumstance in itself to provide a defence against the lack of consultation.

E Ivor Hughes Educational Foundation v Morris[120] concerned a failing school. The number of pupils was declining to the stage where the school might not be viable. One issue was whether the consultation should have begun when the school governors were told of the financial situation with closing the school being an option, or whether it should start when the decision to close was taken and whether there were special circumstances which made it not possible to consult on the earlier occasion. The EAT held that Section 188(7) looked at the actual events which occurred and decides whether or not those events rendered it not reasonably practicable to consult. It provides, according to the EAT, a limited exception to the obligation to consult when the circumstances prevailing at the time, which were out of the ordinary run of events, made it impracticable for consultation to occur. One of the special circumstances put forward by the employer was the need for confidentiality, believing that if the information about the state of the school became known, then it might precipitate the school closure as parents took their children away. The EAT agreed with the Employment Tribunal that it was not inevitable for this information to be released so that it could not provide a special circumstance.

The shedding of employees in an attempt by a receiver to sell the business was not a sufficient justification in GMB v Rankin and Harrison.[121] The facts that the business could not be sold and that there were no orders were common to insolvency situations and not enough in themselves to justify being special. Special circumstances means something out of the ordinary or something that is not common. In any complaint to an employment tribunal, the onus is upon the employer to show that there were special circumstances or that they took all reasonably practical steps towards compliance.[122]

In UK Coal Mining Ltd v NUM[123] a coal mine closed because of damage resulting from sea water entering the mine and it was declared unfit. The employer decided not to go through the consultation procedure because the inrush of water could not have been foreseen. The EAT held that there was still an obligation to consult even when there was to be a closure of an operation; this would include the reasons for the dismissals. The reasons for the closure, rather than the closure itself, were the reasons for the dismissal and the true reasons here were the financial difficulties of the employer.

10.3.4 Failure to comply

Where an employer has failed to comply with the requirements to consult, a complaint may be made to an employment tribunal.[124] If the tribunal finds the complaint well founded, it will make a declaration to that effect and may make a protective award. A protective award to those who have been dismissed as redundant or whom it is proposed to dismiss and the protected period, up to a maximum of 90 days, begins with the date on which the first dismissals take effect or the date of the award, whichever is earlier. The length is that which the tribunal decides is just and equitable.[125] There is a time limit for complaints. They must be presented to the tribunal before the date on which the last of the dismissals takes effect, or during the three months beginning with that date, or within

---

120 [2015] IRLR 696.

121 [1992] IRLR 514; neither were a local authority's financial difficulties a 'special circumstance': see *Middlesbrough Borough Council v TGWU* [2002] IRLR 332.

122 Section 189(6) TULRCA 1992.

123 [2008] IRLR 4.

124 Section 189(1) TULRCA 1992; the onus of showing compliance with respect to questions about the election of appropriate representatives, or whether the employee representative was an appropriate representative, rests with the employer: s. 189(1A)–(1B) TULRCA 1992.

125 Section 189(2)–(4) TULRCA 1992.

such further period as the tribunal considers reasonable if it is satisfied that it was not practicable for the complainant to present their complaint during that period.[126] During the protected period all the employees who are covered will receive a week's pay[127] for each week that he would have been paid by the employer during that period.[128] Parts of weeks are paid proportionately. Tribunals are required to state their reasons for the length of the award made.[129] Protective awards resulting from a claim by a trade union can only be awarded in respect of employees for which the trade union has been recognised. Other employees must make their own complaints.[130] The purpose of the award is to ensure that consultation takes place by providing a sanction against employers who fail to do so properly. The focus of the award is not on compensating the employees but on the seriousness of the employer's failure to comply with their statutory obligations,[131] and the employer's ability to pay is not relevant.[132] An employee may bring a complaint to an employment tribunal if they have not been paid their protective awards in part or entirety. This complaint must be brought within three months of the last date on which the employee claims they were entitled to payment which is likely to be the last day of the protected period,[133] unless the period is extended by the tribunal if it considers that it was not reasonably practicable to do so. If the tribunal finds the complaint well founded, it can order the employer to pay the award.[134]

Employers have an obligation to notify the Secretary of State of their proposals to dismiss employees for redundancy.[135] Proposals to dismiss 100 or more employees within 45 days or fewer are to be notified at least 45 days before any notice is given to employees in respect of any of the dismissals. Proposals to dismiss 20 or more within such a period require at least 30 days' written notice to the Secretary of State.[136] The written notice must contain details of where the employees are employed, identify the representatives to be consulted and when consultation with them began. The Secretary of State may give a written notice requiring more information.[137] There is also a special circumstances defence for the employer if it is not reasonably practicable for the employer to comply with these notification requirements. Failure of a controlling employer to provide the information does not constitute a special circumstance.[138] Failure to comply with these requirements may lead to a fine and individuals can be prosecuted if their actions had led to a corporate body not complying with these statutory requirements.[139]

10.4 Employer insolvency

Many redundancies and transfers of undertakings (see below) are likely to arise out of the insolvency of employers. The precise effect on employees will depend upon the action taken by creditors in

---

126 Section 189(5) TULRCA 1992.

127 A week's pay as defined by Part XIV Chapter II ERA 1996.

128 Section 190 TULRCA 1992; s. 191 deals with certain situations, such as a fair dismissal and offers of alternative employment, which might stop the employee continuing to receive payment.

129 *E Green & Sons v ASTMS* [1984] IRLR 134.

130 *TGWU v Brauer Coley Ltd* [2007] IRLR 207.

131 *Susie Radin Ltd v GMB* [2004] IRLR 400 where the employers unsuccessfully argued that the tribunal should have taken into account a separate decision that consultation would have been futile anyway. The Court of Appeal stated that the futility of the consultation was not relevant to the making of a protective award.

132 In *Smith v Cherry Lewis Ltd* [2005] IRLR 86 the employer was insolvent, but this was held not to be relevant in making the award.

133 *Howlett Marine Services Ltd v Bowlam* [2001] IRLR 201.

134 Section 192 TULRCA 1992.

135 Requirements of arts. 3 and 4 Collective Redundancies Directive.

136 Section 193(1)–(2) TULRCA 1992 as amended by the Collective Redundancies (Amendment) Regulations 2006, SI 2006/2387.

137 Section 193(4)–(5) TULRCA 1992.

138 Section 193(7) TULRCA 1992.

139 Section 194 TULRCA 1992.

order to secure their assets. If a winding-up order is made by a court, the effect is, from the date of its publication, to bring the contracts of employment to an end with immediate effect. If the court were to appoint a receiver, the effect would be the same. Receivers appointed by creditors, by way of contrast, do not constitute a change in the legal identity of the employer and no automatic termination of the contracts of employment takes place. The effect of the appointment of an administrator is the same as a creditor-appointed receiver. This is because they act as agents of the company and do not replace the legal entity.[140] Without statutory intervention such employees, if the insolvent business is not taken over or sold to a new employer, would merely join other creditors hoping to receive at least part of that which is owed to them.

Council Directive 2008/94/EC on the protection of employees in the event of the insolvency of their employer[141] (the Insolvency Directive) is the European Community's attempt to harmonise the approach of Member States. The purpose of the Directive was to add to employee protection by ensuring that each Member State had a guarantee institution which would guarantee, subject to limits, payment of employees' outstanding claims resulting from their contracts of employment and employment relationship.[142] Provisions providing this protection in Great Britain are contained in Part XII ERA 1996.

Section 182 ERA 1996 provides that employees may write to the Secretary of State to apply for payment of debts, owed to them by their insolvent employer, from the National Insurance Fund.

In *Everson and Barrass v Secretary of State for Trade and Industry and Bell Lines Ltd*[143] the Court of Justice was asked to settle the issue as to which country's guarantee institution should compensate the employees of an employer from a different Member State. In this case the Irish courts made a winding-up order on the company in Ireland and the British employees of that company made a claim against the Secretary of State in Great Britain. In a previous case[144] the Court of Justice had held that it was the guarantee institution of the country of the parent company that was liable. This concerned employees who did not work from a registered office in the country where they were employed. In *Everson and Barrass* the Court of Justice held that, because the employees worked from a branch office from which all the employees worked, the guarantee institution of the country in which the branch was established should be liable for the payments. In *Svenska Staten*[145] the Court accepted that modern technology meant that an organisation did not need to have a fixed establishment in another State in order to have a stable economic presence there.

The Secretary of State will need to be satisfied that the employer has become insolvent,[146] the employee's employment has been terminated and that the employee was entitled to be paid the whole or part of the debt. Section 183(3) ERA 1996 provides that an employer which is a company is to be treated as insolvent if:

1. a winding-up order or an administration order has been made; or
2. a receiver or manager has been appointed or possession has been taken of any of the company's property by debenture holders; or
3. there is a voluntary arrangement under Part I Insolvency Act 1986.

---

140 See *In the matter of Maxwell Fleet and Facilities Management Ltd* [2000] IRLR 368 for an example of how administrators tried to use the Transfer of Undertakings Regulations 1981 in order to shed the employees and sell the business without inherited debts.

141 This Directive codified previous directives on this subject, namely Directive 2002/74/EC which amended Council Directive 80/987/EEC on the approximation of the laws of the Member States relating to the protection of employees in the event of the insolvency of their employer.

142 Articles 3 and 4 Insolvency Directive.

143 Case C-198/98 [2000] IRLR 202.

144 Case C-117/96 *Mosbæk (Danmarks Aktive Handelsrejsende) v Lonmodtagernes Garantifond* [1998] IRLR 150.

145 Case C-310/07 *Svenska Staten v Holmqvist* [2008] IRLR 970.

146 Section 183 ERA 1996 defines insolvency for employers who are individuals and for employers who are companies.

If the employee cannot show that one of these events has taken place, then it is unlikely that the individual will be entitled to payment from the National Insurance Fund. Even though, as in *Secretary of State for Trade and Industry v Walden*,[147] the employer is in financial difficulties and the company has been dissolved, this will not be enough in itself. The absence of any one of these three definitions was sufficient to stop the employee from successfully making a claim. In addition the Secretary of State's liability is as at the date of the liquidation. Some employees in *McDonagh* and *Pengelly*[148] were unaware that their employer had entered a Creditor's Voluntary Arrangement (CVA) and continued to work. The period after the employer had entered the CVA was held not to count for the purposes of claims against the National Insurance Fund.

There is only liability for debts which the employee was entitled to receive from the employer.[149] The debts which are protected by statute are:[150]

1. Arrears of pay up to a maximum of eight weeks, although there is likely to be an entitlement to choose the best eight weeks;[151] this includes[152] guarantee payments, payments for time under Part VI ERA 1996[153] and for time off for carrying out trade union duties,[154] remuneration on suspension on medical grounds[155] and any amounts due from a protective award under s. 189 TULRCA 1992.
2. Any amount payable to fulfil the statutory notice requirements in s. 86 ERA 1996.
3. Any holiday pay outstanding at the appropriate date[156] from the previous 12 months, up to a maximum of six weeks.[157]
4. Any basic award of compensation for unfair dismissal.[158]
5. Any reasonable sum by way of reimbursing the whole or part of a fee paid by an apprentice or articled clerk.[159]

In addition, s. 166(1)(b) ERA 1996[160] provides that employees whose employer is insolvent may apply to the Secretary of State for any statutory redundancy payments due.[161]

10.4.1 Occupational pensions

Article 8 of the Directive provides that Member States must ensure that all the necessary measures are taken to protect the interests of employees and ex-employees at the date of the employer's insolvency in respect of rights under occupational pension schemes. This is an important measure because it affects situations where not only the employer becomes insolvent, but also the pension

---

147 [2000] IRLR 168.
148 *Secretary of State for Business, Innovation and Skills v McDonagh and Secretary of State for Business, Innovation and Skills v Pengelly* [2013] IRLR 598.
149 See *Mann v Secretary of State for Employment* [1999] IRLR 566 HL.
150 Section 184(1) ERA 1996.
151 See *Mann v Secretary of State for Employment* [1999] IRLR 566 HL.
152 Section 184(2) ERA 1996.
153 Time off for public duties, looking for work, antenatal care, dependants, occupational pensions and for employee representatives.
154 Section 169 TULRCA 1992.
155 Section 64 ERA 1996.
156 See s. 185 ERA 1996 for the meaning of 'appropriate date'.
157 This includes pay for holidays actually taken and accrued holiday pay: s. 184(3) ERA 1996.
158 Or an award under a designated dismissal procedure, so long as it is not greater than the basic award.
159 A rare event in modern times.
160 See generally Part XI Chapter VI ERA 1996 on the rules regarding these and other payments by the Secretary of State.
161 See *Secretary of State for Trade and Industry v Lassman* [2000] IRLR 411 CA, where employees were mistakenly paid redundancy payments. This was held to break their continuity of employment and they were unable to claim for the same period again when their new employer became insolvent.

scheme. *Robins v Secretary of State*[162] concerned two pension schemes which had a combined deficit of over £140 million. The pensioners therefore faced significant reductions in their pensions from these schemes. The question was whether the UK government had an obligation, under art. 8, to make up the difference between what the funds would pay and what they would have been entitled to if they had not been in deficit. In the event the Court of Justice held that there was no requirement on the government to provide a full guarantee. The Directive allowed a certain latitude to Member States. On the other hand, the amounts guaranteed in this case (between 20 and 49 per cent) did not amount to the minimum degree of protection that the claimants were entitled to. This was also reflected in *Hogan v Minister for Social and Family Affairs*.[163] This case concerned claims which arose out of the insolvency of Waterford Crystal Ltd in Ireland. The claimants had been told that they would receive only 28 per cent of the pension benefits that they were entitled to and they successfully argued that this breached art. 8 of the Insolvency Directive. The Court of Justice held that the Irish government was 'in serious breach of its obligations' by not following the decision in *Robins*.

10.4.2 Controlling directors

One issue concerns individuals who are controlling directors of companies as well as having contracts of employment with those companies. If an individual can have an influence upon whether a company is insolvent or not, is it possible for that same individual to have a claim against the Secretary of State for redundancy pay and other contractual emoluments?[164] In *Fleming v Secretary of State for Trade and Industry*[165] an individual was refused a claim for redundancy and statutory notice payments on the grounds that he was not an employee. He owned 65 per cent of the company's shares and, when the company got into difficulties, he had given personal guarantees to the company's two main suppliers and had elected not to take a salary for a time. This was enough for the employment tribunal to decide that he was not an employee. The appeal courts accepted that the decision as to whether an individual was an employee or not was a question of fact for the tribunal. The Court of Session held, therefore, that the tribunal was entitled to reach the decision that it did, but that the fact that a person was a controlling director was only one of the factors that should be taken into account. The significance to be given to that factor would depend upon the surrounding circumstances.

This view was supported in *Secretary of State for Trade and Industry v Bottrill*[166] which concerned the managing director of a company who held all the shares in that company. In this case he was also held to be an employee as the shareholding was only intended to be temporary. The court confirmed the approach that the controlling shareholding was only one of the factors to be taken into account. Other factors might be the degree of control exercised by the company, whether there were other directors and whether the individual was answerable to himself only and incapable of being dismissed.

10.4.3 Complaints to employment tribunals

The total amount payable in respect of any debt, where that debt refers to a period of time, is, currently, £489 per week[167] and even this is subject to deductions such as national insurance

---

162 Case C-278/05 *Robins v Secretary of State for Work and Pensions* [2007] IRLR 271.

163 [2013] IRLR 668.

164 See *Lee v Lee's Air Farming Ltd* [1961] AC 12 for the classic approach to the relationship between an individual as a controlling director and an individual as an employee; also *McMeechan v Secretary of State for Employment* [1997] IRLR 353 CA, where an employment agency worker established their employee status and was able to claim against the Secretary of State.

165 [1997] IRLR 682.

166 [1999] IRLR 326 CA.

167 Section 186 ERA; this is the figure for 2017/2018.

contributions.[168] If the Secretary of State fails to make a payment that has been claimed, or only makes it in part, then the individual may make a complaint to an employment tribunal. This complaint needs to be submitted within three months, beginning with the date on which the Secretary of State's decision was communicated, or such further period as the tribunal considers reasonable. If the complaint is upheld, the tribunal may stipulate the amount that should be paid.[169]

Where a 'relevant officer' has been appointed in connection with the insolvency, then the Secretary of State may wait for a statement of the employer's debts to employees from that officer before making any payments. The relevant officer is a trustee in bankruptcy, a liquidator, an administrator, a receiver or manager, or a trustee under an arrangement between the employer and the creditors or under a trust deed.[170] The Secretary of State also has the power to require, by giving notice in writing, an employer, or any other person having control of the necessary records, to provide any information necessary for the Secretary of State to deal with the claim. Failure to co-operate or the provision of false information can lead to a fine.[171]

Once the Secretary of State makes a payment, then all the rights and remedies associated with that debt accrue to the Secretary of State. If, for example, an employment tribunal makes an award after the payment has been made, then the debt is paid to the Secretary of State.[172]

10.5 Transfer of undertakings

The Transfer of Undertakings (Protection of Employment) Regulations 2006 (TUPE) replaced previous regulations of the same name from 1981. These have been subsequently amended by the Collective Redundancies and Transfer of Undertakings (Protection of Employment) (Amendment) Regulations 2014 (CRTUPE Regulations 2014).[173] The original Regulations were the focus of much controversy and litigation, especially during a period in the 1980s and 1990s when the government pushed forward with its agenda for the outsourcing of parts of the public sector to the private sector. There was much uncertainty as to whether the Regulations applied to outsourcing.[174] The 1981 Regulations resulted from the transposition of what became known as the Acquired Rights Directive.[175] The Directive was concerned with the potential restructuring of European business as a result of the development of the single market. One way of making the changes consequent upon restructuring more acceptable was to give workers in such situations added protection. Thus workers who work for an economic entity that is transferred from one employer to another are protected in the sense that their contracts of employment are transferred intact and their employment is continuous despite the change of employer.

The purpose of the TUPE Regulations is to be found in reg. 4(1) which describes the effect of a relevant transfer on contracts of employment. It states that:

> Except where objection is made under paragraph (7), a relevant transfer shall not operate so as to terminate the contract of employment of any person employed by the transferor and

---

168 See *Titchener v Secretary of State for Trade and Industry* [2002] IRLR 195.
169 Section 188 ERA 1996.
170 Section 187 ERA 1996.
171 Section 190 ERA 1996.
172 Section 189 ERA 1996.
173 At the time of writing this chapter, these Regulations had not taken effect, but we have included them as the due date for their introduction preceded the publication date of this book.
174 See, for example, decisions of the Court of Justice in the cases of Case 24/85 *JMA Spijkers v Gebroeders Abbatoir CV* [1986] ECR 1119; Case C-392/92 *Schmidt v Spar- und Leihkasse der früheren Ämter Bordesholm* [1995] ICR 237 and Case C-13/95 *Süzen v Zehnacker Gebudereinigung GmbH Krankenhausservice* [1997] IRLR 255.
175 Directive 77/187/EEC on the approximation of the laws of the Member States relating to the safeguarding of employees' rights in the event of transfers of undertakings; subsequently amended by Directive 98/50/EC and consolidated by Directive 2001/23/EC.

assigned to the organised grouping of employees that is subject to the relevant transfer, which would otherwise be terminated by the transfer, but any such contract shall have effect after the transfer as if originally made between the person so employed and the transferee.

Thus, if a transfer which is protected by the TUPE Regulations (a relevant transfer) between employers (the transferor and the transferee) of an economic entity takes place, then the employees' contracts of employment also transfer. It is as if the transferred employees had originally entered into their contracts of employment with the new employer (the transferee). So, if an employee has, say, ten years' service with their employer before the transfer (the transferor), then the regulations will ensure that, after the transfer, he or she will be credited with ten years' service with the new employer (the transferee).

10.5.1 A relevant transfer

The TUPE Regulations apply in two situations: first, they apply to a transfer of an undertaking and, second, they apply to a service provision change.

Regulation 3(1)(a) provides that the Regulations apply to a transfer of an undertaking, business or part of an undertaking or business where there is a transfer of an *economic entity which retains its identity*. This definition results from decisions of the Court of Justice and there has been much litigation on what is meant by an economic entity. In *Kenny v South Manchester College*,[176] for example, the issue was whether the contracts of employment of the teaching staff transferred when a tendering exercise for a teaching contract at a young offender's institution resulted in a change of contractors. A relevant transfer was held to have taken place because the entity, which consisted of teaching certain courses, existed before the transfer and continued after the transfer albeit by a different contractor. There were similar decisions in the courts concerning the outsourcing of cleaning services by a local authority and the transfer of a cleaning contract within an NHS hospital.[177] The courts held that there was an economic entity in existence before the transfer which continued after the transfer. The European Court of Justice then, in the case of *Süzen*,[178] declared that there was a distinction between the transfer of an economic entity and the transfer of an activity. In other words, more was needed than just the transfer of an activity such as contract cleaning. The Court stated that there was also a need for an organised grouping of people, so the relevant workforce also had to be taken over by the transferee. Regulation 3(2) TUPE Regulations therefore defines an economic entity as 'an organised grouping of resources which has the objective of pursuing an economic activity'. Thus a relevant transfer is one where there is a transfer of an economic entity that retains its identity after the transfer; and the economic activity is more than just an activity, but needs to include an organised grouping of resources (which can be people or equipment) to be transferred.

Regulation 3(1)(b) provides that the TUPE Regulations also apply to a 'service provision change'. A service provision change, according to the Regulations, is a situation where

(i)   activities cease to be carried out by a person ('a client') on his own behalf and are carried out instead by another person on the client's behalf ('a contractor');

(ii) activities cease to be carried out by a contractor on a client's behalf (whether or not those activities had previously been carried out by the client on his own behalf) and are carried out instead by another person ('a subsequent contractor') on the client's behalf; or

---

176 [1993] IRLR 265.
177 *Wren v Eastbourne District Council* [1993] ICR 955 and *Dines v Initial Health Care Services and Pall Mall Services Group Ltd* [1994] IRLR 336.
178 Case C-13/95 *Süzen v Zehnacker Gebudereinigung GmbH Krankenhausservice* [1997] IRLR 255.

(iii) activities cease to be carried out by a contractor or a subsequent contractor on a client's behalf (whether or not those activities had previously been carried out by the client on his own behalf) and are carried out instead by the client on his own behalf.

The 2014 amendments[179] clarified that references to activities means activities that are fundamentally the same as those carried out by the person who has ceased to carry them out. The EAT in *Arch Initiatives*[180] stated that it need not be all the activities, and if the activities are divided up, this is only a consideration in deciding whether the activities that ceased to be carried out by the outgoing person were carried out by the incoming person after the relevant date.

Regulation 3(3)(a) makes it clear that there needs to be, immediately before the service provision change, 'an organised grouping of employees' carrying on the activities on behalf of the client; and also that the client intends that the activities will be carried out by the transferee. In *Rynda*[181] the Court of Appeal held that an organised grouping of employees was capable of being interpreted as referring to a single employee. The court set out the stages to be gone through when considering whether a service provision change had taken place. It was necessary, first, to identify the service being provided to the client; second, to list the activities which were performed for the client in order to meet the service requirements; third, to identify the employee or employees that carried out these activities; and, finally, to consider whether the employee or employees were a grouping whose principal purpose was the carrying out of the listed activities.

In contrast the Court of Appeal held that a service provision change did not take place in *Hunter v McCarrick*.[182] The problem here was that the client of a property management company had become insolvent and the administrator appointed a new property manager. Thus the client had changed and this meant that a service provision change had not taken place. A similar situation applied in *SNR Denton UK LLP v Kirwan*[183] where a lawyer failed to show a service provision change when the client had not remained the same. Not only must the client remain the same, but the work carried out must be similar. In *Enterprise Management*[184] a difference of just 15 per cent in the type of work was sufficient for there not to be a service provision change. The CRTUPE Regulations 2014 now make this point explicit by inserting Regulation 5(2A) into the 2006 Regulations. This states that references to activities being carried out instead by another person 'are to activities which are fundamentally the same as the activities carried out previously'.

10.5.2 Effect of a relevant transfer

As explained above, reg. 4(1) provides that a relevant transfer (this includes a service provision change) will not result in the termination of the contract of employment of 'any person employed by the transferor and assigned to the organised grouping of resources or employees' that is transferred. The contract of employment will transfer to the transferee and it will be as if the employee signed the original contract with the transferee employer. There are perhaps three issues here: first, what is meant by 'assigned'; second, what happens if the employee objects to the transfer; and, third, what happens if employees are dismissed prior to the transfer?

Sometimes it may not be clear as to who is part of the group of employees to be transferred – for example, employees working in a centralised function, such as HR or Finance, but who spend all of their time concerned with the group transferred. The Court of Justice dealt with this issue in *Botzen*[185] where it devised the 'assignment test'. The Court held that:

179 The Collective Redundancies and Transfers of Undertakings (Amendment) Regulations 2014 SI 2014/16.
180 *Arch Initiatives v Greater Manchester West Mental Health NHS Foundation Trust* [2016] IRLR 406.
181 *Rynda (UK) Ltd v Rhijnsburger* [2015] IRLR 394.
182 [2013] IRLR 26.
183 [2012] IRLR 966.
184 *Enterprise Management Services Ltd v Connect-Up Ltd* [2012] IRLR 190.
185 Case 186/83 *Arie Botzen v Rotterdamsche Droogdok Maatschappij BV* [1986] 2 CMLR 50.

> An employment relationship is essentially characterised by the link existing between the employee and the part of the undertaking or business to which he is assigned to carry out his duties.

Being assigned to an organised grouping requires more than just an administrative connection, especially with those absent from work at the time of the transfer or service provision change. Temporary absences for sickness or for maternity leave carried an expectation of future participation in the group so could be recognised as being assigned even if absent at the time of the transfer. Someone on long-term sickness with no expectation of returning to work, in contrast, would not have that expectation and so could not be said to be assigned to the organised grouping.[186]

Thus there needs to be a clear link between the employee and the part transferred. *Duncan Web Offset (Maidstone) Ltd v Cooper*[187] concerned three employees who spent some 80 per cent of their time on work connected with the part of the business that was transferred. If they were not also transferred, then there would be insufficient work for them and they would have become unemployed. The court held that they were protected by the Regulations and suggested a number of factors that might be taken into account by tribunals in such situations. These were, for example, the amount of time spent on one part of the business or another by the employee; the amount of value given to each part by the employee; the terms of the contract of employment showing what the employee could be required to do; and how the cost to the employer of the employee's services had been allocated between the different parts of the business.[188]

Regulation 4(7) provides that employees who object to being transferred cannot be made to do so. There is a real problem for such employees, however, because when the transfer takes place, the employee's contract with the transferor will cease. The result is that the employee will not be employed by the transferor or the transferee and will not be treated as being dismissed by the transferor. As a result he or she will not have any claim for unfair dismissal or any other connected remedy.[189] In *Katsikas*[190] the Court of Justice held that to stop someone objecting to the transfer of his employment would undermine the fundamental rights of the employee who must be free to choose his employer and cannot be obliged to work for an employer whom he has not freely chosen.[191]

Regulation 4(3) also provides that it is only persons employed immediately before the transfer and who are assigned to such an organised grouping, or *would have been* had they not been unfairly dismissed, who are protected. The necessity for the words 'would have been' is to avoid the situations where a transferor employer could dismiss the employees before the transfer in order to avoid the effect of the Regulations. This was the situation in *Litster*[192] where the employer did dismiss all the employees that might be affected. In this case the employees would have transferred had it not been for the fact that the employees had been unfairly dismissed prior to the transfer. In group situations, where an employee is employed by one company but spends all his or her time with another, it may be necessary to treat the group company as the employer. This was the situation in *Albron*[193] where all

---

186 BT Managed Services Ltd v Edwards [2015] IRLR 994. See also Jakowlew v Nestor Primecare Services Ltd (T/A Saga Care) [2015] IRLR 813 where it was observed that an absence because of disciplinary action would not have the effect of removing someone from the organised grouping.

187 [1995] IRLR 633; see also Michael Peters Ltd v (1) Farnfield and (2) Michael Peters Group plc [1995] IRLR 190.

188 This issue is not confined to large organisations only as was shown in Buchanan-Smith v Schleicher & Co International Ltd [1996] IRLR 547.

189 Regulation 4(8) TUPE Regulations 2006.

190 Case 132/91 Katsikas v Konstantidis [1993] IRLR 179.

191 See also Hay v George Hanson [1996] IRLR 427 where an individual was held to have objected to being transferred from the employment of a local authority to a contractor; and Capita Health Solutions Ltd v McLean [2008] IRLR 597 where there was confusion as to whether an employee had agreed to be transferred to a contractor by the BBC.

192 Litster v Forth Dry Dock and Engineering Ltd [1989] IRLR 161 HL.

193 Albron Catering BV v FNV Bondgenoten [2011] IRLR 76.

employees of Heineken International were employed by one company but permanently assigned to another group company.

10.5.3 Economic, technical or organisational reason

Regulations 7(1) and 7(2) provide that if the principal reason for an employee being dismissed is the transfer or a reason connected to the transfer that is not an 'economic, technical or organisational reason (ETO) entailing a change in the workforce', then the dismissal is automatically unfair within the terms of Part X of the ERA 1996. Similarly, any variation to the contract of employment where the principal or sole reason for the variation is the transfer itself or a reason connected to the transfer that is not an ETO reason will be void.[194] Variations that are unconnected to the transfer or are for an ETO reason can be agreed between the employer and employee or may be possible if allowed for in the contract of employment. Thus removing an expensive employee from the payroll by an Administrator in order to make the sale of the business more attractive may be a dismissal by reason of the transfer and for an ETO reason to exist there must be an intention to change the workforce and to continue to conduct the business as distinct from the aim of selling it.[195] The 2013 Regulations also provide that 'changes in the workforce' can also mean a change to the place of work.[196]

There is no definition offered in the Regulations as to the meaning of 'economic, technical or organisational', but it is clear that the ETO needs to entail a change in the workforce, so this may include redundancies or a change in the number of employees in the undertaking or part of under-taking as well as a change in the place of work. It is not altogether clear, of course, when a variation of contract is related to the transfer or to an ETO reason. *Wilson v St Helens Borough Council*[197] concerned the transfer of a community home from Lancashire County Council to St Helens Borough Council. Negotiations took place with the trade union concerned and staffing levels were reduced from 162 to 72. In addition, some of the 72 who transferred did so on reduced terms and conditions. All were dismissed for reasons of redundancy by the County Council prior to the move. Subsequently, the employees claimed that the Transfer Regulations applied and that they should have been transferred on the same terms and conditions that they had enjoyed when employed by the transferor. The court concluded that the transfer itself was not the reason for the variation, although deciding when a variation in terms is as a result of a transfer and when it is not seems a difficult question. It stated that:

> It may be difficult to decide whether the variation is due to the transfer or attributable to some separate cause. If, however, the variation is not due to the transfer itself it can in my opinion, on the basis of the authorities to which I have referred, validly be made.

Collective agreements

There has long been an issue with TUPE transfers and the effect of collective agreements. The question was whether the effect of these collective agreements transferred, so if a group of employees, whose terms and conditions were the result of a collective agreement, were transferred to an out-sourcing company, would future negotiated changes to those terms and conditions still apply. This was the situation in a case referred to the Court of Justice by the Supreme Court.[198] The answer was that such a dynamic interpretation was inappropriate given the fact that the transferee employer would not even be involved in the negotiations for the new collective agreement. This has now been

---

194 Regulation 4(4) TUPE Regulation 2006.
195 *Spaceright Europe Ltd v Baillavoine* [2012] IRLR 111.
196 Within the meaning of s. 139 ERA 1996 which deals with the definition of redundancy.
197 [1998] IRLR 706.
198 *Alemo-Herron v Parkwood Leisure Ltd* [2013] ICR 1116.

made clear by the CRTUPE Regulations 2014 which inserted Regulation 4A into the TUPE Regulations and provides now that provisions of a collective agreement that come into force after the date of the transfer and where the employer is not a participant in the bargaining do not transfer.

10.5.4 Insolvency

Many transfers of undertakings take place during insolvencies. When an organisation becomes insolvent, there may be attempts to rescue it all or only those parts that are perceived to be profitable. The original Directive was silent on this issue and problems may have arisen when 'rescues' of insolvent enterprises were hampered by the fact that they may be relevant transfers. This would mean the transfer of all the employees on current contracts of employment which, in turn, would limit the amount of reorganisation that could be done to rescue the enterprise.

The issue was tested in *Abels*[199] where the Court distinguished between different types of proceedings in deciding the applicability of the Directive. There was a difference, according to the Court, between those situations when the insolvency proceedings were aimed at liquidation of the assets and those situations when the aim, at an earlier stage, was to rescue the business.

The 2001 Directive excludes, in art. 5(1), any transfers where the transfer is the subject of bankruptcy proceedings with a view to liquidation of the assets of the transferor. Article 5(2) also gives Member States the option of excluding transfers of liabilities in other types of insolvency proceedings as well as giving them the option of agreed changes to terms and conditions of employees which are 'designed to safeguard employment opportunities by ensuring the survival of the undertaking, business or part of the undertaking or business'. The distinction between insolvency leading to liquidation and insolvencies leading to a rescue are not always easy to make.[200] When an enterprise or undertaking goes into administration, for example, the purpose will be to rescue its business or at least part of it. Thus administration proceedings do not constitute insolvency proceedings leading to liquidation, even though this might be the ultimate outcome.[201]

The rescue of enterprises is assisted therefore by allowing employers and appropriate representatives to agree to variations in contracts when the transferor is subject to insolvency proceedings.[202] This is 'designed to safeguard employment opportunities by ensuring the survival of the undertaking'.[203] In addition the costs for which the government might assume responsibility when an enterprise becomes insolvent (see section 10.5) do not transfer to the transferee. The debts owed to employees by the transferor, to the limits of its statutory obligations, will be guaranteed by the Secretary of State. This includes some arrears of pay, notice periods, holiday pay and any basic award for unfair dismissal compensation.[204] Other debts owed to employees will transfer.

10.5.5 Information and consultation

Regulations 13 to 16 TUPE Regulations 2006 are concerned with the duty to inform and consult employee representatives, how employee representatives are to be elected and the consequences of a failure to inform and consult. Long enough before[205] a relevant transfer the employer must inform the employee representatives of:

---

199 Case 135/83 *Abels v The Administrative Board of the Bedrijfsvereniging voor de Metaal Industrie en de Electrotechnische Industrie* [1987] 2 CMLR 406.
200 *Oakland v Wellswood (Yorkshire) Ltd* [2009] IRLR 250 concerned whether the insolvency proceedings were instituted with a view to liquidation of the assets of the transferor; the court held that this is a matter of fact for the employment tribunal. Where joint administrators continue to trade with a view to a sale as a going concern, then any relevant transfer would fall under the protection of the Regulations.
201 *Key2Law (Surrey) LLP v De'Antiquis* [2012] IRLR 212.
202 Regulation 9(1) TUPE Regulations 2006.
203 Regulation 9(7) TUPE Regulations 2006.
204 See Part XII ERA 1996.
205 Regulation 13(2) TUPE Regulations 2006.

- the fact that the transfer is to take place, the date of the proposed transfer and the reasons for it;
- the legal, economic and social implications of the transfer for any affected employees;
- the measures which the employer envisages it will, in connection with the transfer, take in relation to any affected employees or, if it envisages that no measures will be so taken, that fact; and
- if the employer is the transferor, the measures, in connection with the transfer, which it envisages the transferee will take in relation to any affected employees who will become employees of the transferee after the transfer, or if it envisages that no measures will be taken.

Where the employer has fewer than ten employees and there are no appointed representatives, then the employer may treat the whole workforce as if they were each appointed representatives. In other words, micro businesses may inform and consult the workforce rather than going through any procedure to appoint representatives.[206]

It is clear that the obligation to inform and consult rests upon the transferor employer as well as the transferee one. There has been some litigation on the meaning of the term 'long enough before'. In *Institution of Professional and Civil Servants v Secretary of State for Defence*,[207] the court held that the words 'long enough before' meant as soon as measures are envisaged and *if possible* long enough before the transfer.

The rules on who are appropriate representatives and the requirements are identical to those rules concerning the appointment of appropriate representatives for the purposes of consultation in collective redundancies (see above). The representatives are the independent trade union which is recognised by the employer. If there is no such trade union, then there are employee representatives[208] to be elected or appointed by the affected employees, whether for the purpose of these consultations or for some other purpose.

The employer needs to consult the appropriate representatives 'with a view to seeking their agreement to the measures to be taken'. In the course of these consultations the employer will consider the representations made by the appropriate representatives and, if any of those representations are rejected, the employer must state the reasons for so doing.[209] The obligation on the employer is to inform the employee representatives of what it genuinely believed to be the legal or other implications of the transfer. It is not required to guarantee that its analysis is correct.[210]

The obligation is only to inform and consult the 'affected employees', not the workforce as a whole. The affected employees are those who would be transferred and those whose jobs were in jeopardy as a result of the transfer. It does not include employees whose future careers might be affected by the transfer.[211]

If there is a complaint about the failure of an employer to inform and consult, the employer will need to show:

- that it was not reasonably practicable to do so because there were special circumstances which rendered it not reasonably practicable for the employer to perform the duty;[212]
- that the employer took all such steps as were reasonably practicable in the circumstances.

---

206 Reg. 11 CRTUPE Amendment Regulations 2014.
207 [1987] IRLR 373; this case concerned the introduction of private management into the Royal dockyards at Rosyth and Devonport, a measure which was opposed by the trade unions. Before consultation could take place there needed to be some definite plans or proposals by the employer around which consultation could take place.
208 Regulation 13(3) TUPE Regulations 2006 states that employee representatives are either those who are elected for the purpose of consultation or elected for some other purpose and it is appropriate to consult them.
209 Regulation 13(7) TUPE Regulations 2006.
210 See *Royal Mail Group Ltd v CommunicationsWorkers Union* [2009] IRLR 1046.
211 *Unison v Somerset County Council* [2010] IRLR 207.
212 Regulation 15(2) TUPE Regulations 2006; the courts have traditionally construed special circumstances very narrowly; see collective redundancies above and *GMB v Rankin and Harrison* [1992] IRLR 514, where the dismissal of employees to make a sale more attractive was held not to be a special circumstance.

There is also a defence for the employer if the employees fail to elect representatives. In such a case the duty to consult is fulfilled if the employer gives each employee the necessary information.[213]

Regulations 11 and 12 TUPE Regulations concern the notification of employee liability information and provide a statutory duty for the transferor to pass on to the transferee certain information. This includes the identity and age of the employee; their terms and conditions of employment (as required by s. 1 ERA 1996); disciplinary or grievance action over the previous two years and details of any claims, cases or action brought in the past two years and any future actions that the transferor might have reasonable grounds to believe are possible.

Tribunals are expected to adopt a similar approach to that taken concerning failures in consultation concerning collective redundancies (see above). This means that awards should be concerned with punishing the employer rather than with compensating the employee.[214]

 ## Further reading

McMullen, J. 'Service Provision Change under TUPE: Not Quite What We Thought' (2012) 41(4) *Industrial Law Journal* 471.
Smith, I. and Baker, R. *Smith and Wood's Employment Law* (Oxford University Press, 2017).
www.acas.org.uk – ACAS, for guidance on redundancies and transfers.

---

213 Regulation 13(11) TUPE Regulations 2006.
214 *Sweetin v Coral Racing* [2006] IRLR 252.

Chapter 11

Trade unions

Chapter Contents

11.1 Introduction

For much of its history the trade union movement in Great Britain has struggled to establish a position within the law which would enable it to organise and make use of the power that comes from size. In the nineteenth century the struggle was with the criminal law, which was used to control and limit the activities of workers' organisations, whilst in the twentieth century the struggle was with the civil law as the courts imposed new tortious liabilities upon them.

The Combination Act 1800, for example, made unlawful any contracts or agreements between certain groups of workers which had, as their purpose, the improvement of wages or working hours or almost anything that interfered with an employer's ability to run their own business. The severity of the oppression varied over time but there were important landmarks, such as the Trade Union Act 1871, which adopted the principle of non-intervention in trade union affairs. Section 2 of that Act provided that trade unions were not to be considered as criminal conspiracies just because their rules were in restraint of trade. Nevertheless, unions suffered a series of setbacks as the civil courts continued to regard them with suspicion. The Trade Disputes Act 1906 was adopted by the last Liberal administration and was partly a reaction to the *Taff Vale* case,[1] which had the effect of limiting opportunities to take strike action and threatened the finances of unions. The 1906 Act provided trade unions with immunities from civil actions – for example, the tort of inducing breach of contract when in contemplation or furtherance of a trade dispute.[2]

In more modern times the Conservative government of 1971–74 introduced the Industrial Relations Act 1971, which repealed the 1906 Act and tried to set up a new legal framework for industrial relations. The National Industrial Relations Court was established to administer this process. It failed because of the lack of co-operation from the union movement and because the government lacked the authority to enforce its will. The Trade Union and Labour Relations Acts of 1974 and 1976 repealed the Industrial Relations Act 1971 and returned to the system of immunities. After the 'winter of discontent'[3] the Conservative government came to power in 1979 with the intention of reforming the union movement. Throughout the 1980s and the early 1990s there was a series of Acts of Parliament which limited the freedom of action of trade unions and their members. It is these legislative measures, mostly incorporated into the Trade Union and Labour Relations (Consolidation) Act (TULRCA) 1992, which deal with the right to associate and the rights of members and trade unions in relation to each other. More recently, trade union law has been amended by the Trade Union Act 2016.

11.2 Freedom of association

An important part of the struggle by workers in the past has been to establish the right to associate in unions and not to be discriminated against for doing so. However, over the last few decades the union movement has declined in size and influence. In 1979 it reached its peak membership of over 13.2 million but the latest returns made to the Certification Officer show that this has declined to some 6.9 million.[4]

The right to associate has been a concern of international organisations and is seen as a basic right of workers in a democratic society. For example, art. 11 European Convention on Human

---

1 *Taff Vale Railway Co v Amalgamated Society of Railway Servants* [1901] AC 426.

2 This is a very simplistic description. For those who want a more serious historical analysis there is a wealth of material; see e.g. Paul Davies and Mark Freedland, *Labour Legislation and Public Policy* (Clarendon Press, 1993).

3 The 'winter of discontent' was a description given to the winter of 1978–79, where there was a peak in industrial action by trade unions, especially within the public sector.

4 Annual Report of the Certification Officer 2015–2016.

Rights (ECHR) states that everyone has the right of peaceful association and freedom of association.[5] The European Court of Human Rights has held that in determining the meaning of the Convention it will take into account elements of international law other than the Convention itself, the interpretation of such elements by competent organs and the practice of European states representing their common values. Thus in *Demir v Turkey*[6] it ruled that the right to bargain collectively with the employer has, in principle, become one of the essential elements of the right to form and join trade unions.

The European Charter of the Fundamental Social Rights of Workers[7] 1989 states:

> 11. Employers and workers of the European Community shall have the right of association in order to constitute professional organisations or trade unions of their choice for the defence of their economic and social interests. Every employer and every worker shall have the freedom to join or not to join such organisations without any personal or occupational damage being thereby suffered by him.

It is interesting that the freedom to join a trade union is linked with the freedom not to join. This dual freedom is reflected in the United Kingdom legislation and results from the perceived coercion resulting from the 'closed shop'. Until their existence became impossible as a result of legislation during the 1980s and 1990s,[8] there were two types of closed shop. These were the pre-entry and the post-entry closed shops. In the former there was a requirement for applicants for job vacancies to be members of the recognised trade union or unions.[9] In the latter there was a requirement for successful job applicants to join a recognised union within a specific period of starting employment. This was a widespread practice and one not always opposed by employers. In 1978 about 23 per cent of the workforce (about 5.2 million people) worked in locations where there was a closed shop. The advantage for the management of these companies was that they avoided multi-union situations.

Whether the 'negative right' not to join a trade union can be equated with the 'positive right' to join is debatable. In *Young, James and Webster v United Kingdom*[10] three employees of British Rail lost their jobs because they refused to join one of the unions with whom British Rail had concluded a closed-shop agreement. In total, 54 individuals were dismissed for refusing to join one of the unions, out of a total workforce of about 250,000. The European Court of Human Rights held that art. 11 ECHR had been breached. The majority of the judges concluded that art. 11 did not put the 'negative' aspect of the freedom of association on the same footing as the 'positive' aspect, although a minority of six judges felt that:

> the negative aspect of freedom of association is necessarily complementary to, a correlative of and inseparable from its positive aspect. Protection of freedom of association would be incomplete if it extended to no more than the positive aspect. It is one and the same right that is involved.[11]

This approach is incorporated into s. 137(1) TULRCA 1992, which outlaws the refusal of employment on the grounds that a person is or is not a member of a trade union (see below).

---

5 This article was incorporated into national law by the Human Rights Act 1998.

6 [2009] IRLR 766.

7 Signed by all the Member States of the European Community at the time, except the United Kingdom.

8 Especially the Employment Acts 1980, 1982, 1988 and 1990.

9 In some instances the trade union had the right to put up candidates from its own known unemployed members before any wider recruitment exercise.

10 [1981] IRLR 408 ECHR.

11 Ibid. at p. 419.

11.3 Meaning of a trade union

Section 1(a) TULRCA 1992 defines a trade union as an organisation

> which consists wholly or mainly of workers of one or more descriptions and whose principal purposes include the regulation of relations between workers of that description or those descriptions and employers or employers' associations.

Similarly, it can be an organisation which consists of constituent or affiliated organisations which meet these criteria or an organisation of the representatives of such constituent or affiliated organisations.[12] Thus a trade union is defined by its membership and its purposes. For example, in *Hopkins v National Union of Seamen*[13] the objects of the union were shown to include the promotion and provision of funds to extend the adoption of trade union principles and the improvement of the conditions and protection of the interests of all members. According to the court, this might have been enough to justify payments to the National Union of Mineworkers during the miners' strike of 1984 – either keeping pits open might have supplied more work for the seamen involved in transportation or helping miners' families might have promoted the union principle of solidarity.

A list of trade unions is maintained by the Certification Officer (CO)[14] and being on the list is evidence that an organisation is a trade union.[15] An organisation of workers can apply to be included in the list and will need to supply the CO with various materials, including a copy of its rules and a list of its officers.[16] If the CO is satisfied with the information, then the organisation will be added.[17] Conversely, an organisation may be removed if the CO decides that it is not a trade union or if the organisation so requests it, or if the organisation has ceased to exist (e.g. when two unions merge). The CO is required to give 28 days' notice of the intention to remove a name from the list.[18]

11.3.1 Independence

An advantage of being on the list maintained by the CO is that any trade union on it may apply to the CO for a certificate that it is independent.[19] The statutory benefits accruing to trade unions usually go to those that are independent. For example, workers cannot have action taken against them because they seek to join, have joined or have taken part in the activities of such a union (see below). The CO may withdraw the certificate if he or she is of the opinion that the union is no longer independent.[20] However, whilst in force the certificate is conclusive proof of independence.[21] Section 5 TULRCA 1992 defines an independent trade union. There are two tests to be satisfied:

1. the trade union must not be under the domination or control of an employer or an employers' association or of a group of employers or employers' associations; and
2. the trade union must not be liable to interference by an employer, or any such group or association, which tends towards control.

---

12 Section 1(b) TULRCA 1992. On the need to look at the collective work done by an applicant association, see *Akinosun v Certification Officer* [2013] IRLR 937.
13 [1984] ICR 268.
14 Section 2(1) TULRCA 1992; the CO publishes an annual report containing the list and size of membership; it is available free of charge.
15 Section 2(4) TULRCA 1992.
16 Section 3(1) and (2) TULRCA 1992.
17 Section 3(3) and (4) TULRCA 1992.
18 Section 4 TULRCA 1992.
19 Section 6(1) TULRCA 1992.
20 Section 7(1) TULRCA 1992.
21 Section 8(1) TULRCA 1992. In *Bone v North Essex NHS Trust* [2016] IRLR 295 the Court of Appeal indicated that a certificate is retrospective for a reasonable period before the date of certification.

An organisation that is refused a certificate or has one withdrawn may appeal to the EAT.[22]

In *Blue Circle Staff Association v The Certification Officer*[23] the CO outlined the factors used in assessing the independence of an organisation. These were: finance, and whether there was a direct subsidy from the employer; other assistance received, such as free premises, facilities and time off; employer interference; history and the extent to which it has grown away from being a 'creature of management'; the rules and the extent to which the employer's senior employees are involved in running it; single company unions are more likely to be under the employer's dominance; organisation; attitude, such as a 'robust attitude in negotiation'. The newness of the Blue Circle Staff Association was a major factor in its failure to gain a certificate.[24]

Interference tending towards control might be as a result of providing financial, material or other support. It is not necessary to show that interference actually takes place, nor is it necessary for the CO to decide on the likelihood of such interference tending towards control. The question for the CO is whether there is a possibility of interference by the employer tending towards control. 'Liable to interference' means 'vulnerable to interference' or being 'exposed to the risk of interference'.[25] This was highlighted in *Government Communications Staff Federation v Certification Officer*.[26] Here a staff association was established at GCHQ after the government withdrew recognition of the unions and banned GCHQ employees from union membership. The EAT concluded that the Staff Federation was vulnerable to interference and that its continuing existence depended upon the approval of the Director of the organisation. It therefore supported the CO's refusal to issue a certificate of independence.

11.4 Contract of membership

When an individual joins a trade union, he or she enters into a contract of membership. It has not always been entirely clear whether that contract is one that is between the trade union and its members or whether it is one between the members of the trade union. In *Bonsor v Musicians Union*[27] a musician was expelled from the Musicians Union and thereafter found it difficult to obtain work. It was held that, although the trade union was an unincorporated body, it was capable of entering into contracts and being sued as a legal entity distinct from its individual members. When Bonsor's application to join was accepted, a contract came into existence with the union. The trade union impliedly agreed that the member would not be excluded by the union or its officers otherwise than in accordance with the rules. When the union broke this contract by wrongfully expelling the individual, it could be sued as a legal entity. Thus there was no reason why Bonsor should not be granted all the remedies against the union which were appropriate for a breach of contract.

Section 10 TULRCA 1992 gives trade unions a 'quasi corporate status'. The union is not a body corporate, except that it is capable of making contracts and suing or being sued in its own name. Any proceedings for an offence alleged to have been committed by it may be brought against it in its own name. Section 11 TULRCA 1992 excludes the common law rules on restraint of trade (see Chapter 12).

The contract of membership serves as the constitution of the trade union. The primary source of the contract is the union rule book, which is likely to cover the rights and obligations of individual

22 Section 9(1) TULRCA 1992.

23 [1977] IRLR 20.

24 See *Association of HSD (Hatfield) Employees v Certification Officer* [1977] IRLR 261, where an organisation was able to satisfy the EAT of its independence.

25 See *The Certification Officer v Squibb UK Staff Association* [1979] IRLR 75 CA.

26 [1993] IRLR 260.

27 [1956] AC 104.

members, the power and composition of various bodies within the union, the purposes for which union funds can be expended and the powers of union officers. The contract between all the members is embodied in the rules of the union. As was stated in *Wise v Union of Shop, Distributive and Allied Workers*,[28] which involved a challenge to a decision of the union executive committee concerning elections:

> A decision which is inconsistent with the rules . . . is a decision . . . to which the member has not given his or her consent. The decision has been made or the election held in a manner which contravenes the contract into which the member has entered by joining the union. Accordingly, as it seems to me, the right of a member to complain of a breach of the rules is a contractual right which is individual to that member; although, of course, that member holds the right in common with all other members having the like right.

Thus, by joining a trade union, the member enters into an agreement and joins with all other members in authorising officers or others to carry out certain functions and duties on their collective behalf. The basic terms of the agreement are to be found in the union's rule book.[29]

As with other contracts, the terms may be modified by custom and practice, although not so as to conflict with the union's rules, and terms can be implied with caution.[30] However, the rules are not to be treated as if they were written by parliamentary draftsmen:

> The rules of a trade union are not to be construed literally or like statute, but so as to give them a reasonable interpretation which accords with what, in the court's view, they must have been intended to mean, bearing in mind their authorship, their purpose, and the readership to which they are addressed.[31]

In *Iwanuszezak v GMBATU*[32] an individual tried to argue that a trade union had an implied obligation to use its collective strength to safeguard an individual member's terms and conditions. In this case a new agreement between employers and the union had rearranged work shift patterns to this person's detriment. The Court of Appeal refused to imply the term, accepting the argument that, where there was a conflict between collective and individual interests, the collective interest must prevail. In every contract of membership there is also a statutorily implied right for the individual to terminate their membership, subject to reasonable notice and reasonable conditions.[33]

There are three situations considered here in which members have statutory rights that can be exercised against their union. These relate to union membership and discipline; rights arising if a union does not comply with the statutory provisions on ballots; and rights arising from the application of funds for political objects.

11.5 Rights in relation to trade union membership and discipline

Until the Industrial Relations Act 1971 there was little statutory regulation limiting a union's powers to admit, discipline or expel a member.[34] Section 65 of this Act introduced rules dealing

---

28 [1996] IRLR 609 at p. 613.
29 See *Heatons Transport (St Helens) Ltd v TGWU* [1972] IRLR 25 HL.
30 See *Porter v National Union of Journalists* [1980] IRLR 404 HL.
31 *Jacques v AUEW (Engineering Section)* [1986] ICR 683.
32 [1988] IRLR 219 CA.
33 Section 69 TULRCA 1992.
34 The Trade Union Act 1913 had established a requirement that a trade union could not refuse admission or discipline solely because of a refusal to contribute to the political fund.

with arbitrary exclusions or expulsions and unfair or unreasonable disciplinary action. Although this section was repealed in 1976, it was reintroduced in the Employment Act 1980 as part of the government's attack on the closed shop.

11.5.1 Exclusion and expulsion

Currently, an individual may not be excluded or expelled from a trade union except for the following reasons.[35] (Note that exclusion means not being admitted to membership.[36])

1. If the individual does not satisfy an enforceable membership requirement.
2. If the individual does not qualify for membership on the grounds that the union only operates in a particular part or parts of Great Britain.
3. If the union's purpose is to regulate the relations with one particular employer, or a number of particular employers, and the individual no longer works for any of those employers.
4. If the exclusion or expulsion is entirely attributable to the individual's conduct (other than 'excluded conduct') and the conduct to which it is wholly or mainly attributable is not 'protected conduct'.

In the first of these exceptions, the 'enforceable membership requirement' means a restriction on membership as a result of employment being in one specific trade, industry or profession; or of an occupational description such as a particular grade or level; or of the need for specific trade, industrial or professional qualifications or work experience. 'Excluded conduct' means:

1. Being or ceasing to be, or having been or ceased to be, a member of another trade union or employed by a particular employer or at a particular place.
2. Conduct to which s. 65 TULRCA 1992 applies.

'Protected conduct' consists of the individual being or ceasing to be, or having been or ceased to be, a member of a political party, unless such membership is contrary to a rule or objective of the trade union.[37] Activities undertaken as a member of a political party are not protected.

These rules necessitated a revision of the 'Bridlington Principles'. These were a set of recommendations agreed at the 1939 Trades Union Congress which were designed to minimise disputes over membership questions.[38] They laid down the procedures by which the TUC dealt with complaints by one union against another and were designed to stop inter-union disputes over membership and representation. In the light of the legislation to inhibit unions from excluding members, introduced by the Trade Union Reform and Employment Rights Act 1993, these principles were revised so as to provide that:

1. Each union should consider developing joint working arrangements with other unions to avoid such conflicts.
2. No union should commence activities at an establishment where another trade union had a majority.
3. There should be no industrial action in an inter-union dispute until the TUC had an opportunity to examine the issue.

---

35 Section 174 TULRCA 1992.
36 See *NACODS v Gluchowski* [1996] IRLR 252.
37 See s. 174(4C–4H) TULRCA 1992.
38 For an example of a TUC disputes committee attempting to resolve issues under the Bridlington Principles, see *Rothwell v APEX* [1975] IRLR 375 CA.

The courts have not always been hostile to union autonomy in relation to membership matters. *Cheall v APEX*[39] involved an individual who was excluded from membership on the orders of the TUC's disputes committee. The relevant union rule stated that 'the executive committee may, by giving 6 weeks' notice in writing, terminate the membership of any member, if necessary to comply with a decision of the disputes committee of the TUC'. The House of Lords rejected the view that this was contrary to public policy. Lord Diplock stated that:

> freedom of association can only be mutual; there can be no right of an individual to associate with other individuals who are not willing to associate with him.

This was clearly not the view of the government, as shown by its subsequent legislation.[40] Individuals may present a complaint to an employment tribunal if they have been excluded or expelled in contravention of s. 174.[41] The tribunal is unable to consider the complaint unless it is presented before the end of six months beginning with the date of exclusion or expulsion, unless it is satisfied that it was not reasonably practicable for the claim to be presented in time.[42] Where a tribunal finds the complaint to be well founded, it will make a declaration to that effect. A subsequent application for compensation can be made to a tribunal but, in order to give the union time to act, the claimant may not make the application for compensation until after four weeks beginning with the date of the declaration. There is also a limit of six months after which an application cannot be made.[43] If the applicant has not been admitted or readmitted, there is a minimum amount that will be awarded by the EAT of £9,118 (in 2017).

Compensation can be reduced if the union member is partly at fault. In *Howard v NGA*[44] an individual was dismissed from a job, in a closed-shop environment, for not being a member of a union. The EAT recognised four heads of compensation: loss of earnings during the period of unemployment, the net loss of earnings resulting from his dismissal, loss of earning opportunity generally as a result of being denied union membership, and non-pecuniary loss. However, the individual had contributed by taking the job in a closed-shop organisation whilst an application for union membership was still under consideration. This resulted in compensation being reduced by 15 per cent. In *Saunders v The Bakers, Food and Allied Workers Union*[45] an applicant resigned from the union over a disagreement about an unofficial strike. The individual later reapplied for membership and was refused. An appeal was made to the national executive committee in writing but the individual failed to attend. The application was rejected and, subsequently, an employment tribunal held this action to be an unreasonable refusal of membership. The EAT agreed with the tribunal when it stated that the individual could have done more to help themselves by attending the meeting of the national executive committee. Compensation was reduced as a result. Similarly, in *Day v SOGAT 1982*[46] it was held that a member's failure to pay their subscription did not contribute to the union's refusal to readmit into membership so as to justify a reduction in compensation. However, the individual's failure to tell the union that he had a new job, which might have led to the return of the union card, had contributed to the situation and this led to a reduction in the amount of compensation.

---

39 [1983] IRLR 215 HL; see also *Edwards v SOGAT* [1971] Ch 354, where a person's right to work in a closed shop was supported by the court.
40 In *ASLEF v UK* [2007] IRLR 361 the European Court of Human Rights ruled that there is no general right to join the union of one's choice irrespective of the rules of the union.
41 Section 174(5) TULRCA 1992.
42 Section 175(a) and (b) TULRCA 1992.
43 Section 176(3) TULRCA 1992. On the possible imposition of financial penalties on employers where there has been a breach of employment rights, see Chapter 4, section 4.2 above.
44 [1985] ICR 101.
45 [1986] IRLR 16.
46 [1986] ICR 640.

It is the union's duty to put the member back into the position that they were in before the wrongful expulsion. This might include arranging for the employee to sign a further mandate to authorise the employer to recommence deductions of union subscriptions, rather than placing the onus on the employee to take the initiative.[47]

11.5.2 Discipline

The courts have the role of applying union disciplinary rules, often in favour of the individual, especially where the offence is of a broad nature – for example, acting in a way which was 'detrimental to the interests of the union'. *Esterman v NALGO*[48] involved the following rule: 'a member who disregards any regulation issued by the branch, or is guilty of conduct which, in the opinion of the executive committee, renders him unfit for membership, shall be liable to expulsion'. The member had refused to obey an instruction not to help with local election organisation. The member successfully obtained an injunction on the grounds that, in these circumstances, no committee could find the individual guilty of the offence. The court doubted whether the union had the power in the first place to stop people doing things outside their normal working hours or from volunteering for duties.

Rules which appear to conflict with public policy can be struck out,[49] as can those requiring action in breach of the rules of natural justice. In *Hamlet v GMBATU*[50] an unsuccessful candidate challenged election results using an internal procedure. The individual claimed a breach of the rules of natural justice when an appeal committee was composed of some of the same people as the body against whose decision the appeal was being made. In this case the court held that the individual had expressly agreed to accept a tribunal with this membership and that an individual 'cannot therefore come bleating to the courts complaining of a breach of natural justice when the contract is carried out expressly according to its terms'. In *Losinska v CPSA*,[51] a union president was able to stop the executive committee and its annual conference from discussing matters critical of themselves on the grounds that both played a part in the union's disciplinary process. They could not therefore be allowed to condemn the individual until that process had taken place.

Section 64(1) TULRCA 1992 states that an individual who is, or has been, a member of a trade union has the right not to be 'unjustifiably disciplined' by that union. A person is disciplined by a union if it takes place under the rules or by a union official or by a number of persons which include an official.[52] Section 64(2) TULRCA 1992 identifies six forms of discipline for these purposes. These include expulsion from the union, payment of a sum to the union, depriving them of access to any services or facilities that they would be entitled to by virtue of belonging to the union, encouraging another union or branch not to accept the individual into membership, and subjecting the individual to some other detriment.[53] Suspension of membership can mean depriving someone of access to the benefits of membership. In *Killorn*[54] an individual was suspended from membership for refusing to cross a picket line. The union also sent out a circular naming her, and others, as being suspended for strike-breaking. Both the suspension and the circular were held to be forms of unjustifiable discipline.

---

47 See *NALGO v Courtney-Dunn* [1992] IRLR 114.
48 [1974] ICR 625.
49 See *Lee v Showmen's Guild* [1952] QB 329, where the court could find no evidence that the members had agreed to a rule which gave an internal body exclusive jurisdiction.
50 [1986] IRLR 293; see also *Radford v National Society of Operative Printers* [1972] ICR 484, where the failure to apply such rules was an issue.
51 [1976] ICR 473.
52 Section 64(2) TULRCA 1992.
53 Section 64(2)(a)–(f) TULRCA 1992.
54 *NALGO v Killorn and Simm* [1990] IRLR 464.

The meaning of 'unjustifiably disciplined' is set out in s. 65 TULRCA 1992. This lists[55] ten types of conduct[56] for which any resulting discipline will be 'unjustified'. This includes failing to participate in or support a strike or other industrial action,[57] or indicating a lack of support for, or opposition to, such action; asserting that the union, an official or a representative of it,[58] has contravened, or is planning to contravene, a requirement under union rules or some other enactment or law;[59] or working with, or proposing to work with, individuals who are not members of the union or who are not members of another union.[60]

An individual who claims to have been unjustifiably disciplined may present a complaint to an employment tribunal within three months of the infringement, unless it was not reasonably practicable for the complaint to be presented in that time.[61] Additionally, if there is a delay resulting from an attempt to appeal against the discipline or have it reviewed or reconsidered,[62] the three-month limit may be extended.[63] This happened in Killorn,[64] where a letter to the union branch chair, in which the complainant raised a series of questions about the suspension, was held to be a 'reasonable attempt' to appeal in accordance with this section. The EAT held that the statute did not lay down any specific method of appealing, so an employment tribunal should consider the reality of the events, rather than look for formal appeal proceedings. It is also necessary to wait until the union has made a final determination, such as expulsion, before making the complaint to an employment tribunal. If there is only a recommendation to the general executive committee of a union that an individual be expelled, that cannot be seen as the final decision. It is not possible to make a claim in respect of an act that might never take place, no matter how much the individual thinks it is likely to happen.[65]

The employment tribunal may make a declaration that the complaint is well founded.[66] The applicant may then make an application to the tribunal for compensation and repayment of any money unjustifiably paid to the union.[67] The employment tribunal may award compensation in line with that for cases of expulsion or exclusion under s. 174 TULRCA 1992 (see above).[68] This can include injury to feelings.[69] It should be noted that the complaint cannot be made before four weeks from the date of the tribunal's declaration and not more than six months beginning with that date.[70]

---

55 Section 65(2)(a)–(j) TULRCA 1992.
56 'Conduct' includes statements, acts or omissions; s. 65(7) TULRCA 1992.
57 See *Knowles v Fire Brigades Union* [1996] IRLR 617 CA, where the complainants failed to prove unjustifiable discipline because the pressure exerted on employers by the union did not amount to industrial action.
58 'Representative' means a person acting or purporting to act in their capacity as a member of the union or on the instructions or advice of a person acting, or purporting to act, in the capacity of an official of the union: s. 65(7) TULRCA 1992.
59 A person is not unjustifiably disciplined if the reason is that they made such assertions vindictively, falsely or in bad faith: s. 65(6) TULRCA 1992.
60 See *Santer v National Graphical Association* [1973] ICR 60, where a trade union expelled a member for working for a firm which did not recognise the union.
61 Section 66(1) and (2) TULRCA 1992.
62 In *McKenzie v NUPE* [1991] ICR 155 it was held to be an implied term of the contract between the union and the member that a disciplinary tribunal should be entitled to reopen a case if new evidence came to light.
63 Section 66(2)(b) TULRCA 1992.
64 [1990] IRLR 464.
65 See *TGWU v Webber* [1990] IRLR 462 and *Beaumont v Amicus* [2007] ICR 341.
66 Section 66(3) TULRCA 1992; s. 66(4) TULRCA 1992 prevents any further proceedings relating to expulsion being brought under this section and s. 174 (see above).
67 Section 67(1) TULRCA 1992.
68 Section 67(5)–(7) TULRCA 1992.
69 See *Bradley v NALGO* [1991] IRLR 159.
70 Section 67(3) TULRCA 1992.

11.6 Statutory obligations in relation to union elections

Strict statutory rules were introduced during the 1980s dealing with the election of certain union officials. The rules stipulated which union offices were to be the subject of regular elections and laid down detailed rules about how those elections were to be conducted. The government at the time stated its intentions:

> There must also be a proper balance between the interests of the unions and the needs of the community . . . individual unionists themselves [are] . . . entitled to see minimum standards established to ensure that union power is exercised more responsibly, more accountably and more in accordance with the views of their members.[71]

Section 46(2) TULRCA 1992 lists those positions for which there is a duty to hold elections at least every five years.[72] However, there is no requirement for a ballot if the election is uncontested.[73] The positions are: (i) a member of the executive, or any position held as a result of being a member of the executive; (ii) president; and (iii) general secretary. The executive is defined as the principal committee of the union exercising executive powers.[74] However, a member of the executive includes any person who may attend or speak at meetings of the executive, excluding technical or professional advisers.[75]

According to s. 119 TULRCA 1992, presidents and general secretaries are the people that hold those offices or the nearest equivalent to them. Those who hold the position of president on an annual basis and are not voting members of the executive or employees of the union and have not held the position in the 12 months before taking up the position, are excluded from the elections requirements.[76] Similarly, such office holders may stay in office for up to a further six months if they fail to be re-elected. This is a period which may 'reasonably be required' to give effect to the election result and aid the transition between office holders.[77]

No member of the trade union can be 'unreasonably' excluded from standing as a candidate, although the union can have eligibility conditions that apply to all members.[78] Thus there is a requirement for objective criteria to be applied in relation to eligibility. In *Ecclestone v National Union of Journalists*[79] a rule provided that 'the NEC [National Executive Committee] shall prepare a shortlist of applicants who have the required qualifications'. The union argued that this gave the executive committee a discretion to decide on the qualifications appropriate to the post. In this case they imposed the qualification that the candidates should have the confidence of the NEC. According to the court, this amounted to the exclusion of a class of members which was determined by reference to whom the union chose to exclude. It was essentially a subjective test which was in breach of s.

---

71 *Democracy in Trade Unions* (HMSO, 1983).
72 Section 46(1)(b) TULRCA 1992, although there is an exception in s. 58 for those within five years of retirement age. In *GMB v Corrigan* [2008] ICR 197 the EAT held that the purpose of s. 46(1) TULRCA 1992 was not to oblige a union to hold an election as soon as a position became vacant but to ensure that anyone in fact holding the position was elected.
73 Section 53 TULRCA 1992.
74 Section 119 TULRCA 1992.
75 Section 46(3) TULRCA 1992. There is a definition of 'voting members of the executive' in s. 46(5) TULRCA 1992.
76 Section 46(4)–(4A) TULRCA 1992.
77 See *Paul v NALGO* [1987] IRLR 43 CO, where a retiring president who continued on the executive for a further year was held to be covered by the transitional arrangements.
78 In *UNISON v Bakhsh* [2009] IRLR 418 the EAT ruled that suspended members are not precluded from standing for office for the purposes of s. 47(3) TULRCA 1992.
79 [1999] IRLR 166; see also *Wise v USDAW* [1996] IRLR 609, where it was held that even if much of the rule governing the election of the general secretary was inconsistent with TULRCA, it would be wrong not to give effect to any of it.

47(3) TULRCA 1992. Good practice requires that selection criteria be laid down in advance of applications so as to avoid arbitrary decisions.

No candidate directly, or indirectly, can be required to be a member of a political party.[80] Although it might be understandable for a Conservative government to impose such a rule on trade unions, it does seem rather an odd one. Presidents or general secretaries of large trade unions are likely to play an active part in the political party to which their union is affiliated.

Every candidate may provide an election address and the union will distribute it to all members entitled to vote. This will be done at no expense to the candidates. The union can decide the length of the address, subject to a minimum of 100 words. All candidates are to be treated equally in this matter. Their material cannot be changed without consent and it is the candidate that incurs any civil or criminal liability arising from the contents of the election address.[81] The entitlement to vote should be accorded equally to all members, although the rules can exclude certain classes, such as unemployed members, those in arrears with their subscriptions, new members and students, trainees or apprentices.[82] In NUM (Yorkshire Area) v Millward[83] an election result was challenged when a group called 'limited members', who were mostly people who had taken early retirement, were excluded from participating. The EAT held that their exclusion was permissible within the union rules, as they were not members for the purpose of voting in ballots. Although they were members of the union and received fringe benefits, they had no right to vote on decisions or stand for office and were only indirect beneficiaries of the purpose of the union.

The union will appoint an independent scrutineer[84] to supervise the production of the ballot papers and their distribution to those entitled to vote. As soon as is reasonably practicable after the end of the ballot period the independent scrutineer will make a report to the union.[85] In Douglas v Graphical, Paper and Media Union[86] the independent scrutineer issued a certificate stating that there were no reasonable grounds for believing that there had been any breach of statutory requirements relating to the ballot. Subsequently, the scrutineer examined a complaint and decided that there had been a breach of the union rules which might have influenced the outcome of the ballot. The union then attempted to set the ballot aside and call a fresh election. The High Court held that there was nothing in its rules that permitted it to do this so the union was acting outside its powers. It was also doubtful whether it was possible to cancel a ballot once the scrutineer had issued their report approving the ballot.[87]

There are detailed rules on the voting process contained within s. 51 TULRCA 1992. The essential features are that: it is to be done by marking a ballot paper; as far as is reasonably practicable, the ballot is to be conducted by post and at no cost to the individual member; the ballot should, as far as is reasonably practicable, enable votes to be cast in secret. In Paul v NALGO[88] the union was held to be in breach of the rule that there should be no cost to the member. Arrangements were made for the ballot papers to be collected from the union district organisers. The responsibility of getting their completed ballot paper to the district organiser was placed on the individual. If a member did not wish to use that system, then they incurred the cost of sending in the vote.

---

80 Section 47(1)–(3) TULRCA 1992.
81 Section 48(1)–(7) TULRCA 1992.
82 Section 50(1)–(2) TULRCA 1992.
83 [1995] IRLR 411.
84 Section 49 TULRCA 1992.
85 Section 52 TULRCA 1992.
86 [1995] IRLR 426.
87 See also Brown v AUEW [1976] ICR 147, where a union called a fresh ballot after some irregularities in the voting process. The new election resulted in a different outcome, but the election was held to be outside the union's powers to call.
88 [1987] IRLR 43 CO.

The ballot is to be conducted so as to enable the result to be determined solely by counting the votes cast for each candidate.[89] This does not necessarily mean that those with the highest votes get elected. For example, if there are rules which state that there is a maximum number of elected representatives for each region, then it will be those with the highest votes in that region who are elected. It does not matter that an unsuccessful candidate in one region might have gained more votes than a successful candidate in another.[90] In *AB v CD*[91] two candidates gained identical numbers of votes in an election using the single transferable vote system. The rules did not provide for such an eventuality. The court implied a term into the union's standing orders that the candidate with the most votes in the initial ballot should be declared the winner.

The remedy for a failure to comply with the statutory requirements is for a person who was a member of the trade union at the time of the election, or a person who was a candidate in the election, to make a complaint to the Certification Officer (CO) or to the High Court within one year of the election result being announced.[92] If the application is to the CO[93] in accordance with s. 55 TULRCA 1992, then the CO has an obligation to ensure, so far as is reasonably practicable, that the matter is determined within six months.[94] On receiving the application the CO will make inquiries and give the applicant and the union the opportunity to be heard.[95] The CO may then make a declaration specifying where the union has failed to comply, giving reasons for the decision in writing.[96] This declaration may be accompanied by an enforcement order requiring a new election or rectification of the fault or a requirement to abstain from specified acts in the future.[97] A declaration or enforcement order made by the CO may be relied upon as if it were an order of the court.[98] Appeals arising from complaints dealt with by the CO are to the EAT.[99]

11.7 Rights related to the application of funds for political objects

The funds of a trade union cannot be used for the furtherance of political objects unless a political resolution is in force. The political resolution needs to be supported by a majority of those voting and needs to be approved at least every ten years.[100] The process of the ballot and the rules governing it are similar to those concerned with ballots for the election of union officials (see above).[101] As a result of Section 11 Trade Union Act 2016, those who join a union after the this section came into effect can only contribute to a political fund if they have opted in[102] and, having done so, they can give a month's notice to cancel their contribution.[103] The employee can certify to their employer

---

89 Section 51(6) TULRCA 1992, although s. 51(7) allows for the single transferable vote system to be used.
90 See R v CO, *ex parte Electrical Power Engineers' Association* [1990] IRLR 398 HL.
91 [2001] IRLR 808.
92 Section 54(1)–(3) TULRCA 1992.
93 Similar provisions concerning applications to the court are dealt with in s. 56 TULRCA 1992.
94 Section 55(6) TULRCA 1992.
95 Section 55(2) TULRCA 1992.
96 Section 55(3) and (5) TULRCA 1992.
97 Section 55(5A) TULRCA 1992.
98 Section 55(8) and (9) TULRCA 1992.
99 Section 56A TULRCA 1992.
100 Section 73 TULRCA 1992.
101 See ss 75–81 TULRCA 1992.
102 The Trade Union Act 2016 (Political funds) (Transition period) Regulations 2017 require union membership application forms to indicate that there is a choice as to whether or not to opt in to the political fund and that there is no detriment for members who choose not to opt in. Reminder notices must be provided annually informing members that they have the right to opt out of the political fund at any time.
103 Section 84 TULRCA 1992.

that they are exempted from such contributions and the employer must then ensure that no deductions are made for that part of the subscription which applies to the political fund.[104] If an employer fails to comply with s. 86 TULRCA 1992, the individual may make a complaint to an employment tribunal within three months of the date of the payment, unless the tribunal accepts that this was not reasonably practicable.[105] The tribunal may make a declaration and/or an order to remedy the failure of the employer. If the employer fails to comply with the order, then the individual may make a further complaint to the tribunal after four weeks and before six months. The tribunal may then order the employer to provide the claimant with up to two weeks' pay.[106]

There also need to be provisions in the union rules for the making of such payments out of a separate fund and for the exemption of any member of the union who objects to contributing to that fund.[107] Section 32ZB TULRCA 1992 requires unions which spend more than £2,000 per annum from its political fund to provide detailed information about this expenditure in their annual return to the Certification Officer. Section 72 TULRCA 1992 provides some definitions of expenditure for political objects. These are:

1. Any contributions[108] to the funds of a political party, or the payment of expenses incurred directly or indirectly by a political party.
2. The provision of any service or property for use by, or on behalf of, a political party.
3. In connection with the registration of electors or the candidature of any person, including the holding of a ballot by the union in connection with any election.
4. On the maintenance of any holder of a political office.[109]
5. The holding of a conference or meeting by, or on behalf of, a political party, including any meetings whose main purpose is the transaction of business in connection with a political party; this includes, according to s. 72(2) TULRCA 1992, any expenditure incurred by delegates to the conference or meeting.[110]
6. On the production, publication or distribution of any literature, document, film, sound recording or advertisement concerned with persuading people to vote, or not to vote, for a particular candidate[111] or political party.

A number of these issues were tested in *ASTMS v Parkin*,[112] where decisions of the CO were appealed against. These related to donations made by the union and are indicative of how strictly the line between the union's general funds and the political fund are drawn. The donations considered here were a contribution from the union's general fund towards the development of the property then used by the Labour Party as its headquarters and a donation from the general fund to the Leader of the Opposition's office at Parliament. The contribution towards the Labour Party offices was made at commercial rates and, the union argued, was a commercial investment. The EAT supported the CO's conclusions that, despite their commercial nature, they were still payments to a political party and fell within the political objectives as set out in what is now s. 72 TULRCA 1992. Similarly, the EAT supported the CO in deciding that the donation to the Opposition Leader's office should not

---

104 Section 86 TULRCA 1992; this applies only if the employer is deducting subscriptions on behalf of the trade union.
105 Section 87(1)–(8) TULRCA 1992.
106 Subject to the definition of a week's pay contained in s. 225 ERA 1996.
107 Section 71(1) TULRCA 1992.
108 Contribution includes affiliation fees or loans made to a political party: see s. 72(4) TULRCA 1992.
109 Political office means the office of Member of Parliament, Member of the European Parliament, or a member of a local authority or any position within a political party: see s. 72(4) TULRCA 1992.
110 See *Richards v NUM* [1981] IRLR 247, where this was held to include the cost of sending delegates and a colliery band to a lobby of Parliament organised by the Labour Party to protest at government cuts.
111 Candidate also includes 'prospective candidates': see s. 72(4) TULRCA 1992.
112 [1983] IRLR 448.

have been made out of the general fund. The maintenance mentioned in the legislation refers to the support of someone as a politician. The union had argued that this interpretation gave too wide a meaning to the term but the EAT held that maintenance covered expenses incurred in carrying out the functions of being a Member of Parliament. Thus a grant to an MP to enable them to conduct research for the purpose of carrying out parliamentary functions is maintenance as an MP and should come out of the political fund.

It should be noted that a union having its own views on political issues and campaigning for them may not be involved in political activities as defined in the statute. *Coleman v Post Office Engineering Union*[113] involved an affiliation fee of £8 to a District Trades Council campaign against government cuts. The CO decided that 'political' meant 'party political'. It was difficult to draw the line between these two concepts but the legislation applied to support of some kind to a political party or to candidates of political parties.

11.8 Breach of rules

Apart from any common law action for breach of contract, a member of a union[114] may apply to the CO for a declaration that there has been a breach, or threatened breach, of rules relating to the following matters:[115]

1. The appointment or election (or the removal) of a person from any office.
2. Disciplinary proceedings by the union (including expulsion).
3. The balloting of members on any issue other than industrial action.
4. The constitution or proceedings of the executive committee or any other decision-making committee.[116]
5. Any other matters specified by the Secretary of State.[117]

Specifically excluded are the dismissal of an employee of the union or any disciplinary proceedings against such an employee.[118] The application must normally be made within six months from the day on which the breach or alleged breach took place. Alternatively, if an internal appeals procedure is invoked, within six months of the end of that procedure or within one year of the invocation of that procedure.[119] A person may not make a complaint both to the CO and the court but may appeal to the courts against the CO's decisions[120] and to the EAT.[121]

The CO may refuse to act unless satisfied that the applicant has taken all available steps to make use of the internal complaints procedure. Thereafter the CO may make whatever inquiries the CO thinks fit and give the applicant and the union the right to be heard. The CO may make a declaration with written reasons and may make an enforcement order to remedy the breach and take such action necessary to stop such a breach happening in the future.

113　[1981] IRLR 427.

114　Or was a member at the time of the alleged breach: s. 108(3) TULRCA 1992.

115　Section 108A TULRCA 1992.

116　Definitions are provided by s. 108A(10)–(12) TULRCA 1992.

117　Section 108A(2) TULRCA 1992.

118　Section 108A(5) TULRCA 1992

119　Section 108A(6)–(7) TULRCA 1992.

120　Section 108A(14) TULRCA 1992.

121　Section 108B(9) TULRCA 1992.

11.9 The Certification Officer's powers under the Trade Union Act 2016

Section 32ZC TULRCA allows the Certification Officer to make a declaration that a union has failed to comply with the annual return requirements introduced by the Trade Union Act 2016 and requires him or her to make an enforcement order unless it is inappropriate to do so. In addition, Schedule 3 TUA 2016 allows the Certification Officer to impose financial penalties, Schedule 2 TUA 1996 enables him or her to exercise a number of enforcement powers without having first received an application from a union member and Schedule 1 TUA 2016 provides the Certification Officer with new investigatory powers, including the appointment of an inspector.

11.10 Discrimination against members and officials

11.10.1 Blacklisting

In March 2010 the Employment Relations Act 1999 (Blacklists) Regulations 2010 came into force.[122] Under these Regulations current and former trade union members can claim at an employment tribunal if they are denied employment, subjected to a detriment or unfairly dismissed for a reason relating to a prohibited list.[123] It is unlawful to compile, use, sell or supply blacklists containing details of those who are or have been union members or who are taking part or have taken part in union activities.[124] In addition, an employment agency is unable to refuse to provide a service because a worker appears on a blacklist. Where these Regulations are breached, compensation can be awarded, including damages for injury to feelings.[125]

11.10.2 Refusal of employment

Part III TULRCA 1992 deals with refusal of employment related to membership of any trade union or membership of a particular trade union.[126] This part contains a number of measures designed to prevent employers or unions introducing measures related to a closed shop. Thus it is unlawful to refuse employment for belonging to, or not belonging to, any union or a particular union. Pressure exerted by a trade union may also result in the union being joined to any employment tribunal proceedings and being liable to pay compensation (see below). For these purposes 'employment' means employment under a contract of employment.[127]

There is no rigid dividing line between membership of a union and taking part in its activities. Thus an applicant who is refused employment because of trade union activities with a previous employer may have been refused because of their membership of a union.[128] Any requirements that a person must take steps to join a union or make payments in lieu connected with membership or non-membership are also unlawful.[129] Persons offered employment on these conditions who refuse it because they do not meet the conditions, or are unwilling to meet the conditions, are treated as

---

122 SI 2010/493.
123 See Smith v United Kingdom [2017] IRLR 771.
124 Regulation 3.
125 Regulation 8. On the possible imposition of financial penalties on employers where there has been a breach of employment rights, see Chapter 4, section 4.2 above.
126 Section 143(3) TULRCA 1992.
127 Section 143(1) TULRCA 1992.
128 See Harrison v Kent County Council [1995] ICR 434; also Fitzpatrick v British Railways Board [1991] IRLR 376 CA which concerned dismissal for previous trade union activities (see below).
129 Section 137(1)(b) TULRCA 1992.

being refused employment for those reasons.[130] Previous practices of putting union membership requirements in advertisements or recruiting from union nominations only are also unlawful.[131]

A person is taken to have been refused employment if, in seeking employment of any description, the potential employer: refuses or deliberately fails to entertain and process the application or inquiry; causes the person to withdraw or cease to pursue the application or inquiry; refuses or deliberately omits to offer employment of that description; makes an offer of such employment on terms which no reasonable employer would offer if they wished to fill the post (and the offer is not accepted); makes an offer of employment, but withdraws it or causes it not to be accepted.[132] Section 138 TULRCA 1992 applies similar rules in respect of employment agencies.

Where a person is refused employment for a reason related to union membership, they may make a complaint to an employment tribunal.[133] The claim needs to be made within three months of the date of the conduct which is complained about, unless the tribunal accepts that it was not reasonably practicable to do so.[134] The date of various types of conduct is defined in s. 139(2) TULRCA 1992:

1.   In the case of an actual refusal of employment, it is the date of that refusal.
2.   In the case of a deliberate omission to entertain or process the application, then the date is the end of a period in which it was reasonable to expect the employer to act.
3.   In the case of conduct causing the applicant to withdraw or stop pursuing an application or inquiry, the date is when that conduct took place.
4.   In the case when the offer was made and then withdrawn, the date is when it was withdrawn.
5.   In any other case where an offer is made, but not accepted, then the date is when the offer was made.[135]

If a tribunal finds that a complaint is justified, then it may award compensation and/or make a recommendation that the employer takes action within a specified period which appears to be reasonable to obviate or reduce the adverse effects on the complainant of the conduct complained of.[136]

11.10.3 Subject to detriment

Section 146 TULRCA provides for workers not to be subject to detriment by any act, or deliberate failure to act, if the act or failure to act takes place for the purpose of:

1.   Preventing or deterring them from seeking to become a member of a trade union,[137] or penalising them for doing so.
2.   Preventing or deterring them from taking part in the activities of the trade union or from making use of trade union services at an appropriate time, or penalising them for doing so.[138]
3.   Compelling them to be or become a member of a trade union, or a particular trade union.[139]

---

130 Section 137(6) TULRCA 1992.
131 Section 137(3) and (4) TULRCA 1992; s. 143(1) gives a wide meaning to the term 'advertisement'.
132 Section 137(5) TULRCA 1992.
133 Section 137(2) TULRCA 1992.
134 Section 139(1) TULRCA 1992.
135 Section 138 TULRCA 1992 applies similar provisions to actions and omissions by employment agencies.
136 Section 140 TULRCA 1992; s. 141 applies similar provisions in respect of employment agencies. On the possible imposition of financial penalties on employers where there has been a breach of employment rights, see Chapter 4, section 4.2 above.
137 In *Ridgway and Fairbrother v National Coal Board* [1987] IRLR 80 CA, it was held that this can mean either an individual trade union or any trade union.
138 See *Bone v North Essex NHS Trust* [2016] IRLR 295.
139 Section 146(1) TULRCA 1992.

4. Enforcing a requirement that in the event of their failing to become, or their ceasing to remain, members of any trade union or a particular trade union or one of a number of particular trade unions, they must make one or more payments. For this purpose, any deduction from remuneration which is attributable to the employee's failure to become, or his ceasing to be, a union member will be treated as a detriment.

Where either party claims that the employer acted under pressure from a third party, for example a union, they may request that the third party be joined to the proceedings. In these circumstances the tribunal may require that any compensation be paid by the third party.[140]

It is not always easy to identify when the purpose of an act or omission falls within s. 146. For example, in *Gallagher v Department of Transport*[141] an employee was elected group assistant secretary of a union. The individual was a higher executive officer in the civil service, but, with the employer's approval, the union duties were effectively full-time. When the employee applied for promotion to the next grade, he was turned down. Previously, in an appraisal, the employee had been told of problems with management skills. As a result of being a union assistant secretary, it was said that there was no way of telling whether these skills had improved. The job also required more management experience than could be gained by being a union activist. The employment tribunal agreed that there had been discrimination on the grounds of union membership and activities. However, the Court of Appeal held that the tribunal had confused cause and effect. The purpose of the procedure was to ensure that those promoted had management skills, not to deter the employee from continuing with union activities, although this may have been the effect.[142] More recently, the Court of Appeal ruled that a detriment relating to trade union activities does not include giving an employee a written warning for failing to comply with a management instruction to discuss the process of identifying time off to engage in union activities.[143]

The detriment is to be interpreted as action against employees as individuals rather than as trade unionists. In *FW Farnsworth Ltd v McCoid*[144] the employee was derecognised by the employer as a shop steward and claimed that this breached s. 146(1)(b) TULRCA 1992. The Court of Appeal held that the words 'as an individual' were inserted into the legislation to exclude collective disputes from the scope of the section. The complainant here was an individual who happened to be a shop steward and so the employer's action was held to be against him as an individual and thus unlawful.[145]

'Penalising' is given a wide meaning and is to be interpreted as subjecting an individual to a disadvantage.[146] Indeed, it is specifically provided that penalising a worker because an independent trade union raises a matter on the member's behalf (with or without the member's consent) falls within the ambit of s. 146 TULRCA 1992. 'Activities' can mean the organising of meetings at an appropriate time. In *British Airways (Engine Overhaul) Ltd v Francis*[147] the employee was a shop steward whose members had an ongoing grievance concerning equal pay. They arranged a meeting during their lunch break. It was not a formal meeting of the branch or of a union committee and the discussion was critical of the union. Nevertheless it was held to be an activity of an independent union. 'Trade union services' means the services made available to the worker by virtue of union membership and 'making use' includes consenting to the raising of a matter by the union on his behalf.[148]

---

140 Section 142 TULRCA 1992.
141 [1994] IRLR 231 CA.
142 See also *Southwark London Borough Council v Whillier* [2001] ICR 142, where a union branch secretary was offered promotion, but no salary increase until she had taken up the new duties; this was held to be a detriment because the individual would have to give up her trade union duties in order to take on these responsibilities.
143 *Gayle v Sandwell NHS Trust* [2011] IRLR 810.
144 [1999] IRLR 626 CA.
145 See also *Ridgway and Fairbrother v National Coal Board* [1987] IRLR 80 CA, which was distinguished in this case.
146 See *Carlson v Post Office* [1981] IRLR 158, where the withdrawal of a car parking permit was sufficient to penalise an individual.
147 [1981] ICR 278.
148 Section 146(2A) TULRCA 1992.

'Appropriate time' means either a time outside working hours or a time within working hours where, 'in accordance with arrangements agreed with or consent given' by the employer, it is permissible to take part in union activities or make use of their services. 'Working hours' means any time, in accordance with the contract of employment, that the individual is required to be at work.[149] This does not necessarily require the express agreement of an employer and arrangements can be of an informal nature.[150] If workers are able to converse whilst working and discuss union membership and activities, there is no reason why an employment tribunal could not come to the conclusion that there was implied consent or implied arrangements for them to talk about union activities.[151] Additionally, being at work is not necessarily the same as working. An employee is entitled to take part in union activities whilst on the employer's premises, but not actually working.[152] Thus tea breaks might be occasions when an employee is being paid, but is not necessarily at work.[153]

A worker may make a complaint to an employment tribunal if they have been subjected to a detriment contrary to s. 146 TULRCA 1992.[154] The complaint needs to be made within three months of the act or failure to which it relates. If there is a series of acts or failures, then the three months runs from the last of them.[155] There is the usual proviso that where the tribunal is satisfied that it was not reasonably practicable to do so, then the period may be extended.[156] In the absence of evidence to the contrary, the employer will be taken to have decided on a failure to act when they perform an act inconsistent with the failure or when a period expires when they might reasonably be expected to have done the failed act, if it was going to be done.[157] The burden of proof is on the employer to show the purpose of the act or the failure to act.[158]

If the tribunal finds the complaint well founded, it may award compensation which reflects any loss suffered by the complainant as a result of the act or failure complained of. This loss will include any expenses reasonably incurred as a result of the act or failure plus the loss of any benefit which the complainant may reasonably be expected to have received but for the act or failure. It may also include compensation for injury to feelings.[159] Compensation is for the injury sustained and is not aimed at punishing the employer.[160] The complainant has a duty to mitigate their losses and the tribunal may take into account any contributory action by the worker towards causing the act or failure complained of.[161]

11.10.4 Inducements relating to membership or activities

Employers may try other ways to influence decisions about joining a trade union. In *Associated Newspapers Ltd v Wilson*[162] the employer ceased to recognise the union for negotiating purposes and encouraged employees to agree individual contracts. Those who did not agree were given a smaller

---

149 Section 146(2) TULRCA 1992.

150 See *Marley Tiles Co Ltd v Shaw* [1978] IRLR 238.

151 See *Zucker v Astrid Jewels Ltd* [1978] IRLR 385.

152 See *Post Office v Union of Post Office Workers* [1974] IRLR 23 HL.

153 *Zucker v Astrid Jewels Ltd* [1978] IRLR 385.

154 Section 146(5) TULRCA 1992. However, this does not apply to employees who have been dismissed (see below).

155 In *Adlam v Salisbury and Wells Theological College* [1985] ICR 786 continued weekly payments of a disputed settlement were held not to be a series of similar actions.

156 Section 147(1) TULRCA 1992.

157 Section 147(3) TULRCA 1992.

158 Section 148(1) TULRCA 1992. See *Serco Ltd v Dahou* [2017] IRLR 81.

159 See *Adams v London Borough of Hackney* [2003] IRLR 402 where £5,000 was awarded for injury to feelings after the withdrawal of an offer of promotion.

160 See *Brassington v Cauldon Wholesale Ltd* [1977] IRLR 479. However, note the possible imposition of financial penalties on employers where there has been a breach of employment rights; see Chapter 4, section 4.2 above.

161 Section 149 TULRCA 1992.

162 [1995] IRLR 258 HL; s. 298 TULRCA 1992 also defines act or action as including omission.

pay rise than those who did. The question was whether this omission was action aimed at deterring employees from being members of a union. The Supreme Court held that the action was not for this purpose but was designed merely to end collective bargaining. The European Court of Human Rights,[163] however, disagreed and held that:

> such conduct constituted a disincentive or restraint on the use by employees of union membership to protect their interests.

As a result there was a failure in the State's positive obligation to secure rights under art. 11 of the Convention.

Section 145A TULRCA 1992 now provides workers with the right not to have an offer made to them by their employer for the sole or main purpose of inducing them:

(i) not to be or seek to become a member of an independent trade union, or
(ii) not to take part in the activities of an independent trade union or make use of union services at an appropriate time, or
(iii) to be or become a member of any trade union at a particular time.[164]

In addition, s. 145B TULRCA 1992 gives members of independent trade unions which are recognised or seeking to be recognised the right not to have an offer made to them if acceptance of the offer would have the 'prohibited result' and the employer's sole or main purpose is to achieve that result. The 'prohibited result' is that any of the worker's terms of employment will not (or no longer) be determined by collective agreement. Claims under s. 145A or 145B TULRCA 1992 must be brought within the usual three-month time period and it will be for the employer to show the main purpose in making the offers.[165] If a complaint is upheld, the employment tribunal must make a declaration to that effect and award £3,907 (in 2017) to the complainant.[166] It is also provided that if an offer made in contravention of s. 145A or 145B is accepted, the employer cannot enforce the agreement to vary terms.[167]

11.10.5 Dismissal on grounds related to membership or activities

A dismissal will be unfair if the reason or the principal reason for it was that the employee: (i) was, or proposed to become, a member of a trade union; (ii) had taken part, or proposed to take part, in the activities of a trade union or make use of union services at an appropriate time; (iii) was not a member of a trade union, or had refused or proposed to refuse to become a member; (iv) had failed to accept an offer in contravention of s. 145A or 145B (see 11.10.4 above).[168] Similarly, if one of the reasons in s. 152(1) TULRCA 1992 is a reason for an individual being selected for redundancy, then this is also likely to be an unfair dismissal.[169] Dismissal on the basis of union activities with a previous employer, when that decision was because of a fear that the employee would engage in further union

---

163 [2002] IRLR 568 ECHR.
164 'Appropriate time', 'trade union services' and 'working hours' have the same meaning as in s. 146 TULRCA 1992 (see above).
165 Sections 145C and 145D TULRCA 1992.
166 On the possible imposition of financial penalties on employers where there has been a breach of employment rights, see Chapter 4, section 4.2 above.
167 Section 145E TULRCA 1992.
168 Section 152(1) TULRCA 1992. 'Appropriate time', 'working hours' and 'trade union services' have the same meaning as in s. 146 (see above).
169 Section 153 TULRCA 1992; see *Driver v Cleveland Structural Engineering Co Ltd* [1994] IRLR 636.

activities, may also be a breach of s. 152 TULRCA 1992.[170] Another example of an employee suffering dismissal as a result of their trade union activities is an individual who spoke on behalf of the union at a company recruitment meeting and made derogatory remarks about the company.[171] However, in the more recent case of *Palomo Sanchez v Spain*,[172] the European Court of Human Rights drew a distinction between criticism and insult and ruled that dismissal for publishing an insulting leaflet was not a violation of either art. 10 or 11 of the European Convention on Human Rights.

The reasons in s. 152(1) are inadmissible for the purposes of Part X ERA 1996; therefore such a dismissal will be automatically unfair. Section 108 ERA does not apply so there is no requirement for a qualifying period of service.[173] Where there is a dismissal by virtue of s. 152(1) or 153 TULRCA 1992, then there is a basic minimum award of compensation, before any reductions under s. 122 ERA 1996.[174]

An employee who presents a complaint to an employment tribunal that they have been dismissed by virtue of s. 152 may also apply for interim relief. This application must be made within seven days of the effective date of termination.[175] If the application is in connection with becoming a member of a union or taking part in the activities of a union,[176] then the tribunal will require a certificate signed by an authorised official[177] stating that the individual was or proposed to become a member of the union and there appeared to be reasonable grounds for the complaint.[178] The tribunal has an obligation to determine the application for interim relief as soon as practicable after receiving it and, where appropriate, the certificate.[179] The employer[180] will be given a copy of the notice and certificate at least seven days before the hearing.[181] The tribunal will ask the employer whether they will reinstate or re-engage the employee. If the answer is positive, the tribunal will make an order accordingly. If the employer fails to attend or refuses to reinstate or re-engage, the tribunal can make an order for continuance of the employee's contract.[182] If the employer fails to comply, the tribunal will award compensation to the employee having regard to the infringement of the employee's right to reinstatement or re-engagement and any loss suffered by the employee as a result of the non-compliance.[183]

 ## Further reading

Ewing, K. 'The Function of Trade Unions' (2005) 34(1) *Industrial Law Journal* 1.
Ewing, K. 'The Implications of the ASLEF Case' (2007) 36(4) *Industrial Law Journal* 425.
Hendy, J. and Ewing, K. 'Trade Unions, Human Rights and the BNP' (2005) 34(3) *Industrial Law Journal* 197.
www.ilo.org – International Labour Organization.
www.tuc.org.uk – Trades Union Congress.

---

170 *Fitzpatrick v British Railways Board* [1991] IRLR 376 CA.
171 *Bass Taverns Ltd v Burgess* [1995] IRLR 596.
172 *Palomo Sanchez v Spain* [2011] IRLR 234.
173 Section 154(1) and (2) TULRCA 1992.
174 Section 156 TULRCA 1992 (£5,970 in 2017). If the dismissal is unfair by virtue of s. 153, then s. 156(2) (reduction for contributory fault) applies. On the possible imposition of financial penalties on employers where there has been a breach of employment rights, see Chapter 4, section 4.2 above.
175 Section 161(1) and (2) TULRCA 1992.
176 Section 152(1)(a)–(b) TULRCA 1992.
177 'Authorised official' is an official of the trade union authorised by it to act for these purposes: s. 161(4) TULRCA 1992.
178 Section 161(3) TULRCA 1992.
179 On the 'pretty good chance of success test', see *London City Airport Ltd v Chacko* [2013] IRLR 610.
180 And any party joined to the proceedings: s. 160 TULRCA 1992.
181 Section 162 TULRCA 1992.
182 Sections 163 and 164 TULRCA 1992.
183 Section 166 TULRCA 1992.

Chapter 12

Collective bargaining and industrial action

Chapter Contents

12.1 Collective agreements

Collective bargaining is a means of achieving a collective agreement. In statutory terms it means any agreement or arrangement made between trade unions and employers relating to a number of specific issues.[1] These issues relate to:

1. Terms and conditions of employment.
2. Engagement, non-engagement, termination or suspension of one or more workers.
3. Allocation of work or duties between workers.
4. Matters of discipline.
5. Membership or non-membership of a trade union.
6. Facilities for officials of trade unions.
7. The machinery for negotiation or consultation.

Sometimes these last two items are treated as a separate 'facilities agreement' between management and trade unions. It should be noted that a collective agreement may be as a result of negotiations in a formal setting or it might be the result of deliberations of a joint consultative committee or other committee which makes recommendations.[2]

12.1.1 Legal enforceability and incorporation

For historical reasons, trade unions have been suspicious of the intervention of the law in industrial relations, and although there is the opportunity for trade unions to enter into legally binding agreements with employers, few actually do so. Collective agreements are presumed not to be legally enforceable contracts, unless the agreement is in writing and contains a provision which states that the parties intend the agreement to be a legally enforceable contract.[3] Any agreement which does satisfy these provisions will be 'conclusively presumed to have been intended by the parties to be a legally enforceable contract'.[4] It is also possible to enter into an agreement where only part is designated as being legally enforceable. In such circumstances the part which is not legally enforceable may be used in interpreting the part that is.[5]

The intentions of the parties appear to be crucial, and unless that intention to enter into a legally enforceable agreement is clear, then there is likely not to be such an agreement. The collective agreement needs to show that, at the very least, the parties have directed their minds to the issue of legal enforceability and have decided in favour of such an approach. Without this there will be an insufficient statement of intent for the purposes of the statute.[6] The court may take into account the surrounding circumstances and even the general climate of opinion about this issue when the agreement is made. In *Ford Motor Co Ltd v Amalgamated Union of Engineering and Foundry Workers*[7] the court found the generally unanimous climate of opinion as relevant. It cited (from Flanders and Clegg) an extract[8] which described the general view at the time:

---

1 Section 178(1) TULRCA 1992; the issues included are listed in s. 178(2).
2 See *Edinburgh Council v Brown* [1999] IRLR 208, which concerned a local authority joint consultative committee.
3 Section 179(1) TULRCA 1992.
4 Section 179(2) TULRCA 1992.
5 Section 179(4) TULRCA 1992.
6 See *National Coal Board v National Union of Mineworkers* [1986] IRLR 439, which concerned whether a 1946 agreement on consultation was legally binding; the court held that there would need to be evidence that the parties had at least directed their minds to the question and decided on legal enforceability.
7 [1969] 2 QB 303.
8 A. Flanders and H. Clegg, *The System of Industrial Relations in Britain* (Blackwell, 1954), p. 56.

> This appears to be the case with collective agreements. They are intended to yield 'rights' and 'duties', but not in the legal sense; they are intended, as it is sometimes put, to be 'binding in honour' only, or (which amounts to very much the same thing) to be enforceable through social sanctions but not through legal sanctions.

This view that collective agreements are binding in honour and are subject to social sanctions, rather than legal sanctions, still reflects the climate of opinion.

It is possible for the terms of collective agreements to become legally binding through the route of incorporation into the individual contract of employment (see also Chapter 3). This can be achieved expressly or impliedly. Express incorporation is most effectively achieved by including a term of the contract of employment which refers to the collective agreement.[9] If a collective agreement is not expressly incorporated in this way or by some other form of agreement, then the courts may be prepared to give it legal effect via implied incorporation. It is possible that this may be done on the basis of custom and practice but the collective agreement would need to be well known and established practice and to be 'clear, certain and notorious'.[10]

Garratt v Mirror Group Newspapers Ltd[11] concerned whether there was a term implied by long usage to enter into a compromise agreement as a condition for receiving enhanced redundancy payments. The Court of Appeal relied on *Albion Automotive Ltd v Walker*[12] which set out the factors to be considered in deciding whether a unilateral management policy had become incorporated into the contract of employment. The factors were:

- whether the policy was drawn to the attention of employees;
- whether it was followed without exception for a substantial period;
- the number of occasions on which it was followed;
- whether payments were made automatically;
- whether the nature of the communication of the policy supported the inference that the employers intended to be contractually bound;
- whether the policy was adopted by agreement;
- whether the employees had a reasonable expectation that the enhanced payment would be made;
- whether the terms were incorporated into a written agreement;
- the understanding and knowledge of the employer and the employees.

Alexander v Standard Telephones & Cables Ltd[13] concerned a claim that a redundancy procedure had become incorporated into individuals' contracts of employment. The High Court summarised the principles to be applied in deciding whether there had been incorporation of a part of the collective agreement. These were as follows:

1. The relevant contract is that between the individual employee and the employer.
2. It is the contractual intention of these two parties that needs to be ascertained.

---

9 See *Whent v T Cartledge* [1997] IRLR 153, in which the issue was whether the national agreement had transferred to a new employer as a result of reg. 6 Transfer of Undertakings Regulations 1981, SI 1981/1794 (see Chapter 10). This was subsequently limited to the collective agreement in force at the time of the transfer by the Court of Appeal in *Parkwood Leisure Ltd v Alemo-Herron* [2010] IRLR 298.

10 *Duke v Reliance Systems Ltd* [1982] IRLR 347; in *Henry v London General Transport Services Ltd* [2002] IRLR 472 CA the court held that there is no requirement for 'strict proof' of custom and practice; the burden is on the balance of probabilities.

11 [2011] IRLR 591.

12 [2002] All ER (D) 170 (Jun).

13 [1991] IRLR 286.

3. In so far as that intention is found in the written document, then the document must be construed on ordinary contractual principles.[14]
4. If there is no such document, or if it is unclear, then the contractual intention has to be inferred from other available material, including the collective agreement.

In *Kaur v MG Rover Ltd*[15] it was held that a provision in a collective agreement stating that there would be 'no compulsory redundancy' was not incorporated. According to the Court of Appeal, in conjunction with the words of incorporation, it is necessary to consider whether any particular part of the document is apt to be a term of a contract of employment. Looking at the words in their context, it was decided that they were expressing an aspiration rather than a right. However, the fact that a document is presented as a collection of 'policies' does not preclude their having a contractual effect if, by their nature and language, they are apt to be contractual terms. Thus a provision which is part of a remuneration package may be apt for construction as a contractual term even if couched in terms of information or explanation, or expressed in discretionary terms. Provisions for enhanced redundancy pay would seem to be particularly appropriate for incorporation.[16]

Once the collective agreement has become incorporated into the contract it is not open to the employer unilaterally to alter it.[17] It is only when terms are altered by agreement that individual contracts of employment can be lawfully varied. If the collective agreement is unilaterally varied or the employer withdraws from it, the contracts of employment containing the provisions are likely to remain intact.[18] The possible exception to this is when there are provisions which allow the employer to vary the terms. If there is a collective agreement which allows an employer to vary part of the contents unilaterally, then the fact that it has become part of the contract of employment will not inhibit this option.[19] One issue here is whether the employer's authority is limited as a result of an agreement reached mutually with employee representatives. In *Cadoux v Central Regional Council*[20] an employer introduced rules after consultation with the relevant trade unions. This consultation was different from an agreement and the employers retained the right to alter their own rules.

Employees are assumed to know of the contents of a collective agreement negotiated with a trade union. In *Gray Dunn & Co Ltd v Edwards*[21] an employee was dismissed only three weeks after the signing of an agreement which included the provision that being at work whilst under the influence of alcohol was a serious misdemeanour which could result in summary dismissal. The EAT stated that there could be no stability in industrial relations if an employee could claim that an agreement did not apply to them on the basis that they had not heard of it or its contents. This suggests that the trade union is acting as the agent of the member in reaching an agreement with an employer that becomes part of the contract of employment. The problem with this approach is, of course, that non-union members would not be bound by such an agreement as the trade union could not act as their agent.[22] Such an approach has not been followed, but it does raise an interesting question in relation to employees who are not members of the trade union with whom the

---

14 See also *Lee v GEC Plessey Telecommunications* [1993] IRLR 383, where the court considered whether consideration had passed from the employees for the enhanced redundancy terms contained in a collective agreement which was incorporated into the contract of employment.
15 [2005] IRLR 40.
16 *Keeley v Fosroc Ltd* [2006] IRLR 961.
17 See *Gibbons v Associated British Ports* [1985] IRLR 376.
18 See *Robertson and Jackson v British Gas Corporation* [1983] IRLR 302; also *Gascol Conversions Ltd v JW Mercer* [1974] IRLR 155 CA which concerned conflicting national and local agreements.
19 See *Airlie v City of Edinburgh District Council* [1996] IRLR 516.
20 [1986] IRLR 131.
21 [1980] IRLR 23.
22 See *Heatons Transport (St Helens) Ltd v TGWU* [1972] IRLR 25 HL.

collective agreement is negotiated. In *Singh v British Steel Corporation*[23] a group of employees had not received any document which indicated that their system of working could be changed by the employer without consulting them or by consulting a trade union, whether or not they belonged to it. At the time that the employers negotiated a new shift arrangement these particular employees were not members of the trade union concerned. Neither did the employment tribunal find it possible to imply any term entitling the employer to vary the contract. Without an express or implied term binding the individuals to the collective agreement, the variation in working arrangements could not be said to apply to them. The effect is similar to an employer's unilateral variation.

In certain situations the courts are willing to be assertive in their remedies. *Anderson v Pringle of Scotland Ltd*[24] concerned a decision about whether an agreed 'last in, first out' redundancy procedure should be followed as a result of incorporation or whether the employer could introduce a different selection method. In order to stop the employees being made redundant under the new procedure the court was willing to grant an interdict (injunction) restraining the employers from changing the selection procedure, even though this might amount to an order for specific performance. In this case the court felt that there was still no lack of trust and confidence in the employee by the employer. There may also be some judicial reluctance to fill gaps in collective agreements. Thus, where a collective agreement leaves a topic uncovered, the inference is not that there has been an omission so obvious as to require judicial intervention. The assumption should be that it was omitted deliberately for reasons such as the item being too controversial or too complicated.[25]

12.2 Recognition

Recognition of a trade union or trade unions by an employer or employers is defined in s. 178(3) TULRCA 1992. It means recognition for the purposes of collective bargaining and therefore is likely to be recognition in respect of one or more of the items listed in s. 178(2) (see above). Recognition need not be for the purposes of all these items, but can be partial in the sense that it is only for specific purposes. It appears to require a positive agreement between the parties:

> An act of recognition is such an important matter involving such serious consequences on both sides, both for the employers and the union, that it should not be held to be established unless the evidence is clear upon it, either by agreement or actual conduct clearly showing recognition.[26]

It would be difficult for a trade union to claim implied recognition if the employer had expressly refused recognition for collective bargaining purposes. Recognition is not given because the employer responds to points raised by union representatives, neither is it to be implied from the fact that a union provides health and safety representatives or is a member of a national body, which is not the employer, that is concerned with terms and conditions of employment.[27]

Recognition implies that an employer is willing to recognise a trade union as the legitimate representative of the workforce. There are a number of benefits which accrue to the union as a result of this recognition. There are rights associated with: being given time off for trade union duties and activities;[28] consultation over a number of matters, such as transfers of undertakings, collective redundancies and health and safety matters; and the disclosure of information for collective bargaining purposes.[29]

---

23 [1974] IRLR 131.
24 [1998] IRLR 64.
25 See *Ali v Christian Salvesen Food Services Ltd* [1997] IRLR 17 CA.
26 *National Union of Gold, Silver & Allied Trades v Albury Brothers Ltd* [1978] IRLR 504 CA at p. 506.
27 See *Cleveland County Council v Springett* [1985] IRLR 131.
28 See ss 168–170 TULRCA 1992.
29 See ss 181–184 TULRCA 1992.

Prior to the Employment Relations Act 1999, the decision as to whether to recognise a trade union belonged to the employer.[30] Perhaps as a result of this the majority of workplaces in the United Kingdom have no coverage by collective agreement at all.

12.2.1 A legal framework

There have been previous attempts at government intervention to ensure that recognition disputes were settled without disruption. The Industrial Relations Act 1971 was a Conservative government's attempt to provide a comprehensive legal framework for industrial relations. It allowed employers, trade unions and the government to refer recognition disputes to a Commission for Industrial Relations.[31] This body was able to make recommendations on whether a union should be recognised for a particular bargaining unit. The legislation largely failed because of the unwillingness of the trade unions to co-operate. The Employment Protection Act 1975, passed by a Labour government, changed the approach. Section 11 allowed an independent trade union to apply to ACAS to resolve a recognition dispute. ACAS was allowed to organise a workforce ballot and then make recommendations for recognition.[32] Failure to follow an ACAS recommendation could lead to a referral to the Central Arbitration Committee (CAC), which could then make an award on the terms and conditions that might have been agreed if those negotiations had taken place. This award would be incorporated into the contracts of employment of the employees concerned.[33] This process had only limited success. Between 1976 and 1980 there were 1,610 referrals to ACAS of which some 82 per cent were resolved voluntarily without resort to the s. 11 procedure.

A number of problems were associated with the Employment Protection Act 1975 and inhibited its success. First, some employers refused to co-operate. In one dispute, concerning Grunwick Processing Laboratories Ltd, the employers refused to supply ACAS with the names and addresses of their employees, which resulted in ACAS being unable to carry out its statutory duty under s. 14(1) Employment Protection Act 1975 to ascertain the views of the employees. The result was that the recognition process was thwarted.[34] Second, there were difficulties in dealing with inter-union disputes, where more than one trade union claimed recognition on behalf of a group of workers. In *Engineers' and Managers' Association v ACAS*[35] there was just such a dispute between two unions. ACAS had deferred its decision on recognition and the House of Lords upheld its right to do so if the deferral would help promote good industrial relations. Third, there were problems associated with defining acceptable bargaining units which would also help foster good industrial relations. ACAS had to deal with situations where there was a demand for representation within a particular unit, but fragmentation of larger units into smaller ones might not be conducive to better industrial relations.[36] Finally, there were problems associated with the length of time the process took[37] and with employers attempting to influence the outcome of the recognition ballots.

All these problems have been addressed in the statutory recognition procedures contained in Sch. A1 TULRCA 1992. An awareness of these potential problems is important in understanding the reasons for some of the procedures contained in the Schedule.

---

30 An exception to this is in the Transfer of Undertakings Regulations 2006, SI 2006/246, where reg. 6 provides for any trade union recognition by the transferor to be transferred to the transferee. This seems a rather strange requirement as it is then open to the transferee to exercise the right to derecognise the union.
31 See *Ideal Casements Ltd v Shamsi* [1972] ICR 408 on the effect of the legislation in a dispute over recognition.
32 Sections 14 and 15 Employment Protection Act 1975.
33 Section 16 Employment Protection Act 1975.
34 See *Grunwick Processing Laboratories Ltd v ACAS* [1978] 1 All ER 338 HL.
35 [1980] ICR 215 HL.
36 See *ACAS v United Kingdom Association of Professional Engineers* [1980] IRLR 124 HL.
37 Ibid.

12.2.2 Statutory recognition

Section 70A TULRCA 1992 gives effect to Sch. A1 which is concerned with the recognition of trade unions for collective bargaining purposes. Collective bargaining here has a more limited meaning than that contained in s. 178 TULRCA 1992 (see above). For the purpose of statutory recognition, collective bargaining means, unless otherwise agreed by the parties, negotiations concerned with pay, hours and holidays only.[38] However, 'pay' does not include terms relating to a person's membership of or rights under, or the employer's contributions to, either an occupational or personal pension scheme.[39] What exactly was the scope of 'pay, hours and holidays' was discussed in *BALPA v Jet2.com*.[40] The case concerned whether an airline's rostering schedule for pilots could be included. The employer argued that only those negotiations about proposals affecting specific contractual rights of employees should be included. The rostering schedule included some of these but also included other matters not subject to incorporation into the contract of employment. The Court of Appeal rejected this argument and stated that there was no reason why the phrase 'pay, hours or holidays' should not include negotiations about non-contractual issues.

The schedule was brought into effect on 6 June 2000.[41] The procedures contained in it for claiming recognition are long and complex. Below is a summary of the essentials of part of the recognition process, which shows the underlying principles. The principles underlying the procedures are that:

1. The measures apply to independent trade unions only (see Chapter 11).[42]
2. Trade unions will need to demonstrate 'baseline support'.[43]
3. The subsequent vote must demonstrate widespread support.[44]
4. The bargaining unit needs to be clearly defined.[45]
5. There are exceptions for small businesses.[46]
6. There is a right to derecognition.[47]
7. The time that the process will take should be clear.[48]

12.2.2.1 The request for recognition[49]

The process must begin with the trade union or unions seeking recognition making a request for recognition to the employer.[50] This request must be in writing and it must identify the union or unions concerned and the bargaining unit. It must also state that the request is made under Sch. A1.[51] However, an application is inadmissible if there is already in force a collective agreement under which the employer recognises another union as entitled to conduct collective bargaining on behalf of the workers concerned.[52] This may be the case even if the recognised union is not an 'independent' one as defined in the Act.[53] If more than one union is applying for recognition, the

---

38 Schedule A1 para. 3 TULRCA 1992.
39 Schedule A1 para. 3 TULRCA 1992.
40 *BALPA v Jet2.com* [2017] IRLR 233.
41 Employment Relations Act 1999 (Commencement No 6 and Transitional Provisions) Order 2000, SI 2000/1338.
42 Schedule A1 para. 6 TULRCA 1992.
43 Schedule A1 para. 13(5) TULRCA 1992 for a description of 'the 10% test'.
44 Schedule A1 para. 29 TULRCA 1992.
45 Schedule A1 paras 18–19F TULRCA 1992.
46 Schedule A1 para. 7 TULRCA 1992.
47 See Sch. A1 Part IV TULRCA 1992.
48 See e.g. Sch. A1 para. 10(6) and (7) TULRCA 1992.
49 Derecognition is covered by similar provisions contained in Sch. A1 Parts IV–VI TULRCA 1992.
50 Schedule A1 para. 4 TULRCA 1992.
51 Schedule A1 para. 8 TULRCA 1992.
52 See Sch. A1 para. 35 TULRCA 1992 and *R v Central Arbitration Committee* [2006] IRLR 54.
53 As in *Pharmacists Defence Association Union v Boots Management Services Ltd* [2017] IRLR 355.

applications will not be admissible unless the unions show that they will co-operate with each other and that, if the employer so wishes, they will enter into collective bargaining arrangements which ensure that they will act together.[54]

Schedule A1 para. 7 provides the exception for small businesses. The employer, together with any associated employers, needs to employ at least 21 workers on the day the request for recognition is received, or an average of 21 workers over the 13 weeks ending with this day.

12.2.2.2 Parties agree

There are clearly defined periods of time in which events should take place, which are contained in Sch. A1 para. 10(6) and (7). The first period is one of ten working days commencing on the day after the employer received the request for recognition. The second period commences on the day after the first period ends and lasts for 20 working days or such longer time as the parties agree.

Thus, if before the end of the first period the parties agree on the bargaining unit and that the trade union is to be recognised, then there are no further steps to be taken under this schedule. If the employer informs the union, before the end of the first period, that they do not accept the request, but are willing to negotiate, then they may do so. Provided that they reach agreement before the end of the second period, no further steps will need to be taken under this Schedule.

12.2.2.3 Employer rejects request or negotiations fail

If, by the end of the first period, the employer has either failed to respond to the request or has rejected the request and refused to negotiate, then the union may apply to the CAC[55] for the determination of two questions. These are:

1. Whether the proposed bargaining unit is appropriate.
2. Whether the union or unions has or have the support of the majority of workers in the proposed bargaining unit.[56]

If the negotiations have not succeeded by the end of the second period, then the union or unions may apply to the CAC for the determination of the same two questions. Additionally, if the parties agree the bargaining unit, but fail to agree on whether the union or unions should be recognised to represent it, then the union may only apply to the CAC for an answer to the second question on whether it has the majority support of the workers in that bargaining unit.[57]

There is some pressure on the trade union to negotiate as well as the employer. If, within the first period of ten days, the employer requests the help of ACAS during the negotiations and the unions reject that help or fail to accept the employer's proposal for the help of ACAS, then the union will lose its right to put the questions to the CAC.[58]

12.2.2.4 Acceptance of application[59]

The CAC must give notice of receipt of an application. The CAC must decide, within the 'acceptance period', whether any of the applications received fulfil the 10 per cent test, contained in Sch. A1 para. 14(5) TULRCA 1992. This test is satisfied if at least 10 per cent of the workers constituting a relevant bargaining unit are members of the trade union applying for recognition. The acceptance

54 Schedule A1 para. 37 TULRCA 1992.
55 In the year 2006/7 the CAC received 64 applications concerning trade union recognition under Sch. A1 Part I. See CAC Annual Report 2006/7.
56 Schedule A1 para. 11(1) and (2) TULRCA 1992.
57 Schedule A1 para. 12(1)–(4) TULRCA 1992.
58 Schedule A1 para. 12(5) TULRCA 1992.
59 Schedule A1 paras 13–15 TULRCA 1992.

period is ten working days from the receipt of the last application or such longer period as the CAC specifies, giving reasons. If the 10 per cent test is satisfied by more than one applicant union or none of them, the CAC will not proceed. There is a clear message that there needs to be baseline support for one trade union and that the CAC is not the body to decide which union is to be given recognition where more than one meet this basic test. If the CAC decides that one union meets the test, then it will proceed with that union.

12.2.2.5 Appropriate bargaining unit[60]

Once the CAC has decided to accept an application it has an obligation to try to help the parties to reach agreement as to what the appropriate bargaining unit is, if they have not already agreed. This must be done within 20 working days, starting with the day after that on which the CAC has given notice of acceptance, or a longer period specified by the CAC by notice and with reasons.[61] After the end of this period the CAC has ten days in which it must decide on the appropriate bargaining unit, or a longer specified period by notice and with reasons.[62]

There is a set of criteria contained in Sch. A1 para. 19B(2)–(3), which the CAC must use in arriving at its decision. These are the need for the bargaining unit to be compatible with effective management and, so far as they do not conflict with that need:

1. The views of the employer and the trade union or unions.
2. Existing national and local bargaining arrangements.
3. The desirability of avoiding small or fragmented bargaining units within an undertaking.
4. The characteristics of the workers falling within the proposed bargaining unit and any other workers the CAC considers relevant.
5. The location of the workers.

It is expressly provided that the CAC must take into account the employer's view about any other bargaining unit it considers would be appropriate.[63]

Netjets Management v CAC[64] contained a situation where the employer claimed that it had no workers in the proposed bargaining unit in respect of whom the statutory recognition procedure could apply. The proposed bargaining unit was to include all the pilots employed by the company. The employer submitted that only a minority of its pilots were located in the UK and that, amongst other matters, instructions were issued by the Lisbon headquarters of the company where all HR issues were managed. The High Court disagreed and said that it was not appropriate to take into account the individual characteristics of individual employees when considering collective bargaining rights. The focus should be on the workers as a group. The link with the UK was sufficiently strong for the union to be allowed to use the legislation to seek bargaining rights.

The appeal in *LIDL v GMB*[65] essentially concerned the third of the matters that the CAC needed to take into account (see above), which was the 'desirability of avoiding small fragmented bargaining units'. Recognition as a bargaining unit had been sought by LIDL's warehouse staff in Bridgend. They made up a total of 273 employees – that is, just 1.2 per cent of the employer's 18,203 employees. The employer had argued that 'it was not compatible with effective management to fragment the workforce in this way'. The Court, however, accepted the argument that it was a sole unit – that is, not a large unit being fragmented into parts.

---

60 Schedule A1 paras 18–19 F TULRCA 1992.
61 Schedule A1 para. 18(2) but note also para. 18(3)–(7) TULRCA 1992. Paragraph 18A introduced a duty on employers to supply information to the union.
62 Schedule A1 paras 19(2) and (4) and 19A(2) and (4) TULRCA 1992.
63 Schedule A1 para. 19(4) TULRCA 1992. See *R v Central Arbitration Committee, ex parte Kwik-Fit Ltd* [2002] IRLR 395.
64 *Netjets Management Ltd v Central Arbitration Committee and Skyshare* [2012] IRLR 986.
65 [2017] EWCA Civ 328.

12.2.2.6 Union recognition[66]

Once the issue of the bargaining unit is resolved, the CAC may then move on to the question of recognition. If it is satisfied that the majority of the workforce in the bargaining unit are members of the union or unions, the CAC will issue a declaration that the union or unions are recognised for collective bargaining purposes.[67] However, this will not be done if any one of three qualifying conditions are met. These are that:

1. A ballot will be in the interests of good industrial relations.
2. The CAC has credible evidence from a significant number of union members within the bargaining unit that they do not want the union or unions to conduct collective bargaining on their behalf.
3. Evidence is produced that leads the CAC to conclude that a significant number of union members within the bargaining unit do not wish to be represented by the union or unions.[68]

If any of these qualifying conditions are met, the CAC will give notice to the parties that it intends to organise a ballot to discover whether the workers in the bargaining unit wish the union or unions to conduct collective bargaining on their behalf. The cost of the ballot is to be borne half by the employer and half by the union or unions.

The ballot must be conducted by a qualified and independent person appointed by the CAC.[69] It will take place within 20 working days starting with the day after the independent person is appointed or longer if the CAC so decides. The CAC may decide whether to organise a workplace ballot or a postal ballot, or a combination of the two. It will determine the method by taking into account the likelihood of a workplace ballot being affected by unfairness or malpractice and the costs and practicality of the alternatives, as well as any other factors it considers appropriate.[70]

There are five duties placed upon an employer who has been informed that a ballot is to take place. These are:

1. To co-operate generally in connection with the ballot, with the union or unions and with the person appointed to conduct the ballot.
2. To give the union or unions access to the workforce constituting the bargaining unit for the purposes of informing them about the ballot and seeking their support. The government Code of Practice recommends that the parties reach an access agreement which will include the union's programme for when, where and how it will access the workers and will also provide a mechanism for resolving disagreements.[71]
3. To provide the CAC, within ten working days, with the names and home addresses of the workers concerned and to inform the CAC subsequently of the names and addresses of any new workers or those who cease to be employed.
4. To refrain from making workers an unreasonable offer which has or is likely to have the effect of inducing them not to attend a meeting between the union and the workers in the bargaining unit.

---

66 Schedule A1 paras 20–29 TULRCA 1992.
67 See *Fullarton Computer Industries Ltd v Central Arbitration Committee* [2001] IRLR 752.
68 Schedule A1 para. 22(4) TULRCA 1992.
69 See the Recognition and Derecognition Ballots (Qualified Persons) Order 2000, SI 2000/1306 which names a number of suitable persons, such as the Association of Electoral Administrators.
70 Schedule A1 para. 25 TULRCA 1992.
71 Code of Practice on Access to Workers during Recognition and Derecognition Ballots, issued under s. 203 TULRCA 1992; the Code imposes in itself no legal obligations, but any of its provisions may be taken into account in any proceedings before the CAC or any court or tribunal: s. 207 TULRCA 1992.

5. To refrain from taking any action solely or mainly on the grounds that a worker attended or took part in a meeting between the union and workers in the bargaining unit or indicated an intention to attend or take part in such a meeting.[72]

If the employer fails in any of these duties, the CAC may order the employer to take steps to remedy the situation within a certain time. If the employer fails to comply with this order, then the CAC may cancel the ballot and declare the union or unions recognised for the purposes of collective bargaining in respect of the bargaining unit.[73]

Once the result of the ballot is known the CAC must inform the parties of the result. If the ballot result is that the union is supported by a majority of the workers voting and at least 40 per cent of the workers constituting the bargaining unit, then the CAC will declare the union recognised. If the result is otherwise, the CAC will issue a declaration stating that the union is not recognised.

12.2.2.7 Consequences of recognition[74]

If the CAC has made a declaration for recognition, the parties have a 'negotiation period' to agree a method by which they will conduct collective bargaining. This negotiation period is 30 working days starting with the day after they have been informed of the declaration, or a longer period if the parties agree. If the parties do not agree in the period, then they can ask the CAC for assistance. The CAC will assist for a period of 20 working days or longer, with the agreement of the parties, if the CAC so decides. After this period, if the parties still fail to agree, the CAC will specify the method.[75] Unless the parties agree otherwise, this specified method will have the effect of being a legally binding contract, which can be enforced through an order for specific performance. If, however, the parties negotiate and agree a method of collective bargaining between themselves and one party fails to keep to the agreement, then they may apply to the CAC for assistance. The CAC will then treat the parties in the same way as if they had failed to reach agreement in the first place.[76]

If the CAC has declared that the unions should not be recognised, then those same unions cannot apply again within a period of three years if the bargaining unit remains substantially the same.[77]

12.2.2.8 Changes affecting the bargaining unit

Schedule A1 Part II TULRCA 1992 is concerned with providing the CAC with similar powers for situations where the parties have entered into voluntary arrangements and agreed on recognition and the bargaining unit. Part III is concerned with the issue of a changing bargaining unit which can have important consequences for the recognition process. If the employer or the union or unions believe that the original bargaining unit is no longer appropriate they may apply to the CAC to make a decision as to what is an appropriate unit. The CAC will consider such an application only if it decides that the original unit is no longer appropriate because there has been: a change in the organisation or structure of the business; a change in the activities pursued by the employer; or a substantial change in the number of workers employed in the original unit. The CAC will then decide on whether the original unit is still appropriate. If it decides that it is not, then it will decide which new unit is appropriate. If necessary, it will then repeat the process of assessing whether a union or unions passes or pass the membership test and proceed to a new ballot.

---

72 Schedule A1 para. 26 TULRCA 1992. See Sch. A1 para. 27A TULRCA 1992 on unfair practices in relation to recognition ballots.
73 Schedule A1 para. 27 TULRCA 1992.
74 Schedule A1 paras 30–32 TULRCA 1992.
75 In specifying the method the CAC will take into account in exercising its powers the method specified in the Trade Union Recognition (Method of Collective Bargaining) Order 2000, SI 2000/1300.
76 See UNIFI v Union Bank of Nigeria plc [2001] IRLR 712.
77 Schedule A1 para. 40 TULRCA 1992; the same rule applies to derecognition claims by employers: see Sch. A1 para. 121 TULRCA 1992.

12.2.2.9 Detriment and dismissal

Schedule A1 Part VIII TULRCA 1992 provides protection from detriment by any act, or failure to act, of the employer if it takes place, or fails to take place, on the grounds that the worker:

1. Acted with a view to obtaining or preventing recognition of a union.
2. Indicated support or lack of support for recognition.
3. Acted with a view to securing or preventing the ending of bargaining arrangements.
4. Indicated support or lack of support for the ending of bargaining arrangements.
5. Influenced, or sought to influence, the way votes were cast.
6. Influenced, or sought to influence, other workers to vote or abstain.
7. Voted in such a ballot.
8. Proposed to do, failed to do, or proposed to decline to do any of the above.[78]

A ground does not fall within these categories if it constitutes an unreasonable act or omission by the worker.[79] The only remedy is a complaint to an employment tribunal[80] within three months of the act or failure to act to which the complaint relates, or such further period as the tribunal considers reasonable.[81] If the tribunal finds the complaint well founded, it may make a declaration and award compensation, which may be reduced if the employee contributed in any way to the action complained of.[82]

The same grounds are contained in Sch. A1 para. 161 in relation to dismissal, with the same proviso that a reason does not fall within these grounds if it constitutes an unreasonable act or omission by the employee. Thus a dismissal for any of these reasons will be automatically unfair for the purposes of Part X ERA 1996. If a worker who is not an employee is dismissed, compensation would be subject to the same rules as those for employees who are unfairly dismissed.[83] Similarly, dismissal for reasons of redundancy will be an unfair dismissal if the grounds are any of those listed above.[84]

12.2.2.10 Training

If a trade union has become recognised as a result of the process in Sch. A1 and the method of collective bargaining has been specified by the CAC, then the employer is under an obligation to invite the trade union to send representatives to a meeting to discuss the employer's policy on the training of workers, together with training plans over the next six months, as well as reporting to them on training since the previous meeting.[85] These meetings are to take place at least every six months and there is an obligation to disclose information in advance[86] (see below on disclosure of information generally). The employer is also obliged to take into account any written representations about matters raised at a meeting which are received by the employer within four weeks of the meeting.[87] Failure to fulfil these obligations in relation to a bargaining unit will enable the trade union to make a complaint to an employment tribunal. If it finds the complaint well founded, the tribunal may make a declaration and award compensation up to a maximum of two weeks' pay per individual.[88]

---

78 Schedule A1 para. 156(2) TULRCA 1992.
79 Schedule A1 para. 156(3) TULRCA 1992.
80 Schedule A1 para. 156(5) and (6) TULRCA 1992.
81 Schedule A1 para. 157 TULRCA 1992.
82 Schedule A1 para. 159 TULRCA 1992.
83 Schedule A1 para. 160 TULRCA 1992.
84 Schedule A1 para. 162 TULRCA 1992.
85 Section 70B(1) and (2) TULRCA 1992.
86 Section 70B(3) and (4) TULRCA 1992.
87 Section 70B(6) TULRCA 1992.
88 Section 70C(4) TULRCA 1992; a week's pay is subject to the limit in s. 227(1) ERA 1996.

12.3 Prohibition of union recognition requirements

Despite these new rules enabling a trade union to obtain recognition against an employer's wishes, the provisions stopping recognition being a condition of a contract with a third party remain. Section 186 TULRCA 1992 provides that a term or condition of a contract for the supply of goods and services is void in so far as it requires recognition of a trade union or unions for collective bargaining purposes or to the extent that it requires the other party to negotiate with or consult an official of a trade union or unions. Neither is it permissible to refuse to deal with a supplier or prospective supplier on the grounds that the supplier will not recognise a trade union or negotiate or consult with one.[89] A person refuses to deal with a supplier by failing to include them on a list of approved tenderers, or by excluding them from tendering, or by stopping them from tendering or by terminating a contract for the supply of goods or services.[90] The obligation to comply with this section is to be interpreted as owing a duty to the adversely affected party.[91]

12.4 Disclosure of information

A natural consequence of the recognition of a trade union by an employer is the need for both parties to have sufficient information about the undertaking for them to be able to bargain effectively. That there needs to be a statutory requirement, albeit a weak one, to ensure that information is disclosed to the trade union by the employer is an indication that not all employers have regarded it as important that the trade unions with whom they negotiate should be kept informed. One may equally surmise that there have been trade union negotiators who, at times, have not wished to know about the employer's financial position, in order to press their claims for a pay rise, regardless of the consequences for the employer.

Section 181(1) TULRCA 1992 provides a general duty for an employer, who recognises an independent trade union, to disclose certain information for the purposes of all stages of collective bargaining. The duty relates to the categories of workers for whom the trade union is recognised as representing for collective bargaining purposes. The information must be disclosed to representatives of the union, who are defined as officials or other persons authorised by the union to carry on such bargaining. According to *R v Central Arbitration Committee, ex parte BTP Oxide Ltd*,[92] these provisions contemplate that there may be alternative types of relationship between employers and unions, rather than just collective bargaining, that entitled a union to information. These alternatives might be:

- Bargaining between employers and unions which does not amount to collective bargaining because it does not deal with matters referred to in s. 181(2) TULRCA 1992.
- Dealings between employers or unions which do not amount to collective bargaining because they cannot properly be called negotiations.
- Collective bargaining which does not attract the right to information because it is not about matters in respect of which the union is recognised for collective bargaining. In this case the union concerned unsuccessfully asked for information about a job grading structure for which it had representational rights, rather than negotiating rights.

The information to be disclosed is that which relates to the employer's undertaking and is in its possession.[93] There is a twofold test to decide the relevance of the information. It must be:

---

89 Section 187(1) TULRCA 1992.
90 Section 187(2) TULRCA 1992.
91 Section 187(3) TULRCA 1992.
92 [1992] IRLR 60.
93 Section 181(2) TULRCA 1992; employer also includes associated employers.

1. Information without which the trade unions would be 'to a material extent impeded in carrying out collective bargaining'.
2. Information the disclosure of which 'would be in accordance with good industrial relations practice'.

There is an ACAS Code of Practice on the disclosure of information to trade unions for collective bargaining purposes.[94] Paragraph 11 of this Code provides examples of information which might be relevant in certain collective bargaining situations. These examples are information relating to the undertaking about pay and benefits, conditions of service, manpower, performance and finances. Although the ACAS Code is an important guide, it does not exclude other evidence that might be in accord with good industrial relations practice.[95] The request for information by the trade union must be in writing, if the employer so requests, as must the employer's reply, if requested by the trade union.[96]

An employer is not required to disclose information if the disclosure:[97]

1. Would be against the interests of national security.
2. Could not be disclosed without contravening a statutory prohibition.
3. Has been communicated to the employer in confidence.
4. Relates specifically to an individual, unless the individual has consented.
5. Could cause substantial injury to the undertaking, other than its effect on collective bargaining.
6. Is information obtained for the purpose of bringing, prosecuting or defending any legal proceedings.

This list of exceptions clearly undermines the effectiveness of the legislation. The confidentiality clause, for example, could result in important and relevant information not being disclosed to a trade union. In *Sun Printers Ltd v Westminster Press Ltd*[98] a widely circulated document about the future of a company was held not to be confidential, but it was suggested by Donaldson LJ, *obiter*, that the stamping of the word 'confidential' on the document would have been enough to allow wide circulation, whilst retaining confidentiality. Perhaps of more concern to trade unions is the difficulty in obtaining pay information concerning parts of a business that are put out to competitive tender. In *Civil Service Union v CAC*[99] a trade union was stopped from obtaining information about a tenderer's proposed wage rates on the basis that they were given in confidence and that it was information the lack of which could not be held to impede, to a material extent, the union's ability to carry out collective bargaining.

There are further limitations, on the obligations of employers to disclose information, contained in s. 182(2) TULRCA 1992:

1. An employer is not required to produce any documents or extracts from documents unless the document has been prepared for the purposes of conveying or confirming the information.
2. The employer is not required to compile or assemble any information which would involve an amount of work or expenditure out of proportion to the value of the information in the conduct of collective bargaining.

---

94 Originally introduced in 1977; it was last updated in 1997 and was brought into effect by the Employment Protection Code of Practice (Disclosure of Information) Order 1998, SI 1998/45; for the effect of failing to comply with the Code, see s. 207 TULRCA 1992.
95 Section 181(4) TULRCA 1992.
96 Section 181(3) and (5) TULRCA 1992.
97 Section 182(1) TULRCA 1992.
98 [1982] IRLR 292 CA.
99 [1980] IRLR 253.

All these exceptions place important limitations on the right of trade unions to make employers disclose information. Indeed, it is significant that during the period of the 1980s and early 1990s, when Conservative governments were introducing legislation to limit the power of trade unions, this particular piece of legislation remained untouched.

The remedy for failure to disclose information to trade unions is to make a complaint to the CAC. The CAC will refer the matter to ACAS if it thinks that there is a reasonable chance of a conciliated settlement. If this fails, the CAC will decide whether the complaint is well founded. Where it does so, then the employer is given a period of not less than a week to disclose the information. If the employer still fails to disclose, then the trade union may present a further complaint to the CAC, who will decide if the complaint is well founded and specify the information in respect of which it made that decision.[100] The CAC may then make an award in respect of the employees specified in the claim. This award will consist of the terms and conditions being negotiated and specified in the claim, or any other terms and conditions which the CAC considers appropriate. These terms and conditions can only be for matters in which the trade union is recognised for collective bargaining purposes.[101]

The ineffectiveness of this legislation is illustrated by low numbers of disclosure of information complaints. In the year 2016/17, for example, there were just seven and in the previous year just nine.[102]

12.5 Industrial action – trade union immunities

It is not appropriate in this book to provide a history of the struggles of individuals and groups to be allowed to join trade unions. Nevertheless, it is worth remembering that, until the latter part of the nineteenth century, it was the criminal law that was used against employees who combined and/or took industrial action in defence of their collective rights. Employees were prosecuted for such offences as obstruction, intimidation and conspiracy. The turning point came in the 1870s with the passing of a number of statutes, notably the Trade Union Act 1871 and the Conspiracy and Protection of Property Act 1875, which protected members of trade unions from the common law doctrine of 'restraint of trade'.

The 1875 Act was a landmark in that it provided immunities from prosecution for those involved in trade disputes. Like subsequent legislation, it did not abolish the offences for which one could be prosecuted. Rather it provided immunity from prosecution if the 'offence' was committed 'in contemplation or furtherance of a trade dispute'. Subsequent protection has followed the pattern of providing immunities, rather than offering positive rights to individuals. In some other Member States of the EU, such as France and Germany, there are constitutions which provide a right for individuals to join trade unions and take part in industrial action. These 'positive rights' are to be contrasted with the 'negative rights' approach in the United Kingdom. Workers do not have positive rights to take part in industrial action; rather they have protection if they do so. The distinction is important because it has allowed the courts and various governments to remove or change the degree of protection provided.

A classic example of this was in *Taff Vale Railway Co v Amalgamated Society of Railway Servants*.[103] This case arose out of a strike in support of an individual alleged to have been victimised by the employer. The trade union organised pickets to stop the employer bringing in non-union labour. The

---

100 Section 184 TULRCA 1992.
101 Section 185 TULRCA 1992.
102 See CAC Annual Report 2016/17.
103 [1901] AC 426.

employers applied to the court for an injunction against the union leaders and the union itself. This latter move was a novel one in that it had been assumed that the unions themselves could not be sued in this way for the actions of their officials. Lord Macnaughton stated:

> Has the legislature authorised the creation of numerous bodies of men capable of owning great wealth and acting by agents with absolutely no responsibility for the wrongs they may do to other persons by the use of that wealth and the employment of those agents? In my opinion, Parliament has done nothing of the kind.

Thus trade unions were immediately put at risk if they took industrial action. In this case, damages and fines on the union amounted to £42,000 which, in 1902, amounted to two-thirds of its annual income.

A Royal Commission in 1903 led to the Trade Disputes Act 1906, which provided protection for acts done in 'contemplation or furtherance of a trade dispute'. It provided, in s. 4, that an action in tort could not be brought against a trade union for acts of its members or officials, even though carried out on its behalf. It also provided immunity for a person who induced another to break a contract of employment and immunity against a possible tort of interference with trade, business or employment of another person. This Act was to be the foundation of future legislation on industrial action.

The current situation is simply summed up by Elias LJ in *NURMTW v Serco Ltd*[104] as follows:

> The common law confers no right to strike in this country. Workers who take strike action will usually be acting in breach of their contracts of employment. Those who organize the strike will typically be liable for inducing a breach of contract, and sometimes other economic torts are committed during the course of a strike. Without some protection from these potential liabilities virtually all industrial action would be unlawful.

12.6 Common law torts

The common law has therefore traditionally regarded a strike as a breach of the contract of employment and the calling or organising of a strike as an inducement to another to breach the contract of employment. The courts have developed a number of torts to limit the actions of workers, both individually and collectively. One perspective is to regard the history of the law regarding industrial action as a series of steps by the courts to introduce new torts to make individuals and unions liable, with the State stepping in from time to time to limit the worst excesses of the judiciary by providing some statutory immunity to individuals and unions for actions in contemplation or furtherance of a trade dispute. These liabilities in tort include the following.

12.6.1 Inducing a breach of contract

This tort derives from the case of *Lumley v Gye*.[105] It involved an opera singer, Miss Johanna Wagner, who was induced by a theatre manager to breach her contract with one theatre in order to appear at the defendant's own theatre. The court held that each party has a right to the performance of the contract and that it was wrong for another to procure one of the parties to break it or not perform it.

---

104 *National Union of Rail, Maritime and Transport Workers v Serco Ltd* [2011] IRLR 399.
105 (1853) 2 E & B 216.

An inducement to breach an employment contract is when a trade union, for example, instructs its members to take strike action against their employer. Without further intervention the employer may have a case against the trade union for inducing its employees to breach their contracts of employment. A direct inducement to breach of a commercial contract is when A puts pressure on B not to fulfil a contract with C. Thus, if trade union A were, for example, to apply pressure on employer B, in order to stop employer B making a delivery to employer C, then C, without further intervention, may be able to take action against B for breach of the supply contract. It is also possible for A indirectly to induce B to break its contract with C. If the trade union instructed its members to take strike action against employer B in order to stop them supplying employer C, then they might be liable for indirectly inducing that breach.

DC Thomson & Co v Deakin[106] concerned the delivery of bulk paper from a supplier to a printing firm. The employees of the supplier refused to deliver paper to the printer and an injunction was sought to stop the trade unions concerned from inducing the supplier to breach its contract with the printer. Jenkins LJ listed four categories where there was a direct interference by a third party with the rights of one of the parties to a contract.[107] The four categories were:

1. A 'direct persuasion or procurement or inducement by the third party to the contract-breaker, with knowledge of the contract and the intention of bringing about its breach'.[108]
2. Dealings by the third party with the contract-breaker which, to the knowledge of the third party, are inconsistent with the contract between the contract-breaker and the person wronged.[109]
3. An act done by a third party with knowledge of the contract, which, if done by one of the parties to it, would have been a breach of that contract.[110]
4. The imposition by the third party, who has knowledge of the contract, of some physical restraint upon one of the parties to the contract so as to make it impossible for the contract to be performed.

According to Jenkins LJ, the conditions necessary to show that there had been an actionable interference with one of the parties to the contract were:

1. The person charged with the actionable interference knew of the existence of the contract and intended to procure its breach.
2. The person so charged did persuade or induce the employees to break their contracts of employment.
3. The persuaded or induced employees did break their contract of employment.
4. The breach of contract was a natural consequence of the employees' breaches of their contracts of employment.

In relation to this last point, it needs to be shown that, because of the employees' actions, their employer was unable to fulfil the contract.[111]

The difference between direct and indirect inducement to breach a contract is, according to Neill LJ,[112] one of causation. For direct inducement to take place, as in Lumley v Gye, the persuasion

---

106 [1952] 2 All ER 361 CA; see also Merkur Island Shipping Corporation v Laughton [1983] IRLR 218 HL which approved this approach.

107 The summing up of these categories by Neill LJ in Middlebrook Mushrooms Ltd v TGWU [1993] IRLR 232 CA is relied upon here.

108 Lumley v Gye (1853) 2 E & B 216 is an example of this.

109 Jenkins LJ gave British Motor Trade Association v Salvadori [1949] Ch 556 as an example of this.

110 Jenkins LJ gave GWK Ltd v Dunlop Rubber Co Ltd (1926) 42 TLR 376 as an example, where the defendant's employees had removed the tyres from a car, which belonged to a rival, at a motor show.

111 See Falconer v ASLEF and NUR [1986] IRLR 331 as an example of a court applying these four steps.

112 Note 108 above.

had to be directed at the parties to the contract. In *Middlebrook Mushrooms Ltd v TGWU*[113] the distribution of leaflets by dismissed employees outside a supermarket was aimed at persuading customers not to buy their ex-employer's produce. This amounted to indirect inducement on the parties to the contract, namely the supplier and the shop. There was also the question of knowledge of the contracts. Jenkins LJ concluded that there needed to be knowledge of the contract(s) and an intent to procure its breach.[114] In this case the court held that there was no evidence that contracts existed between the shop and the supplier. It may be possible to infer knowledge, but not in this case.

The knowledge needed, however, may be minimal.[115] In a rather bizarre case in the county court,[116] a railway passenger claimed damages from two rail unions for costs incurred as a result of industrial action. The action had been called without a ballot, resulting in the union being unable to rely on any statutory immunities (see below). The claim was successful because not only did the union know of the existence of contracts between the railway company and passengers, but their intention was to affect the plaintiff and other passengers in order to put pressure on the employer. The county court judge decided that the unions were reckless in their intent, as they knew the effect of the action on the plaintiff, but nevertheless pursued it. More recently, the House of Lords has ruled that for a person to be liable they must know that they are inducing a breach of contract.[117]

There is the possibility of a defence against this tort if the defendant can show that they have an equal or superior right to that of the injured party – for example, where the contract interfered with is inconsistent with a previous contract with the person intervening.[118]

12.6.2 Interference with a contract or with business

This tort is closely connected with the tort of inducing a breach of contract. *Torquay Hotel Co Ltd v Cousins*[119] involved an attempt by a trade union to stop the supply of heating oil to a hotel with whom there was a trade dispute. Lord Denning MR extended the principle expounded in *Quinn v Leathem*[120] that 'it is a violation of legal right to interfere with contractual relations recognised by law if there be no sufficient justification for the interference'. Lord Denning stated that there were three aspects to the principle:

1. There needed to be interference in the execution of a contract.
2. Interference must be deliberate, meaning that the person interfering must know of the contract.
3. The interference must be direct.

Indirect interference would not be enough and might, according to Lord Denning, take away the right to strike. The conditions were satisfied in this case, where there was direct and deliberate interference in the contractual relations between the hotel and oil supplier.[121]

A further example can be found in *Timeplan Education Group Ltd v National Union of Teachers*.[122] This concerned a teachers' union attempting to interfere with the advertising for recruits by a teachers'

---

113 [1993] IRLR 232 CA.
114 *DC Thomson & Co v Deakin* [1952] 2 All ER 361 CA.
115 See *JT Stratford & Sons Ltd v Lindley* [1965] AC 269 HL.
116 *Falconer v ASLEF and NUR* [1986] IRLR 331.
117 See *Mainstream Properties Ltd v Young* [2007] IRLR 608.
118 See *Smithie's case* [1909] 1 KB 310 HL.
119 [1969] 2 Ch 106 CA at p. 510.
120 [1901] AC 495.
121 See also *Merkur Island Shipping Corporation v Laughton* [1983] IRLR 218 HL, where a ship was boycotted. Lord Diplock approved the principle laid down by Denning LJ that interference is not confined to a breach of contract, but includes the prevention or hindering from performing their contract, even though it is not a breach.
122 [1997] IRLR 457 CA.

supply agency. The Court of Appeal held that, in order to establish the tort of wrongful interference with contractual rights, five conditions need to be fulfilled:

1. The defendant persuaded or procured or induced a third party to break a contract.
2. Knowledge of the contract.
3. Intention to procure a breach.
4. The plaintiff suffered more than nominal damages.
5. The plaintiff can rebut a defence of justification.

In this case no tort was committed because there was a failure to show knowledge of contracts or intention to procure a breach of them.[123]

12.6.3 Intimidation

In its direct form[124] this is committed where an unlawful threat is made directly to the plaintiff with the intention of causing loss to the plaintiff. In its indirect form it is where C suffers as a result of action taken by B following an unlawful threat by A to B. An example of this can be seen in *News Group Newspapers Ltd v SOGAT '82*[125] concerning the breakdown of negotiations between the plaintiff and the union over the employment of union members at its new plant in Wapping – the unions called their members out on strike but they were then dismissed. This was followed by picketing, large-scale rallies and demonstrations outside the Wapping plant. According to the High Court, although the tort of intimidation is not complete unless the person threatened succumbs to the threat and damage results, in this case there were sufficient threats of violence and molestation to justify the granting of injunctive relief.[126]

Rookes v Barnard[127] was a landmark case which caused great alarm to trade unionists by deciding that a threat to breach a contract of employment, by threatening to go on strike, was unlawful for the purposes of a tort of intimidation. In this case an airline company had a closed-shop agreement for a part of its operation. The union threatened the airline that it would call its members out on strike if they did not remove an individual employee who had resigned from the union. The House of Lords reacted by making it almost impossible to threaten a strike without being subject to the tort of intimidation. Lord Devlin stated that there was nothing to differentiate a threat of a breach of contract from a threat of physical violence or any other illegal threat. This decision undermined the immunities enjoyed by trade unions in certain circumstances since the 1906 Act. Strikes are often preceded by threats of industrial action which would have fallen foul of the *Rookes v Barnard* decision if immunity had not been restored by the Trade Disputes Act 1965 (see 12.8 below).

12.6.4 Conspiracy

There are two types of conspiracy. One is the conspiracy to injure and the other is the conspiracy to commit an unlawful act.

---

123 See also *Messenger Newspaper Group Ltd v National Graphical Association* [1984] IRLR 397, which concerned pressure on a third party by the union in an attempt to enforce a closed shop and *Union Traffic Ltd v TGWU* [1989] IRLR 127 CA where picketing at a location other than the pickets' own place of work, in an attempt to bring it to a standstill, was considered.

124 See also s. 240 TULRCA 1992 regarding breach of contract involving injury to persons or property and s. 241 on intimidation or annoyance by violence or otherwise.

125 [1986] IRLR 337.

126 See also *Thomas v National Union of Mineworkers (South Wales Area)* [1985] IRLR 136 which partly concerned the intimidatory effect of mass picketing at collieries.

127 [1964] AC 1129 HL; see also *JT Stratford & Sons v Lindley* [1965] AC 269 HL.

A conspiracy to injure occurs when two or more people combine to injure a person in their trade by inducing customers or employees to break their contracts or not to deal with that person, which results in damage to that person.[128] *Huntley v Thornton*[129] was about an individual member of a trade union who failed to support a strike. Thereafter there were various successful attempts made to prevent the individual finding other work, by circulating details to shop stewards and others at alternative places of work. The individual then successfully brought an action for damages and conspiracy against a number of members of the trade union, who were held to have combined to injure the plaintiff in his trade and the acts were not done to further the legitimate trade interests of the defendants. Those acts were held to be done without justification. Of importance is the real purpose of the combination. If the predominant purpose was an intention to injure the plaintiff, then the tort is committed, even if the means used to inflict the damage were lawful and not actionable. In *Crofter Hand Woven Harris Tweed Co Ltd v Veitch*[130] the courts recognised that no liability should be attached to a trade union in a genuine trade dispute. It was held that the real purpose of an embargo on Harris Tweed exported by certain crofters was to benefit the members of the trade union. This contrasts with *Huntley v Thornton* where the motives were deemed to be personal rather than in furtherance of a trade dispute.

A conspiracy to commit an unlawful act is when a combination of persons conspires to inflict damage intentionally on another person by an unlawful act. Even if the primary purpose were to further or protect some legitimate interest, it is enough that this was achieved by the use of unlawful means.[131]

12.6.5 Inducing a breach of a statutory duty

It is possible that industrial action may have the effect of applying pressure on an employer to breach a statutory duty imposed on either the employer or the employee. *Associated British Ports v TGWU*[132] concerned proposed industrial action resulting from the government's decision to abolish the National Dock Labour Scheme. This scheme had the effect of preserving jobs in the docks for registered dock workers. Part of the scheme listed the obligations of workers, which included the requirement to 'work for periods as are reasonable in his particular case'. The issue was whether industrial action would be an inducement to the dock workers to breach a statutory duty to work. The Court of Appeal took the view that this was the case but the House of Lords held that this was incorrect because the relevant provision imposed a contractual duty rather than a statutory one.[133]

12.6.6 Economic duress

Economic duress is when one party is in such a dominant position that they can exercise coercion on the other party. The issue of economic duress has occurred in the context of the boycotting of ships and demands for money and payments to the union or members concerned. *Universe Tankships Inc of Monrovia v ITWF*[134] concerned the boycotting of a ship whilst in a British port and subsequent payments made by the ship owners to obtain the release of the ship. Lord Diplock stated that:

> The use of economic duress to induce another person to part with property or money is not a tort *per se*; the form that the duress takes may or may not be tortious. The remedy to which

---

128 *Quinn v Leathem* [1901] AC 495.
129 [1957] 1 WLR 321.
130 [1942] 1 All ER 142 HL.
131 See *Lonhro plc v Fayed* [1991] 3 All ER 303 HL.
132 [1989] IRLR 399 HL.
133 See also *Barrets & Baird (Wholesale) Ltd v IPCS* [1987] IRLR 3, where it was argued that a series of strikes stopped the employer from carrying out their statutory duties. The argument was rejected as no statutory duty was identified.
134 [1983] AC 366 HL.

> economic duress gives rise is not an action for damages but an action for restitution of property
> or money exacted under such duress . . .

This approach was developed in *Dimskal Shipping Co v ITWF*,[135] which also concerned a ship that was confined to port by an industrial dispute. The employers were forced to issue their employees with new contracts with backdated pay as well as to make a payment to the union. As these payments were induced by illegitimate economic pressure, the employer was entitled to restitution.

12.7 Protection from tort liabilities

There is a potential conflict between an approach which assumes that strikes are unlawful unless certain conditions are fulfilled and the much more positive approach contained in Article 11(1) of the European Convention on Human Rights, incorporated into British law by the Human Rights Act 1998. This Article is concerned with protecting the right of association including the right to form a trade union to protect one's interests. This was recognised by the Court of Appeal in *NURMTW v Serco Ltd*[136] where it was stated that if one starts from the premise that domestic legislation should be strictly construed against those who seek the benefit of the immunities, that would be the same as assuming that Parliament had intended that the interests of the employers should take priority. Elias LJ stated:

> That is not a legitimate approach. The legislation should simply be construed in the normal
> way, without presumptions one way or the other. The starting point should be that the 1992 Act
> should be given a likely and workable construction.

Protection is given against certain potential liabilities in tort by s. 219 TULRCA 1992. The immunity from liability is on the grounds that the act (i) induces another to break a contract or interferes, or induces another to interfere, with the contract's performance and (ii) consists in threatening these actions.[137] Any agreement or combination of two or more persons to do, or procure the doing of, an act in contemplation of furtherance of a trade dispute will not be actionable in tort if the act is one that would not have been actionable if done without any agreement or combination.[138]

There are three requirements in respect of this protection:

1. The act done should be in 'contemplation or furtherance of a trade dispute'.
2. It must be a trade dispute between workers[139] and their employer.
3. It must relate, wholly or mainly, to a number of specific issues. These are:

   (a) Terms and conditions of employment,[140] including physical working conditions.
   (b) Engagement, non-engagement, termination or suspension of employment or the duties of employment.
   (c) Allocation of work or the duties of employment between workers.
   (d) Matters of discipline.

---

135 [1992] IRLR 78 HL.

136 *National Union of Rail, Maritime and Transport Workers v Serco Ltd* [2011] IRLR 399.

137 Section 219(1)(a) and (b) TULRCA 1992.

138 Section 219(2) TULRCA 1992.

139 Section 244(5) TULRCA 1992 defines a worker as either someone employed by the employer or a person no longer employed by the employer, but who was terminated in connection with the dispute or whose termination is one of the circumstances leading to the dispute.

140 Section 244(5) TULRCA 1992 provides that employment includes any relationship where one person personally does work or performs services for another.

(e) Membership, or non-membership, of a trade union.

(f) Facilities for trade union officials.

(g) Machinery for consultation and negotiation in connection with any of the above, including disputes about the right of a trade union to be recognised in representing workers for
the purpose of negotiating any of the above.[141]

The phrase 'relates wholly or mainly to' requires a consideration of more than the event that
caused the dispute and involves analysis of the reasons why it arose.[142] This means investigating
the motives of a trade union and whether there are other reasons which might be perceived as the
real ones.[143]

The term 'in contemplation or furtherance of a trade dispute' requires a subjective judgement
as to how widely it should be interpreted. For example, is the collection of information about an
employer's business performance and the terms and conditions of their employees an act in contemplation or furtherance of a dispute? In *Bent's Brewery Co Ltd v Luke Hogan*[144] a union attempted to collect
such information. The court held that the union was inducing employees to breach their contracts of
employment by revealing confidential information. The union was not entitled to statutory protection, because there was no imminent or existing dispute. There was a possibility of a future dispute,
but no certainty that such a dispute would arise. The court relied upon a judgment given in *Conway v
Wade*,[145] where Lord Loreburn LC discussed the words 'in contemplation or furtherance':

> I think they mean that either a dispute is imminent and the act is done in expectation of and
> with a view to it, or that the dispute is already existing and that the act is done in support of one
> side to it. In either case the act must be genuinely done as described and the dispute must be
> a real thing imminent or existing.

A trade dispute needs to be related to the contractual or other relationship between workers and the
employer. In *British Broadcasting Corporation v DA Hearn*[146] the trade union attempted to stop the employer
broadcasting the football cup final via a satellite which would allow it to be seen in South Africa.
The court held that this could not be seen as a trade dispute in itself. If the unions had requested a
change in the contract of employment to include a term that the union's members would not be
required to take part in broadcasts to South Africa, then a subsequent dispute about whether to
include that term might have been interpreted as a trade dispute about terms and conditions of
employment. Without such a link, the dispute could not qualify for protection.

According to the House of Lords, a dispute about the reasonableness of instructions from an
employer can be a dispute about terms and conditions of employment.[147] In this case an individual
was excluded from school for disruptive behaviour. The school governors allowed the mother's
appeal and reinstated the pupil, and, subsequently, the headmaster issued an instruction that he
should be taught in class. The trade union balloted its members and the union gave notice that it
would not comply with the instruction. The court held that the reality was that the dispute was about
the working conditions of teachers and therefore related to terms and conditions of employment.

---

141 Section 244(1) TULRCA 1992.

142 *Mercury Communications Ltd v Scott-Garner* [1983] IRLR 494 CA.

143 Perhaps a wider political motivation. Such motivation was considered in *University College London Hospital v UNISON* [1999] IRLR 31
CA where the court held that it was possible to have a wider political objective and, simultaneously, a specific objective of
alleviating adverse consequences in a particular situation. See also *UNISON v UK* [2002] IRLR 497 where the ECHR considered the
impact of art. 11 of the European Convention on Human Rights.

144 [1945] 2 All ER 570.

145 [1909] AC 506 HL.

146 [1977] IRLR 273 CA.

147 *P v National Association of Schoolmasters/Union of Women Teachers* [2003] IRLR 307.

The dispute must be between existing workers and their current employer. Thus it is not possible to conduct a dispute, within the protection of s. 219 TULRCA 1992, about the contracts of employment of future workers. This unfortunate outcome was confirmed in *University College London Hospital v UNISON*.[148] Here the trade union balloted its members on a strike over the employer's refusal to guarantee the protection of the Transfer of Undertakings Regulations 1981[149] for the duration of a 30-year PFI[150] scheme. The Court of Appeal held that there were three requirements of a trade dispute: (i) that it must be a dispute between workers and their employer; (ii) that the dispute must relate wholly or mainly to one of the activities in s. 244 TULRCA 1992; and (iii) that the act must be carried out in contemplation or furtherance of a trade dispute. This was a dispute about terms and conditions between workers and a future employer and about workers as yet to be employed. It is difficult to see how this latter point is different from all other industrial disputes, which protect the contracts of not only current workers, but also future ones yet to be employed.[151]

12.8 Exceptions to statutory immunity

There are a number of actions which will not qualify for the immunity provided by s. 219 TULRCA 1992.

12.8.1 Picketing

There is no statutory definition of picketing although the Court in *Thames Cleaning*[152] suggested that, in that case, a working definition could have been the attendance at a workplace by those who are or used to be workers there, for the purpose of preventing or discouraging others from working.

As well as the economic torts, pickets are potentially liable for other torts. Possible torts include: trespass to the highway, which would need to be enforced by the owner of the soil; the tort of private nuisance, which suggests an unlawful interference with a person's right to enjoy or use land or some right in connection with it;[153] and the tort of public nuisance which consists of an act or omission which causes inconvenience to the public in the exercise of their common rights, such as the unreasonable obstruction of the highway.[154]

There is no immunity from actions in tort for acts done in the course of picketing unless they are done in accordance with s. 220 TULRCA 1992.[155] This provides that it is lawful for a person, in contemplation or furtherance of a trade dispute, to attend at or near their own place of work for the purpose of either peacefully obtaining or communicating information, or peacefully persuading any person to either work or abstain from working. The same provision allows an official of a trade union to accompany, for the same purposes, a member of the union, whom the official represents, at or near their place of work.[156] There is no precise definition of what is meant by 'at' or 'near' the place of work. May LJ declined to give one as the number of circumstances that one might have to

---

148 [1999] IRLR 31 CA.

149 SI 1981/1794.

150 Private Finance Initiative to build and run a new hospital.

151 In *Westminster City Council v UNISON* [2001] IRLR 524 CA the court held that a dispute about a proposed transfer was a trade dispute because it was about the change in the identity of the employer, rather than about the public policy issue of privatisation.

152 *Thames Cleaning v United Forces of the World* [2016] IRLR 695.

153 See *Thomas v National Union of Mineworkers (South Wales)* [1985] IRLR 136, which considered mass picketing of collieries and held that the way in which it was carried out amounted to harassment of working miners in using the highway for the purpose of going to work; see also *Mersey Docks v Verrinder* [1982] IRLR 152.

154 See *News Group Newspapers v SOGAT '82* [1986] IRLR 337, which discussed the torts of public and private nuisance.

155 Section 219(3) TULRCA 1992.

156 Section 220(1) TULRCA 1992.

provide for were so variable as to make it impossible to lay down a test.[157] He suggested the use of a commonsense approach, as did Woolf LJ in *R v East Sussex Coroner, ex parte Healy*:[158]

> The word 'near' being an ordinary word of the English language indicating a short distance or at close proximity is to be applied . . . in a common sense manner . . . it seems to me that it is not for the courts to define what is precisely meant by the word.

In *Rayware Ltd v TGWU*[159] the issue had been whether a group of workers picketing at the entrance to a private trading estate, about seven-tenths of a mile from the workplace, were 'at' or 'near' the place of work. According to the Court of Appeal, the word 'near' was an expanding word and not a restraining one – that is, its meaning was to be expanded to give effect to the purpose of the legislation. This purpose was to give a right to picket. This right was not to be taken away by holding that the nearest point where picketing could take place, even though it was seven-tenths of a mile away, was not 'at or near'.[160]

If a person normally works at a number of different locations or at a location where it would be impracticable to picket, then the place of work can be any location at which that employee works or otherwise at the location from which the work is administered.[161] The same rules apply for ex-employees whose termination is related to the dispute. They may treat their last place of work as their location for picketing purposes.[162]

The legislation does not prescribe the number of pickets that are to be allowed at or near the place of work. However, the requirement is for the picketing to be peaceful and it may be that the presence of large numbers of individuals may be too intimidating for it to be seen as peaceful. In *Thomas v NUM (South Wales Area)*[163] there was mass picketing at the gates of a number of collieries in South Wales during the 1984 miners' strike. It was held to be tortious because of its nature and the way that it was carried out. It represented an unreasonable harassment of those miners who were working. Mass picketing by trying to block the entry to the workplace may be a common law nuisance. The court relied on the existing Code of Practice on Picketing[164] which recommended that the number of pickets should be limited to six and issued an injunction restricting the number of pickets to that number.

Section 10 of the Trade Union Act 2016 introduced a further requirement concerning lawful picketing. There is now a need for the picketing to be supervised by a union official or any other union member who is familiar with the Code of Practice on Picketing. This person will need to make themselves known to the police and inform them where he/she can be contacted and where the picketing is to take place. This picket supervisor needs to be present during the picket and be readily contactable by the police.[165]

---

157 See *Rayware Ltd v TGWU* [1989] IRLR 134 CA.

158 [1988] 1 WLR 1194.

159 [1989] IRLR 134 CA.

160 In *Union Traffic v TGWU* [1989] IRLR 127 CA, picketing at a depot some 14 miles away was held to be too far, even though the 'home' depot had closed down.

161 Section 220(2) TULRCA 1992.

162 Section 220(3) TULRCA 1992; if a reason for the dispute is a change of work locations, ex-employees will not be protected if they picket at the new location where they have not worked; they are confined to the old location even if it has been closed down. See *News Group Newspapers v SOGAT '82* [1986] IRLR 337.

163 [1985] IRLR 136.

164 This Code was made by the Secretary of State for Employment and came into force on 1 May 1992; SI 1992/476.

165 Now Section 220A TULRCA 1992.

12.8.2 Action taken because of dismissal for unofficial action

An act is not protected if the reason, or one of the reasons, for it is in connection with the dismissal of one or more employees who are not entitled to protection from unfair dismissal by reason of their taking unofficial action.[166]

12.8.3 Secondary action

Secondary action is not lawful picketing.[167] It is defined as an inducement, or a threat, to break or interfere with a contract of employment where the employer in that contract is not party to the dispute.[168] An employer shall not be regarded as party to a dispute between another employer and the workers of that employer; and where more than one employer is in dispute with its workers, the dispute between each employer and its workers is to be treated as a separate dispute.[169] Finally, a primary action in one dispute, which is protected if in contemplation or furtherance of a trade dispute, cannot be relied upon as secondary action in another dispute.[170]

12.8.4 Pressure to impose a union recognition requirement

An act is not protected if it constitutes an inducement or an attempt to induce a person to incorporate into a contract a requirement to recognise or consult with a trade union[171] or is an act that interferes with the supply of goods and services in an attempt to achieve the same with the supplier.[172]

12.9 Ballots and notices of industrial action

Detailed rules on the need for trade unions to conduct ballots before taking industrial action were introduced by successive Conservative governments during the 1980s and early 1990s and, more recently, in the Trade Union Act 2016. Currently s. 219 TULRCA 1992 provides that if industrial action takes place without a ballot complying with the rules, then there will be no immunity from actions in tort.

An underlying assumption on the need for such ballots was that many strikes were organised and led against the wishes of the majority of members of a particular trade union. Compulsory balloting of the membership would stop this happening. It would also reduce or eliminate 'wildcat' strikes.[173] It was intended to stop public voting at mass meetings where, it was suggested, individuals might feel coerced into showing solidarity and voting for industrial action. The arguments against formalised balloting procedures include: (i) the fact that once a ballot has been held which is in favour of industrial action, then that action may be given greater legitimacy; and (ii) negotiators may have less flexibility to come to a deal with the employer if there is a ballot result which is binding upon them. It is worth noting that although a ballot is required before protected industrial action can take place, no ballot is required to stop the action.

Although there was an unsuccessful attempt to introduce ballots and 'cooling-off' periods in the Industrial Relations Act 1971, the current legislation stems from the Trade Union Act

---

166 See below, s. 237 TULRCA 1992.
167 Section 224(1) TULRCA 1992.
168 Section 224(2) TULRCA 1992.
169 Section 224(4) TULRCA 1992.
170 Section 224(5) TULRCA 1992.
171 As in ss 186 and 187 TULRCA 1992; see above under 12.3.
172 Section 225 TULRCA 1992.
173 A wildcat strike is where members of a group of workers stop work and take industrial action without notice to the employer or, possibly, their own trade union.

1984.[174] The rules were added to and amended in the Employment Acts 1988 and 1990, with the current law contained in TULRCA 1992. There is also a Code of Practice on Industrial Action Ballots and Notice to Employers.[175]

A trade union will lose its protection under s. 219 TULRCA 1992 if it induces a person to take part or to continue to take part in industrial action that is not supported by a ballot and the rules about notifying the employer about the ballot contained in s. 226A TULRCA 1992.[176] This is so even if the inducement is unsuccessful, whether because the individual is not interested or for some other reason.[177]

A failure to hold a ballot will deprive the union of protection against legal action taken by members under s. 62 TULRCA 1992; by employers, or customers or suppliers of that employer, relying on s. 226 TULRCA 1992; or by an individual deprived, or likely to be deprived, of goods and services under s. 235A TULRCA 1992 but relying on s. 62 or 226 TULRCA 1992. Section 62 TULRCA 1992 deals with the rights of members of a trade union who have been, or are likely to be, induced into taking industrial action, which does not have the support of a ballot.[178] Industrial action shall only be seen to have the support of a ballot if all the requirements of ss 226–234A TULRCA 1992 have been fulfilled (see below).[179] The member or members of the trade union concerned may apply to an employment tribunal. If the tribunal finds that the claim is well founded, it may make such orders as are necessary to ensure that the trade union stops inducing members to continue or take part in industrial action.[180]

12.9.1 Notifying the employer of the ballot

The trade union must take such steps as are reasonably necessary to notify the employer of persons entitled to vote in the ballot that the union intends to hold a ballot and the date which the union reasonably believes will be the opening day of the ballot.[181] The notice, which is to be in writing, must also contain: a list of the categories of employee to which the employees concerned belong and a list of their workplaces;[182] the total number of employees concerned, the number in each of the categories listed and the number at each workplace, together with an explanation of how these figures were arrived at. Alternatively, where some or all of the employees concerned have union deductions made from their wages, the union can supply 'such information as will enable the employer readily to deduce': the total number of employees concerned, the categories to which they belong and the number in each of the categories; and the number who work at the workplaces concerned.[183] This notice must be given not later than the seventh day before the opening day of the ballot.[184]

---

174 The Trade Union Act 1984 only withdrew immunity for disputes concerning contractual matters. If the action did not concern contractual matters, then, it could be argued, no ballot was required. This was the argument unsuccessfully used by teachers in *Metropolitan Borough of Solihull v NUT* [1985] IRLR 211, who refused to cover for colleagues' absences and to cover school lunches, amongst other actions. They claimed that these were of a voluntary nature and not contractual, so a ballot was not required.

175 The current Code came into effect on 1 September 2005, SI 2005/2420.

176 Section 226(1) TULRCA 1992.

177 Section 226(4) TULRCA 1992.

178 In ss 226–234A TULRCA 1992, a reference to a contract of employment includes any contract under which one person personally does work or performs services for another; see s. 235 TULRCA 1992.

179 Section 62(2) TULRCA 1992.

180 Section 62(3) TULRCA 1992.

181 Section 226A(2)(a)–(b) TULRCA 1992.

182 See *EDF Energy Powerlink Ltd v National Union of Rail, Maritime and Transport Workers* [2010] IRLR 114 where, even before the ballot was completed, the employer was able to obtain an injunction stopping the union because it had not given a sufficient breakdown of who, in the different trades, would be balloted.

183 Sections 226A(2)(c) and 226A(2A)–(2C) TULRCA 1992. Section 226A(1)(a) TULRCA 1992; s. 226A(4) defines the opening day of the ballot as the first day when a voting paper is sent to any person entitled to vote.

184 [1994] IRLR 227.

It is still unlikely, however, that the statement of an intention to hold a ballot amongst 'all our members in your institution' would fulfil the requirements of the legislation. This statement was contained in *Blackpool and Fylde College v NATFHE*[185] which involved the introduction of flexible contracts for new members of staff. Of the 330 members of staff, 288 were members of the union. Only 109 had subscriptions deducted through the payroll, so it was not possible for the employer to ascertain which employees would be entitled to take part in the ballot.[186] Similarly, in *Metroline Travel Ltd v Unite the Union*[187] a statement that the union intended to ballot 'all members who are drivers; engineering grades and supervisory grades working on the TFL contracts either on a full time or part time basis' was not clear enough for the employers to be able to identify the numbers of employees concerned in the various categories. The rule now is that if the trade union possesses information as to the number, category or workplace of the employees concerned, that is the minimum information that must be supplied. The fact that it is not necessary to give names of individuals to an employer[188] is an important safeguard for employees, both in terms of privacy and in terms of protection from potential harassment by the employer.

Not later than the third day before the opening day of the ballot, the trade union must also submit a sample of the ballot paper to the employer of the persons likely to be entitled to vote.[189] If, for some reason, not all the ballot papers are the same, then a sample of all of the different versions must be given to the employer.[190]

12.9.2 Appointment of a scrutineer

Before the ballot takes place, the trade union needs to appoint a suitably qualified[191] person as a scrutineer. The functions of the scrutineer are to take all the steps necessary to prepare a report on the ballot for the trade union stating whether the ballot was satisfactory or not and providing a free copy to employers and voters on request.[192] This report is to be made as soon as possible after the ballot and, in any event, not more than four weeks after the date of the ballot.[193] There is an obligation for the trade union to comply with all reasonable requests made by the scrutineer in relation to the ballot.[194]

There is an exception for small ballots, as there is no requirement for the appointment of a scrutineer where the number of members entitled to vote does not exceed 50.[195]

12.9.3 Entitlement to vote

The entitlement to vote is to be given only to those members of the trade union who it is reasonable at the time of the ballot for the union to believe will be induced to take part in, or to continue to take part in, the industrial action. No one else has any entitlement to vote.[196] There is a difference between 'taking part in a strike' and 'being on strike'. Section 227 TULRCA refers to the former and,

---

185 See also *National Union of Rail, Maritime and Transport Workers v London Underground* [2001] IRLR 228 CA, where the phrase 'all members of the union employed in all categories at all workplaces' was held not to comply with the Act's requirements; and *British Telecom v CWU* [2004] IRLR 58.

186 Section 226A(2G) TULRCA 1992.

187 [2012] IRLR 749.

188 Section 226A(2G) TULRCA 1992.

189 Section 226A(1)(b) TULRCA 1992.

190 Section 226A(2F) TULRCA 1992.

191 Section 226B(2) TULRCA 1992 provides information on who is a qualified person.

192 Section 231B TULRCA 1992 describes the contents of the scrutineer's report: it is to state whether the ballot met statutory requirements, that the arrangements for the ballot were fair and that the scrutineer has been able to carry out the required duties without interference.

193 Section 226B(1) TULRCA 1992.

194 Section 226B(2), (4) TULRCA 1992.

195 Section 226C TULRCA 1992.

196 Section 227 TULRCA 1992. In *RMT v Midland Mainline Ltd* [2001] IRLR 813 the union omitted to ballot a significant number of members in the grades concerned.

according to the High Court, this means that the ballot is not necessarily restricted to those who will actually go on strike. This occurred in the case of London Underground v ASLEF[197] where the union balloted other people in the same grade as those who would actually be called out on strike.

Subject to exceptions, a separate ballot is to be held for each workplace. If there is a single set of premises, a person's workplace is the premises the person works at, or, in any other case, the premises to which the person's employment has the closest connection.[198] The exceptions to the requirement for separate workplace ballots include, first, if the entitlement to vote is limited to all those members who have an occupation of a particular kind or have any number of particular kinds of occupation; second, where the entitlement to vote is limited to members employed by a particular employer, or by any number of particular employers, with whom the union is in dispute.[199] In University of Central England v NALGO[200] the ballot covered a number of colleges, in which the union had members entitled to vote. As the negotiations were with an employers' association and the vote covered all the colleges concerned, it was held that there was no requirement for separate workplace ballots. The potential absurdity of the rules on separate workplace ballots is shown in Inter City West Coast v NURMTW.[201] In this case there were two railway companies owned by the British Railways Board occupying separate office sites. The dispute concerned train conductors who worked from Manchester Piccadilly station, but the employers claimed that two separate ballots should have been held. The court rejected their arguments and held that the conductors had one place of work – that is, the railway station.[202]

Industrial action will not be regarded as having the support of a ballot if a member of a trade union, whom it was reasonable to assume would be induced to take part in the industrial action, was not accorded their entitlement to vote and was subsequently induced to take part in the action.[203] Small accidental failures in the process are to be ignored if the failure was unlikely to have an effect on the result of the ballot.[204] There are problems for trade unions in organising ballots that meet the statutory requirements. These are connected with maintaining a centralised register of members when membership can be in a state of flux. London Underground v NURMTW[205] involved the recruitment of some 600–700 new members after the ballot for industrial action had been completed. The employers were unsuccessful in their attempt to obtain an injunction, because the Court of Appeal accepted that industrial action was not the action of the individual who voted, but was a collective action in which the individual took part. It is the collective industrial action that must have the support of the ballot.[206] In Balfour Beatty v Unite the Union[207] it was claimed that numbers of members entitled to vote were left out of the ballot, despite the union devoting hundreds of hours of employees' time to try to track down all those entitled to vote. The Court refused the employer's application for an injunction because the union had gone to 'considerable lengths to ensure democratic legitimacy' and it would not have been reasonable to expect more.

---

197 London Underground v Associated Society of Locomotive Engineers and Firemen [2012] IRLR 196.

198 Section 228 TULRCA 1992.

199 Section 228A(1)–(4) TULRCA 1992; s. 228A(5) defines who are the particular members of a trade union affected by different types of disputes.

200 [1993] IRLR 81.

201 [1996] IRLR 583.

202 See also RJB Mining (UK) Ltd v NUM [1997] IRLR 621, where the union decided to hold an aggregate ballot, but then omitted one location.

203 Section 232A TULRCA 1992; see also National Union of Rail, Maritime and Transport Workers v Midland Mainline Ltd [2001] IRLR 813 CA, which concerned the missing out of some of those entitled to vote.

204 Section 232B TULRCA 1992; also National Union of Rail, Maritime and Transport Workers v Serco Ltd [2011] IRLR 399.

205 [1995] IRLR 636 CA.

206 See also British Railways Board v NURMTW [1989] IRLR 349 CA where the number of ballot papers issued appeared to be less than the membership of the union entitled to vote.

207 Balfour Beatty Engineering Services Ltd v Unite the Union [2012] IRLR 452.

12.9.4 The voting paper

We have seen that voting at mass meetings is no longer permissible. Every member entitled to vote must be given a voting paper which must state the name of the independent scrutineer and clearly specify the address to which it is to be sent and the date by which it must be sent. In addition it must have a unique whole number which is one of a series of numbers.[208] The voting paper must also contain at least one of two questions, depending upon the industrial action envisaged. The first question is whether the voter is prepared to take part in, or continue, a strike. The second is whether they are prepared to take part in, or continue, industrial action short of a strike.[209] If the union wishes to pursue both options, then they must ask both questions.[210] The questions need to be in such a form that the members can vote either yes or no. Prior to the ERelA 1999 the only definition of a strike was contained in s. 246 TULRCA 1992, which defined it as 'any concerted stoppage of work'. In *Connex South Eastern Ltd v NURMTW*[211] this was held to include any refusal by employees to work for periods of time for which they are employed to work, provided it was 'concerted'. Concerted was taken to mean mutually planned. Such action could therefore include a ban on rest-day working and overtime when people might normally be working. The ERelA 1999 changed this view and included a section stating that, for the purposes of s. 229(2) TULRCA 1999, an overtime ban and a call-out ban constituted action short of a strike.[212]

In addition, the voting paper must also specify, in the event of a yes vote, who is authorised to call upon members to take industrial action.[213] The person specified must be one of those included in s. 20(2) TULRCA 1992, which defines those whose acts are to be taken as being authorised or endorsed by a trade union. Finally, the following statement needs to appear on the ballot paper:

> If you take part in strike or other industrial action, you may be in breach of your contract of employment.
>
> However, if you are dismissed for taking part in strike or other industrial action which is called officially and is otherwise lawful, the dismissal will be unfair if it takes place fewer than eight weeks after you started taking part in the action, and depending on the circumstances may be unfair if it takes place later.[214]

The second paragraph, perhaps making it less intimidatory, was added by the ERelA 1999.

The Trade Union Act 2016 added further requirements for the ballot paper. Section 229 TULRCA 1992 is amended to require that the voting paper must include a summary of the matters at issue to which the proposed industrial action relates. It must also contain information about the period or periods within which the industrial action will take place, and also if there is a question about action short of a strike, it will need to specify what this means in terms of the types of action proposed.

12.9.5 The ballot

There are also strict rules applied to the ballot itself. As far as is reasonably practicable, voting must be done in secret.[215] Every person who is entitled to vote in the ballot must be allowed to

---

208 Section 229(1) TULRCA 1992.
209 Section 229(2) TULRCA 1992.
210 See *West Midlands Travel v TGWU* [1994] IRLR 578, which considered that each question had to be voted on individually and the majority in respect of each question considered separately.
211 [1999] IRLR 249 CA.
212 Section 229(2A) TULRCA 1992.
213 Section 229(3) TULRCA 1992.
214 Section 229(4) TULRCA 1992.
215 Section 230(4)(a) TULRCA 1992.

do so without interference from the trade union or its officials and must be able to do so, as far as is reasonably practicable, without incurring any direct costs themselves.[216] A further restriction imposed by s. 2 Trade Union Act 2016 was that there needs to be at least a 50 per cent turnout of those entitled to vote before a ballot can be seen as valid. In 'important public services' there is also a further quite onerous requirement that at least 40 per cent of those entitled to vote in the ballot answered yes to the question.[217]

Members must have a voting paper sent to them by post to their home address, or any other address to which the individual has requested the union to send it.[218] *London Borough of Newham v NALGO*[219] involved a strike ballot which the trade union thought would take one month to organise and hold. The union funded a campaign, and provided speakers, to rally support for a yes vote. The courts held that the statute did not require trade unions to adopt a neutral stance. The union is perfectly entitled to be partisan so long as it complies with the legislation.

There is an obligation that the votes in a ballot are to be fairly and accurately counted, although this does not mean that inaccuracies in the counting will necessarily invalidate the result. So long as the inaccuracies are accidental and do not affect the result, they are to be disregarded.[220] As soon as reasonably practicable after the ballot, the union must inform both those entitled to vote and all the employers concerned of the result.[221] The scrutineer will also produce a report on the ballot.[222] In *Metrobus v Unite*[223] the union claimed that there was no need to inform the employer of the ballot result unless the union decided in favour of industrial action, because the need to inform the employer of the result only arose in order for the union to have statutory immunity for the action. The Court of Appeal did not accept this argument, stating that the need to inform the employer of the ballot result was a free-standing obligation. The union could wait for the best part of three weeks before it called industrial action, but there was an obligation to inform the employer of the ballot result as soon as reasonably practicable.

British Airways plc v Unite the Union[224] concerned the requirement to provide information to those who were entitled to vote in the ballot. The employer claimed that the union had failed to carry out this responsibility adequately. It had not communicated with each person individually but had relied upon emails, texts and notices on union notice boards. The employer also alleged that the information supplied did not fulfil all the requirements of s. 231 TULRCA. The Court of Appeal held that this was insufficient to invalidate the whole process and that the temporary injunction previously given, should be discharged.

The ballot will cease to be effective if action has not been called, by a specified person,[225] or taken place within a period of six months from the date of the ballot. This period can be extended to a maximum of nine months if such an extension is agreed between the employer or employers concerned and the trade union.

---

216 See *Paul v NALGO* [1987] IRLR 43 CO. Although this case did not concern industrial action, it did show that even minor costs incurred, i.e. the cost of posting a ballot paper, would be sufficient to breach the requirement that there should be no direct costs falling upon the member.

217 A series of regulations in 2017 have specified who works in an important public service. These were: the Important Public Services (Border Security) Regulations 2017, SI 2017/136; the Important Public Services (Transport) Regulations 2017, SI 2017/135; the Important Public Services (Fire) Regulations 2017, SI 2017/134; the Important Public Services (Education) Regulations 2017, SI 2017/133; the Important Public Services (Health) Regulations 2017, SI 2017/132.

218 Section 230(1) and (2) TULRCA 1992.

219 [1993] IRLR 83 CA.

220 Section 230(4)(b) TULRCA 1992.

221 Sections 231–231A TULRCA 1992.

222 Section 231B TULRCA 1992; see above.

223 [2009] IRLR 851.

224 [2010] IRLR 809.

225 See s. 233 TULRCA 1992 which states that action will only be regarded as having the support of a ballot if called by a specified person; see above.

12.9.6 Notice to the employer

An act done by a trade union to induce a person to take part in, or continue, industrial action will not be regarded as protected unless the trade union gives a relevant notice to the affected employer or employers, within 14 days of having notified the employer of the result as required by s. 231A TULRCA 1992.[226] A relevant notice is one that is in writing and contains: a list of the categories of employee to which the affected employees belong and a list of their workplaces; the total number of affected employees, the number in each of the categories listed and the number at each workplace, together with an explanation of how these figures were arrived at. Alternatively, where some or all of the employees affected have union deductions made from their wages, the union can supply 'such information as will enable the employer readily to deduce': the total number of affected employees, the categories to which they belong and the number in each of the categories; and the number who work at the workplaces concerned.[227] The relevant notice must also state whether the action is going to be continuous or discontinuous; the dates on which continuous action will commence and, if relevant, the dates on which discontinuous action will take place.[228] Discontinuous action is that which takes place on some days only.[229]

One of the problems with the legislation prior to the ERelA 1999 was that the rules were so rigid that if a trade union wished to cease or suspend action in order to negotiate, they were then required to go through the notice provisions again in order to restart the whole process.[230] The ERelA 1999 added subsections (7A) and (7B) to s. 234A TULRCA 1992. These additions have the effect of allowing a suspension of the action and therefore of the requirement to notify the employer again of intended action. These suspensions can take place so that the union can comply with a court order or undertaking or if the employer and the union agree to the suspension.

12.9.7 Industrial action affecting the supply of goods and services

Where an individual claims that, as a result of an unlawful act to induce any person to take part in industrial action, there has been a delay or failure in the supply of goods or that there has been a reduction in the quality of goods or services supplied, that individual may apply to the High Court for an order. An act to induce any person to take part in or continue such industrial action is unlawful if it is actionable in tort and does not have the support of a ballot. The High Court may grant interlocutory relief or make an order requiring that there is no further inducement to take part in industrial action and that no person should engage in conduct after the order as a result of inducement before the order.[231]

12.10 Union responsibility for the actions of their members

Where proceedings in tort are brought against a trade union on the grounds that it is inducing, or threatening to induce, another to break a contract of employment or interfere with its performance,

---

226 Section 234A(1) TULRCA 1992.
227 Section 234A(3)–(3C) TULRCA 1992; see also s. 234A(5A) which describes the information that must be given to the employer, although not giving the names of any employees is not a ground for holding that there has been a breach of the condition. This provision was added by the ERelA 1999; for an example of the position before this amendment, see *Blackpool and Fylde College v NATFHE* [1994] IRLR 227.
228 Section 234A(3)(b) TULRCA 1992.
229 Section 234A(6) TULRCA 1992.
230 See s. 234A(7) TULRCA 1992.
231 Section 235A TULRCA 1992.

then the union is to be treated as liable if it has endorsed or authorised the act in question.[232] One of the perceived problems that this measure attempts to solve is that of unofficial action, where individual groups or parts of a trade union take action without the express approval of their trade union.

Trade unions are to be taken as having endorsed or authorised an act if it was done, or was authorised or endorsed: by any person who is empowered by the rules[233] of the union to authorise or endorse such action; or by the executive committee or the president or general secretary of the union; or by any other committee or official of the union.[234] For the purpose of this latter category, a committee of the union is any group of persons constituted in accordance with the union's rules and an act is to be taken as authorised or endorsed by an official if it was authorised or endorsed by a committee of which the official was a member and the committee had as one of its purposes the organising or co-ordinating of industrial action.[235]

Heatons Transport (St Helens) Ltd v TGWU[236] discussed the derivation of a shop steward's authority in order to assess the union's liability for the shop steward's actions. The court concluded that such authority could come from the rules expressly or by implication; or may come under the rules by express or implied delegation; or by virtue of the office held; or otherwise by such means as custom and practice. There is no need to look for specific authority in a particular case if the authority to act has been expressly or impliedly delegated to different levels of the organisation. A court may grant an injunction requiring the union to ensure that there is no further inducement to take part in industrial action and that no person continues to act as if they had been induced to take part.[237]

It is possible for a trade union to avoid liability for the actions of its members if the executive, president or general secretary repudiates the act as soon as is reasonably practicable after it came to their knowledge. For such a repudiation to be effective, the union must give, without delay, a written notice to the committee or official in question and do its best, without delay, to give the notice to every member that the union believes might be involved in the action and to the employer of every such member.[238] The notice must, according to s. 21(3) TULRCA 1992, contain the following statement:

> Your union has repudiated the call (or calls) for industrial action to which this notice relates and will give no support to unofficial industrial action taken in response to it (or them). If you are dismissed while taking unofficial industrial action, you will have no right to complain of unfair dismissal.

It is only by following this procedure that the union can avoid liability for the act and its consequences. There is a requirement for strict compliance with a repudiation, for the union not to be held liable for further breaches. Section 21(5) TULRCA 1992 provides that an act will not be treated as being repudiated if, subsequently, the executive, president or general secretary of the union acts in a way that is inconsistent with the repudiation. Thus it is not enough to issue a written repudiation and then continue as before. In *Richard Read (Transport) Ltd v NUM (South Wales Area)*[239] there was a failure to comply with an injunction stopping mass picketing. Although the union president

---

232 Section 20(1) TULRCA 1992. See *Gate Gourmet Ltd v TGWU* [2005] IRLR 881.
233 Rules means the written rules of the union or any other written provision between members: s. 20(7) TULRCA 1992.
234 Section 20(2) TULRCA 1992; an official need not be employed by the union; see *Express & Star Ltd v NGA* [1985] IRLR 455 where the West Midlands Secretary was held to be an official for whose actions, in this respect, the union was vicariously liable.
235 Section 20(3) TULRCA 1992.
236 [1972] IRLR 25 HL.
237 Section 20(6) TULRCA 1992; the provisions relating to union liability above also relate to complying with court injunctions; proceedings against the trade union do not affect the liability of any other person in respect of the act: s. 20(5) TULRCA 1992.
238 Section 21(1)–(2) TULRCA 1992.
239 [1985] IRLR 67.

had said that the union would comply, there was no evidence that instructions to pickets had changed at all. The court cited a statement by Sir John Donaldson to the effect that it was not sufficient, when complying with an injunction, to say that one had done one's best (unless that was what was required by the injunction). Strict compliance was necessary.[240] In *Read*, the officials had shown an indifference as to whether or not the injunction was complied with.[241] As a result the union was held liable and fined.[242]

The union will be held not to have repudiated if, within three months of the repudiation, there is a request from a party to a commercial contract (i.e. not an employment contract) whose performance has been, or is being, interfered with and who has not been given the necessary written notification, and the union has not provided written confirmation that the act has been repudiated.[243]

12.11 Prohibition on use of funds to indemnify unlawful conduct

Section 15(1) TULRCA 1992 prohibits trade unions from using their property in the following ways: first, towards the payment of a fine imposed by a court for an offence or for contempt of court; second, towards the securing of any such payment; and, finally, towards indemnifying an individual in respect of such a penalty. This reflects a view of the courts that such payments or indemnities are against public policy. *Drake v Morgan*[244] concerned the ability of the National Union of Journalists to pay the fines that its members incurred on the picket line. The court refused to make a declaration that such payments were not lawful. The resolution indemnifying the pickets had been made after the event and could not be seen as a way of indemnifying future unlawful acts. Thus it was not contrary to public policy because it could not be seen as either an incitement to commit an offence or aiding or abetting the securing of an offence. By way of contrast, in *Thomas v NUM (South Wales Area)*[245] an injunction was granted to stop the union indemnifying pickets against possible future fines. According to the court, even this did not stop the union from considering individual cases of hardship if it was in the interests of the union and the members as a whole. The court distinguished *Taylor v NUM (Derbyshire Area)*,[246] where payments had been made to pickets and striking miners, on the grounds that the strike was not authorised and was in breach of the union's rules.

12.12 Remedies

The remedies that may be available to the courts include specific performance, injunctions and damages.

Specific performance is an order of the court which compels the party in breach of contract to fulfil its obligations under that contract. Like all equitable remedies, it is discretionary and is unlikely

---

240 *Howitt Transport Ltd v TGWU* [1973] IRLR 25.
241 See also *Express & Star Ltd v NGA* [1985] IRLR 455, where the relationship of the statutory provisions on repudiation and contempt proceedings for failure to abide by an injunction were considered.
242 Section 22 TULRCA 1992 provides limits as to the amount of fines that can be levied on trade unions in actions in tort and s. 23 provides that certain property of the union is protected with regard to the enforcement of fines.
243 Section 21(6) TULRCA 1992.
244 [1978] ICR 56.
245 [1985] IRLR 136.
246 [1985] IRLR 99.

to be used in the context of industrial relations. In fact s. 236 TULRCA 1992 stops the courts making orders for specific performance in relation to the contract of employment. It establishes an important statutory principle that an employee cannot be made to work or attend at any place for the purpose of doing so. The dividing line between an order for specific performance and an injunction may sometimes be unclear. It is possible that an injunction stopping an employer from, for example, dismissing an employee with one month's notice, rather than the six months' notice to which they were entitled, has the effect of ordering the continuation of the contract of employment.[247]

Injunctions can be interim or permanent in nature. The advantage of interim injunctions is the speed with which they can be obtained, although s. 221 TULRCA 1992 does place some restrictions on their availability. First, where there is a without notice application for an injunction and the likely defence is that the action was in contemplation or furtherance of a trade dispute, the court cannot grant the injunction unless it is satisfied that all reasonable steps have been taken to give the other side the opportunity of being heard. Second, where there is an application for an interim injunction pending a full trial of the action, and the party against whom the injunction is sought claims that they acted in the furtherance or contemplation of a trade dispute, then the court is to exercise its discretion as to whether it will be possible to establish a defence. Issues to be considered are whether there is a possibility of establishing a defence under ss 219 and 220 TULRCA 1992; whether it can be established that there is a trade dispute;[248] whether there is a serious issue to be tried: where the balance of convenience lies between the plaintiff and the defendant; and whether the granting of an order is in the public interest.

The standard authority for the approach to be taken in granting interim injunctions is set out in *American Cyanamid Co v Ethicon Ltd.*[249] Lord Diplock stated that the object of such an injunction was to protect the plaintiff against injury for which there could not be sufficient compensation in damages, if successful at the trial. However, this protection had to be weighed against the defendant's need to be protected from injury resulting from being stopped from exercising their own legal rights. Thus the test to be used is the balance of convenience. In particular, the court needs to decide whether the granting of an interim injunction is tantamount to giving final judgment against the defendant.[250] The courts will also need to ask whether there is a serious question to be tried.[251] For example, in *Associated British Ports v TGWU*[252] the employers failed to show that a strike by registered dock workers would be in breach of their statutory duty under the National Dock Labour Scheme. Having failed in this argument, there was no serious issue to be tried, so there was no basis for granting an injunction.

An injunction must be complied with by the person to whom it is addressed and must be obeyed from the moment that the defendant knows of its existence. It is not enough to claim that the order was not formally served and therefore could not be followed, as this would open the door to abuse. A telephone call or letter informing the defendant should be enough.[253]

Most disputes are resolved at, or soon after, the interim injunction stage and it is rare for a dispute to go all the way to obtaining a permanent injunction. If proceedings do continue, the appropriate remedy by then is likely to be damages rather than an injunction. In *Messenger Group Newspapers v NGA*[254] the plaintiffs were awarded: sums for liquidated damages for all the expenditure that they had incurred as a result of the tort; compensatory damages for the loss of revenue; aggravated

---

247 Hill v CA Parsons Ltd [1972] 1 Ch 305 CA.
248 See University College London Hospital v UNISON [1999] IRLR 31 CA, which set out three conditions for establishing whether there was a trade dispute (see above).
249 [1975] AC 396 HL.
250 NWL Ltd v Nelson and Laughton [1979] IRLR 478 HL, per Lord Diplock.
251 See Dimbleby & Sons Ltd v NUJ [1984] IRLR 161 HL.
252 [1989] IRLR 399 HL.
253 See Kent Free Press v NGA [1987] IRLR 267, where such an event happened.
254 Messenger Group Newspapers Ltd v National Graphical Association [1984] IRLR 397.

damages as a result of the injury being caused by malice or by the manner of doing the injury; and exemplary damages for the necessity of teaching the wrongdoer that tort does not pay.[255]

12.13 Dismissals during industrial action

An employee who is sacked is only able to claim unfair dismissal in limited circumstances. The circumstances that need to be taken into account are: whether the action is official or unofficial; whether all or some of the employees taking part have been dismissed or re-engaged; and whether the employee is taking part in protected industrial action.

12.13.1 Unofficial action

An employee has no right to complain of unfair dismissal if, at the time of the dismissal, the employee was taking part in unofficial industrial action.[256] Industrial action is unofficial unless the employee is:

1. a member of a trade union and the action is authorised or endorsed[257] by that trade union; or
2. not a member of a trade union, but there are members taking part in the action whose union has authorised or endorsed the action.[258]

There are exceptions to this rule, which include the dismissal being for a reason related to pregnancy, maternity leave, parental leave, time off for dependants, health and safety, being or planning to be an employee representative, or making a protected disclosure.[259]

12.13.2 Official action

Where an employee has a right to complain of unfair dismissal during industrial action or a lock-out, the employment tribunal will not be able to entertain the claim unless:

1. one or more of the relevant[260] employees has not been dismissed;[261] or
2. a relevant employee has been offered re-engagement within a period of three months, beginning with the date of dismissal, and the complainant has not been offered re-engagement.[262] Re-engagement means the same job as before the dispute or in a different reasonably suitable job.[263]

Even a re-engagement made in error might be enough to bring these provisions into effect. In *Bigham and Keogh v GKN Quickform Ltd*[264] an employee working on a site was dismissed as a result of

---

255 See *Rookes v Barnard* [1964] AC 1129 HL, *per* Lord Devlin.
256 Section 237(1) TULRCA 1992.
257 Authorised or endorsed in accordance with s. 20(2) TULRCA 1992 – see note 238 above.
258 Section 237(2) TULRCA 1992.
259 Section 237(1A) TULRCA 1992.
260 Section 238(3) TULRCA 1992 states that a relevant employee is an employee, at the establishment of the employer, who is taking part in the industrial action; in the case of a lock-out, a relevant employee is an employee who was directly interested in the dispute leading to the lock-out.
261 The material time for deciding whether a relevant employee has not been dismissed is at the conclusion of the hearing determining jurisdiction of the complaint; see *P & O European Ferries (Dover) Ltd v Byrne* [1989] IRLR 254 CA and *Manifold Industries v Sims* [1991] IRLR 242.
262 Section 238(1) TULRCA 1992.
263 Section 238(4) TULRCA 1992.
264 [1992] IRLR 4.

going on strike. Less than three months later he applied for and was successful in obtaining a job at the employer's main office elsewhere. He revealed his previous employment but not the dismissal. After two weeks the connection with the dismissal was made and the employee was dismissed from the new position. This was sufficient to bring into effect s. 238(2)(b) TULRCA 1992 as the employer had constructive knowledge of the employee's previous employment, even though they had not connected this to the previous industrial dispute.[265]

There are the same exceptions to this rule as are applied in unofficial industrial action above.

12.13.3 Protected action

A person takes protected industrial action if that person commits an act, or is induced to commit an act, which is protected from action in tort by s. 219 TULRCA 1992 (see above). Such a person will be unfairly dismissed[266] if the reason, or the principal reason, for the dismissal is that the individual took protected industrial action, provided that the dismissal takes place within a basic period of 12 weeks beginning with the day that the employee started to take protected action. This basic period can be extended by the number of days on which an employee is locked out by the employer.[267]

The provisions will continue to apply to dismissals that take place after the protected period if:

1. The employee had stopped the industrial action during or before the end of the period.
2. The employee had not stopped industrial action during that period but the employer had not taken 'such procedural steps as would have been reasonable for the purposes of resolving the dispute to which the protected industrial action relates'.[268]

The protection is linked to applying pressure to both parties to act in a way that might lead to the resolution of the dispute, because, in deciding whether an employer has taken such steps, regard is to be had as to whether:

1. There had been compliance by the union or the employer with any procedures agreed in a collective agreement or other agreement.
2. The employer or the union had offered or agreed to negotiate after the start of the protected action.
3. Either party had unreasonably refused, after the start of the protected action, a request for the use of conciliation services.
4. The employer or union had unreasonably refused mediation services in relation to the procedures to be adopted for ending the dispute.[269]

The remedies for an unfair dismissal in respect of taking protected industrial action are as for other unfair dismissal cases, except that the remedies of reinstatement and re-engagement are not available until the end of the protected industrial action.[270]

---

265 See also *Crosville Wales Ltd v Tracey* [1993] IRLR 60, which concerned the dismissal of an entire workforce and the recruitment of a new one on different terms and conditions; some of the old workforce were recruited into this new workforce.
266 The rules on length of service do not apply in respect of dismissals for taking a protected action: s. 239(1) TULRCA 1992.
267 Section 238A(7A)–(7C) TULRCA 1992.
268 Section 238A(4)–(5) TULRCA 1992.
269 Sections 238A(6) and 238B TULRCA 1992.
270 Section 239(4)(a) TULRCA 1992.

Further reading

Elgar, J. and Simpson, B. 'The Impact of the Law on Industrial Disputes Revisited: A Perspective on Developments over the Last Two Decades' (2016) 46(1) *Industrial Law Journal* 6.

Ewing, K. and Hendy, J. 'New Perspectives on Collective Labour Law: Trade Union Recognition and Collective Bargaining' (2017) 46(1) *Industrial Law Journal* 23.

www.acas.org.uk – Advisory, Conciliation and Arbitration Service.

www.cac.gov.uk – Central Arbitration Committee.

www.ilo.org.uk – International Labour Organization.

www.tuc.org.uk – Trades Union Congress.

Index